third edition

A Global History
THE HUMAN HERITAGE

L. S. Stavrianos

Prentice-Hall, Inc., Englewood Cliffs, New Jersey 07632

Library of Congress Cataloging in Publication Data

STAVRIANOS, LEFTEN STAVROS.

A global history.

Rev. ed. of: Man's past and present. 2nd ed. 1975.

Includes bibliographical references and index.

1. World history. I. Title.
D20.S832 1983   909   82-10183
ISBN 0-13-357152-1

Dedicated to
ROBERT WILSON KELSO AND SUSIE STARR KELSO
*whose lakeside retreat facilitated
the writing of this and other works.*

A Global History: The Human Heritage
is the third edition of a book formerly titled
Man's Past and Present.

Printed in the United States of America

10 9 8 7 6 5 4 3 2 1

ISBN 0-13-357152-1

PRENTICE-HALL INTERNATIONAL, INC., *London*
PRENTICE-HALL OF AUSTRALIA PTY. LIMITED, *Sydney*
PRENTICE-HALL CANADA INC., *Toronto*
PRENTICE-HALL OF INDIA PRIVATE LIMITED, *New Delhi*
PRENTICE-HALL OF JAPAN, INC., *Tokyo*
PRENTICE-HALL OF SOUTHEAST ASIA PTE. LTD., *Singapore*
WHITEHALL BOOKS LIMITED, *Wellington, New Zealand*

Contents

Preface, *xiii*

Part I
BEFORE CIVILIZATION *1*

chapter 1
Humans As Food Gatherers *3*

      I. FROM HOMINIDS TO HUMANS, 4
     II. LIFE OF THE FOOD GATHERERS, 6
    III. APPEARANCE OF RACES, 10
        SUGGESTED READING, 11

chapter 2
Humans As Food Growers *12*

      I. ORIGINS OF AGRICULTURE, 13
     II. SPREAD OF AGRICULTURE, 14
    III. VARIETIES OF AGRICULTURE, 15

iii

IV. LIFE OF THE FOOD GROWERS, 16
V. DEMOGRAPHIC AND RACIAL RESULTS, 19
    SUGGESTED READING, 20

What It Means For Us Today   *21*

THE NATURE OF HUMAN NATURE, 21
SUGGESTED READING, 22

Part II
CLASSICAL CIVILIZATIONS OF EURASIA, TO A.D. 500   *23*

chapter 3
First Eurasian Civilizations, 3500–1000 B.C.   *25*

I. WHAT CIVILIZATION MEANS, 26
II. HOW ANCIENT CIVILIZATIONS BEGAN, 27
III. HOW ANCIENT CIVILIZATIONS SPREAD, 30
IV STYLES OF ANCIENT CIVILIZATIONS, 31
V. NOMADS GAIN POWER, 38
VI. NOMADS DESTROY ANCIENT CIVILIZATIONS, 41

chapter 4
Classical Civilizations Begin Eurasian Unification, 1000 B.C.–A.D. 500   *46*

I. ROOTS OF UNIFICATION, 47
II. COMMERCIAL BONDS, 49
III. CULTURAL BONDS, 52
    SUGGESTED READING, 58

chapter 5
Greco-Roman Civilization   *59*

I. FORMATIVE AGE, 800–500 B.C., 60
II. CLASSICAL AGE, 500–336 B.C., 62
III. CIVILIZATION OF THE CLASSICAL AGE, 64
IV. HELLENISTIC AGE, 336–31 B.C., 69
V. EARLY REPUBLIC, TO 264 B.C., 71
VI. LATE REPUBLIC, 265–27 B.C., 73
VII. EARLY EMPIRE, 27 B.C.–A.D. 284, 75
VIII. LATE EMPIRE, A.D. 284–476, 77
    SUGGESTED READING, 81

chapter 6
Indian Civilization   *82*

      I. ARYAN IMPACT, 83
     II. REFORMATION AND COUNTER-REFORMATION, 85
    III. MAURYA EMPIRE, 86
    IV. INVADERS, TRADERS, AND MISSIONARIES, 88
     V. GUPTA CLASSICAL AGE, 89
        SUGGESTED READING, 91

chapter 7
Chinese Civilization   *92*

      I. AGE OF TRANSITION, 93
     II. PHILOSOPHERS AND CLASSICS, 94
    III. CH'IN EMPIRE, 97
    IV. HAN EMPIRE, 98
     V. IMPERIAL DECLINE, 101
        SUGGESTED READING, 102

chapter 8
End of Classical Civilizations   *103*

      I. DECLINE OF CLASSICAL CIVILIZATIONS, 104
     II. BARBARIAN INVASIONS, 106
    III. GERMAN AND HUNS IN THE WEST, 108
    IV. CONTINUED INVASIONS IN THE WEST, 111
     V. THE GREAT WESTERN EXCEPTION, 112
        SUGGESTED READING, 114

What It Means For Us Today   *115*

      CIVILIZATION: CURSE OR BLESSING?, 115
      SUGGESTED READING, 118

Part III
MEDIEVAL CIVILIZATIONS OF EURASIA, 500–1500   *119*

chapter 9
Medieval Civilizations Complete Eurasian Unification   *121*

      I. COMMERCIAL BONDS, 122
     II. TECHNOLOGICAL BONDS, 124
    III. RELIGIOUS BONDS, 126
    IV. EXPANDING HORIZONS, 127
        SUGGESTED READING, 130

chapter 10
Rise Of Islam   *131*

    I. ARABIA BEFORE ISLAM, 132
    II. MOHAMMED, 132
    III. AGE OF CONQUESTS, 134
    IV. ARAB KINGDOM TO ISLAMIC EMPIRE, 136
    V. ISLAMIC CIVILIZATION, 137
    VI. DECLINE OF THE CALIPHATE, 140
    SUGGESTED READING, 142

chapter 11
Turco-Mongol Invasions   *143*

    I. TURKISH INVASIONS, 144
    II. GENGHIS KHAN'S CONQUESTS, 145
    III. MONGOL EMPIRE, 148
    IV. MONGOL DECLINE, 149
    V. TURKISH REVIVAL, 149
    VI. SIGNIFICANCE OF TURCO-MONGOL INVASIONS, 151
    SUGGESTED READING, 153

chapter 12
Traditional Byzantine Civilization   *154*

    I. EMERGENCE OF BYZANTIUM, 155
    II. BYZANTIUM'S GOLDEN AGE, 156
    III. BYZANTIUM'S DECLINE, 157
    IV. END OF BYZANTIUM, 160
    V. BYZANTIUM'S LEGACY, 162
    SUGGESTED READING, 163

chapter 13
Traditional Confucian Civilization   *164*

    I. SUI AND T'ANG DYNASTIES, 165
    II. SUNG GOLDEN AGE, 168
    III. YÜAN MONGOL RULE, 169
    IV. MING ETHNOCENTRISM AND WITHDRAWAL, 170
    V. CHINESE CIVILIZATION IN JAPAN, 174
    VI. JAPANESE FEUDALISM, 176
    VII. JAPAN'S WITHDRAWAL AND ISOLATION, 177
    SUGGESTED READING, 178

chapter 14
Revolutionary Western Civilization:
Technological And Economic Growth   *179*

    I. PLURALISM IN THE WEST, 180
    II. GEOGRAPHIC BACKGROUND, 181
    III. TECHNOLOGICAL PROGRESS, 182

IV. DEVELOPING ECONOMY, 183
SUGGESTED READING, 186

chapter 15
Revolutionary Western Civilization:
Renaissance, Reformation, And New Monarchs   *187*

I. RENAISSANCE, 188
II. REFORMATION, 191
III. NEW MONARCHS, 194
IV. WESTERN EUROPE'S EXPANSIONISM, 195
SUGGESTED READING, 197

What It Means For Us Today   *198*

DEVELOPED SOCIETIES AND THE "RETARDING LEAD," 198
SUGGESTED READING, 199

Part IV
NON-EURASIAN WORLD TO 1500   *201*

chapter 16
Africa   *203*

I. GEOGRAPHY, 203
II. AGRICULTURE AND IRON, 205
III. ISLAM, 206
IV. SUDAN EMPIRES, 207
V. KINGDOMS AND TRIBES, 209
VI. CONCLUSION, 210
SUGGESTED READING, 212

chapter 17
Americas And Australia   *213*

I. LAND AND PEOPLE, 214
II. CULTURES, 215
III. CIVILIZATIONS, 216
IV. CONCLUSION, 219
V. AUSTRALIA, 221
SUGGESTED READING, 223

What It Means For Us Today   *224*

RACES IN HISTORY, 224
SUGGESTED READING, 226

Maps   *230–259*

Part V
WORLD OF THE EMERGING WEST, 1500–1763 *261*

chapter 18
West European Expansion: Iberian Phase, 1500–1600 *263*

I. ROOTS OF IBERIAN EXPANSIONISM, 263
II. COLUMBUS DISCOVERS AMERICA, 265
III. PORTUGAL IN ASIA, 267
IV. DIVISION OF THE WORLD, 269
V. CONQUISTADORS AND NEW SPAIN, 270
VI. IBERIAN DECLINE, 273
  SUGGESTED READING, 275

chapter 19
West European Expansion: Dutch, French, British Phase, 1600–1763 *276*

I. EARLY NORTHWEST EUROPEAN EXPANSION, 277
II. HOLLAND'S GOLDEN CENTURY, 279
III. ANGLO-FRENCH RIVALRY, 281
IV. ENGLAND'S TRIUMPH, 282
  SUGGESTED READING, 287

chapter 20
Russian Expansion In Asia *288*

I. GEOGRAPHY OF RUSSIAN EXPANSION, 289
II. EARLY RUSSIAN EXPANSION, 290
III. CONQUEST OF SIBERIA, 291
IV. ADMINISTRATION AND DEVELOPMENT OF SIBERIA, 293
V. CONQUEST OF THE UKRAINE, 295
  SUGGESTED READING, 297

chapter 21
Beginning of Global Unity *298*

I. NEW GLOBAL HORIZONS, 298
II. GLOBAL DIFFUSION OF HUMANS, ANIMALS, AND PLANTS, 299
III. GLOBAL ECONOMIC RELATIONS, 300
IV. GLOBAL POLITICAL RELATIONS, 304
V. GLOBAL CULTURAL RELATIONS, 305
VI. EARLY MODERN PERIOD IN HISTORICAL PERSPECTIVE, 307
  SUGGESTED READING, 308

What It Means For Us Today *309*

REGIONAL AUTONOMY VERSUS GLOBAL UNITY, 309
SUGGESTED READING, 311

Part VI
WORLD OF WESTERN DOMINANCE, 1763–1914
Basis of Dominance *313*

chapter 22
Europe's Scientific and Industrial Revolutions *315*

I. ROOTS OF THE SCIENTIFIC REVOLUTION, 316
II. COURSE OF THE SCIENTIFIC REVOLUTION, 318
III. SIGNIFICANCE OF THE SCIENTIFIC REVOLUTION, 320
IV. ROOTS OF THE INDUSTRIAL REVOLUTION, 321
V. COURSE OF THE INDUSTRIAL REVOLUTION, 323
VI. EFFECT OF THE INDUSTRIAL REVOLUTION ON EUROPE, 326
VII. EFFECT OF THE INDUSTRIAL REVOLUTION
ON THE NON-EUROPEAN WORLD, 330
SUGGESTED READING, 334

chapter 23
Europe's Political Revolutions *335*

I. PATTERN OF THE POLITICAL REVOLUTION, 335
II. ENGLISH REVOLUTION, 337
III. ENLIGHTENMENT, 339
IV. AMERICAN REVOLUTION, 341
V. FRENCH REVOLUTION, 344
VI. NATIONALISM, 350
VII. LIBERALISM, 352
VIII. SOCIALISM, 353
SUGGESTED READING, 356

Impact of Dominance *357*

chapter 24
Russia *359*

I. RUSSIA AND EUROPE TO 1856, 359
II. RUSSIA AND EUROPE, 1856–1905, 362
III. RUSSIA AND ASIA TO 1905, 365
IV. FIRST RUSSIAN REVOLUTION AND AFTERMATH, 1905–1914, 369
SUGGESTED READING, 372

chapter 25
The Middle East *373*

I. BALKAN CHRISTIANS, 374
II. TURKS, 375
III. ARABS, 380
SUGGESTED READING, 383

chapter 26
India   *384*

    I. INDIA'S TRADITIONAL SOCIETY, 384
   II. BRITISH CONQUEST, 386
  III. BRITISH RULE, 387
  IV. BRITISH IMPACT, 388
   V. INDIAN NATIONALISM, 390
     SUGGESTED READING, 395

chapter 27
China And Japan   *396*

    I. OPENING OF CHINA, 397
   II. MILITARY AND ECONOMIC IMPACT, 400
  III. SOCIAL AND INTELLECTUAL IMPACT, 401
  IV. POLITICAL IMPACT, 402
   V. JAPAN IN SECLUSION, 404
  VI. MODERNIZATION OF JAPAN, 406
 VII. EXPANSION OF JAPAN, 408
     SUGGESTED READING, 408

chapter 28
Africa   *409*

    I. SLAVE TRADE, 410
   II. AGE OF EXPLORATION, 412
  III. PARTITION OF AFRICA, 413
  IV. EUROPE'S IMPACT, 415
     SUGGESTED READING, 420

chapter 29
The Americas And The British Dominions   *421*

    I. ETHNIC EUROPEANIZATION, 421
   II. POLITICAL EUROPEANIZATION, 425
  III. ECONOMIC EUROPEANIZATION, 426
  IV. CULTURAL EUROPEANIZATION, 427
     SUGGESTED READING, 429

chapter 30
Consolidation Of Global Unity   *430*

    I. EUROPE'S POLITICAL DOMINANCE, 430
   II. EUROPE'S ECONOMIC DOMINANCE, 431
  III. EUROPE'S CULTURAL DOMINANCE, 432
  IV. WHITE MAN'S BURDEN, 433
   V. FIRST CHALLENGES TO EUROPE'S DOMINANCE, 434
     SUGGESTED READING, 436

What It Means For Us Today   *437*

    MARX TURNED UPSIDE DOWN, 437
    SUGGESTED READING, 439

Part VII
WORLD OF WESTERN DECLINE
AND TRIUMPH, 1914-   *441*

chapter 31
World War I: Global Repercussions   *443*

      I. ROOTS OF WAR, 444
     II. SARAJEVO, 445
    III. EUROPEAN PHASE OF THE WAR, 1914–1917, 446
    IV. GLOBAL PHASE OF THE WAR:
        1917 RUSSIAN REVOLUTION, 449
     V. GLOBAL PHASE OF THE WAR:
        AMERICAN INTERVENTION, 454
    VI. ALLIED VICTORY, 456
   VII. PEACE SETTLEMENT, 457
  VIII. WORLD WAR I IN WORLD HISTORY, 459
        SUGGESTED READING, 461

chapter 32
Nationalist Uprisings In The Colonial World   *462*

      I. TURKEY, 462
     II. ARAB MIDDLE EAST, 466
    III. PERSIA, 469
    IV. INDIA, 470
     V. CHINA, 472
        SUGGESTED READING, 475

chapter 33
Revolutions And Settlement In Europe To 1929   *476*

      I. COMMUNISM TRIUMPHS IN RUSSIA, 477
     II. COMMUNISM FALLS IN CENTRAL EUROPE, 480
    III. ITALY GOES FASCIST, 483
    IV. PROBLEMS OF DEMOCRACY IN WESTERN EUROPE, 485
     V. STABILIZATION AND SETTLEMENT IN EUROPE, 487
        SUGGESTED READING, 490

chapter 34
The Five Year Plans And The Great Depression   *491*

      I. FIVE YEAR PLANS, 492
     II. THE GREAT DEPRESSION, 496
        SUGGESTED READING, 504

chapter 35
Drift To War, 1929–1939   *505*

      I. JAPAN INVADES MANCHURIA, 506
     II. DIPLOMATIC REACTIONS TO HITLER, 507
    III. ITALY CONQUERS ETHIOPIA, 510
    IV. ROME-BERLIN AXIS, 511
     V. SPANISH CIVIL WAR, 512

VI. END OF AUSTRIA AND CZECHOSLOVAKIA, 515
VII. COMING OF WAR, 518
SUGGESTED READING, 519

chapter 36
World War II: Global Repercussions   *520*

I. EUROPEAN PHASE OF THE WAR, 521
II. GLOBAL PHASE OF THE WAR, 524
III. WORLD WAR II IN WORLD HISTORY, 533
SUGGESTED READING, 534

chapter 37
End Of Empires   *535*

I. ROOTS OF COLONIAL REVOLUTION, 537
II. INDIA AND PAKISTAN, 537
III. SOUTHEAST ASIA, 539
IV. TROPICAL AFRICA, 541
V. SOUTH AFRICA, 545
VI. NORTH AFRICA, 546
VII. MIDDLE EAST, 547
SUGGESTED READING, 551

chapter 38
Grand Alliance, Cold War, and Aftermath   *552*

I. WARTIME UNITY, 553
II. UNITED NATIONS AND PEACE TREATIES, 554
III. COLD WAR IN EUROPE, 556
IV. COLD WAR IN THE FAR EAST, 559
V. RELAXATION OF THE COLD WAR, 562
VI. EUROPE ITS OWN MASTER, 562
VII. CHINA CHALLENGES RUSSIA, 564
SUGGESTED READING, 566

chapter 39
Age Of "Great Disorder"   *567*

I. GLOBAL CONFRONTATIONS, 567
II. DECLINE AND TRIUMPH OF THE WEST, 570
SUGGESTED READING, 572

What It Means For Us Today   *573*

GOLDEN AGE OR DARK AGE?, 573
SUGGESTED READING, 575

Notes   *576*
Glossary   *583*
Acknowledgments   *588*
Index   *589*

Preface

This book is distinctive in two ways.

First, it connects the past to the present. History is something more than "one damned thing after another," as a famous historian once complained. That type of history is more likely to give intellectual indigestion than intellectual understanding. This does *not* mean that only the study of current affairs is useful and worthwhile. Rather it means that the past should be analyzed in a manner that is meaningful for the present, and that the relationship between past and present should be noted and emphasized. This is why each of the seven parts of this volume ends with an essay entitled, "What It Means For Us Today."

The second distinctive feature of this book is that it is a *world* history. It deals with the entire globe rather than with some one country or region. It is concerned with *all* peoples, not just with Western or non-Western peoples. It is as though you, the reader, were perched upon the moon looking down on our whole vast planet. Your viewpoint would be different from that of an observer living in Washington or London or Paris or, for that matter, in Peking or Delhi or Cairo.

This global approach is a departure from traditional modern history. Since the days of the Enlightenment in the eighteenth century, the emphasis has been on the nation rather than on peoples. But in recent years, interest in world history has been growing, in response to present-day events that are sweeping our globe. With astronauts and cosmonauts encircling the entire planet in a few hours, and with headlines concerned just as much with Asia and Africa as with Europe and the Americas, we must have a wider angle of vision. World history is essential for the understanding of a world that has become "one" in reality as well as in rhetoric.

The need for world understanding is not the only reason for turning to world history. Equally important is the fact that the story of humankind from its very beginnings has a basic unity that must be recognized and respected.

We cannot truly understand either Western or non-Western history unless we have our global overview that encompasses both. Then we can see how much interaction there is between all peoples in all times, and how important that interaction is in determining the course of human history.

At first the interaction was fitful and rather slight. The various human communities prior to 1500 has existed in varying degrees of isolation. Yet this isolation was never absolute. During the long millenia before the European overseas discoveries, the various branches of the human race had indeed interacted one with the other, though the precise degree varied enormously according to time and location. Then Columbus and da Gama set forth on their historic voyages, and their successors brought all parts of the world into direct contact. The intimacy of that contact has grown steadily to the present day.

Modern communication and transportation facilities have been shrinking our world before our eyes, so that we now call it "spaceship earth," and the "global village."

If we accept the fact that all peoples share a common world history, how can we possibly learn about the whole world by taking a single course or reading a single book? Some historians say that world history, by definition, encompasses all civilizations. It is far too broad for classroom purposes. Western civilization, they say, is barely manageable by itself; how can all the other civilizations—including the Chinese, the Indian, and Middle Eastern—also be encompassed? The answer, of course, is that they cannot, and that world history, thus defined, is obviously impractical. But such a definition is inaccurate and misleading. World history is not the sum of histories of the civilizations of the world, just as Western history is not the sum of the histories of the countries of the West.

If the study of Western civilization were simply a series of surveys of British history, German history, French, Italian, Spanish, Balkan history, and the rest, then Western civilization would not be a feasible subject of study. Yet, in fact, it is feasible, and the reason is that the approach is not agglomerative. Rather it focuses on those historical forces or movements that affected the West as a whole, such as Christianity, Islam, the Crusades, the Renaissance, the Reformation, the French Revolution, the scientific and industrial revolutions, and so forth. So it is with world history, though the stage in this case is global rather than regional, and the emphasis consequently is on movements of worldwide influence.

In Paleolithic times, for example, humans emerged in Africa and gradually spread through Eurasia, Australia, and the Americas. The fateful breakthrough to agriculture occurred during the Neolithic period, followed by metalworking and assorted other crafts and leading to earliest urban life and civilization. This in turn led to the development of the great Eurasian civilization—the Chinese, Indian, Middle Eastern, and European—which for millennia developed autonomously along parallel lines. The amount of interaction among Eurasian civilizations varied as a result of powerful interregional historical forces such as Hellenism, Christianity, Buddhism, and the recurring invasions from the Central Eurasian steppes. After 1500 this Eurasian balance gradually gave way to a global unity imposed by an emerging West and culminating in the nineteenth century in an unprecedented worldwide domination by that region. Finally, in the twentieth century world history becomes the story of the growing reaction against this domination and the perilous groping toward a new world balance that was made necessary by the rapid diffusion of Western technology and ideology. This, in a nutshell, is the rationale and structure of world history. It is a structure that is not more complex than that of Western history. The difference is merely that the stage is our planet rather than the continent of Europe.

Finally the reader will note that all the maps are grouped together between pages 230 to 259, with an introductory essay explaining the subject of each map. The reason for the grouping is that it makes clear the overall organization and content of this textbook. In fact, the reader might find it helpful to start off by reading the introductory essay and looking at the maps. This will provide both a preview and a summary of our "Human Heritage".

L. S. STAVRIANOS

Part I

Before Civilization

Part I is concerned with the 4 million years before human *civilization.* The other parts of the book are devoted to history since humans became civilized: less than 6 thousand years ago. Thus, by far the longest phase of human evolution will receive by far the briefest consideration. The reason for the disproportionate emphasis on the story of civilized people is the constantly accelerating tempo of human history. Geologic time is measured in billions of years, and human prehistory in thousands, but since the advent of civilization, the time unit has shrunk progressively to centuries and to decades, until fateful events now daily crowd us, unceasingly and inexorably. Indeed the pace of change has reached such proportions that it is a very real question whether the human species is capable of adjusting quickly enough to avoid obsolescence, or even extinction.

The disparity in the pace of events, and the corresponding disparity in emphasis in this study, should not lead us, however, to minimize the significance of what happened during prehistory. During those millennia, two developments provided the bedrock foundation for all later history. One was the gradual transition from *hominid* to *Homo sapiens,* or thinking human being. The other was the transformation of the human newcomers from a *food gatherer* who was dependent on the bounty of nature to a *food producer* who became increasingly independent of nature—the master of his destiny. These two epochal events—the appearance of human beings and their invention of *agriculture*—are the subjects of the two chapters of Part I.

Anthropology holds up a great mirror to man and lets him look at himself in his infinite variety.

Clyde Kluckhohn

chapter 1

Humans As Food Gatherers

One of the outstanding achievements of our time is the study and reconstruction of early human history. The ancients had little understanding of what had happened before them. Thucydides, the most objective of Greek historians, began his study of the Peloponnesian War by stating that nothing of great importance had happened before his time. His ignorance of history prevented him from recognizing the unique glory and contribution of Athens. By contrast, our age is more history minded than any other. We know more about the early history of the Egyptians, the Greeks, or the Chinese than they themselves knew. Furthermore, scientists in various fields—geology, archeology, anthropology, paleontology, and biology—have extended our knowledge back before the beginning of civilization, even before we had written records. This is very important, for it was only about 5 thousand years ago that humans learned to write, whereas their hominid beginnings have been traced back some 4 million years. In this first chapter we shall consider these long prehistoric millennia when people became human. They existed, as did the other animals, by collecting food wherever it was to be found, rather than by growing it as their agriculturist descendants would learn to do.

3

I. FROM HOMINIDS TO HUMANS

Our earth is a minor planet spinning in a minor galaxy. Compared to the entire universe it is inconceivably small—literally like a speck of dust on the Pacific Ocean. It took form between 12 and 18 billion years ago, and the first life appeared on it about 3 billion years ago in the form of single-celled creatures. This life traditionally has been viewed as qualitatively different from nonlife, but scientists no longer accept this assumed dichotomy between organic and inorganic. Rather they think of living matter as having evolved naturally from nonliving matter. They classify all matter into a hierarchy of states of organization. At a certain level in this hierarchy the transition occurs from inorganic to organic. More specifically, electrons, protons, and neutrons combine to form atoms, and the atoms form molecules. The molecules become more or less well-organized aggregates, and one class of these is living matter.

Organic matter in turn went through a comparable hierarchical evolution: from the original microorganisms to primitive plants such as seaweeds, to animals without backbones such as jellyfish and worms, and to backboned (vertebrate) animals. These vertebrates, with some of their invertebrate and plant cousins, began their successful adaptation to life on land about 300 million years ago. First came the amphibians, then the great army of prehistoric reptiles, followed by the birds, and finally the mammals. For the past 60 million years, mammals have been the dominant form of life on earth.

Almost all scientists accept the proposition that humans belong to the animal kingdom—more specifically to the order of Primates, which they share with the tree shrews, lemurs, tarsiers, monkeys, and apes. Evidence from several fields of study supports this conclusion. Anatomists have found basic similarities between humans and the other higher animals in the general plan of their skeletal, muscular, and organic structures. Embryologists have noted that the human embryo displays, at different stages of its development, characteristics of some of the lower forms of life, such as gill arches at the end of one month and a rudimentary tail at two months. Anthropologists have shown that human fossil remains show a consistent trend away from the general anthropoid type, or hominids, towards Homo sapiens. Other scientists have discovered many similar indications of our ties to the other animals, including close resemblance between the chemical composition of the blood of apes and of humans, possession of common parasites, and similarities in their ways of learning.

The differentiation of the human stock occurred during the *Pleistocene epoch,* which lasted until 11,000 years ago, and which included six or seven glacial and five or six interglacial periods. These drastic environmental changes compelled all animals to adapt and readapt themselves continually to new conditions. Success in this crucial matter depended neither upon brute strength nor upon the ability to resist cold, but rather upon the continuous growth of intelligence and the use of that intelligence to work out satisfactory adaptations. This, of course, is the secret of the unchallenged primacy of human beings on this earth. Humans have been, first and foremost, generalists. They never adapted exclusively to one type of environment, as the gibbon did to the forest with its long lithe arms, or the polar bear to the arctic with its heavy white fur. Rather humans adapted with their brains, which they used to adapt to any environment.

At one time it was assumed that humans and the apes had developed from a common ancestor, and the task of anthropologists was to find the "missing link" between the two. Now it is agreed that Homo sapiens is the product of *natural selection* from a succession of humanlike ancestors, or hominids, some of which were capable of using simple stone tools and weapons. The earliest of these hominids was Australopithecus, believed to have appeared first in the *savannas* of eastern and southern Africa some 4 million years ago. The pelvis and leg of this hominid were strikingly similar to that of modern humans, but the cranial capacity was only about one-third that of a human, or hardly larger than that of living apes. Thus a humanlike bipedal locomotive system was combined with an apelike brain. The low level of intelligence meant a correspondingly low level of speech and of toolmaking. The significance of this sequence is that the human brain did not appear first and then proceed to create human culture. Rather there was interaction back and forth. The development of speech and use of tools were both the causes and the effects of brain development.

The African savannas were ideal for primates at that level of development. The climate was warm enough to make the lack of clothing bearable, and the open grasslands, in contrast to dense forests and deserts, afforded both water and animal foods. Thus, despite their simple pebble tools with their single cutting edges, the australopithecines subsisted on an adequate diet including eggs, crabs, tortoises, birds, rodents, and young antelopes. The latter were easy prey because they ''freeze'' in the grass when faced with danger.

Australopithecus roamed the African plains for over 2 million years, during which time several species of this hominid appeared, flourished, and disappeared. Anthropologists often disagree on the details of this sequence because new finds are made each year, and theories change with these finds. About a half-million years ago, Australopithecus gave way to our immediate ancestor, the hominid Homo erectus. The brain of this species was about twice as large as that of its australopithecine predecessor, or two-thirds that of a modern human. The generalized stone tool of Homo erectus, the fist hatchet, was also more complex. It was the first overall designed tool, usually almond shaped, from six to eight inches long, several inches wide, and about one inch thick. The butt end was rounded for grasping in the palm of the hand, while the other end was pointed and sharpened on one side. It was used for all purposes—hand ax, knife, scraper, or awl. The huge quantities of skeletal remains of large slaughtered animals—deer, rhinos, pigs, elephants, buffalo, hippos, horses, antelopes, and gazelles—demonstrate the effective use made of this tool. Such large-scale hunting of big game also reflects efficient group organization and action, including speech communication. Another indication of social life is the first evidence of reverence for the dead. Fossils of hominid bodies have been found that originally had been covered with earth upon which red ochre or hematite had been scattered. Almost certainly this represented some kind of ritual burial. Along the same lines there is evidence of the dawn of the decorative arts in the beads and perforated teeth and shells that have been found in association with the fossils. Finally there are the all-important telltale signs of fire making—circular dark discs in the soil, five to six inches in diameter.

The mastery of fire had fundamental and far-reaching repercussions. It freed our ancestors from the bondage of the limited energy supply of their own bodies. It helped them to survive the advancing glaciers of the ice ages. It increased their available food supply tremendously because now it was possible for them to cook a great range of roots and seeds that hitherto had been inedible. Fire further improved the hominid diet as the cooking liberated protein and carbohydrate materials. Fire also made it possible for the hominids to break out of the warm savanna in which they had thus far been confined and to begin spreading throughout the globe. The results of their fanning out are being felt to the present day (see Map I, ''Global Distribution of Hominids and Homo Sapiens'').

The evolutionary process culminating in our human species was finally completed about 35,000 years ago with the appearance of Homo sapiens, or ''thinking human being.'' Viewed in broadest perspective, this represents the second major turning point in the course of events on this planet. The first occurred when life originated out of inorganic matter. After that momentous step, all living forms evolved by adapting to their environments through mutation and natural selection. That meant that the genes adapted to the environment, as was evident during the climatic upheavals of the Pleistocene. But with the appearance of humans, the evolutionary process was reversed. No longer did genes adapt to environment; instead, humans adapted by changing the environment to suit their genes. Today, a third epochal turning point appears imminent, as humans' growing knowledge of the structure and function of genes may soon enable them to modify their genes as well as their environment.

Humans, and only humans, have been able to create a made-to-order environment, or culture, as it is called. The reason is that only humans can symbolize, or envision things and concepts divorced from here-and-now reality. Only humans laugh, and only they know that they will die. Only they have wondered about the universe and its origins, about their place in it and in the hereafter.

With these unique and revolutionizing abilities, humans have been able to cope with their environment without mutations. Their culture is the new nonbiological way of having fur in the arctic, water storage in the desert, and fins in the water. More concretely, culture consists of tools, clothing, ornaments, institutions, language, art forms, and religious beliefs and practices. All these have served to adapt humans to their physical environment and to their fellow humans. Indeed, the story of humanity as related in the following chapters is simply the story of a succession of cultures that we have created, from our Paleolithic origins to the present day.

II. LIFE OF THE FOOD GATHERERS

Just as Homo erectus had been able to fashion a more effective overall tool than their australopithecine predecessor, so now Homo sapiens with their superior intelligence developed the so-called ''blade technique.'' They used the long, sharp flakes—or ''blades''—struck off the core of a stone to fashion a variety of new tools as well as ''tools to make tools.'' Some of the new tools were composite, such as spears with hafted heads of bone, antler, or flint, and flint blades set in bone or wooden handles. Another departure was the construction of projectiles such as the bola, sling, spear thrower, and bow and arrow. The latter must have been relatively inefficient at first, but it was gradually improved until it became the most formidable weapon prior to modern firearms. Other inventions of the upper Paleolithic included bone and ivory bodkins, bone needles with eyes, belt fasteners, and even buttons—all of which indicate that the Magdalenian hunters wore sewn skin garments with fitting sleeves and trousers.

Although this technology of the late Paleolithic was advanced compared to that of the early Paleolithic a half-million years earlier, it still was primitive in the sense that *productivity* was low. Food gatherers had no formal political structure with full-time political leaders. Rather they formed autonomous bands that usually numbered twenty to fifty persons. Larger groups were possible, and some did exist in areas that yielded plentiful food supplies, such as the American northwest, with its inexhaustible salmon runs, and the Dordogne valley in southern France, with its great reindeer herds in Magdalenian times. Judging from contemporary hunting societies, authority in Paleolithic times was rigidly limited and lacked an established and recognized power to control people. Leaders arose naturally for specific purposes; an old man might be the accepted planner of ceremonies because of his ritual knowledge, while a younger person with proven skill in the chase might take the lead of hunting parties. But the important point is that all such leaders were more persons of influence than of authority, since there were no institutions for imposing one's will upon others.

Social organization necessarily was as simple as the political, if indeed the two can be distinguished at this stage. The basic unit was the family, consisting of the parents and their immature and unmarried children. Extra wives usually were permitted, but in practice polygamy was rare. Intra- and interfamily relationships rested on kinship ties. Each member of a group had duties towards the others and in turn enjoyed rights and privileges. They helped each other in the quest for food and in providing shelter from the elements and defense from their enemies. Some fighting between tribal groups arose from personal feuds and from competition for hunting and fishing grounds. But Paleolithic society lacked both the manpower and the resources essential for large-scale warfare. This was not possible until the coming of agriculture, with its greatly increased productivity and correspondingly increased population. In short, the essence of Paleolithic social organizations was cooperation. Families and bands were primarily mutual-aid societies, working together in the harsh struggle for existence.

This cooperation was evident in economic matters as well as social ones. No specialization was needed amongst hunters, except on a sex basis. Every man and woman possessed all the knowledge and skills proper to their sex and functioned accordingly. During the early Paleolithic, women collected fruits, nuts, and grains and grubbed up roots and insects, while men caught small game and fish. At that level there was little to choose between the sexes as food gatherers. But as tools improved, the males were able to organize large-scale hunting parties and to kill large animals, while the women remained close to camp to cook, care for the children, and collect available edibles. This step increased the male's importance as a food provider. It may be that this role combined with the extra strength, aggressiveness, and skill that went with it, led near the end of the Paleolithic era to a dominance of men over women, such as we find today amongst the Australian aborigines.

Turning our discussion from social institutions and practices to general beliefs, we find that primitive humans were basically ahistorical and nonevolutionary in their attitudes towards themselves and their society. They assumed that the future would be identical to the present, as the present was to the past. Consequently there was no notion of change, and hence no inclination to criticize or to tamper with existing institutions and practices. Everything, including themselves, their *culture,* and their *habitat,* had appeared with the world's creation and was destined to continue unaltered into the future. The creation myths of hunting peoples are strikingly similar, involving heroes who fashioned the landscape, stocked it with game, brought forth the people, and taught them the arts and their customs.

Primitive humans were very knowledgeable concerning nature. They had to be, for their very existence depended on it. Yet they had little explanatory knowledge; if there were floods or droughts, or if the hunting or fishing was poor, they could give no naturalistic explanation. And not knowing how to cope with nature by naturalistic means meant they had to resort to the supernatural. They turned to magic and spent much time in efforts to persuade or fool nature to yield a greater abundance. By making each useful animal or plant the *totem* of a particular group, and by using images, symbols, and imitative dances, primitive people believed that the animal or food could be encouraged to flourish and multiply. As long as the rules of the totems were strictly observed, the reproduction of the group and of its food supply could be assured.

All group members seem to have participated at first in the ritual ceremonies, but towards the end of the Paleolithic part-time specialists in the form of medicine men or *shamans* seem to have appeared. These people were thought to have peculiar relations with the forces that were supposed to control those parts of the universe or environment that mattered—primarily food and fertility, but also health and personal luck. More and more, as they were relieved from the full-time work of food and tool production, they used their magical arts for the common good. Shamans are still found today in nearly every surviving food-gathering culture, including those of the Bushmen, the Eskimos, and the Australian aborigines.

Paleolithic technology, however, was not productive enough to support anything approaching a *hierarchy* of priests, so no cohesive theology could be developed. Conceptions of gods and spirits were hazy, and much emphasis was placed on individual visions. Religion was not used as a method of social control. Benefits did not depend on the morality of the individual. Instead people begged or bargained with the supernatural through their shamans.

This fear of things that people didn't understand and their desire to bring the supernatural under human control was expressed in art as well as religion. By far the outstanding example of Paleolithic art consists of the extraordinary cave paintings, the best of which are located in southern France and northwestern Spain. The subjects of the drawings are usually the larger game: bison, bear, horses, woolly rhinoceros, mammoth, and wild boar. The best of the drawings are in full color, remarkably alive, and charged with energy. Despite their extraordinary artistic quality, the cave drawings apparently were designed for utilitarian reasons. They were drawn in the darkest and most dangerous parts of the caves, although the people lived only in or near the entrances. Also the artists commonly painted one picture over another, with no apparent desire to preserve their works. Hence it appears that when these Paleolithic artists made their way to the depths of the earth and created as realistic a reproduction as possible of the animals they hunted, they did so in the belief that they thereby gained some sort of magic power over them.

In conclusion, Paleolithic life was in many ways very attractive. Its members were equal with one another. Warm bonds of kinship permeated and determined their social relationships. It offered everyone specific and accepted obligations and rewards. There was no problem of *alienation* or of anxiety in the face of an uncertain or unpredictable future. To the present day, an Australian aborigine can take a piece of broken glass, fashion it skillfully into an arrow head or spear point, fit it to a spear thrower or to a bow that he has strung himself, set forth and kill his game, prepare his dinner with due attention to ceremony, and after dinner, round out the day with storytelling in which he shares the adventures of the day with the stay-at-homes. In this manner the Paleolithic hunter was a complete man to a degree that has not been approached since the agricultural revolution.

But the bonds that held Paleolithic society together were also restricting as well as comforting. The individual was wholly subordinate to the band or tribe, which was viewed as a timeless procession of the dead, the living, and the unborn, attended by all the unseen powers of the spirit world. To this procession of life the individual was completely subject.

Doubtless the overwhelming majority of individuals felt themselves to be participants rather than captives. Yet the fact remains that the result was stagnation along with security. The Paleolithic way of life was psychically satisfying yet it was a dead-end street. Among the Arunta of Australia, the elders arranged with the enemy to kill those individuals who had not been living in accord with tribal tradition. It was this tradition, this stultifying and constraining tradition, that was the historically all-important other side of Paleolithic society.

THE LIFE OF THE FOOD GATHERERS

We may assume that the style of human life during the Paleolithic millenia was basically the same as that of the food gatherers whom the Europeans discovered overseas during their explorations after Columbus. The accounts left by the explorers, and by the settlers and missionaries who followed them, are valuable in giving us a glimpse into our common human past. The following report is by the Jesuit Father Jacob Baegert, who lived between 1750 and 1767 amongst the Indians of California. His description of the "Californians" gives us a picture of Paleolithic ancestors, and also challenges common assumptions about "human nature."*

With all their poor diet and hardships, the Californians are seldom sick. They are in general strong, hardy, and much healthier than the many thousands who live daily in abundance and on the choicest fare that the skill of Parisian cooks can prepare . . . .

For the smallpox the Californians are, like other Americans, indebted to Europeans, and this disease assumes a most pestilential character among them. A piece of cloth which a Spaniard, just recovered from the smallpox, had given to a Californian communicated, in the year 1763, the disease to a small mission, and in three months more than a hundred individuals died . . . .

From what I have already said of the Californians, it might be inferred that they are the most unhappy and pitiable of all the children of Adam. Yet such a supposition would be utterly wrong, and I can assure the reader that . . . they live unquestionably much happier than the civilized inhabitants of Europe. . . . Throughout the whole year nothing happens that causes a Californian trouble or vexation, nothing that renders his life cumbersome and death desirable. . . . Envy, jealousy, and slander embitter not his life, and he is not exposed to the fear of losing what he possesses, nor to the care of increasing it. . . . The Californians do not know the meaning of *meum* [mine] and *tuum* [thine], those two ideas which, according to St. Gregory, fill the few days of our existence with bitterness and unaccountable evils.

Though the Californians seem to possess nothing, they have, nevertheless, all that they want, for they covet nothing beyond the productions of their poor, ill-favored country, and these are always within their reach. It is no wonder, then, that they always exhibit a joyful temper, and constantly indulge in merriment and laughter, showing thus their contentment, which, after all, is the real source of happiness.

* Smithsonian Institution, *Annual Report for 1863* (Washington, D.C.: 1864), pp. 352–369.

We shall see that the agricultural revolution set off a chain reaction of urbanization, class differentiation, and social cleavage that undermined the appealing equality of primitive society. But in doing so it also broke the restricting bonds of tribal traditionalism and thereby launched man, for good or ill, on the fateful course that was to lead from hunting ground to megalopolis, from human muscle to atomic power. Before turning to the agricultural revolution, however, it is necessary to consider the spread of Paleolithic humans throughout the globe and the ensuing repercussions felt to the present day.

III. APPEARANCE OF RACES

It is commonly assumed that population explosion is a phenomenon peculiar to our times, but this is not so. Spectacular population spurts have occurred with each major technological breakthrough, and for the obvious reason that an advance in *technology* leads to increased productivity, which can support a larger number of people. At this time the differential between early and late Paleolithic technology did represent a major advance. This in turn led to a population jump from an estimated 125,000 hominids in the early Paleolithic to 5.32 million Homo sapiens on the eve of the agricultural revolution at the end of the Paleolithic ten thousand years ago. This increase of over forty-two times is thus comparable to the population explosions that, as we shall see, were to accompany each of the later technological revolutions (see Map II, "World Population Growth").

Another *demographic pattern* set at this time and repeated in the future was the disproportionate increase of any population that took the lead in technological innovation, and hence the spread of that population over larger areas. This pattern has prevailed since the first appearance of life on this planet. At all times, the best-adapted species—the most efficient exploiter of the physical environment—is the species that has prevailed and extended its domain. Thus the australopithecines, with their primitive pebble tools and lack of clothing, were unable to extend their range beyond the warm savanna lands. Homo erectus, by contrast, with superior tools and clothing and control of fire, was able to expand north from Africa to the temperate zones of Eurasia—hence the discovery of that species' widely scattered fossil remains such as Java man, Peking man, and Heidelberg man. Finally Homo sapiens, with still more advanced technology and correspondingly more efficient adaptation, was able to push further north into the Siberian tundra, as well as south into the African and Southeast Asian tropical rain forests.

Under these circumstances, Homo sapiens occupied the remaining continents by crossing one land bridge to Australia and another to Alaska. Once in the New World they fanned out in all directions through North America and South America. Thus humans occupied all the continents except Antarctica, thereby becoming, together with the inseparable dog, the most widespread animal in the world.

Hand in hand with the dispersal of Homo sapiens went race differentiation. A variety of so-called races appeared, with distinguishing characteristics in skin color, hair texture, and facial structure. These races are believed to have emerged because of the relative isolation of the various human populations and their adaptation to differing local environments. The significant point concerning this differentiation within the human species is that it occurred so late—well after the emergence of Homo sapiens. All modern races, then, stem from a common stock after it had attained its full human development. This explains why the Europeans were able to interbreed with all races in all the lands they discovered. It also explains why, as virtually all anthropologists agree, there are no significant differences in the innate mental capacity among the living races of mankind. Representatives of late Paleolithic man or of the contemporary Australian aborigines would stand as much chance of graduating from a university as would representatives of any other races.

The details about how the races first appeared in various regions are not known, and probably never will be. But we do know that by the end of the latest Ice Age, about 10,000 years ago, the global distribution of races was beginning to be the same as today. The Caucasoids occupied Europe, North and East Africa, and the Middle East, extending into India and Central Asia. The Negroids were in the Sahara (better watered then) and a bit southward, while the Pygmies and Bushmen, in contrast to later times, occupied the remainder of Africa. Other Pygmies, the Negritos, lived in the forests of India and Southeast Asia, while in the open country of these regions and in Australia were the Australoids. Finally, East Asia and the Americas were inhabited by the Mongoloids (see Map III, "Global Race Distribution").

Although this racial pattern is vaguely similar to the one we know, Map III shows that basic changes had occurred by A.D. 1000, and still more by today. These changes, as we shall note later, came as a direct result of later technological revolutions. It was the failure to keep up with these revolutions that explains the virtual disappearance of the Bushmen and Pygmies and Australoids, as well as the swamping of the American Indians in most of the New World. Put in other words, it explains why 10,000 years ago blonds probably were no more numerous than Bushmen, whereas today there are 100,000 blonds for every living Bushman.

The very different experiences of the Bushmen compared with those of the Caucasoids or other races, had nothing to do with differences in ability. We will return to this important point at the end of Part IV, "Races in History," where we shall consider the reasons for the varied experiences.

SUGGESTED READING

G. Barraclough, ed., *The Times Atlas of World History* (Times Books, 1972); K. W. Butzer, *Environment and Archeology* (Aldine, 1964); R. E. Leakey, *The Making of Mankind* (Dutton, 1981); R. B. Lee and J. DeVore, eds., *Man the Hunter* (Aldine, 1969); J. E. Pfeiffer, *The Emergence of Man* (Harper & Row, 1969); M. Sahlins, *Stone Age Economics* (Aldine, 1972); R. Steel and A. Harvey, *The Encyclopedia of Prehistoric Life* (McGraw-Hill, 1979).

chapter 2

Humans As Food Growers

During Paleolithic times humans became humans by learning to speak, to make tools, and to use fire. This gave them an enormous advantage over the other animals about them, and yet in one fundamental respect humans remained akin to animals. They were still hunters among other hunters. They were still food gatherers as were countless other species that were completely dependent on the bounty of nature. And being dependent on nature, humans were dominated by nature. They had to be constantly on the move in order to follow animals and to locate berry patches or fishing grounds. They had to live in small groups or bands because not many could find enough food to support themselves in a given area. It is estimated that even in fertile areas with mild winters, only one or two food collectors could support themselves per square mile. And as much as twenty or even thirty square miles were needed for each human soul in regions of cold climate, tropical jungle, or desert.

All this changed when humans learned how to grow their own food. Their shift from being food gatherers to being food producers changed every aspect of their lives. Why the shift was made, and what its results were, are the subjects of this chapter.

I. ORIGINS OF AGRICULTURE

When humans became food producers a new world with limitless horizons opened before them. They left behind them the Paleolithic (old stone) age and entered the Neolithic (new stone) age.

Neolithic humans differed from their Paleolithic predecessors in two respects: they made stone tools by grinding and polishing rather than by chipping and fracturing, and, even more important, they obtained food wholly or primarily from agriculture and/or stock raising rather than from hunting animals or gathering plants. The new cutting tools made of ground stone were more durable than earlier tools and facilitated important inventions like the plow and the wheel, which appeared towards the end of the Neolithic period. But still, the trick of grinding a chipped or hewn ax to a smooth polished edge was a rather trivial matter compared to the transformation of humans from food collectors to food producers.

This transformation was not the result of sudden inspiration. It was not a case of some prehistoric Archimedes shouting ''Eureka!'' as he understood how plants grow. Actually people understood the mechanics of plant growth before the agricultural revolution, just as they knew before Columbus's voyage that the earth was round—and just as modern primitives who are wholly without agriculture are nevertheless thoroughly familiar with the nature and behavior of plants in their habitats. Modern primitives know that plants sprout from seeds, that they usually need water and sunshine to flourish, and that they grow better in one type of soil than in another. Such knowledge is acquired naturally by them because their very existence depends on practical understanding of the surrounding flora and fauna. There is no reason for doubting, and plenty of evidence for believing, that prehistoric people acquired the same practical understanding when they were in similar circumstances.

If the basic principles of plant life were known to humans thousands of years before the agricultural revolution, why did they delay so long before putting them into practice? One reason is that there was no incentive to do so. Hunting peoples did not normally live on the brink of starvation. Nor did they increase rapidly in numbers and outstrip the available food supply. Instead they resorted to practices such as infanticide, abortion, and *lactation taboos* in order to keep their numbers low enough to pull through the lean months of each year. Thus hunting societies continued to exist for millennia at a comfortable equilibrium. And consequently they lacked stimulus for radical change.

Not only did the hunters under normal circumstances have plenty to eat, they also had a rich variety of food. This fact can be easily illustrated by a modern example. The Bushmen of South Africa, who live in an unfavorable desert environment, nevertheless collect food from 85 edible plant species and 223 animal species. So their diet is much richer in vitamins, minerals, and protein than the diet of peasants who depend on a few types of grains or tubers that they grow. Likewise, the prehistoric hunters also had a more dependable supply of food because they could draw on such a large number of plants and animals. By contrast, peasants of any period have always faced the danger of starvation if bad weather spoils their crops.

Not only did the early hunters have a better and more dependable food supply than food-growing peasants, but in addition they had to work less for their food. Again today's adult Bushmen, who live in a harsh desert, spend an average of only 15 hours per week hunting or collecting food. This is little more than 2 hours a day. It is not surprising then, that Bushmen are exceptionally healthy, with 10 percent of their adults being over 60 years of age. Their good health is also helped by their nomadic way of life. Since they are always on the move, they are not cut down by diseases from human excreta and other waste materials that pile up in the villages where peasants spend their lives.

For all these reasons, hunters did not shift to agriculture until 10,000 years ago, even though they knew much earlier how to grow things. Another reason for the late beginning of agriculture was the scarcity of plants and animals suitable for domestication. Throughout history humans have been able to domesticate only a few hundred plants and a few dozen animals that happen to possess certain essential characteristics. Plants must be potentially high-yielding and be adaptable to a variety of environments. If these re-quirements are not met, plants will have little effect even though they are domesticated. For example, in the region which today constitutes the United States prehistoric Indians cultivated pigweed, marsh elder, lamb's quarter, and sunflower, but none of these plants yielded enough to affect the Indian way of life significantly. Likewise animals, to be domesticable, must be able to lose their instinctive fear of humans, be able to breed in cap-tivity, and be willing to accept the diet provided by humans. The peoples of the Old World were fortunate in having available a variety of such animals to provide them with meat, milk, wool, and beasts of burden. The development of American Indians, by con-trast, was retarded because they had nothing comparable; they had to do with a half-domesticated group of Andean cameloids: the llama, the alpaca, and the vicuna.

As we can see from this discussion, no breakthrough to agriculture could be expected unless some change occurred to upset the comfortable equilibrium of the hunting societies, and, even then, agriculture could occur only in areas where domesticable plants were available. This is precisely what happened.

During the comparatively short period between 10,000 and 2000 years ago, the great majority of humans on this planet shifted to agriculture. Obviously this was a forced shift, for no hunters would voluntarily leave their easy and secure way of life for the never-ending work of the peasants tied to their fields and their cattle. What forced the change was population pressure. Over tens of thousands of years, the number of humans had in-creased slowly, causing the migrations from Africa to Asia, Europe, Australia, and the Americas. Finally all the continents, except Antarctica, were populated. As the number of humans continued to grow slowly but steadily, hunters were forced to supplement the food they gathered with food they grew. Undoubtedly they were unhappy about staying in one area to grow crops and raise cattle, but the fact is that many more people per square mile can be supported by agriculture than by foodgathering.

Agriculture became a full-time occupation in those few regions where there were plants and/or animals that could be domesticated. In the process of domestication the wild plants and animals became larger and provided more food. Thus the hunters spent more and more of their time as food producers rather than food gatherers, until they ended up as peasants living in villages. From the first few centers of this agricultural revolution, the new way of life gradually spread over most of the globe.

II. SPREAD OF AGRICULTURE

We know with certainty that the Middle East, Mesoamerica and northern China were in-dependent centers of agricultural revolution. In addition, new discoveries now being made yearly suggest that there were other independent centers in Southeast Asia, West

Africa, the Andes, and elsewhere. We know the most about the Middle East and Mesoamerica, the regions which had an especially large number of domesticable plants and/or animals.

In the Middle East, prehistoric people found the ancestors of modern wheat, oats, rye, and barley, as well as those of modern goat, sheep, cattle, and pig. In Mesoamerica dozens of plants were successfully domesticated. The most important ones were maize, amaranths, beans, and squashes.

Over a period of many centuries the various plants were adapted to a variety of environmental conditions, and thus spread to other areas creating thereby a regional complex of multiple-species agriculture. This advanced type of agriculture had two great advantages: a high level of productivity and *"subsistence security."* If one crop failed for climatic reasons, another with different requirements could survive. So it provided the dependable food supply essential for dense populations and for the civilizations they produced.

The transition from the earliest domestication to agricultural revolution, or full dependence on agriculture, was very gradual and prolonged. It is known as the phase of *"incipient agriculture."* In the Middle East this phase lasted from roughly 9500 to 7500 B.C. In the New World it was even longer. One of the earliest centers of domestication in the New World was the Mexican valley of Tehuacán, where incipient agriculture began in approximately 7000 B.C. It was not until about 1500 B.C. that maize and other plants were hybridized to the point where their yield was sufficiently high to provide most of the food, and so to complete the transition from incipient agriculture to the agricultural revolution.

From these two original centers of full-fledged agriculture, as well as from northern China and other centers that remain to be identified in the future, the new mode of living spread to all parts of the globe. The diffusion process was sparked by the inefficiency of early agriculture, which was an intermittent or shifting type of cultivation. The land was cleared and used for crop growing for a few years. Then it was abandoned to natural growth for eight or ten or more years in order to allow the fertility to be restored. As a result, the ratio of abandoned or recuperating land to that under cultivation at any one time was between five and ten to one. This, very extensive, type of agriculture, together with increasing population, required constant extension of the limits of the tilled land into new regions. There was a continual "budding-off" or "hiving-off" from the agricultural settlements into the relatively sparsely populated lands of the food-gathering peoples. In this way agriculture was diffused in all directions from the original centers. Very little is known, however, about the precise details of the spread of agriculture from region to region.

III. VARIETIES OF AGRICULTURE

The worldwide diffusion of agriculture required adaptation of plants to a variety of local conditions and so led to the domestication of a variety of plants suitable to those conditions. In the Middle East wheat and barley had been the most common crops. But as the farmers moved northward they found that these crops did not do as well as rye, which originally had been a weed sown unintentionally with the wheat and barley. Hence there was a shift to rye in Central Europe and for the same reasons, another shift further north to oats.

Likewise, the extension of agriculture to sub-Saharan Africa led to the cultivation of native millets and of one type of rice, while around the shores of the Mediterranean the olive became one of the most important sources of edible oil. Across the Iranian plateau and in northwest India an essentially Middle Eastern type of agriculture was practiced. But a dividing line running north and south through central India marks the transition to an entirely different climatic zone with correspondingly different plants. This is the monsoon world, with heavy seasonal rainfall, constant heat, and dense jungles. Seed-bearing plants of the Middle Eastern variety, which require plenty of sun, cannot thrive here, so in their place we find the yam, taro, banana, and above all, rice. Finally, in the Americas the main crop everywhere was maize, supplemented by beans and squash in North America and by manioc and potatoes of both the sweet and "Irish" varieties in South America.

The net result of the agriculture diffusion described above was, very generally speaking, three great cereal areas: the rice area in East and Southeast Asia; the maize area in the Americas; and the wheat area in Europe, the Middle East, North Africa, and Central Asia as far as the Indus and Yellow River valleys. During the several millennia between the agricultural and industrial revolutions these three cereals were as fundamental for human history as coal and iron and copper were to become following the industrial revolution.

In regions where there was not enough rainfall for agriculture, the local inhabitants turned to stock raising. They depended on domesticated animals rather than domesticated plants. They became *pastoral nomads,* and many continue today to make their living in this way, roaming the vast steppes and desert lands from the Sahara to Manchuria, and in the broad savannas of sub-Saharan Africa. Pastoral nomadism was late in developing because it had to await the domestication of the horse and camel which provided suitable transport in open country. But once pastoral nomadism got under way, between 1500 and 1000 B.C., a variety of forms developed. Some nomads depended on a single animal—camels in Arabia and cattle in East and South Africa—while those of Central Asia had herds of horses, cattle, camels, sheep, and goats.

Yet regardless of the variety of animals, the pastoral nomads were poor compared to those agrarians who lived in the rich valleys of the Tigris-Euphrates, Nile, Indus, and Yellow rivers. In these valleys, a permanent type of irrigation agriculture was developed that was very productive and came to support great and wealthy civilizations. These valley civilizations were irresistable magnets to the comparatively poverty-stricken nomads of the Central Eurasian steppes and of the deserts of the Middle East and North Africa. Thus Eurasian history to modern times has been in large part the history of the rise and fall of great civilizations, with the pastoral nomads always ready to contribute to the fall of any civilization weakened by internal discord.

IV. LIFE OF THE FOOD GROWERS

The most obvious impact of the agricultural revolution was the new sedentary existence. Humans now had to settle down in order to care for their newly domesticated plants and animals. Thus the Paleolithic nomadic band gave way to the Neolithic village as the basic economic and cultural unit. Indeed the village remained the basis for a pattern of life that was to prevail until the late eighteenth century and that persists to the present day in the vast underdeveloped regions of the world.

It is easy to romanticize Neolithic village life, but to do so would be grossly misleading.

Everyone—men, women, and children—had to work, and work hard, to produce food and a few handicraft articles. Productivity was low since people learned slowly and painfully about soils, seeds, fertilizers, and crop rotation. Despite hard labor, famine was common. It followed upon too much or too little rain, or a plague of pests. Epidemics swept the villages repeatedly as sedentary life introduced the problem of the disposal of human excreta and other wastes. While dogs helped with sanitation and personal modesty presumably caused people to deposit stools away from habitation, neither of these was sufficient to prevent the various diseases that follow the route from the bowel to the mouth. Also, malnutrition was the rule because of inadequate food supply or unbalanced diet. Life expectancy under these circumstances was exceedingly low, but the high birth rate increased village populations everywhere until famine, epidemic, or emigration restored the balance between food supply and number of mouths to feed.

Yet Neolithic village life was not all misery and suffering. This was a time when people made technological progress at an infinitely more rapid rate than in the preceding Paleolithic period. The basic reason was not that they had more leisure time than the hunters, because we have seen that this was not so. Rather, the new sedentary life made a richer material existence physically possible. The living standards of the nomadic hunters were limited to what they could carry, whereas the Neolithic villagers could indulge in substantial housing together with furnishings, utensils, implements, and assorted knick-knacks. They learned to make pottery out of raw clay, at first imitating the baskets, gourds, and other containers of preagrarian times. Gradually they grasped the potentialities of pottery materials and techniques and began to fashion objects that no longer resembled the earlier containers. By the end of the Neolithic period, people in the Near East were building kilns or ovens that could fire pottery at a higher temperature and so allowed for glazing. The glazed surface sealed the pottery and prevented seepage or evaporation. The agriculturist then had vessels that could be used not only for storing grain but also for cooking and for keeping liquids such as oil and beer.

Similar progress was made with textiles. Late Paleolithic peoples may have twisted or spun wild mountain sheep, goat, dog, or other animal fibers into coarse threads and may have woven them to make belts, head bands, or even rough blankets. Indeed they probably also modeled clay into crude containers. But it was during the Neolithic that people developed the textile art. They used fibers of the newly domesticated flax, cotton, and hemp plants and spun and wove the fibers on spindles and looms that had gradually evolved. Neolithic villagers also learned to build permanent dwellings, the materials usually being wood or adobe, depending on local resources and climate.

Sedentary life also made possible a tribal political structure in place of the individual bands of the hunting peoples. *Tribes* were made up of inhabitants of the villages of a given region and were identified and distinguished from others by distinctive characteristics of speech and custom. Some tribes, usually those with primitive economies, were so loosely organized that they were almost at the hunting-band level. Others boasted powerful chiefs and primitive nobilities as distinct from the commoners, though the lines were blurred and never reached the class exclusiveness characteristic of later civilizations.

The basic social unit of the Neolithic village customarily was the household consisting of two or more married couples and their children. This *extended family* was more common than the independent *nuclear family* because it was better suited for coping with the problems of everyday living. If an individual food producer was temporarily or permanently disabled, the extended family could absorb the loss. It could function more efficiently during ''choke'' periods when many hands were needed for clearing forest, harvesting, or pasturing livestock. It could also exploit a large area effectively by sending members for long periods to care for distant gardens or grazing herds, while others tended nearby plots and did household chores.

The distinctive feature of the Neolithic village was *social homogeneity*. All families had the necessary skills and tools to produce what they needed, and, equally important, all had access to the basic natural resources essential for livelihood. Every family was automatically a component part of the village community, which owned the farmlands, pastures, and other resources of nature. Hence there was no division between landed proprietors and landless cultivators in tribal society.

Precisely because of this equality, tribal societies, whether of Neolithic times or today, have a built-in brake on productivity. Output is geared to the limited traditional needs of the family, so there is no incentive to produce a surplus. This in turn means that labor is sporadic, diversified, and correspondingly limited. The daily grind—the eight-hour day, five-day week—is conspicuously absent. The typical Neolithic tribesman worked fewer

LEGEND OF INDIAN CORN

When food gatherers became food producers, they changed their religions as well as their ways of making a living. They also developed new myths dealing with growing crops rather than hunting animals. Typical is the following legend of the Wabanaki of Maine, which narrates how the Indians got their staff of life.*

A long time ago, when Indians were first made, there lived one alone, far, far from any others. He knew not of fire, and subsisted on roots, bark, and nuts. This Indian became very lonesome for company. He grew tired of digging roots, lost his appetite, and for several days lay dreaming in the sunshine; when he awoke he saw something standing near, at which, at first, he was very much frightened. But when it spoke, his heart was glad, for it was a beautiful woman with long *light* hair, very unlike any Indian. He asked her to come to him, but she would not, and if he tried to approach her she seemed to go farther away; he sang to her of his loneliness and besought her not to leave him; at last she told him, if he would do just as she should say, he would always have her with him. He promised that he would. She led him to where there was some very dry grass, told him to get two very dry sticks, rub them together quickly, holding them in the grass. Soon a spark flew out; the grass caught it, and quick as an arrow the ground was burned over. Then she said, "When the sun sets, take me by the hair and drag me over the burned ground." He did not like to do this, but she told him that wherever he dragged her something like grass would spring up, and he would see her hair coming from between the leaves; then the seeds would be ready for his use. He did as she said, and to this day, when they see silk (hair) on the cornstalk, the Indians know she has not forgotten them.

*J. Greenway, *The Primitive Reader* (Hatboro, Pa.: Folklore Associates, 1965; distributed by Gale Research Co.), pp. 34, 35.

hours per year than modern man, and, furthermore, worked at his or her pleasure. The basic reason was that each labored and produced in his or her role as a social person—as a husband or father or brother, a wife or mother or sister, or village member. Work was not a necessary evil tolerated for the sake of making a living; rather it was a concomitant of kin and community relations. One helped one's brother in the field because of kinship ties, and not because one might be given a basket of yams.

The new life of the soil tillers also meant new gods—new religions. The spirits and the magic that had been used by the hunters were no longer appropriate. Now the agriculturists needed, and conceived, spirits who watched over their fields and flocks and hearths. Behind all these spirits stood a creator, usually vaguely conceived. But most important, almost everywhere was a goddess of the earth, or the goddess of fertility—the earth mother. She was the source of productivity of plants and animals, and of the fecundity of women. Life and well-being, the annual cycle of death and rebirth, ultimately depended upon her. Hence the creation of many fertility goddess cults. Such cults were symbolized by the numerous clay figurines with exaggerated female characteristics—pendulous breasts and heavy thighs. They reflect the spread of agriculture from the Middle East, and have been found throughout Europe and as far east as India.

V. DEMOGRAPHIC AND RACIAL RESULTS

We have seen that population increase was responsible for the agricultural revolution, but that revolution in turn caused still more population increase. Many more people can be supported per square mile by growing rather than gathering food. And the impact of this new productivity was dramatic: between 10,000 and 2000 years ago, the human population jumped from 5.32 to 133 million, a 25-fold increase within 8000 years (see Map II, ''World Population Growth'').

Not all the scattered peoples of the earth increased to the same degree. Those that switched to agriculture the earliest, grew the fastest. Those that remained food gatherers were left far behind, and soon were pushed aside by the more numerous food growers. Since early agriculture was not very productive, population pressure soon built up in the villages. The surplus population migrated to nearby fresh lands used by the food gatherers. Sometimes the outnumbered gatherers fled to other lands which were not suitable for farming. This happened in Africa to the Bushmen who ended up in the Kalahari Desert, and to the Pygmies who now live in dense jungles (see Map IV, ''Recession of Hunters,'' and Map V, ''Expansion of Agriculturists'').

More commonly, the agricultural immigrants and the local food gatherers intermarried and produced a new hybrid people. Then as population pressure built up again, the new hybrid population would ''bud-off'' in turn into fresh lands, where further interbreeding would take place with native peoples. In this way agricultural techniques and crops were transmitted long distances, and the people who emerged at the end of the line were of an entirely different racial type from the originals. Thus the immigrants who brought wheat, cattle, the wheel, and the plow into north China were thoroughly Mongoloid, even though these materials originated in the Middle East.

The net result of these migrations, which spread agriculture over the globe, was that by A.D. 1000 the hunters, who 10,000 years ago comprised 100 percent of the human race, had shrunk to little more than 1 percent of the population. This occupational shift led in turn to a racial shift. Ten thousand years ago the race map of the globe showed a rough balance amongst six races—the Caucasoid, Mongoloid, Negroid, Bushman, Pygmy, and Australoid (see Map III, "Global Race Distribution"). By A.D. 1000 this balance was drastically changed in favor of the agriculturist Mongoloids, Caucasoids, and Negroids, and against the Bushmen-Pygmies who had remained food gatherers. The only reason the Australoids held their own was that their isolated island home had not yet been discovered by any agriculturists. This had to wait for the European explorers of the eighteenth century, and when the discovery did take place, belatedly, the consequences were all the more catastrophic for the hapless aborigines. Considering the globe as a whole, then, the racial effect of the agricultural revolution was to end the millennia-old racial equilibrium and to establish the Mongoloid-Caucasoid-Negroid predominance that persists to the present.

SUGGESTED READING

L. R. Binford and S. R. Binford, eds., *New Perspectives in Archeology* (Aldine, 1968); R. J. Braidwood and G. R. Willey, eds., *Courses Toward Urban Life* (Aldine, 1962); M. N. Cohen, *The Food Crisis in Prehistory* (Yale University Press, 1977); Ping-ti Ho, "The Loess and the Origin of Chinese Agriculture," *American Historical Review,* LXXV (October, 1969), pp. 1–36; S. Struever, ed., *Prehistoric Agriculture* (Natural History Press, 1971); P. J. Ucko and G. W. Dimbleby, eds., *The Domestication and Exploitation of Plants and Animals* (Aldine, 1970).

What It Means
For Us Today

THE NATURE OF HUMAN NATURE

The world was surprised and excited in 1971 by the discovery of the Tasaday, a tribe of twenty-seven food-gathering people who had been living in complete isolation on Mindanao Island in the Philippines for at least six centuries. The most striking and significant characteristic found among this small band is their complete lack of aggressiveness. They have no words to describe weapon, hostility, anger, or war. They have eagerly adopted the long Filipino knife, the bolo, because it is superior to their stone tools for gathering food, chopping wood, and slashing through jungle brush. But they have turned down the spear and the bow and arrow because they cannot use them for food gathering. And all of the food they collect (yams, fruit, berries, flowers, fish, crabs, frogs) they divide carefully and equally among all members of the band.

The importance of the Tasaday is that they are food gatherers, as were all human beings before the agricultural revolutions—in other words, for over 80 percent of human history. If, during all those tens of thousands of years, people everywhere were as peaceful as the Tasaday, then we cannot accept the common belief that the species Homo sapiens is innately aggressive.

Unfortunately, at the same time that the world was learning about the Tasaday, another isolated band of thirty people, the Fentou, was discovered in New Guinea. These tribesmen are fierce warriors, continually fighting with bows and arrows. Similar contradictions appeared among the American Indians: the Camanches and Apaches raised their children to be fighters, while the Hopis and Zunis raised theirs for peaceful living—and still do.

So where does this leave us about the nature of human nature? The record of history suggests that human beings are born neither peace loving nor war loving—neither cooperative nor aggressive. What determines how human beings act is not their genes but their society. The psychologist Albert Bandura, who has specialized on this subject, has concluded that human nature is "a vast potentiality that can be fashioned by social influences into a variety of forms. . . . Aggression is not an inevitable or unchangeable aspect of man but a product of aggression—promoting conditions within a society."[1]

This puzzle about human nature represents a life-and-death question for us all. With the development of technology, wars have become more deadly. They have also become more frequent. There were few real wars during the Paleolithic period, which covers most of human history, because the small food-gathering bands of that time could only use so much territory. They had nothing to gain by trying to take over the territory of a neighboring band. In fact, they had everything to lose, because bloody wars might very well have destroyed the human race at a time when so few were scattered about the globe.

All this changed with the agricultural revolution. As agriculture became more productive, populations increased, villages grew into cities, and cities into empires with great palaces and temples and accumulated wealth. Now there was plenty to fight over, and wars became more and more frequent. They also became more and more destructive. Of course, homicidal efficiency grew slowly at first. Not that many people were killed by Roman soldiers with their short swords or by medieval knights in their heavy armor. But during the First World War, 8.4 million military personnel were killed, as well as 1.3 million civilians. During the Second World War the score was even higher: 16.9 million military and 34.3 million civilians dead. And a 1978 Washington study concluded that in a hypothetical Third World War a minimum of 140 million people would be killed in the United States, and 113 million in the Soviet Union.

The important lesson that history teaches is that such wars are *not* inevitable. They have occurred not because of human nature but because of human societies, and human societies can be changed by human beings. The great question is whether future societies will create people like the Tasaday or the Fentou, like the Hopis or the Apaches. The significance of this question is obvious in an age when the weapons of war are nuclear bombs and intercontinental missiles, not bows and arrows.

SELECTED READING

The following authors argue that humans are by instinct aggressive creatures: R. Audrey, *African Genesis* (Atheneum, 1961), and his *Territorial Imperative* (Atheneum, 1966); and also D. Norris, *The Naked Ape* (McGraw-Hill, 1968). The opposite view, that human conduct is molded by social environment rather than genes, is presented in the popular work by M.F.A. Montagu, *The Nature of Human Aggression* (Oxford University Press, 1976), and in the technical work by A. Bandura, *Aggression* (Prentice-Hall, 1973).

Part II

Classical Civilizations Of Eurasia, To A.D. 500

We have seen in Part I that after hominids became humans, their first major achievement was the agricultural revolution. This revolution made it possible for the ancient river valley civilizations to develop in the Tigris-Euphrates, Nile, Indus, and Yellow River valleys. Beginning about 3500 B.C., the ancient civilizations lasted to the second millenium B.C., when they were uprooted by nomadic invaders from the steppes of Central Asia and the deserts of the Middle East. Thus the ancient civilizations gave way to the new classical civilizations which were different in several respects.

One difference was in range. Whereas the ancient civilizations had been confined to river valleys, the classical civilizations expanded outward until they all had contact with one another. Civilizations during the Classical Age, then, stretched without interruption across Eurasia, from the Atlantic to the Pacific Oceans. The classical civilizations were distinctive in content as well as in range. Like the ancient civilizations, each of the classical civilizations developed its special style. Each developed its own social, religious, and philosophical systems that persist to modern times. This creativity, it should be noted, was not limited to the Middle East, as it was at the time of the ancient civilizations. Now, during the centuries of the Classical Age, all regions of Eurasia interacted as equals. All made their distinctive contributions which still affect human beings throughout the globe to the present day.

chapter 3

First Eurasian Civilizations, 3500–1000 B.C.

The first light of civilization dawned on a desert plain scorched by the sun and nourished by two great rivers, the Tigris and the Euphrates. Although at one time it was believed that the Nile valley gave birth to civilization, it is now agreed that the earliest centers were in Sumer, the Old Testament's "land of Shinar." This area comprised the barren, wind-swept plains at the head of the Persian Gulf, in the southern part of what used to be known as Mesopotamia and is now the state of Iraq. About 3500 B.C. certain communities of agriculturists that had developed techniques for cultivating this arid wasteland suc-cessfully completed the transition from Neolithic tribalism to civilization.

The date given is an approximation, and it is pinpointed merely for the sake of conve-nience. In fact, no one year, or decade, or even century, can be specified. We have seen that the shift to food production did not suddenly occur when someone hit upon the idea of agriculture. Likewise the transition to civilization did not happen at the moment that someone had the idea of developing urban centers and urban civilization. What hap-pened, in short, was not an event but a process. The purpose of this chapter is to examine the nature and origins of this process.

I. WHAT CIVILIZATION MEANS

Precisely what do we mean by the term civilization? Anthropologists point to certain characteristics found in civilizations that distinguish them from the preceding Neolithic cultures. They include such characteristics as urban centers, institutionalized political authority in the form of the state, tribute or taxation, writing, social stratification into classes or hierarchies, monumental architecture, and specialized arts and sciences. Not all civilizations have possessed all of these characteristics. The Andean civilization, for example, developed without writing, while the Egyptian and Mayan lacked cities as commonly defined. But this cluster of characteristics does serve as a general guide for defining the attributes of the civilizations that emerged at various times in various parts of the world.

The civilizations that arose were not of a uniform type. Rather there was a striking variety of "styles" of civilization. The earlier Neolithic cultures, as noted in the preceding chapter, represented adaptations to specific environments. Hence they differed markedly according to the balance between cultivation and stock breeding, and the varieties of plants cultivated and of animals bred. So now also the various civilizations differed correspondingly. The degree to which each was distinctly different depended on the degree of isolation in which it developed. Thus the Mayan, Aztec, and Inca civilizations, which emerged independently in the Americas, are clearly distinguishable from those which had taken form earlier in Eurasia. The Eurasian group in turn comprised a diversity of individual civilizations whose distinctiveness depended on their distance from the earliest center of civilization in the Middle East. China, being the most isolated behind desert expanses and mountain barriers, has from earliest times to the present been the most divergent of the Eurasian civilizations.

The next question is why the step to civilization was taken in the first place, particularly where the egalitarian Neolithic society held so many attractions. The answer is suggested by the experience in modern times of the Tanala of Madagascar. Their transition to civilization occurred recently enough so that it has been recorded by the anthropologist Ralph Linton. Before they shifted to civilization, the Tanala cultivated dry rice by the slash-and-burn method. This would give them a good crop the first year, but then the yield would progressively decline. Accordingly, the village moved frequently as the fields became exhausted. This mobility prevented individual ownership of land. The village as a whole owned the fields and the village elders parceled out the land as fairly as possible amongst joint families. The several households in each of these joint families worked together and divided the produce amongst themselves according to need. This was, then, a typical *egalitarian* tribal *society,* with no significant economic, political, or social differentiation.

All this changed when some of the families shifted to wet-rice cultivation in imitation of neighbors to the east. Since the naturally wet lands were very limited in area, the labor force of an entire joint family was not needed, so the new type of farming was carried on by individual families. Each family invested so much year-round labor in its rice terraces that it did not return them to the village for reallocation. And since little land was suitable for wet-rice cultivation, the formerly classless Tanala society was now divided into a small class of landowners and a large majority who could not hope to own the more productive type of land.

Class division became actual physical division because the dry-rice farmers were forced to move periodically to fresh lands, while the wet-rice farmers remained on their plots. Warfare also was affected by the new type of economy. The permanently settled villagers were now willing to spend time and effort to build elaborate fortifications that discouraged the traditional raiding parties. Raiders then turned to the capture of stragglers for use as slaves. Slaves had been of little use for the slash-and-burn agriculture, but now they became important because they could be used for year-round work on the terraces. Also in place of the previous democracy there developed a society with an absolute king at the head, nobles who held land by royal assignment, commoners who formed the bulk of the population, and slaves who were war captives or their descendants. Finally, a new set of social values evolved, with property becoming the only means of enhancing one's ego.

It was a far cry, [concludes the anthropologist Ralph Linton] from the mobile, self-contained Tanala villages with their classless society and strong joint families to the Tanala Kingdom with its central authority, settled subjects, rudimentary social classes based on economic differences, and lineages of little more than ceremonial importance . . . The transformation can be traced step by step and at every step we find irrigated rice at the bottom of the change.[1]

This transformation of the Tanala is a replica in miniature of the process of change that undermined Neolithic society in the Middle East during the fourth millennium B.C. and ended finally in the urban revolution and the rise of civilization.

II. HOW ANCIENT CIVILIZATIONS BEGAN

In the hills above the Tigris-Euphrates early peoples had learned to domesticate plants and animals and so brought about the agricultural revolution. There also they now began their next great adventure when they moved down to the river valley and gradually developed a new and more productive irrigation agriculture and new social institutions. The interaction of the new technology and institutions set off a chain reaction that eventually ended in civilization.

To move to the lowlands presented the Neolithic agriculturists with new problems—inadequate rainfall, searing heat, periodic floods, and lack of stone for building. But there were advantages that more than compensated. There were date palms that provided plentiful food and abundant, though poor wood. There were reedy marshes with wild fowl and game, fish that furnished valuable protein and fat for the diet, and, above all, there was fabulously fertile alluvial soil. The potential of this new environment was challenging, and the pioneer agriculturists successfully met the challenge with a remarkable feat of adaptation. Thus one of the great technological advances occurred during the fourth milennium B.C.

Rainfall was barely sufficient for growing crops in the hilly uplands, but in the valleys below it was severely inadequate. Irrigation was necessary to bring the rich alluvial soils under cultivation, so the pioneer farmers dug short canals leading from the river channels to their fields. The rewards of this extra output in human energy far outweighed the effort, since the crops were incredibly large compared to those that they had previously wrested from the stony hillsides. Documents dating to 2500 B.C. indicate that the average yield on a field of barley was eighty-six times the sowing! Food was now available as never before—more abundant, more varied, and, thanks to irrigation, more assured. The increased food meant increased population, which in turn made it possible to have more irrigation canals, more new fields, and still more food.

While the technique of irrigation was being worked out, the new craft of metallurgy was also being mastered. This was particularly valuable for the valley settlements where flint was unavailable. At first native metals were treated just like tough and malleable stones: worked cold by hammering and grinding. True metallurgy did not begin until people learned how to reduce metals from their ores by smelting. Copper seems to have been the first metal so treated, for it was discovered that when it was heated it became liquid and assumed the shape of any container or mold. As it cooled it hardened and could be given as good a cutting edge as stone. By 3000 B.C. it was widely known in the Middle East and India that a more durable alloy could be produced by adding small quantities of other metals to the copper. Finally they hit on the ideal combination of copper and tin. The resulting bronze was decidedly superior to stone. Bronze was sought after for making weapons, since stone was too brittle to be dependable in battle. But bronze was expensive because of the scarcity of both copper and tin so it wasn't available for general uses, like toolmaking.

Equally significant at this time was the invention of the plow. In the beginning a plow consisted simply of a sapling with one lopped and pointed branch left protruding two-thirds of the way down the trunk. A pair of oxen were yoked to the upper end of the trunk while the plowman steered by the lower end as the protruding branch was dragged through the earth. In the light soils of the semiarid Middle East this primitive contrivance was highly functional. By 3000 B.C. it was widely used in Mesopotamia and Egypt and was being introduced in India; by 1400 B.C. it had reached distant China. The significance of the ox-drawn plow is that for the first time people could use something besides their muscles for motive power. In this sense the plow was the precursor of the steam engine, the internal combustion engine, the electric generator, and the fission reactor.

By 3000 B.C., wind also was being harnessed to supplement human muscles—in this case to furnish power for water transport. Clumsy square sails were used first in the Persian Gulf and then on the Nile River. They represented the first successful use of inorganic force to provide motive power. Crude though the early sail boats were, they offered a far more economic means for heavy transport than pack asses or oxcarts, so that much of the commerce of the ancient civilizations was waterborne.

Another basic invention of this creative *millennium* was the wheel. In the earliest Mesopotamian models, the wheel and axle were fastened together solidly and the wheels were disks. By 3000 B.C., the axle had been fixed to the cart with the wheel left separate and able to revolve freely, and shortly thereafter the spoked wheel appeared. Though these early carts were heavy and clumsy, they were preferable to what was available before—human shoulders and the pack animal, usually the ass. The wheel was also used for war chariots and for the potter's wheel, which made it possible to mass produce pottery.

Far-reaching technological advances went hand in hand with far-reaching institutional changes. The increase in population enabled some of the villages to grow into towns dominated by a new elite of religious, and later military and administrative leaders. The increased productivity of agriculture, with its food surpluses, could now support a growing new class of priests, soldiers, and bureaucrats.

The beginning of the class differentiation that distinguished civilization may be seen in the modest village shrines that were centers of socioreligious life. But there was not yet a full-time priesthood. When the villages grew to towns, the shrines likewise grew to temples with retinues of priests and attendants—the first persons ever to be freed from direct subsistence labor. We can see why the priests became the first elite group when we realize that they were the successors of the earlier tribal shamans. The shamans had been most influential because of the importance of group agricultural ceremonies, such as rain making, for Neolithic farmers. Now the new priesthood bore responsibility not only for the traditional supernatural phenomena but also for the growing managerial functions essential for an increasingly complex society.

The growth of technology and the increasing food surplus had made possible the emergence of the new priestly hierarchies, but the latter in turn contributed to both the technology and the economy. The earliest known examples of writing, which in itself was a priestly invention born of the need for keeping records, tell us that the priesthoods supervised a multitude of economic as well as religious activities. They kept the records necessary for calculating the time of the annual floods. They assumed the vital managerial functions necessary for the proper operation of the growing irrigation facilities, including such tasks as the rationing of water and the construction and maintenance of dams and canals. At this time they also provided the main stimulus for crafts, which were designed mainly for the temples rather than for secular markets.

At this point the growing complexity of society, to which the religious elite had contributed so vitally, began to undermine the position of that elite. The larger and the more complex the towns grew, the more ineffective became purely *religious sanctions*. At the same time warfare was growing in scale and in frequency. This may have been due to the fact that population growth was outstripping agricultural resources, and paradoxically the wealth of the temples themselves may have contributed to the disorders by inviting raids. The outcome was a shift of power from the priesthood to a new secular elite.

Previously, the occasional threat of outside attack had been met by the assembly of the community's adult males who selected a war leader for the duration. But as the intervals of peace became shorter, the tenure of these war leaders became longer, until they were ensconced as permanent military chiefs, and eventually as kings. Thus the palaces came to rival the temples, until a working partnership was evolved. The priests normally retained their great landholdings and continued their sacred services, while the palace officials constructed walls around their cities and raised large armies, which they employed against neighboring cities and, eventually, for empire building.

One effect of this rise of *secular states* and empires was a great increase in the output of nonagricultural commodities. The mass production of pottery, the prevalence of metal utensils, and the hordes of assorted objects found in some of the more substantial houses, all suggest a new and significant middle-class market. Also, a great quantity of luxury commodities was absorbed by the growing palace retinues. In addition, increasing militarization required armaments on an unprecedented scale. The armies needed not only metal weapons and armor but also more elaborate equipment such as chariots. All this was a far cry from the relatively limited production of earlier times when crafts were geared mainly to meeting temple needs. But it is important to note that this change was almost exclusively in volume rather than in technique. What was new was the mass production, not a stylistic or technological innovation.

Mass production had important implications for foreign affairs. Most of the crafts were dependent on raw materials brought from the outside, since the lowlands were almost totally lacking in minerals and quality timber. Copper, for example, came from Oman, south of the Persian Gulf, silver and lead from the Taurus Mountains in Asia Minor, and timber from the Zagros Mountains of Iran and from Lebanon on the Mediterranean coast. In order to pay for such imports, the various crafts had to expand production and to provide exports in exchange. The alternative was to conquer the sources of the needed raw materials. This alternative was not overlooked as is evident from the career of Sargon, King of Akkad, in the middle of the third millennium B.C. An epic poem, "The King of Battle," describes how Sargon led his army across unknown mountain passes into the heart of Asia Minor in support of Akkadian merchants who were being maltreated by the local ruler. Eventually Sargon's empire extended "from the Lower to the Upper Sea"—from the Persian Gulf to the Mediterranean—and he thereby controlled the sources of metals, stone, and timber.

The combined cost of the military and palace establishments was so expensive for the early city-states that it undermined the traditional assemblies. They balked against the onerous levies necessary to meet the rising expenditures. As a result, the assemblies were increasingly bypassed and replaced by permanent, hereditary royal authority.

The centralization of political power led to increased *class differentiation.* We can see the growing differentiation in the differences in grave offerings. During the early period the disparity was minimal, but the more time passed, the more pronounced it became. The great majority of the graves had only a few pottery vessels or nothing at all, reflecting the poverty of the commoners. Those of the well-to-do exhibited "conspicuous consumption" in the form of copper vessels and beads of precious metal. The royal tombs, by contrast, were luxuriously furnished with beautifully wrought weapons and precious ornaments, and included large numbers of palace attendants—men-at-arms, harem ladies, musicians, charioteers, and general servants—who were sacrificed in order to accompany the royal occupant and attest to his power and wealth.

III. HOW ANCIENT CIVILIZATIONS SPREAD

Such is the story of the millennia-long evolution from autonomous farm villages to small *theocratically-controlled states,* and finally to dynastic empires with all of the attributes of civilization as we have defined it above.

Once civilization took root in Mesopotamia and later in the several other regions of Eurasia and the New World, it spread out in all directions. Just as the agricultural revolution had replaced hunting societies with tribal ones, so now the tribal societies in turn were replaced by civilization. By the time tribalism had reached the boundaries of Eurasia, it was being superseded in its core areas. The displacement process continued inexorably as civilization spread out of the original river valleys and across adjacent uncivilized areas, until by the time of Christ it extended with virtually no interruption from the English Channel to the China Sea (see Map VI, "Ancient Civilizations of Eurasia, 3500–1500 B.C.").

If 3500 B.C. is accepted as the approximate date for the emergence of civilization in Mesopotamia, then corresponding dates may be given for the other centers of civilization: in Egypt, about 3000 B.C.; in the Indus valley, about 2500 B.C.; in the Yellow River valley of China, about 1500 B.C.; and in Mesoamerica and Peru, about 500 B.C. These dates are rough estimates and are constantly being revised as new findings are made. Indeed, radiocarbon dating, on which much prehistoric chronology has been based, has been found recently to be off by several centuries. Hence some scholars now question the traditional assumption that culture spread from the Eastern Mediterranean to Western Europe.

The New World civilizations, like New World agriculture, are believed to have developed independently of any Eurasian influences. Whether the beginnings of Chinese civilization were indigenous or stimulated indirectly from the Middle East cannot be answered at present. In the Nile and Indus valleys, civilization got under way as a result of stimulus diffusion from Mesopotamia. *Stimulus diffusion* means that it was not specific techniques and institutions that were adopted, but rather the underlying ideas or principles. For example, the idea of writing was taken from Sumer, but distinctive writing systems were evolved in Egypt and India; likewise with state organization, monumental architecture, and so forth. This is the traditional diffusionist view, but again we should note that it is now being questioned. Some scholars, for example, now believe that the Minoan-Mycenaean civilization of prehistoric Greece emerged independently of Mesopotamian or Egyptian influences.

Whatever the precise sequence, the end result was several civilizations that shared a common general pattern but that nevertheless had their own distinctive characteristics or styles. These styles gradually took form and crystallized during long millennia of autonomous development, so that to a considerable degree they persist to the present day.

IV. STYLES OF ANCIENT CIVILIZATIONS

Mesopotamia

The style of the pioneer civilization of Mesopotamia was urban. The first center was at Sumer, which by 3000 B.C. consisted of twelve separate city-states. The cities fought each other continually, so that they were easily conquered by Indo-European invaders from the north and Semitic invaders from the south. Indeed the history of Mesopotamia was in large part a centuries-long struggle between the Indo-European and Semitic invaders for control of the fertile river valley.

The first great empire builder was the Semite, Sargon the Great (c. 2276–2221 B.C.), whose conquests stretched from Akkad in the middle of the valley, to the Persian Gulf in the south and the Mediterranean in the West. Another empire builder was also a Semite, Hammurabi (c. 1704–1662 B.C.), who, as we shall see, is most famous for his law code. This pattern of successive invasions continued to modern times, with Hammurabi followed by Hittites, Assyrians, Persians, Macedonians, Romans, Arabs, and Turks.

Despite the parade of empires, the cities remained the basic units of ancient Mesopotamia. Most citizens earned their livelihood as farmers, craftsmen, merchants, fishermen, and cattle breeders. Each city had a section reserved for the craftsmen—the masons, smiths, carpenters, potters, and jewelers. They sold their handicrafts in a free town market and were paid in kind or in money that consisted of silver ingots or rings which were weighed after each transaction.

Outside the city walls were the fields upon which the urban inhabitants were dependent. Most of the land was held in the form of large estates that belonged to the king or the priests or other wealthy persons. The workers on these estates were allotted individual plots along with seed, implements, and draft animals. In return they provided the labor and, through a variety of arrangements, gave their surplus produce to the temple or palace or landowner. The basic crops were barley and wheat; the milk animals were goats and cows; sheep supplied the wool that was the chief textile fabric of Mesopotamia. The most common vegetables were beans, peas, garlic, leeks, onions, radishes, lettuce, and cucumbers; the fruits included melons, dates, pomegranates, figs, and apples.

The management of the estates required keeping the accounts of the rents received from the tenant farmers, the size of the herds, the amount of fodder needed for the animals and of seed for the next planting, and the intricate details regarding irrigation facilities and schedules. Management and accounting records were inscribed with a reed stylus on clay tablets that were then baked in order to preserve them. This earliest form of writing, known as *cuneiform,* was obviously invented as an instrument of administration, not for intellectual or literary purposes.

At first the cuneiform consisted of *pictographs,* so that the scribe drew simplified pictures of oxen, sheep, grain, fish, or whatever was being recorded. Soon the pictographs were conventionalized rather than being left to the artistic fancy of each scribe. This assured uniform writing and reading of records, but a basic problem remained; pictographs could not be used to depict abstract concepts. Sumerian scribes met this difficulty by adding marks to the pictographs to denote new meanings, and, more important, by selecting signs that represented sounds rather than objects or abstractions. This was the essence of the phonetic alphabet that was evolved centuries later, but the Sumerians failed to apply the phonetic principle systematically and comprehensively. They reduced their signs from an original number of about two thousand to some six hundred by 2900 B.C. This was a substantial improvement, but cuneiform remained far more cumbersome than the alphabet developed later by the Phoenicians and the Greeks. Hence there was a need for scribes, since they alone had mastered the difficult art of writing and therefore enjoyed high status and privilege.

Although the origins of writing are to be found in the new circumstances arising from the production of economic surplus, it had other far-reaching and fateful effects. It stimulated intellectual development because factual data could now be collected, recorded, and passed along to successive generations. Equally significant, writing helped to define and consolidate individual cultures. It gave permanent written form to religious traditions, which thereby became sacred books, to social customs, which became law codes, and to oral myths and stories, which became classics. Thus writing became the chief means for the cultural integration of the various civilizations.

The Sumerians developed sciences and mathematics, as well as writing, in response to the concrete needs of their increasingly complex society. Their earliest mathematical documents were accounts of flocks, measures of grain, and surveys of fields. Their chief contribution was the development of the first systems for measuring time, distance, area, and quantity. Also, as early as 3000 B.C., they were carefully studying and recording the movements of heavenly bodies, and their motive again was utilitarian. They believed that the will of the gods determined celestial movements, and that knowledge of those movements would enable their people to know the divine will and act accordingly. Thus Mesopotamian astrologers in the course of many centuries accumulated an enormous amount of data that later was used to develop scientific astronomy.

The religious beliefs of the Sumerians and their successors were profoundly affected by their physical environment, and particularly by the annual flooding of the Tigris-Euphrates. The coincidence of heavy rains in the northern areas and deep snow in the Zagros and Taurus mountains frequently produced disastrous floods that devastated farmlands instead of filling irrigation canals. Fear of the annual floods, together with the ever-present danger of outside invasion, left the Sumerians with a deep feeling of helplessness in a world of uncontrollable forces. ''Mere man—his days are numbered,'' reads a Sumerian poem, ''whatever he may do, he is but wind.''

The Mesopotamian view of life was tinged with an apprehension and pessimism reflecting the insecurity of the physical environment. Humans, it was felt, had been made only to serve the gods, whose will and acts were unpredictable. Hence a variety of techniques were employed to foresee the uncertain future. One was the interpretation of diverse omens, and especially dreams. Another was hepatoscopy or divination by inspecting the livers of slaughtered animals. Still another was astrology, which, as already noted, involved the study of the planets for their imagined influence upon, or predictions about the destinies of individuals. Finally, each person had his or her personal god as a sort of private mentor. Through this personal god, one could make one's wishes and needs known to the great gods who were much too remote for direct communication.

The Mesopotamians also sought to ease the insecurity prevailing between one person and another by compiling detailed codes of law. The most outstanding of these was that of Hammurabi, which tried to regulate all social relationships, clearly and for all time. The code sheds as much light upon the society it regulated as it does upon the legal system of ancient Babylon. The following are some of its typical features:

1. The application of the principle of an eye for an eye, a tooth for a tooth: "If a man has knocked out the eye of a patrician, his eye shall be knocked out. If he has broken the limb of a patrician, his limb shall be broken." (*Laws* 196, 197)

2. Class discrimination, so that the lower orders received less compensation: "If a man has smitten the privates of a patrician of his own rank, he shall pay one mina of silver. If the slave of anyone has smitten the privates of a freeborn man, his ear shall be cut off." (*Laws* 203, 205)

3. The strict requirement of a business society that property be safeguarded: "If a man has stolen goods from a temple, or house, he shall be put to death; and he that has received the stolen property from him shall be put to death." (*Law* 6)

4. The multitude of "welfare state" provisions, including annual price fixing for basic commodities, limitation of interest rate to 20 percent, minute regulation of family relationships, assurance of honest weights and measures, and responsibility of the city for indemnifying victims of unsolved robbery or murder. "If the highwayman has not been caught, the man that has been robbed shall state on oath what he has lost and the city or district governor in whose territory or district the robbery took place shall restore to him what he has lost." "If a life [has been lost], the city or district governor shall pay one mina of silver to the deceased relatives." (*Laws* 23, 24)

5. A static view of the past, present, and future, typical of premodern peoples. Thus the code is presented as part of the divine order for the benefit of mankind under justice, and any later ruler who dares alter the code is colorfully and explicitly cursed: "a reign of sighing, days few in number, years of famine, darkness without light, sudden death, . . . the destruction of his city, the dispersion of his people, the transfer of his kingdom, the extinction of his name and memory from the land . . . his ghost [in the underworld] is to thirst for water." (*Laws,* Epilogue)

Egypt

The style of Egypt's civilization, in contrast to Mesopotamia's, was imperial rather than urban. It was a united river valley ruled by long-lasting dynasties. The main reason for the security and continuity was the geography of the country. The Nile valley is well protected against foreign invasion by the Libyan Desert on the west, the Arabian Desert in the east, the Nubian Desert and the cataracts on the south, and the harborless coast of the Delta on the north. The Egyptian people were left free in their sheltered valley to work out their own destiny without interference from the outside. There was not the constant rise and fall of empires, as there was in Mesopotamia because of foreign invaders. Also the Nile River provided a natural cohesion that held the entire valley together as a stable and functioning unit. Its slow but steady current carried northbound traffic effortlessly, while the prevailing north-to-northwest winds made the return trip almost as simple. Thus the Egyptians were provided with a priceless means for reliable communication and transportation that helped to unify the valley about 3100 B.C.

During the twenty-five hundred years between the unification in 3100 B.C. and the conquest of the country by the Persians in 525 B.C., only three empires ruled Egypt. The intervening periods between the three empires were comparatively short. The civilization of Egypt therefore was stable and conservative. It was also a confident and optimistic civilization, partly because the Nile was gentle and predictable compared to the Tigris-Euphrates with its devastating and unpredictable floods. Whereas the Mesopotamians regarded their flood god as harsh and merciless, the Egyptians viewed theirs as a god "whose coming brings joy to every human being."

A predominant feature of Egyptian religious belief concerned death and the physical preparations for the afterlife, especially that of the king. Since his death was not final, his body was embalmed and placed in a gigantic tomb or pyramid, along with food and other necessities. The greatest of these pyramids was that of the Pharaoh Khufu, or Cheops. It covered 13 acres, rose to a height of 481 feet, and contained some 2.3 million blocks, each weighing an average of 2.5 tons. And this was done with the simplest tools—ramps, rollers, and levers; no pulleys and no iron!

It has been said that the Egyptian peasants worked enthusiastically on these pyramids, believing that they were constructing the dwellings of a god on whom their collective well-being would depend. Whatever the justification for this statement—and it may be assumed that, enthusiastic or not, they had little choice in the matter—it does point up the supposed divinity of Egyptian kingship. From beginning to end the pharaoh was a god-king. No distinction was made between the sacred and the secular; indeed the notion was unthinkable. So there was an absence in Egypt of anything corresponding to the Mesopotamian law codes. All law was the expression of the divine authority of the god-king.

Royal authority was enforced by a bureaucracy headed by the vizier—"the steward of the whole land," "the eyes and ears of the king." Other officials included the Royal Sealbearer, who controlled the Nile traffic, the Master of Largesse, who was responsible for all livestock, and the head of the Exchequer, who maintained branch offices and storehouses throughout the kingdom for the collection of taxes. In bad years, the head of the Exchequer probably also took care of the distribution of seeds and livestock. There were governors or monarchs to rule each province, or nome, and below them came the mayors of the towns and villages.

A final distinctive feature of Egyptian civilization was the overwhelming state domination of economic life. Individual property and enterprise were not unknown, but neither were they as common as in Mesopotamia. The state not only controlled most production, both agricultural and handicraft, but also directed distribution. Huge government warehouses and granaries were filled with the taxes collected in kind—grains, animals, cloths, and metals. These were used for state expenses and also provided reserves for years of scarcity. The king, it was said, is "he who presides over the food supplies of all." In addition to the taxes, each community had to provide men for the *corvée*, or forced labor. The pyramids are the best known examples of their work, but these laborers were also used for quarrying and mining and maintaining the irrigation canals.

Egyptian craftsmen were universally recognized for their skills, particularly in luxury products. Their jewelry can scarcely be excelled today; their enamel work and ivory and pearl inlay were superb; they discovered how to make glass in many colors; they were the first to bark-tan leather in the manner still followed in most of the world; and their linen cloth was as fine as has ever been woven. Egyptian technology was very advanced in creating artificial beauty aids. Papyri were written to describe medical procedures for removing wrinkles and darkening gray hair. Among the substances used for cosmetic purposes were kohl for lengthening the eyebrows and lining the outer corners of the eyes, malachite and lead ore for green and gray eye shadow respectively, red ocher for rouge, henna for dyeing the nails, the palms of the hand and the soles of the feet, and human hair for making wigs over which melted beeswax was poured. Ladies who wished to be in the height of fashion gilded their breasts and painted their nipples blue.

Crete

The style of the Minoan civilization of the island of Crete is summed up by the Greek word *thalassocracy,* or sea civilization. The prosperity of Crete depended on its trade with countries from one end of the Mediterranean to the other. The storms in the landlocked Mediterranean are not as fierce as in the open Atlantic, so Cretan merchants could sail, almost always in sight of land, to all the countries on the Mediterranean Sea. Also the mountains of Crete were covered with forests, which provided timber for building the single-masted trading ships. In these ships the Minoans carried back and forth the foodstuffs, ivory, and glass of Egypt, the horses and wood of Syria, the silver, pottery, and marble of the Aegean Isles, the copper of Cyprus, and their own olive oil and pottery.

This trade affected all aspects of the Minoan civilization. None of the cities were fortified because Minoan sea power was strong enough to protect the island. Cretan communities seem to have been socially and economically more egalitarian than their counterparts on the mainland. In place of a few great temples and palaces surrounded by relative slums, the pattern on Crete was the open village, with its outdoor shrine as the center for community life. Families as a rule lived in individual houses built of timber and stucco. Domestic slaves probably were held, though not in large numbers. No buildings that may have been slave quarters have been found, so that the Cretan galleys presumably were rowed by freemen.

Minoan artists did not try to impress by mere size, nor did they concern themselves with remote and awful deities or divine kings. Instead they reproduced the life about them on their household utensils, on the walls of their houses, and in their works of art. They found models everywhere: in natural objects such as birds, flowers, sea shells, and marine life of all types; and in scenes from their own everyday life, such as peasants returning from their fields, athletes wrestling with bulls, and women dancing in honor of the Great Goddess. In architecture the Minoans were more interested in personal comfort than outward appearance. The royal palace at Knossos was a sprawling complex that apparently had grown over several centuries. It included not only a throne room, reception chambers, and living quarters, but also storehouses and workshops that occupied most of the complex, as befitted a trading people. Outstanding was an elaborate plumbing and sanitation system that was not surpassed until modern times. The drains were arranged so that the rain water flushed the sewers and kept them clean, and manholes enabled workmen to enter the sewers for repairs.

Women appear to have enjoyed a freedom and social status equal to that of men. Frescoes show them crowding the bleachers at the bull arena and actually participating in the bull wrestling. Some even took part in war, in contrast to the feminine homebodies of Mesopotamia and Egypt, and, for that matter, of classical Greece.

Indus

The style of the civilization in the Indus River valley was conservative, religious, and highly planned. We can see this in the cities which were carefully built according to a common design. Each city at its height extended over six to seven square miles. Each was laid out on the grid pattern, with wide main streets encompassing large rectangular city blocks some four hundred yards in length and two hundred yards in width, far larger than the average city blocks of today. The buildings were constructed of bricks hardened in kilns, in contrast to the stone used in Egypt and the sundried bricks in Mesopotamia. The bricks everywhere were molded in two standard sizes (11 by 5.5 by 2.5 inches, and 9.2 by 4.5 by 2.2 inches), and weights and measures likewise were uniform throughout the Indus lands. Such orderliness and organization seem to have been all pervasive in this civilization. After it reached its maturity about 2500 B.C., it remained virtually static during the following millennium. Even when cities were destroyed by floods the new cities were built to duplicate the old. Such undeviating continuity of tradition has had no equal, even in Egypt, and has given rise to the theory that the authority regulating this disciplined society may have been spiritual. This hypothesis is supported also by the absence of military equipment and fortifications.

Like all the other ancient civilizations, that of the Indus was predominantly agricultural. Wheat and barley were the staples, but field peas, melons, sesame, and dates were also grown, as well as cotton, which was first used for cloth making in this valley. There was also considerable trade with the outside world, the items exported including peacocks, apes, pearls, cotton textiles, copper, ivory, and ivory articles such as combs. Combs were fashioned in the same pattern as those still used in India today, and still indispensable for combing lice out of the hair. Most foreign trade was with Mesopotamia and was carried on with sailing boats that followed the coast to the Persian Gulf. If their ships were driven out of sight of land, the sailors released crows that always flew toward the nearest point of coast. According to the Bible, this is precisely the method followed by Noah in the Ark, when he wished to find out where the land lay.

The causes and circumstances of the decline of the Indus civilization remains obscure. Hitherto it has been widely believed that Aryan invaders who came down from Central Asia about 1500 B.C., were primarily responsible. But it has recently been suggested that the civilization may have been literally drowned in mud. Subterranean volcanic activity, according to this theory, caused a huge upswelling of mud, silt, and sand that dammed the river and formed a huge lake that swamped the capital, Mohenjo-daro. After several decades the dam was worn down, the water drained through, and the river resumed its normal course, but in the meantime the city had been ruined. Judging from the multiple layers of silt found in Mohenjo-daro, some such disaster occurred at least five times and perhaps more. The net result was irreparable damage to the heart of the Indus civilization, which left the outlying regions in the north too weak to resist assimilation by native cultures.

Much of this is guesswork and cannot be proven because the Indus script has not yet been deciphered. The script is pictographic and is read from left to right on one line and from right to left on the following line. This is the practice followed in Early Greek and is known as boustrophedon—"as the ox plows."

Shang

The style of the Shang civilization of the Yellow River of north China was the most different from all the other Eurasian civilizations. To the present day, Chinese civilization is the most distinctive and unique of all major civilizations, and the main reason is the geographic isolation of the country. China is located at the eastern tip of Eurasia, separated from the rest of the continent by great mountains, deserts, and steppes.

Although China was isolated it was not completely cut off from outside influences. The founders of the Shang dynasty about 1500 B.C. were a small group of Mongoloid invaders from the northwest steppes. They were able to conquer north China because they had gotten, indirectly from the Middle East, a knowledge of bronze and of war chariots. Using this military technology, they became the masters of the scattered Neolithic communities of north China. But now the same thing happened to the Shang as did to the many other later invaders of China. Because of the great numbers of the Chinese people, the Shang were assimilated, and people remained distinctively Chinese. But China was enriched by elements from the Middle East, such as barley, wheat, sheep, cattle, horses, bronze, and the wheel. These innovations did not change China fundamentally. Whereas the ancient Egyptian civilization has long since disappeared, and likewise the ancient civilizations of Mesopotamia and the Indus, by contrast China's civilization continued uninterrupted. Today China can boast the oldest continuous civilization.

China's civilization is not only the oldest, but also the most unique. It was the first to raise silkworms and to weave their delicate fibers into fine silk cloth. It was the only major civilization which did not use animal milk and milk products for human consumption. Indeed the Chinese had the same reaction towards animal milk as Westerners did towards eating worms and ants. Also ancestor worship was a prominent and unique feature of Chinese religion from earliest times. Closely related was the importance attached to one's family name, which always preceded the personal name instead of following it as in the West. This custom reflected the traditional primary role in Chinese society of the family rather than of the individual, the state, or the church. The familiar Chinese style of architecture with the ornate roof supported by rows of wooden pillars also dates back to earliest times, as does the use of chopsticks rather than forks and spoons. Most significant for the later history of China and all East Asia was the complex *ideographic script* found in Shang remains. This is the direct ancestor of modern Chinese writing, illustrating again the continuity of Chinese civilization. For millennia, the hieroglyphics and cuneiform have meant nothing to the people of the Middle East, but the Shang script is recognizable to modern Chinese.

As with the other Eurasian civilizations, the peasants were required to yield a portion of their crops to support the nobles, scribes, and officials gathered in the towns. Also they were obliged to serve under their lords in time of war as a light-armed infantry. Only the ruling warrior class could afford the two-horse chariots and the bronze helmets and plate mail that they wore into battle. The monopoly of bronze metallurgy by the ruling class enhanced the sharp class differentiation within Shang society. The gap is reflected in the contrast between the elaborate palaces and royal tombs on the one hand, and the crude pit dwellings of the common people on the other. It shows also in the costly offerings that were placed in the tombs—bronze ritual vessels, fine silks, jades, marbles, musical instruments, and elaborate weapons.

V. NOMADS GAIN POWER

During the second millenium B.C., all the ancient civilizations collapsed, whether in the Middle East or India or far-off China. Was it internal rot or external force that was primarily responsible for political and social demolition throughout Eurasia? It is hard to answer such a broad question with certainty and precision. We cannot determine exactly the relative importance of internal and external factors in the several regions involved. But it is certain that both were important in determining the course of events.

Beginning with the internal weaknesses, there was first the scarcity and costliness of copper and bronze, which prevented their general use in making weapons and tools. Hence monarchs and their political and military allies had a virtual monopoly of armaments and so strengthened their privileged position at the top of the social pyramid. But this meant that only a small percentage of the total population was armed, a serious weakness when the old centers of civilization had to face the assault of nomads who were all armed. The high cost of copper and bronze also deprived the peasantry of metal tools, and perforce they had to rely on stone axes and hoes, and on flint knives and sickles. Since stone tools were less efficient and durable than metal, productivity was reduced.

TRIBESMEN AND PEASANTS

One of the costs of civilization was the division of people into rulers and ruled. This was discovered by Dutch officials in New Guinea. The Papuan tribesmen of that island country, who had never known civilization, refused to bow and scrape because they considered themselves to be free men. But the Indonesian peasants who had lived in a class society were ready to accept the Dutch as masters. The following report by an American correspondent reveals how civilization affected relations amongst human beings.*

A Dutch official walked into an office in Hollandia [New Guinea]. Seated at a table were an Indonesian official, still in the Netherland's service, and two Papuan village headmen. The Indonesian jumped to his feet and stood still. The Papuans looked up, smiled and remained seated.

In the bar of a grimy Government hotel, about 9 o'clock one night, a Dutch official asked the Papuan bartender for a beer. The bartender, after five minutes, produced it. He also produced a pointed look at a wristwatch and asked the Dutchman how long he intended to stay.

A Dutch destroyer pulled into a south New Guinea coastal port. Local Dutch officials thought it would be a good idea to show some people from the jungles, still in the head-hunting stage, some real weapons.

Jungle people trekked down, wandered about the ship, and one of them gave the verdict:

Weakened by this rot inside, the ancient civilizations were easy targets for the nomads outside. Three principal nomadic groups did the work of empire smashing: the Semitic tribesmen in the southern deserts, the Indo-Europeans in the Eurasian steppes to the west, and to the east the Mongol-Turkish peoples.

The Indo-Europeans, a cultural rather than a racial group, appear to have originated in the region of the Caspian Sea where they tended their herds of cattle and did a little farming on the side. Primarily pastoralists, they were ever ready to pack their belongings into their great oxcarts and move on to more promising lands. Entire tribes participated in these migrations—women and children as well as the warriors. Thus they pushed westward to southern Russia and southeastern Europe, so that by 2000 B.C. they ranged in the broad belt from the Danubian Plain to the Oxus and Jaxartes valleys. From this far-flung base they increasingly threatened the centers of civilization that were geographically accessible to them—the Middle East, the Balkan peninsula, and the Indus valley.

The original dividing line between the Indo-European peoples in the western part of the steppes and the Mongol-Turkish in the eastern part consisted of the Altai and the Tien Shan mountains. To the east of this line the steppes are higher and drier, and the climate generally harsher. The pastures here are not as rich as in the west and can support sheep, camels, and horses, but not cattle. The discrepancy between the relatively poor eastern and the richer western geographic areas explains why the peoples of the eastern steppes were attracted to the west, both as refugees and as conquerors. A succession of tribes followed one upon the other—Scythians migrated from the Altai to the Ukraine. Turkish tribes replaced them in Central Asia but later followed them westward. Finally the Mongols kept pushing from the rear until they erupted in the thirteenth century and overran most of Eurasia. These eastern nomads, because of their geographic location, had access not only to Europe, the Middle East, and India, but also to China, where they broke through periodically when the opportunity presented itself.

Because of the East-to-West migrations, the racial composition of the peoples of the western steppes gradually changed from predominantly Caucasoid to predominantly Mongoloid, at least as far west as the Caspian Sea. The racial shift began in the first millennium B.C. and continued until the end of the medieval period. Then the tide was reversed by the Slavic Russians who were armed with the weapons and transport of Western technology—muskets and cannon at first, and later machine guns and railroads.

Finally the Semites occupied roughly the area from the Mediterranean to the Tigris and from the Taurus to Aden. Successive waves have appeared through history, emerging apparently from the deserts of Arabia. They used the donkey for transportation until about 1100 B.C., when the domestication of the camel transformed their culture as the domestication of the horse did that of the steppe nomads. With the rise of civilization many Semitic tribes lived on the edges of the cities, with the urban dwellers, but were always ready to seize any chance for raid and plunder.

The old centers of civilization on the periphery of Eurasia were irresistible magnets for the surrounding tribespeople. The abundant crops, the barns swollen with grain, and the dazzling luxuries of the cities, all beckoned to the hungry nomads of steppes and deserts. Hence the periodic raids and invasions, particularly of the Mesopotamian cities, which were more vulnerable than those of Crete or the Nile or the Indus.

It was not until the second millennium B.C. that the balance of power throughout Eurasia shifted, and for the first time the nomads threatened the very existence of the great civilizations. The new military capabilities of the nomads rose from two fateful developments—the domestication of the horse, and, later, the smelting of iron. So far as is known, the earliest domestication of animals took place in the Middle East, where people first learned to ride animals. Both these events took place about 5000 B.C., but there was little riding at that early date for the simple reason that the only animals available were the ox, which was too slow, and the onager, or wild ass, which was too small. The practice of animal domestication, however, spread northward to southern Russia where both the onager and the wild horse were to be found. These two animals were domesticated there by 2500 B.C., and soon the horse became favored because it was larger, stronger, and faster. Furthermore, with selective breeding the horse gradually increased in size. A wild horse averages 13 hands (a hand equals 4 inches), whereas a modern domestic horse averages 15 to 16 hands. When allowed to breed indiscriminately for a few generations, domestic horses soon return to a smaller size, as illustrated by the mustang of the American West.

The first military use that the nomads made of their horse was to harness it to a light-bodied chariot with two spoked wheels, which they developed as an improvement on the clumsy Mesopotamian cart with four solid wheels. The combination of the large horse and easily maneuverable chariot gave the nomads a formidable weapon—the war chariot. The first wave of nomadic invasions in the second millennium B.C. were invasions of charioteers. They rode hard into battle with one warrior in the chariot in charge of the horses and the others shooting arrows from their powerful compound bows. Few infantrymen could stand up for long to the volleys of arrows, let alone to the massed chariot charges that followed.

Towards the end of the second millennium the nomads further increased their military effectiveness by shifting from chariot to cavalry warfare. Their horses were now large and strong enough to bear the direct weight of the rider. Also the nomads developed the bridle and bit for guiding the horse, and the horned saddle and stirrup, which enabled them to ride with both hands free and to launch a shower of arrows at full gallop. Hence the Eurasian nomads had unprecedented mobility, and were able to outride and outfight armies defending the urban centers. The riding process was the basis of nomadic military power through the Classical and Medieval ages, and culminated in the extraordinary conquests of Genghis Khan in the thirteenth century. The centers of civilization were under constant threat of nomadic invasion until superior Western firearms were brought to bear.

The counterpart of the horse for the desert nomad was the camel. There were two varieties—the one-humped Arabian, which is adapted to hot desert conditions, and the two-humped Bactrian relative, which is adapted to cold desert conditions. Both can live off land where even the ass would starve, and both can go for weeks on fat stored in their humps and on water stored in their multiple stomachs. Where and when the camel was first tamed is not clear, but by 1000 B.C. transportation and communication across the deserts of Central Asia and the Middle East were dependent on the "ship of the desert."

The discovery of the technique for smelting iron ore also enhanced nomadic military strength. The technique was developed in the middle of the second millenium B.C. in northeast Asia Minor. But it was not until the destruction of the Hittite Empire about 1200 B.C. that the local ironsmiths became scattered over wider areas and their technique became generally known. Iron ore, in contrast to copper and tin, is very widespread and correspondingly cheap. Ordinary peasants could now afford iron tools. Agricultural productivity rose as fields were extended into heavily wooded areas that previously resisted the old stone axe. Equally significant was the effect of the cheap new metal on the Eurasian military balance. Up to now the poverty-stricken nomads had not been able to afford as many of the expensive bronze weapons as could the rulers of the urban centers. But now iron ore was available in almost every region, and every village smith could forge new weapons that were both superior to, and cheaper than, the old. Thus nomadic warriors now enjoyed not only superior mobility but also iron weapons that were as good and as plentiful as those of the soldiers guarding the civilized areas.

VI. NOMADS DESTROY ANCIENT CIVILIZATIONS

With their horses and iron weapons, the nomads launched two great waves of invasion that overwhelmed the centers of civilization. During the first, between roughly 1700 and 1500 B.C., the invaders usually arrived with horse-drawn chariots and bronze weapons; by the second wave, between about 1200 and 1100 B.C., they commonly rode on horses and fought with iron weapons. These invasions were not vast incursions of hordes that displaced native stock and completely changed ethnic patterns. Instead there were rather small numbers of invaders who used their superior military technology to establish themselves as military elites ruling over subject peoples that far outnumbered them.

The end result was the uprooting of civilization everywhere except in the Middle East. Empires rose and fell in rapid succession. But civilization in the Middle East, because of its geographic accessibility, endured the largest number of invasions and survived, with its cities, palaces, temples, scribes, merchants, and government officials. One reason was that civilization had been established for a longer period in the Middle East and had sunk deeper roots. Also such large expanses of the Middle East had become civilized by 1700 B.C. that they could not all be overwhelmed and destroyed. Finally, invaders in the Middle East usually were not raw barbarians fresh from the steppes or desert, but rather semicivilized barbarians who had settled earlier in surrounding lands and who consequently were already partially assimilated by the time of conquest.

Middle East

Considering first the Middle East, the invasions began there about 2000 B.C. when the Indo-European Hittites filtered into Asia Minor. Together with the native peoples, the Hittites organized a large empire, including Asia Minor and much of Syria, though not Mesopotamia. The Hittites were followed by two other Indo-European invaders, the Kassites and the Hurrians. Even well-protected Egypt was overrun by a mixed, though mostly Semitic group of invaders, the Hyksos. By 1500 B.C. the first wave of invasions ended, leaving the Middle East controlled by the three major powers: the Hittites in the north, the Egyptians in the south, and the Semitic Assyrians in the east.

This triangular balance was upset by the second wave of invasions which began about 1200 B.C. A long series of wars between the Hittites and Egyptians had weakened both empires. Three Semitic invaders moved into the vacuum: the Phoenicians to the Mediterranean coast, the Arameans to Syria, Palestine, and northern Mesopotamia, and the Hebrews to Palestine and Syria. About 1100 B.C. the powerful second Assyrian Empire began to expand, with its iron weapons, disciplined army, efficient bureaucracy, and iron battering rams mounted on wheels. By the seventh century the Assyrian empire, with its capital at Nineveh, included all Mesopotamia, Asia Minor, Syria, Palestine, and Egypt. But overextension of the empire and the deep hostility of its subject peoples finally led to disaster. In 612 B.C. a coalition of enemies destroyed Nineveh and ended forever the role of the Assyrians in history.

The Assyrians were followed by the Persians, who now organized the greatest empire to that date. Under their King Cyrus (550–529 B.C.), and using Assyrian military techniques, the Persians conquered all the lands from the Nile River in the west to the Indus River in the east. For the first time the entire Middle East was under one rule and the barbarian invaders were firmly shut out.

Greece

In contrast to the Middle East, civilization in Greece, India and China did not survive the barbarian invasions. In these peripheral areas, civilization lacked depth in time and space, and therefore was plowed under. Thus it was in those regions that new classical civilizations emerged, with new religious, social, and philosophical systems.

In Greece, the first invaders were the Indo-European Achaeans who came in the twentieth century B.C. They were charioteers with bronze weapons, and their general level of development was far behind that of the Minoan Cretans. But by 1600 B.C. the newcomers had absorbed much of the Minoan culture that had been transplanted to the mainland, and they had established a number of small kingdoms from Thessaly down to the southern tip of the Peloponnesus.

The most-advanced settlements were those in the Peloponnesus, which was closest to Crete. Mycenae was the outstanding center in the Peloponnesus, and it has given its name to the emerging civilization. In contrast to the cities of Crete, all settlements in Mycenaean Greece were strongly fortified. Massive hilltop citadels were constructed, where the king and his retainers lived. The commoners built their dwellings outside the citadel but in time of danger sought refuge within its walls.

Unlike the other Indo-European invaders who had established themselves in the Middle East and the Indus valley, the Mycenaeans took to the sea after the fashion of the Minoans and developed a formidable maritime power. They raided, or traded as opportunities dictated, and they founded overseas colonies in Rhodes, Cyprus, and the west coast of Asia Minor. The Mycenaeans soon undermined the former economic hegemony of Crete in the Mediterranean, and by the fifteenth century B.C. they were raiding the great island itself. The unwalled cities, including the capital of Knossos, were taken and destroyed. These disasters, together with a series of devastating earthquakes, led to the virtual extinction of the formerly great Minoan civilization by 1150 B.C.

Meanwhile the Mycenaeans were experiencing a similar fate at the hands of new invaders, the Dorians. Appearing about 1200 B.C. and armed with superior iron weapons, the Dorians captured the Mycenaean citadels and towns one by one. Administrative systems disintegrated, rural populations scattered, foreign trade withered, and Greece reverted to an agrarian and pastoral economy. A Dark Age descended and obscured Greece until the rise of the city-states about 800 B.C.

The main Dorian settlements were in the Peloponnesus, from which the invaders pushed on overseas and founded colonies in Crete, in Rhodes, and on the adjacent coast of Asia Minor. Other Greeks, perhaps Mycenaean refugees, crossed from Athens to the Cyclades Islands and on to the central part of the west coast of Asia Minor. There they established settlements that became known as Ionia, which for a period was the most advanced region of the entire Greek world. Still further north other bands speaking the Aeolic dialect sailed from Thessaly and central Greece to the island of Lesbos and thence to northern Asia Minor. These new Greek colonies in Asia Minor were never able to expand into the interior because of the resistance of the large local population. They were confined to the coastal areas, yet they prospered and were destined to play a major role in the general history of the Greek people.

Much more is known of this Dark Age in Greece than of the corresponding postinvasion period in India. This is due largely to the precious heritage of the four great poems left by the Greeks—Homer's *Iliad* and *Odyssey,* and Hesiod's *Works and Days* and *Birth of the Gods.* Homer wrote of war, adventure, and the life of nobles and kings, while Hesiod described the life and lore of the farmer, and the genealogies of the gods. Between them they have left a vivid picture of the primitive agricultural and pastoral society of these centuries. Households were largely self-sufficient, growing their own food and making their cloth with wool from their flocks of sheep. The only full-time traders were foreigners— Phoenicians or Cypriots—who appeared sporadically with trinkets for the commoners and more valuable goods for the nobles. The monotony of the farm work was broken by the occasional visit of a bard who sang of the glories of war and of the exploits of illustrious ancestors.

Each community consisted of the noble families that governed and led in war, and of the commoners, including freehold peasants, tenant farmers, and a few craftsmen, hired laborers, and slaves. At the top was the king, whose authority depended on his prowess in war and his ability to exercise leadership in the meetings of the council of nobles. Occasionally the king called a meeting of the assembly that included all adult males, but the purpose usually was to mobilize popular support for decisions already reached in conjunction with the nobles. These simple institutions, typical of the Indo-European tribes at this level of development, represented the embryo from which the Greek city-state was to develop its organs of government.

India

In India, the Indus valley civilization experienced the same fate as the Minoan civilization of Crete. About 1500 B.C., it was overrun by tribespeople who had the military advantage of iron weapons and horse-drawn chariots, and they easily overwhelmed the copper weapons and ox-drawn carts of the natives. The invaders called themselves Aryans, and the land in which they settled, Aryavarta, or land of the Aryans. They were of the Indo-European family of peoples, of which the western branches had invaded Mesopotamia and Greece. Infiltrating in small groups, the Aryans easily overthrew the decaying Indus valley civilization, so that a primitive new society emerged in the latter half of the second millennium B.C. Information concerning this society is scanty. The Aryans left no concrete remains, for they used wood or mud for their dwellings and had no large cities. Thus material available for the reconstruction of Aryan life is the direct opposite of that available for the Indus civilization. The latter left a wealth of material remains and no decipherable written records, whereas the Aryans left practically no remains and a wealth of literature in the form of Vedas.

The word *veda* means knowledge, and for the Hindus the Vedas are a primary source of religious belief as the Bible is for Christians and the *Koran* for Muslims. There were originally four Vedas, but the most important is the oldest, the Rigveda. In the course of time other works were added to the four Vedas and acquired a similar sacred status. The Rigveda is a primary source for study of the early Aryans as Homer's epics are for Mycenaean Greece. It is in essence a collection of 1028 hymns arranged in ten books, and is as bulky as the *Iliad* and *Odyssey* combined.

The Aryans were tall, with blue eyes and fair skin, and very conscious of these physical features in contrast to those of the indigenous people whom they conquered. The latter are referred to in the Vedas as short, black, noseless, and as *dasas*, or slaves. The image of the Aryans that emerges from the Vedic literature is that of a virile people, fond of war, drinking, chariot racing, and gambling. Their god of war, Indra, was the ideal Aryan warrior: he dashed into battle joyously, wore golden armor, and was able to consume the flesh of three hundred buffaloes and drink three lakes of liquor at one time.

When they first arrived in India the Aryans were primarily pastoralists. Their economic life centered around their cattle, and wealth was judged on the basis of the size of the herds. As the newcomers settled in the fertile river valleys, they gradually shifted more to agriculture. They lived in villages consisting of a number of related families. Several villages comprised a clan, and several clans a tribe, at the head of which was the king. As in Greece, the king's authority depended on his personal prowess and initiative, and it was limited by the council of nobles and, in some tribes, by the freemen.

The outstanding characteristic of this early Aryan society was its basic difference from the later Hinduism. Cows were worshipped but eaten. Intoxicating spirits were not forsaken but joyously consumed. There were classes but no castes, and the priests were subordinate to the nobles rather than being at the top of the social pyramid. In short, Aryan society resembled the other contemporary Indo-European societies much more than it did the classical Hinduism that was to develop in later centuries.

China

About 1500 B.C. charioteers with bronze weapons also invaded the distant valley of the Yellow River in north China. There they found the flourishing Neolithic culture of the Shang, to which they made contributions, but by which they were absorbed. As has always been true in China, invaders did not make a complete break with the past, as they did in Greece and India. Hence the distinctively Chinese civilization has continued uninterrupted from the early Shang period to the present, sometimes modified, but never destroyed or transformed.

The pattern of continuity is apparent in the transition from the Shang to the Chou dynasty in 1027 B.C. The Chou people had for long lived in the Wei valley on the fringes of civilization, so that they shared the language and basic culture of the Shang at the same time that they borrowed military techniques from the sheep-herding ''barbarians'' to the north and west. Consequently when the Chou overran north China there was no interruption in the evolution of Chinese civilization. The writing system continued as before, as did ancestor worship, the methods of divination, and the division of society into aristocratic warriors and peasant masses. Political decentralization also persisted, and indeed became more pronounced as the Chou rulers assigned the conquered territories to vassal lords. The vassal lords journeyed periodically to the Chou court for elaborate ceremonies of investiture, but gradually this practice lapsed. So eventually the lords, ensconced in their walled towns, ruled over the surrounding countryside with little control from the capital.

In 771 B.C. the Chou capital was captured by ''barbarians'' allied with rebellious lords. The Chou dynasty resumed its rule from a center further to the east that was not so vulnerable to attacks from the borderlands. Thus the dynastic period before 771 B.C. is termed by the Chinese the Western Chou, and the period thereafter, the Eastern Chou. During the Eastern Chou period the kings were rulers in name only. They were accorded certain religious functions and some ceremonial respect, but their domains were smaller than those of their nominal vassals, and their power correspondingly weaker. Indeed they managed to survive until 256 B.C. only because they provided spiritual leadership. The dynasty was also a royal priesthood, and as such it was preserved as a symbol of national unity.

Although the Eastern Chou was a period of political instability, it was also a period of cultural flowering. It was a dynamic and creative age when the great works of literature, philosophy, and social theory were written. This was the time when the classical Chinese civilization was taking form. And it corresponded to the classical Greek and Indian civilizations that were evolving at roughly the same time. The origin and nature of these classical civilizations is the subject of the following chapters.

SUGGESTED READING

R. M. Adams, *The Evolution of Urban Society* (Aldine, 1966); C. H. Kraeling and R. M. Adams, eds., *City Invincible: A Symposium on Urbanization and Cultural Development in the Ancient Near East* (University of Chicago, 1960); B. M. Fagan, ed., *Avenues to Antiquity* (W. H. Freeman, 1976); A. Guha, ed., *Central Asia: Movement of Peoples and Ideas* (Harper & Row, 1972); M. H. Fried, *The Evolution of Political Society* (Random House, 1967); C. Renfrew, *Before Civilization: The Radiocarbon Revolution and Prehistoric Europe* (Knopf, 1973).

chapter 4

Classical Civilizations Begin Eurasian Unification, 1000 B.C.–A.D. 500

The most striking feature of the age of the classical civilizations was the beginning of the unification of Eurasia. A comparison of the map of Eurasia about 1500 B.C. with that of about A.D. 200 makes clear the extent of this unification (see Maps VI and X). The empires of the early period were almost entirely restricted to their respective river valleys, and they give the appearance of tiny islands in a vast sea of barbarism. By the first century A.D., however, the Roman, Parthian, Kushan, and Han empires spanned the breadth of Eurasia from the Scottish Highlands to the China Seas. This made possible a modest degree of interaction amongst empires. Of course there had always been certain interregional contacts even at the time of the ancient civilizations, as evidenced by the nomadic invasions in all directions. But now in the Classical Age these interregional contacts were substantially closer, more varied, and more sustained. And yet, even by the end of the classical period the Roman and Chinese empires at opposite ends of Eurasia had not been able to establish direct official contact and possessed no specific or reliable knowledge of each other. Thus Eurasian unity remained at the beginning stage throughout those centuries. The origins, nature, and significance of this first stage in the process of unification is the subject of this chapter.

I. ROOTS OF UNIFICATION

Technological advance was at the root of the new Eurasian unity. This was not surprising, since from the very beginning of history the range of human activities had always depended on the level of technology. When people were at the food-gathering stage, the range of the individual band was its hunting ground. As people learned agriculture and metallurgy and shipbuilding, we have seen that their range broadened to encompass, for example, the valley empires of Sargon and of the pharaohs. But now further technological advance allowed for a much greater extension of agriculture and civilization. Regional empires were organized and stretched contiguously across the breadth of Eurasia. The basic technological advance responsible for all this was the discovery and ever more widespread use of iron.

Iron smelting was developed first in Asia Minor in the middle of the second millennium B.C., and it spread from there after the destruction of the Hittite Empire about 1200 B.C. As we have seen, the discovery made possible the second wave of barbarian invasions at the end of the second millennium B.C. But some centuries passed before the new metal was available in sufficient quantities for everyday use. When hoes and axes and plows, as well as weapons, could be made of iron, then the economic, social, and political repercussions were immediate and far reaching.

This stage was reached slowly—about 800 B.C. in India, 750 B.C. in Central Europe, and 600 B.C. in China. In these and other regions the use of cheap iron led first and foremost to the cutting down of heavy forests hitherto invulnerable to stone-edged axes and wooden plows. But farmers now were able to use their strong and sharp iron axes and their iron-shod plows to extend agriculture from the Middle East eastward across the Iranian plateau and westward across the Mediterranean lands and into Central and Northern Europe. Likewise in India the Aryan newcomers pushed eastward and cut down the forests of the Ganges valley. At the same time agriculturists in China were extending their operations from the Yellow River valley southward to the great Yangtze basin.

The expansion of the frontiers of agriculture made possible a corresponding expansion of the frontiers of civilization. They grew more in the half-millennium from 1000 to 500 B.C. than in the preceding three millennia from 4000 to 1000 B.C. The basic reason for this was the tremendous increase in productivity that now took place. Not only was agriculture practiced in much larger areas, but the combination of soils and climate in Central Europe and in the monsoon Ganges and Yangtze basins was much more productive than in the comparatively arid Middle East and Indus and Yellow River valleys.

The jump in agricultural productivity meant that a *surplus* was now available for economic development and for state-building purposes. Trade increased in volume, especially along the rivers that constituted ready-made highways. Craftsmen appeared in increasing numbers to provide the services needed in the new agricultural communities and the products in demand for the new trade. At first goods and services were exchanged by barter, with obvious inconvenience for both buyer and seller. Then media of exchange were developed, such as measures of grain or, more common, bars of metal. But with every transaction the weight and purity of the metal had to be checked against fraudulent clipping and debasing.

About 700 B.C., the Lydians of western Asia Minor began stamping and guaranteeing pieces of metal as to both quality and weight. Various Greek city-states soon improved on this by stamping flat circular coins on both sides. Thus gold and silver coins now helped large-scale wholesale or interregional trade. Also copper coins enabled farmers to sell rather than barter their produce, and artisans to work for wages rather than foodstuffs. The net effect was a great boost for all kinds of commerce, a corresponding boost for manufacturing and agriculture, and an overall increase in efficiency and productivity. Now, for the first time the manufacturer of cheap goods had a mass market available. The small landholder could turn from subsistence agriculture to specialized farming, whether the specialty were the mulberry and silkworm in China or wine and olive oil in Greece.

The new iron tools also made it possible to build better and larger ships, which, in turn, led to longer voyages and to more trade and *colonization*. Overseas expansion was hindered at the outset by piracy, which was regarded as normal an activity as brigandage on land. The *Odyssey* describes the half-piractical, half-commercial expeditions of Menelaus and Odysseus in the Aegean Sea, and relates how all participants as a matter of course asked those whom they met whether or not they were pirates. But gradually maritime trade was developed on a regular large-scale basis, with great economic advantage. Transport by sea was many times cheaper than by land, and it remained so until the development of an efficient horse harness in the Middle Ages and the building of good roads in the eighteenth century.

By the end of the Classical Age, trade routes encircled all of Eurasia, in contrast to the local self-sufficiency of most regions following the invasions of the second millennium B.C. In addition to the caravan routes across the interior of Eurasia, there were sea routes around the circumference—from the North Sea to the western Mediterranean, from the western Mediterranean to the Levant, from the Red Sea to India, and from India to Southeast Asia and, to a lesser degree, to China. This maritime commerce was accompanied by colonization, especially in the Mediterranean by the Phoenicians and Greeks, and later in Southeast Asia by the Indians.

Side by side with these economic developments came equally significant social and political changes. The military aristocracy that had risen to prominence with the invasions of the second millennium B.C. was being undermined by the new class of merchants, craftsmen, and mariners. The old tribal society was being transformed by the use of money; personal services and allegiances were being replaced by the demands of the market place.

Equally disruptive was the political consolidation made possible by the economic growth. Tribal chiefs and their advisory councils and assemblies were replaced by kingdoms and then by *empires*, whether in Italy or India or China. Nor was it a one-way process of economic development stimulating political centralization. A reverse process also operated, for the great new regional empires spanning the Eurasian land mass enforced order and security so that long-distance trade by land and sea was possible. Regional empires also were able to build and maintain regional road networks that facilitated commerce.

In the Persian Empire, for example, the so-called Royal Road ran 1677 miles from Susa, located to the north of the Persian Gulf, westward to the Tigris, and thence across Syria and Asia Minor to Ephesus on the Aegean coast. The route was divided into 111 post-stations, each with relays of fresh horses for the royal couriers. Caravans took ninety days to travel this road from end to end, while the royal couriers traversed it in a week. As the empire was enlarged, branch lines were constructed southwest to Egypt and southeast to the Indus valley. A few centuries later the Romans constructed their well-known system of roads that were so well engineered that some of them, along with their bridges, are still in use.

At the other end of Eurasia, the Chinese built an elaborate network of both roads and canals. They were able to transport goods from present-day Canton to the Yangtze valley by an all-water route, thereby promoting their overseas trade. To the northwest they built roads that linked up with the long silk route, which, as will be noted in the following section, crossed the whole of Central Asia to the Middle East. The main highways were lined with trees and provided with stations and guest houses. Road construction and maintenance was the responsibility of central and local officials who were punished if they did not carry out their duties properly. Likewise in India the Royal Highway ran from the Ganges delta to Taxila in the northwest, near the Khyber Pass, where it connected with the caravan routes west to the Middle East and north to Central Asia.

All these developments involved profound changes in social relationships, in political organizations, and in ways of living and earning a livelihood. Such basic and all-inclusive disruption was unsettling and uncomfortable. It led to soul searching—to the posing of new questions and the seeking of new answers. Thinkers had to reconsider their respective traditions and to either abandon them or adapt them to the requirements of an age of transition. People speculated about such questions as the moral basis of ideal government, the functioning of the social order, and the origin and purpose of the universe and of life.

About the sixth century B.C. such questions were being posed and discussed all over Eurasia. The answers made up the great *philosophical systems* and religious and social systems of the Classical Age. It was not happenstance, then, that the spokesmen for these systems were all contemporaries—Confucius in China, Buddha in India, Zoroaster in Persia, and the rationalist philosophers in Greece. In all these regions the disruption and the challenge was the same, but the answers varied greatly, and the several Eurasian civilizations set off in decidedly different directions. Indeed it was at this time that these civilizations developed their distinctive philosophical attitudes and social institutions that continued through the centuries to the present day.

The specific nature of these attitudes and institutions will be analyzed in the following chapters devoted to each of the classical civilizations. The remainder of this chapter will be devoted to an examination of the interrelationships amongst these civilizations. Contemporary Eurasians were very much aware of these interrelationships. They were definitely aware that the historical stage was expanding—that life was becoming more complex and that many new domestic and external forces were pressing in on them. Thus the Greek historian Polybius, when starting his history of events from 220 to 145 B.C., observed that, "during this period history becomes, so to speak, an organic whole. What happens in Italy and in Libya is bound up with what happened in Asia and in Greece, all events culminating in a single result."

Two aspects of this new "organic whole" were particularly clear, even to contemporaries. These were interregional *commercial bonds* and interregional cultural bonds, the subjects of the following two sections.

II. COMMERCIAL BONDS

The principal interregional bonds of a material nature were commercial in character, though not exclusively so. This was a time when not only goods moved from one region to another, but people also moved about, taking with them their technological skills and their plants. We can see how wide-ranging this interchange was by the fact that cotton, sugar cane, and chickens, all first domesticated in India, spread to both China and Western Eurasia during this period. Likewise the Chinese during these centuries obtained for the first time the grape vine, alfalfa, chive, cucumber, fig, sesame, pomegranate, and walnut. In return the Chinese gave to the rest of Eurasia the orange, peach, pear, peony, azalea, camellia, and chrysanthemum. There was a similar interchange of technology, as is evident in the case of that fundamental invention, the waterwheel.

The first waterwheel in Western Asia was that of Mithridates, King of Pontus, on the south shore of the Black Sea, about 65 B.C. The first waterwheel in China was built soon after, about 30 B.C. The difference between the two dates is much too small for direct diffusion in either direction, and this strongly suggests diffusion in both directions from some unknown intermediate source. Such interaction between the various regions of Eurasia was the result of a great increase in local and long-distance trade during the centuries of the Classical Age.

Trade was conducted both by land across Central Eurasia and by sea around the coasts of the land mass. These two general routes were by no means exclusive or independent of each other. A large proportion of the goods were moved along some combination of the two routes, usually by sea between Egypt and India, and by one of several overland routes between India and China. Furthermore, the land and sea routes were competitive, so that excessively high charges or intolerable lack of security in one route normally shifted the trade to the other.

The maritime trade had gotten under way first at the time of the ancient civilizations. Egyptian traders ventured down the Red Sea to East Africa and along the Levant coast to Lebanon. Likewise, Sumerian merchants sailed down the Persian Gulf, along the Arabian peninsula, while their counterparts from the Indus valley worked their way westward until contact was established, perhaps at the Bahrain Islands in the Persian Gulf. But all of these early seafarers were mere landlubbers compared to the Minoans of Crete. They were the great maritime traders of ancient times, plying the Mediterranean from end to end as the unrivaled sailors of that inland sea.

With the invasions of the Achaeans and Dorians this far-flung commerce dried up and the eastern Mediterranean people sank back to an agrarian and isolated type of existence. The first to resume the *mercantile activities* of the Cretans were the Phoenicians. A Semitic-speaking people who had settled along the narrow coastal plains of the eastern Mediterranean, they soon developed a flourishing trade as middlemen. In the eleventh century B.C. the Phoenicians began to spread out over the Aegean, and by the end of the ninth century B.C. they had entered the western Mediterranean. They founded trading posts and colonies on the northwest coast of Africa, the south coast of Spain, and on Sicily, Malta, and the Balearic Islands. They even ventured beyond Gibraltar as far afield as Cornwall, England, where they traded for valuable tin.

From about 1100 B.C. until the late eighth century B.C. the sailors and merchants of Phoenicia controlled most of the maritime trade of the Mediterranean. Then the Greeks appeared as competitors, spurred on by the same pressure of overpopulation. First they established trading posts, which later developed into agricultural settlements wherever the land resources made this possible. The settlements were quite independent of the mother city whence they sprang, even though the colonists established the same institutions and copied the same religious practices that they had left behind. Greek colonization then took the form of many independent city-states rather than one centrally controlled empire. The principal areas of Greek settlement were in Sicily, south Italy, southeastern France, northeastern Spain, and the Black Sea basin, which by the fifth century B.C. was ringed with flourishing Greek trading posts and settlements.

While the Greeks were prospering on the sea, the Persians were building an empire that eventually extended from the Nile valley to the Indus. Although Persians were a mountain people and had little maritime knowledge, they wanted nevertheless to open sea routes and so facilitate communications between their eastern and western provinces. For this purpose they made use of their subjects, the Phoenicians and Asia Minor Greeks who were experienced seagoers. They appointed a Greek mariner, Scylax, to head an expedition that sailed about 510 B.C. from the Indus to Arsinoë at the head of the Red Sea. The Persians also had plans for cutting a canal from the Nile to the Red Sea and appear to have done considerable work toward that goal. Trade flourished and surpassed anything previously known in volume and in geographic range. Greek, Phoenician, Arab, and Indian mariners sailed back and forth between India, the Persian Gulf, Egypt, and the numerous ports of the Mediterranean. Alexander and his successors continued the work of the Persians by sending more expeditions, which increased geographic knowledge. They also constructed a series of ports along the Red Sea, through which goods could be transported overland to the Nile then shipped down the river to Alexandria.

All this was only the prelude to the great expansion of trade between East and West that blossomed shortly before the Christian era and lasted for about two centuries. One reason for this increase in trade was China's great westward expansion. The Chinese not only opened overland trade routes but made it easier to obtain silk, the most important item in interregional commerce. The precise role of China will be considered shortly in the analysis of overland trade. The other main factor behind the booming trade was the consolidation of the Roman Empire which encompassed the entire Mediterranean basin and much of Central and Northwestern Europe. The establishment of *Pax Romana* eliminated brigandage and piracy, which hitherto had hindered trade, and removed almost all tolls and exactions. The wealth of the empire also stimulated trade, particularly since the wealthy Roman ruling class had both the taste and the funds for exotic foreign products.

The Romans carried on a flourishing trade with all neighboring lands—with Scandinavia to the north, Germany across the Rhine, Dacia across the Danube, and Africa south of the Sahara. Most significant in its general Eurasian repercussions was commerce with the East. Eastern commerce was greatly expanded sometime in the first century B.C. when a Greek mariner discovered that the monsoon winds could be used to speed the sailing back and forth across the Indian Ocean. (This was more likely a rediscovery, since Arab sailors appear to have preceded the Greeks—monsoon is derived from the Arab word "Mauzim," or "season.") The northeast, or winter, monsoon blows from India towards East Africa from October to April, and the southwest, or summer, monsoon blows in the opposite direction from June to September. No longer was it necessary for the sailors to hug the coasts in a wide, time-consuming arc; now they could scud before the wind directly across the ocean. A merchant could journey from Rome to India in sixteen weeks, including the land stage through Egypt.

"Roman" merchants, mostly Greeks and Syrians, not only undertook such journeys, but a few settled permanently in Indian cities, as we know from Indian literary sources. A few of the more adventurous "Roman" traders made their way further east beyond India. In the second and third centuries A.D. they reached Burma, Malaya, Sumatra, and passed on through the Malacca Straight to Kattigara (Hanoi), from which they at last made direct contact with China. At the same time Indian merchants traded and settled throughout Southeast Asia. They brought with them Hindu religion and customs and established Indian kingdoms on the islands and mainland.

As far as overland trade was concerned, much depended on the degree to which order and security could be maintained. When large sections of the land routes were under the firm control of some authority, trade could flourish; when *anarchy* prevailed, trade withered. This pattern is clearly apparent in surveying commercial trends through these centuries. A general upward trend is evident in the volume of trade, the result of the technological advances and the expansion of civilization and of empires. But within this overall trend there are dips and rises as a result of political conditions. For example, the centuries of the Scythian Empire in Western Eurasia, the Chinese empires in Eastern Eurasia, and the Mongol Empire embracing most of the continental land mass, were all centuries of safe trade routes and increasing commerce.

The Scythians, for example, carried on a lively trade with the Greek cities on the north shore of the Black Sea. They exchanged slaves, cattle, hides, furs, fish, timber, wax, and honey, for Greek textiles, wine, olive oil, and various luxury goods. Likewise the Chinese traded goods back and forth along the famous Silk Road from northwest China across Central Asia to the Black Sea and Levant ports. The Chinese exported mostly silk, but they also brought cinnamon, rhubarb, and high-grade iron. In return they received furs, woolens, jade and livestock from Central Asia, amber from the Baltic, and from the Roman provinces, glass, corals, pearls, linen and wool textiles, and, above all, gold.

This flourishing land trade declined gradually with the growing troubles and anarchy in the Roman and Chinese empires after the second century A.D. The great blow came when the Moslem Arabs conquered the entire Middle East in the seventh century and then pushed into Central Asia. After the Arabs defeated the Chinese in the battle of Talas in 751, all Central Asia was converted to Islam. The huge Moslem Empire now was a barrier rather than a bridge between China and the West, or between China and India. Finally the overland routes were closed and trade shifted to the surrounding seas where the Arabs were becoming the leading mariners and merchants. It was not until the thirteenth century, when the Mongols conquered all Eurasia from the Pacific Ocean to the Baltic and Black seas that overland routes could be reopened, clearing the way for Marco Polo and his fellow merchants of medieval times.

Despite the various shifts in the direction of trade, one basic fact emerges from this survey—the fact that there was a huge increase in both the range and volume of commerce during the Classical Age as compared to the preceding ancient period. No longer was the scope of commerce confined to individual regions, whether in the Mediterranean Sea or the Arabian Sea or some segment of the Eurasian steppes. Rather trade now became interregional with goods being carried from one end of Eurasia to the other by sea and by land.

III. CULTURAL BONDS

Commercial and cultural bonds were not unconnected or independent of each other. The Greek merchants who followed Alexander's armies spread their Hellenistic culture throughout the Orient. Likewise the spread of Buddhism from India to China can be traced along the well-known Silk Road. Cultural movements, however, had their own internal force and were by no means entirely caused by merchants and their trade routes. A fundamental factor affecting cultural developments in the classical world, exclusive of China, was the invention of a simple alphabetic script in the late second millennium B.C. Prior to that time only a handful of professional scribes had been able to read and write the complicated cuneiform script of Mesopotamia and the hieroglyphics of Egypt. The first alphabetic system was devised by Semitic traders in the Sinai peninsula who adapted the Egyptian signs, with which they had become familiar, to indicate consonantal sounds. But they continued to use many additional symbols for words and syllables and therefore failed to develop a strictly phonetic alphabet. The Phoenicians completed the transition in the thirteenth century B.C. by developing an alphabet of twenty-two signs denoting simple consonants. The Greeks improved the Phoenician alphabet by using some of its signs to indicate vowels. This Greek alphabet, with some modifications, was spread by the Romans westward and by the Byzantines eastward.

The significance of the alphabet is that it extended intelligent communication far beyond the narrow circle of the priests and officials of the old days. The scribes of Egypt and Mesopotamia naturally shunned the new style of writing and continued to use their traditional scripts almost until the Christian era. China also, in its isolation, continued with its combination phono-pictographic system that has been maintained with modifications to the present day. But elsewhere in Eurasia, alphabets were adopted with slight adjustments to fit the different languages. Everywhere the effect was to reduce somewhat, though by no means entirely, the gap between urban ruling circles and peasant masses that had developed with the appearance of civilization. By challenging the monopoly of privileged intellectual cliques that generally supported the status quo, the simplified scripts generated a certain ferment. And the ferment affected both politics and culture.

The overall cultural pattern noticeable amongst all Eurasian civilizations during these centuries of the Classical Age was the breakdown of local cultures, which were integrated into new regional civilizations with distinctive languages, religions, and social systems. It was much easier for these civilizations to exchange material goods than culture traits. Textiles, spices, and luxury products were universally usable and desirable, whereas ancestor worship, the caste system, and the city-state were irrelevant and unacceptable outside their places of origin. Thus the commercial interregional bonds during this period of reorganization were generally more extensive and influential than the cultural.

Cultural bonds did develop, however, and in some cases they were of first-rate historical significance. The first outstanding instance was that of *Hellenism,* which spread from the Greek world eastward to the Orient and westward to Europe. Toward the end of the classical period there were also the great universal religions, especially Christianity and Buddhism, with their claims to the allegiance of all humankind rather than of any one group.

Let us first consider Hellenism, which is derived from the Greek word Hellas, meaning Greece. Its diffusion throughout the Middle East was made possible by Alexander's famous conquest eastward to Central Asia and the Indus valley. As will be noted in the following chapter, this empire lasted for only a few years during Alexander's lifetime. On his death in 323 B.C. it was divided among his generals, and later it was partitioned between Rome in the West and the Parthians in the East. During these fourth and third centuries B.C. the military dominance of the Greek soldiers paved the way for the hundreds of thousands of Greek merchants, administrators, and professional people who flocked to the numerous cities built by Alexander and his successors. From the first and most famous Alexandria in Egypt to the farthest Alexandria—Eschata (Kojand) in Afghanistan—these cities served as centers for the diffusion of Greek culture.

Many of the Greek emigrants married local women. Alexander himself set an example by taking a Persian noblewoman as wife. He then arranged for the mass marriage of three thousand of his soldiers with Persian women after their return from the Indian campaign. He also enlisted Persian soldiers in his regiments, and adopted the costume of the Persian king and the etiquette of his court. Even though the majority of its inhabitants usually were non-Hellenic, the typical city was basically Greek, with elected magistrates, a council, and an assembly of the citizens. A new form of the Greek language, the Koine, or common tongue, was used widely throughout the Middle East.

Despite this impressive diffusion, Hellenism did not leave a permanent imprint on the Middle East. The basic reason was that its influence had been restricted to the cities where Greek settlers lived and where Greek *dynasties* had courts. Some of the native peoples were affected, but they were almost exclusively of the small upper classes. The great majority in the countryside, and even in many of the cities, continued to speak their own languages and worship their own gods. Thus Hellenism did not sink deep roots and was incapable of surviving through the centuries. When the Islamic conquerors appeared during the Middle Ages, they had little difficulty in overwhelming the little islands of Hellenistic culture, so that today the Greek language and culture survive only in the Greek homeland on the southern tip of the Balkan peninsula.

Hellenism was slower to take root in the Western Mediterranean because the indigenous populations had not yet reached a sufficiently affluent and sophisticated level of civilization. But for that very reason there was less competition from the local culture and the long-run impact of Hellenism in that region was more durable.

As early as the sixth century B.C., the Romans were being influenced by the Greek colonies in southern Italy. But it was not until the third century onward, when the Romans conquered the heartland of Hellenism in the Balkans and the Levant, that they felt the full force of Greek culture. Roman soldiers and officials now came into direct contact with highly educated Greek rulers and administrators, while among the hostages and slaves brought to Rome were many Greeks who served in every capacity—from moral philosopher to contortionist, from laudatory poet to master chef. New intellectual horizons opened for upper-class Romans as they heard the dazzling rhetoric and high-level discussions of their sophisticated subjects.

Greeks served as tutors for the leading families, offering instruction in Greek language, rhetoric, philosophy, and literature. By the first century B.C. it was common for young Romans to be sent to Athens or Rhodes for training in the philosophical schools. In the field of literature, the Romans at first translated or imitated Greek originals, though gradually they turned to Roman themes.

Greek influence also was clear in the physical appearance of Rome and the other cities of the Empire. All three Greek architectural forms were used—the Doric, Ionic and Corinthian—though Roman buildings tended to be larger and more ornate. Thus towns and cities in Italy, as in the Middle East, began to take on a uniform physical appearance under the influence of Greek art and architecture. Indeed a basic contribution of the Romans to civilization was to appropriate and adapt Greek culture and then to spread it to diverse peoples who had never experienced direct contact with it—Gauls, Germans, Britons, and Iberians.

Much more durable than the impact of Hellenism was that of the two great universal religions, Christianity and Mahayana *Buddhism.* They began their expansion in the late classical period from their respective places of origin in the Middle East and India. During the course of the following centuries they won over all Europe in the one case, and most of Asia in the other. The reason for their success is to be found in certain characteristics that they shared in common. One was their emphasis on salvation and their promise of an afterlife of eternal bliss. Another was their egalitarianism, so that their brotherhood was open to all who sought admittance—women as well as men, rich and poor alike, slave or free. Finally, both religions stressed a high code of ethics, the observance of which was essential for salvation. This requirement, together with efficient ecclesiastical organization, enabled these two religions to have an important influence on the daily lives of the faithful.

The features of these religions were particularly appealing in the later centuries of the Classical Age. These were times of social unrest and moral confusion, especially in the large urban centers. The multitudes in the cities felt uprooted and drifting. For such people, Christianity and Mahayana Buddhism offered solace, security, and guidance. When Pilate, voicing the despairing mood of the times, asked "What is truth?," religion provided an answer. It was not accidental that the earliest converts to Christianity were the lowly and dispossessed. Likewise, the greatest triumph of Mahayana Buddhism was in China during the time of troubles following the collapse of the Han dynasty, when there seemed to be no solution to humanity's worldly problems.

Indeed, these satisfying characteristics of the two religions were evolved precisely in response to the needs of the times. They were present neither in the Judaism from which Christianity had emerged nor in the original Buddhism from which developed the later Mahayana variant.

Judaism was the parochial faith of the Jewish people who about the twelfth century B.C. adopted a national god, Jehovah. "I am Jehovah, thy God. . . . Thou Shalt have no other gods before me." This first of Jehovah's Ten Commandments did not say that Jehovah was the only god in the world. It said, rather, that he was the only god for the children of Israel. Also this Judaistic faith was at this time more social and ethical than mystical and otherworldly. In the words of one of the Jewish prophets, Jehovah cares nothing for ritual and sacrifice; he cares only that men should "seek justice, relieve the oppressed, judge the fatherless, plead for the widow."

But from the sixth century B.C. onward, the Jews changed their religious ideas under the influence of the religions of the Persians and other of their rulers. Also they were affected by the many Jews who lived outside Palestine where, exposed to the tenets of Hellenism, they sought to interpret Judaism in terms of Greek philosophy. Thus the Jews gradually adopted a belief in an afterlife—obedience to God's will would bring eternal happiness in heaven, and disobedience would bring eternal punishment in hell.

Nevertheless, Christianity was a Jewish cult during the lifetime of Jesus and immediately after his crucifixion. But it was universalized by Paul, a Hellenized Jew who lived in the city of Tarsus in Asia Minor. Paul boldly denied that Jesus was sent merely as the redeemer of the Jews. A loving Father had sent His only Son to atone for the sins of all humanity. Therefore Christianity was not a sect of Judaism. It was a new church, a church for Gentiles as well as for Jews. Paul's approach meant that Christianity henceforth could appeal not only to a handful of Jews, but to the millions of Gentiles throughout the Roman Empire.

The new religion grew despite steady persecution by Roman officials. Finally, in 313 Christianity was tolerated by Emperor Constantine's Edict of Milan, and in 399 it was made the official state religion of the Roman Empire. Then, after the fall of the empire, Christian missionaries carried the faith to the English and German peoples between 600 and 800, and to the Scandinavian and Slavic peoples between 800 and 1100. With the expansion of Europe, both missionaries and emigrants spread Christianity to all parts of the globe.

The evolution of Buddhism was somewhat similar in that it began, as will be noted in chapter 6, as a distinct Indian reaction against the injustice of the caste system and the exploitation by the Brahman priestly class. The founder, Siddhartha (c. 563–483 B.C.), of the Gautama clan, was of noble rank, but he became so distressed by the suffering he saw about him that he gave up his family and material comforts for the life of a wandering ascetic. Finally, in a moment of revelation, he achieved enlightenment and thenceforth was known as Buddha, or the Enlightened One.

The four great truths of Buddhism are: (1) life is sorrow; (2) the cause of sorrow is desire; (3) escape is possible only by stopping desire; and (4) this can only be done by the ''eight-fold path'' consisting of right belief, right ambition, right speech, right conduct, right living, right effort, right thoughts, and right pleasures. The objective of all this effort was *Nirvana,* literally meaning ''emptiness,'' the ''blowing out of the flame.''

Buddha had not intended to establish a new religion, but after his death his disciples preached his teachings and founded monastic communities that came to dominate the religion. The ideal of these communities was mental and physical discipline culminating in the mystic experience of Nirvana. Satisfying as this was for the monks, it failed to meet the needs of the everyday life of laymen. Hence the evolution of Mahayana, or the Greater Vehicle, as opposed to the Hinayana, or Lesser Vehicle. The Greater Vehicle was ''greater'' in the sense of its all-inclusiveness. It incorporated more of the concepts of pre-Buddhist Indian thought as well as the religious ideas of the people it converted. In doing so, it turned somewhat from its original contemplative bent and adopted precepts that were easier to comprehend and observe. Salvation now could be attained through faith, even an unthinking act of faith such as the mouthing of the name of Buddha. Also Nirvana changed, at least for the less sophisticated believers, to mean an afterlife in Paradise, and attainment of Paradise was more likely through good works that helped others.

This shift of emphasis from monasticism, asceticism, and contemplation to charity, faith, and salvation made Mahayana Buddhism more palatable to non-Indian peoples than the original religion had been, though both forms of the faith won foreign converts. Buddhism spread first to Ceylon and to northwest frontier regions of India in the third century B.C. Then in the first century B.C. it was carried into Central Asia and China, first by traders, then by Indian missionaries and, most effectively, by Chinese converts who studied in India and then returned to win over their fellow countrymen. So successful were they that by the late fourth century A.D., nine-tenths of the population of northwest China was said to have been converted, and by the sixth century south China had followed suit. From China, Buddhism spread still further: to Korea in the fourth century A.D., to Japan in the sixth century, and later to Tibet and Mongolia. Meanwhile Buddhism in both its Hinayana and Mahayana forms had been penetrating into Southeast Asia. This did not occur at any particular period; rather it represented one aspect of the general Indianization of the region that took place over many centuries.

After these successes Buddhism declined in many countries. In China it reached its peak about 700 but thereafter suffered from internal decay and governmental hostility. Its great landholdings, its vast treasures, and the large numbers of monks and nuns it withdrew from the national economy, all aroused official envy and displeasure and brought on persecution. Between 841 and 855, according to official accounts, 4600 monasteries and 40,000 shrines were destroyed; 260,000 monks and nuns were defrocked

BUDDHISM IN INDIA AND CHINA

The unification of Eurasia began in classical times. The bonds were partly commercial and partly cultural. Buddhism played an important role in the cultural interaction. This is evident in the following experiences of a Chinese Buddhist monk, Hsüan-tsang, who spent the years from 629 to 645 visiting monasteries in India. While at the Nolanda monastery he announced his decision to return to China. The reaction of the monks is revealing. *

The monks of Nalanda [monastery], when they heard of it, begged him to remain, saying: "India is the land of Buddha's birth, and though he has left the world, there are still many traces of him. What greater happiness could there be than to visit them in turn, to adore him and chant his praises? Why then do you wish to leave, having come so far? Moreover China is a country of . . . unimportant barbarians, who despise the religious and the [Buddhist] Faith. That is why Buddha was not born there. The mind of the people is narrow, and their coarseness profound, hence neither sages nor saints go there. The climate is cold and the country rugged—you must think again."

The Master of the Law (the Chinese Buddhist) replied, "Buddha established his doctrine so that it might be diffused to all lands. Who would wish to enjoy it alone, and to forget those who are not enlightened? Besides, in my country the magistrates are clothed with dignity, and the laws are everywhere respected. The emperor is virtuous and the subjects loyal, parents are loving and sons obedient, humanity and justice are highly esteemed, and old men and sages are held in honour. Moreover, how deep and mysterious is their knowledge; their wisdom equals that of spirits. They have taken the Heavens as their model, and they know how to calculate the movements of the Seven Luminaries; they have invented all kinds of instruments, fixed the seasons of the year. . . . How then can you say that Buddha did not go to my country because of its insignificance?"

* J. Needham, *Science and Civilization in China* (London: Cambridge University Press, 1954), 1, pp. 209–210.

and, together with their 150,000 slaves, returned to the tax registers. Buddhism never recovered from this blow, and thereafter it was merely one of "the three religions" (along with Taoism and Confucianism) in which the syncretic Chinese were interested. Likewise, in India, Buddhism eventually gave way to a revival of Hinduism, so that virtually no followers are to be found today in its own birthplace. In Ceylon and in many parts of Southeast Asia, however, Buddhism of the Hinayana variety remains predominant to the present.

Despite this relative decline after its period of greatness, the fact remains that Buddhism in late classical and early medieval times was the predominant religion of Asia. It prevailed in the whole continent except for Siberia and the Middle East, thus giving that vast area a degree of cultural unity unequaled before or after. In doing so, it functioned as a great civilizing force in Asia as Christianity did at the same time in Europe. To many peoples Buddhism brought, not only a religion and a set of ethics, but also a system of writing, a type of architecture, and all the other attributes of the great civilizations of India and China that the missionaries spread together with their religion. In the same way, at the other end of Eurasia Christian missionaries were bringing to the barbaric Germanic and Slavic peoples the civilizations of Rome and of Constantinople, as well as the teachings of Christ. Such was the impact and historical significance of these powerful "cultural bonds" for the Eurasian peoples.

During the millennia of the ancient civilizations, the Middle East had been the center of initiative. It was the Middle East that during that period had made the fundamental contributions to human society—contributions such as agriculture, metallurgy, urbanism, and imperial organization. But now in classical times this Middle Eastern predominance faded away, except in one area—that of religion. Not only Judaism but also Zoroastrianism have their roots in the Middle East. The latter religion, although observed today by only a handful of Parsis in India, had considerable influence in the Middle East when the Persian Empire was at its height. Furthermore, it stands out in the history of religions as a lofty faith that sought to replace the prevailing gross practices and superstitions of the Persian people with the principles of light, truth, and righteousness.

Yet the fact remains that apart from these religions and other related sects, the Middle East no longer was the vital source of innovation during the Classical Age. The new ideas and institutions which took shape in classical times, and which have persisted in many cases to the present, were the products of what formerly had been the peripheral regions of Eurasia. Accordingly, the following three chapters are devoted to the civilizations of these regions: the Greco-Roman, the Indian, and the Chinese.

SUGGESTED READING

G. Barraclough, ed., *The Christian World* (Abrams, 1981); J. N. Hillgarth, ed., *The Conversion of Western Europe 350–750* (Prentice-Hall, 1969); G. F. Hudson, *Europe and China: A Survey of Their Relations from the Earliest Times to 1800* (Arnold, 1931); J. Needham, *Science & Civilization in China* (Cambridge University Press, 1954–); H. G. Rawlinson, *Intercourse Between India and the Western World* (Cambridge University Press, 1916); C. G. F. Simkin, *The Traditional Trade of Asia* (Oxford University Press, 1969); E. Zurcher, *Buddhism: Its Origin and Spread* (St. Martin's Press, 1962).

chapter 5

Greco-Roman Civilization

Of the three chapters dealing with the three classical civilizations—the Greco-Roman, the Indian, and the Chinese—this one on the Greco-Roman civilization is the longest. One reason is that two distinct though related civilizations are involved. The historical development at this time of the West was basically different from that of the unitary civilizations of India and China. All three civilizations spread out from restricted centers of origin to encompass entire surrounding regions—from the Greek peninsula to the western Mediterranean, from the Indus River valley to south India, and from the Yellow River valley to south China. As noted in Chapter 4, section I, iron tools made this possible because they facilitated the extension of agriculture into forested regions and of commerce and colonization into new coastal areas. But at this point the common pattern ends. The newly civilized regions in India and China remained generally subservient to the original core areas, whereas in the West, Rome developed a military superiority that enabled it to conquer not only the Greek homeland in the Balkans but also the western portions of the ancient Middle East—Asia Minor, Palestine, Syria, and Egypt. In doing so, Rome began a new phase of the history of the West and launched a new, though related, Western civilization. The history and nature of these two sister civilizations, the Greek and the Roman, is the subject of this chapter.

I. FORMATIVE AGE, 800–500 B.C.

With the Dorian invasions of the twelfth century B.C., Greece lapsed into a "Dark Age" (see Chapter 3, section VI). The Greece of this period was tribal, aristocratic, agricultural, and confined to the Aegean basin. By the end of the sixth century B.C. all this had changed. The tribe had given way to the *city-state;* other social classes had risen to challenge the nobility; industry and commerce had come to play a considerable role; and Greek colonies were scattered upon all the Mediterranean shores. These changes transformed the Greek world during the formative age and cleared the way for the Classical Age (see Map VII, "Classical Age Empires in the Middle East and Europe").

A basic factor behind these developments was the geography of the Greek lands. Greece had no rich natural resources—no fertile river valleys or broad plains that, when properly developed and exploited, could support elaborate empires like those of the Middle East, India, and China. In Greece and on the Asia Minor coast there were successive mountain chains that restricted agricultural productivity and divided the countryside up into compartments. Consequently the Greeks had no *natural geopolitical center* that could provide a basis for regional integration. Instead, after the invasions, they settled down in isolated villages, usually located near some easily defended high point that provided both a refuge in time of danger and a location for a shrine to the gods. The settlement as a whole was called the *polis,* and the place of refuge the acropolis, literally "high town." If the polis was strategically situated near fertile lands or communication routes, it attracted more settlers and became the leading city of the region. In this manner dozens of little city-states emerged, relatively isolated and fiercely independent.

At the outset the city-states depended primarily on subsistence agriculture, herding, and fishing. But by the beginning of the eighth century B.C. economic self-sufficiency was undermined by population pressure. Land-hungry peasants were forced to take to the sea, to become pirates or traders or colonists, or, as often happened, some combination of the three. By the fifth century the entire Mediterranean basin, including the Black Sea, was ringed with prosperous Greek colonies that were overseas replicas of the mother cities (see Chapter 4, section II).

The founding of colonies set off a chain reaction that in the end transformed the Greek world. The colonies shipped raw materials, especially grain, to overpopulated Greece and in return received wine, olive oil, and manufactured goods, such as cloth and pottery. This trade pattern triggered an economic boom in the homeland. The Greek soil was better suited for olive orchards and vineyards than for wheat fields, and, now that wheat could be imported, rocky hillsides could be planted to grape vines and olive trees. Hence the amount of land under cultivation increased substantially. The shift to *commercial agriculture,* therefore, made it possible to support a population three to four times larger than under the former subsistence agriculture. Likewise manufactures increased, as we can see by the large quantities of Greek pottery unearthed not only around the Mediterranean but also far into the hinterland—into central Russia, southwest Germany, and northeast France. At the same time the Greek merchant marine prospered as it carried these goods back and forth. Indeed this was the first time in history that bulky commodities, as distinct from luxury items, were traded and transported on such a large scale. All this economic activity was efficiently lubricated by the growing use of coin money in which the Greeks pioneered.

The commercialization of agriculture meant debts as well as profits, especially for the small landholder. Formerly the nobles had collected rent in the form of a portion of the crop, so that in bad years the people pulled in their belts for the duration. But now the combination of foreign markets, money economy, and new luxuries left the small farmers vulnerable to mortgages, foreclosures, and even loss of personal freedom. Inevitably this led to bitter class conflict and to popular clamor for debt cancellation and redistribution of land. Likewise in the cities new wealthy families emerged and wanted political recognition commensurate with their economic strength. They could count on the support of the urban poor—artisans, stevedores, and sailors. All these discontented elements, then, struck out against the traditional political system where all power lay in the hands of the landowning aristocracy.

Change was greatly hastened in the seventh century when the aristocratic cavalryman, once the main figure on the battlefield, was replaced by the heavily armored infantryman, the hoplite. Massed together in a solid block or phalanx, with a shield in the left hand and a long spear in the right, the hoplites were trained to act in unison and could execute bristling sweeps through the hitherto invincible horsemen. This innovation undermined the military basis of aristocratic political authority. At the same time it raised the status and influence of the independent farmer and artisan who could afford to equip himself for phalanx service.

The combination of economic and military change brought about corresponding political change. The city-states that had started out as monarchies in the "Dark Age," gradually changed to aristocratic *oligarchies.* Then, in the seventh century they came under the rule of dictators, or tyrants as they were called. These ambitious leaders, usually of noble birth, championed popular demands, won mass support, and seized personal power. The word "tyrant" referred to one who ruled without legal right, but it carried with it no sense of moral reproach. Indeed, tyrants commonly favored the interests of the common people against the privileged classes, and often, though not always, hastened the advent of democracy.

Sparta, in the southern Peloponnesus, was the classic example of the opposite trend—away from democracy. About 1000 B.C. the Dorian forefathers of the Spartans had overrun the rich valley of the Eurotas and reduced the native population to the status of *helots,* or serfs. Later in the eighth century the Spartans conquered the rich plains of neighboring Messenia, so they had no need for overseas expansion. But the price paid was heavy and inevitable. Sparta was deprived of the economic and intellectual stimulus of foreign contacts and condemned to a static rural existence. In addition the Spartans were forced to organize their state like a military camp in order to keep down the large subject population. Everything was subordinated to military needs. Only healthy infants were allowed to live, the sickly ones were left to die of exposure in the wilderness. From the age of seven, boys lived and trained in the barracks. Until age sixty all men remained under military discipline. Private life was all but abolished and luxury was frowned upon. This routine made the Spartan the best infantryman in all Greece. But it left him no time or inclination for writing plays or carving statues or formulating philosophy.

Meanwhile the Athenians had been developing an altogether different type of society. Far from being a band of invaders camped amidst a hostile population, the Athenians prided themselves on being native inhabitants of Attica. Like the Greeks of other city-states, they began with a monarchy which gave way to an oligarchy of nine archons who were the chief executive officers and who were invariably aristocrats. But in contrast to Sparta, the evolution of Athens was towards increasing democracy. The burgeoning trade created a strong middle class that joined forces with the dispossessed peasantry and demanded political reform. In 594 B.C. all parties agreed upon the appointment of the archon Solon as chief magistrate with full powers for reform. In addition to ending enslavement for debts, this legendary lawgiver admitted propertyless citizens for the first time to the Athenian Assembly, made wealthy businessmen eligible to become archons, and diluted the power of the aristocratic Areopagus, or chief judicial body, by establishing new and more popular courts of justice. This social reform and political liberalization was continued by Pisistratus who became the first tyrant of Athens about 560 B.C., and later by Cleisthenes who created a new Council of Five Hundred for which all male citizens were eligible. By 500 B.C. Athens had emerged as a democracy while Sparta remained a militarized and regimented society.

II. CLASSICAL AGE, 500–336 B.C.

In his famous funeral speech commemorating the Athenian soldiers who had fallen in battle against the Spartans in 431, Pericles declared, "Our city is open to the world. . . . Athens is the school of Greece." This boast was fully justified. During the fifth century B.C. Athens overshadowed Sparta and all other Greek cities. This "golden age" of Periclean Athens was simultaneously the golden age of all classical Greece.

One reason for the dazzling preeminence of Athens was its leading role in the fateful defeat of the great Persian Empire. The root of the war was the Persian conquest of the Greek city-states in Asia Minor during the mid-sixth-century B.C. Heavy-handed Persian interference in their domestic affairs led the cities to revolt in 499. They appealed to the homeland cities for aid and received a positive response, partly because the Persian Empire at this time was expanding into Southeastern Europe and menacing Greece from the north. Despite the naval assistance from across the Aegean, the Asia Minor cities were overwhelmed by 494. The Persian Emperor Darius now resolved to chastise the obstreperous Greeks and sent out an expedition that landed at Marathon, to the northwest of Athens, in 490. Although the Athenians fought almost alone, thanks to inter-city rivalries, their phalanxes inflicted a stunning defeat on the invaders. The effect on Greek morale was enormous. "These were the first Greeks," wrote the historian Herodotus, "who had the courage to face up to Persian dress and the men who wore it, whereas up to that time the very name of the Persians brought terror to a Greek."

Ten years later the Persians came again with much larger forces, and this time by land through Thrace and Thessaly. A mixed force under Spartan command fought gallantly to the last man at the pass of Thermopylae. The Persians pressed on to Athens, which they sacked, but the Athenian fleet destroyed the Persians in nearby Salamis. An allied Greek fleet followed the retreating Persians across the Aegean and won another naval victory. Soon the Asia Minor cities were freed from Persian rule, and the Greeks emerged as the victors over the greatest empire in the world.

The repercussions of the Greek triumph were tremendous. First and foremost, it saved the Greeks from being engulfed in an oriental despotism, thereby allowing them to preserve their identity and to make their unique contribution to human civilization. The success of the Greeks, and especially of the Athenian fleet, also furthered the cause of democracy, for the rowers who drove the ships into battle were citizens who could not afford to equip themselves as hoplites. Thus the urban poor now assumed a military role even more important than that of the propertied hoplites. This naturally strengthened the movement for more democracy, which reached its height during the Age of Pericles (461–429 B.C.).

Although an aristocrat by birth, Pericles was an earnest democrat who completed the transference of power to the Assembly. All adult male citizens were members of this body which was the sovereign power in the affairs of Athens. Pericles also introduced pay for service in most public offices so that the poor could afford to assume such offices. In addition he established an array of popular courts in which final decisions were rendered by juries on which all citizens could serve if chosen by lot. In giving his funeral oration in honor of the Athenian heroes who fell in battle with Spartans in 431, Pericles was quite justified, then, in proudly stating that, ''Athens is the school of Hellas.''

PERICLES'S FUNERAL ORATION

The Athenian leader, Pericles, has left the classic description of the culture of his city during its great golden age. He gave the following famous account during his funeral oration commemorating the Athenian soldiers who had fallen in battle against Sparta in 431 B.C.*

Our form of government does not enter into rivalry with the institutions of others. We do not copy our neighbours, but are an example to them. It is true that we are called a democracy, for the administration is in the hands of the many and not of the few. But while the law secures equal justice to all alike in their private disputes, the claim of excellence is also recognized; and when a citizen is in any way distinguished, he is preferred to the public service, not as a matter of privilege, but as the reward of merit. Neither is poverty a bar, but a man may benefit his country whatever be the obscurity of his condition. There is no exclusiveness in our public life, and in our private intercourse we are not suspicious of one another, nor angry with our neighbour if he does what he likes. . . . We are lovers of the beautiful, yet simple in our tastes, and we cultivate the mind without loss of manliness. Wealth we employ, not for talk and ostentation, but when there is a real use for it. To avow poverty with us is no disgrace; the true disgrace is in doing nothing to avoid it. An Athenian citizen does not neglect the state because he takes care of his own household; and even those of us who are engaged in business have a very fair idea of politics. We alone regard a man who takes no interest in public affairs, not as a harmless, but as a useless character; and if few of us are originators, we are all sound judges of policy. The great impediment to action is, in our opinion, not discussion, but the want of that knowledge which is gained by discussion preparatory to action. For we have a peculiar power of thinking before we act and of acting too. . . .

To sum up: I say that Athens is the school of Hellas. . . .

I have paid the required tribute, in obedience to the law, making use of such fitting words as I had. The tribute of deeds has been paid in part; for the dead have been honourably interred, and it remains only that their children should be maintained at the public charge until they are grown up: this is the solid prize with which, as with a garland, Athens crowns her sons living and dead, after a struggle like theirs.

*B. Jowett, trans., *The History of Thucydides* (New York: Tandy-Thomas, 1909), book 2, pp. 35–46.

Finally the prominent role of Athens in the Persian Wars led the city to a course that eventually ended in *imperialism*. Whereas Sparta was immobilized by its static economy and the constant threat of a helot revolt, Athens took the lead in organizing a confederacy of Asiatic Greeks and islanders. Known as the Delian Confederation because its headquarters were originally on the small island of Delos, its purpose was collective security against possible further Persian attacks. It was theoretically an alliance of equals, for the constitution provided each member with only one vote in the periodic meetings. But from the start Athens provided the executive leadership. The generals were Athenians and Athens also collected tribute from cities unable or unwilling to furnish ships. Step by step Athens tightened its hold, until by 450 B.C. the Confederation had become an empire, and the power of Athens extended, in the words of Euripides, from Ionia "to the outward Ocean of the West"—that is, to the Atlantic.

Almost inevitably, the sea power of Athens clashed with the land power of Sparta. The fighting dragged on indecisively for ten years. The Spartan armies raided Attica each year but could not penetrate the long walls that joined Athens to the sea and protected its supplies. The Athenians for their part were badly hurt by the great plague of 429 B.C. which carried off almost half the population, including Pericles. They could only make random raids on the coast of the Peloponnesus. Then in 415 the fatal decision was made to send the Athenian fleet to capture Sicily and cut off Sparta's grain supply. "Fleet and army," wrote Thucydides, "perished from the face of the earth, nothing was saved." Athens's allies now revolted; the Spartans finally destroyed the long wall; and Athens was starved into capitulation in 404 B.C. Athens was left shorn of its fleets, its empire, and even its vaunted democracy, for the Spartan victors imposed a short-lived oligarchic regime.

This ruinous war left the Greek world exhausted and solved none of its problems. Spartan high-handedness caused Thebes and Athens to unite together in a new league for mutual protection. In 371 the Thebans inflicted on the Spartans their first major military defeat in two hundred years. For the next decade Thebes was supreme on the Greek mainland, but then intercity rivalries prevailed again and the city-states once more were engulfed in a confused anarchy of shifting alliances and petty wars. The stage was set for a foreign power to subjugate and forcibly unify Greece. In 388 B.C. Philip of Macedon smashed the combined armies of Thebes and Athens at Chaeronea. He deprived the Greek cities of most of their autonomy, but before he could proceed further he was assassinated in 336 B.C. His successor was his world famous son, Alexander the Great.

The Classical Age was over; the Hellenistic Age was beginning. Before turning to the latter we shall pause to consider the civilization of the Classical Age, an age that is generally accepted as one of the great triumphs of the human mind and spirit.

III. CIVILIZATION OF THE CLASSICAL AGE

The "Golden Age of Pericles," "the Greek Miracle," "the Glory That Was Greece"—these are some of the tributes commonly used in referring to the civilization of fifth-century Greece.

We shall see that this civilization had its shortcomings, yet these extravagant praises are understandable and largely deserved. Why is this so? What was the basis of the Greek "genius"? It may be safely assumed that it was not literally a matter of genius—that the Indo-Europeans who migrated to the south Balkans did not happen to be genetically superior to those who migrated to the Middle East or India or Western Europe. The answer must be sought in the comparison of the historical development of the Greeks with that of the other Indo-Europeans who settled in other regions of Eurasia.

Such a comparison suggests two explanations for the extraordinary achievements of the Greeks. In the first place they lived near enough to the earliest centers of civilization in Egypt and Mesopotamia to profit from their pioneering accomplishments. But they were not so close that they lost their individuality. Indeed, the main significance of the outcome of the Persian Wars was precisely that it allowed the Greeks to have their cake and eat it too.

The second factor behind the Greek achievement was the emergence and persistence of the polis which provided the essential institutional framework for the cultural blossoming. The polis, of course, was not a uniquely Greek institution. In India, for example, the Aryan immigrants in the earlier stage of their development also had what amounted to city-states in certain regions. But these were eventually absorbed by the territorial monarchies that came to dominate the Indian peninsula. The Greeks alone were able to preserve their city-states for several centuries.

One reason was the mountainous terrain, which did not afford a geopolitical base for a regional empire (see section I of this chapter). Another was the direct access to the sea enjoyed by most of the Greek city-states, which gave them economic strength as well as intellectual stimulation. It is true that the Greeks paid a heavy price for their polis fragmentation in the form of continual wars. And war led eventually to unification imposed from without, first by Macedon and then by Rome. But in the meantime they enjoyed centuries of freedom within their respective states, and this freedom was a prerequisite for the great creative outburst of the fifth century.

The classical Greek civilization was not purely original. Like all civilizations, it borrowed heavily from what had gone before, in this case the Middle Eastern civilizations. But what the Greeks borrowed, whether art forms from Egypt or mathematics and astronomy from Mesopotamia, they stamped with the distinctive quality of their minds. And this distinctive stamp was, in the final analysis, an openmindedness, an intellectual curiosity, an eagerness to learn, and a commonsense approach. When the Greeks traveled abroad, as they did very often as traders, soldiers, colonists, and tourists, they did so with a critical eye and skeptical mind. They questioned everything and tested all issues at the bar of reason. In Plato's *Apology,* Socrates maintains that the individual must refuse, at all costs, to be coerced by human authority or by any tribunal, to do anything, or think anything, which his own mind condemns as wrong—". . . the life which is unexamined is not worth living. . . ."

This sort of free thinking was uniquely Greek, at least in such a strong and pervasive form. Unique also was the secular view of life, the conviction that the chief business of existence was the complete expression of human personality here and now. This combination of rationalism and secularism enabled the Greeks to think freely and creatively about human problems and social issues. And they expressed their thoughts and emotions in their great literary, philosophical, and artistic creations, which are relevant and compelling to the present day.

These unique qualities of the Greeks are clearly reflected in their religious thought and practices. The Greeks viewed their gods as similar in nature to themselves, differing only in superior power, longevity, and beauty. By believing in such divinities the Greeks felt secure and at home in a world governed by familiar and comprehensible powers. The relationship between people and their gods was essentially one of give and take. In return for prayers and sacrifices the gods were expected to demonstrate their good will. The religious tie consisted of "common shrines and sacrifices" as Herodotus stated, rather than of an organized church or a common faith. The Greek religion never formulated a common body of doctrines or a sacred book, though Homer's *Iliad* and Hesiod's *Theogony* summed up prevailing religious concepts. The quality of Greek religion becomes evident when contrasted with that of the Mesopotamians. According to Mesopotamian explanations of the origins of things, the human race had been specifically created to build temples for the gods and to feed them with offerings. Such duties, in fact, were the whole reason for human existence. How different was the conception of the sixth-century Greek philosopher Xenophanes:

> Mortals think that the gods are begotten, and wear clothes like their own, and have a voice and a form. If oxen or horses or lions had hands and could draw with them and make works of art as men do, horses would draw the shapes of gods like horses, oxen like oxen; each kind would represent their bodies just like their own forms. The Ethiopians say their gods are black and flat-nosed; the Thracians, that theirs are blue-eyed and red-haired.[1]

Religion in classical Greece was an integral part of polis life and accordingly affected every aspect of that life. Religion offered an interpretation of the natural world, a consecration of daily work and of social institutions, and it was also one of the chief sources of inspiration for poets and artists. Every Greek temple was a focus of local and national culture. Many temples specialized, more or less accidentally, in the development of particular arts. A brotherhood of miracle workers grew up around the worship of the legendary Aesculapius on the island of Cos. These miracle workers became the first scientific physicians. Outstanding was the renowned Hippocrates, whose medical treatises were resolutely clinical in tone. He diagnosed each case on the basis of objective observation, rejecting magical causes or cures for disease. Regarding the "sacred" disease, epilepsy, he wrote,

> It seems to me that the disease called sacred is no more divine than any other. It has a natural cause, just as other diseases have. Men think it divine because they do not understand it. . . . In Nature all things are alike in this, that they can all be traced to preceding causes.[2]

Likewise round the worship of Dionysus, the wine god, there grew up a company of actors who went from dramatizing the ritual cult of the god to creating profound tragedy and uproarious comedy. This literature cannot be imagined apart from its setting in fifth-century Athens. Plays were produced before the assembled citizens at regularly held religious festivals organized and financed by the state. The close contact and relationship between the author and his audience was responsible for the balance and normality of Athenian drama. Aeschylus, in his *Persians,* presented a dramatized version of the victory at Salamis before the very citizens who had won that victory. Sophocles in his tragedies referred frequently to the gods, yet he was not interested primarily in religious problems. Rather he was chiefly concerned with human beings, noble and admirable, confronted with forces beyond their control, committing awful deeds, and suffering terrible retribution. The heroism and suffering of Oedipus in the face of overwhelming adversity are the essence of tragedy. His tragedy expresses something of the meaning of human life and of the problems common to all men.

If Sophocles was not deeply interested in conventional religion, Euripides was positively skeptical. He wrote plainly and without mincing words of the weakness of the gods and satirized those who deemed them superior to men. Euripides was generally critical and a dedicated fighter for unpopular causes. He championed the rights of the slave and the foreigner, urged the emancipation of women, and attacked the glorification of war. The same is even more true of Aristophanes, whose comedies were filled with social satire. Himself a conservative who yearned for the good old days, he ridiculed democratic leaders and policies. In the *Lysistrata* he presented a group of women who, appalled by the endless bloodshed, refused to sleep with their husbands until they stopped their wars.

Greek art also was the distinctive product of a polis civilization. Art and architecture found their highest expression in the temples, the civic and religious core of polis culture. The temples were the revered dwelling places of the protecting gods and goddesses. A famous example is the Parthenon in Athens which was built as a shrine to the protecting goddess, Athena. Sculpture, the handmaiden of architecture, served to decorate the houses of the gods. Master sculptors, such as Phidias and Praxiteles, worked on temple walls and pediments and also carved statues for the interiors. All of Greek art embodied the basic Greek ideals of balance, harmony, and moderation. This is evident if we compare the Parthenon with an Egyptian pyramid or a Mesopotamian ziggurat, or a Greek statue with the relatively crude and stilted sculptures of most Middle Eastern peoples of that time.

We find a similar contrast when we compare the philosophical speculation of the Greeks with that of other peoples. The sixth-century rationalist philosophers of Ionia on the Asia Minor coast were the first to challenge the traditional supernatural explanations of the nature of the world. They posed the basic question, "What is the stuff of which the world is made?" Thales speculated that everything originally was water, because this substance is found in liquid, solid, and vapor form. Heraclitus thought fire was the prime element because it was so active and could transform everything. Anaximenes believed it was air, arguing that it became fire when rarefied, and wind, cloud, water, earth, and stone when condensed. In the light of modern science these efforts may appear naive, but what is important is that the question was asked and the answer was sought by the free use of reason, not by resorting to intervention of the gods.

As Greek society grew more complex, philosophers about the mid-fifth-century B.C. turned their attention from the physical universe to human beings and their problems. Protagoras, the outstanding spokesman of the Sophists, reflected the interest in human beings. "Man is the measure of all things," he maintained, by which he meant that there are no absolute truths since everything is relative to the needs of man himself. This emphasis on the value of the individual human led the Sophists to condemn slavery and war and to espouse most popular causes of the time. On the other hand many Greeks, especially those of conservative persuasion, feared that the relativism of the Sophists endangered social order and morality. Typical was Socrates (c. 470–399 B.C.), who was profoundly disturbed by the political corruption of his day and by the absence of any certain guide to correct living. Out of his never-ending conversations with his friends he evolved the science of *dialectics*. Provisional definitions were tested by questions and answers until universally recognized truths were reached. In this way, Socrates maintained, concepts of absolute truth or absolute good or absolute beauty could be discovered. These would provide enduring guides for personal conduct, in contrast to the relativism of the Sophists, which often provided rationalizations for private and public corruption.

Socrates's disciple Plato (427–374 B.C.) was an aristocrat who shared with his friends a great pride in Athens, but also a distrust of the Athenian people. Distrust deepened into hatred when Athenian democracy condemned Socrates to death. Plato's goal was a society that preserved aristocratic privileges and yet was acceptable to the poorer classes. Accordingly he divided the citizens of his ideal Republic into four grades: guardians, philosophers, soldiers, and the masses that did the work. This class differentiation was to be permanent, and it was to be justified by a myth, or "noble lie," about God creating men of four kinds: gold, silver, brass, and iron.

The other great thinker of this period was Aristotle (384–322 B.C.), who began as Plato's disciple but who, following his master's death, founded the Lyceum where his own unique approach to understanding the world soon found a forum. Aristotle was a collector and rational thinker rather than a mystic, a logician and scientist rather than a philosopher. He took all knowledge for his province, so that he ranged more widely than anyone before or since. His outstanding contributions were in logic, physics, biology, and the humanities; indeed he established these subjects as formal disciplines. As a great encyclopedist, he sought orderliness in every aspect of nature and of human life. Thus he correlated the human social classes of the world with corresponding orders in the natural world, beginning with minerals at the bottom, then vegetables, animals, and finally man at the top. This gradation justified the division of human beings into born masters and born slaves.

No account of classical Greece would be complete without reference to Herodotus and Thucydides who related the stirring events of their times and in so doing created a new form of literature, namely, history. Herodotus had lived first among the Asia Minor Greeks who had fallen under Persian rule. He then lived in Athens where the Persians had suffered their great defeat. Herodotus wrote that the cause for the defeat was the democratic constitution of the Athenians, so that his *History* is the first great tribute to democracy. The moral of his tale may be illustrated by the words he attributes to a Greek who speaks of his countrymen to the Persian king:

> For though they be free men, they are not in all respects free; Law is the master whom they own, and this master they fear more than your subjects fear you. Whatever it commands they do; and its commandment is always the same; it forbids them to flee in battle, whatever the number of their foes, and requires them to stand firm, and either to conquer or die.[3]

Thucydides's history was very different, being of the Peloponnesian War in which Athens, after twenty-seven years of bitter struggle, was finally beaten to its knees. Whereas Herodotus wrote about victory and glory, Thucydides analyzed defeat and suffering. His sympathies were unquestionably with Athens, whose armies he had led as a general. But he sternly suppressed his emotions and set for himself the task of determining objectively the causes of the disaster. Although he did not use the phrase, he nevertheless said in effect that he was seeking to create a science of society.

> Of the events of the war I have not ventured to speak from any chance information, nor according to any notion of my own; I have described nothing but what I either saw myself or learned from others of whom I made the most careful and particular enquiry. The task was a laborious one, because eyewitnesses of the same occurrences gave different accounts of them, as they remembered or were interested in the actions of one side or the other. And very likely the strictly historical character of my narrative may be disappointing to the ear. But if he who desires to have before his eyes a true picture of the events which have happened, and of the like events which may be expected to happen hereafter in the order of human things, shall pronounce what I have written to be useful, then I shall be satisfied. My history is an ever-lasting possession, not a prize composition which is heard and forgotten.[4]

Now that we have described the remarkable achievements of the Greeks in so many fields, we have also to point out certain failings. Women were accorded inferior status; slaves were exploited; and these slaves, together with the metics, or resident aliens, were denied Athenian citizenship, even though they made up the majority of the population. All this is true but largely irrelevant, for we must judge classical Greece by the standards of that time, not by present-day practices, or by some perfect utopia.

As regards citizenship, the Athenians, like all other Greeks, regarded themselves as a kinship group, so that one became a citizen only by descent and not by residence, however long. The metics, as voluntary immigrants, were free to leave whenever they wished. Yet many lived permanently in Athens and made generous gifts to their adoptive city, suggesting a certain degree of contentment and loyalty. Likewise, slavery, despite its many bad effects, which will be analyzed in the last section of this chapter, was not as widespread as commonly assumed. The great majority of citizens—two-thirds to three-fourths—had no slaves and worked for their living as farmers, artisans, shopkeepers, and sailors. The popular notion that the average male Athenian spent his days watching plays, serving on public bodies, and discussing philosophy and politics, while his slaves supported him, is pure fiction.

Classical Greece, then, should be judged not by what it failed to do but by what it did. If this be the criterion, then the contributions and their historical significance stand out clearly and overwhelmingly. The spirit of free inquiry, the theory and practice of democracy, the major forms of art and literature and philosophical thought, and the emphasis on individual freedom and individual responsibility—these are the splendid legacy of Greece to humanity.

IV. HELLENISTIC AGE, 336–31 B.C.

The Hellenistic Age derives its name from the new civilization that emerged as classical-Greek culture spread throughout the Middle East in the wake of Alexander's conquests (see Chapter 4, section III). On succeeding his father, Philip, in 336 B.C., Alexander first crushed a revolt in Thebes with such severity that the other Greek cities were persuaded to accept his rule. Then in 334 B.C. he led his Macedonian soldiers eastward against the Persians. Crossing the Hellespont, he overran first Asia Minor, then Syria, Egypt, Mesopotamia, and Persia itself, capturing Darius's capital, Persepolis, in 330 B.C. Next year the conqueror pushed on to the Hindu Kush and Bactria, and from there marched on into India, penetrating as far as the Punjab. Only the refusal of his men to advance any further persuaded Alexander to return to Babylon where he died of malarial fever in 323 at the age of thirty-three.

Rival generals now fought for control of the great empire until by the beginning of the third century three succession states emerged: Macedon in the Balkan peninsula, Egypt under the Ptolemies, and the Asian provinces under the Seleucids. Although Alexander's empire proved short-lived, the succession states survived more or less intact for three centuries, during which time the Middle East became Hellenized. Thousands of Greek merchants, administrators, teachers, professional men, and mercenary soldiers emigrated from their city-states to Egypt and the Asian provinces, attracted by the unprecedented opportunities afforded by those rich lands. Thus the foundations were laid for the new Hellenistic civilization, a hybrid creation that differed from the classical parent stock in virtually every respect.

The political framework changed radically because the traditional structure of the independent polis was undermined and made sterile. The Greek city-states tried to survive by experimenting with federal unions—the Achaean League and the Aetolian Federation—but they proved ineffective and eventually succumbed to the Roman legions. As for the cities in the succession states, they never resembled the classical polis. They were divided internally by the distinctions between the Greek immigrants and the native people. Furthermore they were always completely subordinate to one or another imperial structure. If the citizens suffered from tyrannical, or weak kings, they could do very little about it. The real decisions were made in the courts or on battlefields rather than in meetings of popular assemblies. Thus the citizens understandably concentrated on accumulating wealth and enjoying life, leaving the poor and the slaves to shift for themselves as best they could. The civic spirit and social cohesion of the old polis gave way to self-centeredness and class strife.

Economic conditions and institutions also changed fundamentally. The Greek homeland suffered economic as well as political eclipse. It had depended on the export of wine, oil, and manufactured goods in return for foodstuffs and raw materials from the overseas colonies. But by the fourth century these colonies had taken root and developed their own industries and vineyards and olive orchards.

Although the Greek lands suffered economic decay, many Greeks grew rich by emigrating to the Middle East, which was now open to them. They had much to contribute with their enterprising spirit and their advanced commercial and banking methods. They discovered and circulated the huge gold and silver hoard of the Persian dynasty. Also they introduced, or put to wider use, technological inventions such as the suction and piston pumps, the water mill, the worm screw, and a hydraulic machine. The Greeks also directed large-scale public works and state enterprises, including irrigation systems, mines, quarries, salt pans, ''royal lands,'' and workshops for luxury fabrics and ceramics. The net result was increased economic integration which brought about a corresponding increase in commerce and productivity. The proceeds, however, were grossly maldistributed. Speculators took advantage of rising profits to reap great fortunes, while slaves increased in number and free workmen declined in status. It was a period, in short, of greater productivity but also of greater economic inequality and social strife.

The common people during this Hellenistic Age were buffeted not only economically but also psychologically. Many felt lost in the large new cities with their teeming multitudes uprooted from their traditional environment. In the old polis, life had been relatively simple. Law, morality, religion, and duties were all clearly defined and generally accepted. Now all this was gone and citizens found themselves in a formless world. Furthermore the Hellenistic cities frequently were torn by racial and cultural as well as class divisions. The rulers tried to cultivate a mystique of personal loyalty, adopting titles such as Savior and Benefactor. But such expedients offered no lasting solution. Each person remained confronted with the question of how to conduct himself in the face of the impersonal and overwhelming forces of the time.

The response of intellectuals tended to be to withdraw from worldly affairs and turn from reason to mysticism. Their withdrawal was reflected in the vogue for romantic adventure and utopian literature. It was reflected also in the philosophies of the day—*Cynicism, Skepticism, Epicureanism,* and *Stoicism*—which though very different in many respects, were generally concerned with the pursuit of personal happiness rather than of social welfare. Their underlying motive was to reconcile the individual to the uncertainties of life in an economically insecure and war-ridden world.

If philosophy was the religion of the cultivated upper classes, the religion of the lower classes was very different. They turned to cults of oriental origin—Mithraism, Gnosticism, the Egyptian mother-goddess Isis, and the astral religion of the Chaldeans. All these promised salvation in after-life. All satisfied the emotional needs of the harried masses with comforting assurances of a paradise to come. Thus the secularism and *rationalism* of classical Greece now gave way to mysticism and otherworldliness.

In view of these trends in philosophy and religion, it is surprising that more progress was achieved in science in the Hellenistic Age than in any other period prior to the seventeenth century. This was due in part to the economic opportunities afforded by Alexander's conquests. The greatly expanded markets provided incentive to improve technology in order to increase output. Also the continual wars amongst the succession states, and between them and outside powers, created a demand for more complex war engines. Equally stimulating was the direct contact between Greek science and that of the Middle East—not only of Mesopotamia and Egypt, but also, to a certain extent, of India. Finally, the Macedonian rulers of the Hellenistic states, brought up to value the prestige of Greek learning, generously supported scientific research. This was particularly true in Egypt, where the Alexandria Museum and Library was in effect the first state-supported research institute in history. It included astronomical observatories, laboratories, and dissecting rooms, botanical and zoological gardens, and a library of from 500,000 to 700,000 volumes. All these factors explain the galaxy of outstanding scientists during these centuries—Euclid in geometry, Archimedes in mechanics, Ptolemy in astronomy, Eratosthenes in geography, and Galen in medicine.

In conclusion the historical significance of the Hellenistic Age is that it brought the East and West together, breaking the separate molds that had been formed through history. Now for the first time people thought of the entire civilized world as a unit. At first the Greeks and Macedonians went to the East as conquerors and rulers, and imposed a pattern of Hellenization. But in the process they themselves were changed, so that the resulting Hellenistic civilization was a blend rather than a transplantation. And in the long run the religions of the East made their way West and contributed substantially to the transformation of the Roman Empire and medieval Europe.

V. EARLY REPUBLIC, TO 264 B.C.

Meanwhile the city-states in Greece continued to fight each other as they had in the past. They organized unions such as the Achaean League and the Aetolian Federation, but none proved lasting and effective. Despite many warnings, the divided Greeks ignored the rising power of the Romans. After destroying the Carthaginians, their great rivals in the western Mediterranean, the Romans turned eastward. First they conquered Macedon and the divided Greek cities, and then they overran the entire Hellenistic East.

Why were the Romans able to become the masters of the entire Mediterranean, and eventually of all Europe? Actually there were many similarities between the early histories of the Greeks and the Romans. Both were of the same ethnic stock, for just as the Indo-European Achaeans and Dorians filtered down the Balkan peninsula to Greece, so the Indo-European Latins filtered down the Italian peninsula to the south bank of the Tiber River. Among the Latin communities formed at the time was Rome. Rome was located on the Tiber at the lowest point that could be conveniently crossed, and at the highest to which small ships could go. This strategic position, similar to that of London on the Thames, made Rome from the very beginning both more mercantile and more open to foreign influences than other Latin settlements.

The chief foreign influences came from two civilized peoples who had come from overseas to settle in Italy—the Etruscans and the Greeks. The Etruscans, who arrived about 800 B.C., probably from Asia Minor, settled to the north of the Tiber and then conquered the Latins to the south. The Greeks, who appeared shortly after the Etruscans, established colonies in southern Italy and Sicily, including Tarentum, Syracuse, and Naples.

About 500 B.C. Rome expelled its last Etruscan king and began its career as an independent city-state. Within a few years it had conquered the surrounding peoples and controlled the entire Latin plain from the Apennine Mountains to the sea coast. Roman institutions during this formative period were similar to those of the early Greek cities. The king originally held the imperium, or sovereign power. He was restrained only by an advisory council of aristocrats and a popular assembly that had power only to approve or disapprove legislation. Then, as in Greece, the monarchy was abolished and the patricians became the dominant element in society. The sovereign power formerly held by the king was now delegated to two consuls who were elected for one-year periods and who were always patricians. The Senate, which was the principal legislative body, was also an aristocratic body and remained so even after a few commoners, or *plebeians,* were admitted.

The development of Rome diverged from that of the Greek city-states when Rome accomplished what was beyond the capacity of the Greek cities—the conquest and unification of the entire peninsula. Why was it that Rome could master the Italian peninsula whereas no Greek city was able to unify even the Greek lands, let alone the whole of the Balkan peninsula? One reason was the marked difference in terrain. The Balkans are a jumble of mountains, whereas in Italy there are only the Appenines which are not as difficult to cross and which run north and south without transverse ranges. Consequently the far less compartmentalized Italian peninsula is easier to unite and keep united. There was no Balkan counterpart to the system of Roman roads that knitted Italy into one unit.

Another reason for the success of the Romans was their enlightened treatment of the other Italian peoples. Athens had levied tribute and never extended its citizenship. Rome granted full citizenship to about a fourth of the population of the peninsula. The rest were granted Latin citizenship, which carried substantial but not complete privileges. Autonomy was enjoyed by all. The only restrictions were the loss of control over foreign relations and a compulsory manpower levy for military service. This farsighted policy saved Rome, for its Italian allies remained loyal during the critical years when Hannibal was rampaging up and down the length of the peninsula. Finally, the Romans prevailed because of the superior military force and strategy that they developed. In contrast to the traditional phalanx of 8000 men, which had proved too large and unwieldy, the Roman legions were trained to disperse and fight in small units.

By 295 B.C. the Romans had won central Italy and pushed south against Tarentum, the prosperous Greek city in the "instep" of the peninsula. The Tarentines called in the help of the Greek king Pyrrhus of Epirus, ranked by Hannibal as second only to Alexander in generalship. Pyrrhus won two "Pyrrhic victories." But he could not afford his heavy losses, whereas the Romans, though they lost even more, could draw from a pool of 750,000 Italian fighting men. So Pyrrhus withdrew in 272 B.C. with the prophetic observation "What a battleground I am leaving for Rome and Carthage!" Only eight years later in 264 B.C., Rome and Carthage were at war in Sicily.

VI. LATE REPUBLIC, 265–27 B.C.

The transformation of Rome from an Italian republic to a great empire was sudden and spectacular, rather like the conquests of Alexander. Indeed certain common basic factors help to explain the explosive expansions of both Macedon and Rome. Each had evolved superior military instruments and techniques. Each enjoyed the vital advantage of social vigor and cohesion in contrast to the social decrepitude and fragmentation of the Persian Empire and the Hellenistic succession states.

Rome's great rival, Carthage, had started as a Phoenician colony about 850 B.C. Thanks to its near monopoly of the transit trade in the western Mediterranean, Carthage had become rich and powerful. With its wide-ranging fleets and mercenary troops it dominated Northwest Africa, southern Spain, Sardinia, Corsica, and western Sicily. At first there was no direct conflict between Rome and Carthage for the simple reason that one was a land power and the other a sea power. But they finally did clash when the Romans conquered southern Italy. The Romans feared Carthage's growing influence in Sicily, which was all too close to their newly won possessions.

The First Punic War (264–241 B.C.) forced the Romans for the first time to turn to the sea. They built a fleet and by turning naval battles into boarding operations they doggedly wore down the Carthaginians and conquered Sicily. The struggle to the death between the two great powers was now inevitable. Rome spent the next twenty years subduing the Celtic tribes in the Po valley, thereby increasing its reserve of peasant soldiers. Carthage, to compensate for the loss of Sicily, consolidated its hold on Spain. From this base the great Carthaginian strategist, Hannibal, launched his daring invasion of Italy, crossing the Alps in 218 and thus beginning the Second Punic War (218–201). He defeated the Romans in battle after battle, particularly in his great triumph of Cannae (216). But the loyalty of Rome's allies robbed him of victory. When a Roman army landed near Carthage, Hannibal, undefeated in Italy, was recalled only to be defeated on his home ground. Once again Rome had exhausted its opponent, and in 201 Carthage was forced to accept a peace leaving the former empire only its small home territory, its walls, and ten ships—enough to chase off the pirates. Despite this catastrophic defeat, the Carthaginians made a remarkable recovery. But this so alarmed the Romans that they ruthlessly provoked the Third Punic War (149–146 B.C.). Carthage itself was captured, the city completely destroyed, and the populace enslaved.

With these Punic Wars, Rome was caught in a chain reaction of conquest leading to further conquest. One reason was its overwhelming strength; with Carthage out of the way Rome was now the number-one power in the Mediterranean. Also conquest was manifestly profitable, as booty, slaves, and tribute poured in from each new province. Finally, there were the inevitable commitments and challenges associated with far-flung imperial frontiers. For example, Philip V of Macedon had aided Hannibal during the Second Punic War, so Rome, after having disposed of Carthage, turned on Macedon. The ensuing war proved to be the first of a series in which the Romans skillfully played off against each other the several Middle Eastern powers—Macedon, Seleucid Syria, Ptolemaic Egypt, and the rival Aetolian and Achaean leagues of Greek city-states.

Thus the Romans overran and annexed in quick succession Macedon, Greece, the Asia Minor states of Pergamum, Bithynia, and Cilicia, then Seleucid Syria, and finally Egypt in 31 B.C. In this manner the Romans took over the Hellenistic succession states of the East. In Asia though, they acquired only the provinces along the Mediterranean coast. All the interior had fallen to Parthia, which henceforth was to be Rome's chief rival in the East. Meanwhile Julius Caesar had gained fame by conquering (58–49 B.C.) all of Gaul between the English Channel and the Mediterranean. Finally the permanent occupation of Britain was begun in the first century of our era and was consolidated with the construction of a line of fortifications between the firths of Clyde and Forth. This marked the limits of Roman rule in Northern Europe.

Rome did not treat its newly acquired provinces as generously as it had its earlier Italian allies. The Senate appointed governors who were given a free hand so long as they kept sending back home an adequate flow of tribute, taxes, grain, and slaves. The result was shameless exploitation and extortion. The maladministration of Governor Gaius Verres in Sicily (73–71 B.C.), described in the following indictment by Cicero, was neither exceptional nor atypical:

Countless sums of money, under a new and unprincipled regulation, were wrung from the purses of the farmers; our most loyal allies were treated as if they were national enemies; Roman citizens were tortured and executed like slaves; the guiltiest criminals bought their legal acquittal. . . . Famous and ancient works of art, some of them the gifts of wealthy kings . . . this same governor stripped and despoiled every one of them. Nor was it only the civic statues and works of art he treated thus; he also pillaged the holiest and most venerated sanctuaries; in fact, he has not left the people of Sicily a single god whose workmanship he thought at all above the average of antiquity or artistic merit.[5]

These policies affected the Roman homeland almost as adversely as it affected the subject territories. Many of the small farmers in Italy had been ruined by the ravages of Hannibal's campaigns and by the long years of overseas service during the following wars. Then came the influx of cheap grain and of droves of slaves from the conquered provinces. The peasants were forced to sell out to the new class of the very rich. They were especially eager to accumulate large estates because agriculture was still considered the only respectable calling for gentlemen. Thus the second century B.C. saw the growth in Italy of large plantations (*latifundia*) worked by slaves and owned by absentee landlords. The dispossessed peasantry drifted to the towns where they lived in squalid tenements and once again had to compete with slaves for such work as was available. The authorities took care to provide them with ''bread and circuses'' (panis et circenses) in order to keep them quiet. Despite the insecurity and rootlessness, city life at least was exciting and alluring. Poets were loud in their praise of rustic virtues, but the peasants themselves thought otherwise and continued to flock to Rome—the ''common cesspool'' as the contemporary historian Sallust, termed it.

The political fruits of empire were as bitter as the economic. The earlier trend towards democratization was reversed because the Senate had directed the victorious overseas campaigns and gained greatly in prestige and power. Also the new urban mobs offered no basis for popular government since they were always ready to sell their votes or to support any demagogue who promised relief from their troubles. Equally disruptive was the changing character of the armed forces. Imperial obligations required a large standing army. It no longer sufficed to call up property owners for short-term militia service. So the ranks were opened to volunteers, and dispossessed peasants enlisted for long periods. Rome's legions accordingly changed from a citizen army to a professional one. The soldiers' first loyalty was not to the state but to their commanders to whom they looked for a share of the booty and of any land that might be available for distribution. The generals increasingly came to regard the legions entrusted to them as their own armies and used them to advance their personal fortunes.

Imperial expansion also disrupted Roman culture. The traditional Roman virtues had been those of poor, hard-working peasants. But when wealth began to pour into the capital, the ancient values of thrift, abstinence, and industry were soon forgotten. The last days of the Republic were marked by a wild scramble for money, the sort of ostentatious waste to be expected from the newly rich, and a callous indifference to all human values. "Rome," grumbled a contemporary, "has become a city where paramours fetch a better price than plowlands, and pots of pickled fish than plowmen."

In light of the above, it is understandable that the period from the end of the Punic Wars in 146 B.C. to the end of the Republic in 27 B.C. was one of crisis—of class war, slave revolts, and increasing military intervention in politics. A gallant reform was made at the outset by Tiberius Gracchus and his brother Gaius. They sought to use their elective positions as tribunes to push through a moderate program of land distribution. But the oligarchs would have none of it and resorted to violence to gain their ends. Tiberius was murdered in 133 B.C. along with three hundred of his followers. Twelve years later Gaius was driven to suicide, and the senatorial class resumed its sway.

The fate of the Gracchi brothers made clear the impossibility of orderly reform. The empire now was torn by generals competing for power at the top, and by slave revolts from below. The most serious of the revolts was that of Spartacus which broke out in 73 B.C. For a while the entire imperial system tottered, but in the end Spartacus was defeated, and the roads to Rome were lined with his crucified followers.

The final victor was Julius Caesar, the conqueror of Gaul, who had built up a powerful and devoted army. In 49 B.C. he crossed the river Rubicon, which separated Gaul from Italy, and in a series of brilliant campaigns defeated the forces of the Senate under his rival Pompey. Caesar was now the undisputed master of the empire. Precisely what he would have done with his mastery cannot be known, for he was murdered in 44 B.C. by representatives of the old oligarchy.

His death was followed by another thirteen years of political jockeying and armed strife between his adopted son and heir Octavian and the political adventurer Mark Antony. This interlude ended in the naval defeat of Antony and Cleopatra at Actium (31 B.C.), when Octavian finally grasped supreme power. He was only thirty-three years old at the time, the age at which the great Alexander had died. But Octavian had forty-four years of life ahead of him, during which he laid the foundations for two golden centuries of imperial peace and stability.

VII. EARLY EMPIRE, 27 B.C.–A.D. 284

In 27 B.C. the Senate conferred upon Octavian the titles of Augustus and Imperator, symbolizing the transformation of Rome from republic to empire. Octavian professed to prefer the republican title of "First Citizen" (*Princeps*), but in practice he acted like an emperor. He created a centralized system of courts under his own supervision and assumed direct control over provincial governors, punishing them severely for graft and extortion. He standardized taxes and made their collection a state function rather than a private business operated by greedy tax farmers. He kept close check on the army and saw to it that the soldiers were well provided for and swore allegiance directly to him. He also created a permanent navy that suppressed piracy and safeguarded the transportation of both commodities and troops to all parts of the empire.

By these measures Augustus, as he came to be known, created an efficient administrative system that ensured the *Pax Romana* that was to prevail for two centuries. The four emperors following Augustus—Tiberius (A.D. 14–37), Caligula (37–41), Claudius (41–54), and Nero (54–68)—were unworthy of their high office. But the empire weathered their misrule and then blossomed under a succession of "five good Emperors"—Nerva (96–98), Trajan (98–117), Hadrian (117–138), Antonius Pius (138–161), and Marcus Aurelius (161–180). During these reigns the Roman Empire reached its height, both in geographic extent and in the quality of its civilization.

In the extreme north, the imperial frontier was set by the fortifications built from the Forth to the Clyde. In the northeast, the Rhine and the Danube provided a natural frontier, which further east curved north of the Danube to include Dacia (modern Rumania). Both Asia Minor and Egypt were Roman possessions, but between the two the frontier ran close to the Mediterranean coast, leaving the interior to the Parthians and, after A.D. 224, to the Sassanians. Likewise in North Africa the Romans controlled the coastal territories between Egypt and the Atlantic, with the Sahara as their southern limit.

This huge area, with its strong natural frontiers, constituted a prosperous and virtually self-sufficient economic unit. Various factors contributed to the flourishing imperial economy during these centuries—honest and efficient administration, monetary stability, large-scale public works, and extensive trade, both within and without the empire. Thanks to the thriving domestic and foreign trade, staples and luxuries poured into the capital from as near as Gaul and as far as China—enough staples to feed and clothe over a million people, and enough luxuries to satisfy the extravagances of the rulers of the Western world.

In the cultural field, a basic achievement of the Romans was the extension into Central and Western Europe of urban civilization with all that that entailed. In this respect their role in the West was similar to that of the Greeks in the Middle East. In the third century B.C., after Alexander, the Greeks founded dozens of cities from which Hellenistic culture spread as far as India and Central Asia. So now the Romans founded cities such as London and Colchester in Britain, Autun and Vaison in Gaul, and Trier and Cologne in Germany. These cities, varying from 20 to 500 acres in size, were a distinct improvement on the relatively squalid hill-top forts and villages of the Celts and Germans. Even the slaves' quarters in these cities were more hygienic than the hovels of the contemporary native villagers. Furthermore the cities possessed public bathhouses for the comfort of the body and public theaters for the pleasures of the mind, as well as residential blocks and public markets and shops. These cities were the basic cells of the imperial culture as well as of the imperial political system.

The great city of the empire, of course, was Rome. It sprawled over 5000 acres and its population during the second century A.D. is estimated at a little over 1 million. This was gigantic for a period when there was little of the technology that makes modern cities viable. This lack would doubtless be very impressive to a modern visitor to ancient Rome. Such a visitor would have noticed the complete absence of street lighting and of sanitary facilities in the crowded tenements of the poor. Equally impressive would have been the teeming streets reverberating with the noise of hawkers bawling their wares, money changers ringing their coins, tinkers pounding their hammers, snake charmers playing their flutes, and beggars rehearsing their misfortunes to passersby. Life under such conditions was made tolerable by mass state facilities and entertainments—chariot races, gladiatorial contests, and sumptuous baths with exercise quarters, lounging halls, gardens, and libraries.

Finally the Rome of these centuries was also the center of imperial culture. This culture, as noted earlier, was essentially Greek-derived, particularly in such fields as literature, art, and philosophy. But in engineering and law, the Romans, with their bent for practicality, had important contributions of their own to make. Typically, the Romans achieved little in abstract science but excelled in the construction of aqueducts, sewer systems, bridges, and roads, the latter being so well built that they continued to be used through the Middle Ages, and in some cases even to the present day. Likewise, Roman architecture, in contrast to the Greek, was concerned primarily with secular structures such as baths, amphitheaters, stadia, and triumphal arches. And new Roman building materials—concrete, brick, and mortar—made possible vaulting on the grand scale necessary for their large buildings.

Perhaps the most important single intellectual contribution of the Romans was their body of law based on reason rather than custom. Their original laws, as set down in the Twelve Tablets about 450 B.C., were simple and conservative, typical of a peasant people. With the growth of commerce and of empire, life became more complicated and these laws no longer sufficed. Hence the formulation of a new body of law—the *jus gentium,* or law of the peoples—which they accepted and applied both to themselves and to others. The Romans also evolved the legal concept of *jus naturale,* or natural law. This stemmed not from judicial practice but from the Stoic idea of a rational god ruling the universe. Or, in Cicero's words, it was law above mere custom or opinion, "implanted by Nature, discoverable by right reason, valid for all nations and all times." While jurists did not regard this as an automatic limitation upon Roman civil law, they did view it as an ideal to which human legislation should conform. This basic principle represents one of Rome's great contributions and remains operative to the present day. In fact, Roman law, as systematized later in Justinian's Code in the mid-sixth century, constitutes the basis for the present legal systems of the Latin countries of Europe, of the Latin American states, of the Province of Quebec, and of the state of Louisiana.

VIII. LATE EMPIRE, A.D. 284–476

The great days of Rome came to an end with the death of Marcus Aurelius in 180. His son, Commodius, avoided his duties as head of the empire and spent most of his time at chariot races and gladiatorial contests. After his assassination in 193 he was followed by rulers who were for the most part equally incompetent. The Praetorian Guard, a highly trained and well-paid body created by Augustus to protect the security of the capital, now got out of control. An emperor could remain in power only while he had the support of this body. During the period from 235 to 284 there were almost two dozen emperors, and only one of them died a natural death. Such disintegration at the center inevitably weakened the frontier defenses. Outlying provinces were overrun by the German tribes in the West and by the revived Persian Empire of the Sassanians in the East.

The imperial decay of the third century was checked with the advent of the strong and capable emperors Diocletian (284–305) and Constantine (312–317). Among the policies they adopted to hold the empire together was a rigid regimentation, including controls of prices and interest rates, and export prohibitions on "strategic products" such as iron, bronze, weapons, army equipment, and horses. These controls were extended to the point where they virtually became a caste system. Constantine required every soldier's son to be a soldier unless unfit for service. Similarly agricultural laborers were tied to the land on a permanent and hereditary basis. The tendency was to extend this to all crafts and professions that were deemed indispensable or that had recruitment difficulties.

Another policy during this time of troubles was decentralization, which became necessary as the imperial economy deteriorated. Diocletian divided his realm in two, keeping the eastern half for his own administration and appointing a coemperor for the western. This division was hardened when Constantine built a new capital on the site of the old Greek colony of Byzantium on the Bosphorus. Constantinople, as the new city soon came to be called, became one of the great cities of the world. It served as the proud capital of the East Roman, or Byzantine Empire, for centuries after Rome and the Western empire had passed away.

Another policy of these later centuries that was to affect the future profoundly dealt with relations between Christianity and the imperial government. Constantine made the fateful decision to seek stability and cohesion through cooperation with Christianity rather than its suppression. This was the end of a centuries-old trend in religious attitudes and practices. The hardships of daily life during this later imperial phase caused increasing numbers to turn for solace to salvation religions, as had happened earlier in the Hellenistic East (see section IV of this chapter). Spiritual needs no longer were satisfied by the cult of emperor and the official polytheism. Brotherhoods that celebrated the mysteries of Oriental gods now provided satisfying explanations of the world, rules of conduct, and release from evil and from death.

The most successful of the new religions was Christianity. It offered the doctrine of One God, the Father Omnipotent, in place of the polytheism of the Greco-Roman gods and the monotheism of the oriental cults. It brought the solace of a Redeemer, Jesus, who was not an ambiguous figure in a mythological labyrinth, but who miraculously lived an earthly life, even though he was the Son of God. Christianity also guaranteed salvation to the believer, but instead of a starry eternity, it restored him to life through a personal resurrection foreshadowed by the Resurrection of Christ himself. Perhaps most important of all, Christianity provided fellowship when times were disjointed and common people felt uprooted and forsaken. All Christians were brothers, and their meetings were often called agape, meaning "love" in Greek. They assisted one another, and by their devotion and self-denial they set an inspiring and contagious example. Thus at a time when the laws and philosophy of the old order were becoming irrelevant and unviable, Christianity offered relevance and hope for the meek and the humble.

By the time of the great fire of 64 the Christians had become so numerous that Nero thought it was wise to blame them for the disaster and to begin the first of numerous persecutions. But this merely hallowed the memory of the martyrs and spurred the proselytizing efforts. After a final major persecution early in the fourth century, Emperor Constantine issued the Edict of Milan (313) excusing Christians from pagan rituals and granting their religion the same toleration accorded to all others. Finally Emperor Theodosius (379–395) made Christianity in effect the state church. The old Roman aristocracy and the apostate Emperor Julian (361–363) fought a stubborn rearguard action to preserve pagan practices, but by the end of the fourth century Christianity reigned supreme.

Just as the emperors adopted Christianity with the aim of furthering social cohesion, so they adopted the pomp and circumstance of oriental court etiquette. In contrast to Augustus who had dubbed himself "First Citizen," Diocletian took the name of Jovian, the earthly representative of Jupiter, while Constantine, after his conversion to Christianity, assumed sacred status. The power of the emperor henceforth was considered to be derived from the gods rather than delegated by citizens. Accordingly, court ritual now made the emperor remote and unapproachable. Bedecked in a jeweled diadem and a robe of purple silk interwoven with gold, all subjects were required to prostrate themselves. Only a privileged few were allowed to kiss the border of the emperor's robe.

With these measures the emperors of the third and fourth centuries strove valiantly to halt the imperial decline. If resolve and effort alone were needed, they would have been spectacularly successful. In fact they did stabilize the situation somewhat, but only temporarily. The net effect of their herculean endeavors was to postpone rather than to avert the end. Beginning in 406 the West Roman emperors were powerless to prevent permanent large-scale invasions of Franks, Burgundians, Visigoths, and Vandals in Gaul, Spain, and Africa. Nor could they prevent the ultimate indignity of the sack of Rome by barbarians in 410 and again in 455. Finally in 476 Romulus Augustulus, the last of the West Roman emperors, was forced to abdicate by Odoacer, the German (or Hunnic) leader of a band of mercenary soldiers.

Though this incident is generally taken to mark the end of the West Roman Empire, it attracted little attention at the time for it was merely the culmination of a process of disintegration that had extended over two centuries. To understand the reason for the "fall of Rome," if this traditional cataclysmic phrase may be used, it is necessary to determine the dynamics of the prolonged but inexorable descent to oblivion.

The instrument responsible for the "fall" was, of course, the German barbarians. Thus a French historian has concluded, "Roman civilization did not die a natural death. It was murdered."[6] There is some justification for this verdict, yet it was not a case of irresistible hordes sweeping everything aside by sheer weight of numbers. Historians estimate that only about 100,000 Ostrogoths invaded Italy, and an equal number of Visigoths subjugated Spain and southern France. The Vandal force that crossed the Straits of Gibraltar to North Africa totaled about 80,000 men, or 1 percent of the native population of that province.

So the question still remains—why the "fall"? An American historian has recently stated that "though war was the apparent cause of death . . . the organic disease of the Empire was economic."[7] In fact, this "organic disease" is discernible not only in the Roman Empire but in the Hellenistic states, in classical Greece, and even in the earlier ancient civilizations. All were afflicted by the same basic problem of low productivity. This stemmed from the failure to advance technology significantly after the Neolithic age, which had produced such core inventions as metallurgy, the plow, the wheel, the sail, and the solar calendar.

The underlying cause for the technological retardation appears to have been the institution of slavery, which was an integral and universally accepted part of all these civilizations. Even in classical Greece, where slavery never was as rampant as in Rome, Aristotle asserted that some men were born to rule and some to be ruled, and if the latter refused to accept their preordained fate, then it was "naturally just" that they should be hunted down as though they were "wild beasts."

The repercussions of the institution of slavery were manifold and pernicious. The institution deprived the slave of any incentive to improve on the traditional operations of his or her craft. It also deprived the master of any incentive for technological innovation so long as plenty of slave labor was available. Thus during the reign of Vespasian when an obelisk was to be erected in the present-day Piazza San Pietro in Rome, an inventor of the time suggested an engineering technique that would have made the operation much easier. But the emperor preferred manual slave labor so as not to leave the slaves unemployed. Likewise the water-mill, though known in the eastern provinces of the empire as early as the first century B.C., was not adopted in Rome until the fourth century when the supply of slaves had shrunk.

Equally harmful was the natural tendency of a slave-owning society to associate manual labor with slaves and hence to regard such labor as beneath the dignity of freemen. Thus the Greek essayest Plutarch stated that the great Archimedes

. . . did not think the inventing of military engines an object worthy of his serious studies, but only reckoned them among the amusements of geometry. . . .

The first to turn their thoughts to mechanics, a branch of knowledge which came afterwards to be so much admired, were Eudoxus and Archytas, who confirmed certain problems, not then soluble on theoretical grounds, by sensible experiments and the use of instruments. But Plato inveighed against them, with great indignation, as corrupting and debasing the excellence of geometry, by making her descend from incorporeal and intellectual, to corporeal and sensible things, and obliging her to make use of matter, which requires much manual labor, and is the object of servile trades. Mechanics were in consequence separated from geometry, and were for a long time despised by philosophers.[8]

In these various ways, then, the institution of slavery tended to inhibit technological innovation during the millennia following the egalitarian Neolithic age. Slavery also depressed the internal economic market because domestic purchasing power was restricted since slaves obviously could not purchase the fruits of their labor.

For some time these basic structural weaknesses were masked by imperial expansion, with the resulting flood of booty, tribute, foodstuffs, and slaves. But there were limits to the expansion of empires at that level of technological development—limits set by logistical and communications requirements. Thus Rome, like China, was able to advance just so far and no further. When that point was reached, the imperial frontiers became fixed, or even began shrinking, and the hitherto hidden structural defects came to light.

The army, which previously had been a profitable source of slaves and material wealth, now became a heavy but inescapable burden. Likewise the bureaucracy had become swollen during the period of expansion and was impossible to support in a period of contraction. The excessive expenditures led to inflation that eventually reached runaway proportions. In Egypt, for example, a measure of wheat that cost 6 drachmai in the first century A.D. rose to 200 drachmai in 276, 9000 in 314, 78,000 in 334, and to more than 2 million drachmai soon after 334. With such inflation, coinage became worthless and there was some reversion to barter. This trend was hastened by the growing diffusion of industry to the countryside and to the provinces. The diffusion occurred for a number of reasons such as the deterioration of imperial communication facilities and the drop in the supply of slaves which made it necessary to tap new labor pools. The shift of industry from the cities to villages and large country estates meant the agrarianization of the empire. The large estates became increasingly self-sufficient, boasting craftsmen of every kind as well as agricultural laborers. And the more self-sufficient they became, the more the imperial economy disintegrated into *autarchic units*.

Economic decentralization inevitably was accompanied by political decentralization.

With the decline of trade and the shrinkage of state revenues, the imperial edifice no longer could be supported and slowly it began to crumble. Diocletian and Constantine made desperate efforts to buttress the structure by imperial fiat. But the disease was ''organic'' rather than superficial, so all the regimentation, with its propping and bracing, was of no avail in the long run. Regimentation, however, was not the cause of imperial decay, but an ineffective remedy that was tried to halt the decay. ''Crisis preceded regimentation,'' as an economic historian has pointed out.[9]

It follows that a major reason why the West Roman Empire ''fell'' and the East did not was precisely because the economy of the West was less advanced and weaker. Italian agriculture was never as productive as that in the rich river valleys of the Middle East. The grain harvest in Italy was on an average no more than four times the sowing. The rich soils of Central and Northern Europe had to await medieval technological advances for effective exploitation. Likewise industry in the West was of relatively recent origin and generally lagged behind that in the East. Thus although the whole Roman Empire was wracked by ''organic disease,'' the western part, being the least robust, was the first to succumb. The eastern part survived to live on for another millennium.

Despite its demise, the West Roman Empire did leave a rich legacy. Most apparent are the material remains—the amphitheaters, arenas, temples, aqueducts, roads, and bridges. Equally obvious is the linguistic bequest in the form of the Romance (or Romanized) languages of Europe. Roman law, as noted above, is very much alive in the legal systems of numerous countries in Europe and the Americas. The organization and ritual of the Catholic church owe much to Roman imperial structure and religious traditions. Finally the Pax Romana, which had brought two centuries of relative peace and prosperity, left a tradition of imperial unity in place of the city-state particularlism of the Greeks. It was this tradition during the following centuries that fired the imagination and ambition of barbarian princes throughout Europe to become imperator or basileus or tsar.

SUGGESTED READING

J. Ferguson, *The Heritage of Hellenism* (Harcourt Brace Jovanovich, 1973); M. Grant, *History of Rome* (Scribner's, 1978) and *The Etruscans* (Scribner's, 1981); T. B. Jones, *From the Tigris to the Tiber: An Introduction to Ancient History* (Dorsey, 1969); D. Kagan, ed., *Decline and Fall of the Roman Empire* (D. C. Heath, 1962); C. Roebuck, *The World of Ancient Times* (Scribner's, 1966); M. Rostovtzeff, *Social and Economic History of the Hellenistic World,* 3 vols. (Clarendon, 1941); R. Sealey, *A History of the Greek City States* (University of California Press, 1976); W. W. Tarn and G. T. Griffith, *Hellenistic Civilization* (Arnold, 1952); T. B. L. Webster, *Athenian Culture and Society* (University of California Press, 1973).

chapter 6

Indian Civilization

Turning from Greece and Rome to India, we enter an altogether different world. The differences are not simply those that might naturally emerge from contrasting physical environments—differences in occupations, diet, habitation, dress, and the like. The differences were much more far reaching and fundamental. There was nothing in the West remotely resembling basic Indian concepts and institutions such as *caste, ahimsa,* or nonviolence, reincarnation, and karma, or the law of moral consequences. These were not just eccentric or abstract ideas. They constituted the bedrock of Indian civilization, molding the thought and daily lives of all Indians. The pattern that resulted was so distinctive and so enduring that Indian civilization to the present day has distinguishing characteristics that mark it off from all other Eurasian civilizations.

Distinctiveness also characterizes the civilization of China, as will be noted in the following chapter, but this is natural because of the unparalleled geographic and historical isolation of that country. In India, by contrast, the beginnings appeared to be basically similar to those of the other regions to the west where Aryan invaders had settled—the Iranian plateau and the Balkan and Italian peninsulas. As noted earlier (chapter 3, section VI), the Aryan tribes that descended upon India about 1500 B.C. possessed the same physical features, the same pastoral economy, the same social institutions, the same gods, and the same epics as did, for example, the Achaeans and the Dorians. Furthermore the Indo-Aryans were not isolated in their subcontinent to anywhere near the degree that the Chinese were on the eastern extremity of Eurasia. The mountain ranges of northwest India are not impassable, so that armies and merchants and pilgrims crossed back and forth through the centuries. In fact, during much of the time there was more interaction between northern India and the Middle East and Central Asia, than between northern India and the southern part of the peninsula.

The question naturally arises, then, why the Indo-Aryans should have developed a civilization so basically different from those of their kinsmen to the west. The scanty evidence available does not allow for a specific or definitive answer, but the most simple and likely explanation is that the Indo-Aryans were Indianized. In contrast to the Achaeans or Dorians or Latins, who settled in relatively uncivilized areas, the Indo-Aryans encountered in the Indus valley a highly developed civilization with large urban centers and a dense population. The native population, although subjugated and despised, was too numerous and too advanced to be exterminated or pushed aside or assimilated, leaving few traces of the original culture. Instead, as the Aryan pastoralists settled down and took up agriculture, they perforce lived in close proximity with the prior inhabitants of their new land. After some centuries of such coexistence and intermarriage, the inevitable result was a cultural synthesis. The nature and consequences of this synthesis are the subject of this chapter.

I. ARYAN IMPACT

Following their penetration into the Indus valley, the Aryans concentrated in the more rainy parts of the Punjab where the pasture was adequate for their herds. Gradually they began to spread into the heavily forested basin of the Ganges. Their expansion was slow at first, since only stone, bronze, and copper axes were available. But after iron was introduced about 800 B.C. their pace quickened. The main occupation now shifted from pastoralism to agriculture. Furthermore, the monsoon climate of the Ganges valley was good for rice cultivation, which was much more productive than the wheat and barley grown in the Punjab. Thus the center of population density shifted from the northwest to the east, which then became the seat of the first powerful kingdoms.

The shift to agriculture stimulated various crafts necessary for the new villages, including carpentry, metallurgy, weaving, and tanning. Agriculture also promoted trade, with the river serving as the natural highway for transporting surplus foodstuffs. Barter was the common practice at first, with the cow as the unit of value in large-scale transactions. When coins appeared, the earliest weight standards, significantly enough, were exactly those of the pre-Aryan Indus civilization. Towns grew out of villages that were strategically located for trade or that had specialized in particular crafts.

This economic growth in turn facilitated political consolidation. Originally the Indo-Aryans, like their relatives in the West, were organized under tribal chiefs assisted by councils of elders and general assemblies. With economic development the tribes gave way to kingdoms in the Ganges plain and to republics in the Punjab and in the foothills of the Himalayas. Of these early states the kingdom of Magadha in the lower Ganges soon rose to preeminence because of its location on two main trade routes and its control over rich iron-ore deposits. With these advantages Magadha was to serve as the base for the formation of both the Maurya and Gupta empires.

The Nanda dynasty in the fourth century B.C. was the first to exploit systematically the resources of Magadha for state-building purposes. They built canals, organized irrigation projects, and established an efficient administrative system for the collection of taxes. The Nandas have been described as the earliest empire builders of India. In fact, they laid the foundations of empire but were not destined to actually fashion the first imperial structure. This was to be the historic role of Chandragupta Maurya, the young adventurer who usurped the Nanda throne in 321 B.C. and went on to build the famous empire named after him.

Economic and political developments were paralleled by fateful changes in social structure. Originally the Indo-Aryans, like other Aryans, were divided into three classes, the warrior nobles, the priests, and the common people. They had none of the restrictions associated with caste, such as hereditary professions, rules limiting marriages to people of the same caste, and taboos as to dining companions. But by 500 B.C. the caste system was functioning with all its essential features. Although many theories have been advanced as to its origins, it is generally agreed that color was a basic factor. Indeed the Sanskrit word for caste, varna, means color.

The Aryan newcomers were very conscious of the difference in complexion between themselves and the dark natives, and dubbed them Dasas, or slaves. With their strong sense of racial superiority, the Aryans strove to prevent mixture with their despised subjects. Accordingly they evolved a system of four hereditary castes. The first three comprised their own occupational classes, the priests (Brahmans), the warrior nobles (Kshatriyas), and the farmers (Vaishyas). The fourth caste (Shudras) was reserved for the Dasas, who were excluded from the religious ceremonies and social rights enjoyed by their conquerors.

This arrangement ceased to correspond to racial reality with the passage of time. Aryan tribes frequently made alliances with Dasa tribes to wage war against other Aryan tribes. Also Aryan settlers mingled with the natives who then adopted Aryan speech and customs. In such cases the Dasas' priests became Brahmans, and their chiefs, Kshatriyas. Thus today black south-Indian Brahmans are no less aristocratic by reason of their dark skin, nor are the light-skinned, grey-eyed untouchables of certain northern Indian regions any more elevated because of their pale complexion. In response to these realities, traders and some landowners were classified as Vaishyas, while cultivators and general laborers became Shudras.

A bewildering variety of castes have grown up within these four broad divisions. The castes have four basic features in common. One is characteristic employment, so that bankers and merchants often belong to the Vaishya caste. Another feature of caste is the hereditary principle, expressed in complex marriage regulations and restrictions. Caste also involves further restrictions as to food, water, touch, and ceremonial purity. Finally each caste has its *dharma,* or moral code, which stipulates such duties as maintenance of the family unit and performance of prescribed ceremonies at marriage, birth, and death.

Outside this system are the pariahs, or untouchables, comprising today about a seventh of the Indian population. They are condemned to trades or crafts regarded as unclean because their function involves some ritual defilement or the taking of human or animal life. These occupations include hunters, fishermen, butchers, executioners, gravediggers, undertakers, tanners, leather workers, and scavengers. Involvement in these occupations has led in turn to social segregation. Untouchables live in isolated villages or in quarters outside town limits, and are required to use their own temples and wells. They have to be most careful to avoid polluting members of the castes by any kind of physical contact or, in extreme cases, by even coming within their sight. For this reason, until recent decades they never moved outside their quarters or villages without striking a pair of clappers together to warn others of their approach.

The untouchables are further subjected to psychological disabilities that are as crippling and degrading as the physical. The doctrine of karma holds that one's status in present life has been determined by the deeds of previous lives. The untouchables therefore deserve their low position because of past sins, and their only hope for improved status in future lives is the dutiful performance of their present duties.

This combination of social and religious sanctions has enabled caste to function to the present day. Of course, with its manifold provisions for mutual aid, caste does provide security so long as one follows its rules. So it continues to serve as the steel framework of Hindu society. And although it has been attacked by reformers and undermined by the pressures of modern industrial society, caste nevertheless still operates in rural India where three-fourths of the total population continues to live.

II. REFORMATION AND COUNTER-REFORMATION

Caste, with its basic tenets of dharma, karma, and reincarnation, is part and parcel of the Hundu religious system. Originally the Aryans had typical tribal gods personifying natural forces, such as Indra, god of thunder and war, Agni, god of fire, and Soma, god of their sacred intoxicant of the same name. Gods of this nature were appropriate for pastoralists, but as the Aryans settled down to agriculture they perforce turned to new deities. Hence the advent of the "great gods" of Hinduism—Brahma, the Creator, Vishnu, the gracious Preserver, and Shiva, the Mighty and the Destroyer. It is not accidental that these new gods, particularly Shiva, bear striking resemblances to finds in the Indus valley sites. At this time, the Aryans naturally appropriated native religious ideas and practices that had evolved through the millennia in the ancient agriculture-based civilization.

With the new gods there came also a growing concentration of power in the hands of the priestly class, or Brahmans. This also was probably derived from pre-Aryan religious tradition. The Brahmans, who in some regions were in contact with native religious leaders, presumably learned of the magical claims and practices of their counterparts in the Indus civilization. Whatever the historic prototypes in the distant past, the Brahmans effectively exploited their mastery of the Vedas, or hymns, that were recited aloud during rituals and sacrifices. These were transmitted orally through the generations and were considered so sacred that they were memorized word for word, sound for sound. As the custodians and transmitters of this precious heritage, the Brahmans were able to assert and enforce their claims as the leaders of Hindu society, superior to the Kshatriya, or secular heads.

The Brahmans enjoyed numerous prerogatives and exemptions because of the sacred nature of their functions. Donors of gifts to the Brahmans were assured definite reward in this, as well as in subsequent, lives. "Gift of land" was rated most highly for it "liberated from all sin." Thus the Brahmans acquired vast estates, including entire villages. Also they were exempt from all taxes since they were deemed to have discharged such debts through "acts of piety." And being sacrosanct, the Brahmans could not be sentenced to death or to any type of corporal punishment. Finally the doctrines of karma, reincarnation, and dharma provided virtually irresistible means for Brahman control of the mind. There was little chance for individuals to assert themselves when a person's station in life was the inescapable result of one's own past actions, and when hope for a better life in the future depended entirely on one's faithful observance of specific caste duties, regardless of how onerous or degrading they might be.

The Brahman pretensions and exactions were one factor in the religious reformation in India in the sixth and fifth centuries B.C. Another was the economic growth noted above, which created a wealthy merchant, or Vaishya, caste that resented the special privileges enjoyed by the two upper castes. Finally there was the tension between the Brahmans and the non-Aryans who had been admitted to the Hindu fold but who resented the priestly domination. Thus the Shakya tribes in the Nepal hills from which the Buddha came are thought to have been of Mongolian stock. This combination of factors lay behind the ferment in Indian religious and intellectual circles during these centuries. The demand arose for moshka, or freedom—for something more meaningful and satisfying than prescribed rituals and rigid doctrines.

One manifestation of the unrest was a trend toward asceticism. Some of the most active minds, alienated by the society about them, concentrated on pure introspection. They developed techniques for disciplining or ''yoking'' (yoga) the senses to an inward focus, ending in a state of trance or ecstasy which mystics describe as ''enlightenment'' and sceptics call ''self-hypnotism.'' Out of this inward searching and speculating came many reform movements, of which the most important was Buddhism. The new religion had no place for caste or for Brahmans. It required that the scriptures should be understood by all believers and not merely by a few at the top. Buddhism also banned all magic, sacrifices, and obscure writings (see Chapter 4, section III).

Buddhism became a powerful force, not only in India, but also in Central Asia and East and Southeast Asia. After A.D. 600, however, it lost ground within India. Eventually it existed in only a few localities in the land of its birth. One reason for the decline of Buddhism at home was that it failed to provide for the usual crises of life. It offered no ceremonies for birth, marriage, death, and other critical turns in the lives of the laity. By contrast the Brahmans were ready with their rites, and their survival was assured despite the attacks of the reformers. More important, the Brahmans themselves embraced reform. In their philosophical texts, the Upanishads, they set forth their own paths to moshka—to freedom and release.

They taught that the supreme spirit permeating the universe was Brahman, a being capable of all knowledge and feeling. He was the universal soul and the all-pervading breath; all else was illusion. The individual soul—Atman—was a spark of the supreme being. By transmigration it passed from state to state until it attained release by reabsorption into Brahman, the Soul of the Universe. This identification of the individual soul and the Soul of the Universe was the ultimate goal that holy men sought to reach by discipline, meditation, and withdrawal from the world of the senses. Seekers after truth could now abandon the world and rest within the folds of Hinduism. Although Buddhism as a practicing faith disappeared in India, it has survived to the present because its basic tenets have been incorporated in the Hindu counter-reformation.

III. MAURYA EMPIRE

Turning from religious movements to political developments, the outstanding political event was the emergence of India's first imperial structure, the Maurya Empire. As noted earlier in this chapter, the migration of the Aryans to the Ganges valley had shifted the center of gravity to that region, and particularly to the kingdom of Magadha. Meanwhile the northwest provinces had been going their own way, isolated from the rest of India because of their close ties with Persian civilization. In fact, Emperor Darius crossed the Hindu Kush mountains about 518 B.C. and made the western Punjab the twentieth province of his empire. Two centuries later, in 327 B.C., Alexander the Great also invaded India from the northwest. But he stayed only two years, and, soon after he left, Greek rule in Punjab ended. Despite his short stay, Alexander did have considerable influence on India.

One effect was the growth of the east-west trade from northwest India through Afghanistan and Iran to Asia Minor and Levant ports. The Greek colonies planted throughout the Middle East by Alexander doubtless contributed much to this trade, and the Hellenistic states that followed Alexander promoted it for two centuries.

Most important for Indian history was Alexander's role in creating a political vacuum in northwest India by overthrowing several local kingdoms and republics. Chandragupta Maurya promptly filled the void and founded the empire named after him. In 322 B.C., three years after Alexander's departure, Chandragupta, then an ambitious young general, unseated the Nanda dynasty of Magadha and founded his own. In the following years he extended his rule steadily northwestward until his empire extended from the Ganges to the Indus, including the deltas of both rivers. At the same time he organized a powerful army and an efficient administration to sustain his realm. Thus when Seleucus became king of the Middle East as one of the successors to Alexander and attempted to recover Alexander's Indian provinces, Chandragupta easily repelled the Greek forces. Chandragupta's son conquered the Deccan in the south, while his grandson, the famous Ashoka (273–232 B.C.), conquered Kalinga, or eastern India. Thus the Maurya Empire under Ashoka included the whole Indian peninsula except for the southern tip (see Map VIII, ''Classical Age Empires in India'').

India under the Mauryas was wealthy and well governed, like the Roman Empire at its height. Numerous highways were crowded with merchants, soldiers, and royal messengers. The conquest of Kalinga on the east coast stimulated trade, and an admiralty department maintained waterways and harbors. The capital, Pataliputra, known as the ''city of flowers,'' was famous for its parks, its public buildings, and its river frontage of over nine miles. Its educational institutions were crowded with students from all parts of the empire and from abroad.

All this was supported by ''the king's sixth'' of the harvest, which in practice was more commonly raised to a fourth, leaving the peasants with barely enough for existence. Law was severe and order ruthlessly maintained. The army reputedly numbered 700,000 men, with 9000 elephants and 10,000 chariots. Spies were efficient and numerous, sending in a stream of reports to the capital by messenger and carrier pigeon. Torture was frequently used as a means of punishment and to extort confessions. All in all, it was an efficient, harsh, bureaucratic society, based on the principle that ''Government is the science of punishment.''

Ashoka's reign differed radically from this traditional type of imperial rule. Having conquered the kingdom of Kalinga in a particularly bloody campaign, Ashoka underwent a spiritual experience. He himself described how over 100,000 prisoners were killed, and how he felt ''profound sorrow and regret.'' From then on, Ashoka tried to apply the gentle teachings of the Buddha. He issued edicts based on Buddhist principles: simplicity, compassion, mutual tolerance, and respect for all forms of life. He ordered many public works that benefited his people rather than his government. These included hospitals and medical care at state expense, orchards and resting places on highways, alms that were distributed to all sects, and Buddhist missions to several foreign countries.

Ashoka did not make Buddhism the state faith, nor did he persecute the other sects. To the contrary, he helped the worthy of whatever denomination. It was not a change of religion, then, but of general attitude. He laid most stress on toleration and nonviolence, not only because they were morally desirable but also because they would promote harmony in his huge and diverse empire. This proved successful during his reign, for Ashoka ruled with great popularity for forty-one years. But within half a century after his death his dynasty was overthrown and his empire destroyed.

This has been the pattern of Indian history to modern times. In contrast to China, where imperial unity was interspersed with short intervals of fragmentation, in India it was precisely the opposite—brief unity and prolonged fragmentation. This is not to say that India had no unity. It did, but that cohesiveness was cultural rather than political. And this culture emphasized loyalty to the social order rather than to the state, as we see by the fact that higher status was accorded to caste than to any political institution. Thus the culture that enhanced unity in one sphere undermined it in another.

IV. INVADERS, TRADERS, AND MISSIONARIES

With the end of the Maurya Empire early in the second century B.C. there followed five hundred years of confusion and obscurity. But one constant factor is clear throughout this period. This is the increasing interaction between India and the outside world, with manifold repercussions in all areas—political, economic, and cultural.

First there were the numerous invaders. Beginning with Alexander and his Greeks, there followed the Parthians, the Scythians and the Kushans, to mention only the most important. The empires of all these peoples were based at least as much in Central Asia or the Middle East as in India. Their linking of India with foreign lands stimulated trade overland and overseas. Roman traders went to southern and western India, while Indian traders settled in large numbers in Southeast Asia. Just as the Greeks traded and colonized all through the Mediterranean, so did the Indians all through Southeast Asia.

In the realm of culture, Indian Buddhist missionaries during these centuries were carrying their message to all the surrounding countries. The begging priest could move among hostile or disordered peoples with safety since he was too poor to be worth robbing and also was respected as a man of religion. There was little incentive for robbing or injuring such a man, since the only return was the possibility of retribution from above. Hence the diffusion of Buddhism and Brahmanism from India to the surrounding countries, with all the culture that went along with such transfer of religions. Nor was the culture flow exclusively one-sided. The succession of invaders from the north brought with them a variety of Greek, Persian, and Central Asian influences. And by sea there came to India in the first century A.D. a new religion—Christianity. According to legend St. Thomas arrived about A.D. 52 on the Malabar coast of southwest India where he established a number of churches. Thence he traveled overland to the east coast. His preaching, however, was strongly opposed, and he was killed in A.D. 68 near Madras. His work in the Malabar region, however, bore fruit, for considerable Christian communities exist there to the present day.

V. GUPTA CLASSICAL AGE

In the fourth century A.D. the great Gupta Age began—a time when the invaders of the preceding centuries were assimilated and when various cultural trends reached fruition. This was the classical period of Indian civilization, comparable to the Early Empire or Augustan Age in the West. The Gupta Empire, like the Maurya, had as its base the Magadha state in the Ganges valley. This state had managed to preserve its independence following the Maurya collapse, and then, with the end of the Kushans, it began to expand once more into the resulting vacuum.

The Gupta era began with the accession of Chandragupta I about 320, and reached its height under his grandson, Chandragupta II, who reigned from 375 to 415. He expanded his empire until it stretched from the Indus to the Bay of Bengal, and from the northern mountains to the Narbada River. The Gupta Empire was a north-Indian empire and did not include the entire peninsula. Indeed south India at this time was in many ways a world apart, with the Vindhya range still an effective barrier dividing the peninsula in two. The peoples of the south spoke Dravidian or pre-Aryan languages—Tamil, Telugu, and Kanarese—in contrast to the Indo-Aryan speech of the north. On the other hand, the south had accepted the Hindu and Buddhist religions and social customs and used Sanskrit as its language of scripture and learning. Thus a single civilization bound together the diverse peoples despite their disparate ethnic and linguistic backgrounds and the existence in the south of several independent kingdoms.

The Gupta Empire enjoyed much prosperity, especially after Chandragupta II introduced standard gold and silver coins. The volume of trade reached new heights, both within the peninsula and with outside countries. The degree of security under Gupta rule is reflected in the drop of interest rates on loans for overseas trade from 240 percent during the Maurya period to 20 percent at this time. One of the chief industries was textiles—silk, muslin, calico, linen, wool, and cotton—which were produced in large quantities for both domestic and foreign markets. Other important crafts included metallurgy, pottery, carving, and the cutting and polishing of precious stones.

Judging from the reports of Chinese Buddhist pilgrims, Gupta rule was milder than that of the Maurya. Fa-hien, who spent the years 401 to 410 in India, traveling from monastery to monastery, was impressed by the state services and by the general prosperity. Although the dynasty was Hindu, he found no discrimination against Buddhists. The countryside was peaceful and prosperous, and not overrun by police and spies as under the Maurya.

In linguistics and literature, this was the period of the triumph of Sanskrit. Hitherto the learned and rather archaic language of the Brahmans, Sanskrit now staged a comeback, and spread to administration and to secular literature. Poetry and prose flourished with the stimulus of lavish royal patronage. Outstanding were the works of Kalidasa, "the Indian Shakespeare," who rendered ancient legends and popular tales in both dramas and lyrics. Perhaps the greatest cultural achievement of the Gupta era was the reduction into final form of the two great national epics, the Mahabharata and the Ramayana. Dating back to many centuries before Christ, the early versions of these works have been entirely lost. Today they are known only in the form in which they are left by Gupta writers. In this form they have remained the classics of Hindu literature and the repositories of Hindu tradition. Their heroes and heroines are a part of the life of the people; their mine of stories has been used by generations of writers and their philosophical poem, the *Bhagavad Gita,* is the supreme scripture of the Hindus.

A CHINESE VIEW OF INDIA

Chinese Buddhist pilgrims have left valuable descriptions of India in its classical age. The most famous was Hsüan-tsang who visited all parts of the country between 629 and 645, and left the following vivid picture.*

The towns and villages have inner gates; the walls are wide and high; the streets and lanes are tortuous, and the roads winding. The thoroughfares are dirty and the stalls arranged on both sides of the road with appropriate signs. Butchers, fishers, dancers, executioners, and scavengers, and so on, have their abodes without the city. In coming and going these persons are bound to keep on the left side of the road till they arrive at their homes. Their houses are surrounded by low walls, and form the suburbs. The earth being soft and muddy, the walls of the towns are mostly built of brick or tiles. The towers on the walls are constructed of wood or bamboo; the houses have balconies and belvederes, which are made of wood, with a coating of lime or mortar, and covered with tiles. The different buildings have the same form as those in China: rushes, or dry branches, or tiles, or boards are used for covering them. The walls are covered with lime and mud, mixed with cow's dung for purity. At different seasons they scatter flowers about. Such are some of their different customs. . . .

They are very particular in their personal cleanliness, and allow no remissness in this particular. All wash themselves before eating; they never use that which has been left over (*from a former meal*); they do not pass the dishes. Wooden and stone vessels, when used, must be destroyed; vessels of gold, silver, copper, or iron after each meal must be rubbed and polished. After eating they cleanse their teeth with a willow stick, and wash their hands and mouth.

Until these ablutions are finished they do not touch one another. Every time they perform the functions of nature they wash their bodies and use perfumes of sandalwood or turmeric. The most usual food is milk, butter, cream, soft sugar, sugar-candy, the oil of the mustard-seed, and all sorts of cakes made of corn are used as food. Fish, mutton, gazelle, and deer they eat generally fresh, sometimes salted; they are forbidden to eat the flesh of the ox, the ass, the elephant, the horse, the pig, the dog, the fox, the wolf, the lion, the monkey, and all the hairy kind. . . .

There is no lack of suitable things for household use. Although they have saucepans and stewpans, yet they do not know the steamer used for cooking rice. They have many vessels made of dried clay; they seldom use red copper vessels: they eat from one vessel, mixing all sorts of condiments together, which they take up with their fingers. They have no spoons or cups, and in short no sort of chopstick.

* Si-Yu-Ki, *Buddhist Records of the Western World,* trans. S. Beal (Kegan Paul, 1884), I, pp. 70–89. Reprinted by Paragon Reprint Corp., New York (1968).

In the field of science the Gupta period was outstanding. Contact with Greeks resulted in mutually beneficial exchanges of ideas. Aryabhata, born in A.D. 476 at Pataliputra, is one of the greatest figures in the history of astronomy. He taught that the earth is a sphere, that it rotates on its own axis, that lunar eclipses are caused by the shadow of the earth falling on the moon, and that the length of the solar year is 365.3586805 days—a calculation with a remarkably slight margin of error.

The greatest achievement doubtless was the formulation of the theory of zero and the consequent evolution of the decimal system. The base could have been any number; the Hindus probably chose ten because they counted on their fingers. With this system, individual numbers were needed only for 0, 1, 2, . . . 9. By contrast, for the ancient Greeks each 8 in 888 was different. And for the Romans, 888 was DCCCLXXXVIII. The difficulty of division and multiplication with these systems is apparent. The simple Hindu numerals were carried westward by Arab merchants and scholars, and so became known as ''Arabic numerals.'' Despite their obvious advantage they were long scorned as pagan and as too vulnerable to forgery; one stroke could turn 0 into 6 or 9. It was not until the late fifteenth century that Hindu-Arabic numerals prevailed in the West and the door was opened to modern mathematics and science. In retrospect, this Indian contribution stands out as comparable to the invention of the wheel, the lever, or the alphabet.

SUGGESTED READING

A. L. Basham, *The Wonder That Was India* (Sidgwick, 1956); W. T. deBary, et al., *Sources of Indian Tradition* (Columbia University Press, 1958); B. S. Cohan, *India: The Social Anthropology of a Civilization* (Prentice-Hall, 1971); M. Edwardes, *Everyday Life in Early India* (Batsford, 1969); P. Spear, *India: A Modern History* (University of Michigan Press, 1961); R. Thapar, *A History of India,* Vol. I (Penguin, 1966).

chapter 7

Chinese Civilization

Chinese civilization is characterized by cohesion and continuity as compared with the looseness and discontinuity of Indian civilization. There has been no sharp break in China's evolution comparable to that caused in India by the appearance of the Aryans or the Moslems or the British. There were, of course, numerous nomadic invasions of China, and even a few dynastic takeovers. But it was not the Chinese who were forced to adopt the language or the customs or the pastoralism of the invader. Rather it was the invaders themselves who invariably became Chinese, quickly and completely.

One reason for this was the greater isolation of China, so that it was invaded only by the nomads of the northwest. It did not have to cope with the succession of peoples who invaded India and who, with their relatively sophisticated cultures, were able to retain in varying degrees their *ethnic group* and cultural identity. The Chinese were all Mongoloids to begin with, as were their nomadic invaders and the relatively primitive tribes that they assimilated in the course of their expansion eastward to the Pacific and southward to Vietnam. Thus the Chinese enjoyed racial and cultural homogeneity throughout their history. During the Classical period this homogeneity was further cemented, as we shall see, by the standardization of the writing system, which enabled speakers of widely differing dialects to communicate with each other. In India, by contrast, there are today fourteen "national languages," one of which is English, and that imported tongue serves, in Nehru's words, as "the link" amongst the other thirteen.

The remarkable political unity that has persisted through the ages in China has been as important as its cultural homogeneity. This unity results in large part from the unique secularism of Chinese civilization—the only great civilization that has at no time produced a priestly class. To be sure, the emperor was also a priest who made sacrifices to heaven in behalf of all his subjects, but his religious function was always secondary to the business of governing. Consequently, there was no place in China for the great division between religious and laity, between church and state, which existed in the other Eurasian civilizations. Nor was there any counterpart to India's epics, steeped in metaphysics and concerned with personal salvation. Rather the Chinese classics emphasized the life of man in society, and particularly the relations between the members of a family and between a king and his subjects. This strong secular characteristic provided a firm underlying foundation for political organization and stability. This was further cemented during these centuries by a unique Chinese institution—a civil service recruited on the basis of public competitive examinations. It was two thousand years before anything comparable appeared in the West, or anywhere else for that matter.

These then, are some of the background factors that will help explain the Chinese civilization and history that will be analyzed in this chapter.

I. AGE OF TRANSITION

The period of the Eastern Chou (771–256 B.C.) was on the surface inauspicious, with its powerless dynasty and its feudal lords constantly at war with one another (see Chapter 3, section VI). Yet it was also a period of basic socioeconomic change that determined the course of China's evolution decisively and permanently. The root cause for this change here, as in India, was the introduction of iron. Iron came late in China. It was not a significant factor until about 600 B.C. But by the fifth and fourth centuries B.C. it was making its mark on Chinese society and government.

The pattern of its impact was familiar. New and more efficient iron tools allowed agriculture to spread from the original Yellow River place of origin southward towards the heavily wooded Yangtze basin (corresponding to the spread in India from the Indus to the Ganges). Iron tools also facilitated extensive drainage projects in the valleys, canal building for long-distance hauling of bulky commodities, and well digging for irrigation purposes in the dry northwest lands.

All this meant a very substantial increase in productivity, which in turn stimulated trade and industry and ended in the use of money in much of the economy. Money had been used earlier, usually in the form of cowrie shells. Now copper coins appeared and were increasingly used in all branches of the economy. A new class of free and wealthy merchants and craftsmen were most involved in the growing use of money. They were no longer dependent on feudal lords as they had been in the past. Instead they now formed a new monetary aristocracy that soon challenged the leadership of the feudal lords.

With the use of money, land became a form of property that was bought and sold. Wealthy merchants purchased large estates, and nobles sought to increase their revenues by appointing agents to collect more rent. The agents collected the increased rent directly from the peasants instead of in the traditional way, from the village headman.

This economic change was accompanied by political change—by a fundamental shift from feudal decentralization to state centralization. The economic growth and use of money provided the rulers of the various feudal states with the financial resources needed for centralization. Since the newly reclaimed lands could be administered outside feudal relationships, rents were contributed directly to the princes' exchequers. Also the princes set up more and more profitable monopolies to produce and distribute iron and salt. The result was that the princes of the feudal states were able to change fiefs they had formerly parceled out to nobles into administrative units staffed by officials of their own central government. This was a gradual development, but, where it did occur, it greatly increased the resources and power of the ruler and, correspondingly, weakened the Chou dynasty in the capital. Indeed a basic reason for the success of the rulers of Ch'in in conquering all China was precisely that they pioneered in these measures and reaped the profits. We will discuss this in section III of this chapter.

II. PHILOSOPHERS AND CLASSICS

The disruption and reorganization that we have described profoundly affected Chinese thinkers. It forced them to take a new look at their traditions and to either abandon them or adapt them to the requirements of a period of transition. Thus the Eastern Chou period was a time of great intellectual ferment and creativity, reminiscent of the achievements under comparable circumstances of the rationalist philosophers in Greece and of the Buddha and other religious reformers in India. So intense was this intellectual activity that the Chinese refer to this as the period of the "Hundred Schools." Here we shall consider a few of these schools that persisted through the centuries and had an important influence on the evolution of Chinese civilization.

Although the founders of the various schools often were bold innovators, almost all of them looked for inspiration in a supposedly golden age in the distant past. A similar tendency is found in most civilizations, but consciousness and veneration of the past was exceptionally strong amongst the Chinese. Hence they carefully preserved and studied the writings of earlier ages and considered them indispensable for the conduct of both private and public affairs.

The most important of these ancient works were the *Five Classics* consisting of poems, popular traditions, and historical documents. The *Classics* were studied and used by philosopher-teachers, of which the most outstanding by far was Confucius. His influence has been so overwhelming and lasting that the Chinese way of life during the past two thousand years can be summarized with one word—*Confucianism.* Born in 551 B.C. to a poor family of the lower aristocracy, Confucius (the Latinized form of K'ung-fu-tzu, or Master Kung) had to make his own way in the world. And the world he faced was harsh. There was runaway feudal anarchy and no higher power, spiritual or temporal, to attract national loyalty. Confucius was moved by this to wander from court to court seeking a ruler who would adopt his ideas for successful government. He did hold a few minor posts, but his influence in the world of practical politics was slight. So he turned to the teaching of young men who, he hoped, might be more effective in carrying out his ideas.

Confucius at last had found himself. He proved to be a teacher of rare enthusiasm and skill. Surviving records describe him as an attractive and magnetic person—sensible, kindhearted, distressed by the folly of his age, convinced that he could restore tranquility, and blessed with a saving sense of humor. Confucius's teachings were fundamentally

TEACHINGS OF CONFUCIUS

Confucianism was above all a practical moral system concerned with the problems of everyday life. The main emphasis was on propriety and social responsibility, as evident in the following selections.*

The Individual

It is by the rules of propriety that the character is established.

The rules of propriety serve as instruments to form men's characters. They remove from a man all perversity and increase what is beautiful in his nature. They make him correct, when employed in the ordering of himself; they ensure for him free course, when employed toward others.

The Family

The superior man while his parents are alive, reverently nourishes them; and when they are dead, reverently sacrifices to them. His chief thought is how, to the end of life, not to disgrace them.

There are three degrees of filial piety. The highest is being a credit to our parents; the next is not disgracing them; and the lowest is merely being able to support them.

The services of love and reverence to parents when alive, and those of grief and sorrow for them when dead—these completely discharge the duty of living men.

Government

Good government obtains when those who are near are made happy, and those who are far are attracted.

The people are the most important element; . . . the sovereign, least important.

If the people have plenty, their prince will not be left to want alone. If the people are in want, their prince will not be able to enjoy plenty alone.

When rulers love to observe the rules of propriety, these people respond readily to the calls upon them for service.

The ruler must first himself be possessed of the qualities which he requires of the people; and must be free from the qualities which he requires the people to abjure.

Education and Arts

In providing a system of education, one trouble is to secure proper respect for the teacher; when such is assured, what he teaches will also be regarded with respect; when that is done, the people will know how to respect learning.

A scholar should constantly pursue what is virtuous and find recreation in the arts.

Music produces pleasure which human nature cannot be without.

*M. M. Dawson, *The Ethics of Confucius* (Putnam's, 1915), pp. 2–5, 167–168, 255–257.

conservative. He did not want to tamper with the existing social order and relationships. ''Let the ruler be a ruler and the subject a subject; let the father be a father and the son a son.'' But while insisting on the right of the rulers to rule, he was equally insistent that they should do so on the basis of sound ethical principles. Like Plato, he wanted the kings to be sages, and this they could be if they possessed the five virtues of a gentleman—integrity, righteousness, loyalty, altruism, and love, or human-heartedness.

Confucius also was a rationalist in an age of gross superstition and fear of the supernatural. People firmly believed in the prophetic significance of dreams, in the arts of divination, and in the dread power of the spirits of the dead. But Confucius, though he recognized spirits and Heaven, largely ignored them in his teachings. ''If you do not know about the living, how can you know about the dead?''

Confucius's teachings were far from being generally accepted, let alone applied, during his lifetime. Yet in the end they prevailed and became the official creed of the nation. One reason was his basic conservatism, his acceptance of the status quo, which naturally appealed to those at the top. Another was his emphasis on ethical principles, which he insisted were essential for the proper exercise of authority. Finally Confucius provided a philosophy for officialdom, for the bureaucrats who became indispensable with the establishment of imperial government two and a half centuries after his death. In the second century B.C. Confucianism was declared the official dogma or faith of the empire. The *Classics* became the principal study of scholars and statesmen. Until the fall of the Manchu dynasty more than two thousand years later, in 1911, the teachings of Confucius were unchallenged in China.

After Confucianism, the most influential Chinese philosophy was *Taoism*. This is understandable, for the two doctrines supplement each other neatly. Between them they satisfy both the intellectual and emotional needs of the Chinese people. While Confucianism emphasized decorum, conformity, and social responsibility, Taoism stressed individual whim and fancy, and conformity to the great pattern of nature. This pattern was defined as Tao, or the Road or Way, so that the Disciples are known as Taoists. The key to conforming with Tao was abandonment of ambition, rejection of honors and responsibilities, and a meditative return to nature. According to this philosophy, the ideal subject had big bones, strong muscles, and an empty head, while the ideal ruler ''keeps the people without knowledge and without desire . . . and fills their stomachs. . . . By nonaction nothing is ungoverned.''

Altogether different from both Confucianism and Taoism were the doctrines of the *Legalists*. The Legalists were practicing statesmen rather than philosophers, and they were interested in reorganizing society in order to strengthen the princes they served and to enable them to wage war and unite the country by force. They viewed the nobility as a useless hangover from the past, who should be replaced by state military forces. They also believed that the mass of the people should be forced into productive work. They regarded merchants and scholars as nonessential and therefore not to be tolerated. All aspects of life were to be regulated in detail by laws designed to promote the economic and military power of the state. Rulers were to be guided, not by the traditional virtues of humanity and righteousness extolled by the Confucianists, but by their need for power and wealth.

These Legalists doctrines were used successfully by the Ch'in rulers to conquer other princes and to establish the first empire. They then extended their regimentation ruthlessly to the entire country, but the result, as we shall see, was a reaction that led to the overthrow of the empire a few years after the death of its founder. Legalism was discredited and Confucianism became the permanent official creed.

III. CH'IN EMPIRE

China's long history has been marked by three great revolutions that triggered fundamental change in its political and social structure. The first in 221 B.C. ended the feudal system and created a centralized empire; the second in 1911 ended the empire and established a republic; while the third in 1949 put the present Communist regime in power.

The first of these revolutions was the work of the leaders of the northwest state of Ch'in in the Wei valley. This location contributed to the victory, for the valley is largely inaccessible and easy to defend. The Ch'in rulers were able to attack the other states to the east without fear of any enemy action in their rear. The frontier location also helped to keep the Ch'in military forces in fighting trim because of the constant wars against the barbarian nomads. In fact the Ch'in were amongst the first Chinese to use iron in place of bronze weapons, and cavalrymen in place of charioteers. Important also in the Ch'in triumph was the conquest in 318 B.C. of the great food-producing plain of Szechwan. This added greatly to the area and strength of Ch'in, placing it in somewhat the same relationship to the other Chinese states as Macedonia had been to the Greek cities. Finally the Ch'in rulers were able and ambitious realists who pioneered in applying Legalist doctrines and in concentrating all power in their hands (see Map IX, "Classical Age Empires in China").

With these advantages, the Ch'in leaders extended their possessions steadily, overcoming the surrounding states one by one. Contemporaries referred fearfully to the "wild beast of Ch'in" and compared its steady expansion to that of a "silkworm devouring a mulberry leaf." By 221 B.C. the Ch'in ruler was master of all China, and he adopted the title of "Shih Huang-ti," or "First Emperor." His successor would be "Second Emperor," and so on down the generations for "ten thousand years," meaning forever.

The new emperor applied to all China the Legalist doctrines that had succeeded so brilliantly in his home state. He abolished all feudal states and kingdoms. He reorganized his vast realm into administrative areas, or commanderies, each with a set of officials appointed by, and responsible to, the central government. Also he disarmed all soldiers except his own, required the old aristocratic families to reside in his capital where they could be kept under watch, and planted Ch'in garrisons throughout the country. The new emperor also imposed economic centralization by standardizing weights, measures, and coinage.

In the light of future history, one of the most important innovations was the scrapping of the numerous ways of writing the characters of the language that had been developed in the kingdoms. In their place a standardized script was substituted that was understandable from one end of China to the other. This proved to be a most effective and enduring bond of unity because of the nature of Chinese script. It is not based on a limited number of signs expressing the phonetic elements of a word. Rather, it consists of a large number of symbols or characters, each one of which denotes an object or an abstract concept. The system is precisely that used in the West for figures. All Westerners know what the symbol "5" means, even though they call it five, funf, cinque, or cinq. So it is with Chinese characters, or ideographs, which have meaning but no sound. They are ideas, like numerals, which all readers can sound according to their own dialects. Thus the new Ch'in standardized script, which has continued with modifications to the present, could be read and understood by all educated Chinese, even though they spoke dialects that often were mutually unintelligible. For the same reason, the script was equally comprehensible to foreign peoples, so that educated Japanese, Koreans, or Vietnamese can read Chinese without being able to speak a word of it. The significance of this for future Chinese national unity and for Chinese cultural influence throughout East Asia can well be imagined.

These changes made by the Ch'in dynasty hurt many vested interests and aroused passionate opposition. This was especially true of the scholars, who hated the Legalist doctrines and policies. The First Emperor accordingly decided to deprive them of their intellectual props by ordering the "Burning of the Books." All the *Classics* were consigned to the flames, except those dealing with subjects of utilitarian value, such as medicine, agriculture, and divination. The plan failed, for scholars hid their books at great risk or else memorized entire texts before surrendering them. Later, after the fall of the dynasty, the greater part of the traditional literature was recovered from the hidden books and from the memories of old men. The persecution, however, effectively dampened the intellectual ferment that had characterized the Chou period; the Golden Age of Chinese thought was over.

This intellectual loss should be balanced against the economic progress that was made through more efficient use of human and natural resources. The standardization of weights, measures, and coinage promoted economic growth. Also a network of trunk roads was built, radiating from the capital to the most distant frontiers. To make the roads as useful as possible, the emperor standardized the length of the axles of the two-wheeled Chinese carts—an essential measure because the wheels cut deep ruts in the sandy soil, so that every cart had to follow the existing ruts or be fitted with new axles. The emperor also used the new national unity and strength to expand the frontiers southward to present-day Vietnam. To the northwest the nomads were beaten back. To keep them back the famous Great Wall was built, running 1400 miles from Inner Mongolia to the ocean. So great was the loss of life on this stupendous project that even today, more than two thousand years later, people still speak of the fact that a million people perished at this task, and that every stone cost a human life. Just as the scholars cursed the emperor for the "Burning of the Books," so the common people cursed him for the building of the Great Wall.

It was this widespread resentment, together with the lack of a competent successor, that explains the popular revolt and the end of the dynasty in 207 B.C., only four years after the death of the First Emperor. But although Ch'in rule was so short-lived, it left a deep and permanent imprint on China. The country had been transformed from a loose collection of feudal states into a centralized empire, which it remained until the twentieth century. It is only appropriate that the occidental name for China is derived from the Ch'in.

IV. HAN EMPIRE

The First Emperor had abolished feudalism in one stroke, but the succeeding Han emperor, more practical and cautious, first restored feudalism a bit and then whittled it away to insignificance (through restrictions on size and inheritance of hereditary fiefdoms). The imperial structure erected by the First Emperor was gradually restored, though without the original terror and oppression. Thus the Han Empire flourished for four centuries, about the same length of time as the Roman Empire.

The Han Empire also resembled the Roman Empire in its vast size. During the first sixty years the Han rulers concentrated on national recuperation and dynastic consolidation. But under the "Martial Emperor," Wu Ti (141–87 B.C.), the imperial frontiers were greatly expanded in all directions. Tribal territories in the south were conquered, though several centuries of Chinese immigration and assimilation of the local peoples were necessary before this part of the empire became predominantly Chinese-speaking. The greatest expansion occurred to the west, where Chinese expeditions drove across Central Asia, establishing contact with the Kushan Empire in northwest India and vastly increasing the volume of trade along the Silk Road (see Chapter 4, section II).

The Han Empire was comparable to the Roman Empire in population as well as territorial extent. A census taken in the year A.D. 1, and believed to be reasonably accurate, showed the empire to have 12.2 million households with a total of 59.6 million people. By contrast the population of the Roman Empire at the time of Augustus (27 B.C.–A.D. 14) is estimated at 30 to 50 million people in Europe, somewhat fewer in Asia, and not quite 20 million in Africa.

At the head of the Han realm stood the emperor, who had full political power and who was responsible for the physical well-being and prosperity of his subjects. Below the emperor were two senior officials corresponding to a modern prime minister and a head of civil service. These men were in constant touch with the emperor and were responsible for the actual operation of government. Beneath them were nine ministries entrusted with the following functions: religious ceremonials, security of the palace, care of the imperial stables, punishment of criminals, receipt of homage and tribute from foreign leaders, maintenance of records of the imperial family, collection of state revenues, and management of the imperial exchequer.

In addition to the central government there was a provincial bureaucracy that administered, in descending order, commanderies, prefectures, districts, and wards. Officials at the grass roots level were assigned such basic tasks as collection of tax in grain, textiles, or cash; arresting of criminals; maintenance of roads, canals, and granaries; and upkeep of the imperial post, with its horses and chain of stations.

In the first century B.C. this *bureaucracy* is said to have comprised some 130,000 officials, or only one for every 400 or 500 inhabitants. This small number in relation to the total population was typical throughout Chinese history and is to be explained by the restricted role of the imperial government. "Governing a country," according to a Chinese proverb, "is like cooking a small fish: neither should be overdone." Consequently Chinese governments did not assume responsibility for the social services taken for granted in the modern world, as is evident from the ministerial duties listed above. Rather the main role of government was collection of revenue and defense of the country against external attack, and of the dynasty against internal subversion.

The bureaucracy was a privileged, but not hereditary, elite. During the Han period, a unique system was originated for the selection of civil service personnel by means of competitive public examinations. In principle the examinations were open to all, but such prolonged study was needed to become a candidate that only the sons of the well-to-do could qualify. On the other hand, poor boys were quite often given village, clan, or guild endowments so that they could study. Since the examinations were based on the Confucian *Classics,* the empire in effect was run by Confucianists and according to Confucian principles. Each official was assigned to a post outside his home province to ensure that he would not use his position to build up local family power. The result was an administrative system that was far more efficient and responsive than any other until modern times. Indeed this civil service based on merit was a major factor in the continuity of the Chinese imperial system from the time of the First Emperor to the twentieth century. There was another side, however, to this examination system. Since it was based on total acceptance of a single body of doctrine, it produced a rigid orthodoxy and an intellectual arrogance that was to hurt China centuries later when Western merchants and gunboats appeared.

Although China was to suffer grievously in modern times because it lagged in science and industry, during the Han period it was a very different story. China then caught up technologically with the rest of Eurasia, and in many fields it took a lead that it was to maintain until recent centuries. Some of the more important Chinese inventions of these centuries were the water-powered mill, the shoulder collar for horses, which greatly increased their efficiency, and the techniques for iron casting, paper making, and pottery glazing. Rag paper, dating from about A.D. 100, soon replaced cumbersome wooden and bamboo slips for writing. But paper is not as durable as wood, and since it was developed by the Chinese long before printing, oddly enough, we must blame the use of paper for the loss of certain books. Pottery glazes, however, which were eventually developed into porcelain or china, were an undiluted blessing. They not only reached the level of true art, but they also represented a major advance in hygiene, since smooth porcelain was more sanitary than the rough pottery or wooden utensils hitherto available.

The outstanding Han contribution in literature was in the field of historical writing. This was to be expected from a people who looked to the past for guidance in dealing with the present. Their *Five Classics* contained a good deal of assorted historical materials. But now in the first century B.C., a history appeared that was much more comprehensive and sophisticated than any to that date. This was the *Shih chi,* or *Historical Records,* written by a father-son team, though authorship is commonly attributed to the son, Ssu-ma Ch'ien, who wrote the major part. As court astrologer, he had access to the imperial library and archives. Also he had the advantage of extensive traveling throughout the empire where he used the resources of local libraries. The history he wrote was not so much an original work as a compilation of all available historical materials. As he explained modestly, ''My narrative consists of no more than a systematization of the material that has been handed down to us. There is therefore no creation; only faithful representation.''

This method had obvious disadvantages, especially the lack of dramatic quality and stylistic unity found in early historians such as Herodotus. On the other hand it did assemble and preserve for posterity a tremendous quantity of historical material from contemporary books and archives. The *Historical Records* was in effect a universal history. It was equal to a work of approximately 1.5 million words. Its 130 chapters included chronological records and tables of the various dynasties, biographies of Han notables, and essays on varied topics such as rituals, music, astrology, astronomy, economic matters, and foreign peoples and lands. Future Chinese historians paid Ssu-ma Ch'ien the tribute of copying his method. As a result Chinese historiography has transmitted through the millennia a mass of data unequaled by that of any other country over so long a period.

All Chinese historians also shared a belief in the ''Mandate of Heaven'' concept. They held that a king ruled as the deputy of Heaven only so long as he possessed the virtues of justice, benevolence, and sincerity. When he no longer demonstrated these virtues and misruled his kingdom, he was automatically deprived of the Mandate of Heaven, and rebellion against him was not a crime but a just punishment from Heaven through the medium of the rebels. Thus Chinese historians, although often aware of the social and economic factors behind dynastic decline, subordinates them to what they considered to be a more basic underlying consideration—the moral qualifications of the ruler. Chinese historiography, then, was based on the rise and fall of dynastics interpreted in accordance with the workings of the Mandate of Heaven.

V. IMPERIAL DECLINE

This traditional interpretation of Chinese history views it as a succession of dynastic cycles that repeated each other. But the cyclical facade obscures some fundamental changes. It is true, of course, that dynasties did rise and fall. The founder of a line naturally was a man of ability, drive, and action. But his descendants, after a few generations of living in a court atmosphere, were likely to be effete and debauched. Sometimes a strong ruler or a capable and devoted minister managed to halt the deterioration. But the overall trend was downhill, until successful revolt removed the dynasty and started the familiar cycle again.

More fundamental than the dynastic cycle, however, was what might be termed the economic-administrative cycle. This began with the security and prosperity common at the outset of every major dynasty. The restoration of peace led to population increase, greater production, correspondingly greater revenues, and full government coffers. But a combination of personal ambitions, family influences, and institutional pressures inevitably led the emperors sooner or later to overextend themselves. They squandered their human and financial resources on roads, canals, fortifications, palaces, court extravagances, and frontier wars. Thus each dynasty began to experience financial difficulties about a century after its founding.

To meet the deficits the government raised taxes, which bore most heavily on the small peasant proprietors that were the backbone of Chinese society. At the beginning of each dynasty small proprietors constituted the majority of the peasantry. But as taxes increased, more and more of them lost their plots to the large landowners and became tenants. The landowners had political influence to commensurate with their wealth and paid negligible taxes. So, the more their holdings increased, the more the government revenues declined, and the more the taxes rose for the diminishing number of small peasants. Thus a vicious circle was set in motion—rising taxes, falling revenues, neglected roads and dikes, and declining productivity. Eventually this ended up with famines, banditry, and full-scale peasant uprisings. Meanwhile frontier defenses were likely to be neglected, inviting raids across the frontiers by the nomads. Often it was the combination of internal revolt and external invasion that brought down the tottering dynasty and cleared the way for a new beginning.

This was essentially the pattern of the Earlier Han dynasty. The "Martial Emperor," Wu Ti (141–87 B.C.), had won great victories and extended China's frontiers deep into Central Asia. But in doing so he overstrained the imperial resources. He resorted to a variety of measures to cope with the crisis, including currency debasement, sale of ranks, and reinstitution of government monopolies on salt, iron, and liquor. Although he managed to remain solvent for the duration of his reign, his successors sank deeper into trouble as the number of tax-paying small peasants declined. Large-scale revolts broke out, and even at the court various omens were interpreted as portents from Heaven that the end of the dynasty was drawing near.

In fact the dynasty was briefly ousted (A.D. 9–25) by Wang Mang, a powerful minister who had already dominated the court for some three decades. He boldly tackled the basic economic problem by nationalizing the great private estates and distributing them amongst the tax-paying peasants. This and other reforms alienated the wealthy families, who opposed the usurper bitterly. At the same time a disastrous change in the lower course of the Yellow River made millions homeless and drove the uprooted peasants into banditry and rebellion. The nomads took advantage of the disorders to invade the country and sack the capital, where Wang Mang died at their hands in A.D. 23. He was succeeded on the throne by a distant cousin of the former Han emperor.

The history of the Later Han (A.D. 25–222) was basically the same as that of its predecessor. During the lengthy wars many of the old aristocrats and landowners had been wiped out. Tax returns, therefore, were adequate at the beginning of the revived dynasty. But again the tax-paying peasantry began to be squeezed out, and the downward spiral once more was under way. Great rebellions broke out and the situation resembled that of the last days of Rome. The decimation of the small peasants had also destroyed the original peasant draft army. This was replaced by professional troops, whose first loyalty was to their generals. The generals, therefore, could ignore the central government. Great landowners also defied the government by evading taxes and enlarging their holdings by various legal and extralegal means. Helpless peasants, fleeing the barbarian invaders or government tax collectors, became the virtual serfs of these landowners in return for economic and physical security. The great families converted their manors into fortresses, virtually taking over the functions of government in their respective localities. Their estates were largely self-sufficient, so that trade declined and cities shrank correspondingly. Thus the Han dynasty disappeared in A.D. 222 from the stage of history, in a swirl of peasant revolts, warlord coups, and nomadic raids. China then entered a prolonged period of disunity and disorder similar to that in the West following the collapse of the Roman Empire

SUGGESTED READING

H. G. Creel, *Confucius, the Man and the Myth* (Day, 1949); G. B. Cressey, *Land of the 500 Million: A Geography of China* (McGraw-Hill, 1955); W. T. deBary, et al., *Sources of Chinese Tradition* (Columbia University Press, 1960); M. Loewe, *Everyday Life in Early Imperial China* (Putnam, 1968); J. Needham, *Science and Civilization in China* (Cambridge University Press, 1954); E. O. Reischauer and J. K. Fairbank, *East Asia: The Great Tradition* (Houghton Mifflin, 1958); J. Spence, *Emperor of China: Self-Portrait of K'ang-hsi* (Knopf, 1974).

chapter 8

End Of Classical Civilizations

The great civilizations of Greece, Rome, India, and China dominated Eurasia in classical times. Yet in the end, the nomads and pastoralists of the frontier regions overran these civilizations and fundamentally altered the course of global history. Beneath the seeming invulnerability of the empires lay roots of decline that brought on decay and eventual disintegration. Essentially, technology was at a standstill, so productivity was low. These two factors—static technology and lagging production—combined to make the classical civilizations vulnerable to the barbarian attacks from the third to the sixth centuries.

The effect of the nomadic invasions varied from region to region. Northern China and northern India were overrun but retained their distinctive civilizations. Southern China and southern India escaped invasion because of their distance from the lands of the nomads. Byzantium and Persia proved powerful enough to repel the invaders. The West, however, suffered repeated attacks by Germans, Huns, Moslems, Magyars, and Vikings, so that the old order was uprooted to a degree unequaled anywhere else in Eurasia. Ironically, however, this destruction was a principal reason for the primacy of the West in modern times. A new civilization was able to emerge out of the ashes of the old, a civilization better adapted to the demands of a changing world. The purpose of this chapter is to analyze why the classical civilizations declined, and why the West was the exception as it started out on a new road leading to world domination.

I. DECLINE OF CLASSICAL CIVILIZATIONS

The basic reason for the decline of the classical civilizations was as noted above: that their technology was relatively stagnant, and therefore their productivity remained low. John Maynard Keynes described the technological slowdown:

> The absence of important technological inventions between the prehistoric age and comparatively modern times is truly remarkable. Almost everything which really matters and which the world possessed at the commencement of the modern age was already known to man at the dawn of history. . . . At some epoch before the dawn of history . . . there must have been an era of progress and invention comparable to that in which we live today. But through the greater part of recorded history there was nothing of the kind.[1]

Keynes's observation is fully justified. The Neolithic age preceding civilization had been, in fact, remarkable for its technological progress. It was then that humans invented the wheeled cart, the sailboat, and the plow, discovered the chemical processes involved in metallurgy, worked out an accurate solar calendar, and learned how to harness the power of animals and of the wind. After the urban revolution, this headlong advance was arrested. During the following millennia only three discoveries were made that compared in significance with those of the earlier period. These were iron, the alphabet, and coinage. All three, significantly enough, were discovered, not in the old centers of civilization along the Nile and Tigris-Euphrates, but rather in peripheral and less restricting environs—the Caucasus frontier regions and the Aegean commercial cities.

Apart from these three great inventions, the advances made at this time were based on the earlier discoveries, merely refining the skill with which they were used or applying them on a much larger scale. Since labor productivity was not raised by new inventions, wealth could be increased only by bringing new areas under cultivation, or by conquest and exploitation. But virgin lands were not limitless. Instead, extensive fertile regions throughout the Mediterranean basin were now being eliminated as sources of food because of large-scale erosion that was becoming a serious problem. Likewise empires could not expand indefinitely, for there were strict limits beyond which they could not extend because of the level of their military technology. Thus there had to be a point of diminishing returns when the pressure of military and bureaucratic establishments became too much for productive capacities. A vicious circle then set in, as noted above. A good example is the case of the fall of the Han and Roman empires, societal collapses on which we have more information. Rising taxes and increasing poverty caused uprisings in the cities and countryside, these invited nomadic incursions and ultimately led to successful internal revolt or invasion from the outside or a combination of the two. Hence the cyclical nature of imperial history in premodern times. A historian, analyzing the decline of the Roman Empire, emphasized, in conclusion, technological backwardness:

> The Roman Empire, we must not forget, was technically more backward than the Middle Ages. In agriculture a two-field system of alternate crops and fallow was usually followed, and the potentially richest soils were little exploited. The horse collar had not been invented, so that oxen had to be employed for plowing and for carting. Water-mills existed, but seem to have been relatively rare, and corn was generally ground by animals or by human labor in hand querns. Yet with this primitive technique, agriculture had to carry an ambitious superstructure far heavier than that of any medieval state. No medieval kingdom attempted, as did the Roman Empire, to support, as well as a landed aristocracy and the church, a professional standing army, and a salaried bureaucracy.[2]

In retrospect it is clear that the cycle could have been broken only by technological advances that would have provided the economic support necessary for the expensive imperial organizations. But technology was stagnant, and the basic reason was that the ruling establishments everywhere knew how to expropriate existing wealth but did not know how to create more wealth. They were capable of siphoning off astonishingly large surpluses from their peasant subjects, as evident in the stupendous amounts of capital and labor invested in pyramids, ziggurats, cathedrals, and palaces. But technological innovation required something more than efficient organization and coercion, and all the agricultural civilizations failed to achieve this *something more*—which was why they remained agricultural.

The widespread presence of slavery was one reason for the technological standstill. It was usually simpler and cheaper to put slaves to work than to design and construct new machines. Thus the inventors of the time usually produced gadgets intended not to save labor but to amuse or to carry on religious ritual. Hero of Alexandria in the first century A.D. used his knowledge of steam power to construct a machine that opened temple doors. Likewise, in the same century, Emperor Vespasian in Rome forbade the use of a machine that would erect columns inexpensively, commenting, ''Let me provide food for the common folk.'' Laudable though this sentiment might be, the fact remains that it made the cities of the classical empires parasites of the countryside rather than centers of productive industry.

Slavery also inhibited technology by fostering a negative attitude toward work. Since labor was the lot of the slaves, it came to be regarded as beneath the dignity of any free citizen. Even in civilizations where slavery was not so widespread, this attitude toward labor existed; witness the cult of the long fingernail in China. Division into sharply distinct social classes promoted upper-class contempt for work and workers, and slavery accentuated this attitude. The Roman philosopher Seneca, in a letter to Lucilius in A.D. 65, expressed scorn for manual labor, which, he said, should be proffered with ''bowed body and lowered eyes'':

> Some things we know to have appeared only within our own memory; the use, for example, of glass windows which let in the full brilliance of day through a transparent pane, or the substructures of our baths and the pipes let into their walls to distribute heat and preserve an equal warmth above and below. . . . Or the shorthand which catches even the quickest speech, the hand keeping pace with the tongue. All these are the inventions of the meanest slaves. Philosophy sits more loftily enthroned: she doesn't train the hand, but is instructress of the spirit. . . . No, she's not, I say, an artisan producing tools for the mere everyday necessities.[3]

It was the isolation of the philosopher from the artisan that blocked the technological growth of the Eurasian civilizations. And it was the interaction between the two—the ordered speculation of the philosopher and the practical experience and traditional lore of the artisan—that enabled the West to achieve its great scientific and industrial revolutions in modern times and thereby make its unique contribution to human development. Such interaction was impossible in the classical civilizations because of the sharp social cleavages and the resulting social attitudes. The lofty intellectual lacked interest, and the lowly artisan lacked incentive.

Technological stagnation explains the cyclical nature of Eurasian imperial history during the premodern millennia. Empires rose and fell in a basically similar pattern. None was able to break through to a new level of development. Hence the repetitive cycles that contrast sharply with the dynamism of modern industrialized societies. W. W.

Rostow has described this common feature of the agricultural civilizations in the times before Britain took off with its epochal and pioneering industrial revolution.

> . . . limitations of technology decreed a ceiling beyond which they could not penetrate. They did not lack inventiveness and innovations, some of high productivity. But they did lack a systematic understanding of their physical environment capable of making invention a more or less regular current flow, rather than a stock of *ad hoc* achievements inherited from the past. . . .
>
> It followed from this productivity ceiling that food production absorbed 75 per cent or more of the working force and that a high proportion of income above minimum consumption levels was spent in non-productive or low-productive outlays: religious and other monuments, wars, high living for those who controlled land rents; and for poorer folk there was beggar-thy-neighbor struggle for land or the dissipation of the occasional surplus in an expensive wedding or funeral. Social values were geared to the limited horizons which men could perceive to be open to them; and social structures tended to hierarchy. . . .[4]

II. BARBARIAN INVASIONS

The period from the third to the sixth centuries was one of Eurasia-wide invasions comparable to the bronze and iron invasions of the second millennium B.C. And just as the earlier invasions were responsible for the transition from the ancient to the classical civilizations, so these later invasions ended the classical civilizations and cleared the way for the medieval (see Map XI, ''Barbarian Invasions in Eurasia, 4th and 5th Centuries A.D'').

The general direction of nomadic movement was from east to west because of the lure that the better watered and more fertile lands of the western steppes held for the nomads of the East (see Chapter 3, section V). The main invasion routes followed the corridor of grassland that stretched across Central Eurasia, beginning near Peking and ending in the Hungarian plains of Central Europe. This is why so many of these nomadic peoples ended their wanderings in present-day Hungary, which became their base for raids into the surrounding European countries.

A basic factor behind the invasions was the constantly increasing interaction between the centers of civilization and the surrounding nomads. In many of the centers, nomads were used as slaves or mercenary soldiers, a practice that was often the entering wedge either for a military coup in the imperial capital or for an invasion by the fellow-tribesmen of the barbarian mercenaries. Another factor was the gradual settling down of nomadic peoples, often in regions adjacent to imperial frontiers. This shift from nomadism to agriculture normally led to population growth and to greater economic and military strength. And if imperial weakness was great enough to hold out the promise of success, the new military strength was used. Invasions also were often the end result of a series of shock waves. A defeat before the Great Wall of China or a stumbling block such as the formation of an aggressive tribal confederacy in Mongolia, frequently turned the nomads westward. A series of invasions, like a train of shocks moving ever further west, ended finally in nomadic incursions across the Oxus or Danube or Rhine rivers.

Because of the Eurasia-wide scope of the invasions, a great variety of peoples were involved. Han China, Gupta India, and Sassanian Iran usually were assaulted by Turco-Mongols, often referred to as Huns. But the Roman Empire, being at the western end of the invasion route, was the object of attack, at one time or another, of all the peoples along that route, as well as of surrounding barbarians. The procession included assorted Germanic tribes, Iranians, Balto-Slavs, and Vikings, as well as the Turco-Mongols.

THE HSIUNG-NU BARBARIANS

Between the third and the sixth centuries A.D. the classical civilizations of Eurasia were overthrown by barbarian invaders. The following selection from the Chinese historian, Pan Ku, describes the Hsiung-nu nomads that overwhelmed the Han Empire.*

The Hsiung-nu live in the north and are a nomadic people. They raise a variety of animals, most of which are horses, cattle, and sheep. Other animals such as camels and donkeys are comparatively small in number. They move constantly to seek water and grass; they have no cities, houses, or crop fields. Land, however, is divided among different tribal groups.

The Hsiung-nu do not have any written language; consequently all agreements or promises are made in oral form. Small children are taught to ride sheep and shoot birds and squirrels. When they grow older, they begin to shoot foxes and rabbits. Meat, instead of grain, is their staple food. All able-bodied men are expert archers and are members of the cavalry in their respective tribes.

Under normal circumstances when life is comparatively easy, the Hsiung-nu earn their livelihood by tending their herds and augment it by hunting. When life becomes difficult, all men are taught the art of warfare, preparing ardently for the launching of attacks. This, you might say, is the nature of the Hsiung-nu. They rely on bows and arrows if the enemy is at a distance and switch to knives and spears in close combat. They attack when they are certain of victory, but are not ashamed to run away from the battlefield if they think that the odds are heavily against them. They go wherever there are profits to be realized; they do not know of such things as righteousness and propriety. . . .

From the king down, all the Hsiung-nu people eat animals' meat, wear their skins and convert their furs into garments. The young and the strong have priority to the best food; the elderly have to be satisfied with the leftovers. They highly value youth and strength, and look down upon the old and the weak. After the death of his father, a man will marry his step-mother. Likewise he takes his brother's wife as his own when and if his brother dies. . . .

The khan worships the rising sun early in the morning and the moon in the evening. In seating arrangement the person who sits on the left and faces the north is the most honored among the group. The dead are buried in coffins, accompanied with gold, silver, and clothing. But the graves are not marked with trees, nor do the mourners wear mourning clothes. Upon the death of a khan approximately one hundred of his favorite ministers and concubines will be put to death so that their spirits will be able to follow his.

During a military campaign the Hsiung-nu watch closely the size of the moon. They attack when the moon is large and bright and withdraw when it becomes small and dim. A Hsiung-nu soldier who kills an enemy will be awarded one goblet of wine plus whatever material goods he has taken from his victim. If he captures a man or woman alive, the latter becomes his slave. Thus on the battlefield all Hsiung-nu soldiers fight valiantly for their own material ends, they disintegrate quickly and disperse like flying clouds. Their favorite strategy is to entice their enemy to a pre-arranged place and then encircle him. After a battle, the warrior who brings home the body of a dead comrade will inherit all of the latter's worldly possessions.

* From Dun J. Li, *The Essence of Chinese Civilization* (D. Van Nostrand, 1967), pp. 211–213. By permission of the author.

The outcome of the invasions varied as much as their personnel. In China, the Han Empire finally succumbed to Turco-Mongol invaders in A.D. 222. Three separate kingdoms emerged, Wei, north of the Yangtze, Wu, in the south, and Shu, in the west. After decades of warfare, Wei defeated its rivals and established in 265 a new dynasty, the Chin. This dynasty ruled all China until 316, when a new wave of invaders overran the entire northern half of the country. The Chin court fled south to Nanking, whence it ruled the Yangtze valley and those regions of the south settled by the Chinese. China remained divided in two in this manner until finally reunited by the Sui dynasty in 589. It is easy to understand why the Chinese historians called these centuries the ''Age of Confusion.''

We shall see later that the West Roman Empire, under similar circumstances, was completely changed as to its politics, culture, and race. But north China was spared such a complete transformation, primarily because the native Chinese population greatly outnumbered the nomadic invaders. The north at that time was still by far the most populous part of the country, and therefore it was able to absorb the nomads without undergoing radical change. In fact large numbers of Chinese migrated from north to south during these troubled centuries to escape the barbarians, so that not only did the north remain Chinese, but the south became more Chinese. Consequently, the partial barbarization of the north was counterbalanced by the southward expansion of Chinese culture, providing an enormous depth to China from north to south. Thus with reunification of the entire country by the Sui dynasty in 589, China resumed its normal course as distinctively Chinese as during the Han period.

Turning to India, the invasions there occurred much later, for the Gupta Empire was at its height when China already was beset with its ''Age of Confusion.'' During the fifth century, however, the eastern branch of the Huns, or the ''White Huns'' as they are called, crossed the Oxus River and drove south to India, while the western branch advanced over the Russian steppes to Europe. Under the impact of the Hun onslaught the Gupta Empire disintegrated during the first half of the sixth century. Very little is known of events during the following centuries, except that the periodic invasions continued. Also there were migrations into India on a large enough scale to form new cultural and social groups. An outstanding example is that of the Rajputs, a sturdy and brave people who gave their name to the area known as Rajputana in northwest India. They were a military aristocracy who were soon absorbed into the Hindu caste of Kshatriyas, or warriors. They became intensely proud of their Hinduism and for some time dominated north and central India. In fact they were still prominent in the nineteenth century, and to some extent even to the present day.

Their experience is significant because it helps explain why India, despite the long centuries of turmoil and invasions, was not fundamentally changed. The newcomers were assimilated into the prevailing caste system. It was much more a case of their adapting to India's civilization than the other way around. Thus India, like China, emerged from its time of troubles with the civilization that it had evolved during classical times modified but not transformed.

III. GERMANS AND HUNS IN THE WEST

In Europe, however, the pattern of events was precisely the opposite; there it was transformation rather than modification. The most numerous invaders were the Germans who occupied the Central and East European lands from the Baltic to the Danube, and from the Rhine to the Russian plains. They were organized in tribes. The more important were the Franks, Vandals, Lombards, and the Ostrogoths and Visigoths. All shared the same general religious beliefs and institutions, and all spoke closely related dialects, so that they could understand each other. Fortunately for the Romans, however, they were not united. They were as ready to fight against each other as against the Romans, thus allowing the Roman Empire to survive as long as it did.

The social organization of the Germans consisted of three main elements. At the top were the nobles whose status was usually hereditary and who were the large landholders. Most Germans were freemen who customarily owned their own plots of land. Those who did not were obliged to work for the nobles as share-croppers. At the bottom was a class of people neither free nor slaves. They were bound to the land but could not be sold apart from it. This form of bondage was the basis for the institution of serfdom that prevailed in Western Europe in medieval times.

The main source of authority in these tribes was the assembly of freemen. It selected the king, if there was one, and also the military leader for each campaign. Tacitus noted that the Germans usually chose their kings on the basis of inheritance. But their war chiefs were selected for their valor and ability on the battlefield. Young men were given the right to carry a sword after solemn rites that were the origin of the later medieval ceremony by which a squire was raised to knighthood. Each outstanding warrior leader had a retinue of young followers, or *comitatus,* who fought beside him in battle and owed him loyalty and obedience. In return the chief provided arms and subsistence as well as a share of the war booty. This institution contributed to the later system of feudalism, which was based on the loyalty of knights to their feudal lords.

Tacitus described the Germans as great eaters, heavy drinkers, and confirmed gamblers. On the other hand he praised their high moral standards, which he held up as a model for his fellow Romans. He also stressed their hospitality as universal and unstinted. During the winter season groups would go from house to house, staying at each until the owner's supplies were exhausted. This is reminiscent of the later medieval arrangement by which a king or noble was entitled, as a part of his feudal dues, to so many days of entertainment for himself and his entourage.

Such were the people who began to press upon the imperial frontiers as early as the first century B.C. At that time the Roman legions were strong enough to hold the line with little difficulty. But with the decline of the empire the army also became weaker, and the Romans were hard pressed to keep control. They resorted to diplomacy, playing off one tribe against another. Also, since they had no choice, they allowed whole bands of German warriors to settle on the Roman side of the border in return for their aid against the tribes on the other side. This policy worked so long as the Romans were able to keep their allies in check. But by the fourth century they could no longer do so and the floodgates burst.

The onslaught was triggered by dread new invaders that the Europeans had never seen before—the Huns. Their appearance and their deliberate policy of frightfulness terrorized both the Romans and the Germans. The contemporary Roman historian, Ammianus Marcellinus, described them as "almost glued to their horses," and "so monstrously ugly and misshapen that you might suppose they were two-legged animals. . . ."[5] Apparently displaced from their original pasture lands in Central Asia by other nomads, the Huns headed westward and crossed the Volga in 372. There on the Russian steppes they quickly defeated the easternmost German tribe, the Ostrogoths, and then terrorized the neighboring Visigoths into seeking refuge across the Danube

River on Roman territory. The Visigoths under Alaric marched to Italy and sacked Rome in 410, an event that shocked the imperial world at the time but that soon was to be repeated.

Eventually the Visigoths settled in southern Gaul and northern Spain where they founded the first German kingdom on Roman territory. Behind the Visigoths came the Huns who established their base on the Hungarian plains whence they raided both the eastern and western provinces of the empire. Under their feared leader, Attila, they appeared in 452 before the undefended gates of Rome, where, according to an implausible tradition, Pope Leo I persuaded the Hun chieftain to spare the capital. In any case Attila turned northward without sacking the capital, and with his death, a year later, his empire collapsed and the Huns disappeared from European history.

The Hunnic devastations, however, shattered Roman control over the western provinces, and German tribes now migrated across the frontiers virtually at will—the Vandals to North Africa, the Franks to Gaul, and the Angles, Saxons, and Jutes to England. Thus it was that the West Roman Empire passed under the control of new German succession kingdoms, a passing symbolized by the deposition of the last emperor, Romulus Augustulus, by the German Odoacer, in 476.

To this point the course of events in Europe repeated a familiar pattern. The West Roman Empire had succumbed to the barbarians as had the Han and Gupta empires in China and India. Furthermore it appeared in the sixth century that the aftermath of imperial disintegration in the West would be the same as that in China. Just as the Sui dynasty had finally united China in 589, so Europe at about the same time seemed to be on the road to reunification by the Frankish kings and the East Roman emperors.

The Franks had originated in the lower Rhine valley whence they had emigrated in the fifth century to northern Gaul. There they played a modest role in the turbulent history of the times until, under the leadership of the Merovingian kings, they became the most powerful people in the West. The most outstanding of the Merovingians was Clovis (481–511), who united the Frankish tribes, defeated the Romans, Byzantines, and Visigoths, and organized a kingdom stretching from the Pyrenees across Gaul and well into Germany. A principal reason for Clovis's success was his conversion to Catholicism, which won him the support not only of the Pope but also of the local Gallo-Roman population. It appeared that the Merovingians might be able to recreate the West Roman Empire, enlarged by the addition of the Frankish lands on the eastern bank of the Rhine.

This imperial ambition was shared by the rulers at Constantinople. While the West Roman Empire had been falling apart, the East Roman Empire remained intact, thanks to its naval power, its superior financial resources, and the natural strength of its capital located on the straits between Europe and Asia. Thus Constantinople survived the barbarian invasions which overwhelmed Rome, and, in fact, endured another half-millennium before falling to the Turks in 1453. During those centuries the empire developed a distinctive civilization, a mixture of Greek, Roman, Christian, and Eastern elements. To emphasize this distinctiveness, the empire is commonly referred to as the Byzantine Empire, so named after the original Greek colony on the site of Constantinople.

After the western provinces had become German kingdoms, the rule of the Byzantine emperors was restricted to the eastern half of the original empire—that is, to the Balkan peninsula, Asia Minor, Syria, and Egypt. This contraction was unacceptable to Justinian the Great (527–565) who was an Illyrian by birth and a westerner at heart. He spoke and thought in Latin and was determined to recover the western lands and to restore the original Roman Empire. One of his generals, Belisarius, with a small number of heavily armed troops, conquered the Vandal kingdoms in North Africa in one year. Southeast Spain also was recovered from the Visigoths, but eighteen years of bitter fighting was needed to subdue the Ostrogoths in Italy. Thus within two decades almost all the Mediterranean had become once more a Roman lake, and Justinian expressed the hope "that God will grant us the remainder of the empire that the Romans lost through indolence."

IV. CONTINUED INVASIONS IN THE WEST

But this was not to be. The West did not follow the path of China. Instead a new wave of invasions smashed the fragile new imperial structures of the Franks and the Byzantines and left the West once more in confusion and disunity. Again it was turmoil in Mongolia that pushed hordes of refugees westward along the invasion route to Europe. Like their Hunnic predecessors, these Avars, as they came to be known in the West, used the Hungarian plains as a base from which they launched raids in all directions. They forced the Germanic Lombards into Italy (568) where they drove out the Byzantines from most of the peninsula, thus blasting Justinian's hopes for an imperial restoration. The Avars also pushed Slavic tribes southward into the Balkan peninsula where they occupied a broad band from the Adriatic to the Black Sea.

In the eighth century hopes were rearoused for western imperial unity by the spectacular successes of the Carolingian dynasty, which had replaced the Merovingians. The successors of Clovis were weak rulers, being known as "do-nothing kings." The kingdom was held together, however, by strong-willed ministers who held the office of "mayor of the palace." The most outstanding of these was Charles Martel, the Hammer, who was the power behind the throne from 714–741. His greatest achievement was the defeat at the Battle of Tours (732) of the Moslems who had overrun North Africa and Spain and had advanced into southern France.

Martel's son, Pepin the Short, was not content to remain the minister of "do-nothing" kings and in 751 deposed the last Merovingian and established what came to be known as the Carolingian dynasty. The name is derived from Charlemagne, the son of Pepin, and the most famous of the line. During his long reign from 768 to 814 Charlemagne campaigned ceaselessly to extend his frontiers. He conquered the Saxons in northwest Germany, dispersed the Avars in Hungary, annexed the Lombard kingdom in Italy, and forced the Moslems back over the Pyrenees. By the end of the eighth century he was the undisputed master of the West, his empire extending from the North Sea to the Pyrenees and from the Atlantic Ocean to the Slavic lands in Eastern Europe. In recognition of his supremacy, Pope Leo III crowned him as emperor on Christmas Day in the year 800. And the assembled multitude, according to Charlemagne's secretary and biographer, shouted, "To Charles Augustus, crowned of God the great and pacific Emperor of the Romans, life and victory!"

The scene shows that the dream of imperial unity had not yet died. But it was destined to remain a dream, for soon after Charlemagne's death Europe was swamped by new waves of attacks from the south, the east, and the north. In the south, Moslem pirates and adventurers conquered the islands of Crete and Sicily and also raided all the Mediterranean coasts with devastating effect on maritime trade. In the east, still another nomadic force from Central Asia, the Magyars, reached the Hungarian plains in 895 and followed the example of the preceding Huns and Avars in raiding the surrounding lands.

Most wide ranging were the raids of the Norsemen, or Vikings. They were the equivalent on sea of the nomads on land. In place of horses they built fast ships with shallow draught that gave them unrivaled speed and mobility. The Vikings from Norway sailed westward to Iceland, Greenland, and North America. With their comrades from Denmark they raided the British Isles and the west coast of Europe, and even forced their way through the Straits of Gibraltar to ravage both shores of the Mediterranean. Since Sweden faces eastward, the Vikings from that country crossed the Baltic to the Russian rivers and followed them to their outlets in the Caspian and Black seas.

Thus the whole of Europe was overrun by these daring raiders. At first, in the late eighth and ninth centuries, they were interested only in plunder, and they destroyed countless monasteries and towns. In the tenth and eleventh centuries the Vikings began to settle down in the overseas territories, thus occupying and ruling large parts of northern France and the British Isles. But wherever they settled they were eventually absorbed into the existing Christian state. The king of France, for example, in the hope of forestalling further depredations by the Vikings, recognized their leader in 911 and gave him the title of duke of what came to be known as Normandy, a name derived from the Norsemen who settled there. One of the descendants of this Duke Rollo of Normandy was William the Conqueror who successfully invaded England in 1066.

The triple assault of Moslems, Magyars, and Vikings destroyed the Carolingian Empire. Western Europe once more was in a shambles. The lowest point was reached in the tenth century. At no time since the end of the Roman Empire did the present seem so wretched and the future so bleak (see Map XII, ''Continued Barbarian Invasions in the West, 9th and 10th Centuries'').

V. THE GREAT WESTERN EXCEPTION

From this survey of the invasions marking the transition from the classical to the medieval eras, it is apparent that the various regions of Eurasia were affected quite differently. South China and south India were unscathed because they were geographically too remote to be reached by the invaders. Through the centuries, the Byzantine Empire, with its resourceful diplomacy and its financial and naval strength, successfully repelled a long succession of assailants—Germans, Huns, Avars, Slavs, Persians, and Arabs. Persia was equally successful under its Sassanian dynasty, which replaced the Parthians in A.D. 226. The Sassanians united the country by appealing to Persian pride, by reviving Zoroastrianism as a state religion, and by organizing a force of heavily armored cavalrymen. Thus Persia was able to repel waves of nomads along the Oxus River while fighting Byzantium to an exhausting standstill that left both empires easy prey for the oncoming Moslem Arabs.

China and India, as noted earlier, did not fare so well in their northern regions. Both were overrun by barbarians, yet both were able to preserve the distinctive civilizations that they had developed during the Classical Age. Thus a Chinese of the first century B.C. Han period would have felt quite at home had he or she been resurrected in the early eighth century A.D. The visitor from China past would have found the contemporary T'ang dynasty essentially the same as the Han and would have noted the same language, the same Confucianism, ancestor worship, and imperial administration, and so forth.

This points up the uniqueness of the historical experience of the West. If a Roman of the first century B.C. had been resurrected in Europe of 1000 or 1500 or 1800, he would have been astonished by the German peoples in many parts of the old empire and by the strange new ways of life. He would have found the Latin language replaced by several new Germanic and Romance languages; the Roman togas replaced by blouses and trousers; the ancient Roman gods cast aside for the new Christianity; the Roman imperial structure superseded by a conglomeration of new nation-states; and the old ways of earning a living rivaled by new agricultural techniques, by commerce with hitherto unknown parts of the globe, and by new crafts with strange machines that saved labor and that ran without the traditional human or animal power.

The explanation, of course, is that only in the West was a classical civilization permanently submerged and succeeded by something fundamentally new. Everywhere else in Eurasia the various regional civilizations either escaped the invaders (south China and south India), or repeled them (Byzantium and Persia), or endured and survived them (north China and north India). Only in the West was the classical civilization shattered beyond recall despite repeated attempts at restoration over several centuries.

Since it was precisely this uniqueness that made it possible for the West to attain worldwide supremacy in modern times, we must pay special attention to its origins. As noted in section I of this chapter, technological stagnation was a basic structural weakness of the classical civilizations. But since this was true of all of them, why did only the West European civilization founder?

A comparison of West European institutions and experiences with those of the rest of Eurasia leads to certain conclusions. In the first place Western Europe was not as productive in classical times as, for example, China. The monsoon winds provide most of East Asia with plenty of rainfall during the summer growing months, in contrast to Europe where most of the rain comes in the sterile winter months. This, together with the greater solar heat in the lower latitudes, allows more intensive and prolonged cultivation in East Asia, including two crops per year in many localities. Furthermore, rice, the principal crop of East Asia, produces a much larger yield per acre than wheat, rye, and the other cereals grown in the West. According to one estimate, rice on a given plot of land yields caloric value that is five times as great as that of wheat on the same land. The net result was a far greater productivity in China than in the West, which led to the correspondingly denser population found in China from the beginnings of agriculture to modern times. This superiority in productivity and in population in turn made China more capable of supporting the empire's bureaucratic and military establishments, and of resisting, or, if necessary, absorbing, barbarian invaders.

Another was the absence in the West of anything comparable to the Chinese writing system, which provided lasting cultural homogeneity, and to the Chinese examination system, which provided administrative efficiency and stability. Finally, the Roman Empire had to cope with more formidable enemies on its frontiers. Being located on the western receiving end of the steppe invasion route, Europe bore the brunt of attacks by virtually all the nomadic peoples. Furthermore, the Roman Empire's Germanic neighbors were more numerous than the nomads on China's northwestern frontier. Also the neighboring Persians and Arabs were more advanced, and a more serious and lasting military threat, than China's nomadic neighbors. For all these reasons the invasions in the West dragged on centuries longer than in the rest of Eurasia. Hence the unique denouement in the West—the absolute and final dissolution of the Roman imperial structure and of its classical civilization.

This outcome is of such significance that it can fairly be described as a major turning point in world history. It was such a fateful turning point because the wholesale destruction cleared the way for innovation that was long overdue. The conclusion drawn by historian Robert Lopez concerning the end of the Roman Empire that opened this chapter bears repeating here: ''All in all, the invasions gave the *coup de grace* to a culture which had come to a standstill after reaching its apogee and seemed doomed to wither away. We are reminded of the cruel bombings in our own day which destroyed ramshackle old buildings and so made possible the reconstruction of towns on more modern lines.''[6] But this ''culture'' was no different from all the others of Eurasia, which also were at a ''standstill.'' Those others, however, managed to survive the invasions and to gain a new lease on life. But it was the old life that was prolonged, while the West, with the death of the Roman Empire, was able to start a new life—to make a new beginning.

The significance of this new beginning becomes clear if it is recalled that during the ancient period the Middle East had been the center of initiative from which had diffused the fundamental innovations of those millennia. But during the classical period it was Europe, India, and China that generated most of the innovations, while the Middle East lagged behind. And the reason was precisely that the ancient civilization of the Middle East had survived the invasions of the second millennium B.C., while the ancient civilizations of the peripheral regions had gone under, leaving the way clear for a fresh start—for the emergence of the new classical civilizations.

So it was during the transition from the classical to the medieval civilizations. But this time the existing classical civilizations survived everywhere except in the West. For this reason the West alone was free to strike out in new directions and to evolve, during the medieval age, a new technology, new institutions, and new ideas—in short, a new civilization. And in modern times this new civilization proved its superiority over the ''standstill'' civilizations of the rest of Eurasia—indeed of the entire world—as inevitably and completely as the agricultural civilizations had triumphed over tribal cultures at an earlier time.

SUGGESTED READING

C. M. Cipolla, ed., *The Economic Decline of Empires* (Methuen, 1970); S. W. Eisenstadt, ed., *The Decline of Empires* (Prentice-Hall, 1967); M. Grant, *Dawn of the Middle Ages* (McGraw-Hill, 1981); G. Jones, *A History of the Vikings* (Oxford University Press, 1968); F. Lot, *The End of the Ancient World and the Beginning of the Middle Ages* (Knopf, 1931); O. J. Maenchen-Helfen, *The World of the Huns* (University of California Press, 1973); S. Mazzarino, *The End of the Ancient World* (Faber, 1966); E. A. Thompson, *A History of Attila and the Huns* (Clarendon, 1948); and his *The Goths in Spain* (Oxford University Press, 1969); F. W. Walbank, *The Awful Revolution* (University of Liverpool Press, 1969).

What It Means
For Us Today

CIVILIZATION: CURSE OR BLESSING?

In all civilizations there have been poets and thinkers who have looked to the past with longing. They have regarded prehistoric man as the "noble savage," untainted by the corrupting influence of civilization. Long ago, "in the beginning," during that wonderful first chapter of humanity's existence, there was paradise on earth. In the Hindu epics there are passages extolling an idyllic past in which castes were absent and humankind could enjoy life in freedom and security. Likewise Hesiod, an eighth century B.C. Greek poet, described a Golden Age of long ago, and then traced man's declining fortunes through the Silver and Iron ages to the deplorable present in which the author lived.

This concept of original bliss had some basis in historical fact. So far as economic and social relationships were concerned, the tribesmen before the advent of civilization had enjoyed free and equal access to the natural resources necessary for livelihood. Economic equality and social homogeneity had been the hallmark of their Neolithic villages. But when the tribesmen became peasants they no longer had free access to land and they no longer enjoyed the full product of their labor. Their specific obligations varied from region to region, but the net result was everywhere the same. After making the payments required by the state, the priest, the landlord, and the moneylender, they were left almost invariably with only enough for sheer existence. In contrast to the egalitarianism of the

Paleolithic hunting bands and the Neolithic villages, all the ancient civilizations have divided people into haves and have-nots.

What this has meant in human terms was expressed as early as the third millennium B.C. by an Egyptian father taking his son to school. He tried to convince his son to study hard and urged him to compare the wretchedness of both peasants and workers with the blessings of learned scribes and officials.

> Put writing in your heart that you may protect yourself from hard labor of any kind and be a magistrate of high repute. The scribe is released from manual tasks; it is he who commands. . . . Do you not hold the scribe's palette? That is what makes the difference between you and the man who handles an oar.
>
> I have seen the metal-worker at his task at the mouth of his furnace, with fingers like a crocodile's. He stank worse than fish-spawn. . . . The stonemason finds his work in every kind of hard stone. When he has finished his labors his arms are worn out, and he sleeps all doubled up until sunrise. His knees and spine are broken. . . . The barber shaves from morning till night; he never sits down except to meals. He hurries from house to house looking for business. He wears out his arms to fill his stomach, like bees eating their own honey. . . . The farmer wears the same clothes for all times. His voice is as raucous as a crow's. His fingers are always busy, his arms are dried up by the wind. He takes his rest—when he does get any rest—in the mud. If he's in good health he shares good health with the beasts; if he is ill his bed is the bare earth in the middle of his beasts. . . .
>
> Apply your heart to learning. In truth there is nothing that can compare with it. If you have profited by a single day at school it is a gain for eternity.[1]

The coming of civilization brought drastic change in political relationships as well as economic. The Neolithic villagers had been subject to only a few controls, whether internal or external. But tribal chiefs and elders now were replaced by king or emperor, and by an ever-present bureaucracy, including palace functionaries, provincial and district officials, judges, clerk, and accountants. Working closely with this imperial administration was the ecclesiastical hierarchy that was also an essential feature of civilization. In place of the former shaman who had been a "leisure-time specialist," there was the priest, a "full-time specialist."[2] Now it was possible to develop an official theology and a priestly hierarchy. Both the theology and the hierarchy served to buttress the existing social order. They gave political institutions and leaders divine sanction and attributes. For example, the Egyptian pharaoh was not only the ruler of his country but also the "living god." This coupling of divine and secular authority provided most powerful support for the status quo. It was a rare individual who dared risk swift punishment in this life and everlasting punishment in the afterlife.

The transformation of culture wrought by civilization was fundamental and enduring. The culture of a Neolithic village had been autonomous and homogeneous. All members had shared common knowledge, customs, and attitudes, and they had been independent of outside sources for the maintenance of their way of life. But with civilization, a new and more complex society emerged. In addition to the traditional culture of the village agricultural people there was now the new culture of the scribes, who knew the mysterious art of writing, of the priests, who knew the secrets of the heavens, of the artists, who knew how to paint and carve, and of the merchants, who exchanged goods with lands beyond deserts and seas. So there was no longer a single culture. Instead there developed what has been called *high culture* and *low culture.* The high culture was to be found in the schools, temples, and palaces of the cities; the low culture was in the villages. The high culture was passed on in writing by philosophers, theologians, and literary men; the low culture was passed on by word of mouth among illiterate peasants.

The high and low cultures of the various civilizations differed in details but were all similar in essentials. They were all based on "sacred books," such as the Indian Vedas, the Buddhist Canon, the Chinese *Classics,* and the Christian Old and New Testaments. Since these texts were the basis of knowledge, they dominated education. Anyone who wished to get ahead had to memorize large portions of these texts. The sacred books also were used to enforce loyalty and obedience. Repudiation of official teachings or challenge to the social order were branded as crimes punishable in this world and in the next. The "hells" which were so prominent in all high cultures were eternal concentration camps for those who dared resist their secular or religious leaders.

The low cultures of all civilizations also were essentially the same. Peasants everywhere had a considerable body of factual information concerning the care of animals and plants. They all regarded hard work as a virtue and looked down upon townsmen as weaklings who tired easily. Also all peasants had a common passion to own a plot of land, a few animals, and the simple tools of field and shop. This meant independence and security, and to attain this all peasantries stubbornly resisted outside intervention, whether by a landlord or by a present-day collective. The "rugged individualism" of the peasant was balanced, however, by the communal life and relationships of the village. The good neighbor was always ready to offer aid and sympathy when needed, as well as to participate in house raisings, warmings, harvest festivals, and other community affairs.

Relations between the high and low culture usually were strained. On the one hand the peasants felt superior, regarding country life and agricultural work as morally "good," in contrast to urban life and professions. On the other hand they were economically and politically subject to the city. The landlords, the tax collectors, the church officials, and the soldiers all came from the city. Their arrogance and arbitrariness made it crystal clear who were the rulers and who the ruled. Whereas the elite viewed their rich life as the product of their own superior mental and moral qualities, their good life was actually made possible by the exploitation of the peasantry. Inevitably, in the source of millennia, the peasants internalized the attitudes of the elite toward them and became servile and obsequious.

It is clear that the coming of civilization was a setback for equality between human beings. On the other hand civilization also brought great gains and achievements. Viewed in the light of historical perspective, it was a major step forward despite all the injustice and exploitation. In this respect it resembled the industrial revolution, which at first caused painful social disruption and human suffering, but which in the long run advanced decisively human productivity and well-being. So it was with the coming of civilization. The average Neolithic tribal member probably led a more rounded and satisfying life than the average peasant or urban worker. But precisely because tribal culture was comfortable and tension-free, it was also relatively unproductive. The demands of the tax collector, the priest, and the landowner were harsh, but they were also effective in stimulating output. Positive proof of the increased productivity was the enormous population increase in the river valleys. Living standards also rose along with population figures. Certainly the monarchs and the top officials, both secular and ecclesiastical, enjoyed a variety of food and drink, along with richness in clothing and housing that no tribal chieftain could ever have imagined. The new middle classes—merchants, scribes, lower officials, and clergy—also were able to lead lives that probably were as pleasant and refined as those enjoyed by their counterparts today. Even the masses may in some cases have been better off in the material sense, if not the psychosocial.

Civilization, with the new art of writing, made it possible to accumulate more and more knowledge and transmit it to successive generations. Various sciences, including mathematics, astronomy, and medicine, were able to take root and to flourish. Also the appearance of wealthy upper classes gave opportunities for the creativity of architects, sculptors, painters, musicians, and poets. The results of this creativity we can see today in masterpieces such as the Parthenon, the Taj Mahal, and the Notre Dame Cathedral.

These precious gains benefited the few much more than the many who, in the final analysis, bore the costs of the high culture. But the important point so far as the whole history of humanity is concerned is that the advances *were* made. And it was these advances, accumulating through the millennia, that finally allowed us to gain such mastery over nature and to attain such productivity through science and technology, that the many are now benefiting along with the few.

It is true that many millions of people are still illiterate and diseased and hungry. But that is very different from the mid-fourteenth century when a third to a half of Europe's total population was wiped out by the Black Death. It is different also from 1846 when a million Irish died of hunger because of the potato blight, and from 1876 when 5 million Indians starved to death when their crops failed. These victims of plague and famine could not possibly have been saved because the people of those times lacked the necessary knowledge.

Today we have that knowledge, and therefore we have the potentiality to free ourselves from millenia-old scourges. It is tragic that the potentiality has not yet been realized, but the fact remains that it does exist. And it exists because of the advances made possible in the past by the different civilizations of the human race. Therefore the answer to the question of whether civilization was a curse or a blessing is that in the past it has been both. What it will be in the future depends on whether the knowledge accumulated from past civilizations is used for destructive or constructive purposes.

SUGGESTED READING

Archeologists and anthropologists have written thought-provoking books on this subject: V. Gordon Childe, *Man Makes Himself* (Mentor, 1951); R. Redfield, *Peasant Society and Culture: An Anthropological View to Civilization* (University of Chicago Press, 1956); L. A. White: *The Evolution of Culture: The Development of Civilization to the Fall of Rome* (McGraw-Hill, 1959); and W. Goldschmidt, *Man's Way* (Holt, Rinehart and Winston, 1959). Also noteworthy are the views of the distinguished philosopher K. Jaspers, *The Origin and Goal of History* (Yale University Press, 1953), and his *Man in the Modern Age* (Doubleday Anchor, 1957). Other viewpoints are presented by W. W. Wagar, *Building the City of Man* (Grossman, 1971); and H. Baudet, *Paradise on Earth: Some Thoughts on European Images of non-European Man* (Yale University Press, 1965).

Part III

Medieval Civilizations Of Eurasia, 500-1500

Like the Classical Age, the Medieval Age was heralded by invasions—by the Dorians, Aryans, and Chou in the first case and by the Germans, Huns, and Turks in the second. There the parallel ends, however, for the medieval centuries, unlike the classical, suffered continued invasions that affected virtually all regions of Eurasia. Beginning in the seventh century, there were the invasions of the warriors of Islam who overran, not only the entire Middle East where they originated, but eventually North Africa, Spain, the Balkans, India, Southeast Asia, and much of Central Asia. Even more extensive were the conquests of the Turks and the Mongols during the half-millennium between 1000 and 1500. They encompassed the great bulk of the Eurasian land mass from the Baltic Sea to the Pacific Ocean.

Despite their fury and range, these great conquests did not uproot civilization in most of Eurasia as did the earlier incursions of the Dorians, Aryans, and Chou. By medieval times most civilizations had sunk roots too deep to be pulled up so easily. Thus the traditional civilizations everywhere survived. In China, for example, the native Ming dynasty replaced the Mongol Yuan, and the country returned with a vengeance to ageold ways. In the sprawling Moslem world the indigenous Greco-Roman, Iranian, Semitic, and Egyptian traditions were not wiped out but rather fused into the civilization of Islam. Likewise the East Roman Empire continued without interruption for a full millennium as the Byzantine Empire, so that its inhabitants referred to themselves in modern times as "Romaioi," or Romans.

The one exception to this general pattern, as noted in the preceding chapter, was in the West. There, and there alone, the prevailing classical civilization was torn up root and branch. Only in the West, therefore, was the ground sufficiently cleared for a new civilization to emerge. In contrast to the traditional civilizations of the rest of Eurasia, the new civilization was free to develop along fresh lines.

It was this unique feature of the West that enabled it to develop the economic vigor, the technological skills, and the social dynamism to expand overseas and to gain control of the sea routes of the world. With this fateful development the Medieval Age came to an end. But it ended, it should be noted, not with land invasions by Eurasian nomads, as did the ancient and classical periods, but rather with the maritime enterprise of the West. The overseas activities of Western explorers, merchants, missionaries, and settlers marked the transition from medieval to modern times, and from the Eurasian to the global phase of world history.

What has emerged is a sense of the remarkable complexity of the interplay between the Occident and East Asia from Roman and Han times onward. This involved a two-way traffic, in many items, along many routes, and of varying density in different periods. . . . Despite difficult communication, mankind in the Old World at least has long lived in a more unified realm of discourse than we have been prepared to admit.

Lynn White, Jr.

Medieval Civilizations Complete Eurasian Unification

Just as an emerging Eurasian unity differentiated the Classical Age from the Ancient Age, so now a full-fledged Eurasian unity differentiated the Medieval Age from the Classical Age. The early stage had been attained as a result of improved technology, particularly the large-scale production of iron, with its manifold repercussions in all aspects of life (see Chapter 4). Likewise full unity was now made possible by further technological advance, especially in shipbuilding and navigation. But more significant during these centuries was a political consideration—the existence for the first time of tremendous empires. These empires did not include river valleys as in the Ancient Age, nor entire regions as in the Classical Age. They reached across several regions to embrace a large proportion of the entire Eurasian land mass.

As we have seen, the great Alexander knew nothing of the Ganges valley or of China. Virtually no direct relations existed between the Roman and the Han empires at the opposite ends of Eurasia. The reason is that Alexander's empire was pretty much confined to the Middle East, while the Roman and Han empires were for all practical purposes restricted to the western and eastern tips of Eurasia. In striking contrast, during the medieval period the Islamic Empire by the mid-eighth century stretched from the Pyrenees to the Indian Ocean, and from Morocco to the borders of China. In later centuries Islam expanded much further into Central Asia, Southeast Asia, and Africa's interior. Even more impressive was the thirteenth-century Mongol Empire that included Korea, China, all of Central Asia, Russia, and most of the Middle East—the greatest

Eurasian empire to that time and even since (see Map XIV, "Mongol Empire at the Death of Kublai Khan, 1294'').

Empires of such unprecedented size eliminated the age-old regional isolation. Direct contact and interaction amongst the various parts of the land mass were now possible. This chapter will consider the nature of the resulting new bonds—commercial, technological, religious, and intellectual.

I. COMMERCIAL BONDS

In classical times, the existence of the large Roman and Han empires at the opposite ends of the Eurasian trade routes stimulated commerce all along the line. Conversely, the disintegration of these empires undermined and reduced this commerce. It revived, however, and reached new heights during medieval times with the appearance of the Islamic, and later the Mongol, Empire.

The Moslem conquests unified the entire Middle East, through which ran all the trans-Eurasian trade routes—both the land routes that terminated at various Black Sea and Syrian ports and the sea routes that ran through the Red Sea and the Persian Gulf. Particularly flourishing was the trade across the Arabian Sea with the Malabar coast of southwest India. Sizeable settlements of Moslem merchants, mostly Arabs and Persians, grew up in the ports of India and Ceylon. Horses, silver, wrought iron objects, and linen, cotton, and woolen fabrics were shipped from west to east where they were exchanged for silks, precious stones, teak, and assorted spices.

Moslem merchants went on from India and Ceylon to Kalah Bar (Kedah) on the Malay coast. From there, some sailed on to Sumatra and Java, while others went through the Malacca Straits and then north to Kanfu (Canton) in South China. The customary schedule was to leave the Persian Gulf in September or October, sail with the northeast monsoon to India and Malaya, and arrive in the China Sea in time for the southern monsoon to Canton. There the Moslem merchants spent the summer and then returned with the northeast monsoon to the Malacca Straits and across the Bay of Bengal, arriving back in the Persian Gulf in the early summer—making a round trip of a year and a half.

After the first Moslem reached Canton in 671, considerable numbers settled there and prospered as middlemen between China and the overseas world. With the advent of the Sung dynasty (960–1127), the Chinese made considerable progress in shipbuilding and navigation. By the end of the twelfth century they were replacing the Moslems in the waters of East and Southeast Asia. When the Mongols conquered China and founded the Yuan dynasty (1279–1368), Chinese ships were the largest and best equipped, while Chinese merchants were settling in various ports in Southeast Asia and India. Marco Polo, who in 1291 accompanied a Mongol princess around southeast Asia to Iran, witnessed and described the vigor of Chinese maritime enterprise. So did the Arab traveler Ibn Battuta, who fifty years later chose to make his way from India to China on a Chinese junk.

During the Ming dynasty (1368–1644), Chinese maritime activity reached its height, ending in a remarkable but short-lived naval domination of the Pacific and Indian Oceans in the early fifteenth century. For example, a series of seven expeditions was sent out between 1405 and 1433 under the superintendency of the chief court eunuch, a certain Cheng Ho. These expeditions were unprecedented in their magnitude and in their achievements. The first was made up of 62 ships and 28,000 men, and sailed as far as

Java, Ceylon, and Calicut. On the return a flotilla of Sumatran pirates tried to block the way but they were completely annihilated. The later expeditions pressed on further, reaching as far as the east coast of Africa and the entrances to the Persian Gulf and the Red Sea. More than thirty ports in the Indian Ocean were visited by the Chinese, and everywhere they persuaded or compelled the local rulers to recognize the suzerainty of the Ming emperor. And all this at a time when the Portuguese were just beginning to feel their way down the coast of Africa where they did not reach Cape Verde until 1445! (see Map XVII, "Early 15th-Century Chinese and Portuguese Voyages").

These extraordinary Chinese expeditions were suddenly halted by imperial order in 1433. The reasons for their beginning as well as for their ending remain a mystery. It is believed that the expeditions may have been launched to compensate for the loss of foreign trade over the land routes when the Mongol Empire disintegrated. Or they may have been sent to enhance the prestige of the imperial court, or to find the emperor's predecessor who had disappeared underground as a Buddhist monk. Some think that the expeditions may have been halted because of their excessive cost or because of the traditional rivalry between court eunuchs and Confucian bureaucrats. In any case the withdrawal of the Chinese left a power vacuum in the waters of East and South Asia. Japanese pirates harried the coasts of China, while in the Indian Ocean the Moslem Arabs regained their former primacy. But adept though they were as merchants, the Arabs lacked the unity and the resources to develop naval power as had the Chinese. Thus when the Portuguese sailed around Africa into the Indian Ocean in 1498, they encountered no effective resistance, and proceeded to establish their domination.

Meanwhile a great revolution in land trade had occurred with the rise of the Mongol Empire. For the first and only time in history one political authority extended across the breadth of Eurasia—from the Baltic Sea to the Pacific, and from Siberia to the Persian Gulf. A mid-fourteenth-century Italian handbook summarized the commercial significance of this *Pax Mongolica* in describing a trade route running across Central Asia from its beginning point at Tana at the mouth of the Don River.

> The road you travel from Tana to Cathay [China] is perfectly safe, whether by day or by night, according to what the merchants say who have used it. . . . You may reckon that from Tana to Sarai [on the Volga] the road is less safe than on any other part of the journey; and yet even when this part of the road is at its worst, if you are some sixty men in the company you will go as safely as if you were in your own house.[1]

When Kublai Khan in 1264 moved his capital from Karakorum in Mongolia to Peking, China was automatically opened to the European merchants trading along the trans-Eurasian routes. The first Europeans to arrive at Kublai's new court were not diplomatic emissaries but two Venetian merchants, Nicolo and Maffeo Polo. Of greater economic importance than access to China was access for the first time to the source of spices in India and the East Indies. Hitherto spice had reached Europe via two routes: through the Red Sea and Egypt, or to the Persian Gulf and then by caravan routes to ports on the Black Sea or the eastern Mediterranean. The first route was controlled by the Arabs who shipped the spices to Egypt, and by the Venetians who loaded cargoes at Alexandria for distribution in Europe. The second route was dominated by the Mongol ruler (Ilkhanate) of Persia and Mesopotamia, and by the Genoese who awaited the spices at the port terminals.

The Genoese, however, were not content only to sail the Black Sea. They ascended the

Don River from the Azov Sea in small, light vessels, which they transported, probably on ox-wagons, across the narrow neck of land to the Volga and thence to the Caspian Sea and to Persia. Thus the Genoese were able to reach the Persian Gulf and to go directly to India and the East Indies where they discovered how cheap the spices were in their places of origin and what fabulous profits had been made during the past centuries by the succession of middlemen between the producers in Southeast Asia and the consumers in Europe.

This revival of overland trade during the *Pax Mongolica* proved short-lived. One reason was the expulsion of the Mongols from China in 1368 and the general disintegration of the Mongol Empire. This led to fragmentation in Central Asia and hence to the disruption of trans-Eurasian trade. More important was the conversion of Ilkhan Ghazan (1295–1304) to Islam, which automatically barred to European merchants the transit route to the spice islands. Almost all spices henceforth were shipped along the Red Sea–Nile route, with golden profits for the Arab and Venetian middlemen. But other Europeans were unwilling to continue paying exorbitant prices, particularly since they now knew from where the spices came and at what cost. Hence the search for a new sea route around the Moslem barrier—a search that was to end with da Gama's great voyage around Africa.

II. TECHNOLOGICAL BONDS

The great Moslem and Mongol empires quickened not only the flow of trade within Eurasia but also the diffusion of technology. An outstanding example is the lateen sail, a tall, triangular, fore-and-aft sail that has always been used on Arab craft. In the Mediterranean, by contrast, the Egyptians, Phoenicians, Greeks, and Romans had used a square sail which is easier to handle in bad weather. But the Arab sail is much more maneuverable, being able to keep closer to the wind and to tack on rivers and narrow waters. For this reason it soon replaced the square sail in the Levant, and by the eleventh century it had become the normal rig throughout the Mediterranean. Today this triangular sail is still known as the "Latin," or "lateen," sail, though it was the Arabs who, with the Moslem invasions, introduced it into the Mediterranean. And from there it spread to the Atlantic where, during the fifteenth century, Portuguese and Spanish ship designers combined the square sail on the foremast with the lateen on the main and mizzen. The resulting hybrid three-masters were capable of sailing in all reasonable weathers, and thus made possible the long ocean voyages of Columbus and da Gama.

The Moslem Empire, straddling North Africa, the Middle East, and South Asia, had contact with all regions of Eurasia and thus served as an intermediary in the interchange of knowledge and techniques as well as of articles of trade. An example of this interchange may be seen in the following account left by an Arab physician and scientist who lived in Baghdad between 850 and 925. This shows how the Chinese learned from the Moslems about Galen, a Greek physician of A.D. 130 to 200, whose numerous writings had been translated into Arabic.

A Chinese scholar came to my house and remained in the town about a year. In five months he learnt to speak and write Arabic, attaining indeed eloquence in speech and calligraphy in writing. When he decided to return to his country, he said to me a month or so beforehand, "I am about to leave. I would be very glad if someone would dictate to me the sixteen books of Galen before I go." I told him that he had not sufficient time to copy more than a small part of it, but he said, "I beg you to

TABLE 1. TRANSMISSION OF TECHNIQUES AND INVENTIONS*

Technique or Invention	Approx. lag in centuries
From China to the West	
Square-pallet chain-pump	15
Edge-runner mill	13
Edge-runner mill with application of water-power	9
Metallurgical blowing-engines, water-power	11
Rotary fan and rotary winnowing machine	14
Piston-bellows	14
Draw-loom	4
Silk-handling machinery (a form of flyer for laying thread evenly on reels appears in the + 11th century, and water-power is applied to spinning mills in the + 14th)	3–13
Wheelbarrow	9–10
Sailing-carriage	11
Wagon-mill	12
Efficient harness for draught-animals: Breast-strap (postilion)	8
Collar	6
Cross-bow (as an individual arm)	13
Kite	12
Helicopter top (spun by cord)	14
Zoetrope (moved by ascending hot-air current)	10
Deep drilling	11
Cast iron	10–12
"Cardan" suspension	8–9
Segmental arch bridge	7
Iron-chain suspension-bridge	10–13
Canal lock-gates	7–17
Nautical construction principles	10
Stern-post rudder	4
Gunpowder	5–6
Gunpowder used as a war technique	4
Magnetic compass (lodestone spoon)	11
Magnetic compass with needle	4
Magnetic compass used for navigation	2
Paper	10
Printing (block)	6
Printing (movable type)	4
Printing (metal movable type)	1
Porcelain	11–13
From the West to China	
Screw	14
Force-pump for liquids	18
Crankshaft	3
Clockwork	3

*Adapted from J. Needham, Science and Civilization in China *(London: Cambridge University Press, 1954), 242–43.*

give me all your time until I go, and to dictate to me as rapidly as possible. You will see that I shall write faster than you can dictate.'' So together with one of my students we read Galen to him as fast as we could, but he wrote still faster. We did not believe that he was getting it correctly until we made a collation and found it exact throughout. I asked him how this could be, and he said, ''We have in our country a way of writing which we call shorthand, and this is what you see. When we wish to write very fast we use this style, and then afterwards transcribe it into the ordinary characters at will.'' But he added that an intelligent man who learns quickly cannot master this script in under twenty years.[2]

This revealing account is unusual because during the medieval period the Chinese usually were the donors rather than the recipients in the Eurasian interchange. In earlier times, it is true, it had been the other way around. During the ancient and classical periods such basic inventions as the wheel, windlass, and pulley diffused in all directions from Mesopotamia, the swape and crank from Egypt, the windmill from Persia, and iron smelting from Asia Minor. But during the first fourteen centuries of the Christian era, China was the great center of technological innovation and transmitted to the rest of Eurasia a multitude of inventions. These included such important inventions as gunpowder, the magnet, printing, paper, the stern-post rudder, the foot stirrup, and the breast-strap harness. How much greater the technological flow was from east to west than west to east is clear from the list of technology transfers in Table 1. The Chinese also domesticated numerous fruits and plants which spread throughout Eurasia. These include the chrysanthemum, the camellia, the azalea, the tea rose, the Chinese aster, the lemon, and the orange. The orange is still called ''Chinese apple'' in Holland and Germany.

III. RELIGIOUS BONDS

The medieval period was characterized not only by an unprecedented trans-Eurasian exchange of goods and technologies, but also by an unprecedented diffusion of religious creeds. In the case of Christianity and Buddhism, this began towards the end of the classical period and continued during the medieval (see Chapter 4, section III). But by all odds the outstanding religious change during the medieval centuries was the appearance of *Islam*. Apart from its teachings, which will be noted in the following chapter, the new religion profoundly affected extensive regions of Eurasia and Africa as it burst out from the Arabian peninsula following the death of Mohammed in A.D. 632.

The spread of Islam (the details of which will be noted later) occurred in two stages. During the first, from 632 to 750, it flooded over the Middle East and then west to the Pyrenees and east to Central Asia. The net effect was the virtual transformation of the Mediterranean into a Moslem lake. But the second stage of expansion between 1000 and 1500 made the Indian Ocean also a Moslem preserve, for during these centuries Islam expanded much further—into India, Southeast Asia, and Africa.

The vast extension of the domains of Islam naturally alarmed the rulers of Christendom who were now isolated on the western tip of Eurasia. This explains their ambivalent reaction to the appearance of the Mongols in the thirteenth century. They were terrified by the slaughter inflicted by the Mongol horsemen. But the picture was not all black, because the Mongols also crushed the Moslems in Persia and Mesopotamia. The Christian rulers therefore hoped they might be able to convert the pagan Mongols to Christianity, as they had earlier converted the pagan Magyars and Vikings.

The Pope sent two missions to the court of the Grand Khan in Karakorum in northern Mongolia. They tried to persuade the Khan to adopt Christianity and to join the Pope in a crusade against the Moslems. But the traditional magicians or shamans were very influential at the court, and the missions failed to win any converts. They were successful, however, in gathering the first reliable information about Mongol customs and military tactics. They also learned that twenty days' journey east from Karakorum was the mysterious land of Cathay, or China. It was known to be not only wealthy but also non-Islamic and, therefore, a possible ally against the Moslems.

Since China was a part of the great Mongol Empire, Kublai Khan moved his capital in 1264 from Karakorum to Cambaluc, or modern Peking. The first Europeans to arrive in the capital were two Venetian merchants, Nicolo and Maffeo Polo. Kublai welcomed them warmly, questioned them about Europe, and gave them letters to deliver to the Pope. In 1289 Pope Nicholas IV sent John of Montecorvino, a veteran of fourteen years' missionary work amongst the Moslems in the Levant to the Mongol court. He was allowed to remain in Peking and to preach, so that within six years after his arrival in 1292 he had built a church with a campanile and with a choir of 150 boys whose Gregorian chants pleased the imperial ear. When the Papacy learned of this success it sent reinforcements, enabling Friar John to start another mission in Canton. By the time of the friar's death in 1328 several thousand converts had been won over in China.

This progress was made possible by the positive attitude of the Mongol rulers. They deliberately encouraged all alien religions, whether Moslem, Buddhist, or Christian in order to counteract the dominant Confucian establishment in China. Accordingly the Christian missionaries received liberal allowances from the imperial treasury, as well as luxurious apartments in which they lived on a scale far above anything in their past. Their affluence proved short-lived because it depended entirely on the generosity of the Mongol emperors. When the emperors were expelled from China in 1368, the various foreign missionaries that they had patronized were expelled along with them. Thus the Catholics were forced to leave, and Western Christianity disappeared in China until da Gama's voyage around the Cape in 1497–98. This established the first direct sea route between Western Europe and China and paved the way for the arrival of new Catholic missions—by sea rather than by land.

IV. EXPANDING HORIZONS

Although the Europeans did not win over the Mongols as allies or as coreligionists, they did, thanks to the Mongol Empire, broaden immeasurably their own horizons and gain a new Eurasian perspective. This was very different from the early medieval period when the collapse of the Han and Roman empires cut the trans-Eurasian ties of classical times. Parochialism set in, and in the West this was accentuated by the teachings of Christianity. The Bible became the main source of geographical knowledge, so that Jerusalem was regarded as the center of the earth, while the Nile, Euphrates, and Ganges were believed to have a common source in the Garden of Eden.

The expansion of Islam in the seventh and eighth centuries further narrowed European horizons by erecting a barrier across North Africa and the Middle East. It was not until the twelfth century when the Crusaders began to return from the Levant that first-hand information of the outside world was again available. Yet even then the Mediterranean remained the axis of the world, and knowledge of the lands to the east and south was very meager.

The great breakthrough came with the Mongol Empire. Its existence brought about the transition from a Mediterranean to a Eurasian perspective, just as the voyages of Columbus and da Gama later brought about a transition from a Eurasian to a global perspective. The travels of merchants, missionaries, and prisoners of war revealed the existence of a great empire in the Far East that not only equaled but surpassed Europe in population, wealth, and level of civilization. Nor was this a one-way process, for the East now became aware of the West, and vice versa. Marco Polo, who opened the eyes of the West to Cathay, had his counterparts in China and the Middle East.

We know of Chinese trading colonies in Moscow, Tabriz, and Novgorod during this period. Chinese engineers were employed on irrigation projects in Mesopotamia. Also there are records of Chinese bureaucrats who accompanied Genghis Khan on his campaigns and inspection tours from one end of Eurasia to the other. In addition there was the Christian Nestorian monk Rabban Bar Sauma, who was born in Peking and who traveled in 1278 to the Moslem court in Baghdad. From there he was sent by the Mongols to Europe to seek Christian help against Islam. Starting out in 1287, he traveled to Constantinople, Naples, Rome, Paris, and London, meeting en route both Philip IV of France and Edward I of England. The most wide ranging of these medieval travelers was the aforementioned Moslem Ibn Battuta (1304–1378). Starting from his native Morocco, he made the pilgrimage to Mecca and journeyed on through Samarkand to India where he served as judge and also as ambassador to China. Returning later to Morocco, he resumed his travels, crossing north to Spain and then south to the interior of Africa, where he reached Timbuktu. When he finally returned to Morocco and settled down, he had traveled no less than 75,000 miles.

By all odds the most important traveler for the Western world was the famous Marco Polo. Accompanying his father and his uncle on their second journey to China, he arrived at Kublai Khan's court in 1275. He favorably impressed the Khan and served him for seventeen years in various ways that required him to travel throughout the country. As an official he carefully observed the inhabitants and resources of the lands through which he journeyed, noting such things as "a kind of black stone, which is dug out of the mountains like any other kind of stone and burns like wood." In 1292 he escorted a Mongol princess on a voyage around southeast Asia and across the Indian Ocean to Persia where she was to be the bride of the Moslem ruler. Marco Polo then continued westward to his native Venice, arriving there in 1295 after an absence of twenty-five years. Shortly afterward he was captured in a battle with the Genoese, and while in prison he dictated his account of his travels.

He told of the Grand Khan's palace with its gardens and artificial lakes, its elephants with harnesses of silver and precious stones. He told also of roads that were paved and raised above the surrounding ground so that they might drain easily, of the Grand Canal through which merchant vessels passed each year, of ports with ships larger than any known in Europe, and of lands which produced spices, silk, ginger, sugar, camphor, cotton, salt, saffron, sandalwood, and porcelain. Marco Polo described also all the fabulous countries he visited and heard about while escorting the Chinese princess to Persia— Singapore, Java, Sumatra, Ceylon, India, Socotra, Madagascar, Arabia, Zanzibar, and Abyssinia.

The title of Marco Polo's book is significant—*The Description of the World*. In fact this work had suddenly doubled the size of the known world for Westerners, as shown in Map XV "Eurasian Unification about 1300." Marco Polo opened up new vistas for his contemporaries fully as much as Columbus was to do two centuries later. Indeed it was his

MARCO POLO'S NEW WORLD

Medieval Eurasia was united primarily by merchants who traveled back and forth from the Mediterranean Sea to China and Southeast Asia. The following selections from Marco Polo's great travel account make clear how much the horizons of the medieval world were opening up.*

As regards the size of this city [Cambaluc, or modern Peking], you must know that it has a compass of 24 miles, for each side of it hath a length of 6 miles. . . . There are 12 gates, and over each gate there is a great and handsome palace. . . . The streets are so straight and wide that you can see right along them from end to end and from one gate to the other. And up and down the city there are beautiful palaces, and many great and fine hostelries, and fine houses in great numbers. . . .

And first let us speak of the [Chinese] ships in which merchants go to and fro amongst the Isles of India. These ships, you must know, are of fir timber. They have but one deck, though each of them contains some 50 or 60 cabins, wherein the merchants abide greatly at their ease, every man having one to himself. The ship hath but one rudder, but it hath four masts; and sometimes they have two additional masts, which they ship and unship at pleasure. . . . Each of their great ships requires at least 200 mariners [some of them 300]. They are indeed of great size, for one ship shall carry 5000 to 6000 baskets of pepper.

Chipangu [Japan] is an Island towards the east in the high seas 1500 miles distant from the Continent; and very great Island it is. The people are white, civilized, and well-favoured. They are Idolaters, and are dependent on nobody. And I can tell you the quantity of gold they have is endless.

When you sail from Chamba [Indochina], 1500 miles in a course between south and south-east, you come to a great Island called Java. And the experienced mariners of those Islands who know the matter well, say that it is the greatest Island in the world, and has a compass of more than 3000 miles. It is subject to a great King and tributary to no one else in the world. The people are Idolaters. The Island is of surpassing wealth, producing black pepper, nutmegs, spikenard, galingale, cubebs, cloves, and all other kinds of spices. . . .

When you leave the Island of Seilan [Ceylon] and sail westward about 60 miles, you come to the great province of Maabar which is styled India the Greater; it is best of all the Indies and is on the mainland. . . . The people are Idolaters, and many of them worship the ox [sacred cow], because it is a creature of such excellence. They would not eat beef for anything in the world, nor would they on any account kill an ox.

* H. Yule, ed. and trans., *The Book of Ser Marco Polo* (Scribner's, 1903), vol. 1, 423–26, vol. 2, 249–50, 253–54.

tantalizing picture of Cathay and the Spice Islands that beckoned the great explorers on-ward as they sought a direct sea passage after the Moslems had blocked the overland routes.

SUGGESTED READING

G. F. Hourani, *Arab Seafaring in the Indian Ocean in Ancient and Early Medieval Times* (Princeton University Press, 1951); G. F. Hudson, *Europe and China: A Survey of Their Relations from the Earliest Times to 1800* (Beacon Press, 1961); D. F. Lach, *Asia in the Making of Europe* (University of Chicago Press, 1965); R. E. Latham, trans., *The Travels of Marco Polo* (Penguin, 1958); J. Needham, *Science and Civilization in China* (Cambridge University Press, 1954); C. G. F. Simkin, *The Traditional Trade of Asia* (Oxford University Press, 1969); A. Toussaint, *History of the Indian Ocean* (University of Chicago Press, 1966).

The burden of the desert of the sea. As whirlwinds in the south pass through; so it cometh from the desert, from a terrible land.

Isaiah 21:1

We have revealed to thee an Arabic Koran, that thou mayest warn Mecca, the Mother of Cities, and those who are about her; that thou mayest give warning of the Day of Judgement, of which is no doubt— when part shall be in Paradise and part in the flame.

Koran, Sura XLII

chapter 10

Rise Of Islam

The centuries between 600 and 1000 saw the emergence of Islam, a major turning point in Eurasian and world history. The spectacular conquests of the Moslem warriors united the entire Middle East as Alexander the Great had done almost a millennium earlier. The subsequent disruption of Alexander's empire was followed by the imposition of Roman rule in Asia Minor and Syria. This led to the division of the Middle East into two parts with the Euphrates River as the dividing line. The eastern part was the center of Persian civilization and consisted of Iran and Iraq, while the western part, the center of Byzantine civilization, encompassed the Balkans, Asia Minor, Syria, Egypt, and North Africa. The Islamic conquests of the seventh and eighth centuries ended this division and united, under the star and crescent, all the territories from the Pyrenees to India and from Morocco to Central Asia.

More remarkable than these military exploits were the cultural achievements of Islam. Although the conquered territories were the centers of humanity's most ancient civilizations, nevertheless, by the eleventh century, the Arabs had affected both their language and their culture. Arabic became the language of everyday use from Persia to the Atlantic. And a new Islamic civilization emerged that was an original synthesis of the preceding Judaic, Perso-Mesopotamian, and Greco-Roman civilizations. This linguistic and cultural transformation has lasted to the present day, so that an Iraqi and a Moroccan now have as strong linguistic and cultural ties as a Briton and an Australian.

I. ARABIA BEFORE ISLAM

The Middle East on the eve of the Moslem invasions was dominated by two great empires: the Byzantine and the Sassanian. The Byzantine, from its center at Constantinople, controlled the lands of the eastern Mediterranean, while the Sassanian, with its capital at Ctesiphon, ruled the Tigris-Euphrates valleys and the Iranian plateau. The hostility between these two states was chronic, for one was Christian with a Greco-Roman culture and the other, Zoroastrian with Perso-Mesopotamian traditions. Between 603 and 629 they fought a series of exhausting wars that left both of them vulnerable to the storm that was gathering in the Arabian deserts.

Arabia at this time was regarded by its civilized neighbors as an obscure land of nomadic barbarians. Yet it had become economically important in the second half of the sixth century because of a shift in the routes of trade. The traditional Red Sea–Nile Valley and Persian Gulf–Red Sea routes had become unusable because of disorders in Egypt and the Byzantine-Persian wars. The traders accordingly turned to the more difficult but tranquil route from Syria through western Arabia to the Yemen. Their vessels then transported the goods back and forth across the Indian Ocean. Mecca, situated halfway down the coast of Arabia, profited from the new route since it was located at the crossing of the new trade routes.

Apart from the south where agriculture and monarchical government were feasible, the rest of Arabia was pastoral and tribal. The *skeikhs,* or elective tribal leaders, were merely the first among equals, and they were bound by the same traditional custom that governed all. Their principal functions were to lead in time of war and to serve as custodians of holy places. Most of the tribes were pagan and worshiped trees, fountains, and stones that were regarded as the dwelling-places of vaguely defined powers. There was also a belief in more personal gods, which were subordinate to a high deity called Allah. Both Judaism and Christianity had penetrated Arabia from the north, winning over entire tribes in the border region as well as isolated groups in the remainder of the peninsula. Compared to these faiths, idolatry and the belief in many gods, tribal warfare, and the political disunity of Arabia must have seemed shamefully primitive to thoughtful Arabs. One reason for Mohammed's success was that his teachings satisfied the needs and longings of his people.

II. MOHAMMED

Mohammed, the most influential historical personality of the Medieval Age, was born in 569. Since his father died before he was born, and his mother when he was six, Mohammed was brought up first by his grandmother and then subsequently by his uncle. Little is known of his youth, though tradition has it that at the age of twelve he was taken by his uncle on a caravan to Syria. In the course of that journey he may have picked up some Jewish and Christian lore. At the age of twenty-five he married a wealthy widow who bore him several daughters and two sons who died in infancy.

About his fortieth year Mohammed went through a period of intense spiritual tension, in the course of which he became convinced that God had chosen him to be a prophet, a successor to Abraham and Moses and Jesus. Asked to describe the process of revelation, he answered that the entire text of the Koran existed in Heaven and that one fragment at a time was communicated to him, usually by the archangel Gabriel who made him repeat every word. Others who were near Mohammed on some of these occasions neither saw nor heard the archangel. The convulsions that shook him at these times may have been epileptic seizures, particularly since he reported hearing sounds like the ringing of bells—a frequent occurrence in epilepsy. In any case Mohammed now believed that he had received a divine call to teach of the unity and supreme power of Allah, to warn his people of the Day of Judgment, and to tell them of the rewards for the faithful in Paradise and the punishment of the wicked in Hell.

His teachings were written down soon after his death and became the sacred scripture of the new religion known as Islam, meaning "submission to God's will." Mohammed did not establish an organized priesthood nor did he prescribe specific sacraments essential for salvation. But he did call on his followers to perform certain rituals known as the Five Pillars of Islam. These are: (1) Once in his life the believer must say with full understanding and absolute acceptance, "There is no God but Allah; Mohammed is the Messenger of Allah." (2) Five times daily the believer must pray—at dawn, at noon, in mid-afternoon, at dusk, and after it has become dark. Facing in the direction of Mecca, the worshiper prays on a carpet, with shoes removed and head covered. (3) The Moslem must give alms generously, as an offering to Allah and an act of piety. (4) The Moslem must fast from daybreak to sunset during the whole month of Ramadan. (5) Once in his or her life the Moslem, if able, must make the pilgrimage, or Hadj, to Mecca.

These rituals provided the believers with an extraordinarily powerful social cement. They prayed and fasted together, they assumed responsibility for their less fortunate fellow Moslems, and they journeyed to Mecca together—rich and poor, yellow, white, brown, and black. Furthermore the Koran provided guidance for all phases of the life of the faithful—for manners and hygiene, marriage and divorce, commerce and politics, crime and punishment, peace and war. Thus Islam was not only a religion but also a social code and a political system. It offered to its followers both religious commandments and specific guidance for private and public life. There was no split between the secular life and the religious, between the temporal and the spiritual, as there was in the Christian world. What is Caesar's, in Islam, is God's, and what is God's is also Caesar's. The *Shari'a*, or Holy Law, was until recently the law of the land throughout the Moslem world, and it is still the basic law in individual countries.

Mohammed slowly won converts to these teachings. The first were members of his immediate family and personal friends, who later enjoyed great prestige as "Companions of the Prophet." As the little band of converts grew, the wealthy merchants of Mecca became alarmed for fear that Mohammed's teachings would undermine the older religious beliefs and discourage pilgrims from coming to worship at the shrine of the Black Stone in their city. Because of the growing opposition, Mohammed accepted an invitation to go to Medina, an oasis town on the trade route nearly three hundred miles north of Mecca. His emigration to Medina, known as the hegira, took place in 622, and the Moslem calendar is dated from the beginning of the year in which this event occurred. Gradually Mohammed persuaded the Medina Arabs to accept his religion and he organized a theocratic state based on his teachings.

From his base in Medina, Mohammed organized attacks on the Mecca caravans. Such raiding was an accepted and popular economic activity amongst Arab nomads, who now flocked to the banner of the Prophet in the hope of winning booty, and incidentally salvation. By 630 the Moslems were strong enough to capture Mecca, whereupon Mohammed made the Black Stone, housed in the Ka'ba, the chief shrine of his religion. Thus he effected a compromise by which he preserved the basic tenets of his faith and yet rooted it in traditional Arab custom. By the time of his death in 632, most—though by no means all—of the Arab tribes had recognized his overlordship and paid him tribute.

Mohammed had found his native land divided with many local idolatrous practices. He left it with a religion and a book of revelation, and with a community and a state sufficiently well organized and armed to dominate the entire peninsula. Within a century his followers were to march on from victory to victory, building an imposing empire across the breadth of Eurasia and spreading his creed, which today boasts half a billion followers, throughout the world.

III. AGE OF CONQUESTS

Precisely because the Moslem community was the product of Mohammed's genius, it now seemed likely with his death to break up into its component elements. To forestall this, foreign raids were undertaken—and enthusiastically supported by Bedouins eager for booty. These raids, then, did not begin as religious crusades to propagate the faith. Mohammed did not think of Islam as a universal faith and did not believe that God had chosen him to preach to any other people than his own Arabs. So the Arab raids grew out of the need to keep the turbulent Bedouins preoccupied and loyal to Medina.

The leader of the raids was the caliph, or deputy, who was chosen to represent the Prophet in his secular role. There was no possibility, of course, of a successor to Mohammed as Prophet, but a secular chief of the community was essential. Thus when Abu Bakr, Mohammed's father-in-law, was selected as caliph, it meant that he was the defender of the faith rather than religious leader.

Under Caliph Omar, who succeeded Abu Bakr in 634, the early raids blossomed into full-fledged campaigns of conquest. They did so because the outwardly powerful Byzantine and Persian empires were soon found to be hollow shells. They had been weakened by the series of wars between them, and their subjects were very dissatisfied because of heavy taxation and religious persecution. Furthermore the Moslem forces now were growing from raiding parties to large-scale armies as entire tribes from all Arabia migrated northward, attracted by reports of dazzling riches. Thus the great conquests that followed represented the expansion not of Islam but of the Arab tribes, who on many occasions in earlier centuries had pushed northward into the Fertile Crescent. The unprecedented magnitude of the expansion at this time can be explained by the exceptional weakness of the two empires and by the unity and élan engendered by the new Islamic faith.

Once the invasions were under way the Arabs made good use of their experience in desert warfare. Mounted on camels, instead of horses like the Byzantines and Persians, they were able to attack at will and, if necessary, to retreat back to the safety of the desert. Just as the Vikings later were to be able to ravage the coasts of Europe because of their command of the sea, so now the Arabs used their "ships of the desert" to attack the wealthy empires. It was not accidental that in the provinces they conquered the Arabs established their main bases in towns on the edge of the desert. They used existing cities like Damascus when they were suitably located and, when necessary, created new ones like Kufa and Basra in Iraq, and Fustat in Egypt. These garrison towns met the same need for the emerging Arab Empire that Gibraltar, Malta, and Singapore later did for the British sea empire.

CHRISTIAN-MOSLEM MUTUAL SLANDER

Christians and Moslems were mortal enemies in the Middle Ages, fighting on battlefields in Europe, the Middle East, and overseas. They also had a low opinion of each other, as evident in the following two statements. The first is by a Moslem judge of Toledo, Spain, who placed Northern Europeans at the bottom of his category of nations.* The second is by a Christian bishop who expressed the common Western belief in Moslem moral degeneracy.†

Judge Sa'id al-Andalusi...As for the rest of this category which cultivated no sciences, they are more like animals than human beings. Those of them who live deep in the north—between the end of the seven climates and the confines of the habitable world—have been so affected by the extreme distance from the sun from the Zenith above their heads, resulting in cold climate and thick atmosphere, that their temperaments have become chilly and their humors rude. Consequently their bodies are huge, their color pale and their hair long. For the same reason they lack keenness in intelligence and perspicacity, are characterized by ignorance and stupidity. Folly and mental blindness prevail among them as among Slavs, Bulgars and other neighboring peoples.

William of Adam, Bishop of Sultaniyah In the Muslim sect any sexual act at all is not only not forbidden, but allowed and praised. So, as well as the innumerable prostitutes that there are among them, there are many effeminate men who shave the beard, paint their own face, put on women's dress, wear bracelets on the arms and feet....The Muslims, therefore, forgetful of human dignity, are shamelessly attracted by those effeminates, and live together with them as with us husband and wife live together publicly.

* From *Islam and the West* by P. K. Hitti © 1962 by Litton Educational Publishing Inc. Reprinted by permission of D. Van Nostrand Company.
† N. Daniel, *Islam and the West* (Edinburgh University Press, 1960), p. 144.

In 636 the Arabs won a decisive victory over the Byzantines in the ravines of the Yarmuk River, a tributary of the Jordan. Attacking in the midst of a blinding sandstorm they almost annihilated a mixed force of Greek, Armenian, and Syrian Christians. Emperor Heraclius fled to Constantinople, abandoning all of Syria to the victors. Caliph Omar now turned against the neighboring rich province of Iraq. Its Semitic, partly Christian, population was alienated from its Persian and Zoroastrian masters. This split contributed to the great victory won by the Arabs in the summer of 637 at Qadisiya. The Persian emperor hastily evacuated his nearby capital Ctesiphon and fled eastward.

The astonishing triumphs at Yarmuk and Qadisiya left the Moslems with unheard of riches, which further swelled the flood of Bedouin tribesmen from the southern deserts.

Their pressure on the frontiers was irresistible, and the Arab armies rolled onward, westward into Egypt and eastward into Persia. Within two years (639–641) they had overrun the whole of Egypt, but in Persia for the first time they encountered stiff resistance. Although the imperial leadership was incompetent and unpopular, nevertheless the nation was ready to fight for its freedom and its Zoroastrian religion against the despised Arab nomads who had always been looked down upon as "desert vermin." As the Moslems advanced, local resistance bands fought fiercely against the invaders. Not until 651 was the country subdued, and long before then, in 644, Omar had been assassinated by a Persian captive.

Omar's successors in the caliphate bore the banners of Islam still further afield, driven on by the momentum of victory, of religious enthusiasm, and of nomadic greed. In North Africa the Arab forces, supplemented by native Berber converts, fought their way clear across to Morocco and then crossed the Straits of Gibraltar into Spain. In 711 they defeated Roderick, the last Visigothic king of Spain, and advanced to the Pyrenees and on into France. There, however, they were defeated by Charles Martel at Tours in 732. This battle is often described as a major turning point in the history of Western Europe, though it is doubtful that the Moslems, even if successful, could have advanced much further in a region so distant from their home base. The same is true of the expansion of the Moslems to the east. In 715 they conquered the province of Sind in northwest India but were unable to push further into the great Indian subcontinent. Likewise in 751 the Moslems defeated the Chinese at Talas in Central Asia but again were unable to advance further towards China. Thus Talas, Sind, and the Pyrenees marked the limits for Moslem expansionism because of the existing level of their military technology.

This points up the exceptional significance of the Arab failure to take Constantinople after a full year's siege in 717–18. Since this city was so close to the center of their empire, they presumably would have been able to overrun much of Eastern Europe had they won at Constantinople. This, of course, is precisely what the Moslem Turks did in the fifteenth century, but, if it had occurred nearly a millennium earlier, much of Eastern Europe would have been Arabized and Islamized and would today be an integral part of the Moslem Middle East.

Despite these setbacks, the fact remains that what had started out as a simple desert religion had grown in little more than one century into a great Eurasian empire. By 750 Islam ruled over the vast territories stretching from the Pyrenees to Sind, and from Morocco to the frontiers of China (see Map XIII, "Expansion of Islam to 1500").

IV. ARAB KINGDOM TO ISLAMIC EMPIRE

With the first phase of expansion completed, the Arabs now settled down to enjoy the fruits of victory. They were virtually an army of occupation in their subject lands. They lived mostly in the strategically located camp cities, from where they controlled the surrounding countryside. Since Caliph Omar had decided at the outset that his followers should not be given fiefs in the conquered provinces, they now were supported by government pensions. The funds for these pensions were obtained from lands confiscated by the Islamic state and from taxes which were levied at a higher rate upon non-Moslems than upon Moslems. Apart from this discriminatory taxation, the non-Moslems were left virtually undisturbed. No effort was made to convert them; indeed conversion was not at all welcomed for it involved under the circumstances a decline in revenue. Thus Islam was in effect a privilege of the Arab warrior-aristocracy that ruled over the much more numerous subject peoples.

This arrangement was soon disturbed by the appearance in increasing numbers of the *Mawali,* or non-Arab Moslems. These converts flocked to the cities where they served the needs of the Arab aristocracy as servants, artisans, shopkeepers, and merchants. Being Moslems they claimed equality with the Arabs but this was not granted. Although the Mawali fought in the armies of Islam, they were usually restricted to the infantry, which received a lower rate of pay and less booty than the Arab cavalry.

As the empire expanded and wealth poured into the cities from the subject provinces, the Mawali increased in numbers and wealth. But they were still excluded from the ruling circles, so they became a disaffected urban element, determined to gain status equal to their economic power. Thus the Arab Umayyad dynasty of caliphs, which had moved the capital from Medina to Damascus in 661, came to be regarded with much justification as a parasitic clique that had outlived its usefulness once the conquests were completed. The opposition to the Arab aristocracy, therefore, was both a national and a social movement of protest.

A disputed accession to the throne set off a decade of civil strife that ended in the accession of the Abbasid caliphate in 750. This represented much more than a mere change of dynasty. The Mawali, and particularly the Persians, now replaced the old aristocracy. The Arabs no longer were a privileged salaried soldiery but were replaced by a royal standing army that was at first largely Persian. The former garrison cities became great commercial centers under Mawali control. Some of the Arabs became absorbed into the mass of townspeople and peasants, while others reverted to nomadism.

The imperial structure also changed radically, especially with the shift of the capital from Damascus eastward to Baghdad in 762. In effect this meant that the Abbasid caliphate was turning its back on the Mediterranean and looking to Persia for traditions and support. The caliph no longer was an Arab sheikh but a divinely ordained autocrat—the "Shadow of God upon Earth." His authority rested not on tribal support but on a salaried bureaucracy and standing army. Thus the caliphate became an oriental monarchy similar to the many that had preceded it in Ctesiphon and Persepolis and Babylon. Under the order and security imposed by this monarchy, a syncretic civilization that was a mixture of Judaic, Greco-Roman, and Perso-Mesopotamian traditions evolved during the following centuries. Islam ceased to be merely the creed of a ruling warrior-aristocracy and became instead a new and distinctive civilization.

V. ISLAMIC CIVILIZATION

Within a century after Caliph Mansur had selected Baghdad as the Abbasid capital, it numbered about a million people. In the center was a citadel some two miles in diameter in which were the caliph's residence and the quarters of his officials and guards. Beyond the citadel walls a great commercial metropolis sprang up, supported by the plentiful produce of the fertile Mesopotamian valley. The main crops were wheat, barley, rice, dates, and olives. The Abbasids increased the output when they extended the area of cultivated land by draining swamps and by enlarging the irrigation works. They also were less extortionist at the outset than the previous rulers in their tax and labor levies on the peasants.

The provinces contributed rich supplies of metals—silver from the Hindu Kush, gold from Nubia and the Sudan, copper from Isfahan, and iron from Persia, Central Asia, and Sicily. Precious stones came from many regions of the empire, while the waters of the Persian Gulf yielded pearls. Industry also flourished, textiles being the most important in the number of workers employed and the value of the output. Linen, cotton, and silk goods were produced in many parts of the empire, both for local consumption and for export. Carpets also were made almost everywhere. Those of Tabaristan and Armenia were considered the best. The art of papermaking, learned from Chinese prisoners taken at Talas in 751, spread rapidly across the Islamic world, reaching Spain by 900. Other industries included pottery, metalwork, soap, and perfumes. Such a rich economy, stretching across the breadth of the far-flung Abbasid Empire, greatly increased interregional trade. Moslem merchants, as noted in the preceding chapter, traded overland through Central Asia, and overseas with India, Ceylon, Southeast Asia, China, and Africa. The large-scale trade stimulated a highly developed banking system with branches in all leading cities, so that a check could be drawn in Baghdad and cashed in Morocco.

With this solid economic base, the Abbasid caliphs were able to enjoy themselves in their dazzlingly luxurious palaces. The *Thousand and One Nights* describes Harun al-Rashid (786–809), the best known of these caliphs, as a gay and cultured ruler, surrounded by poets, musicians, singers, dancers, scholars, and wits. Among the popular indoor games were chess, dice, and backgammon, while outdoor sports included hunting, falconry, hawking, polo, archery, fencing, javelin throwing, and horse racing. Harun was contemporary with Charlemagne, but their respective capitals, Baghdad and Aix-la-Chapelle, were quite incomparable—as incomparable as Baghdad and Paris today, but in the reverse sense.

The Abbasid caliphate was noted not only for its affluence and splendor but also for its relative toleration in religious matters in an age when this quality was markedly absent in the West. The explanation is to be found partly in the religious law of Islam. The sacred law recognized the Christians and Jews as being, like the Moslems, People of the Book. Both had a scripture—a written word of revelation. Their faith was accepted as true, though incomplete, since Mohammed had superseded Moses and Jesus Christ. Islam therefore tolerated the Christians and Jews. It permitted them to practice their faith, with certain restrictions and penalties. Despite this moderate discrimination, their position was clearly superior to that of comparable dissenters in the West. They could practice their faith, enjoy normal property rights, and belong to craft guilds. They were often appointed to high state office and were spared the martyrdom or exile endured, for example, by Jews and Moslems in Spain following the Christian conquest.

The Abbasid caliphate also was noteworthy for its achievements in the field of science. It is true that the tendency here was to preserve and to pass on rather than to create something new. One of their greatest scientists, al-Biruni (973–1048), stated, "We ought to confine ourselves to what the Ancients have dealt with and to perfect what can be perfected."[1] On the other hand, the sheer size of the empire, its contacts with literally all regions of Eurasia, and its rich legacy from the several great centers of civilization that it encompassed, all contributed to the very real achievements of Islamic science. Baghdad, for example, boasted a "House of Wisdom" consisting of a school of translators, a library, an observatory, and an academy. The scholars associated with it translated and studied the works of Greek scientists and philosophers, as well as scientific treatises from Persia and India.

In astronomy the Moslems generally accepted the basic tenets of their Greek predecessors and made no significant advances in theory. But they did continue without interruption the astronomical observations of the ancients, so that the later Renaissance astronomers had available some nine hundred years of records which provided the basis for their crucial discoveries. Mathematics was of great interest to Moslems because it was needed both in astronomy and in commerce. Thanks to Babylonian and Indian influence, the Moslems made important advances, especially in popularizing the Hindu system of numbers based on the decimal notation. Misleadingly called Arabic numerals, this system did for arithmetic what the discovery of the alphabet had done earlier for writing. It democratized mathematics, making it available for everyday use by nonspecialists.

In geography, as in astronomy, the Moslems made little theoretical progress, but the extent of their empire and of their commerce enabled them to accumulate reliable and systematic data concerning the Eurasian land mass. Al-Biruni's famous book on India, for example, described not only the physical features of the country, but also the social system, religious beliefs, and scientific attainments of the Hindus in a manner that was not to be equaled until the eighteenth century. The Moslems also prepared charts and maps in which they naturally located Mecca in the center, as the contemporary Christian cartographers did for Jerusalem.

Islamic medicine also was based on that of the Greeks, but the greater geographical spread of Islam made it possible to learn of new diseases and drugs. Moslems established the first apothecary shops and dispensaries, founded the first medieval school of pharmacy, required state examination and certification for the practice of medicine, and operated well-equipped hospitals, of which some thirty are known. The great Islamic doctors, such as Muhammad al-Razi (844–926) and Abu Ali al-Husein ibn Sina (980–1037), famous in Europe as ''Rhazes'' and ''Avicenna,'' were brilliant men of wide knowledge ranging from astronomy through botany to chemistry and wrote texts that were used in European medical schools until the seventeenth century.

Even more significant for the general advance of science were the Moslem contributions in chemistry. To the traditions and practices of the Babylonians, Egyptians, and Greeks, the Moslems added the extensive chemical knowledge of the Indians and Chinese. They spent much talent and energy in the quest for the two ancient will-o'-the-wisps: the philosopher's stone for transforming base metals into precious ones, and the elixir for prolonging life indefinitely. Yet their treatises show that they were the first to evolve sophisticated laboratory techniques for handling drugs, salts, and precious metals. Thus they were able to develop localized chemical industries for the production of soda, alum, iron sulphate, nitrates, and other salts for industrial purposes, especially in textiles.

The highest achievement of the Arabs in their own estimation was their poetry. In pre-Islamic times it had a public and social function, with the poet often serving as a eulogist or a satirist. The main themes were war, valor, love, praise of a patron, abuse of an enemy, and glorification of one's tribe or camel or horse. Under the Abbasids, Arabic poetry was enriched by the contributions of many non-Arabs, especially Persians. But there was no borrowing from Greco-Roman literature, which explains why Arabic literature remained strange and unknown to the West. Moslem scientists became familiar to Westerners, but not Moslem poets. Yet to the present day the Arabs find much pleasure and inspiration in their poetry with its intoxicating verbal effect and the hypnotic power of its monotonous rhyming.

In addition to their own original achievements, the Moslems made an invaluable contribution in translating and transmitting ancient works. The Umayyad caliphs had distrusted all non-Arabs and were uninterested in their civilizations. The Abbasids, by contrast, had been strongly supported by Christians, Jews, and Zoroastrian Persians and were much more tolerant and broad-minded. The "House of Wisdom" in Baghdad included a large staff of translators, one of the outstanding ones being a Christian, Hunain ibn-Ishaq (809–873). He visited Greek-speaking lands to collect manuscripts, and with his assistants he translated a large number of them, including works of Hippocrates, Galen, Euclid, Ptolemy, Plato, and Aristotle. Another great translation center was in the city of Toledo in Moslem Spain, where the translators during the twelfth and thirteenth centuries included Jews, Spaniards, and foreign scholars from all over Europe. This activity was of utmost significance, for Western Europeans had lost direct acquaintance with Greek learning and for long were unaware even of its existence. Thus Moslem scholarship preserved the Greek works until Western Europe was ready once more to resume their study.

In conclusion it should be emphasized that two basic bonds held together the diverse peoples of the sprawling caliphate: the Arabic language and the Islamic religion. Much more remarkable than the Arab conquests was the diffusion of the Arabic language. By the eleventh century Arabic had superseded the old Greek, Latin, Coptic, and Aramaic languages and prevailed from Morocco to Persia, as it does to the present day. This common language explains the feeling of common identity prevailing in this region, even though it includes Negroid Sudanese as well as the prevailing Semites, and Christian Lebanese and Coptic Egyptians as well as the prevailing Moslems. Even beyond this vast area that was permanently Arabized, Arabic exerted a profound influence on other Moslem languages. Arabic words are as common in these other languages as Greek and Latin words in English, and some of these languages (Urdu, Malay, Swahili, and Turkish until World War I) are written in Arabic script.

The Islamic religion also is a powerful bond—much more powerful than Christianity in this respect because it is not only a religion but also a social and political system and a general way of life (see section II of this chapter). Religion thus provides the basis for Islamic civilization as language does for the Arabic world. We have seen that the Islamic civilization evolved during the centuries following the conquests as a fusion of Christian, Jewish, Zoroastrian, and Arab religious elements, and Greco-Roman and Perso-Mesopotamian administrative, cultural, and scientific elements. The end-product was not a mere mosaic or agglomeration of previous cultures, but rather a fusion that represented a new and original civilization. It was diverse in its origins and strands, yet uniquely molded by the distinctive imprint of Arabic Islam.

VI. DECLINE OF THE CALIPHATE

The Abbasid caliphate reached its height during the reign of Harun al-Rashid, and then it declined in much the same way as did the Roman Empire. There was first the matter of sheer size—a very real problem in an age when communications were dependent on horse and sail. The outlying provinces were three thousand miles distant from the capital, so that it is not surprising that they should be the first to break away: Spain in 756, Morocco in 788, and Tunisia in 800.

Also, as in the case of Rome, there was the problem of imperial expenditures that were excessive and could not be supported by the prevailing economy and technology. The rampant luxury of the Baghdad court and the heavy weight of the inflated bureaucracy were not matched by technological progress. The resulting financial crisis forced the caliphs to appoint provincial governors as tax farmers in the areas they administered. With the revenues they collected, these governors maintained the local soldiery and officials and remitted an agreed sum to the central treasury. This arrangement left the governors-farmers the real rulers of the provinces, together with the army commanders with whom they soon reached working agreements. By the mid-ninth century the caliphs were losing both military and administrative control, and they were being appointed and deposed at will by Turkish mercenaries.

Imperial weakness, as usual, invited barbarian attacks. Just as the Roman Empire had been invaded across the Rhine and the Danube, so the caliphate now was assaulted from the north, south, and east. From the north came the Crusaders who overran Spain, Sicily, and Syria, aided by Moslem discord in all three areas. In Sicily the end of the local dynasty in 1040 was followed by civil war, which facilitated the invasion of the island by the Normans from southern Italy. By 1091 the whole of Sicily had been conquered, and the mixed Christian-Moslem population came under the rule of Norman kings.

Likewise in Spain the Umayyad dynasty was deposed in 1031, and the country was split up into numerous petty states ruled by "parties" or factions reflecting diverse ethnic groups. These included the Arabs, the Berbers, the indigenous pre-Moslem Iberian stock, and the "Slavs," or European slaves. This fragmentation of Moslem Spain enabled the Christian states of the north to expand southward. By 1085 they captured the important city of Toledo, and by the end of the thirteenth century only Granada on the southern tip of the peninsula was left to the Moslems.

The loss of Sicily and Spain to Christendom proved permanent, but such was not the case with Syria. Here also the warring of several Moslem states enabled the Crusaders from 1096 onward to advance rapidly down the coast of Syria into Palestine. They established four states, Edessa (1098), Antioch (1098), Jerusalem (1099), and Tripoli (1109), all organized along Western feudal lines. But these states lacked roots. They never assimilated their Moslem Arab subjects. Their existence depended on the sporadic arrival of recruits from Europe. Also they were all confined to the coastal areas and hence vulnerable to resistance movements organized in the interior. These states could exist only so long as the surrounding Moslem world remained divided. The disunity was ended by Salah ad-Din, better known in the West as Saladin. By uniting Moslem Syria and Egypt he surrounded the Crusader principalities and began the counterattack in 1187. By the time of his death in 1193 he had recaptured Jerusalem and expelled the Westerners from all but a narrow coastal strip. During the following century this also was overrun and the Moslem reconquest was completed.

In addition to these Crusader onslaughts from the north, the caliphate was attacked by Berbers from southern Morocco and the Senegal-Niger area, and by the two Arab Bedouin tribes of Hilal and Sulaim from Upper Egypt. These tribes swept across Libya and Tunisia, wreaking havoc and devastation. It was this attack rather than the earlier seventh-century Arab invasion that ruined civilization in North Africa.

Finally the third group of invaders were the Turks and Mongols from the East. Their incursions, lasting for several centuries and taking in virtually the entire Eurasian land mass, constitute a major chapter of world history. The Turco-Mongol invasions are comparable to the Arab-Islamic conquests in scope and impact. Indeed the two are intimately related, for many of the Turco-Mongols were converted to Islam, and they then extended the frontiers of their faith into distant new regions. The course and significance of these Turco-Mongol invasions is the subject of the following chapter.

SUGGESTED READING

T. Arnold and A. Guillaume, eds., *The Legacy of Islam* (Clarendon, 1931); F. Gabrieli, *Muhammad and the Conquests of Islam* (World University Library, 1968); H. A. R. Gibb, *Mohammadanism: An Historical Survey* (Home University Library, 1953); P. K. Hitti, *History of the Arabs from the Earliest Times to the Present,* 5th ed. (St. Martin's Press, 1951); A. Lewis, ed., *The Islamic World and the West* (John Wiley, 1970); R. A. Nicholson, *A Literary History of the Arabs* (Cambridge University Press, 1969).

chapter 11

Turco-Mongol Invasions

By all odds the most spectacular development during the half-millennium from 1000 to 1500 was the great swarming of Turco-Mongol peoples from the vast racial hive of Central Asia. These nomads overran literally the whole of Eurasia except for its distant extremities: Japan, Southeast Asia, southern India, and Western Europe.

The nomadic expansion during these centuries occurred in three stages. The first, between 1000 and 1200, marked the emergence of the Turks, first as mercenaries and then as masters of the Abbasid caliphate. They infused vigor and aggressiveness into the now sickly world of Islam and extended its frontiers into Asia Minor at the expense of Byzantium and into northern India at the expense of Hindustan. The second stage, during the thirteenth century, saw the Mongols overrun not only Central Asia, East Asia, and Russia, but also the Moslem Middle East, thereby halting the expansion of the Moslem Turks. The final stage, between 1300 and 1500, involved the disintegration of the Mongol Empire, which cleared the way for the resurgence of the Turks and the resumption of the Turkish-Islamic advance into Christian Europe and Hindustan.

This chapter will consider each of these stages in turn, and their implications for general world history.

I. TURKISH INVASIONS

The Turks are a linguistic rather than an ethnic group. Their common bond is that they all speak one form or another of a Turkish family of languages. Although an ethnically mixed people, they are generally Caucasoid in appearance rather than Mongoloid. By the mid-sixth century they dominated the extensive steppe lands from Mongolia to the Oxus, or Amu Darya. From the eighth century onward they came increasingly under Islamic influence as a result of the Arab conquest of Persia and defeat of the Chinese at Talas (751).

The response of the Turkish tribes to the brilliant Abbasid caliphate across the Oxus River was very similar to that of the Germans to the Roman Empire across the Rhine. First there was the cultural impact as the primitive Turkish pagans succumbed to the teachings of Islam and to the lures of a sophisticated civilization. At the same time the tribesmen were entering the military service of the caliphate, as the Germans earlier had entered that of Rome. As mounted bowmen of great mobility, they soon demonstrated their superior military qualities and increasingly replaced the Arabs and Persians in the caliph's armed forces.

As the caliphs became weaker, the Turkish mercenaries, like their German counterparts, became masters rather than servants. They made and unmade successive caliphs in Baghdad. About 970 a branch of the Turkish people known as the Seljuks were crossing over unhindered into Moslem territory and soon had gathered power into their hands. This was formally recognized in 1055 when the caliph proclaimed the Seljuk leader, Tughril Beg, the "sultan," or "he who has authority." Although the caliphs remained the nominal heads of the empire, the real rulers henceforth were the Turkish sultans. Under their aggressive leadership, the frontiers of Islam now were further extended into two regions.

One was Asia Minor, which had remained for centuries a center of Christian Byzantine power against repeated attacks by Arabic Islam. But in 1071 the Seljuks won a crushing victory at Manzikert in eastern Asia Minor, taking prisoner the Byzantine Emperor Romanus IV. This proved to be a decisive turning point in Middle Eastern history. The Asia Minor peasants, who had been exploited by corrupt Byzantine officials, now welcomed the Turks with relief. Thus between the eleventh and the thirteenth centuries the larger part of Asia Minor was transformed from a Greek and Christian to a Turkish and Moslem region, and it remains so to the present day. Furthermore Byzantium was gutted by the loss of Asia Minor, a province that hitherto had provided the bulk of the imperial revenue and army manpower. Constantinople now was like a huge head atop a shriveled body. The roots of the fall of Constantinople in 1453 go back to 1071.

While the Seljuks had been pushing westward into Asia Minor, other Turks had been fighting their way southward towards the vast treasure house of India. Outstanding was a certain Mahmud (997–1030), who, from his base at Ghazni in Afghanistan, raided the Indian lands almost annually and finally annexed the Punjab, which has ever since remained Moslem. Mahmud's zeal in destroying Hindu temples and smashing their idols, a zeal that was based on the Islamic tenet that any visible representation of the deity was sinful, earned him the epithet "the image breaker."

Mahmud was followed by other Turkish invaders from Afghanistan. They advanced southward to Gujarat and eastward into the Ganges valley. In 1192 they captured Delhi and made it the capital of the Turkish sultanate in India. During these campaigns,

Buddhist monasteries were destroyed and Buddhist monks were slaughtered on such a scale that Buddhism never recovered in its place of origin.

The relative ease with which the Turks conquered a land in which they were hopelessly outnumbered is to be explained partly by the outdated Indian military tactics. They were the same as those that had proven inadequate against Alexander fifteen hundred years earlier. The infantry were usually an undisciplined rabble, while their vaunted elephants were useless against the Moslem cavalry. Equally damaging, and a more fundamental weakness, was the Hindu caste system, which left the fighting to only the Kshatriya, or warrior caste. The rest of the population was untrained and largely indifferent, particularly because class differentiation separated oppressive landlords from their peasants and so added to the fragmentation of the caste system. Thus the masses either remained indifferent or else welcomed the invaders and embraced their faith. This pattern was to be repeated frequently in the future and explains why in modern times the British were able to rule from Delhi just as the Turkish Sultans had before.

II. GENGHIS KHAN'S CONQUESTS

While the Turks were becoming the masters of the Moslem world, an obscure chieftain in far-off Mongolia was beginning his career of conquest that was to culminate in the greatest empire of history. Genghis Khan (spelled also Chinggis, Chingis, Jenghiz, etc.), whose personal name was Temujin, was born about 1167, the son of a minor clan leader. When Temujin was twelve years old his father was poisoned and as a result the future Khan spent a childhood of misery. He was able to overcome these humble beginnings by mastering the complicated art of tribal politics, which called for a mixture of loyalty, cunning, and ruthless treachery, as well as physical prowess. After turning against his overlord and eliminating various rivals he finally was able to combine the various Mongol-speaking tribes into a single unit. An assembly of Mongol chieftains, held in 1206 proclaimed him the supreme head of his people with the title Genghis Khan, signifying "ruler of the universe."

He was now in a position to satisfy his nomadic impulse for conquest and booty. "Man's highest joy," he reportedly said, "is in victory: to conquer one's enemies, to pursue them, to deprive them of their possessions, to make their beloved weep, to ride on their horses, and to embrace their wives and daughters." In this respect Genghis Khan was no different from the long line of steppe conquerors who had gone before him. Why then was he alone destined to become the master of the greater part of Eurasia? This question is particularly intriguing because, as a Mongol, Genghis Khan did not have the manpower resources of other nomad conquerors, who were almost invariably Turks. All the Mongol tribes together numbered about a million men, women, and children, which gave Genghis Khan a maximum of 125,000 warriors. With such limited resources, how was he able to come so close to becoming literally the "ruler of the universe"?

Genghis Khan began with the built-in advantage enjoyed by all nomad warriors—the fact that their daily life was a continuous rehearsal of campaign operations. Leading extra horses as remounts, these warriors were capable of riding several days and nights in succession with a minimum of rest and food. They carried leather bags for water, which when empty could be inflated for use in swimming across rivers. Normally they lived off the countryside, but if necessary they drank the blood of their horses and the milk of their

MARCO POLO ON MONGOL MILITARY STRATEGY

During his seventeen years service with Kublai Khan, Marco Polo gained an un-equaled first-hand knowledge of the Mongols, or Tartars as he called them. The following selection describes the nature and operation of their military machine.*

All their harness of war is excellent and costly. Their arms are bows and arrows, sword and mace; but above all the bow, for they are capital archers, indeed the best that are known. On their backs they wear armour of cuirbouly, prepared from buffalo and other hides, which is very strong. They are excellent soldiers, and passing valiant in battle. They are also more capable of hardships than other nations; for many a time, if need be, they will go for a month without any supply of food, living only on the milk of their mares and on such game as their bows may win them. Their horses also will sub-sist entirely on the grass of the plains, so that there is no need to carry store of barley or straw or oats; and they are very docile to their riders. . . .

When they are going on a distant expedition they take no gear with them except two leather bottles for milk; a little earthenware pot to cook their meat in, and a little tent to shelter them from rain. And in case of great urgency they will ride ten days on end without lighting a fire or taking a meal. On such an occasion they will sustain themselves on the blood of their horses, opening a vein and letting the blood jet into their mouths, drinking till they have had enough, and then staunching it.

They also have milk dried into a kind of paste to carry with them; and when they need food they put this in water, and beat it up till it dissolves, and then drink it. (It is prepared in this way; they boil the milk, and when the rich part floats on the top they skim it into another vessel, and of that they make butter; for the milk will not become solid till this is removed. Then they put the milk in the sun to dry. And when they go on an expedition, every man takes some ten pounds of this dried milk with him. And of a morning he will take a half pound of it and put it in his leather bottle, with as much water as he pleases. So, as he rides along, the milk-paste and the water in the bottle get well churned together into a kind of pap, and that makes his dinner.)

When they come to an engagement with the enemy, they will gain the victory in this fashion. (They never let themselves get into a regular medley, but keep perpetually rid-ing round and shooting into the enemy.) [And] as they do not count it any shame to run away in battle, they will [sometimes pretend to] do so, and in running away they turn in the saddle and shoot hard and strong at the foe, and in this way make great havoc. Their horses are trained so perfectly that they will double hither and thither, just like a dog, in a way that is quite astonishing. Thus they fight to as good purpose in running away as if they stood and faced the enemy, because of the vast volleys of arrows that they shoot in this way, turning round upon their pursuers, who are fancying that they have won the battle. But when the Tartars see that they have killed and wounded a good many horses and men, they wheel round bodily, and return to the charge in per-fect order and with loud cries; and in a very short time the enemy are routed. In truth they are stout and valiant soldiers, and inured to war. And you perceive that it is just when the enemy sees them run, and imagines that he has gained the battle, that he has in reality lost it; for the Tartars wheel round in a moment when they judge the right time has come. And after this fashion they have won many a fight.

* H. Yule, ed. and trans., *The Book of Ser Marco Polo* (Scribner's, 1903), Vol. 1, pp. 256–63, 331.

mares. Their skills in the hunt, acquired from boyhood, enabled them to coordinate the operations of flying horse columns over long distances. Their favorite tactic was feigned flight, during which the enemy might pursue the fleeing Mongols for days, only to be lured to ambush and destruction. Other tactical maneuvers included the tying of branches to the tails of horses to stir up dust in order to give the impression of large forces on the march, and also the mounting of dummies on spare horses for the same purpose.

The basic Mongol weapon was the compound large bow, more powerful than the English longbow and capable of killing at 600 feet with its armor-piercing arrows. This was a fearful weapon in the hands of Mongol horsemen who were able to carry a supply of thirty arrows and shoot all thirty at full gallop. Other equipment included a steel helmet, light body armor made of hide, a saber, and sometimes a lance with a hook and a mace. The Mongol horses grazed only on the open range, with no shelter during the long bitter winter and no hay or grain for supplementary feed. This made them somewhat stunted in size but very tough and adaptable. Genghis Khan further strengthened his forces by adding new skills and equipment learned mostly from the Chinese. These included powerful catapults, battering-rams, and sappers who tunneled under walls and blew them up with gunpowder. Thus Genghis Khan supplemented his incomparable mounted bowmen with the siege weapons necessary for capturing fortified cities.

The Mongols were also masters of espionage and psychological warfare. Before undertaking a campaign they collected all possible intelligence regarding the enemy's roads, rivers, fortifications, and political and economic conditions. They also used agents to spread demoralizing stories about the size of the Mongol forces and the uselessness of resistance. In the course of the campaigning they used terror tactics to undermine enemy morale. Prisoners of war were forced to lead the assault against their own people, and entire populations were put to the sword when any resistance was offered.

Finally Genghis Khan's grand strategy was unique in that he was careful to overcome his nomadic neighbors before assaulting the great empires. He was familiar with the traditional Chinese strategy of divide and rule, or as they put it, "Use barbarians to control barbarians." Thus many nomad chieftains in the past had been destroyed by simultaneous attacks by imperial armies and rival tribesmen. Genghis Khan's strategy, therefore, was first to unite "all the people of the felt-walled tents."

Even with his military genius and superb fighting machine, Genghis Khan could not have become a world conqueror had he not appeared at the right historical moment. A strong and united China, such as had existed under the Han and the T'ang, could have stopped him with ease. So could the Moslem Arabs at the height of their power. But the Eurasian balance of power was quite different in the early thirteenth century. China was divided then into three fragments, with the Chin dynasty ruling the north, the Sung the south, and the Tibetan Tanguts controlling the northwest with their kingdom of Hsi Hsia. To the west was the state of Kara-Khitai based on oasis cities such as Bokhara and Samarkand. Beyond that, on the Oxus River, was the Moslem kingdom of Khorezm, and still further west the Abbasid caliphate at Baghdad, both far past their prime.

Genghis Khan first subjugated the Hsi Hsia state between 1205 and 1209 and forced it to a tributary status. In 1211 he attacked north China, first overrunning the region north of the Great Wall and then in 1213 piercing the Wall and penetrating to the Yellow River plain. By 1215 he had captured and pillaged Peking and also gained the services of Chinese who knew how to besiege cities and others who knew how to administer and exploit agricultural societies. In accordance with his overall strategy, Genghis Khan now turned to the surrounding nomadic territories. Manchuria fell in 1216, Korea in 1218, and Kara-Khitai in the following year. These conquests brought him to the frontiers of Khorezm, which he overran in 1219–1221. Rich and ancient cities such as Bokhara, Samarkand, and Balkh were pillaged and their inhabitants massacred. The only exceptions were the skilled artisans who were sent to Mongolia.

Not content with these spectacular triumphs in the Far East and Middle East, the Mongols swung north to the Caucasus where they defeated the Georgians. Advancing on to the Ukraine they crushed a numerically far superior army of 80,000 Russians in 1223. Meanwhile Genghis Khan had returned to Mongolia to direct another victorious campaign against the Hsi Hsia kingdom, which had revolted against his rule. This was his final exploit, for he died soon after in 1227.

III. MONGOL EMPIRE

After a two-year interval, Genghis Khan's son, Ogodai, was selected as successor. During his reign from 1229 to 1241 the campaigning was resumed in the two extremities of Eurasia—China and Europe—some five thousand miles apart. In China the remnants of the Chin state in the north were liquidated by 1234 and then the Sung in the south were immediately attacked. They resisted stoutly, but the war which lasted forty-five years ended in their complete destruction. At the same time Genghis Khan's grandson, Batu, was sent with a force of 150,000 men to the European West. Crossing the middle Volga in the fall of 1237 he fell upon the principalities of central Russia. Town after town was captured, including the then comparatively unimportant town of Moscow. By March 1238 Batu was approaching Novgorod near the Baltic Sea, but he feared that the spring thaw would mire his horsemen in mud and so he withdrew suddenly to the south.

Two years later, in the summer of 1240, the Mongols attacked southern Russia again, this time from their bases in the Caucasus. By December they had captured the ancient Russian capital of Kiev. Such was Mongol frightfulness that a contemporary monk recorded that the few survivors "envied the dead." The following year the Mongols pressed on into Poland and Hungary, defeated a German army of 30,000 at Liegnitz in Silesia, crossed the frozen Danube, captured Zagreb, and reached the Adriatic coast. Thus Mongol armies now were operating across the breadth of Eurasia from the Adriatic to the Sea of Japan. In the spring of 1242 came news of the death of Ogodai Khan in Mongolia, so Batu withdrew through the Balkans to the lower Volga valley where he laid the foundations of the khanate known as the Golden Horde, a name derived from the golden tent of its khan.

Ogodai's successors decided to complete the conquest of south China and to take over the Abbasid caliphate of Baghdad. In China, the Mongols were bogged down in decades of fighting before finally capturing the great southern port of Canton in 1277. The new Khan, Kublai, moved his capital from Karakorum to Peking in north China. Kublai then launched new campaigns on land against Indochina and Burma, and overseas against Java and Japan.

Meanwhile other Mongol armies had been rampaging through the Middle East, capturing in 1258 the Abbasid capital, Baghdad. Most of its 800,000 are reported to have been massacred, with the exception of a few skilled artisans who were sent to Kublai's court. It seemed that nothing could prevent the Mongols from advancing on to Egypt and North Africa and completing the conquest of the entire Moslem world. In 1260, however, the Egyptian Mamelukes unexpectedly defeated the advancing Mongols in Palestine. The defeat marked the high-water mark of the Mongol Empire in the Middle East, just as similar defeats in Japan and Java marked its high point in the Far East. Unable to expand further, the Mongol Empire fell apart almost as rapidly as it had been built up.

IV. MONGOL DECLINE

The basic reason for the decline of the Mongols was that they were too few in number and too primitive in relation to their subject peoples. The Mongols, as Pushkin put it, were "Arabs without Aristotle and algebra." This left them vulnerable to assimilation as soon as they dismounted from their horses and settled down to enjoy their conquests. In this respect they differed fundamentally from the Arabs who had both a language and a religion that their subjects were willing to adopt and that served as strong bonds for imperial unity. The Mongols, being less advanced than the Arabs, enjoyed no such advantage. Rather the opposite was the case with them, for they adopted the languages, religions, and cultures of their more advanced subjects and thereby lost their identity. This was the root reason why their empire dissolved so soon after its creation.

Indicative of the assimilation process was Kublai Khan's decision to move the Mongol capital from Karakorum to Peking. Inevitably he became a Chinese-style emperor, ruling from a palace of Chinese design, conducting elaborate Confucian ceremonies, and building new Confucian temples. As the Grand Khan, he was nominally the suzerain of all the Mongol khanates. Actually his authority did not extend beyond China. His brother, Arikboga, had contested his election as Grand Khan. Kublai Khan had prevailed only after a four-year struggle. Then he was challenged by his cousin, Kaidu, who controlled Turkestan, and the ensuing forty-year civil war ended in stalemate. Thus the Mongol Empire was shattered by internal dynastic rivalries as well as by cultural assimilation.

While Kublai Khan was becoming a Chinese emperor, Hulagu was becoming a Persian ruler. With Tabriz as his capital he established the so-called Ilkhanate. (The term Ilkhan means "subject Khan," and was applied to the Mongol rulers of Persia as subordinates to the Grand Khan.) His successor's adoption of Islam in 1295 as the official religion both reflected and accelerated the Mongol's assimilation into their Iranian-Islamic milieu. Likewise the Golden Horde across the Caucasus went its own way, influenced by the native Christian Orthodox culture and by the official Islamic creed. Before long the only remaining pure Mongols were those in ancestral Mongolia where they came under the influence of Buddhism and sank into impotent obscurity.

V. TURKISH REVIVAL

Since the Mongols were so few in numbers, they had taken an ever-increasing proportion of Turks into their armies. Then with the break-up of the empire these Moslem Turks quickly came to the fore, as they had earlier in the caliphate before the Mongol onslaught. A succession of military adventurers now rose and fell in the struggle for control of the Central Eurasian steppes. The most remarkable of these was Timur, known to Europe as Tamerlane. He seized Samarkand in 1369, and from there struck out in all directions.

First he destroyed the Ilkhanate in Persia and Mesopotamia, then defeated the Golden Horde in Russia and the Ottoman Turks in Asia Minor, and he even invaded India and sacked Delhi. He was determined to make his capital, Samarkand, the finest city in the world, and after each campaign he sent back caravans loaded with booty, together with craftsmen, artists, astrologers, and men of letters. At its height, his empire extended from the Mediterranean to China, and Timur was preparing to invade the latter country when he died in 1405. His empire then disintegrated even more rapidly than that of the Mongols.

After Timur, the outstanding development was the extension of Moslem Turkish power in India and in Byzantium. During the thirteenth century the Turkish sultans of Delhi, under the pressure of the Mongol threat, had confined themselves to strengthening their position in north India. In the fourteenth century, with the threat removed, they expanded two-thirds of the way down the peninsula to the Kistna River. Then in the aftermath of Timur's raid, north and central India were reduced to a few small Turkish-ruled states with none strong enough to revive the Delhi sultanate. Meanwhile the expansion of Islamic power over a large part of India had provoked a reaction from the Hindus. They set up the large Hindu state of Vijanagar, comprising the whole of India south of the Kistna River. Such was the fragmented condition of the Indian peninsula when unity was imposed from without during the sixteenth century by another Moslem Turkish dynasty, the Mughal.

Meanwhile in the Middle East the frontiers of Islam were being extended at the expense of Byzantium by the Ottoman Turks. These newcomers from Central Asia had entered the Seljuk Empire in its decline and settled in the northwest corner of Asia Minor, less than fifty miles from the strategic straits separating Asia from Europe. In 1299 the leader of these Turks, Uthman, declared his independence from his Seljuk overlord, and from these humble beginnings grew the great Ottoman Empire, named after the obscure Uthman.

The first step was the conquest of the remaining Byzantine portion of Asia Minor. This was accomplished by 1340, thanks to the disaffection of the Christian peasantry and the plentiful supply of ghazis or warriors of the faith, who flocked in from all parts of the Middle East to battle against the Christian infidels. Next the Turks crossed the straits, winning their first foothold in Europe by building a fort at Gallipoli in 1354. They hardly could have selected a more favorable moment for their advance into Europe. The Balkan peninsula was divided by the strife of rival Christian churches and by the rivalries of the Byzantine, Serbian, and Bulgarian states, all past their prime. Also the Christian peasants of the Balkans were as disaffected as their counterparts in Asia Minor. And Western Christendom was too divided to go to the aid of the Balkans even if there was the will to do so, which there was not, because of the ancient antipathy between Catholic and Orthodox Christians. Thus the way was clear for the Ottoman Turks, and they took full advantage of the opportunity.

They surrounded Constantinople by taking Adrianople in 1362 and Sofia in 1384. Then they were diverted for some decades when their sultan was defeated and captured by Timur in 1402. But Timur was a flash in the pan, and his death in 1405 left the Ottomans free to rebuild and to resume their advance. Finally in 1453 they took Constantinople by assault and the Ottomans were the masters of the entire Balkan peninsula to the Danube River, with the exception of a few Venetian-held coastal fortresses. (For details, see chapter 12, section IV.)

VI. SIGNIFICANCE OF TURCO-MONGOL INVASIONS

One result of the Turco-Mongol invasions between 1000 and 1500 was the emergence of a new Eurasian balance of power in which Islam was the central and decisive force. When the West began its overseas expansion in the late fifteenth century, Islam already was expanding overland in all directions. The Ottomans were crossing the Danube into Central Europe; Central Asia was completely won over with the exception of the eastern fringes; and the Mughals were about to begin their conquest of virtually the entire Indian peninsula. Beyond Eurasia, Islam was spreading steadily into the interior of the continent of Africa from two centers. From the North African coast it advanced across the Sahara to West Africa where a succession of large Negro Moslem kingdoms flourished. Likewise from the Arab colonies on the East African coast, Islam spread inward over lands that included the Christian kingdom of Nubia, which was conquered and converted.

Islam also was carried by Arab and Indian merchants to Southeast Asia. Here, as in Africa and other regions where the local peoples had not reached a high level of civilization, conversion was easy because of the simplicity and adaptability of the new faith. All one had to do to become a Moslem was to repeat the words, "I bear witness that there is no God but Allah and that Mohammed is the Messenger of Allah." Local practices and traditions usually were accepted and made holy simply by the addition of Islamic ritual. Thus the faith was spread, not by the sword, but by the unobtrusive work of traders who won over the populace by learning their language, adopting their customs, marrying their women, and converting their new relatives and business associates. By the end of the fifteenth century, Islam had spread as far east as Mindanao in the Philippines. Taking Southeast Asia as a whole, the main Moslem centers, as might be expected, were those areas with the most active trade contacts: the Malay peninsula and the Indonesian archipelago.

This diffusion of Islam throughout Eurasia during these five centuries almost tripled the area that accepted the Moslem faith, with important repercussions on the course of world history. The initial stage of Islamic expansion in the seventh and eighth centuries had made the Mediterranean a Moslem lake; this later stage of expansion made the entire Indian Ocean a Moslem lake. This meant that virtually all the goods reaching Europe from Asia now were carried along Moslem-controlled land or sea routes, especially after the Persian Ilkhanate embraced Islam in 1295. Thus the several decades after 1240 during which the Mongol Empire permitted safe travel and trade across Eurasia were only an interlude between earlier and later eras when Arab-Turkish control of Central Asia and the Middle East raised a barrier between China and the West. The continued expansion of the Moslem faith also served to make Islam by 1500 a world force rather than simply a Middle Eastern power. This has affected profoundly the course of world affairs to the present day. It explains why today the Indian peninsula is divided into two parts, why Moslem political parties are so influential in Southeast Asia, why Islam is a powerful and rapidly growing force in Africa, and why it is now the faith of one-seventh of the people of the world.

The Turco-Mongol invasions are significant also because of the cross-fertilization that they stimulated within Eurasia. In the technological field *Pax Mongolica* was responsible for the transmission of a cluster of Chinese inventions, including gunpowder, silk, machinery, printing, and the blast furnace for cast iron. Another example of cross-fertilization is the case of Ilkhanid Persia, which, by its location, was exposed to influences from both East and West. We know of Chinese artillerymen who reached Persia in the service of the Mongol armies. We also know of one Fu Meng-chi who spread the principles of Chinese astronomy, of Chinese physicians at the Ilkhan's court, and of Chinese artists who left an indelible impression on Persian miniature painting. From the opposite direction, European influence was mostly in the field of trade and diplomacy. A colony of Italian merchants flourished in the capital of Tabriz, and from their numbers the Ilkhans recruited the ambassadors and interpreters for their various missions to Europe. And then there was, of course, Marco Polo, who escorted from China to Persia a Mongol princess to be the Ilkhan's bride, and then proceeded on to Venice.

Finally, the opportunities offered by this cross-fertilization were fully exploited only by the new civilization developing in Europe—a profoundly significant fact that was to mold the course of world history to the present day. All the other Eurasian civilizations were too set in their ways. At first it seemed as though the Islamic world would have no difficulty in adapting and changing. Despite the primitive background of Arabia from which it had emerged, Islam had proven itself remarkably adept at borrowing from the great established civilizations and creating something new and impressive. But there was too great a gulf between the dogma of the Islamic faith and the rationalist philosophy and science of the Greeks. In the early years the Caliph al-Mamum (813–833) had generously supported the translation of the ancient classics and had accepted the rationalist doctrine that the Koran was created and not eternal. But his successors were quite different. They supported conservative theologians who rejected all scientific and philosophical speculation as heresy and atheism.

This was the triumph of *scholasticism,* in the sense that seeking God was more important than understanding nature. Such scholasticism had prevailed also in the early medieval West following the barbarian invasions. The Papacy had then dominated the intellectual life of the age, and theology was the accepted queen of the sciences. The same development occurred now in the Islamic world following its series of barbarian invasions—Crusaders, Berbers, Bedouins, Seljuks, and Mongols. Here, as in the West, people turned to religion for succor and consolation in the face of material disaster. But whereas in the West scholasticism eventually was challenged and replaced, in the Moslem world it remained dominant through the nineteenth century.

In his *Incoherence of Philosophy,* the outstanding theologian of Islam, al-Ghazzali (1058–1111), strongly attacked the whole secular school. He argued that the ultimate source of truth is divine revelation and that the intellect should be used to understand that self-trust must be destroyed and replaced by trust in the divine. The extent of orthodox reaction is reflected in the work of the great historian and father of sociology Ibn Khaldun (1332–1406). He was the first to view history not as the conventional chronicles or relating of episodes, as it was viewed in his time, but as the science of the origin and development of civilizations. And yet this learned and creative thinker rejected philosophy and science as useless and dangerous:

It should be known that the opinion the philosophers hold is wrong in all its aspects. . . . The problems of physics are of no importance to us in our religious affairs or our livelihoods. Therefore we must leave them alone. . . . Whoever studies it [logic] should do so only after he is saturated with the religious law and has studied the interpretation of the Koran and jurisprudence. No one who has no knowledge of the Moslem religious sciences should apply himself to it. Without that knowledge, he can hardly be safe from its pernicious aspects. [1]

Thus intellectual growth and innovation in the Moslem world ceased, and, at a time when Europe's universities were in full ferment, the Islamic madrasas were content with rote memorization of authoritative texts. Whereas the Moslem world had been far ahead of the West between 800 and 1200, by the sixteenth century the gap had disappeared, and thereafter it was the West that boomed ahead while Islam stood still and even went backwards.

A similar disparity developed between the West and the other Eurasian civilizations, for the simple reason that only the West made the fateful transition to modernism. Both India and Byzantium were conquered by Islam and affected by its stagnation. China, re-acting against the Mongols who were expelled in 1368, developed a strong *ethnocen-trism*—an almost instinctive hostility and scorn for all things alien and hence barbarian. Russia also succeeded in 1480 in throwing off the Mongol yoke, but permanent scars re-mained. The country had been closed to fresh winds from the West for two and a half cen-turies, and both Mongol ideas and usages had paved the way for the absolutism of the Muscovite state and of the Orthodox church.

The West alone was the exception to this general pattern. Only there occurred the great mutation—the emergence of modern civilization with a new technological base that quickly proved its superiority and diffused not only throughout Eurasia but the entire globe. This uniqueness of the West stems, as noted earlier (Chapter 8, section V), from the shattering impact of the barbarian invasions, which plowed under the classical civilizations and allowed new concepts and institutions to take root and flourish. The following chapters will consider first the traditional Byzantine and Confucian civiliza-tions that flanked the Islamic world on each side, and then will analyze the contrasting revolutionary civilization of the West.

SUGGESTED READING

J. A. Boyle, ed., *The Cambridge History of Iran,* Vol. 5, *The Seljuk and Mogol Periods* (Cambridge University Press, 1931); C. Cahen, *Pre-Ottoman Turkey* (Sidgwick, 1968); H. Inalcik, *The Ottoman Empire: The Classical Age 1300–1600* (Weidenfeld & Nicolson, 1972); E. D. Phillips, *The Mongols* (Thames, 1969); T. T. Rice, *The Seljuks* (Thames, 1961); J. J. Saunders, ed., *The Mongols on the Eve of Europe's Expansion* (Prentice-Hall, 1966) and his *The History of the Mongol Conquests* (Harper & Row, 1972).

chapter 12

Traditional Byzantine Civilization

Byzantium was one of the traditional Eurasian civilizations that survived the barbarian invasions and continued without interruption from the Classical Age to modern times. But this unbroken sweep of one thousand years of history eventually meant obsolescence and extinction, especially in the political sense. Because it was the most vulnerable, the Byzantine civilization was the first to suffer this fate. China, for example, faced nomadic invasions only from the northwest and was so far out of the way on the eastern tip of Eurasia that the aggressive West was not able to break in until the mid-nineteenth century. Byzantium, by contrast, faced a succession of barbarian invasions from across the Danube, which were comparable to those menacing China. Byzantium also had to bear the onslaught of the expanding West in the form of Venetian merchants and Norman knights. At the same time a resurgent East assaulted Byzantium. First came the Sassanian Persian attack, and then the Moslem Arab and Turkish invasions. Thus, whereas the traditional Chinese civilization endured to 1912, the Byzantine collapsed first in 1204, was partially revived in 1261, and survived in a crippled state until the death blow in 1453 (see Map XVIII, ''Decline of the Byzantine Empire'').

I. EMERGENCE OF BYZANTIUM

No Western capital approaches the proud record of the Byzantine capital, Constantinople, either in continuity or in the scope of its imperial rule. It was already an old city when rebuilt by Constantine in A.D. 330 to be the new Rome. In the following centuries it stood impregnable before the barbarian assaults to which the first Rome eventually succumbed. After the overthrow of Romulus Augustulus in Rome in A.D. 476, the Eastern emperors in Constantinople continued to regard themselves as the heirs of the Caesars. Justinian tried to make this imperial myth a reality by winning back from the barbarians North Africa, Italy, and a part of Spain (see Chapter 8, section IV). But the revived empire proved short-lived. Soon after Justinian's death, a new barbarian tribe, the Lombards, overran most of Italy. Likewise on the Danube frontier the Avars and Slavs were pouring southward into the Balkans, while in the East the Persians overran Syria, Palestine, and Egypt and camped on the shores of the Bosphorus opposite Constantinople.

Under the great Emperor Heraclius (610–641), Byzantium took the offensive against the surrounding enemies. In 627 Heraclius defeated the Persians and forced them to return all their conquests. Turning to the Danube frontier, Heraclius discovered that in the meantime the Slavs had occupied and sunk roots in large parts of the northern Balkans. Making a virtue of necessity, he assigned definite areas to them, and in return they acknowledged his suzerainty and agreed to pay annual tribute. Thus the Slavic newcomers changed gradually from invaders into settlers. With the passing of a few centuries these widely scattered Balkan Slavs had developed along different lines and crystalized into four major groups: the Slovenes at the head of the Adriatic, the Croatians between the Drave River and the Adriatic, the Serbs in the central Balkans between the Adriatic and the Danube, and the Slavs, who shortly were to adopt the name of their Bulgarian conquerors, in the remaining territory to the Black Sea.

Later in the seventh century the Byzantine Empire again was threatened, this time by the combination of Moslem sea raids and Bulgar land attacks. The Arabs developed a naval power with which they conquered Cyprus and Rhodes, and then they besieged Constantinople on several occasions, beginning in 669. At the same time Byzantium was threatened from the north by the Bulgars, who had occupied the territory between the Danube and the Balkan Mountains and from there were threatening Constantinople.

Once more Byzantium was saved by inspired imperial leadership, this time in the person of Leo III the Isaurian (717–741). A military commander of Syrian origin, he seized power when Constantinople was under siege by the Arabs. He not only lifted the siege but drove the Arabs back out of Asia Minor. By the end of his reign the imperial frontiers were secure, but they were drastically shrunken frontiers compared to those of Justinian. Italy had been lost to the Lombards, the northern Balkans to the Slavs and the Bulgars, and Syria, Palestine, Egypt, and North Africa to the Arabs.

This reduced empire, however, was a more homogeneous empire. It was strengthened rather than weakened by withdrawal to the Taurus Mountains that separated Greek Asia Minor from what was now becoming the heartland of the Islamic world. This separation was reinforced by internal convulsions in the Moslem world that culminated in the accession of the Abbasid Caliphate (750). The Islamic capital was moved from Damascus to Baghdad so that the orientation of Islam now was to the East rather than towards the

155

Mediterranean. In this way the Byzantine and Moslem empires were able to coexist peacefully until the appearance of the militant Turks in the eleventh century.

A separation similar to that between Byzantium and Islam was developing between Byzantium and the West. With the Lombard invasion the Roman popes had looked to Constantinople for protection, but to no avail because Byzantine was preoccupied with the Arabs. So the popes turned to the Franks, and the partnership resulted in the famous papal coronation of Charlemagne in 800. In 812, Constantinople reluctantly conceded the title of *Basileus* to Charlemagne and thus recognized the West as a political entity. During the following centuries Byzantium and the West drifted apart not only in politics but also in language, in ecclesiastical matters, and in general culture.

The emerging Byzantine Empire of the eighth century was much smaller than Justinian's short-lived creation, but it was also much more homogeneous. It had shed the diverse racial, cultural, and religious elements of the eastern and western provinces, and the remaining core was basically, though not exclusively, Greek. In this manner, then, the transition was made from the East Roman Empire of the sixth century to the Byzantine Empire of the eighth—an empire with a culture clearly distinct from both that of Islam to the east and from that of the new Europe to the west.

II. BYZANTIUM'S GOLDEN AGE

The Byzantine Empire reached its height during the period between the early ninth and early eleventh centuries. Imperial administration was soundly based on the *themes,* or provinces, each headed by a *strategos,* or general. The general was in charge of both civil and military affairs. Heraclius had militarized the administration so that he could act quickly at a time of imminent foreign danger. Imperial lands in the themes were divided amongst the peasants in return for military service. Under strong emperors this theme arrangement provided good administration, a reliable military reserve, and a well-filled treasury, since the peasants assumed much of the tax burden.

Byzantium's economy also was solidly based on free peasant communities that functioned alongside the estates of the great landowners. In the urban centers that had survived since Greco-Roman classical times, craftsmen worked at a high level of competence. Arab writers described the quality of Byzantine handicrafts, especially the luxury products, as being equaled only by those of China. Equally important was the great volume of goods that passed through Constantinople from all regions of Eurasia—slaves and salt from the Black Sea lands, spices, perfumes, and precious stones from India, papyrus and foodstuffs from Egypt, silk and porcelain from China, and silver, wrought iron objects, and linen, cotton, and woolen fabrics from the West.

This political, economic, and military strength allowed the Byzantine emperors to launch reconquest campaigns that were more realistic if not as ambitious as those of Justinian. Crete and Cyprus were recovered, thereby curbing Arab naval raids in the Aegean waters. The imperial frontiers were extended also into northern Syria, Armenia, and Georgia. In the northern Balkans where the Bulgars were a constant threat to the empire, Basil II won such a crushing victory in 1014 that he was known thereafter as Bulgaroktonus, or ''the Bulgar-Slayer.''

In cultural matters this was a period of stability and homogeneity. The Byzantines still called themselves Romaioi, or Romans, but Greek, in either its literary or popular forms, was the universal language of the empire. Religious homogeneity also had been promoted with the conversion of the Moslems on reconquered Crete, and of the Slavs in the northern Balkans. In 865 the Bulgarian Khan Boris accepted Christianity from Constantinople in return for imperial recognition of his conquests. In the following years Byzantine missionaries provided the Bulgarians with an alphabet, translated the Scriptures into their language, and prepared a Slavonic liturgy. About the same time the Serbian tribes were converted to Orthodoxy, as were the Russians of the Kievan state.

Imperial stability was strengthened by the intimate, mutually supporting relationship between emperor and patriarch. The principle of a subservient state church was traditional and accepted. The emperor called himself not only "autokrator" but also "isapostolos," or the equal of the apostles. The emperor dominated the election of the Patriarch of Constantinople, and in the installation ceremony the new head of the church was pronounced patriarch "by the will of God and Emperor."

In conclusion, Byzantium during these centuries was stable, powerful, wealthy, self-satisfied, and rather inward looking now that a reasonable coexistence had evolved with both the Western and Moslem worlds. These characteristics are reminiscent of China under the Ming dynasty, as will be noted in the following chapter.

III. BYZANTIUM'S DECLINE

When Basil ("the Bulgar-Slayer") died in 1205 the Byzantine Empire seemed to be secure and unchallenged in its splendid eminence. The northern frontier rested solidly on the Danube. Arabic Islam was divided and was no longer a threat. And whatever was emerging in the West was patently primitive and insignificant in comparison to the Second Rome on the Bosphorus. Yet within half a century after Basil's death the empire was in serious trouble, and less than two centuries later, in 1204, its capital had fallen to the despised barbarians of the West.

One reason for the dramatic reversal was the undermining of the imperial military system by the growing insubordination of the strategoi, or generals, in charge of the themes, or provinces. Basil II had been strong enough to keep the military in check, but his weak successors were unable to do so, especially when the strategoi joined forces with the great provincial landowners. Repeatedly the strategoi rebelled against civilian authority in Constantinople, using the peasant levies (military forces conscripted from the peasants) that were originally intended for frontier defense. In retaliation the bureaucrats disbanded the peasant levies and collected cash payments in place of their military service. The funds thus collected were used to hire mercenaries, including foreign Normans, Germans, Patzinaks, and Armenians. But in comparison with the former peasant forces, these mercenaries proved notoriously unreliable. When their pay was not forthcoming they often turned against the empire they were supposed to defend.

A closely related cause for imperial decline was the political problem of the feudalization of society. The strategoi and the local landowners accumulated vast estates, so that entire provinces fell under the domination of a few families. The emperors issued frequent orders against this trend, but to no avail, and for the simple reason that the orders had to be implemented by the very class against which they were directed. After Basil II even these efforts largely ceased, and instead the emperors began to grant state properties to those who had rendered valuable service. These grants, or pronoia, became associated with military service, and thus came to resemble in certain respects the fiefs of the West. Indeed when the Latins conquered Byzantium in 1204 and divided it into fiefs, the Greek aristocracy recognized the fiefs as the Latin version of their own pronoia.

The empire was plagued also by serious economic ailments. The large private and monastic estates reduced imperial revenues, especially when Basil's successors relieved the large landowners of most taxes. At the same time imperial expenditures were rising because of court extravagances and the cost of the mercenary army. Equally serious were the mounting raids of Patzinaks and Seljuk Turks, which left certain regions devastated and unproductive. The Byzantine gold solidus, which had remained stable for seven centuries, now went through a series of devaluations.

In Byzantium as in many other empires, internal weakness attracted external aggression. In the West were the Norman adventurers who originally had served as Byzantine mercenaries. But now they turned against the weakened empire and overran its possessions in southern Italy that had survived since the time of Justinian's conquests. Likewise in the east were the Seljuk Turks who had infiltrated from their Central Asian homeland into the Islamic Empire. There they were employed as mercenaries by the Baghdad caliphs. Gradually the mercenaries became masters, and in 1055 they captured Baghdad and founded the Seljuk Empire. These Turks brought new life into the moribund Islamic world, reuniting the lands between India and the Mediterranean and pressing upon the Taurus Mountain frontier that for centuries had separated the Byzantine and Islamic worlds.

This was the background of the two disasters that befell Byzantium in 1071, marking the beginning of centuries of decline. The first disaster occurred at Bari in southern Italy where the Normans conquered the sole surviving Byzantine foothold. The other, and much more decisive setback, was at Manzikert in Asia Minor. There the Seljuks defeated the Byzantine emperor in a fateful battle that began the transformation of Asia Minor from a Greek to a Turkish stronghold. Following this battle two rival emperors fought for the Byzantine throne, using Turkish forces against each other. Thus Turkish tribes were able to enter at will, gradually changing Asia Minor from the bedrock of Greek Byzantine power to the heartland of the Turkish nation.

The Byzantine Empire was saved from what appeared to be imminent dissolution by the shrewdness and tenacity of Emperor Alexius Comnenus (1081–1118). He granted valuable commercial concessions to the Venetians in return for their support against the Normans who were threatening to attack Constantinople. He also appealed to Western Christendom for assistance against the Moslem Seljuks. Instead of the few mercenaries he had hoped for he got hordes of undisciplined Crusaders. Some were led by the Normans that Alexius had excellent reason to distrust. This contact between eastern and western Christendom resulted in mutual suspicion and open hostility. Greeks and Latins disliked each other's languages, religions, politics, and ways of life.

Alexius adroitly encouraged the Crusaders to cross over to Asia Minor where, together with the Byzantines, they recovered some regions from the Seljuks. But relations between Greeks and Latins became increasingly strained during the Second and Third Crusades. Also the Byzantines suffered a disastrous setback when they rashly set out to attack the Seljuk capital of Konia in central Asia Minor. On the way they were crushed by the Turks at Myriocephalon (1176), a defeat that ended whatever possibility that might have remained for a Byzantine comeback in Asia Minor. Meanwhile the Venetians were undermining the economic foundations of Byzantium with the commercial privileges they had extracted from the hard-pressed emperors. They had complete freedom from

LATIN CONQUEST OF CONSTANTINOPLE

A major event in the decline of Byzantium was the capture of Constantinople by the Latins of the Fourth Crusade in 1261. The following description by the contemporary Byzantine historian, Nicetas Choniates, is as revealing of Greek hatred for the Latins as it is of what actually happened.*

. . . How shall I begin to tell of the deeds wrought by these nefarious men! Alas, the images, which ought to have been adored, were trodden under foot! Alas, the relics of the holy martyrs were thrown into unclean places! Then was seen what one shudders to hear, namely, the divine body and blood of Christ was spilled upon the ground or thrown about. They snatched the precious reliquaries, thrust into their bosoms the ornaments which these contained, and used the broken remnants for pans and drinking cups,–precursors of Anti-christ, authors and heralds of his nefarious deeds which we momentarily expect. Manifestly, indeed, by that race then, just as formerly, Christ was robbed and insulted and His garments were divided by lot; only one thing was lacking, that His side, pierced by a spear, should pour rivers of divine blood on the ground.

Nor can the violation of the Great Church [Santa Sophia] be listened to with equanimity. For the sacred altar, formed of all kinds of precious materials and admired by the whole world, was broken into bits and distributed among the soldiers, as was all the other sacred wealth of so great and infinite splendor.

When the sacred vases and utensils of unsurpassable art and grace and rare material, and the fine silver, wrought with gold, which encircled the screen of the tribunal and the ambo, of admirable workmanship, and the door and many other ornaments, were to be borne away as booty, mules and saddled horses were led to the very sanctuary of the temple. Some of these which were unable to keep their footing on the splendid and slippery pavement, were stabbed when they fell, so that the sacred pavement was polluted with blood and filth.

Nay more, a certain harlot, a sharer in their guilt, a minister of the furies, a servant of the demons, a worker of incantations and poisonings, insulting Christ, sat in the patriarch's seat, singing an obscene song and dancing frequently. Nor, indeed, were these crimes committed and others left undone, on the ground that these were of lesser guilt, the others of greater. But with one consent all the most heinous sins and crimes were committed by all with equal zeal. Could those, who showed so great madness against God Himself, have spared the honorable matrons and maidens or the virgins consecrated to God?

Nothing was more difficult and laborious than to soften by prayers, to render benevolent, these wrathful barbarians, vomiting forth bile at every unpleasing word, so that nothing failed to inflame their fury. Whoever attempted it was derided as insane and a man of intemperate language. Often they drew their daggers against anyone who opposed them at all or hindered their demands.

No one was without a share in the grief. In the alleys, in the streets, in the temples, complaints, weeping, lamentations, grief, the groaning of men, the shrieks of women, wounds, rape, captivity, the separation of those most closely united. Nobles wandered about ignominiously, those of venerable age in tears, the rich in poverty. Thus it was in the streets, on the corners, in the temple, in the dens, for no place remained unassailed or defended the suppliants. All places everywhere were filled full of all kinds of crime. Oh, immortal God, how great the afflictions of the men, how great the distress!

* D. C. Munro, trans., *Translations and Reprints from the Original Sources of European History*, rev. ed., series I, Vol. III, No. 1 (University of Pennsylvania Press, 1912), pp. 15, 16.

tolls or duties throughout the empire, a concession that gave them a decisive advantage over Byzantine merchants who had to pay heavy taxes. Thus not only did the Italians get a stranglehold on the empire's trade, but the treasury at Constantinople lost much revenue. The contrast between Venetian affluence and Byzantine poverty provoked riots in 1183 in which many Latins abroad were killed and their Byzantine properties looted.

Such was the background of the Fourth Crusade, appropriately nicknamed the ''businessmen's crusade.'' Because of the economic plans of Venetian merchants, the quest for loot and lands by Western adventurers, the blandishments of a Byzantine pretender, and the long pent-up grievances harbored by Latins against what they considered to be the cunning, effeminate, grasping, and heretical Greeks, the Fourth Crusade was deflected from its original goal of liberating Jerusalem. Instead the Crusaders attacked Constantinople. A mixed force of French, Venetians, Flemings, and Germans stormed the capital in the spring of 1204 and subjected it to three days of merciless looting and slaughter. ''Even the Saracens,'' observed a Byzantine chronicler, ''would have been more merciful.'' Paradoxically, the end result of the Fourth Crusade was to pave the way for Islamic domination of the entire Middle East. Although the Byzantine Empire was restored in 1261, it never recovered from the traumatic shock of the Latin conquest, and it remained in helpless impotence until the Ottoman capture of Constantinople in 1453.

IV. END OF BYZANTIUM

The victorious Latins set up their feudal states on the ruins of Byzantium. They established a Latin empire at Constantinople, a Latin kingdom at Thessaloniki, and several Latin states in Greece. The commercially minded Venetians occupied a whole quarter of Constantinople and annexed numerous islands and ports strategically located on their route to the Levant. These new states, however, were doomed from the outset. The native Greek Orthodox populations were bitterly hostile to the end. Furthermore the Latin conquerors had won only a few isolated toeholds on the fringes of the Balkan peninsula and were surrounded on all sides by enemies. They faced not only the Serbian and Bulgarian kingdoms in the Balkan interior, but also three Greek succession states located at Arta in Epirus, at Trebizond on the southern shore of the Black Sea, and at Nicaea in western Asia Minor. The first of these Greek states was too poor to provide effective leadership, and the second was too isolated. So it was Nicaea, with its strategic location, adequate resources, and able leadership, that organized Greek resistance to Latin rule.

By skillful diplomacy and force of arms the Nicaean rulers steadily reduced the Latin empire until only the city of Constantinople itself remained. Finally in 1261 the Latin emperor and the Venetian settlers fled from Constantinople without offering resistance. The Nicaean emperor, Michael Palaeologus, then made his solemn entry into the capital and, amidst popular acclamation, took up his residence in the imperial palace.

The final phase of Byzantine history took place in the period between 1261, when Michael Palaeologus recovered Constantinople, and 1453, when his successor, Constantine Palaeologus, was killed at a gate of the capital fighting the Turks. During these two centuries the restored empire consisted merely of the cities of Constantinople and Thessaloniki, with small fluctuating areas around each, and two separate appendages: Mistra, in the Peloponnesus, and Trebizond, in northern Asia Minor.

The outlook for this pitiful remnant of empire was scarcely more promising than that of its Latin predecessors. In Asia it faced the formidable Turks, and in Europe it was surrounded by small Latin states that remained in Greece, and by the Serbians and Bulgarians to the north. To these external dangers were added internal difficulties. Economically the empire was bankrupt. The Italian stranglehold on commerce continued unbroken, so that in the mid-fourteenth century the Genoese quarter in Constantinople was collecting seven times as much as the imperial government in customs revenues. The emperors were reduced to debasing their currency and pawning their crown jewels with Venetian bankers. Increased taxes commonly were avoided by the politically influential rich. The poor rose in revolt against the aristocracy of birth and wealth, so that cities were torn by social strife.

Between 1342 and 1349 the city of Thessaloniki was ruled by revolutionary leaders known as the Zealots. They reduced taxes on the poor, canceled their debts, confiscated and distributed monastery lands, and introduced participatory democracy with mass rallies and popularly elected officials. Their political program appears to have been influenced by the example of the republican city-states in Italy. But a dying Byzantine Empire could not support the political and social innovations then emerging naturally in the vigorous and expanding West. With Serbian and Turkish aid the emperor suppressed the Zealots and ended their republic. The episode was symptomatic, however, of the deep and widespread discord.

The empire was weakened also by religious dissension. Hoping to obtain Western aid against the approaching Turks, the emperors on three separate occasions had agreed to the submission of the Orthodox Church to the Papacy (Unions of Lyons, 1274; Rome, 1369; and Florence, 1439). These agreements proved meaningless, for the West gave insignificant aid, while Byzantium was further torn by the bitter popular opposition to granting any concessions to the hated Latins. "Better Islam than the Pope" was the defiant popular response to the barbarities of the Fourth Crusade and to the exploitation by Italian merchants.

The cry of preference for the Turks had been heard frequently in the past, but in the mid-fifteenth century the situation was unique because the Turks then were in a position to accept the invitation. As noted in chapter 11, section V, the Ottoman Turks had taken over from the Seljuks, conquered the remaining Byzantine enclaves in Asia Minor, crossed the Straits to Europe, defeated the Bulgars and Serbs, and finally by 1453 were ready to close in on the beleaguered Byzantine capital.

Constantinople's population by this time had shrunk to between fifty and seventy thousand. The total force available for the defense of the city, including a small number from the West, amounted to no more than nine thousand. This was totally inadequate to man the extensive series of walls and to repair the breaches pounded by the enemy cannon. The Ottoman army, led by the capable Sultan Mohammed II, numbered at least eighty thousand. Yet the defenders, under the courageous leadership of Emperor Constantine, repulsed the attackers from April 2 when the siege began to May 29 when the final assault prevailed. The city was then given over to the soldiery for the promised three-day sack. The contemporary Byzantine historian Ducas describes as follows this ending of a thousand years of Byzantium.

Three days after the fall of the city he [Muhammed] released the ships so that each might sail off to its own province and city, each carrying such a load that it seemed each would sink. And what sort of a cargo? Luxurious cloths and textiles, objects and vessels of gold, silver, bronze and brass, books beyond all counting and number, prisoners including priests and lay persons, nuns and monks. All the ships were full of cargos, and the tents of the army camps were full of captives and of the above enumerated items and goods. And there was to be seen among the barbarian host one wearing the sakkon of an archbishop, another wearing the gold epitrahelion of a priest, leading their dogs clothed instead of with the usual collars with gold brocaded amnous (ecclesiastical vestments). Others were to be seen seated at banquets, with the holy discs before them containing fruit and other foods, which they were eating, and with the holy chalices from which they drank their wine. And having loaded all the books, reaching unto a number beyond numbering, upon carts, they scattered them throughout the east and west. For one nomisma ten books could be bought (and what kind of books), Aristotelian, Platonic, theological, and every other kind. There were gospels which had every type of embellishment, beyond number, they smashed the gold and silver from them and some they sold, others they threw away. And all the icons were thrown into the flame, from which flame they broiled their meat. [1]

V. BYZANTIUM'S LEGACY

In the light of retrospect Byzantium obviously made significant contributions in various fields. One was in its role as a protective shield behind which the West was left free to develop its own civilization. The full meaning of this became clear when, after the fall of Constantinople in 1453, the Turks within barely half a century reached the heart of Europe and besieged Vienna. Equally important was Byzantium's stimulus to trade and general economic development. For centuries Byzantium was the economic dynamo for the entire Mediterranean basin, while its currency served as the standard international medium of exchange. Its merchants and its commodities did much to lift Western Europe out of its feudalized self-sufficiency and to start the Italian city-states on the road to commercial domination of the Mediterranean. In the realm of culture, Byzantium salvaged the intellectual and artistic treasures of antiquity and transmitted them to posterity along with its own legacy. From Byzantium came Roman law codified by Justinian, a religious art that only recently has been properly understood and appreciated, and the literary and scholarly masterpieces of classical and Hellenistic times as compiled, annotated, and preserved by conscientious scholars.

Finally, Byzantium was for the eastern Slavs what Rome had been for the Germans—the great educator and the source of both religion and of civilization. The early Russian principalities strung out along river routes carried on a flourishing commerce with Byzantium. Through Kiev on the Dnieper River were funneled raw materials gathered from the Russian countryside—furs, hides, grains, timber, and slaves—and in return the Byzantine traders delivered luxury goods such as fine cloths, glassware, spices, jewelry, and wine.

With Greek material goods came Greek cultural institutions. Most important was Orthodox Christianity, adopted by Prince Vladimir about 988. This involved much more than a mere change of religion. An ecclesiastical hierarchy based on the Byzantine model was now organized. The head was the Metropolitan of Kiev, appointed by, and subject to, the jurisdiction of the Patriarch of Constantinople. *Orthodox Christianity* also brought with it a new religious and legal literature, including translations of the Bible, Byzantine collections of the writings of the church fathers, lives of saints, and law books. Byzantine art also was now introduced in the form of stone churches, mosaics, frescoes, paintings, and particularly icons, in which the Russians excelled and developed their distinctive Russo-Byzantine style. The Orthodox Church also brought with it Byzantine ecclesiastical law and established ecclesiastical courts. As in Western Europe, these courts had very wide jurisdiction, including all cases involving morals, beliefs, inheritance, and matrimonial matters.

In the realm of politics the new church served to strengthen the authority of the prince. Just as in Western Europe the Papacy had transformed the Frankish kings from tribal chieftains to the Lord's anointed, so now Russian Orthodoxy transformed the heads of the principalities from mere leaders of bands of personal followers to "servants of the lord" and hence rulers by divine right. Furthermore the Russian church, in accordance with Byzantine tradition, accepted secular authority and control. There was no counterpart in Moscow, as there had been none in Constantinople, of Gregory VII or Innocent III in Rome, demanding and exacting obedience from emperors and kings alike. This tradition continued after the disappearance of Byzantium. The Russian Orthodox Church transferred its loyalty and subservience to the Russian emperor, until the Tsarist empire followed the Byzantine to extinction.

In conclusion, Byzantine civilization stands out for its historic role and achievements. Yet Byzantium did lack the freshness and luster of classical Athens, even though, by comparison, Athens was insignificant in size and in time. The reason is that the role of Byzantium was conservative in the proper sense of the word. This is not to say that Byzantium was static. From beginning to end it was adjusting itself to changing times and circumstances. But the fact remains that its destiny was to conserve rather than to create. It was born an aged state within the Roman Empire. It lived in the shadow of past power and glory which it sought to maintain or recover. It produced a remarkable succession of outstanding leaders—administrators, generals, scholars, and theologians—but because of the context in which they worked very few of them were genuinely creative.

The fact that the East Roman Empire survived that of the West by a full millennium constituted a great advantage at the outset. Between the fifth and the eleventh centuries the West was primitive and insignificant in comparison to the Second Rome on the Bosphorus. But these were centuries when the West, precisely because it had to start afresh, was laying the foundations for a new civilization, while Byzantium was living on its splendid but overpowering patrimony. This is why from the eleventh century onward the West was able to forge ahead with its booming economy, rising national monarchies, new intellectual horizons, and a dynamic expansionism that manifested itself first in local crusades and then in an overseas thrust that was to lead within a few centuries to global hegemony. And, in pitiful contrast, during these later centuries Byzantium was incapable of breaking the bonds to the past and thus became an obsolete anachronism that fought a gallant but doomed holding action to the ignominious and inevitable end in 1453.

SUGGESTED READING

J. Blum, *Lord and Peasant in Russia from the Ninth to the Nineteenth Century* (Princeton University Press, 1961); *Cambridge Medieval History,* Vol. IV (Cambridge University Press, 1966); M. T. Florinsky, *Russia: A History and an Interpretation,* 2 vols. (Macmillan, 1947); D. A. Miller, *The Byzantine Tradition* (Harper & Row, 1966); G. Ostrogorsky, *History of the Byzantine State* (Rutgers University Press, 1957); G. Vernadsky, *The Mongols and Russia* (Yale University Press, 1953); S. Vryonis, *Byzantium and Europe* (Harcourt Brace Jovanovich, 1967); and his *The Decline of Medieval Hellenism in Asia Minor and the Process of Islamization from the Eleventh through the Fifteenth Century* (University of California Press, 1971.)

chapter 13

Traditional Confucian Civilization

The fact that the Han dynasty eventually was succeeded by the Sui and T'ang dynasties ensured that civilization in China was to continue along traditional lines. Hence the course of China's civilization contrasts sharply with the unique change that was taking form in the West following Rome's collapse (see Chapter 8, sections III–V). The ensuing millennium was a great Golden Age for the Chinese people. During the Han period China had succeeded in catching up to the other Eurasian civilizations, but now, during the medieval period, China forged ahead. China remained the richest, most populous, and, in many ways, the most culturally advanced country in the world.

The millennium between the sixth century, when the Sui dynasty restored imperial unity, and the sixteenth, when the Westerners began their intrusion by sea, was for China an era of unparalleled political, social, and cultural stability. But this stability paradoxically proved to be a curse as well as a blessing. It was a blessing because Chinese society during this millennium provided more material advantages and more psychological security for more people than any other society in the world. But the stability was also a curse because it was so successful and comfortable that China remained relatively unchanged, though not completely static. At the same time, however, as we shall see in the following chapter, the West was being transformed by its technological achievements, its economic vitality, and its social and political pluralism. All this engendered a dynamism that culminated in the West's domination of the entire globe. The end result, then, was the disruption of the beautifully balanced but conservative Chinese society by the irresistible expansionism of the West. Despite this outcome, we should not overlook the fact that for a full millennium the civilization of China led the world by its sheer viability and by its contributions to the human heritage.

I. SUI AND T'ANG DYNASTIES

The Sui dynasty (589–618) played the same role in Chinese history as the Ch'in dynasty some eight centuries earlier. Both dynasties reunited China after long periods of disorder, and both then proceeded to make fundamental contributions to the development of the country. But in doing so they drove their people so hard and antagonized so many vested interests that both scarcely survived their founders.

The great contribution of the Ch'in rulers was the imperial unity they forced upon China through road and canal building, construction of the Great Wall, standardization of weights, measures, and script, and extension and strengthening of the frontiers. The efforts of the Sui emperors were very similar and equally exhausting. They reconstructed the Great Wall, parts of which had fallen into disrepair. They built the main sections of the gigantic canal system that came to be known as the Grand Canal. This met a pressing need by linking the Yangtze valley, which had become the economic center of the country, with the north, which remained the political center. But so heavy was the cost in treasure and lives that the Sui emperor responsible for the undertaking lost popular support and undermined his dynasty.

Equally exhausting were the series of campaigns that extended the imperial frontiers to include Formosa, Annam, and Champa in Indochina and Kansu in the northwest. But the attempts to conquer the most northern of the three kingdoms into which Korea was then divided proved disastrous. Four successive invasions were repulsed by the resolute Korean defenders. The disaffected soldiers mutinied, while the overtaxed peasants rose in rebellion in various parts of the country. The emperor fled to south China where he was assassinated in 618. The victor in the ensuing struggle among several pretenders established the T'ang dynasty, regarded by many Chinese and Western historians as the most outstanding of them all.

A striking accomplishment of the T'ang dynasty was its expansion of the empire. In a series of great campaigns, it extended the frontiers even beyond those of the Han emperors. In Central Asia it established Chinese suzerainty over the Tarim basin and beyond the Pamirs to the states of the Oxus valley and even to the headwaters of the Indus in modern Afghanistan. Other vast territories that now were forced to accept Chinese suzerainty were Tibet in the south, Mongolia in the northwest, and Korea and Manchuria in the northeast. The only other comparable empire in the world at the time was that of the Moslem Arabs in the Middle East.

China's foreign conquests were made possible by the reestablishment of strong central government at home. The Han dynasty had been undermined by powerful local families that had accumulated huge, self-sufficient and tax-free estates. They built fortresslike manor houses on these estates and so could successfully defy central authority. Disintegration was also furthered by the appearance of Buddhist monasteries, which, with their extensive and growing landholdings, offered another challenge to the imperial government. The Sui and T'ang dynasties developed an antidote to this political fragmentation. It consisted of the *equal-field system* by which the central government assigned plots of about nineteen acres to all able-bodied peasants. This did not deprive the powerful families of their holdings, for the land assigned to the peasants was obtained from other sources, such as reclamation projects and fields that had been abandoned during the wars. Also only the free peasants received the land grants, and, in actual practice, by no means all of them got land. Nevertheless the equal-field system did help somewhat to loosen the grip of the great families and to strengthen the T'ang regime. It halted for some time the growth of the large semifeudal estates. It increased government revenues, since the small peasants paid taxes whereas the politically powerful great landholders did not. Furthermore the peasants were given military training and organized into a regular militia, thereby strengthening the military position of the imperial government.

The T'ang dynasty strengthened its authority also by developing a competent bureaucracy to administer the empire. The Sui earlier had reinstated the Han system of civil service based on competitive public examinations. The T'ang continued and expanded this system, following the basic Confucian tenet that matters of state are best resolved by recruiting men of talent. It rejected the typical Western practice of handling state affairs by changing laws and institutions. When fully developed, the Chinese civil service system was based on a series of examinations held amidst an elaborate series of rituals. The initial qualifying examinations, in the district and prefectural cities, occurred every two or three years, and the approximately 2 percent of the candidates who passed these took the prefectural exams a few weeks later. Survivors (about half the candidates) became eligible for appointment to minor posts and for further examinations held every three years in the provincial capitals. Success here entitled one to take the imperial examinations at the capital. Only about 6 percent passed this hurdle and became eligible for appointment to high office; and only a third of these normally passed the final palace examination in the presence of the Emperor himself. They were then admitted to membership in the most exalted fraternity of Chinese scholarship, the Hanlin Academy. Historiographers and other high literary officers were selected from the Academy.

At first the examinations were fairly comprehensive, emphasizing the Confucian *Classics* but including also subjects like law, mathematics, and political affairs. Gradually, however, they came to concentrate on literary style and Confucian orthodoxy. The net result was a system that theoretically opened offices to all male Chinese of talent, but that in practice favored the classes with enough wealth to afford the years of study and preparation. This did not mean that a hereditary aristocracy ruled China; rather, it was a hierarchy of the learned, a "literocracy." On the one hand, it provided China with an efficient and stable administration that won the respect and admiration of Europeans. But on the other hand, it was a system that stifled originality and bred conformity. So long as China remained relatively isolated in East Asia, it made for stability and continuity. But with the intrusion of the dynamic West it prevented effective adjustment and response. It was finally abolished altogether in 1905.

The capital of the T'ang Empire was Ch'ang-an, a magnificent city of probably over a million people. Its broad thoroughfares, crisscrossing in checkerboard fashion, often were crowded with Persians, Indians, Jews, Armenians, and assorted Central Asians. They came as merchants, missionaries, and mercenary solidiers, for China under the T'ang was more open to foreigners than at any other time except for the short-lived Mongol Yüan interlude.

Freedom of thought was most apparent in matters of religion. The extension of imperial frontiers and the reopening of land and sea trade routes brought in many foreign religious ideas and missionaries. This was the case with Buddhism, which first entered China from India during the Han dynasty and began to seriously challenge the official Confucianism during the chaos following the collapse of the Han. In that time of trouble Confucianism was increasingly questioned because its emphasis on filial piety and family loyalty appeared to weaken an already weak state. Consequently Buddhism gained rapidly and reached the height of its influence during the early T'ang, which is sometimes called the "Buddhist period" of Chinese history.

Eventually the imperial government turned against Buddhism and resorted to outright persecution. The Buddhist emphasis on the salvation of the individual rather than on his obligation to the family was too contrary to basic Chinese traditions. The complete withdrawal from society of monks and nuns was not only contrary to tradition but was considered unnatural and antisocial. Most important, the government coveted the vast treasures and estates that the monasteries had accumulated through the centuries. Hence the series of persecutions that crippled Buddhism in China, though it did not disappear altogether as it did in India. The persecution was restricted to the institutions and their clergy and did not include the rank-and-file believers, as happened in comparable situations in the West. The end result of this Buddhist interlude was minimal so far as the overall evolution of Chinese civilization was concerned. Buddhism made significant contributions to Chinese philosophy, metaphysics, art, and literature. But it did not remold Chinese society as a whole, as Christianity had remolded the European.

During the last century and a half of their reign, the T'ang rulers were faced with the usual problems of a dynasty in decline. Imperial expenses outstripped revenues. Population growth likewise outstripped land supply, so that peasant families no longer could be provided with individual plots. The equal-field system broke down, and the wealthy families once more enlarged their estates at the expense of the peasants. Since the revenue system was based on per-capita taxes, the burden of paying for the mounting imperial expenses fell on the peasants at a time when their holdings were shrinking.

The government responded by shifting increasingly from per-capita to land taxes. This produced more revenue, but it did not halt the decline in the number of free peasants. The decreasing number of free peasants meant a corresponding decline in the supply of manpower for militia and corvée duty. The defense of the empire was entrusted more and more to mercenaries and border "barbarian" tribes who were not as dependable as the former militia. Thus in 751 Chinese armies were defeated both in Yunnan in the south and at Talas in Central Asia. The battle at Talas was particularly decisive for it enabled the Moslem Arab victors to begin the Islamization of a vast area that had been one of the earliest strongholds of Buddhism.

The T'ang emperors managed to hang on for another century and a half, but it was a period of steady deterioration. Incompetence and provocative luxury in the capital along with successive droughts and widespread famine provoked rebellions in many provinces. The dynasty enlisted the support of local military leaders and assorted "barbarian" border peoples. But these soon were out of control. They disregarded court orders and fought amongst themselves for the succession to the obviously doomed dynasty. The end came in 907, when one of the rebel leaders deposed the last T'ang ruler and sacked Ch'ang-an. The empire now broke into fragments, and the ensuing half-century is known as the period of the "Five Dynasties." An able general finally was able to restore unity and to found a new dynasty, the Sung, which, like its predecessor, endured for about three centuries (960–1279).

II. SUNG GOLDEN AGE

The Sung emperors were much more passive in their external relations than their Han and T'ang predecessors. They did not begin with great campaigns reestablishing imperial frontiers in the heart of Eurasia. Instead the second Sung emperor merely tried to regain from nomad control the territory between Peking and the Great Wall. But he was disastrously defeated, and his successor gave up claim to this region. He even paid the nomads an annual "gift," which in fact was thinly veiled tribute. Thus the Sung never recovered the northeast territories in Manchuria, nor the northwest territories that provided access to the overland routes to the west.

This was a grave weakness for the Sung dynasty, leaving it vulnerable to nomadic invasions. The policy of paying "gifts" worked well for a century and a half, but disaster came when a Sung emperor made a rash attempt to recover the northeastern lands. When newcomers from north Manchuria defeated the ruling nomads in that region the emperor took advantage of what appeared to be an opportunity and sent his armies into Manchuria. Instead of easy victory they suffered a crushing defeat that was followed by massive invasion of north China. The Sung defenses crumpled and the dynasty was left with only the Yangtze valley in central China, and the lands to the south. Consequently the second half of the dynasty, from 1127 to 1279, is known as the Southern Sung; the first half, between 960 and 1127, is called the Northern Sung.

This dynasty was much berated by later Chinese historians because it failed at the outset to regain the outlying provinces and then suffered the loss of the entire northern half of the country. We cannot deny this criticism, but it is also true that in many respects Chinese civilization reached its height during the centuries of the T'ang and the Sung. This was particularly so in the field of culture. During these centuries the vast encyclopedias of Buddhist texts and Confucian *Classics* appeared as well as the comprehensive dynastic histories written by teams of scholars; the masterpieces of scores of great poets and artists; the art of calligraphy, depicted on scrolls prized as highly as paintings; the beautiful porcelain as thin as glass and almost as transparent; the priceless invention of printing that was utilized for the mass duplication and distribution of Buddhist scriptures; and the extraordinary advances in science and technology which are only now being adequately understood (see Chapter 9, section II).

In addition to its cultural attainments, the Sung period is noteworthy for a commercial revolution that was quite significant for all Eurasia. The roots are to be found in a marked increase in the productivity of China's economy. Steady technological improvements raised the output of the traditional industries. Agriculture likewise was stimulated by the introduction of a quickly maturing strain of rice that allowed two crops to be grown each season where only one had been possible before. Also new water-control projects undertaken by the Sung greatly expanded the acreage of irrigated paddy fields. Thus it is estimated that the rice crop doubled between the eleventh and twelfth centuries.

Increasing productivity made possible a corresponding increase in population, which in turn further stimulated production in circular fashion. The volume of trade also rose with the quickening tempo of economic activity. For the first time there appeared in China large cities that were primarily commercial rather than administrative centers.

Even more marked than this spurt in domestic trade was the increase in foreign trade. Considerable overseas commerce had been carried on since Han times, but during the T'ang, and more especially during the Sung, the volume of foreign trade far surpassed all previous records. The basis for this burgeoning trade was, of course, the unprecedented productivity of China's economy. Important also were the improvements in maritime technology, including the use of the compass, of an adjustable centerboard keel, and of cotton sails in place of bamboo slats. Finally overseas trade was stimulated by the initiative of Moslem merchants and mariners who were the great entrepreneurs in Asian seas at this period.

The end result was that for the first time the seaports rather than the old overland routes became China's principal contact with the outside world. Indicative of China's economic leadership at this time is the fact that its exports were mostly manufactured goods such as silk, porcelains, books, and paintings, while the imports were mostly raw materials such as spices, minerals, and horses. Finally it should be noted that during the Sung the Chinese themselves for the first time engaged in overseas trade on a large scale. They no longer depended on foreign intermediaries. In conclusion, China during the Sung was well on the way to becoming a great maritime power. But the all important fact, for world history as well as for Chinese, is that this potentiality was never realized. And, equally significant, this commercial revolution of the Sung era had none of the explosive repercussions on Chinese society that a corresponding commercial revolution had on Western society (see section IV of this chapter).

III. YÜAN MONGOL RULE

The rule of the Southern Sung, though confined to only half the country, was exceptionally peaceful and prosperous. Meanwhile north China was under the Chin, a people of Manchurian origin. About 1215 they appealed to the Southern Sung for help against the formidable Mongols who had driven them out of Peking. The Sung, not aware of the deadly power of the Mongols, supported them by sending infantry skilled in siege warfare and by 1234 the Chin were overwhelmed. The Sung emperor rashly attempted to secure north China for his own empire. The Mongols retaliated by promptly invading south China. The war dragged on for decades because the Mongols were preoccupied elsewhere, but the end came in 1279 when the last Sung ruler perished in a naval battle. A new Mongol dynasty that took the name Yüan now began its rule that was to last until 1368.

This was the first and only time that China was ruled by full nomads who had not already been partly Sinicized by earlier contact with the empire. The first reaction of the rude conquerors was to level the cities and to incorporate their new subjects into the traditional Mongol tribal society. But they soon learned that this was impossible and that a more lucrative alternative was feasible. They established an administrative apparatus essentially similar to that of their Chinese predecessors. At the same time they were able to preserve their identity because their nomadic background separated them from their subjects as regards language, customs, and laws. They also took care to employ many foreigners in their service in order to counterbalance the Chinese majority whom they did not trust. Marco Polo is the best known of these foreign-born bureaucrats, though most of them were Central-Asian Moslems.

Kublai Khan, who moved the Mongol capital from Karakorum to Peking and became essentially a Chinese emperor, dutifully performed the traditional Confucian imperial rites. Also he sought to appease the Confucian literati by exempting them from taxation, but they remained largely alienated. They resented the large number of foreigners that had turned their civil service into an international service. They also resented the Mongol toleration and patronage of various foreign religions, including Islam and Nestorian Christianity (see Chapter 11, section IV).

Because of its nature and relatively short duration, Mongol rule in China did not leave a deep imprint on the country. Perhaps the most lasting contribution was the selection of Peking as the capital. Situated in the north China plain on the routes leading westward to Central Asia and eastward to Manchuria, Peking has remained an important military, economic, and administrative center to the present day. Mongol rule also brought about a sharp rise in overland trade since China now was part of a huge empire encompassing most of Eurasia. Commerce was facilitated by the widespread use of paper money, which was introduced by the Sung but developed further by the Mongols. Marco Polo repeatedly expressed his astonishment at the use of paper money, as did a fellow Italian merchant in the following words:

> Whatever silver the merchants carry with them to Cathay the lord of Cathay takes from them and puts in his treasury and gives that paper money of theirs in exchange. . . . And with this money you can readily buy silk and whatever other merchandise you desire to buy, and all of the people of the country are bound to receive it, and you shall not pay a higher price for your goods because your money is of paper.[1]

The able Kublai Khan died in 1294 at the age of eighty and was succeeded by his equally able grandson, Timur. But Timur died young, and the following Khans were incompetent and debauched by palace life. Fratricidal conflicts broke out within the dynasty, and frequent flooding of the Yellow River produced widespread famine in north China. Rebellions broke out in most of the provinces, and only the rivalry amongst the rebel leaders enabled the Mongols to hold out as long as they did. Finally the turmoil was ended by an able commoner who, like the founder of the Han, rose through sheer ability, in a time of crisis and opportunity, to become the Son of Heaven. Thus the Chinese Ming dynasty was established in 1368 and remained in power to 1644.

IV. MING ETHNOCENTRISM AND WITHDRAWAL

Two dynasties, the Ming (1368–1644) and the Ch'ing (1644–1912), ruled China during the more than half-millennium between the overthrow of the Mongols and the advent of the republic. These centuries comprise one of the great eras of orderly government and social stability in human history. A main reason for this unusual durability was the complete primacy of a new Confucian metaphysics known as *Neo-Confucianism*. This renaissance of Confucian thought took place mostly during the time of troubles following the collapse of the T'ang dynasty, when the needs of the age clearly called for something more than the mere memorization of Confucian *Classics*. Accordingly a number of scholars undertook a searching reappraisal of the problems of man and of the universe.

A leader in this undertaking was Chu Hsi (1129–1200), who in his youth had studied both Buddhism and Taoism. Satisfied with neither, he turned to the Confucian *Classics*, and with his remarkable talent for synthesis he worked out an interpretation that combined elements of Buddhism and Taoism with Confucianism and that was more satisfying and relevant for his time. His approach was essentially that of the empirical rationalist. He taught that the universe is governed by natural law, which should be understood and respected. He also believed in the goodness of humanity-and in its ability to become more perfect. He compared human kind to a mirror covered with dust which, if cleaned, will be as bright as ever. Evil, therefore, was the result of neglect and of defective education, and hence it could be corrected.

Chu Hsi's influence in the Confucian world was comparable to that of Thomas Aquinas in Western Christendom. Just as Aquinas soon was to weave Aristotle and St. Paul into the official scholastic philosophy, so Chu Hsi now integrated contemporary Chinese thought into Neo-Confucianism. And by his very comprehensive and persuasive ideas Chu Hsi, like Aquinas, discouraged further philosophical development. This was particularly true during the Ming period when, as a reaction against the preceding foreign Mongol domination, there was a pronounced ethnocentrism and a looking backward to past traditions. In such an atmosphere, Chu Hsi came to be regarded as the absolute and final authority. "Ever since the time of the philosopher Chu," declared a Ming scholar, "the Truth has been made manifest to the world. No more writing is needed: what is left to us is practice."[2]

Since the Confucian *Classics,* with Chu Hsi's commentaries, became the basis of the civil service examinations, this Neo-Confucianism became the official orthodox view of the empire until the late nineteenth century. Its effect was to provide the growing social rigidity with an intellectual reason for its existence. It contributed fundamentally to the unique and long-lasting continuity of Chinese civilization, but the cost was stultifying conformity that squashed all originality or new ideas from the outside.

Chinese society owed its stability not only to Neo-Confucianism but also to the entrenched power of the so-called gentry ruling class, a power based on its combined possession of land and office in an agrarian-based bureaucratic empire. As landlords and as money lenders the gentry dominated the economic life of the villages and towns. Shortage of land and of capital enabled them to impose extortionate rents and interest rates. Frequent natural disasters bankrupted people with mortgages, and they virtually became

ROOTS OF CHINESE STABILITY

Foreign observers invariably were impressed by the antiquity and stability of Chinese civilization. T. T. Meadows, a British consular officer who served in China in the mid-nineteenth century, gave the following explanation based on first-hand observation.*

The real causes of the unequalled duration and constant increase of the Chinese people, as one and the same nation, . . . consist of *three doctrines,* together with an *institution.* . . . The doctrines are

I. *That the nation must be governed by moral agency in preference to physical force.*

II. *That the services of the wisest and ablest men in the nation are indispensable to its good government.*

III. *That the people have the right to depose a sovereign who, either from active wickedness or vicious indulgence, gives cause to oppressive and tyrannical rule.*

The institution is
The system of public service competitive examinations. . . .
The institution of Public Service Examinations (which have long been strictly competitive) is *the* cause of the continued duration of the Chinese nation: it is that which preserves the other causes and gives efficacy to their operation. By it all parents throughout the country, who can compass the means, are induced to impart to their sons an intimate knowledge of the literature which contains the three doctrines above cited, together with many others conducive to a high mental cultivation. By it all the ability of the country is enlisted on the side of that Government which takes care to preserve it in purity. By it, with its impartiality, the poorest man in the country is constrained to say, that if his lot in life is a low one it is so in virtue of the "will of Heaven," and that no unjust barriers created by his fellow men prevent him from elevating himself. . . .

The normal Chinese government is essentially based on moral force: it is not a despotism. A military and police is maintained sufficient to crush merely factious risings, but totally inadequate, both in numbers and in nature, to put down a disgusted and indignant people. But though no despotism, this same government is in form and machinery a pure autocracy. In his district the magistrate is absolute; in his province, the governor; in the empire, the Emperor. The Chinese people have no right of legislation, they have no right of self-taxation, they have not the power of voting out their rulers or of limiting or stopping supplies. *They have therefore the right of rebellion.* Rebellion is in China the old, often exercised, legitimate, and constitutional means of stopping arbitrary and vicious legislation and administration.

* T. T. Meadows, *The Chinese and Their Rebellions* (London: Smith, Elder, 1856), pp. 23, 24, 401–403.

serfs under contract to local gentry families. It was common for these families by late Ming times to have several thousand indentured peasant households of this sort.

The gentry also were degree holders; indeed this is what the Chinese term for "gentry" literally means. Landowning was almost a necessity for financing the years of study necessary to become a degree holder and, hence, to be eligible for a post in the bureaucracy. Thus the association between the local gentry and the imperial bureaucracy was intimate and mutually supporting. Frequently the government official who appeared at his provincial post found the native dialect quite incomprehensible, so he was completely dependent on the local gentry for orientation and guidance.

Ming and Ch'ing China were ruled by the bureaucracy and the gentry together, if a meaningful distinction can be made between the two. Both the imperial establishment and the local gentry were interested in preserving the mutually beneficial status quo, and they cooperated to that end. Whereas earlier dynasties occasionally had attempted to force through land redistribution and other such reforms, the Ming and the Ch'ing carefully avoided any challenges to the gentry's control of the countryside.

By contrast, it is revealing and significant that the Ming government took the initiative in controlling and repressing the merchant class. This was a basic and most meaningful difference between the Western and Chinese societies. In the West, as we shall note in the following chapter, the bourgeoisie from the start enjoyed considerable autonomy and was able to increase it with the passage of time. In China there was a corresponding merchant class which during the Sung enjoyed a real commercial revolution. Furthermore China made most of the basic technological inventions of medieval times. Yet the commercial revolution and the technological advances together were not enough to cause the revolutionary repercussions in China that completely transformed society in the West. The basic reason for this, as noted in Chapter 8, section V, was the continuity of Chinese history—the fact that the Han dynasty was continued in essentials by the Sui, and the Sui in turn by the T'ang and the Sung, and so on in unbroken succession until the end of the imperial history in 1912. Thus the traditional bureaucracy-gentry ruling establishment, propped up by the ideas of Neo-Confucianism, was able to absorb and blunt the effects of the new technology and of economic growth. But in the West, Rome came to an end with no imperial successor. Instead, a new pluralistic civilization emerged in which gunpowder, the compass, the printing press, and the oceangoing ship were not muffled but rather exploited to their full potential with explosive consequences, first for Europe, and then for the entire world, including China.

Explosive repercussions were impossible in China because the imperial establishment there was too enveloping and restricting. For example, Chinese merchants and industrialists customarily organized themselves into local guilds headed by chiefs. But guild chiefs were certified by the government which held them responsible for the conduct of individual members. Boat traders were organized under harbor chiefs who were also responsible to the government. More important were the government monopolies in the production and distribution of many commodities that the court and the administration consumed, including arms, textiles, pottery, leather goods, apparel, and wine. The government also completely controlled the production and distribution of basic commodities such as salt and iron that were necessities for the entire population. Such restraints deprived Chinese merchants of the opportunity for free enterprise and restricted economic growth. The restraints also promoted official corruption, for members of the imperial court used their privileged positions to manipulate the state monopolies for personal gain.

Another example of the restrictive, inward-looking policies of China's ruling establishment was its active opposition to overseas enterprise. Chinese emigrants had trickled down to Southeast Asia before the arrival of the Europeans. Probably at no time were there as many Spaniards as Chinese in the Philippines. In 1603, thirty-two years after the founding of Manila as a Spanish settlement, the Chinese population there was about 20,000, compared with perhaps 1000 Spaniards. And these Chinese virtually controlled the economic life of the settlement and were extending their control to the other islands of the archipelago. When in that year, 1603, the Manila Chinese suffered one of the massacres which they and their compatriots in Southeast Asia have periodically endured to the present day, an official of the nearby mainland province of Fukien condoned the massacre and denounced all overseas Chinese as deserters of the tombs of their ancestors and men who were unworthy of the emperor's concern. Likewise an imperial edict of 1712 forbade Chinese to trade and reside in Southeast Asia. Five years later another edict allowed those already abroad to come home without fear of punishment, and in 1729 still another edict set a deadline after which those overseas could not be allowed to return. What a striking contrast between this Chinese policy and that of the West. The Western states would soon be actively promoting overseas settlements and trading companies and would be ready to take up arms against any threats to these enterprises.

The bizarre history of the early fifteenth-century Ming voyages provides the most dramatic example of the negative official Chinese attitude toward overseas activities. These voyages had an astonishing range and showed a technological superiority that proved conclusively China's world leadership in maritime undertakings. Then came the imperial order forbidding further overseas expeditions and the immediate enforcement of that order (see Chapter 9, section I).

Although the precise motives behind this edict are unknown, the significant fact is that it was possible to issue it only because Chinese merchants lacked the political power and social status of their Western counterparts. This fundamental difference in institutional structure and outward-thrusting dynamism deflected Chinese energies inward at this fateful turning point in world history, and it left the oceans of the globe open to Western enterprise. The inevitable result was the eclipse within a few centuries of the great ''Celestial Kingdom.'' The barbarians of the West now came to the fore.

V. CHINESE CIVILIZATION IN JAPAN

Since the Chinese civilization and Chinese empires persisted in unbroken continuity to modern times, they have dominated East Asia in a way that no Western country has dominated the West. Consequently there did not develop in East Asia the political and cultural diversity that has characterized the West since the fall of Rome. The only exception has been in the steppes and deserts of the far north and west, where agriculture is climatically impossible and where the nomads accordingly developed a distinctive, non-Chinese, pastoral way of life. By contrast, in the neighboring Vietnamese, Korean, and Japanese lands, there was no climatic obstacle to the development of agriculture and hence to the spread of Chinese civilization. Of these three lands, Japan was able to remain the most independent of the Chinese colossus, both politically and culturally, and hence it played a correspondingly more significant role in both East Asian and world history. The remainder of this chapter, therefore, will concentrate on the evolution of Japan to the eve of the Western penetration.

Japanese history has been shaped to a considerable degree by the influence of geographic location. In this respect there is a close parallel with the British Isles at the other end of the Eurasian landmass. The Japanese islands, however, are more isolated than the British Isles; 115 miles separate them from the mainland, compared with the 21-mile width of the English Channel. Thus before their defeat by the United States, the Japanese had been seriously threatened by foreign invasion only in the thirteenth century by the Mongols. The Japanese, therefore, have been close enough to the mainland to benefit from the great Chinese civilization, but distant enough to be able to select and reject as they wished. In fact, the Japanese have been unusually sensitive and alert to what they have imported from abroad. Although popularly regarded as a nation of borrowers, they have independently evolved, because of their isolation, a larger proportion of their own culture than have any other people of comparable numbers and level of development.

The Japanese are basically a Mongoloid people who migrated from Northeast Asia, but the hairy Caucasoid Ainu who originally inhabited their islands contributed to their racial composition. Malayan and Polynesian migrants from the south probably did also. Early Japan was organized into a large number of clans, each ruled by a hereditary priest-chieftain. Toward the end of the first century after Christ, the Yamato clan established a loose political and religious domination over the others. Its chief was the emperor, and its clan god was made the national god.

This clan organization was undermined by the importation of Chinese civilization, which began on a large scale in the sixth century. Buddhism, introduced from Korea, was the medium for cultural change, playing the same role here as Christianity did in Europe among the Germans and Slavs. Students, teachers, craftsmen, and monks crossed over from the mainland, bringing with them a new way of life as well as a new religion. More went to the "Celestial Kingdom" and returned as ardent converts. The forces for change produced the Taika Reform, which began in 645 and sought to make Japan into a centralized state on the model of T'ang dynasty China. In accordance with the Chinese model, the country was divided into provinces and districts ruled by governors and magistrates who received their power from the emperor and his council of state. Also, all land was nationalized in the name of the emperor and given to peasant households. The new owner-cultivators were responsible for paying to the central government a land tax in the form of rice and a labor tax that sometimes included military service.

These and other changes were designed to strengthen imperial authority, and they did so in comparison with the earlier clan structure. But in practice, the Japanese emperor was far from being the undisputed head of a highly centralized state. The powerful hereditary aristocracy forced certain changes in this Chinese-type administration that finally brought about its downfall. Although officials supposedly were appointed, as in China, on the basis of merit through examination, actually the old aristocracy succeeded in obtaining positions of status and power. Likewise, they kept many of their large land-holdings, which were usually tax exempt and became manors outside the governmental administrative system. During this period the Fujiwara family perfected the *dyarchy,* or dual system of government. They did the actual work of ruling, furnishing the consorts for the emperor, and filling the high civil and military posts. Meanwhile, the emperor passed his life in luxurious seclusion, not bothered by affairs of state or contacts with common men. His chief responsibility was to guarantee that his dynasty would continue forever. This dyarchical system of government, which had no parallel in China, remained the pattern in Japan until the country was opened up by the Europeans in the nineteenth century.

In cultural matters there was the same adaptation of Chinese models. The Japanese borrowed Chinese ideographs but developed their own system of writing. They borrowed Confucianism but modified its ethics and changed its political doctrines to suit their social structure. They accepted Buddhism but adapted it to satisfy their own spiritual needs, while keeping their native Shintoism. They built new imperial capitals, first at Nara and then at Kyoto, that were modeled after the T'ang capital, Ch'ang-an. But there was no mistaking the Japanese quality of the temples, pavilions, shrines, and gardens. The imperial court became the center of highly developed intellectual and artistic activity. Court life is delightfully described in Lady Murasaki's famous eleventh-century novel, *The Tale of Genii.* But this novel also reflects a society grown effeminate and devoted almost exclusively to aesthetic and sensual pleasures. This degeneration, which worsened in the next century, contributed to the coming of the new age of feudalism, when political power shifted from the imperial court to virile rural warriors.

VI. JAPANESE FEUDALISM

The Chinese system of imperial organization introduced by the Taika Reform of 645 worked effectively for a long period. By the twelfth century, however, it had been undermined and replaced by a Japanese variety of feudalism. One reason was the tendency of provincial governors, who were too fond of the entertainments of Kyoto, to give their powers and responsibilities to local subordinates. Another was that powerful local families and Buddhist communities were always hungry for land and often able to seize it by force. They were willing to bring new land under cultivation so long as the incentive of tax exemption was maintained. These trends reduced the amount of tax-paying land, which meant an increased tax load for the peasant owner-cultivators. They in turn either fled to the northern frontier areas where the Ainu were being pushed back by force of arms, or else commended themselves and their lands to lords of manors. This freed them of taxes and provided them with protection, but at the cost of becoming serfs. The net result of this process was that by the end of the twelfth century, tax-paying land amounted to 10 percent or less of the total cultivated area, and local power had been taken over by the new rural aristocracy.

At the same time, this aristocracy had become the dominant military force because of the disintegration of the imperial armed forces. The Taika Reform had made all males between the ages of twenty and sixty subject to military service. But the conscripts were required to furnish their own weapons and food and were given no relief from the regular tax burden. This arrangement proved unworkable and was abandoned in 739. Government military posts usually were filled by effeminate court aristocrats. As a result, the campaigns against the Ainu were fought by the rural aristocrats. They became mounted warriors and gradually increased their military effectiveness until they completely overshadowed the imperial forces. A feudal relationship now developed between these rural lords and their retainers, or samurai (literally, "one who serves"). This relationship was based on an idealized ethic that was known as bushido, or "way of the warrior." The samurai enjoyed special legal and ceremonial rights, and in return they were expected to give unquestioning service to their lords.

By the twelfth century, Japan was controlled by competing groups of feudal lords. For some time the Fujiwara were able to maintain a balance of power by throwing what strength they had on one side or another. In the end, one of these lords, Minamoto Yoritomo, emerged victorious. In 1192 the emperor commissioned him *Seii-Tai-Shogun* (Barbarian-Subduing-Generalissimo), with the right to name his own successor. As Shogun, Yoritomo was commander-in-chief of all the military forces and was responsible for the internal and external defense of the realm. From his headquarters at Kamakura, Yoritomo controlled the country in the name of the emperor, who continued to remain in seclusion in Kyoto. It was during this Kamakura Shogunate that the Mongols made their two attempts to invade Japan, in 1274 and 1281. On both occasions the Mongols were able to land, were fiercely resisted by the Japanese, and then were scattered by great storms that destroyed the invading forces. The Japanese, believing they were saved by the intervention of the gods, called these storms "divine winds," or kamikaze.

In 1333 the Kamakura Shogunate was brought to an end, largely as a result of intrigues at the imperial court as well as growing disaffection among the warrior class. The Ashikaga family now obtained the title of Shogun, but their authority never extended far beyond the capital of Kyoto. In the rest of Japan, local lords struggled to gain control of as much land as possible. The outcome was the rise of great territorial magnates known as *daimyo* (''great name''). At the beginning of the sixteenth century there were several hundred of these daimyo, each seeking to attain hegemony over all Japan.

VII. JAPAN'S WITHDRAWAL AND ISOLATION

The period of daimyo control was one of rapid economic growth, with important repercussions for Japanese society. Important technological advances were made in agriculture as well as in handicrafts. Production per acre apparently doubled or even tripled in some parts of the country. The increased productivity stimulated more trade and a shift from a barter to a money economy. Towns gradually developed in the fifteenth and sixteenth centuries at strategic crossroads or coastal harbors or major temples. In these towns appeared the Japanese guilds, or za, which, like their Western counterparts, sought to gain monopoly rights in the production or transportation of certain goods, or in the exercise of certain trades or professions. They obtained these monopoly rights by paying fees to certain local authorities, thereby gaining greater freedom and higher status for their members.

Foreign and domestic trade quickened with the rising productivity of the Japanese economy. As early as the twelfth century enterprising Japanese had crossed overseas to Korea and then to China, prepared both for trade and for piracy. Gradually they extended their operations, so that by the late fourteenth century these pirate-traders were active throughout Southeast Asia. Japanese settlers and soldiers of fortune also were widely scattered, especially in Indochina, Siam, and the Philippines.

These socioeconomic developments began to undermine feudalism in Japan, as they had done earlier under similar circumstances in the West. If this trend had continued without interruption, Japan presumably would have followed the West European example and developed into a modern unified nation-state with an overseas empire. But Japan did not do so; instead it withdrew into seclusion.

A prime reason for this appears to have been the penetration of the Western powers into the waters of Southeast and East Asia. This blocked the natural course of Japanese expansionism. If the Westerners had not appeared, the Japanese probably would have won footholds in Formosa and in various parts of Southeast Asia. But now the Japanese were alarmed by the obvious superiority of Western military technology on the seas, as well as by the surprising effectiveness of Western missionaries on the home islands. Their response was to withdraw into the almost complete seclusion adopted in the early seventeenth century by the Tokugawa Shogunate.

All missionaries were forced to leave and their converts required to renounce their faith. Eventually all foreigners had to depart, with the exception of a few Chinese and Dutch who were allowed to trade under restricted conditions on the Deshima islet in Nagasaki harbor. In addition, Japanese subjects were forbidden to go abroad on penalty of death. Thus began over two centuries of seclusion for Japan.

The end result, then, was not a modern expansionist nation-state. Rather, Japanese feudalism was preserved and shielded from outside influences by the Tokugawa walls of seclusion. The cost for Japan, as for China, was institutional rigidity and obsolescence. Yet there was a fundamental difference between the two countries. Japan was not saddled with a monolithic, overpowering imperial structure as was the case in China. Rather the Tokugawas had merely papered over the cracks, so that when the West intruded in the nineteenth century, Japan, unlike China, was able to respond positively and creatively.

SUGGESTED READING

On China, see bibliography for Chapter 7 and also the following studies: E. Balazs, *Chinese Civilization and Bureaucracy* (Yale University Press, 1964); W. Bingham, *The Founding of the T'ang Dynasty* (Waverly Press, 1941); M. Elvin, *The Pattern of the Chinese Past* (Stanford University Press, 1973); C. O. Hucker, *The Traditional Chinese State in Ming Times, 1368-1644* (University of Arizona Press, 1961).

On Japan, there are the following: D. Keene, *Japanese Literature: An Introduction for Western Readers* (Grove Press, 1955); and his *Anthology of Japanese Literature from the Earliest Era to the Mid-Nineteenth Century,* 2 vols. (Grove Press, 1955); E. O. Reischauer, *Japan Past and Present,* rev. ed. (Knopf, 1953); G. B. Sansom, *Japan: A Short Cultural History,* rev. ed. (Appleton, 1944), and the same author's three-volume *A History of Japan* (Stanford University Press, 1958-64); R. Tsunoda, et al., *Sources of the Japanese Tradition* (Columbia University Press, 1958).

The chief glory of the later
Middle Ages was not its
cathedrals or its epics or its
scholasticism: it was the building
for the first time in history of a
complex civilization which rested
not on the backs of sweating
slaves or coolies but primarily on
non-human power.

Lynn White, Jr.

chapter 14

Revolutionary Western Civilization: Technological And Economic Growth

"We should note the force, effect, and consequences of inventions which are nowhere more conspicuous than in those three which were unknown to the ancients, namely, printing, gunpowder, and the compass. For these three have changed the appearance and state of the whole world."[1] This statement by the British philosopher-scientist Francis Bacon (1561–1626) is especially significant because all three of the inventions that he so wisely selected originated in China. Yet they had little effect on that country in comparison with their explosive repercussions in the West. Chinese civilization was too deeply rooted and Chinese imperial organization too all-embracing to allow such inventions to disrupt traditional institutions and practices. Thus printing was used to disseminate old ideas rather than new; gunpowder reinforced the position of the emperor rather than of emerging national monarchs; and the compass, despite the remarkable expeditions of Cheng Ho, was not used for world trade and exploration and empire building like the Westerners.

The root of this fateful difference is to be found in the unique characteristics of the new Western civilization—pluralistic, adaptable, and free of the shackles of tradition that bound all the other Eurasian civilizations. The new civilization brought about a historic change, not only in the West, but also, as Bacon foresaw, in the entire globe as it came under the influence of the revolutionary new society.

I. PLURALISM IN THE WEST

"In order to escape the evils which they saw coming, the people divided themselves into three parts. One was to pray God; for trading and ploughing the second; and later, to guard these two parts from wrongs and injuries, knights were created."[2] This analysis by the secretary of Philip VI of France describes simply but accurately the basic division of medieval Western society into priests, workers, and warriors. Although these three classes were to be found in all Eurasian civilizations, their status and interrelationships were unique in the West because of the disintegration of the Roman Empire and the failure to reconstruct the empire. Precisely how the classes functioned under these circumstances will be considered now in relation to the three institutions they represented: feudalism, manorialism, and the church.

Feudalism was a system of government in which those who possessed landed estates also possessed political power. State authority was replaced by contractual agreements between lords and vassals. Feudalism appeared when the German kings who had taken over Roman imperial authority lacked the funds to maintain a bureaucracy, a judiciary, and armed forces. Their only alternative was to grant estates as reward for service. But the recipients, or vassals, tended to rule them as private realms. Charlemagne was strong enough to exact and enforce oaths of loyalty from his vassals. But under his weak successors political power shifted to the vassals, and their estates or *fiefs* became virtually private property. These powerful lords in turn subdivided their holdings into lesser fiefs which they allocated to followers that were dependent on them rather than on the king. The feudal contract between these lords and vassals specified certain mutual obligations. The most important were that the lord should provide protection as well as the estate, while the vassal rendered military service for as long a time each year as local custom required—usually about forty days.

This process of feudalization proceeded rapidly within each of the feudal kingdoms that took form following the disintegration of Charlemagne's empire. Since the legal justification for the fiefs of the great lords was supposed to come from royal authority, the lords were careful to select a suitable king even though they had no intention of respecting his sovereignty. But as Western Europe settled down after 1000 and the foreign invasions ceased, the rulers gradually were able to assert their feudal rights and to begin the building of strong monarchies. The ensuing struggle between kings and nobles was the essence of Western political history during the following centuries.

Just as feudalism emerged when large-scale political organization collapsed, so manorialism emerged with the collapse of large-scale economic organization. Consequently the manor was a self-sufficient village that was worked by serfs who were not free to leave, and who by dint of their labor supported a hierarchy of lay and clerical lords. The size of the manor varied considerably, its inhabitants numbering in the scores or hundreds. Unlike slaves, serfs had recognized rights as well as responsibilities. They were entitled to protection, each family was assured a plot for the support of itself, and serfs enjoyed many religious holidays and harvest festivals that gave them relief from toil. In return they were required to till strips of land in the cultivated fields that were reserved for the lord, to perform other domestic and farm chores for the lord, and to give him a portion of any income from any source.

The *manor* had to fill almost all its own needs because of the virtual disappearance of long-distance trade, of centralized handicraft production, of imperial currencies, and the like. Despite, or perhaps because of, this self-sufficiency, manorial technology was not at all primitive compared to that of Roman times. When the economy of the empire disintegrated, there was a loss of luxury crafts, irrigation works, aqueducts, and road systems. But the self-sufficient villages, just because they were self-sufficient, had no need for imperial organization. They functioned, and with steadily improving efficiency, on a local, village-to-village basis. The manors kept and improved the mills and smithies and used more iron than ever before, since it could be produced locally. Thus agricultural technology in the medieval West, as will be noted in section III of this chapter, advanced substantially beyond Greco-Roman standards; and had far-reaching effects on all aspects of life.

Turning to the church, we find a similarly paradoxical development: that is, the pope emerged with more power precisely because of the fall of Rome. He did not have to fight against imperial domination as did the bishops of Constantinople, Alexandria, and Antioch who had to contend with the dictates of the Byzantine emperor. When one of these emperors sought to control the church in the West, Pope Gelasius (492–496) sent him a famous letter in which he asserted that "bishops, not the secular power, should be responsible for the administration of the church." Furthermore, the Byzantine emperors were distracted by the attacks of the Moslems and of other enemies. The popes were left free to strengthen their position in the West, and they did this in two ways. First, they made an alliance with the rising Franks, which culminated in the crowning of Charlemagne by Pope Leo III in 800. Secondly, the Papacy sent out missions to convert the pagans in Northern Europe. They succeeded in organizing new churches which accepted the pope's authority—churches such as the English in 597, the Lombard and Frisian in the seventh century, and the German in the eighth.

Such, then, were the components of the new pluralistic society emerging in the West: an independent church instead of dictation by the emperor; feudal kings and lords in place of imperial authority; autonomous manors working individually to tame the wilderness instead of the slave plantations of Roman times; and, before long, a rising merchant class operating effectively from its urban bases against nobles, prelates, and ultimately, against monarchs. How this society, alone in all Eurasia, evolved and adapted during the half-millennium after 1000 and how it eventually developed the strength and dynamism for overseas expansion is the subject of the following sections.

II. GEOGRAPHIC BACKGROUND

Geographic considerations are a significant factor in Europe's thrust forward ahead of other regions during the medieval period. One of these considerations was an advantageous location. Being on the western tip of the Eurasian landmass, Europe escaped most of the great invasions after the year 1000. The importance of the remote location of Western Europe is evident when we look at events in the rest of Eurasia—the disastrous Mongol conquest of Russia in the thirteenth century, the Ottoman Turkish conquest of the Balkan peninsula in the fifteenth and sixteenth centuries, and the repeated Berber assaults in North Africa. Spared such ravages, Western Europe certainly had a substantial advantage over the more vulnerable regions to the east.

Equally important were Europe's exceptionally good natural resources. A large part of Northern Europe is a great plain that begins at the western end of the Pyrenees and flares out to the north and east, becoming wider as it progresses until eventually it extends uninterruptedly from the Black Sea to the Baltic. The prevailing westerly winds from the Atlantic sweep unhindered over these plains across all Europe and deep into Russia. Hence Europe north of the Mediterranean basin enjoys a relatively moderate climate and constant rainfall which along with fertile soils provide an ideal combination for productive agriculture. Rivers usually run ice free and full, providing convenient means of transportation and communication. The deeply indented coastline gives inland regions relatively easy access to coastal outlets. Some plateaus and mountain ranges interrupt the sweep of the great plains, but they are not so high or massive that they interfere seriously with the transportation. Rather these mountains are an asset, being rich in minerals that historically have been quite important.

These natural resources had, of course, always been available, but they could not be effectively exploited until a certain level of technological competence had been reached. This need to have adequate skills has existed everywhere and at all times. The United States, for example, has profited tremendously during the past century from the vast iron-ore deposits in the Mesabi Range of northern Minnesota. But for thousands of years Indians had fished and hunted in that area without exploiting the ore, or even being aware of its existence. The same is true currently of the rich oil fields now being tapped in the Middle East, in northern Alaska, and on various ocean floors. And so it was in medieval Western Europe where, for the first time, advancing technology made it possible to exploit local resources effectively. The resulting increase in productivity had profound effects, including the shift of the economic and political center of Europe northward from its traditional site in the Mediterranean basin.

III. TECHNOLOGICAL PROGRESS

More technological progress was made in medieval Western Europe than had been made during the entire history of classical Greece and Rome. One reason for this was the absence of slavery, a practice that tended to inhibit new technology. Another was that the frontier conditions that existed in many areas called for labor-saving devices. The manorial system of the medieval West also contributed to technological progress. The social scale under this system ranged not from a "divine" emperor to a subhuman slave, but from a serf with very definite rights and duties to a manorial lord who kept in touch with his serfs and had some real knowledge of the processes of production. Accordingly manual labor acquired a status and respect that were unknown in the old slave-based civilizations.

Finally technology in the West was stimulated by the humanitarian ethic of Christianity, which itself began as a revolt against the inhumanity of the old imperial society. The monks in the monasteries insisted that manual labor was part of spiritual life. Or, as they put it, "to work is to pray"—*laborare est orare.* These monks have gone down in history as the first intellectuals to get dirt under their fingernails. They were the first to combine brainpower and sweat, and, in doing so, they aided technological advance. In their monasteries they pushed the frontiers of settlement into the forests of Northern and Eastern Europe, and they also introduced advanced methods of agriculture. It was not accidental that it was a friar, Roger Bacon, who in the thirteenth century foresaw many of the technological achievements of the future.

Machines may be made by which the largest ships, with only one man steering them, will move faster than if they were filled with rowers; wagons may be built which will move with unbelievable speed and without the aid of beasts; flying machines can be constructed in which a man may beat the air with mechanical wings like a bird . . . ; machines will make it possible for men to go to the bottom of the rivers. . . .[3]

The specific technological achievements of the West included basic inventions in the primary occupation of agriculture. One was the ''three-field'' rotation system of farming, which was gradually adopted from the eighth century onward and which raised productivity, since only a third of the land lay fallow at any one time instead of the half left by the former ''two-field'' system. Another was the development of a heavy wheeled plow with a sharp iron point that made possible the cultivation of the rich but heavy soils of Central and Northern Europe. More effective use of horsepower also aided agriculture. The invention of a new type of collar enabled the horse to pull without choking, so its pulling capacity increased four to five times. Hence the horse, fast and efficient compared to the ox that had formerly been used, became an essential source of power in farming operations. The invention of horseshoes was also significant because it increased the usefulness of the horse for hauling as well as for plowing.

Finally, note should be made of the all-important water-mill and wind-mill. Both of these were known in Greco-Roman times but little used because of the abundance of slave labor and the scarcity of streams dependable the year around. These obstacles were absent in the northern lands so the mill and the miller soon were to be found in almost every manor. And whereas the water wheel had been employed in the Mediterranean basin as a specialized device for grinding grain, in the course of the Middle Ages it was developed into a generalized prime mover. Thus water power came to be used for forge hammers and forge bellows, for saw-mills and lathes, and for fulling mills making cloth, pulping mills making paper, and stamping mills crushing ore. Indeed 5000 mills were listed in England's *Domesday Book* of 1086. This represented one for every fifty households, certainly enough to affect living standards substantially.

IV. DEVELOPING ECONOMY

Technological advance was matched by corresponding economic advance. There was steady economic growth from 900 to 1300. Then came the fourteenth-century slump, brought on by a combination of factors: first, there was a series of crop failures and famines, especially during 1315 and 1316; then came the Black Death, which carried off between one-third and two-thirds of the urban populations when it first struck in 1349, and which recurred periodically thereafter for generations; finally there were the Hundred Years' War between England and France, and other conflicts in Germany and Italy. Shortly after 1400, however, a revival set in, and the trend from then on was generally upward.

Overall economic progress naturally was related to the technological advances which stimulated productivity in agriculture and handicrafts. Complete relief from foreign invasion during these centuries also contributed to economic growth. Also there was a population increase of about 50 percent between the tenth and fourteenth centuries. This rate of increase seems insignificant in the present age of global population explosion, but it was unmatched at the time in any world area of the same size. The demographic spurt made it necessary to improve agriculture to support the growth of population. And the increased food supply in turn made further population increase possible.

Europe's economic development was evident in all fields. New mining methods led to rising output of salt, silver, lead, zinc, copper, tin, and iron ore in Central and Northern Europe. Likewise the rich timber and naval stores of Britain, Scandinavia, and the Baltic now were exploited more extensively than ever before. The same was true of the northern fisheries, particularly the cod of Iceland and Norway, and the herring of the Baltic. Most important, of course was the rising productivity in agriculture in which most of the population was engaged. Peasants first began to cultivate the wastelands around their own villages, of which there was plenty because in the twelfth century only about half the land of France, a third of the land of Germany, and a fifth of the land of England was under cultivation. Peasants not only cultivated unused lands that were nearby, but with population growth they emigrated to the vast underpopulated frontier regions. Just as the United States had its westward movement to the Pacific Ocean, so Europe had its eastward movement to the Russian border. By 1350 in Silesia, for example, there were 1500 new settlements farmed by 15,000 to 200,000 colonists. Not only were there German colonists moving beyond the Elbe at the expense of the Slavic and Baltic peoples of Eastern Europe, but other colonists were pushing into Moslem Spain, while Anglo-Saxon colonists were advancing into the Celtic lands of Wales, Scotland, and Ireland.

The combination of population increase and rising output in agriculture, mining, fishing, and forestry stimulated a corresponding growth of commerce and of cities. In the tenth century, merchants were to be found in Europe, but they traded mostly in luxuries. By the fourteenth century, however, commerce had advanced from the periphery to the center of everyday life. Goods exchanged included raw wool from England, woolen cloth from Flanders made from English wool, iron and timber from Germany, furs from Slavic areas, leather and steel from Spain, and luxury goods from the east. Although this commerce never engaged more than a small minority of the total population, nevertheless its great expansion in late medieval times had important repercussions for the whole society. Towns slowly appeared, starting out as centers of local trade and local administration. The lead was taken in Italy where the inhabitants of such centers as Venice, Amalfi, and Naples were cut off from their hinterland by the Lombard invaders and so took to the sea for a living. Later other cities appeared along inland trade routes and along the Baltic coast. The great fairs that developed along the trade routes were also important for the distribution of goods. The most outstanding of the fairs were held in the county of Champagne, located strategically equidistant from Flanders, Italy, and Germany.

RISE OF COMMERCE AND OF TOWNS

Medieval technological progress increased productivity and left a growing surplus for commerce. Hence the rise of trading centers or towns. The following contemporary description of twelfth-century London reflects the vigorous life of that city and the pride of its citizens.*

Among the noble and celebrated cities of the world that of London, the capital of the kingdom of the English, is one which extends its glory farther than all the others and sends its wealth and merchandise more widely into distant lands. Higher than all the rest does it lift its head. It is happy in the healthiness of its air; in its observance of Christian practice; in the strength of its fortifications; in its natural situation; in the honour of its citizens; and in the modesty of its matrons. It is cheerful in its sports, and the fruitful mother of noble men. . . .

Everywhere outside the houses of those living in the suburbs, and adjacent to them, are the spacious and beautiful gardens of the citizens, and these are planted with trees. Also there are on the north side pastures and pleasant meadow lands through which flow streams wherein the turning of mill-wheels makes a cheerful sound. Very near lies a great forest with woodland pastures in which there are the lairs of wild animals: stags, fallow deer, wild boars and bulls. The tilled lands of the city are not of barren gravel, but fat Asian plains that yield luxuriant crops and fill the tillers' barns with the sheaves of Ceres....

Immediately outside one of the gates there is a field which is smooth both in fact and in name. On every sixth day of the week, unless it be a major feast-day, there takes place there a famous exhibition of fine horses for sale. Earls, barons and knights, who are in the town, and many citizens come out to see or to buy. It is pleasant to see the high-stepping palfreys with their gleaming coats, as they go through their paces, putting down their feet alternately on one side together. Next, one can see the horses suitable for esquires, moving faster though less smoothly, lifting and setting down, as it were, the opposite fore and hind feet: here are colts of fine breed, but not yet accustomed to the bit, stepping high with jaunty tread; there are the sumpter-horses, powerful and spirited; and after them there are the war-horses, costly, elegant of form, noble of stature, with ears quickly tremulous, necks raised and large haunches....

By themselves in another part of the field stand the goods of the countryfolk: implements of husbandry, swine with long flanks, cows with full udders, oxen of immense size, and woolly sheep. There also stand the mares fit for plough, some big with foal, and others with brisk young colts closely following them.

To this city from every nation under heaven merchants delight to bring their trade by sea. The Arabian sends gold; the Sabaean spice and incense. The Scythian brings arms, and from the rich, fat lands of Babylon comes oil of palms. The Nile sends precious stones; the men of Norway and Russia, furs and sables; nor is China absent with purple silk. The Gauls come with their wines....

I do not think there is a city with a better record for church-going, doing honour to God's ordinances, keeping feast-days, giving alms and hospitality to strangers, confirming betrothals, contracting marriages, celebrating weddings, providing feasts, entertaining guests, and also, it may be added, in care for funerals and for the burial of the dead. The only plagues of London are the immoderate drinking of fools and the frequency of fires.

* From *English Historical Documents, 1042–1189,* Second Edition, edited by George Greenaway and David C. Douglas. © 1953, 1981 by Eyre Methuen Ltd. Reprinted by permission of Oxford University Press, Inc.

Western European cities were insignificant in medieval times compared to those of China, India, or the Middle East, both as regards population and volume of trade. But they were quite unique because of their growing autonomy and political power. Precisely because they were starting afresh, and within the framework of a politically fragmented Europe rather than a monolithic empire, the burghers from the beginning exhibited a self-confidence and independence that had no parallel anywhere else in Eurasia.

As they acquired power and financial resources, the people could usually get the king to give them a royal charter licensing them to unite in a single commune. The commune had the right to act as a corporation, to make agreements under its corporate seal, and to have its town hall, court of law, and dependent territory outside the walls. The charter also permitted merchants and craftsmen to organize into guilds, voluntary associations designed for protection and mutual aid, including the regulation of manufacturing standards, prices, and working hours. Thus towns gradually came to be recognized as a new element in society, with inhabitants who were outside feudal law. For example, the custom was that if a serf escaped to a town and lived there for a year and a day without being apprehended, he became a free man. A saying at that time was, ''Town air makes a man free.''

In certain regions, groups of cities banded together to form leagues which became powerful political, as well as economic, entities. When the Hohenstaufen emperors attempted to force the wealthy cities of northern Italy—Milan, Brescia, Parma, Verona, and others—to pay taxes and accept imperial administration, they organized themselves into the Lombard League. Aided by the pope, the League successfully waged war against the emperors. Likewise various Baltic towns—Bremen, Lubeck, Stettin, Danzig, and others comprising a total of ninety in 1350—organized themselves into the Hanseatic League which fought against pirates, pressed for trading privileges in foreign countries, and virtually monopolized the trade of Northern Europe.

This evolution gave the European merchant status and power that were unique in Eurasia. In China, government was carried on by scholars; in Japan, by soldiers; in the Malay lands and in the Rajput states of India, by the local nobility; but nowhere by merchants. Nowhere, that is, except in Europe, where they were steadily gaining in political as well as economic power. There they were becoming lord mayors in London, senators in the German Imperial Free Cities, and grand pensioners in Holland. Such social status and political connections meant more consideration and more consistent state support for mercantile interests and, later on, for overseas ventures.

SUGGESTED READING

R. H. Bautier, *The Economic Development of Medieval Europe* (Harcourt Brace Jovanovich, 1971); M. Grant, *Dawn of the Middle Ages* (McGraw-Hill, 1981); R. S. Lopez, *The Birth of Europe* (Lippincott, 1966); R. L. Reynolds, *Europe Emerges: Transition Toward an Industrial World-Wide Society 600–1750* (University of Wisconsin Press, 1961); B. H. Slicher van Bath, *The Agrarian History of Western Europe, 500–1850* (Arnold, 1963); L. White, Jr., *Medieval Technology and Social Change* (Clarendon, 1962).

chapter 15

Revolutionary Western Civilization: Renaissance, Reformation, And New Monarchs

In the late Middle Ages the Islamic, Byzantine, and Confucian empires were becoming increasingly ossified and even withdrawing into themselves. The western tip of Eurasia, by contrast, was experiencing an unprecedented and thoroughgoing transformation. This involved not only the technological and economic growth noted in the preceding chapter, but also profound changes in culture, in religion, and in politics. These changes provided the Europeans not only with superior economic and military power but also with superior sociopolitical cohesion and dynamism. For example, a handful of British merchants and soldiers were able to conquer and rule the great Indian subcontinent more because of its sociopolitical fragility than because of British military technology. Conversely it is significant that there never has been any speculation about the possibility of a reverse course of events—the landing in England of Indian soldiers and merchants with the designs for trade and booty that had motivated the English nabobs.

The notion that the Indians might have been able to do in England what Robert Clive and Warren Hastings did in India seems so preposterous as to never be considered even as a remote possibility. But it is preposterous precisely because of the difference between English and Indian societies—the latter hopelessly fragmented, with an infinitely greater gulf between rulers and ruled than in the former. Whereas Clive and Hastings had been able to play off Moslem against Hindus, prince against prince, and local potentates against imperial officials, while the peasant masses remained inert in their villages, any

Indian counterpart of Clive and Hastings doubtless would have encountered a united front of Protestants and Catholics and of government and citizens including the gentry, the townspeople, and the peasants. Such was the chasm, so fateful for world history, separating traditional societies from the European, which was transformed not only by technological and economic growth, but also by the Renaissance, the Reformation, and the new monarchs.

I. RENAISSANCE

The term *Renaissance* is polemical. It means new birth or revival, and was coined by fifteenth-century intellectuals who believed that their age represented the rebirth of classical culture following an intervening ''age of darkness'' as they termed the medieval period. This interpretation was accepted through the nineteenth century, but historians today no longer consider it to have been a case of medieval pitch darkness as against Renaissance dazzling light. The fact is that interest in the classics was by no means completely absent during the Middle Ages, and, conversely, certain characteristics associated with medievalism were very much in evidence during the Renaissance. So modern historians, while not discarding the familiar term Renaissance, now define it as connoting not a sharp break or turning point, but rather an age of transition from medieval to modern civilization—roughly from 1350 to 1600.

The Renaissance got under way first in Italy and hence reflected the conditions and values of contemporary Italian society. This was a bustling urban society based on flourishing industries and on the profitable commerce between Western Europe and the wealthy Byzantine and Islamic Empires. Prosperous cities such as Venice, Genoa, Florence, Milan, and Pisa were dominated by the great merchant families who controlled politics as well as trade and crafts. It was these families that were the patrons of Renaissance artists and writers. Their needs, interests, and tastes colored the Renaissance cultural revival, even though the patrons included ducal families such as the Sforza of Milan, as well as popes such as Nicholas V, Pius II, Julius II, and Leo X. Hence the secularism and humanism of the Renaissance—its concern with this world rather than the hereafter, its focus on pagan classics rather than Christian theology.

At the center of most Renaissance art and literature was the human being—the new Renaissance being who was the molder of his own destiny rather than the plaything of supernatural forces. A person did not need to be preoccupied with forebodings of supernatural forces; rather the purpose of life was to develop one's innate potentialities. ''Men can do all things if they will,'' wrote Leon Battista Alberti (1404–1472), and his own attainments attest to the truth of his maxim. Alberti, Florentine patrician, was an architect, mathematician, and archeologist, as well as playwright, poet, art critic, organist, singer, and in his youth a well-known runner, wrestler, and mountain climber. He was an example of the ideal person of the age, the ''homo universale,'' or what is termed today the ''Renaissance person.''

The secularism and individualism of the Renaissance was reflected in its scholarship and education. The so-called father of Renaissance literature, Francesco Petrarca or Petrarch (1304–1374), stressed the value of the classics as a means for self-improvement and a guide to social action. Likewise the new board schools of the Renaissance trained not priests but the sons of merchants. The curriculum emphasized classical studies and physical exercise and was designed to educate the students to live well and happily and to function as responsible citizens.

The Renaissance spirit is most strikingly expressed in its art. Since the church no longer was the sole patron of the arts, artists were encouraged to turn to subjects other than the traditional Biblical themes. Such themes continued to appear quite commonly, but in the works of such masters as Leonardo da Vinci, Michelangelo, Raphael, and Titian the emphasis shifted more and more to portraits designed to reveal the hidden mysteries of the soul, and to paintings intended to delight the eye with striking colors and forms.

THE RENAISSANCE GENIUS

The supremely talented Leonardo da Vinci was an outstanding Renaissance figure. He personified his age, not only because of his achievements in so many fields, but also because of his readiness to advertise his genius. At the age of 30 he wrote the following letter to the Duke of Milan, who was sufficiently impressed to hire the young man.*

1. I have plans for bridges, very light and strong and suitable for carrying very easily, with which to pursue and at times defeat the enemy; and others solid and indestructible by fire or assault, easy and convenient to carry away and place in position. And plans for burning and destroying those of the enemy.

2. When a place is besieged I know how to cut off water from the trenches, and how to construct an infinite number of bridges, mantlets, scaling ladders, and other instruments which have to do with the same enterprise. . . .

4. I have also plans for making cannon, very convenient and easy of transport, with which to hurl small stones in the manner almost of hail, causing great terror to the enemy from their smoke, and great loss and confusion.

5. Also I have ways of arriving at a certain fixed spot by caverns and secret winding passages, made without any noise, even though it may be necessary to pass underneath trenches or a river.

6. Also I can make armored cars, safe and unassailable, which will enter the serried ranks of the enemy with their artillery, and there is no company of men at arms so great that they will not break it. And behind these the infantry will be able to follow quite unharmed and without any opposition. . . .

9. And if it should happen that the engagement is at sea, I have plans for constructing many engines most suitable either for attack or defense, and ships which can resist the fire of all the heaviest cannon, and powder and smoke.

10. In time of peace I believe that I can give you as complete satisfaction as anyone else in architecture in the construction of buildings both public and private, and in conducting water from one place to another. . . .

And if any of the aforesaid things should seem impossible or impracticable to anyone, I offer myself as ready to make trial of them in your park or in whatever place shall please Your Excellency, to whom I commend myself with all possible humility.

*J. P. and I. A. Richter, eds., *The Literary Works of Leonardo da Vinci* (Oxford University Press, 1939), pp. 92, 93.

The Renaissance was not an exclusively Italian phenomenon. Its innovations spread to Northern Europe in the sixteenth century. Two factors that were responsible for the spread were the Italian diplomats and generals who were employed by northern monarchs and the printing press which speeded up the circulation of books and ideas. Printing was particularly influential in Northern Europe because literacy was more widespread there than in the southern and eastern regions of Europe. The flood of printed matter fomented popular agitation concerning political and religious issues and so contributed substantially to the Reformation and ensuing religious and dynastic wars.

In conclusion, what is the significance of the Renaissance in the perspective of world history? It is apparent that new emphasis on human beings and on what they could accomplish obviously was more conducive to overseas expansion than the preceding medieval outlook. But this point can easily be exaggerated and needs serious modification. The fact is that Renaissance Europe was not science-oriented. The leading figures tended to be more aesthetic and philosophical than objective and skeptical. They retained in various degrees certain medieval patterns of thought. They persisted in admiring and believing the incredible and the fantastic. They continued to seek the philosopher's stone that would convert other metals into gold. They still believed in astrology and confused it with astronomy.

The Iberian pioneers of overseas expansion definitely were not Renaissance men. Prince Henry the Navigator, for example, was described by his contemporaries as a rigid, pious, and chivalrous ascetic rather than as a humanist. Although a generous patron of sailors and cartographers, he was not interested in learning and the arts. The story that he allegedly supported a school of astronomy and mathematics at Sagres is a myth. "However Renaissance be defined," states a distinguished historian of European expansion, ". . . the early process of discovery began independently, with medieval motives and assumptions. Prince Henry and his captains were, in the main, men of the Middle Ages. Even Columbus . . . embarked on his famous enterprise with an intellectual equipment which was mainly medieval and traditional."[1]

The "Renaissance ferment," then, does not explain the origins of European expansion before 1500 as much as it accounts for the impetus and irresistible power of the expansion after 1600. Though there are other significant factors involved in expansion after 1600, the fact remains that there was an intellectual ferment in Western Europe and that it had no counterpart in the rest of Eurasia. This is a fundamental difference of enormous import.

In the Ottoman Empire, for example, the Moslem medressehs (colleges) emphasized theology, jurisprudence, and rhetoric at the expense of astronomy, mathematics, and medicine. The graduates of these schools knew nothing about what was being done in the West and were not interested in finding out. No Moslem Turk believed that a Christian infidel could teach anything of value. Now and then, a rare, far-sighted individual warned of the dangers of this intellectual iron curtain that separated the Ottoman Empire from neighboring Christendom. One of these voices was Katib Chelebi, the famous Turkish bibliographer, encyclopedist, and historian who lived in the first half of the seventeenth century. Coming from a poor family, he was unable to obtain a formal higher education. This was a blessing in disguise. He was spared the superficial, hair-splitting concentration on Moslem sacred studies that was typical of Ottoman education at this time. The fact that he was self-taught explains in large part his open-mindedness towards Western learning.

One of Chelebi's works was a short naval handbook that he wrote following a disastrous defeat of the Ottoman fleet in 1656. In the preface of this work, Chelebi emphasized the need for mastering the science of geography and map-making.

> For men who are in charge of affairs of state, the science of geography is a matter of which knowledge is necessary. They may not be familiar with what the entire globe is like, but they ought at least to know the map of the Ottoman State and of those states adjoining it. Then, when they have to send forces on campaign, they can proceed on the basis of knowledge, and so the invasion of the enemy's land and also the protection and defense of the frontiers becomes an easier task. Taking counsel with individuals who are ignorant of that science is no satisfactory substitute, not even when such men are local veterans. Most such veterans are entirely unable to sketch the map of their own home regions.
>
> Sufficient and convincing proof of the necessity for learning this science is the fact that the heathen, by their application to and their esteem for those branches of learning, have discovered the New World and have overrun the markets of India.[2]

Chelebi saw the connection between Europe's intellectual advance and its overseas expansion. In his last work before his death in 1657, Chelebi warned his countrymen that, if they did not abandon their dogmatism, they would soon "be looking at the universe with the eyes of oxen." His prediction proved prophetic. The Turks continued to be steeped in their religious obscurantism, and, like other non-Western peoples, they paid a high price. The Christian infidels with their new learning eventually became the masters not only of the New World, but of the ancient empires of Islam and of Confucianism.

II. REFORMATION

From the viewpoint of European history the *Reformation* stands out as the great religious upheaval that shattered irrevocably the unity of Western Christendom. But from the perspective of world history the Reformation is significant for its role in transferring power from church to state, and thereby providing the Western monarchies with the political and economic dynamism that powered Europe's overseas drive.

Considering first the Reformation as a religious movement, it got under way with Martin Luther's protest against the selling by the Papacy of a particularly blatant indulgence that promised absolution "from all thy sins, transgressions, and excesses, how enormous soever they may be . . . so that when you die the gates of punishment shall be shut, and the gates of the paradise of delight shall be opened. . . ." It was in protest against this "unbridled preaching of pardons" that Luther, then a priest at the University of Wittenberg, posted his ninety-five theses on the church door. Such a gesture was not unprecedented in the history of the church. Many reformers and rebels had taken similar stands in the past, only to be silenced by the Papacy through persuasion or force. Thus Pope Leo X dismissed Luther's protest as a "squabble amongst monks." But the course of events was to demonstrate that Luther was destined for a role infinitely more fateful than that of a squabbling monk.

One reason was the weakening of the church during the fourteenth century "Babylonian Captivity" when two popes, one in Rome and one in Avignon, each claimed to be the legitimate successor of Saint Peter and excommunicated the other. At least as important was the growth of national feelings in Northern Europe, so that both monarchs and subjects increasingly viewed the popes as foreigners with no right to meddle in national affairs or to raise revenue within national frontiers.

This sentiment explains the enthusiastic popular response to Luther's stand. The ensuing public debate led Luther to spell out the revolutionary implications of his basic doctrine of justification by faith—that is—that the priestly offices and ministrations of the Church were unnecessary intermediaries between the individual and God. In October 1520 Luther burned a papal bull of excommunication, and the following year, when summoned to appear before an Imperial Diet, he refused to recant "unless I am convinced by the testimony of the Scriptures or by clear reason." The Emperor secured passage of an edict condemning the obstinate friar as a heretic, but the sympathetic Elector Fredrick of Saxony provided refuge in his castle and saved Luther from the fate of Hus.

In this place of exile Luther busied himself in the following years translating the Bible into German and building an independent German church. Emperor Charles V was unable to move decisively against the spreading heresy because he was involved in wars with the French and the Turks. By 1546 he was free of these distractions so he set out to crush the Lutheran princes and restore the unity of the Roman church. He was encouraged in this by the pope who provided money and troops. But the Lutherans banded together in the Schmalkaldic League and won support from the Catholic French king who was more concerned with dynastic than religious considerations. The fighting dragged on inconclusively until the signing of the Peace of Augsburg (1555) which granted each German prince the right to select either the Catholic or Lutheran faith and to impose it on his subjects. Thus the end result of the Reformation in Germany was the roughly equal division of the country into Lutheran and Catholic states.

The Peace of Augsburg opened the gates to the rising flood of heresy, or rather heresies. The settlement at Augsburg had recognized only Lutheranism as a possible alternative to the Catholic faith. But Protestantism by its very nature lent itself to a continual proliferation of new sects. Luther's fundamental doctrine of individual interpretation of the Scriptures led inevitably to different interpretations and hence to new varieties of Protestantism. In Switzerland, for example, John Calvin joined Luther in rejecting salvation by "works," but he rejected also Luther's doctrine of salvation by "faith". Instead Calvin preached predestination—each individual's fate was decreed by God before birth. The availability of printing presses enabled Calvin to make Geneva the headquarters of a proselytizing drive that profoundly affected such countries as Bohemia, Hungary, the Netherlands, Scotland, England, and the thirteen American colonies overseas.

An entirely different form of Protestantism was that of the Anabaptists, whose religious and social radicalism earned them persecution by Catholics, Lutherans, and Calvinists alike. Carrying to its logical conclusion Luther's doctrine that every person should follow the dictates of his or her conscience, they demanded full religious liberty, including separation of church and state. Equally radical were their social teachings—their opposition to individual accumulation of wealth, to class or status differentiation, to military service, and to payment of taxes for warmaking purposes. It is not surprising that these tenets, undermining the authority of all religious and political establishments, led to the persecution and wholesale massacre of Anabaptists throughout Europe. The Hutterites and Mennonites are their survivors who have managed to hold out to the present day.

The prevailing factor determining the religion of a state almost invariably was the decision of its prince. If he favored a break with Rome, the Reformation triumphed; if he opposed a break, the Reformation was doomed. Very substantial benefits awaited the prince who opted in favor of Protestantism. His political power increased for he became the head of his national church rather than having to accept the ecclesiastical suzerainty of the international Papacy. His economic position also improved as he could confiscate Catholic church lands and movable wealth, and also check the flow of revenue to Rome. Despite these advantages of turning against the pope, as many princes remained loyal as chose to break away. One reason was the threat of attack by the imperial forces of Charles V supported by the pope. Also many princes found they could extract as many political and economic concessions from the Papacy by remaining Catholic as they were likely to obtain as Protestant princes. Finally the Catholic Reformation organized and strengthened the Catholic forces in Europe, thereby helping to block the advancing tide of Protestantism.

The Catholic Reformation got under way with Pope Paul III (1534–1549), who was the first pontiff to grasp the significance and threat of Protestantism. He summoned the Council of Trent which met intermittently from 1545 to 1563, and he approved the founding of the Jesuit order, the Society of Jesus in 1540. The main achievements of the Council of Trent were the reaffirmation of traditional Catholic doctrine in firmly anti-Protestant terms, and the adoption of practical measures to eliminate abuses and restore church discipline. These measures included a ban on the sale of indulgences, the prohibition of any bishop from holding more than one benefice, the stipulation that every diocese should establish a seminary to train priests, and the publication of an *Index* of books that Catholics would be forbidden to read. Implementation of the Trent reforms was ensured by the discipline and militancy of the Jesuits. Viewing themselves as soldiers of Christ, they founded schools for training a new generation of priests and laymen, and they rooted out heresy wherever it appeared. They also extended their operations all over the world to spread the gospel amongst the heathen in Asia, Africa, and the Americas. The nature and extent of their activities are indicated by the careers of such men as St. Francis de Xavier in Japan, Matteo Ricci in China, Robert de Nobili in India, and Father Jacques Marquette in America.

The legacy of the Reformation is ambiguous. It promoted doctrinal dissension and intolerance which culminated in a series of bloody religious wars. But the resulting fragmentation of Western Christendom compelled the rival sects to accept the fact that the hegemony of any universal church was not feasible. Hence the gradual acceptance and implementation of religious toleration—a process so slow and contested that it is not yet fully complete. The Reformation was equally ambiguous concerning the status of the individual. Luther championed individual interpretation of the Scriptures, but when this led to the radicalism of the Anabaptists and to peasant revolts, he called on the civil authorities to destroy the "murdering, thieving hordes." Yet the emphasis on the reading of the Bible did lead to greater literacy which opened doors to books and ideas other than religious.

So far as the immediate legacy of the Reformation was concerned, it shattered the universal medieval Roman church into a large number of local territorial churches— some national, some princely, some provincial, and some confined to a single city. The common feature of all these local churches was their control by secular rulers. Regardless of whether the church remained Catholic in doctrine or adhered to one of the Protestant faiths, it was the secular authority that controlled ecclesiastical appointments and church finances. The immediate and decisive legacy of the Reformation was the transfer of power from church to state. In this sense, the Reformation represents a stage in the evolution of the modern nation-state—the subject of the following section.

III. NEW MONARCHS

Western Europe by the tenth century had become a mosaic of petty feudal states that had gradually acquired the land and authority of the defunct Carolingian Empire. During the following centuries several traditions and interests operated at cross purposes. There were feudal kings engaged in continual conflict with their feudal vassals who often held larger fiefs and wielded more power. There were city-states that sometimes combined in powerful organizations such as the Lombard and Hanseatic leagues. And in opposition to the particularist interests of these groups, there was the striving for a united Latin Christendom headed by the pope in Rome, or by a "Roman" emperor as the successor to Charlemagne and his predecessors. This complex of conflicting interests produced an infinite variety of constantly changing alliances and alignments at all levels of political life.

In very broad terms, the political evolution of Western Europe after Charlemagne may be divided into three stages. Between the ninth and eleventh centuries, popes and emperors generally cooperated. The popes helped the emperors against the German secular lords, and in return were supported in preference to the Byzantine opponents of papal authority. In 1073 a period of papal supremacy began with the accession of Pope Gregory VII. By the thirteenth century Pope Innocent III was involved in the affairs of virtually every European state, making and breaking kings and emperors. "Nothing in the world," he declared, "should escape the attention and control of the Sovereign Pontiff." For over two centuries, the Papacy generally was recognized as the head of Latin Christendom.

The period of papal supremacy ended suddenly and dramatically when Pope Boniface VIII issued the bull *Unam sanctam* (1302) in which he set forth uncompromisingly the doctrine of papal authority: ". . . we declare, state, define and pronounce that it is altogether necessary to salvation for every human creature to be subject to the Roman pontiff." But what had been acceptable in previous centuries was no longer so. The monarchs and their councilors now were placing the welfare of their kingdoms ahead of the wishes of popes. Boniface was subjected to threats and mistreatment by an agent of the French king, and he died soon after his humiliation. In 1305 a French archbishop was elected pope as Clement V, and instead of going to Rome he took up residence at Avignon in southeastern France. During the next seventy years the Avignonese popes were the pawns of the French monarchy and lost their predecessors' commanding position in Latin Christendom.

The new power of the European kings was derived in large part from their informal alliance with the rising merchant class. The burghers provided financial support to the monarchs. They also supplied managerial talent in the form of chamberlains, overseers, keepers of the king's accounts, managers of the royal mint, and so forth. The people who held these positions originally were members of the king's household in charge of the monarch's private affairs. Now an enlarged royal court developed into a fiscal, judicial, and administrative system which gradually managed the entire realm with the help of aristocratic, ecclesiastic, and commercial representatives.

The new monarchs provided the burghers with protection against the frequent wars and arbitrary demands of the feudal lords and bishops. They also served merchant interests by doing away with some of the crazy-quilt pattern of autonomous local authorities, each with its own customs, laws, weights, and currencies. As late as the end of the fourteenth century there were thirty-five toll stations on the Elbe, over sixty on the Rhine, and so many on the Seine that the cost of shipping grain 200 miles down the river was half its selling price. With the removal of such encumbrances and the enforcement of royal law and order, the new monarchs emerged. By the fifteenth century, they ruled over roughly the territories of modern England, France, Portugal, and, after the marriage of Ferdinand and Isabella, also of Spain.

The power of the new monarchs was strengthened by the Reformation, as noted above. It was also defended and rationalized by political theorists, of whom the best known was Niccolo Machiavelli (1459–1527). A product of the ruthless struggle for survival amongst the competing city states of Renaissance Italy, Machiavelli viewed politics as a struggle for power in which the end justifies the means. In his book *The Prince,* he set forth guidelines for the ruler who aspired to unite the fragmented Italian peninsula and to rid it of the French and Spanish invaders. With cool and relentless realism he rejected moral restraints and spelled out the difference between politics and religion or philosophy.

The states of the new monarchs proved essential for the mobilization of the human and material resources needed for overseas enterprise. It was not accidental that although most of the early explorers were Italian navigators, their sponsors were the new national monarchies rather than their minuscule home city-states. The Spanish and Portuguese courts provided the backing for Columbus and da Gama, and the English and French courts quickly and eagerly followed up with backing for Cabot, Verrazano, and many others.

IV. WESTERN EUROPE'S EXPANSIONISM

Between the fourth and tenth centuries Europe was invaded by Germans, Huns, Magyars, Vikings, and Moslems. But from the tenth to the fourteenth centuries this situation was dramatically reversed as Europe took the offensive on all fronts (see Map XVI, "Expansionism of the Medieval West"). Assorted Crusaders pushed back the Moslems in Spain, southern Italy, Sicily, and the Holy Land, and they even overran the Christian Byzantine empire. Meanwhile in Northeast Europe, German frontier lords were winning lands east of the Elbe. As German expansion continued east of the Oder it was carried on as a crusade by the Teutonic Knights against the pagan Prussians. The Knights built strongholds and around them settled Germans, who provided the supplies and manpower for further expansion. German merchants soon appeared and founded towns at strategic points along the coasts and along river routes. Thus by the end of the fifteenth century large areas formerly occupied by Slavic and Baltic peoples had become thoroughly German from top to bottom: lords, bishops, townsmen, and peasants.

These crusades were considered at one time to have been responsible for starting practically every constructive development in the later Middle Ages, including the growth of trade and towns, and the advances in culture. This interpretation is no longer accepted. Instead it is generally agreed that the crusades were the consequence rather than the cause of this progress. Without the preceding technological advances, commercial revival, demographic upsurge, and general exuberance of spirit, the crusades would have been quite impossible. This dynamism continued and picked up speed after the fourteenth-century slump. The result was to extend the expansionist drive of the Crusaders to overseas territories.

The uniqueness of this West European dynamism is apparent in the variety of Eurasian responses to the expansion of the Moslem world in the fifteenth century. As noted in Chapter 11, section V, Islam at that time was fanning out from the Middle East in all directions. The Turks, after capturing Constantinople, overran the Balkan peninsula and then crossed the Danube and pushed through Hungary to the walls of Vienna. Likewise in the east the Turks under the colorful Babur were striking southward from Afghanistan, beginning their founding of the great Mogul Empire that was to rule India until the British takeover in the nineteenth century. In Africa also, Islam was spreading steadily into the interior from its bases on the northern and eastern coasts of the continent. Finally Moslem merchants dominated the Eurasian sea routes running from the Red Sea and the Persian Gulf across the Indian Ocean and around Southeast Asia to the China seas.

With these advances by its soldiers, merchants, and preachers, the world of Islam had become the heartland of Eurasia. It occupied the strategic center of the great landmass, and the more it expanded, the more it isolated the Chinese at the eastern end of Eurasia and the Europeans at the western. The completely different responses of the Chinese and the Europeans to this encirclement profoundly influenced the course of world history from that time to the present.

The Chinese, as noted earlier, withdrew voluntarily, even though their Cheng Ho expeditions had demonstrated conclusively that they possessed both the technology and the resources to dominate the oceans (see Chapter 13, section IV). But during this Ming period, after the interlude of Mongol domination, the Chinese were turning their backs to the outside world. And their merchant class, lacking the political power and social status of its Western counterpart, was unable to challenge imperial edicts banning overseas enterprise. Thus the Chinese turned their formidable talents and energies inward, thereby deliberately relinquishing a lead role in Eurasia, and ultimately, world affairs.

The response of the Europeans was precisely the opposite. Their geographic horizons and commercial ambitions had been immeasurably broadened by *Pax Mongolica* so that the sudden disintegration of the Mongol empire had left them with acute frustration and yearning. Likewise the loss of the Crusaders' outposts in the Levant, the Islamization of the ilkhanate in Persia, and the Turkish conquest of the Balkans, all served to deprive the Europeans of access to the Black Sea, to the Persian Gulf, and to the Indian Ocean. Thus the Europeans were effectively fenced in on the western tip of Eurasia. It is true that the all-important spice trade still flourished, as Italian merchants continued to meet Arab traders in the ports of the Levant and to pick up cargoes for transshipment to the West. This arrangement was satisfactory for the Italians and the Arabs who reaped the golden profits of the middleman. But other Europeans were not so happy, and they sought earnestly for some means to reach the Orient to share the prize.

Their search was bound to succeed, given their technical skills, their economic strength, and their political pluralism. There was no emperor in Europe to issue restraining orders; instead there were rival national monarchies competing strenuously in overseas enterprises. Also there was in Europe a genuine need and strong demand for foreign products, and the merchants were sufficiently powerful to ensure satisfaction of the need. Thus if Columbus had not discovered America and if da Gama had not rounded the Cape, then others assuredly would have done so within the next few decades. In short,

Western society had reached the take-off point. It was ready to burst out, and when it did it found the ocean ways clear, and it spread irresistably over the globe.

SUGGESTED READING

M. W. Baldwin, *The Medieval Church* (Cornell University Press, 1953); M. Bloch, *Feudal Society,* 2 vols. (University of Chicago Press, 1961); G. R. Elton, *Reformation Europe* (Harper & Row, 1966); W. K. Ferguson, *The Renaissance* (Torchbook, 1940); D. Knowles, *The Evolution of Medieval Thought* (Helicon, 1962); J. R. Levenson, ed., *European Expansion and the Counter-Example of Asia* (Prentice-Hall, 1967).

What It Means
For Us Today

The most surprising and significant development during the thousand years of Eurasian medieval history was the rise of Western Europe from poverty and obscurity. During most of this period between roughly 500 and 1500, the West was the underdeveloped region of Eurasia. We have seen that this underdevelopedness proved an advantage in contrast to the developedness of China, which acted as a brake on that country. The Chinese enjoyed a sophisticated culture, advanced crafts, large-scale commerce, an efficient bureaucracy based on merit, and the creed of Confucianism which provided social cement and intellectual rationale. Very naturally the Chinese considered their civilization to be superior to any other, and they regarded foreigners as "barbarians." When the first Westerners appeared on their coasts, the Chinese assumed there was nothing important they could learn from those particular "long-nosed barbarians."

This attitude, understandable though it was, left the Chinese unchanging in a time of change. By contrast, the Western Europeans, precisely because of their relative backwardness, were ready and eager to learn and to adapt. They took Chinese inventions, developed them to their full potential, and used them for overseas expansion. This expansion, in turn, triggered more technological advances and institutional changes. The end result was the transition from medieval to modern civilization, with the Europeans serving as the pioneers and the beneficiaries.

198

This was not the first time that a backward peripheral region had led in the transition from one historical era to another. During the period of the Ancient Civilizations (3500–1000 B.C.), the Middle East had been the developed core that made the basic innovations in agriculture, metallurgy, writing, and urban life. But this highly developed center fell behind during the transition from the Ancient to the Classical Civilizations. It was the peripheral and comparatively backward regions of China, India and Europe that pioneered in the creative innovations of the Classical Age, including effective exploitation of iron metallurgy, coinage, and the alphabet, as well as the new religions of Confucianism, Hinduism, and Christianity.

This pattern suggests that in history, nothing fails like success. Anthropologists refer to this as the *Law of Retarding Lead,* which holds that the best-adapted and most successful societies have the most difficulty in changing and retaining their lead in a period of transition. And conversely, the backward and less successful societies are more likely to be able to adapt and to forge ahead.

The significance of this law is obvious for us today, when the West is not the underdeveloped region of Eurasia but rather the most highly developed part of the globe. Furthermore we are living in an age of transition when the tempo of history has speeded up immensely in comparison with the Middle Ages. In such a period of constantly accelerating change, adaptability is the key to personal and national success—or perhaps we should say, personal and national survival. President Lyndon B. Johnson summarized it best with this warning to his fellow-Americans: ''We must change to master change.''

SUGGESTED READING

The full implications of the ''retarding lead'' concept are set forth by the anthropologist Elman R. Service in: M. D. Sahlins and E. R. Service, eds., *Evolution and Culture* (University of Michigan Press, 1960); and E. R. Service, *Cultural Evolutionism: Theory in Practice* (Holt, Rinehart & Winston, 1971).

Part IV

Non-Eurasian World To 1500

Thus far we have dealt exclusively with Eurasian history. Now we turn to the history of the non-Eurasian part of the globe. The reason for this separate treatment is that the histories of the people involved were in fact largely separate. Before 1500 there was little interaction between the Eurasian and non-Eurasian segments of the world. Human history during those millennia was essentially regional rather than global in scope. Once human beings scattered to all the continents, the primitive level of their technology restricted the range of their operations and communications. For example, when they crossed over the Bering Sea, they settled down in various parts of the Americas and lost contact with the peoples they had left behind in Siberia. The same thing happened when other bands crossed over from Southeast Asia to Australia. Thus the various human societies, especially those outside Eurasia, lived largely in isolation. The degree of isolation varied from region to region. The peoples of Australia and of the Americas were completely cut off on their respective continents, while those of Africa were largely, though not entirely, so.

The fragmentation of human communities continued until about 1500, when Western Europeans crossed all the oceans of the world and brought all the peoples of the world into direct contact with one another. Because the Europeans took the lead in overseas exploration, history textbooks have focused on Columbus and da Gama and Magellan and on their discoveries and the repercussions that followed. Such an approach is inadequate for global history. A global perspective requires consideration not only of the expanding West but also of the regions into which the West expanded. The peoples of these regions, after all, made up a considerable proportion of the human race, so that their evolution must not be ignored. Also the lands and peoples and institutions of the non-Eurasian world were as significant in determining the outcome of Western expansionism as were the Westerners themselves. For these reasons, then, the following two chapters are devoted to Africa, to the Americas, and to Australia.

Geographers, in Africa's maps,
With savage creatures
filled the gaps;
And o'er unhabitable downs
Placed elephants for want
of towns.

Dean Swift

chapter 16

Africa

A glance at the map suggests that the people of Africa should not have been as isolated from Eurasia as in fact they were. To the north, Africa is separated from Europe by the Mediterranean, a body of water that is narrow, easy to cross, and historically has functioned more as a highway than as a barrier. To the east the Sinai peninsula provides a bridge to Asia, while the Red Sea is even narrower and easier to cross than the Mediterranean. Finally the great expanses of the Indian Ocean are neutralized by the monsoon winds, which facilitate communication back and forth between East Africa and South Asia.

Yet historically Africa has been much more cut off from Eurasia than these impressions would indicate. The isolation has had an important and direct effect upon the history of the people of Africa. This chapter will consider first the geography behind their isolation, and then the nature of their historical experiences.

I. GEOGRAPHY

Africa, as defined in this study, refers to the part of the continent south of the Sahara Desert. The reason for this definition is that the Sahara is the great barrier, the great divider, while the Mediterranean by comparison is a connecting boulevard. This explains why historically the people of North Africa have had more interaction with the other peoples around the Mediterranean basin than with those to the south of the desert barrier. Thus sub-Saharan Africa, the subject of this chapter, is in effect an island, the northern shore of which is the Sahara Desert rather than the Mediterranean.

The Sahara is by no means the only obstacle to contact with the outside world. On the east of the great desert, along the upper reaches of the Nile, are the enormous swamps of the Sudd, which historically have constituted a formidable barrier. Also contributing to Africa's inaccessibility is a coastline unbroken by bays, gulfs, or inland seas. Consequently this coastline is shorter than Europe's, though Africa has thrice the area. The lack of anything corresponding to the Mediterranean, the Baltic, or the Black Sea means that Africa's interior is relatively closed to the outside world.

Other effective barriers are the thousand-mile-long sandbars along the east and west coasts, and the tremendous swells on both coasts, which made landing in a small boat very difficult. And if the bars and breakers are successfully passed, there is still another obstacle—the rapids and waterfalls created by the rivers tumbling down a succession of escarpments from the interior plateau to the low coastlands. Africa's profile is like that of an inverted saucer which today provides a tremendous hydroelectric potential. But historically the coastal waterfalls meant that there was no counterpart in Africa either to the smooth-flowing St. Lawrence and Amazon, which provide easy access to the interior of the Americas, or to the Rhine and Danube, which do the same for Europe. The approaches to Central Africa are made still more dangerous by the hot, humid climate of the low-lying coastal areas and by the tropical diseases accompanying such a climate. The interior uplands generally have a healthy bracing climate, but the coastal regions have presented a serious health hazard to those seeking to penetrate inland.

As significant as this external inaccessibility has been the internal inaccessibility—that is, the difficulty of crossing from one part of Africa to another. Viewing the continent as a whole, it begins with small fertile strips at the extreme northern and southern tips. These soon yield to the great desert expanses of the Kalahari in the south and the Sahara in the north. Next are the rolling grasslands or savannas, known in the north as the Sudan, the Arab term meaning "the country of the black people." Then come the tropical rain forests, which in their densest parts are more difficult to penetrate than the deserts.

These extremes of nature, together with the absence of nearby coastal outlets and of unencumbered river systems, have combined to restrict interaction amongst the various regions of the continent. Inevitably this has retarded the overall development of its peoples and explains the simultaneous existence of large and complex empires in the savannas and of hunting bands in remote desert and forest areas.

This geographic setting also helps to explain the paradoxical difference in the timing of European penetration of Africa compared to that of the Americas. Africa, in contrast to the Americas, has maintained through the millennia an unbroken, though at times tenuous, contact with Eurasia. Yet the Europeans were much slower in penetrating into neighboring Africa than into the distant Americas. Africa remained the "Dark Continent" centuries after the New World had been opened up and colonized. As late as 1865, when the Civil War was ending in the United States, only the coastal fringe of Africa was known, together with a few insignificant portions of the interior. Even by 1900 about a fourth of the continent remained unexplored The imperviousness of Africa to Europe's dynamism was due in part to the geographic conditions that combined to make the continent unusually resistant to outside intrusion. But geography was not the only factor involved. At least as important was the African Negro's general level of social, political, and economic organization, which was high enough to effectively block the Europeans for centuries.

II. AGRICULTURE AND IRON

Until modern times, Africans were largely isolated from the rest of the world. Yet they always did have certain contacts with Eurasia, and these contacts gave the Africans advantages denied to the American Indians and the Australian aborigines. One was immunity against the European diseases, which so devastated the American Indians as we shall see in the following chapter. By contrast, it was the Europeans who were struck down by diseases in Africa. "It seems," wrote a Portuguese chronicler in the sixteenth century, "that for our sins or for some inscrutable judgement of God, in all the entrances of this great Ethiopia [Africa], He has placed a striking angel with a flaming sword of deadly fevers who prevents us from penetrating into the interior . . . . "[1]

Long contact with Eurasia also gave the Africans the important advantage of being able to borrow technology. Archeologists disagree over the basic issue of diffusion versus autonomous development—over what came from abroad and what originated independently at home. Some believe that agriculture spread from Western Asia into the Nile valley and thence to West Africa. Others hold that West Africa was one of the world's originators of agriculture, along with the Middle East, Middle America, and China.

Whichever theory is correct about the beginnings of African agriculture, there is no question that certain plants were brought in from the outside. Examples are wheat and barley from the Middle East, and bananas, Asian yams, and cocoa-yams (or taros) from Southeast Asia. The latter group of plants were important because they made it possible to extend agriculture from the savannas to the rain forests. Also certain types of cattle, such as the Zebu shorthorned humpbacked cow, came from the outside. These imported animals gave the Africans a supply of protein and a source of power that the American Indians lacked.

Archeologists disagree also about the beginnings of iron metallurgy in Africa. Some believe that it came across the Sahara from Carthage or up the Nile valley from the Assyrians. Others maintain that West African communities learned independently to smelt iron. There is also a third possibility—that both diffusion and independent development occurred, depending on whether the people concerned were located close or far from the routes of Eurasian diffusion.

Again, whichever of these theories may be correct, the appearance of iron had as wide repercussions in Africa as we noted in Eurasia. Iron-tipped hoes and iron-shod axes made it possible to extend agriculture into the forests of Africa, just as earlier the use of iron brought agriculture into the forests of Central Europe and of the Ganges and Yangtze valleys. The resulting increase in agricultural output left a surplus available for trading purposes. As in Eurasia, this in turn led to social differentiation—to the division of peoples into rulers and ruled in place of the former simple kinship relationships. Hence the appearance about the ninth century A.D. of definite state structures with military and administrative services and with the revenue sources necessary for their support.

Technological advances in Africa affected the ethnic composition of the continent. It was the accessible Negroes rather than the inaccessible Pygmies and Bushmen who adopted and profited from agriculture and iron metallurgy. Consequently, it was they also who increased disproportionately in number and who were able, with their iron tools and weapons, to push southward at the expense of the Bushmen and Pygmies. This explains why the Negroes were the predominant ethnic group by the time the Europeans arrived, whereas a millennium earlier they had shared the continent fairly evenly with the Caucasoids, Bushmen, and Pygmies.

III. ISLAM

The Africans benefited from Eurasian cultural influences as well as technological ones. A prime example was the impact of the Moslem Arabs who overran all North Africa in the seventh century and later extended their control down the east coast as merchants and as colonists. From these coastal bases, Islam had profound influence on the African peoples.

The impact of Islam was most obvious in the externals of life—names, dress, household equipment, architectural styles, festivals, and the like. It was evident also in the agricultural and technological progress that came with wider contact with the outside world. In East Africa the Arabs introduced rice and sugar cane from India.

Islam also stimulated commerce by linking the African economy to the far-flung network of Eurasian trade routes controlled by Moslem merchants. From their bases in North Africa the Moslems used the camel much more than had the Romans, and they increased the number of trans-Saharan trade routes and the volume of trade. Southward they transported cloth, jewelry, cowrie beads, and, above all, salt, which was in urgent demand throughout the Sudan. In return the Africans provided ivory, slaves, ostrich feathers, civet for perfumes, and, most important, gold from the upper Niger, Senegal, and Volta rivers. Much of this gold ultimately found its way to Europe, and in such large quantities that it became important for doing away with medieval Europe's unfavorable balance of trade with the East. The trade between the Sudan and North Africa was so profitable for both sides that by 1400 the whole of West Africa was crisscrossed with trading trails and dotted with market centers.

Meanwhile a similar trading pattern had been developing in East Africa. Moslem middlemen on the coast sent agents into the interior who bought ivory, slaves, and gold from Rhodesia, and copper from Katanga. These commodities then were exported through Indian Ocean trade channels, controlled at the time by Moslem merchants. In later centuries iron ore also was obtained from the interior, shipped to southern India, and made into the so-called Damascus blades. In return for these products, Africans received Chinese and Indian cloth, and various luxury goods, especially Chinese porcelain, remains of which still can be found along the coast. This trade was the basis for the string of thriving ports and city-states along the East African coast.

Returning to the role of Islam in Africa, it served also to stimulate the intellectual life of the Sudan. Literacy spread with the establishment of Koranic schools. Scholars could pursue higher learning at various Sudanese universities, of which the University of Sankore at Timbuktu was the most outstanding. This institution was modeled after other Moslem universities at Fez, Tunis, and Cairo. It was the custom for scholars to move about freely among these universities and others in the Moslem world, to study at the feet of particular masters.

The adoption of Islam also strengthened the political organization of the Sudanic kingdoms. Traditionally Sudanic rulers could claim the allegiance only of their own kinship units or clans, and of such other related kinship units that recognized descent from a great founding ancestor. But when the kingdoms were enlarged into great empires, the kinship relationship obviously became inadequate as the basis for imperial organization. The greater the extent of an empire, the more alien its emperor appeared to a large proportion of the subjects. Local chiefs could not be depended upon to serve as faithful vassals; they tended instead to lead their own people in resistance to imperial rule. Islam helped to meet this institutional problem by strengthening the imperial administration. Moslem schools and colleges turned out a class of educated men who could organize an effective imperial bureaucracy. These men were not dominated by their kinship alliances; their own interests were tied to imperial authority, and they normally could be counted upon to serve that authority loyally.

IV. SUDAN EMPIRES

The combination of agricultural and metallurgical progress, corresponding growth in economic productivity, flourishing interregional trade, and the stimulus from Islam, explains the process of state building that went on in Africa from the eighth century onward. Not surprisingly, the most complex political structures appeared in the Sudan, where long-distance trade was most highly developed and where Islamic influence was the strongest. Hence the emergence in that region of three great empires: Ghana (700–1200), Mali (1200–1500), and Songhai (1350–1600) (see Map XX, "African Empires and Trade Routes").

These empires had certain fundamental characteristics in common. They were all based primarily upon trade, so that each extended its authority northward to control the import of salt, and southward to control the purchase of gold. Each derived most of its revenues from levies on the buying and selling of these and other commodities. The revenues from these duties allowed for progressively greater sophistication in imperial administration. Thus the Songhai Empire was more complex than its two predecessors. It was divided into definite provinces, each with a governor on long-term appointment. It also boasted the beginnings of a professional army and even of a number of ministries—for finance, justice, home affairs, agriculture, and forests, as well as for "White People," that is, the Arabs and Berbers on the Saharan frontiers of the empire.

The Mali and Songhai empires owed much to Islam for furthering trade, providing a trained bureaucracy, and stimulating intellectual life. Islam also transformed the Sudan from an isolated African region to an integral part of the Moslem world. Thus the fourteenth-century Arab traveler Ibn Battuta included Mali in his journeys which ranged as far east as China. Arriving at the Mali capital in June 1353 he was favorably impressed by the imperial administration and by the habits of the people.

The negroes possess some admirable qualities. They are seldom unjust, and have a greater abhorrence of injustice than any other people. Their sultan shows no mercy to anyone who is guilty of the least act of it. There is complete security in their country. Neither traveller nor inhabitant in it has anything to fear from robbers or men of violence. They do not confiscate the property of any white man who dies in their country, even if it be uncounted wealth. On the contrary, they give it into the charge of some trustworthy person among the whites, until the rightful heir takes possession of it. They are careful to observe the hours of prayer, and assiduous in attending them in congregations, and in bringing up their children to them. On Fridays, if a man does not go early to the mosque, he cannot find a corner to pray in, on account of the crowd.[2]

Although Islam played a key role in the formation and functioning of the Sudanic empires, it should be noted that it was primarily an urban faith. It was the merchants and townspeople who became Moslems, while the country folk by and large remained loyal to their traditional pagan gods and beliefs. Thus the reliance of many of the emperors and of their imperial establishments on Islam was a source of weakness as well as of strength. Islam, as we have seen, had much to contribute, but its base was narrower than it seemed to contemporary observers who naturally visited urban centers and traveled along trade routes. Thus in times of crisis the town-centered empires proved unexpectedly fragile and quickly fell apart.

Another weakness of the Sudanic empires was their vulnerability to attack from the North by Berbers looking for the source of African gold or seeking to impose their particular version of the true faith. The fanatical Almarovids were responsible for the overthrow of Ghana in 1076, and likewise an invasion from Morocco destroyed Songhai in 1591. The latter catastrophe marked the end of the Sudanic imperial era. In the words of a seventeenth-century Timbuktu historian: "From that moment everything changed. Danger took the place of security; poverty of wealth. Peace gave way to distress, disasters, and violence. . . . "[3]

TIMBUKTU IN THE SIXTEENTH CENTURY

Al Hassan Ibn Muhammad, known in the West as Leo Africanus, was a famous North African scholar and traveler. In 1513, he journeyed through the Sudanic states along the Niger and lived for some time in Timbuktu. He was much impressed by the wealth and intellectual life of that city, as evident in the following passage from his account.*

Here are many shops of artificers and merchants, and especially of such as weave linen and cotton cloth. And hither do the Barbary merchants bring cloth of Europe. All the women of this region, except the maid-servants, go with their faces covered, and sell all necessary victuals. The inhabitants, and especially strangers there residing, are exceedingly rich, insomuch that the king that now is, married both his daughters to rich merchants. Here are many wells containing most sweet water; and so often as the river Niger overfloweth, they convey the water thereof by certain sluices into the town. Corn, cattle, milk, and butter this region yieldeth in great abundance: but salt is very scarce here; for it is brought hither by land from Taghaza which is 500 miles distant. When I myself was here, I saw one camel's load of salt sold for 80 ducats. The rich king of Timbuktu hath many plates and sceptres of gold, some whereof weigh 1300 pounds: and he keeps a magnificent and well-furnished court. When he travelleth any whither he rideth upon a camel which is led by some of his noblemen; and so he doth likewise when he goeth forth to warfare, and all his soldiers ride upon horses. Whoever will speak unto this king must first fall down before his feet, and then taking up earth must first sprinkle it upon his own head and shoulders: which custom is ordinarily observed by . . . ambassadors from other princes. He hath always 3000 horsemen, and a number of footmen that shoot poisoned arrows, attending upon him. They have often skirmishes with those that refuse to pay tribute, and so many as they take, they sell unto the merchants of Timbuktu. Here are very few horses bred, and the merchants

V. KINGDOMS AND TRIBES

The three empires noted above are the best-known African medieval political creations. In the rest of the continent, however, there existed a great variety of other political structures. In Southeast Africa, for example, there were certain similarities to the situation in the Sudan. Just as the Sudan was famous in the Mediterranean basin for its gold exports, so Southeast Africa was famous for the same reason in the Indian Ocean basin. And just as the Sudanic empires and North African states were nourished by the one-trade pattern, so by the fifteenth century the Monomotapa empire in the interior and the Kilwa city-state on the coast were supported by the other.

Monomotapa (a word adapted by the Portuguese from the royal title Mwenemutapa) included much of modern Zimbabwe and Mozambique. It controlled the sources of the gold and the routes to the coast, after the fashion of the Sudanic empires. The monarchs of Monomotapa raised the Great Temple of Zimbabwe, a massive enclosure with walls 32-feet high, constructed to provide an appropriate setting for the conduct of royal ceremonial rites. On the coast, the merchant rulers of the port of Kilwa controlled the flow of goods from Monomotapa to the Moslem trading ships that ranged the Indian Ocean and even beyond to the China seas. "Kilwa is one of the most beautiful and well-constructed towns in the world. The whole of it is elegantly built," wrote Ibn Battuta—the same Battuta who was impressed also by Mali.[4]

Just as the Sudanic kingdoms were ravaged by Berber invaders from the north, so Monomotapa and Kilwa were destroyed by Portuguese intruders from overseas. Within a decade after Vasco da Gama's rounding of the Cape of Good Hope in 1497, the Portuguese had plundered many of the coastal cities of southeast Africa and were carrying on in the Indian Ocean as though it were a Portuguese lake. Later the Portuguese made their way up the Zambezi river and similarly undermined the Monomotapa empire. They settled in various strategic locations along the river and extended their influence in all directions until the inevitable showdown in 1628. With their firearms the Portuguese easily defeated two Monomotapa armies, but several substantial kingdoms survived on the ruins of the former empire.

In addition to these kingdoms there were many others, outstanding being that of Ethiopia. Its monarchs were converted to Byzantine or Coptic Christianity in A.D. 333. Since that time, Christianity has remained the official religion and has permeated all phases of Ethiopian life.

In this sampling of diverse African societies—and it is a mere sampling rather than a comprehensive survey—the most primitive should not be overlooked. Their continued existence reflected the extreme physical compartmentalization of the continent. The Pygmies and Bushmen, restricted and isolated in inaccessible deserts and rain forests, remained at the food-gathering stage of development. The world passed them by as they continued with the original mode of human livelihood as hunters and food collectors. But this does not mean that their cultures are of no significance or interest. Those few who have closely observed the Pygmies report highly developed talents in dancing, choral song, acting, mimicry, and storytelling. Likewise the Bushmen are famous for their rock-paintings and engravings, executed with natural and easy rhythmical lines, and depicting animals, hunting and battle scenes, and dancing ceremonial activities. Also, these early ''ecologists'' carefully preserved their environment, preventing overhunting or excessive exploitation of wildlife.

VI. CONCLUSION

Allowing for the difference between the Moslem and the Christian intellectual climates, a citizen of fourteenth-century Timbuktu would have found himself reasonably at home in fourteenth-century Oxford. In the sixteenth century he would still have found many points in common between the two university cities. By the nineteenth century the gulf had grown very deep.[5]

This point made by the British Africanist, Thomas Hodgkin, describes a process that is certainly not unique to Africa. It is clear from the preceding chapters that this is a worldwide process, and for the simple reason that the West pioneered in modernization and consequently pulled ahead of all other societies. Yet the fact remains that the gap between the West and Africa opened much wider than those between the West and other Eurasian regions. Constantinople, Delhi, and Peking did decline in relation to London, Paris, and Berlin, but they did not decline to virtual extinction as did Timbuktu. The problem as to why the West took the lead in modernization and forged ahead of other regions has been considered in Chapter 14. But we face here another problem—namely, why did Africa fall behind not only the West but also Eurasia in general?

This question has scarcely been posed, let alone answered. The preceding chapters analyzing the evolution of various Eurasian civilizations suggest certain factors that may be relevant and that are here presented tentatively for consideration. Their relative significance, if indeed they are significant, cannot be assessed without much more research and reflection.

One distinctive feature of Africa's development that quickly comes to mind is that the general stimulus generated by agriculture, metallurgy, and long-distance trade soon reached a plateau and failed to develop further. There was no counterpart in Africa to the chain-reaction upsurge that occurred in Northern Europe and in the Ganges and Yangtze valleys, when they were opened up and exploited with iron tools. Perhaps one reason was the absence in Africa of regions of corresponding fertility and potential productivity. The combination of poor soils, climatic extremes, and the tsetse fly made it impossible for the African agriculturalists and craftsmen to be as productive as their Eurasian counterparts.

Even the favored Sudan was excessively dependent on the export of gold and slaves, which could not provide a broad enough base for continued economic growth.

Africa's development appears to have been stunted also by the external and internal isolation, described in the first section. For example, Africa did not have anything comparable to Europe's rivers and coastal outlets, nor did it enjoy the advantages of being near the advanced Byzantine and Islamic civilizations as Europe did. Instead there were deserts and rain forests within, and oceanic expanses without. This prevented effective exploitation of even the limited output that the natural resources allowed. It is true that Africa, unlike the Americas, was close enough to Eurasia to benefit from the diffusion of basic technology such as agriculture and metallurgy. But Africa was too remote to receive, for example, the long series of inventions that were exchanged in the course of millennia amongst the Eurasian regions, to their mutual advantage.

Finally Africa suffered from vulnerability to outside attack, for retarded development means weakness, and weakness everywhere invites aggression. The disastrous effects of Berber invasions of the Sudan, and of the Portuguese onslaught on southeast Africa have been described above. They are particularly relevant in view of the fact that Western Europe, by contrast, suffered no invasions whatsoever during the critical five centuries prior to 1500 when it rose to global prominence. This vulnerability factor was to manifest itself in Africa in particularly virulent form with the later infliction of the slave trade, which not only depopulated certain areas but also caused economic and political chaos.

These various factors may explain why Africa's development stopped far short of the levels reached by the Eurasian societies. This retardation is reflected in the continued collective ownership of land and in the failure of urban centers to dominate the economies of any African regions. On the other hand this, in turn, made possible the preservation of the appealing egalitarianism and leisurely pace of life that prevail where kinship ties and communal land ownership remain in force. The British Africanist Basil Davidson has concluded that " . . . comparison between Africa and Europe is likely to be in Africa's favor . . . . So far as the comparison has any value, daily life in medieval Europe was likely to be far more hazardous or disagreeable for the common man and his wife."[6]

This positive judgment doubtless is justified, but from the perspective of world history the noteworthy point is that the appealing features of African society had survived precisely because it lacked the dynamism and continued growth of Eurasian societies. So long as the Africans remained relatively isolated from the outside world, they could preserve and enjoy a way of life that had long since been lost in the Eurasian civilizations. But when Western expansionism reached the African shores, a heavy price had to be paid. For the greater the underdevelopment, the greater the vulnerability and the resulting disruption. This was true when Bantu agriculturists expanded throughout Africa at the expense of "underdeveloped" hunting peoples. It was equally true in modern times when the representatives of the industrialized West burst out over the globe at the expense of "underdeveloped" agriculturists, and especially of those who had remained at a Neolithic level of organization.

Finally, it should be noted that although the Africans had not kept up with the Eurasians, they surpassed the more isolated American Indians and Australian aborigines. This explains to a large degree why the Europeans were so much slower in penetrating into the interior of Africa than into the Americas or Australia. Geographic factors also were involved here, as noted in section I, but more basic was the higher level of development reached by the Africans, particularly those with whom the Europeans had dealings. They were naturally the most advanced, because that meant they were also the most productive, and hence offered the most opportunity for profitable trade.

The commerce that developed with the coming of the Europeans was novel for the advanced Africans only in its scale. Mercantile activity was not, in itself, something strange, since they for a long time had maintained trade ties with areas as far removed as Morocco and Egypt. It follows that the Africans reacted to the Portuguese very differently from the manner in which the American Indians were reacting to the Spaniards at the same time. It is true that the forest dwellers, who had not had direct contact with the Arabs, were astonished by the white skin of the Europeans, by the loud noise of their firearms, and by the fact that these newcomers came from the sea, which was much revered by the coastal peoples. Yet the fact remains that the arrival of the Portuguese did not produce the demoralization and disintegration in Africa that the Spaniards did in the Americas. Accordingly, the Africans traded with the Europeans on terms that they themselves dictated. For centuries the coastal chieftains refused to allow the Europeans to penetrate inland because they wished to maintain their profitable position as middlemen between the European buyers and the producers in the interior. A British official wrote in 1793 that Africa remained an unknown continent ''rather from the jealousy of the inhabitants of the sea coasts, in permitting white men to travel through their country, than from the danger or difficulty attending the penetration.'' This jealousy he attributed to the middlemen's fear ''that the advantages of their trade with Europe should be lessened and transferred from them to their neighbors; or that the inland kingdoms by obtaining European arms'' would become dangerous rivals.[7]

Adam Smith, writing in 1776, was aware of this difference between the American Indians and the African Negroes in their capability for resisting European penetration.

Though the Europeans possess many considerable settlements both upon the coast of Africa and in the East Indies, they have not yet established in either of those countries such numerous and thriving colonies as those in the islands and continent of America. Africa, however, as well as several of the countries comprehended under the general name of the East Indies, are inhabited by barbarous nations. But those nations were by no means so weak and defenceless as the miserable and helpless Americans; and . . . they were besides much more populous. . . . In Africa and the East Indies, therefore, it was more difficult to displace the natives, and to extend the European plantations over the greater part of the lands of the original inhabitants.[8]

SUGGESTED READING

B. Davidson, *The African Past: Chronicles from Antiquity to Modern Times* (Little, Brown, 1964); and his *The African Genius: An Introduction to African Social and Cultural History* (Little, Brown, 1970); J. D. Fage, *An Atlas of African History* (Arnold, 1965); R. Grey and D. Birmingham, eds., *Pre-Colonial African Trade* (Oxford University Press, 1970); R. Hallett, *Africa to 1875* (University of Michigan Press, 1970); R. A. Lystad, *The African World: A Survey of Social Research* (Praeger, 1965); G. P. Murdock, *Africa: Its Peoples and Their Culture History* (McGraw-Hill, 1959); R. Oliver and J. D. Fage, *A Short History of Africa* (Penguin, 1962); J. S. Trimingham, *The Influence of Islam Upon Africa* (Praeger, 1968).

To the nations, however, both of the East and West Indies, all the commercial benefits which can have resulted from these events [the expansion of Europe] have been sunk and lost in the dreadful misfortunes which they have occasioned.

Adam Smith

chapter 17

Americas And Australia

The Vikings stumbled upon North America in the eleventh century, and for about one hundred years they tried to maintain settlements there, but without success. In the fifteenth century Columbus likewise stumbled upon the New World, but this time the sequel was altogether different. Instead of failure and withdrawal, Columbus's discovery was followed by massive and overwhelming penetration of both North and South America. The contrast shows how much European power and dynamism had increased during the intervening half-millennium.

Equally striking was the contrast between the rapid European penetration and exploitation of the Americas and the centuries that elapsed before the same could take place in Africa. One reason was geography: the New World was physically more accessible and inviting. The other reason, as noted by Adam Smith, was "the miserable and helpless" plight of the Indians. Although by no means all of them were at the same level of development, the overall nature of the Indian cultures was such that effective resistance was impossible. And if this was true of the American Indians, it was much more so of the Australian aborigines who were still at the food-gathering stage. In this chapter we shall consider the physical setting and the cultural background of the fateful developments that followed the landing of Columbus in the West Indies and of Captain James Cook in New South Wales.

213

I. LAND AND PEOPLE

The Americas, in contrast to Africa, were exceptionally open to newcomers from Europe. No sandbars obstructed the approaches to the coasts. There were many more harbors available along the indented coastline of the Americas than along the unbroken coastline of Africa. Also the Americas had a well-developed pattern of interior waterways that were relatively free of impediments and offered easy access to the interior. There is no counterpart in Africa to the majestic and smooth-flowing Amazon, Plata, Mississippi, or St. Lawrence. The explorers soon learned the use of the native birchbark canoe, and they discovered that with comparatively few portages they could paddle from the Atlantic up the St. Lawrence, along the Great Lakes, and thence south down the Mississippi to the Gulf of Mexico. Or they could paddle north down the Mackenzie to the Arctic Ocean, or west down the Columbia or the Fraser to the Pacific Ocean.

The climate of the Americas, too, is generally more attractive than that of Africa. The Amazon basin, it is true, is hot and humid, and the polar extremities of both continents are bitterly cold. But the British and the French settlers flourished in the lands they colonized north of the Rio Grande, and the Spaniards likewise felt at home in Mexico and Peru, which became their two principal centers. The climate there is not much different from that of Spain, and certainly a welcome contrast to the sweltering and disease-ridden Gold and Ivory coasts of Africa.

The Indians that the Europeans found in the Americas were the descendants of the bands that had crossed the Bering Sea from Siberia to Alaska. Until recently it was believed that the Indians first began crossing over to the Americas about 10,000 years ago. New archeological findings, together with the use of carbon-14 dating, have forced drastic revision of this estimate. It is now generally agreed that humans were in the New World 20,000 years ago, and probably 20,000 years or more before that. The last major migration of Indians took place about 3,000 years ago. Then came the Eskimos, who continued to travel back and forth across the Straits until modern political conditions forced them to remain on one side or the other. In any case, by this time the parts of America closest to Asia were densely enough populated so as to discourage further migration.

The actual crossing to the New World presented little difficulty to these early newcomers. The last of the Ice Ages had locked up vast quantities of sea water, lowering the ocean level by 460 feet and thus exposing a 1300-mile-wide land bridge connecting Siberia and Alaska. A "bridge" of such proportions was, in effect, a vast new subcontinent, which allowed ample scope for the transfer of plants and animals that now took place. Herds of game crossed over to the New World and were followed by the hunters that depended on them for food. Even after rising temperatures lifted the sea level and submerged the connecting lands, the resulting narrow straits could easily have been crossed in crude boats without even losing sight of shore. Later and more-advanced migrants probably traveled by boat from Asia to America and then continued along the northwest coast until they finally landed and settled in what is now British Columbia.

Most of those who crossed to Alaska moved on into the heart of North America through a gap in the ice sheet in the central Yukon plateau. They pressed forward because of the same forces that led them to migrate to America—the search for new hunting grounds and the continual pressure of tribes from the rear. In this manner both the continents were soon peopled by scattered tribes of hunters. Definite evidence has been found that indicates that the migrants from Asia reached the southern tip of South America by 11,000 years ago.

214

As regards racial traits, all Indians may be classified as Mongoloids. They have the characteristic high cheekbones and straight black hair, sparse on the face and body. Not all Indians, however, look alike. Those on the Northwest coast have flatter faces and noses, and narrower eyes (Mongoloid fold) than do those of the Southwest. The explanation for this difference is twofold. One is the date of arrival in the Americas. The earliest immigrants are much less Mongoloid in appearance because they left Asia before the Mongoloids, as we know them today, had fully evolved. The other reason is that the immigrants at once spread out and settled in small, inbred groups in a variety of climates. This led to the evolution of a great variety of physical types, even though they are all of the same Mongoloid family.

II. CULTURES

The migrants to the New World brought little cultural baggage with them since they came from northeast Siberia, one of the least advanced regions of Eurasia. They were, of course, all hunters, organized in small bands, possessing only crude stone tools, no pottery, and no domesticated animals, except perhaps the dog. Since they were entering an uninhabited continent they were completely free to develop their own institutions without the influences from native populations that affected the Aryans when they migrated to the Indus valley, or the Achaeans and Dorians when they reached Greece.

During the ensuing millennia the American Indians did develop an extraordinarily rich variety of cultures, adapted to one another as well as to the wide range of physical environments they encountered. Some remained at the hunting band stage while others developed kingdoms and empires. Their religions encompassed all known categories, including monotheism. They spoke some 2000 distinct languages, some as different from one another as Chinese and English. This represents almost as much variation in speech as in the entire Old World, where about 3000 languages are known to have existed in A.D. 1500. Nor were these languages primitive, either in vocabulary or in any other respect. Whereas Shakespeare used about 24,000 words, and the King James Bible about 7000, the Nahuatl of Mexico used 27,000 words, while the Yahgans of Tierra del Fuego, considered to be one of the world's most retarded peoples, possess a vocabulary of at least 30,000 words.

Taking all types of institutions and practices into account, anthropologists have defined some twenty-two culture areas in the New World—the Great Plains area, the Eastern Woodlands, the Northwest Coast area, and so forth. A simpler classification, on the basis of how food was obtained, involves three categories: hunting, gathering, and fishing cultures; intermediate farming cultures; and advanced farming cultures. This scheme is not only simpler but is also meaningful from the viewpoint of world history, for it helps to explain the varied responses of the Indians to the European invaders.

The advanced farming cultures were located in Mesoamerica (central and southern Mexico, Guatemala, and Honduras) and the Andean highland area (Ecuador, Peru, Bolivia, and northern Chile). The intermediate farming cultures were generally in the adjacent regions, while the food-gathering cultures were in the more remote regions—the southern part of South America, and the western and northern part of North America.

This geographic distribution of culture indicates that, in contrast to Africa, the most advanced regions in the Americas were not located closest to Eurasia. One reason is that northeast Siberia was not a great center of civilization, as was the Middle East and the

Mediterranean basin that contributed so much to the Africans. Also, climatic conditions in Alaska and the Canadian Arctic obviously were not favorable for rapid cultural development as was the case in the Sudan savannah zone. Thus the tempo of advance in the Americas depended not on proximity to Eurasia but rather on suitability for the development of agriculture. It is significant, then, that agriculture was first developed in the Americas in regions that were strikingly similar to the Middle East where agriculture originated in Eurasia—that is, highland regions not requiring extensive clearing of forests to prepare the fields for crops, with enough rainfall to allow the crops to mature, and with a supply of potentially high-yielding native plants available for domestication.

Chapter 2, section I describes the origins of agriculture in Mesoamerica about 7000 B.C. and the long stage of "incipient agriculture" to 1500 B.C. before food growing finally became the determining factor in society. The Indians domesticated over one hundred plants, or as many as were domesticated in all Eurasia, a truly extraordinary achievement. More than 50 percent of the farm products of the United States today are derived from crops grown by the Indians. The chief plants domesticated by the Indians were corn, potatoes, and beans. Other important plants were squashes, potatoes, tomatoes, peanuts, chocolate, and tobacco. Among the medicinal plants bequeathed by the Indians were cascara, cocaine, arnica, inepcac, and quinine. The fact that none of the plants grown in America was cultivated in the Old World before the discoveries proves conclusively that the origins of agriculture were independent in the two hemispheres.

The regions where the Indians began agriculture were also the regions where they first developed large empires and sophisticated civilizations comparable in certain respects to those of West Africa. Unfortunately, these indigenous American civilizations were suddenly overwhelmed by the Spaniards. Thus they left behind them little but their precious domesticated plants.

III. CIVILIZATIONS

The three major Amerindian civilizations were the Mayan, in present-day Yucatan, Guatemala, and British Honduras; the Aztec, in present-day Mexico; and the Inca, stretching for 3000 miles from mid-Ecuador to mid-Chile (see Map XXI, "Amerindian Empires"). The Mayans created the oldest civilization in the Americas, and were outstanding for their remarkable development of the arts and sciences. They alone evolved an ideographic form of writing in which characters or signs were used as conventional symbols for ideas. They also studied the movements of the heavenly bodies in order to measure time, predict the future, and set favorable dates for sacrifices and major undertakings. So extensive was the astronomical knowledge compiled by highly trained priests that it is believed to have been at least equal to that of Europe at that time. The intricate sacred calendar of the Mayans was based on concurrent cycles merging into greater cycles as their multiples coincided in time. Some of their calendrical computations spanned millions of years, a particularly impressive concept of the dimension of time when we remember how recently in Europe the creation of the world was fixed at 4004 B.C.

Maya cities, if they may be so called, were ceremonial centers rather than fortresses or dwelling places or administrative capitals. This was so because the Mayans practiced slash-and-burn agriculture, which exhausted the soil within two or three years, requiring constant moving of the village settlements. To balance this transitory mode of life, the Maya cultivators expressed their social unity by erecting large stone buildings in centers that were devoted primarily to religious ceremonies. These buildings were large temple pyramids and also community houses in which the priests and novices probably lived. The architecture, produced entirely with stone tools, was decorated with sculpture that was unsurpassed in the Americas and that ranks as one of the great world arts.

The Maya civilization flourished between the fourth and tenth centuries, but then it declined for reasons that remain obscure. It may have been soil exhaustion, or epidemic disease, or peasant revolutions against the burden of supporting the religious centers and their priestly hierarchies. In any case the great stone structures were abandoned to decay and were swallowed by the surrounding forest. They have been unearthed only in recent decades by archeological excavations.

The Aztecs were brusque and warlike compared to the artistic and intellectual Mayas—a contrast reminiscent of that between the Romans and the Greeks in the Old World. The Aztecs actually were latecomers to Mexico, where a series of highly developed societies had succeeded one another through the centuries. They were vulnerable to attacks by barbarians from the arid north who naturally moved down in response to the lure of fertile lands. The last of these invaders were the Aztecs, who had settled on some islands on Lake Texcoco, which then filled much of the floor of the valley of Anáhuac. As their numbers grew and the islands became overcrowded, the Aztecs increased their arable land by making chinampas, floating islands of matted weeds, covered with mud dredged from the lake floor, and anchored to the bottom by growing weeds. To the present day, this mode of cultivation is carried on in certain regions. Before each planting the farmers scoop up fresh mud and spread it over the chinampa, whose level steadily rises with the succession of crops. The farmers then excavate the top layers of mud, which they use to build a new chinampa, thus beginning a new cycle.

The chinampas enabled the Aztecs to boom in numbers and wealth. Early in the fifteenth century they made alliances with towns on the lake shore, and from that foothold they quickly extended their influence in all directions. Raiding expeditions went out regularly, forcing other peoples to pay tribute in kind and in services. By the time the Spaniards appeared on the scene, Aztec domination extended to the Pacific on the west, to the Gulf of Mexico on the east, almost to Yucatan on the south, and to the Rio Grande on the north. The capital, Tenochtitlán, was by then a magnificent city of 200,000 to 300,000 people, linked to the shore by causeways. The conqueror Cortes compared the capital to Venice and judged it to be "the most beautiful city in the world."

Aztec power was based on constant war preparedness. All men were expected to bear arms, and state arsenals were always stocked and ready for immediate use. With their efficient military machine the Aztecs were able to extract a staggering amount of tribute from their subjects. According to their own records, they collected in one year fourteen million pounds of maize, eight million pounds each of beans and amaranth, and two million cotton cloaks in addition to assorted other items such as war costumes, shields, and precious stones.

The splendor of the capital and the volume of tribute pouring into it naturally led the Spaniards to conclude that Montezuma was the ruler of a great empire. Actually this was not so. The vassal states remained quite separate, practicing full self-government. Their only tie to Tenochtitlán was the tribute, which they paid out of fear of the Aztec expeditions. None of the Amerindian states, except for that of the Incas in Peru, was organized on any concept wider than that of the city-state. The Aztecs, in contrast to the Incas, made no attempt to adapt their subjects to the Aztec way of life in preparation for full citizenship.

AZTEC MARKET PLACE

Bernal Diaz, the conquistador who accompanied Cortes in the conquest of Mexico, was a gifted and objective observor. His description of the market place in the Aztec capital reflects the productivity and wealth of the great Indian empire.*

The moment we arrived in this immense market, we were perfectly astonished at the vast numbers of people, the profusion of merchandise which was there exposed for sale, and at the good police and order that reigned throughout. The grandees who accompanied us drew our attention to the smallest circumstance, and gave us full explanation of all we saw. Every species of merchandise had a separate spot for its sale. We first of all visited those divisions of the market appropriated for the sale of gold and silver wares, of jewels, of cloths interwoven with feathers, and of other manufactured goods; besides slaves of both sexes. This slave market was upon as great a scale as the Portuguese market for negro slaves at Guinea. To prevent these from running away, they were fastened with halters about their neck, though some were allowed to walk at large. Next to these came the dealers in coarser wares—cotton, twisted, thread, and cacao. In short, every species of goods which New Spain produces were here to be found; and everything put me in mind of my native town Medino del Campo during fair time, where every merchandise has a separate street assigned for its sale. In one place were sold the stuffs manufactured of nequen; ropes, and sandals; in another place, the sweet maguey root, ready cooked, and various other things made from this plant. In another division of the market were exposed the skins of tigers, lions, jackals, otters, red deer, wild cats, and of other beasts of prey, some of which were tanned. In another place were sold beans and sage, with other herbs and vegetables. A particular market was assigned for the merchants in fowls, turkeys, ducks, rabbits, hares, deer, and dogs; also for fruit-sellers, pastry-cooks, and tripe-sellers. Not far from these were exposed all manner of earthenware, from the large earthen cauldron to the smallest pitchers. Then came the dealers in honey and honey-cakes, and other sweetmeats. Next to these, the timber-merchants, furniture-dealers, with their stores of tables, benches, cradles, and all sorts of wooden implements, all separately arranged. What can I further add?

In this market-place there were also courts of justice, to which three judges and several constables were appointed, who inspected the goods exposed for sale. I had almost forgotten to mention the salt, and those who made the flint knives; also the fish, and a species of bread made of a kind of mud or slime collected from the surface of this lake, and eaten in that form, and has a similar taste to our cheese. Further, instruments of brass, copper, and tin; cups, and painted pitchers of wood; indeed, I wish I had completed the enumeration of all this profusion of merchandize. The variety was so great that it would occupy more space than I can well spare to note them down in; besides which, the market was so crowded with people, and the thronging so excessive in the porticoes, that it was quite impossible to see all in one day. . . .

* J. I. Lockhart, trans., *The Memoirs of the Conquistador Bernal Diaz de Costillo* (London: Hatchard, 1844), I, 228–230.

The Spaniards were not only dazzled by the wealth and magnificence of the Aztec state but also horrified by the wholesale ritual massacre of a continual procession of human victims. These were slaughtered at the top of the ceremonial pyramids that abounded everywhere, and the Spaniards soon realized that the pyramids functioned as altars for human sacrifice. Sacrificial cults were common in Mesoamerica, but nowhere did they lead to the obsessive slaughtering practiced by the Aztecs. Indeed the reasons for Aztec expeditions were not only to collect tribute for their capital but to take captives for sacrifice as well. They considered the taking of captives as even more important than getting tribute, for their priests taught that the world was in constant danger of cataclysm, especially the extinguishing of the sun. Hence the need for offering human victims to appease the heavenly deities.

Turning finally to the Incas of Peru, they were one of the numerous tribes of Quechua stock and language who raised llamas and grew potatoes. In the twelfth century they established themselves in the Cuzco valley, which they soon dominated. At this early stage they built up a dynasty made up of their war chiefs, and their tribesmen constituted an aristocracy amongst the other tribal peoples. The combination of a hereditary dynasty and an aristocracy was unique in the New World and was an effective empire-building instrument. From their imperial city of Cuzco in the Peruvian highlands, the Incas sent forth armies and ambassadors, west to the coastal lands, and north and south along the great mountain valleys. By the time of the Spanish intrusion they had extended their frontiers some 2500 miles from Ecuador to central Chile. Thus they ruled much more territory than did the Aztecs, and furthermore they ruled it as a genuine empire.

This empire was held together physically by a road system which can still be traced for hundreds of miles and which included cable bridges of plaited aloe fibre and floating bridges on pontoons of buoyant reeds. Equally important was an extensive irrigation system, parts of which are still in use, and which made the Inca empire a flourishing agricultural unit. Communications were maintained by a comprehensive system of post-stations and relays of runners who conveyed messages swiftly to all parts of the empire.

Imperial unity was furthered also by elaborate court ritual and by a state religion based on worship of the sun. The Inca was held to be a descendant of the sun, he played an essential role in its ceremonial worship. Other techniques of imperial rule included state ownership of land, mineral wealth, and herds, careful census compilations for tax and military purposes, the deposing of local hereditary chieftains, forced population resettlement in order to assimilate conquered peoples, and mass marriages under state auspices. Not surprisingly, the Inca empire is considered to be one of the most successful totalitarian states the world has ever seen.

IV. CONCLUSION

Impressive as were these attainments of the American Indians, the fact remains that a handful of Spanish adventurers was easily able to overthrow and completely uproot all three of the great New World civilizations. And this despite the fact that the Aztec empire had a population of over 10 million and the Inca empire over 6 million. The explanation for the one-sided Spanish triumph is to be found ultimately in the isolation of the Americas. As in the case of Africa, this isolation, it should be noted, was internal as well as external. That is to say, not only were the American Indian civilizations cut off from stimulating interaction with civilizations on other continents, but also they were largely isolated from each other.

> With respect to interrelations between Peru and Mesoamerica [reports an archeologist] it is sufficient to state that not a single object or record of influence or contact between these areas had been accepted as authentic from the long time span between the Formative period [about 1000 B.C.] and the coming of the Spaniards. . . .[1]

In other words, there is no reliable evidence of interaction between the Mesoamerican and Peruvian civilizations over a span of 2500 years. And during those millennia, as we have seen, the various regions of Eurasia, and to a lesser extent sub-Saharan Africa, were in continual contact. The end result was that the American Indians—even those of the Andes and Mesoamerica—lagged far behind the Eurasians and especially behind the technologically precocious Europeans. By A.D. 1500 the New World had reached the stage of civilization that Egypt and Mesopotamia had attained about 2500 B.C.

Precisely what did this mean when the Spaniards arrived and confrontation occurred? It meant, in the first place, that the Indians found themselves economically and technologically far behind the civilization represented by the invaders. The highly developed art, science, and religion of the Indians should not be allowed to obscure the fact that they lagged seriously in more material fields. The disparity was most extreme in Mesoamerica, but it also prevailed in the Andean area. In agriculture, the Indians were brilliantly successful in domesticating plants but much less effective in actual production. Their cultivation techniques never advanced beyond the bare minimum necessary to feed populations that rarely reached the numbers of those of the Old World. Their tools were made only of stone, wood, or bone. They were incapable of smelting ores, and though they did work with metal, it was almost exclusively for ornamental purposes. The only ships they constructed were canoes and sea-going rafts. For land transportation they made no use of the wheel, which they knew but used only as a toy. With the exception of the llama and the alpaca, which were used in the Andes but could not carry heavy loads, only the human back was available for transportation.

The immediate significance of this technological lag should not be exaggerated. The Indians obviously were at a grave disadvantage with their spears and arrows against the Spaniards' horses and guns. But after the initial shock, the Indians became accustomed to firearms and cavalry. Furthermore, the Spaniards soon discovered that the Indian weapons were sharp and durable, and they came to prefer the Indian armor of quilted cotton to their own.

This suggests that technological disparity was not the only factor that lay behind the Spanish victories. Another was the lack of unity amongst the Indian peoples. In both Mexico and Peru the Spaniards were able to use disaffected subject tribes that had been alienated by the oppressive rule of Cuzco and Tenochtitlán. The Indians were also weakened by overregimentation and overdependency. They had been so indoctrinated and were so accustomed to carrying out orders without question that when their leaders were overthrown they were incapable of organizing resistance on their own. Once Montezuma and Atahuallpa had fallen into Spanish hands, the Aztec and Inca empires became bodies without heads, and resistance was paralyzed.

This passivity was increased by religious inhibitions. The natives thought that both Cortes in Mexico and Pizarro in Peru were gods returning in fulfillment of ancient prophecies. This explains the suicidal vacillations of Atahuallpa in Cuzco and of

Montezuma in Tenochtitlán. To Atahuallpa the Spaniards were the creator-god Viracocha and his followers, and for this reason the ruler waited meekly for Pizzaro, who with his 180 men quickly seized control of the great empire. Likewise, to Montezuma, Cortes was the god Quetzalcoatl who was returning to claim his rightful throne, so that again the ruler waited listlessly for the Spaniards to ensconce themselves in his capital.

Equally disastrous for the Aztecs was their concept of war as a short-term ritual endeavor. Their main interest in war was to capture prisoners, whose hearts they offered to their gods. Accordingly their campaigns frequently were ceremonial contests during which prisoners were taken with minimal dislocation and destruction. This type of military tradition obviously was a serious handicap. The Spaniards killed to win; the Aztecs simply tried to take prisoners.

If the great civilizations of the New World lacked the power and the cohesion to resist the Europeans, this was even more true of the less developed food-gathering and intermediate-farming culture areas. Precisely because they were less developed, they also had smaller populations, though the range of estimates varies greatly. Taking the traditional lower figures, there were, as against the 6 million in the Inca empire, only about 1 million in the rest of South America. Likewise, only another million lived north of the Rio Grande as against the 10 million to the south. When the Europeans appeared, the American Indians in these less developed regions simply lacked the numbers to hold their ground. Weakness due to small numbers was made worse by the diseases that the first explorers brought with them. The Indians, lacking immunity, were decimated by the epidemics, so that the early colonists often found abandoned fields and deserted village sites that they would take over.

Later, when the full flood of immigration from Europe got under way, the Indians were hopelessly overwhelmed. First, came the traders who penetrated throughout the Americas with little competition or resistance, for the Americas, unlike Africa, had no native merchant class. Then appeared the settlers who, attracted by the combination of healthful climate and fertile land, came in ever-increasing numbers and inundated the hapless Indians. When the latter occasionally took up arms in desperation, they were foredoomed to failure because they lacked both unity and the basic human and material resources. Thus, the unequal contest ended relatively quickly with the victorious white man in possession of the choice lands and the Indians relegated to reservations or to the less desirable regions that did not interest the new masters.

It is apparent that the balance of forces was quite different in America from what it was in Africa. Geography, relatively small population, and a comparatively low level of economic, political, and social organization all worked against the Indian and made it possible for the Europeans to take over the Americas at a time when they were still confined to a few toeholds on the coasts of Africa. Adam Smith was indeed justified in referring to the Indians as "miserable and helpless Americans" in contrast to the Africans.

V. AUSTRALIA

Australia is the most isolated large landmass in the world. It is so isolated that archaic forms of life have survived to modern times, including plants such as the eucalyptus family and mammals such as the monotremes and the marsupials. In Australia archaic human types also survived that were still in the Paleolithic stage when the first British settlers arrived in the late eighteenth century. As in the case of the American Indians, the date of the first appearance of the aborigines in Australia has not been determined. Archeological excavations have led to pushing the date farther and farther back. The latest findings indicate an arrival date of at least 31,000 years ago. Three different ethnic groups ferried over to Australia at that time when only narrow straits separated the continent from the Indonesian archipelago. These three strains can still be detected in the present-day aboriginal population. The majority are slender, long-limbed people with brown skins, little body hair, and wavy to curly head-hair and beards. They have survived in substantial numbers because they live in desert areas that are of little use to the white man. In the cool and fertile southeastern corner of the continent, there are a few survivors of a very different native stock—thick set, with light brown skin, heavy body hair, and luxuriant beards. Along the northeastern coast, in the only part of Australia covered with dense tropical rain forest, lives the third ethnic group. Part of the Negroid family, they are small, of slight build, and with woolly hair and black skins.

The culture of these peoples was by no means uniform. The most advanced were those in the southeast, where rainfall was adequate for permanent settlements. But throughout the continent, the aborigines, thanks to their complete isolation, had remained Paleolithic food gatherers. Their retardation was particularly evident in their technology and in their political organization. They wore no clothing except for decorative purposes. Their housing consisted, in dry country, of simple, open windbreaks, and, in wet country, of low, domed huts thrown together of any available material. Their principal weapons were spears, spear throwers, and boomerangs, all made of wood. They were ignorant of pottery, their utensils consisting merely of a few twined bags and baskets and occasional bowls made of bark or wood. As food gatherers and hunters they were highly skilled and ingenious. They had a wide range of vegetable, as well as animal, foods, and an intimate knowledge of the varieties, habits, and properties of these foods. They did all in their power to keep up the rate of reproduction of the plants and animals on which they depended. But since they were not food producers, their method of ensuring an adequate food supply was one of ritual rather than of cultivation. A typical ceremony was the mixing of blood with earth in places where the increase of game or plants was desired.

The poverty of Australian technology was matched by an almost equal poverty of political organization. Like most food-gathering peoples, the aborigines lived in bands, groups of families who normally camped together and roamed over a well-defined territory. They had no real tribes, but only territorial divisions characterized by differences in language and culture. Consequently, they did not have chiefs, courts, or other formal agencies of government. Yet these same aborigines had an extraordinarily complex social organization and ceremonial life. The hunter who brought in game or the woman who returned from a day of root digging was required to divide his take with all his kin according to strict regulations. Among the northern Queensland natives, when a man sneezed, all those within hearing slapped themselves on their bodies, the place varying according to their precise relationship to the sneezer.

So involved were these nonmaterial aspects of Australian society that they have been a delight to students of primitive institutions. But precociousness in these matters was of little help to the aborigines when the Europeans appeared in the late eighteenth century. If the American Indians with their flowering civilizations and widespread agricultural communities were unable to stand up to the white man, the Paleolithic Australians obviously had no chance. They were few in numbers, totaling about 30,000 when the Europeans arrived. This meant one or two persons per square mile in favorable coastal or river-valley environments, and only one person every 30 to 40 square miles in the arid interior. In addition to this numerical weakness, the aborigines lacked both the arms and the organization necessary for effective resistance. And unlike the American Indians and the African Negroes, they showed little inclination to secure and use the white man's "fire stick." Thus the unfortunate aborigines were brutally decimated by the British immigrants, many of whom were lawless convicts shipped out from overcrowded jails. The combination of disease, alcoholism, outright slaughter, and wholesale land confiscation has reduced the native population to 45,000 today, together with some 80,000 mixed breeds. The treatment accorded to the Australians is suggested by the following typical observation of a Victorian settler in 1853: "The Australian aboriginal race seems doomed by Providence, like the Mohican and many other well known tribes, to disappear from their native soil before the progress of civilization."[2]

SUGGESTED READING

A. A. Abbie, *The Original Australians* (Muller, 1969); A. F. Aveni, *Skywatchers of Ancient Mexico* (University of Texas Press, 1981); R. M. and C. H. Berndt, *The World of the First Australians* (University of Chicago Press, 1964); P. Farb, *Man's Rise to Civilization as Shown by the Indians of North America. . . .* (Dutton, 1968); A. M. Josephy, Jr., *The Indian Heritage of America* (Knopf, 1968); Reader's Digest staff and consultants, *America's Fascinating Indian Heritage* (Reader's Digest Press, 1978).

What It Means
To Us Today

RACES IN HISTORY

When the Western Europeans began their voyages of exploration, they found peoples scattered around the world living at very different levels of development. The Chinese, for example, had a civilization that was so wealthy, sophisticated, and well governed that many of the early European visitors considered it superior to their own. Other overseas people were naked, nomadic food gatherers whom the Europeans looked down upon as barely human. So they pushed them aside into deserts or jungles, or enslaved them, or hunted them down and exterminated them. In doing these things, the Europeans justified their actions on the ground that they were a superior people bringing the light of their superior civilization to the inferior (and therefore backward) peoples of the world.

This argument raises a question which is still a matter of dispute today. Are the various human races genetically equal, or are some inherently superior, and others inferior? The great majority of scientists, though not all, agree that races are genetically equal. Typical is the statement issued at an international conference of physical anthropologists and geneticists in September 1952:

> Available scientific knowledge provides no basis for believing that the groups of mankind differ in their innate capacity for intellectual and emotional development. . . . Genetic differences are of little significance in determining the social and cultural differences between different groups of men.[1]

224

If genes do not explain the great differences that European explorers found overseas, then what does? The distinguished anthropologist, Franz Boas, has offered a theory that seems to fit in with actual historical experience.

The history of mankind proves that advances of culture depend upon the opportunities presented to a social group to learn from the experience of their neighbors. The discoveries of the group to others and, the more varied the contacts, the greater the opportunities to learn. The tribes of simplest culture are on the whole those that have been isolated for very long periods and hence could not profit from the cultural achievements of their neighbors.[2]

In other words, the key to different levels of human development has been accessibility. Those with the most opportunity to interact with other people have been the most likely to forge ahead. Indeed they were driven to do so, for there was selective pressure as well as opportunity. Accessibility involved the constant threat of assimilation or elimination if opportunity was not grasped. By contrast, those who were isolated received neither stimulus nor threat, were free from selective pressure, and thus could remain relatively unchanged through the millennia without jeopardizing their existence.

If this hypothesis is applied on a global scale, the remote Australian aborigines should have been the most retarded of all major groups; next, the American Indians in the New World; then the Negroes of sub-Saharan Africa; and finally, the least retarded, or the most advanced, the various peoples of Eurasia who were in constant and generally increasing contact with each other. This, of course, is precisely the gradation of culture levels found by the European discoverers after 1500. The Australian aborigines were still at the Paleolithic food-gathering stage; the American Indians varied from the Paleolithic tribes of California to the impressive civilizations of Mexico, Central America, and Peru; the African Negroes presented comparable diversity, though their overall level of development was higher; and finally, at quite another level, there were the highly advanced and sophisticated civilizations found in Eurasia—the Moslem in the Middle East, the Hindu in South Asia, and the Confucian in East Asia.

We may conclude, then, that the western domination of the globe after 1500 did not mean Western genetic superiority. It meant only that, *at that period of history,* the Western Europeans were in the right place at the right time. At other periods of history, the situation was very different. For example, at the time of the Classical Civilizations, it was the people of the Mediterranean who were in the center of things, and therefore the most accessible and the most developed. By contrast, the Northern Europeans were then on the periphery, and therefore isolated and underdeveloped. Thus we find Cicero writing to a friend in Athens in the first century B.C.: "Do not obtain your slaves from Britain because they are so stupid and so utterly incapable of being taught that they are not fit to form a part of the household of Athens."[3]

Likewise during the period of the Medieval Civilizations, the Mediterranean still was the center, and Northern Europe still an isolated region of backward peoples. Thus a Moslem in Toledo, Spain, wrote in the eleventh century: "Races north of the Pyrenees are of cold temperament and never reach maturity; they are of great stature and of a white color. But they lack all sharpness of wit and penetration of intellect."[4]

Both Cicero and the Toledo Moslem appeared in their times to have been justified in looking down on Northern Europeans as "stupid" and lacking in "wit" and "intellect." But Nordic "backwardness" in classical and medieval times had no more to do with genes than did the "backwardness" of Africans or American Indians or Australian aborigines in the times of the discoveries—or the "backwardness" of the underdeveloped peoples of the world today.

SUGGESTED READING

The most useful book on the nature, significance, and results of race is by P. Mason, *Race Relations* (Oxford University Press, 1970). UNESCO has a collection of essays by an international group of scientists: *The Race Question in Modern Science* (Morrow, 1956). All these contributors agreed that race achievement is determined by historical and social backgrounds rather than by genes. The opposite view has recently been set forth in A. R. Jensen, *Genetics and Education* (Harper & Row, 1972), and in his *Bias in Mental Testing* (Free Press, 1980). Jensen's findings have been rejected by L. J. Kamin, *The Science and Politics of IQ* (John Wiley, 1974); by N. J. Block and G. Dworkin, eds., *The IQ Controversy* (Pantheon, 1976); and by S. J. Gould, "Jensen's Last Stand," *New York Review,* May 1, 1980, pp. 38–44. Finally, a fascinating account of the richness and variety of human cultures is presented in I. C. Brown, *Understanding Other Cultures* (Prentice-Hall, 1963).

Maps

The range of human activity throughout history has been determined by the level of technological development. The more primitive the technology, the more constricted the range; and, conversely, the more advanced the technology, the more extensive the range. Thus in *Map I, Global Distribution of Hominids and Homo Sapiens,* the Australopithecines with their primitive pebble tools and lack of clothing are restricted to the warm African savannas; Homo erectus with their superior tools and clothing and control of fire has expanded into the temperate zones of Eurasia; while Homo sapiens with their still more complex technology has pushed further into Northern Eurasia, the Americas and Australia.

Technological advance has involved not only range extension but also population growth. The more advanced the technology, the more efficient the exploitation of the physical environment and, hence, the larger the population that can support itself in a given region. *Map II, World Population Growth,* presents the population "explosions" resulting from each technological revolution from Paleolithic times to the present.

The population explosions were naturally limited to those races that participated in the technological revolutions. Consequently, as shown in *Map III, Global Race Distribution,* certain races have increased to their present dominant status, while others have dwindled to insignificance.

With the agricultural revolution, the disparity in population growth not only resulted in the rise of certain races and the fall of others, but also caused an increase of agriculturists and a decrease of hunters. The agriculturists, possessing the more-advanced technology, far outstripped the hunters, as depicted in *Map IV, Recession of Hunters,* in *Map V, Expansion of Agriculturists,* and also in *Map V-a, Dispersal of Agriculture.*

The agricultural revolution made possible the rise of civilizations, which were at first limited to the fertile river valley where agriculture was most productive. Thus the early civilizations, as shown in *Map VI, Ancient Civilizations of Eurasia, 3500–1500 B.C.,* were small islands in the surrounding seas of barbarism. These ancient civilizations were overwhelmed during the second millennium B.C. by Indo-European and Semitic nomadic invasions, which thereby cleared the ground for the succeeding classical civilizations.

The classical civilizations and empires covered entire regions rather than isolated river valleys. The development of these regional empires in Europe, India, and China is presented in *Maps VII, VIII,* and *IX.* These regional empires together comprised a new Eurasian unity—a continuous belt of civilizations and imperial structures across the breadth of Eurasia. The political, religious, and economic components of this new entity are depicted in *Map X, Early Eurasian Unification About A.D. 200.*

The classical civilizations, like the ancient ones, were in many cases overthrown by a new wave of Eurasian-wide invasions, as pictured in *Map XI, Barbarian Invasions in Eurasia, 4th and 5th Centuries A.D.* In most of Eurasia, imperial structures eventually were reconstituted and stabilized, but in the West the short-lived Carolingian Empire was overthrown by a new wave of invasions by Moslems, Magyars, and Vikings (*Map XII, Continued Barbarian Invasions in the West, 9th and 10th Centuries*). Two other great waves of invasions profoundly affected medieval Eurasia—that of Islam beginning in the seventh century and that of the Mongols in the thirteenth century (*Map XIII, Expansion of Islam to 1500* and *Map XIV, Mongol Empire at the Death of Kublai Khan, 1294*).

Destructive though these invasions were initially, they did forge bonds and create a Eurasian unity more closely knit than that of the classical period (*Map X*). This new medieval world, with its network of trade routes and wide-ranging travelers, is depicted in *Map XV, Eurasian Unification About 1300.*

In the late Middle Ages, Western Europe passed from an attitude of self-defense, as shown in *Map XII,* and took the offensive. This expansionism was the product of a combination of factors, including technological advances, economic growth, population upsurge and religious militancy. The result was a series of Crusades, motivated at least as much by secular considerations as by religious ones, and launched in all directions, as depicted in *Map XVI, Expansionism of the Medieval West, 11th to 15th Century.*

Because of Western Europe's lead in global exploration, it is often overlooked that in the early fifteenth century the Chinese undertook a series of expeditions that were far more ambitious and wide-ranging than anything in the West at that time, as illustrated in *Map XVII, Early 15th Century Chinese and Portuguese Voyages.*

As striking as the difference between the Chinese and Portuguese voyages was the contrasting fate in Eastern Europe of the Byzantines and the Russians. The Byzantine Empire, which had controlled the Mediterranean basin under Justinian I, shrank during the following centuries, though with periodic comebacks, until by the 15th century it comprised only two small footholds, one in the Peloponnesus and the other around the city of Constantinople. This shrinking is depicted in *Map XVIII, Decline of the Byzantine Empire.* To the north, by contrast, the gathering of the Russian lands was being achieved under the leadership of Muscovy. *Map XIX, The Growth of Muscovy,* depicts this unifying process to the end of Ivan III's reign in 1505.

Meanwhile developments comparable to those in Eurasia had been unfolding in the non-Eurasian world, though at a slower pace. The advent of agriculture and iron metallurgy in sub-Saharan Africa stimulated economic growth, commerce and empire building (*Map XX, African Empires and Trade Routes*). In the Americas, agriculture was developed independently and most successfully, as reflected in the large number of plants that were domesticated. But the Americas suffered from isolation, so that iron metallurgy never reached the New World as it did sub-Saharan Africa from Eurasia. Nevertheless, the flourishing agriculture did provide a base for state structures comparable to those of sub-Saharan Africa, as shown in *Map XXI, Amerindian Empires on the Eve of the Spanish Conquest.*

As a result of the historical evolution shown in the above maps, the various regions of the world had reached different levels of development by 1500, when the Europeans began their overseas expansion which for the first time brought all the regions into direct contact with each other. This disparity in development, as shown in *Map XXII, Culture Areas of the World About 1500,* is of basic historical significance, for it determined the course and speed of European expansion during the following centuries. The more retarded the overseas territories, the more swift and overwhelming the European intrusion, and, conversely, the more advanced the overseas territories, the more effective and prolonged their resistance to the Europeans.

Until the fifteenth-century Iberian discoveries, man had lived in regional isolation. Australia and the Americas had been completely isolated, Africa largely so, and even the various regions of Eurasia had interacted only intermittently. With European overseas expansion this regional compartmentalization gave way to global unity, as illustrated in *Map XXIII, Western Man's Knowledge of the Globe, A.D. 1 to 1800.* Since the West took the lead in overseas expansion, it dominated world trade routes and established colonies in the underdeveloped portions of the globe (*Map XXIV, World of the Emerging West, 1763*).

The industrial revolution, in which the West also pioneered, further increased Western Europe's power and influence in world affairs. One result was the extension of European political domination throughout the world, as described in *Map XXV, Russian Expansion in Europe and Asia,* and *Map XXVI, World of Western Dominance, 1914.*

This Western global hegemony of the nineteenth century stimulated a reaction in the twentieth century that culminated in national and social revolution in the colonial territories. Thus the world of today is altogether different from that of the pre-World War I era, as illustrated in *Map XXVII, World of New Global Relationships, 1980.*

GLOBAL DISTRIBUTION OF HOMINIDS AND HOMO SAPIENS

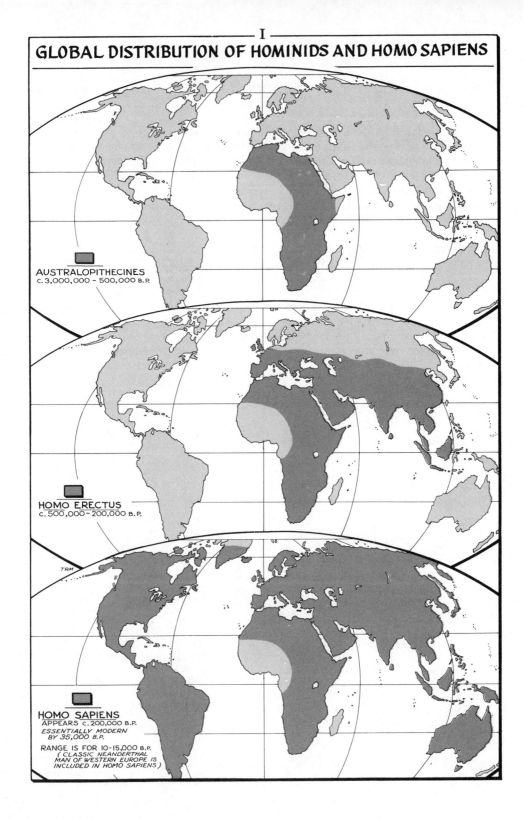

AUSTRALOPITHECINES
c. 3,000,000 – 500,000 B.P.

HOMO ERECTUS
c. 500,000 – 200,000 B.P.

TRM

HOMO SAPIENS
APPEARS c. 200,000 B.P.
ESSENTIALLY MODERN BY 35,000 B.P.
RANGE IS FOR 10–15,000 B.P.
(CLASSIC NEANDERTHAL MAN OF WESTERN EUROPE IS INCLUDED IN HOMO SAPIENS)

II
WORLD POPULATION GROWTH

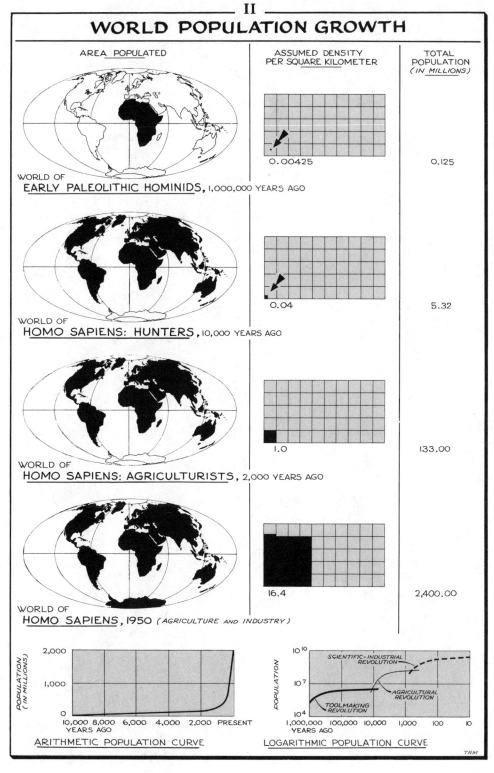

AREA POPULATED	ASSUMED DENSITY PER SQUARE KILOMETER	TOTAL POPULATION (IN MILLIONS)
	0.00425	0.125

WORLD OF
EARLY PALEOLITHIC HOMINIDS, 1,000,000 YEARS AGO

	0.04	5.32

WORLD OF
HOMO SAPIENS: HUNTERS, 10,000 YEARS AGO

	1.0	133.00

WORLD OF
HOMO SAPIENS: AGRICULTURISTS, 2,000 YEARS AGO

	16.4	2,400.00

WORLD OF
HOMO SAPIENS, 1950 (AGRICULTURE AND INDUSTRY)

ARITHMETIC POPULATION CURVE

LOGARITHMIC POPULATION CURVE

TRM

231

III
GLOBAL RACE DISTRIBUTION

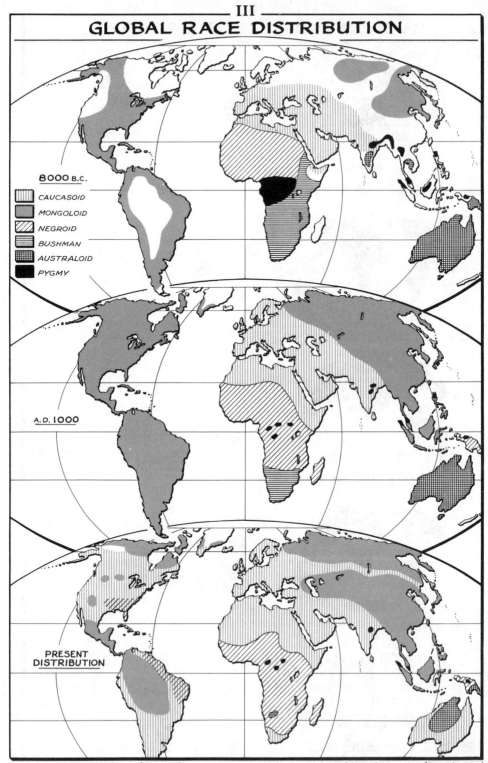

8000 B.C.

CAUCASOID
MONGOLOID
NEGROID
BUSHMAN
AUSTRALOID
PYGMY

A.D. 1000

PRESENT DISTRIBUTION

Adapted from W.W.Howells, "The Distribution of Man," *Scientific American* (September, 1960).

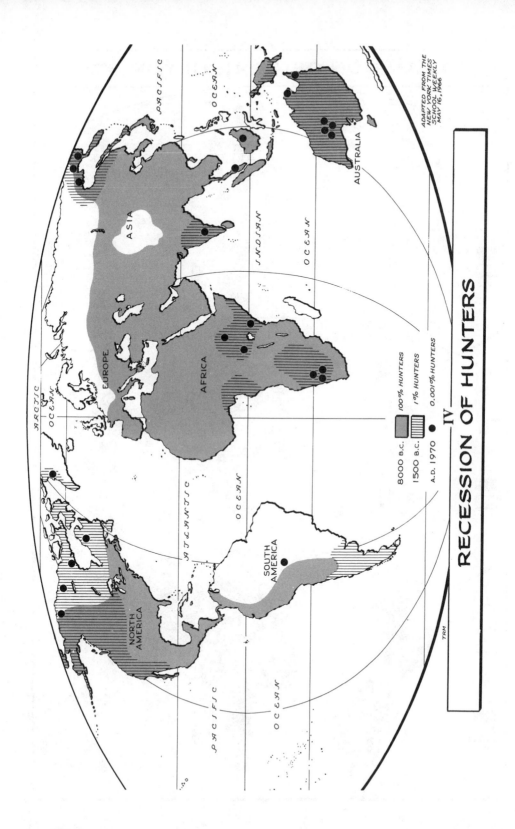

RECESSION OF HUNTERS

8000 B.C. · 100% HUNTERS
1500 B.C. · 1% HUNTERS
A.D. 1970 · 0.001% HUNTERS

IV

ADAPTED FROM THE
NEW YORK TIMES
SCHOOL WEEKLY
MAY 16, 1966

233

EXPANSION OF AGRICULTURISTS

EXPANSION OF
AGRICULTURE

■ 3000 B.C.

▥ 3000 – 500 B.C.

■ 500 B.C.

▥ 500 B.C.–A.D. 1500

■ A.D. 1500

▥ A.D. 1500 – 1970

TRM

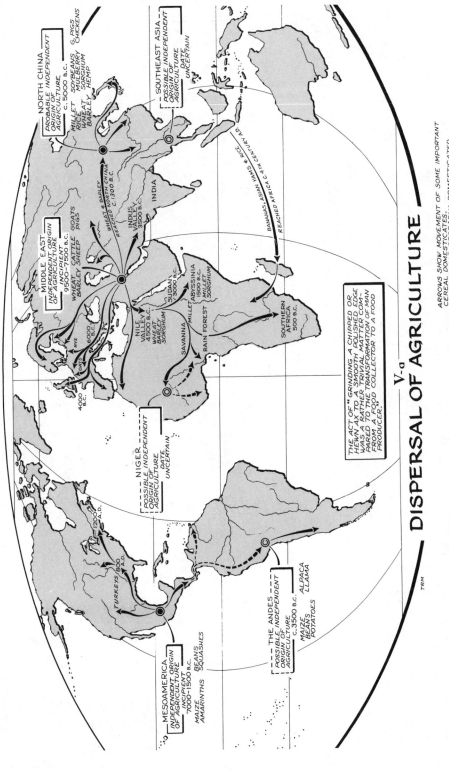

DISPERSAL OF AGRICULTURE

V-a

NORTH CHINA
PROBABLE INDEPENDENT
ORIGIN OF
AGRICULTURE
c. 5000 B.C.

MILLET
RICE
WHEAT
BARLEY
SOYBEANS
MULBERRY
SORGHUM
HEMP
G, PIGS
CHICKENS

SOUTHEAST ASIA —
POSSIBLE INDEPENDENT
ORIGIN OF
AGRICULTURE
DATE
UNCERTAIN

MIDDLE EAST
INDEPENDENT ORIGIN
OF AGRICULTURE
INCIPIENT
9500-7500 B.C.

WHEAT CATTLE GOATS
BARLEY SHEEP PIGS

WHEAT & BARLEY
REACHED NORTH CHINA
c. 1300 B.C.

INDIA

INDUS
VALLEY
3500 B.C.

6,600
B.C.

RYE

4,000
B.C.

OATS

NILE
VALLEY
4500 B.C.

WHEAT
BARLEY
SORGHUM

SUDAN
3000 B.C.

ABYSSINIA
1500 B.C.
MILLET
SORGHUM

MILLET

SAVANNA

RAIN FOREST

SOUTHERN
AFRICA
500 B.C.

BANANAS, ASIAN YAMS & RICE A.D.
REACHED AFRICA C. 4TH CENTURY A.D.

NIGER —
POSSIBLE INDEPENDENT
ORIGIN OF
AGRICULTURE
DATE
UNCERTAIN

1200 A.D.

TURKEYS 800
A.D.

THE ANDES —
POSSIBLE INDEPENDENT
ORIGIN OF
AGRICULTURE
c. 3500 B.C.

MAIZE
BEANS
POTATOES

ALPACA
LLAMA

MESOAMERICA
INDEPENDENT ORIGIN OF
AGRICULTURE
INCIPIENT
7000-1500 B.C.

MAIZE
AMARANTHS

BEANS
SQUASHES

"THE ACT OF "GRINDING A CHIPPED OR
HEWN AX TO A SMOOTH POLISHED EDGE
WAS A RATHER TRIVIAL MATTER COM-
PARED TO THE TRANSFORMATION OF MAN
FROM A FOOD COLLECTOR TO A FOOD
PRODUCER.""

ARROWS SHOW MOVEMENT OF SOME IMPORTANT
CEREAL DOMESTICATES.
MILLET WAS PROBABLY DOMESTICATED
IN SUBSAHARAN AFRICA AFTER THE
DISPERSAL OF AGRICULTURE FROM
THE NORTH.

DATES INDICATE ACHIEVEMENT
OF A "SETTLED FARMING"
WAY OF LIFE BY SOME PEOPLE
IN THE REGION.

TRM

235

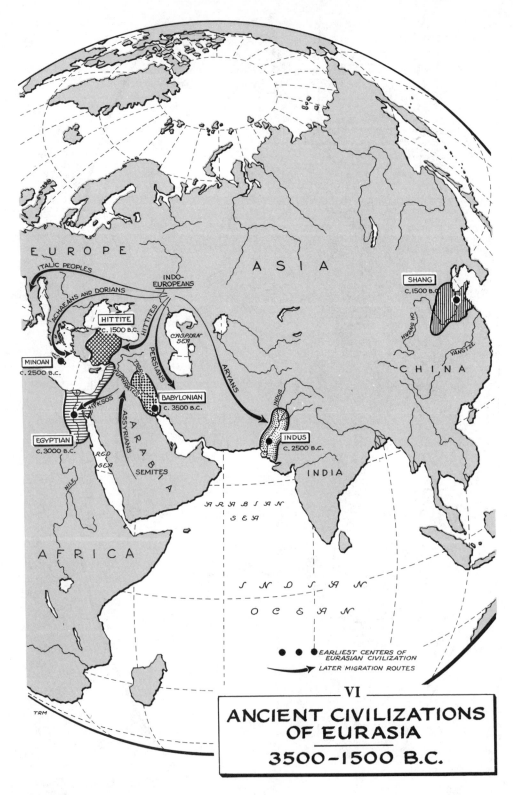

EUROPE

ITALIC PEOPLES

ACHAEANS AND DORIANS

INDO-EUROPEANS

ASIA

SHANG
c. 1500 B.C.

HITTITES

HITTITE
c. 1500 B.C.

MINOAN
c. 2500 B.C.

CASPIAN
SEA

PERSIANS

HUANG HO

ARYANS

YANGTZE

CHINA

EUPHRATES

TIGRIS

HYKSOS

BABYLONIAN
c. 3500 B.C.

ASSYRIANS

INDUS

EGYPTIAN
c. 3000 B.C.

A R A B I A

INDUS
c. 2500 B.C.

RED
SEA

NILE

SEMITES

INDIA

A R A B I A N

S E A

AFRICA

I N D I A N

O C E A N

• • • EARLIEST CENTERS OF
EURASIAN CIVILIZATION

⟶ LATER MIGRATION ROUTES

TRM

VI

ANCIENT CIVILIZATIONS
OF EURASIA

3500–1500 B.C.

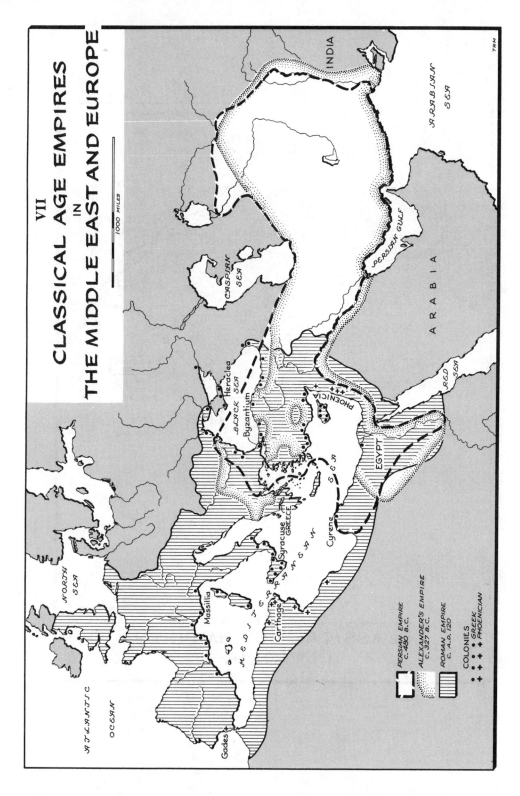

CLASSICAL AGE EMPIRES
IN
THE MIDDLE EAST AND EUROPE

VII

1000 MILES

INDIA

ARABIAN SEA

ARABIA

PERSIAN GULF

CASPIAN SEA

RED SEA

Heraclea

BLACK SEA

Byzantium

PHOENICIA

EGYPT

GREECE

Syracuse

Cyrene

AEGEAN SEA

Massilia

MEDITERRANEAN SEA

Carthage

NORTH SEA

ATLANTIC OCEAN

Gades

PERSIAN EMPIRE
C. 480 B.C.

ALEXANDER'S EMPIRE
C. 327 B.C.

ROMAN EMPIRE
C. A.D. 120

COLONIES
GREEK
PHOENICIAN

TRM

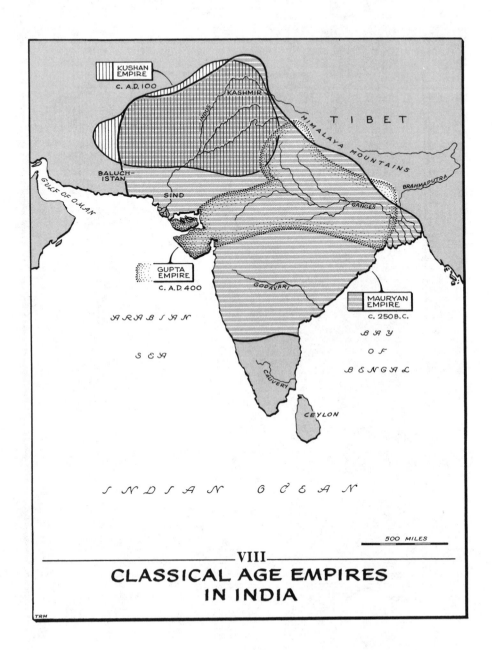

KUSHAN
EMPIRE
C. A.D. 100

GUPTA
EMPIRE
C. A.D. 400

MAURYAN
EMPIRE
c. 250 B.C.

TIBET

KASHMIR

HIMALAYA MOUNTAINS

BRAHMAPUTRA

INDUS

BALUCH-
ISTAN

SIND

GANGES

GODAVARI

ARABIAN

SEA

BAY

OF

BENGAL

GULF OF OMAN

CAUVERY

CEYLON

INDIAN OCEAN

500 MILES

TRM

VIII

CLASSICAL AGE EMPIRES
IN INDIA

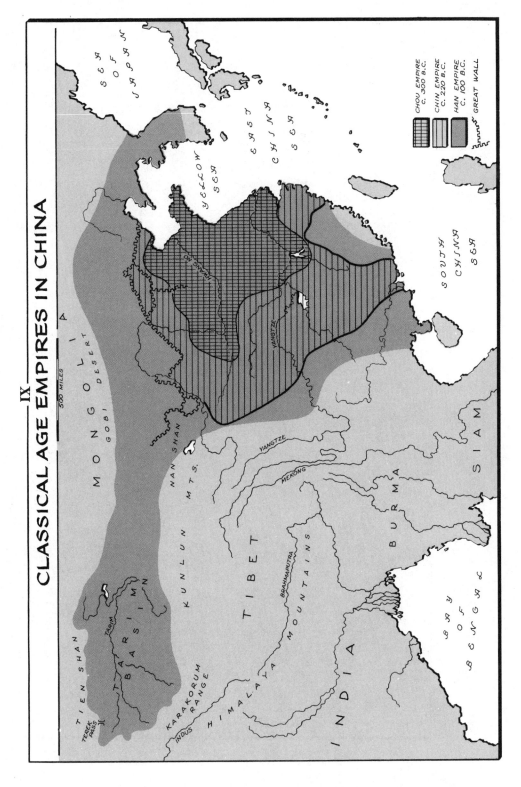

IX

CLASSICAL AGE EMPIRES IN CHINA

CHOU EMPIRE
C. 300 B.C.

CHIN EMPIRE
C. 220 B.C.

HAN EMPIRE
C. 100 B.C.

GREAT WALL

500 MILES

SEA OF JAPAN

EAST CHINA SEA

YELLOW SEA

SOUTH CHINA SEA

MONGOLIA

GOBI DESERT

HWANG HO

YANGTZE

NAN SHAN

KUNLUN MTS.

TIEN SHAN

TARIM

TARIM BASIN

TEREK PASS

KARAKORUM RANGE

INDUS

HIMALAYA MOUNTAINS

TIBET

BRAHMAPUTRA

YANGTZE

MEKONG

INDIA

BURMA

SIAM

BAY OF BENGAL

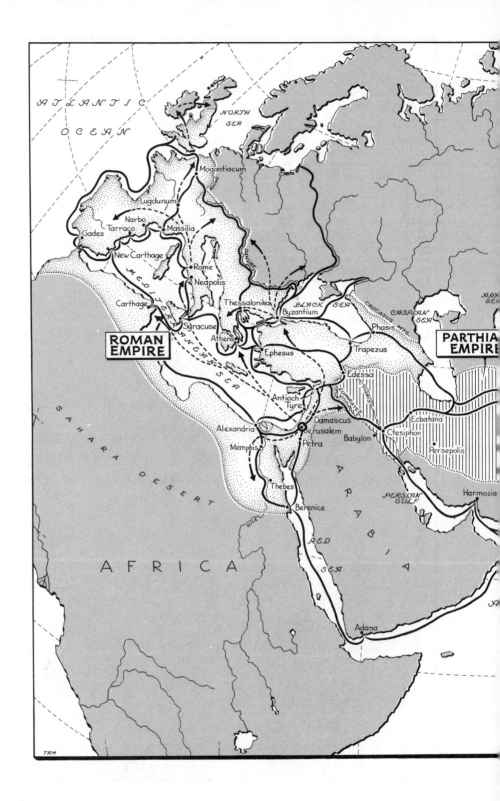

ATLANTIC OCEAN

NORTH SEA

Mogontiacum

Lugdunum

Narbo
Tarraco
Gades
New Carthage

Massilia

Rome

Neapolis

Carthage

MEDITERRANEAN SEA

ROMAN EMPIRE

Thessalonika

Byzantium

BLACK SEA

CAUCASUS MTS.

CASPIAN SEA

ARAL SEA

PARTHIAN EMPIRE

Syracuse

Athens

Ephesus

Trapezus

Phasis

Edessa

EUPHRATES

TIGRIS

Ecbatana

Antioch
Tyre

Damascus

Ctesiphon

Persepolis

Alexandria

Jerusalem

Petra

Babylon

Memphis

SAHARA DESERT

Thebes

Berenice

NILE

RED SEA

ARABIA

PERSIAN GULF

Harmozia

AFRICA

Adana

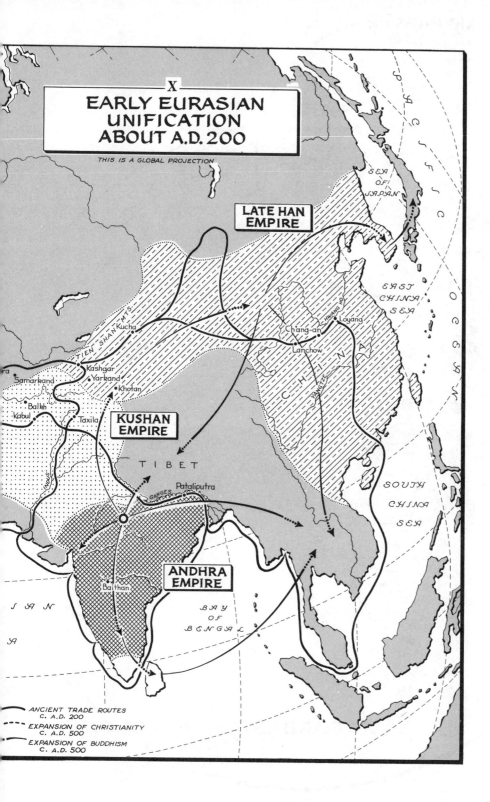

X
EARLY EURASIAN UNIFICATION ABOUT A.D. 200

THIS IS A GLOBAL PROJECTION

LATE HAN EMPIRE

KUSHAN EMPIRE

ANDHRA EMPIRE

TIBET

CHINA

PACIFIC OCEAN

SEA OF JAPAN

EAST CHINA SEA

SOUTH CHINA SEA

BAY OF BENGAL

TIEN SHAN MTS.

Kucha

Chang-an

Loyang

Lanchow

HWANG HO

YANGTZE

Kashgar

Yarkand

Khotan

Samarkand

Balkh

Kabul

Taxila

INDUS

GANGES

Pataliputra

Baithan

ANCIENT TRADE ROUTES
C. A.D. 200
EXPANSION OF CHRISTIANITY
C. A.D. 500
EXPANSION OF BUDDHISM
C. A.D. 500

241

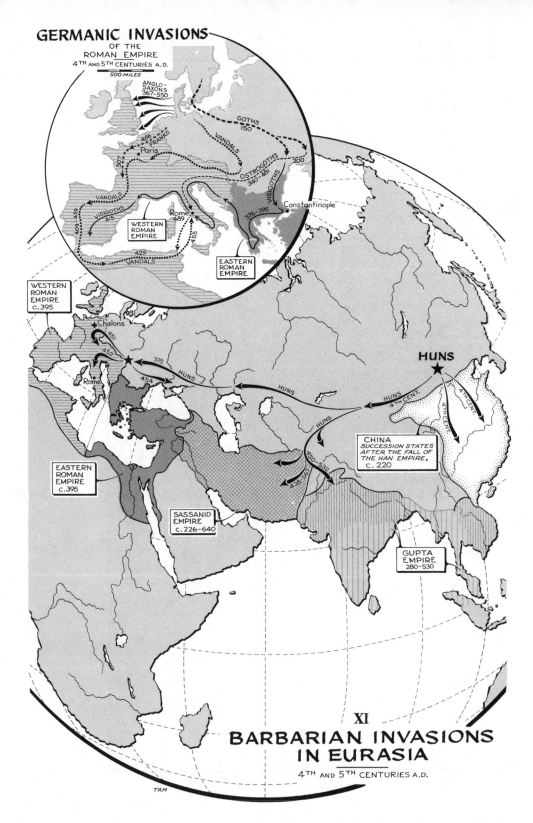

GERMANIC INVASIONS
OF THE
ROMAN EMPIRE
4TH AND 5TH CENTURIES A.D.

500 MILES

ANGLO-SAXONS 367-550

GOTHS 150

VANDALS

FRANKS 486

Paris

507

OSTROGOTHS 340-481

VISIGOTHS

200

Constantinople

VANDALS

VISIGOTHS 415

409-429

WESTERN ROMAN EMPIRE

Rome 489

455

376-395

VANDALS 429

EASTERN ROMAN EMPIRE

WESTERN ROMAN EMPIRE c. 395

Chalons 451

452

375

HUNS

454

Rome

HUNS

HUNS

HUNS

HUNS 4TH CENT.

4TH CENT.

4TH CENT.

HUNS

CHINA *SUCCESSION STATES AFTER THE FALL OF THE HAN EMPIRE,* c. 220

EASTERN ROMAN EMPIRE c. 395

350-535

428-567

SASSANID EMPIRE c. 226-640

GUPTA EMPIRE 280-530

XI

BARBARIAN INVASIONS IN EURASIA
4TH AND 5TH CENTURIES A.D.

TRM

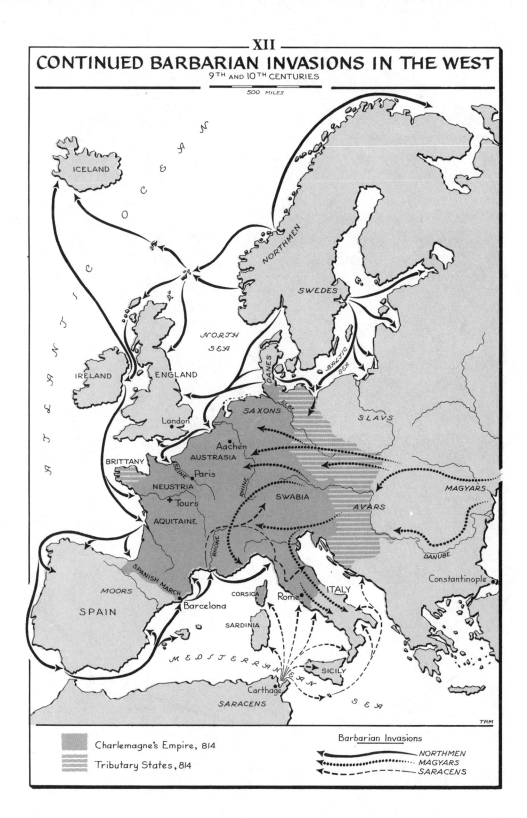

CONTINUED BARBARIAN INVASIONS IN THE WEST
9TH AND 10TH CENTURIES

500 MILES

ICELAND

NORTHMEN

SWEDES

NORTH SEA

BALTIC SEA

IRELAND

ENGLAND

DANES

London

SAXONS

SLAVS

ELBE

Aachen

AUSTRASIA

BRITTANY

SEINE

Paris

RHINE

NEUSTRIA

SWABIA

AVARS

MAGYARS

+ Tours

AQUITAINE

RHONE

DANUBE

SPANISH MARCH

ITALY

Constantinople

MOORS

CORSICA

Rome

SPAIN

Barcelona

SARDINIA

MEDITERRANEAN

SICILY

Carthage

SEA

SARACENS

TRM

Charlemagne's Empire, 814

Tributary States, 814

Barbarian Invasions

NORTHMEN
MAGYARS
SARACENS

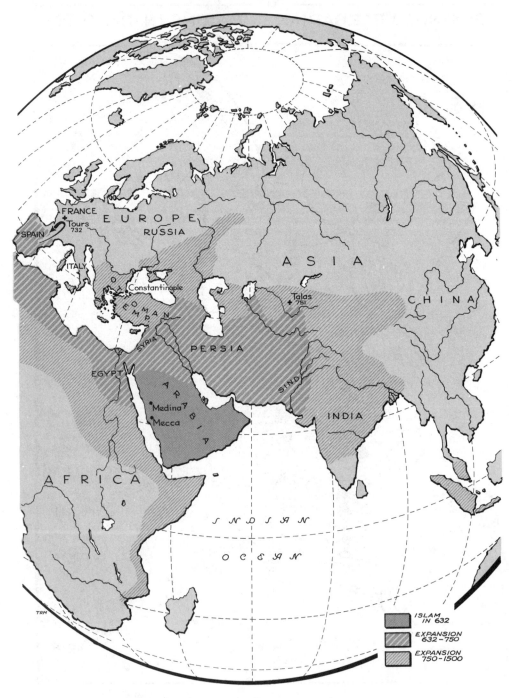

FRANCE
Tours
732
SPAIN
EUROPE
RUSSIA
ITALY
ASIA
CHINA
Constantinople
Talas
751
PERSIA
SYRIA
EGYPT
A R A B I A
Medina
Mecca
SIND
INDIA
AFRICA
I N D I A N
O C E A N

ISLAM
IN 632

EXPANSION
632-750

EXPANSION
750-1500

XIII
EXPANSION OF ISLAM TO 1500

EUROPE

HUNGARY

RUSSIAN
STATES
• Kiev

• Vladimir

GREAT SIBERIAN PLAIN

KHANATE OF
KIPCHAK

GOLDEN HORDE

• Sarai

Constantinople

Karakorum

• Shangtu

• Khanbaligh

KHANATE OF
THE GREAT KHAN

KHANATE OF
CHAGHADAI

CHINA

Samarkand

• Kashgar

• Balkh

Baghdad •

KHANATE OF
PERSIA

ILKHAN

TIBET

Foochow

ARABIA

• Mecca

RED
SEA

INDIA

ARABIAN
SEA

AFRICA

INDIAN

OCEAN

TRM

XIV

MONGOL EMPIRE

AT THE DEATH OF KUBLAI KHAN

1294

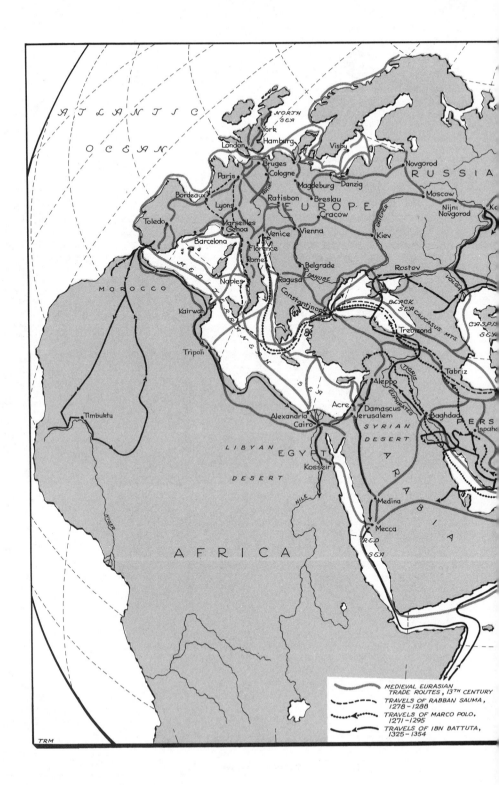

ATLANTIC OCEAN

NORTH SEA

York
London
Hamburg
Visby
Novgorod
RUSSIA

Bruges
Cologne
Paris
Magdeburg
Danzig
Moscow

Bordeaux
Ratisbon
Breslau
EUROPE
Cracow
Nijni Novgorod

Lyons
Venice
Vienna
Kiev

Toledo
Marseilles
Genoa
Rostov

Barcelona
Florence
Rome
Belgrade
VOLGA

MOROCCO
Naples
Ragusa
DANUBE
Constantinople
BLACK SEA
CAUCASUS MTS
CASPIAN SEA

Kairwan
MEDITERRANEAN SEA
Trebizond

Tripoli
Tabriz

TIGRIS

Aleppo
EUPHRATES
Baghdad
PERS
Ispaha

Alexandria
Acre
Damascus
Jerusalem
SYRIAN DESERT

Cairo

Timbuktu
LIBYAN DESERT
EGYPT
Kosseir
A
R
A
B
I
A

DESERT

NIGER
NILE
Medina

AFRICA
Mecca
RED SEA

TRM

MEDIEVAL EURASIAN
TRADE ROUTES, 13TH CENTURY

TRAVELS OF RABBAN SAUMA,
1278-1288

TRAVELS OF MARCO POLO,
1271-1295

TRAVELS OF IBN BATTUTA,
1325-1354

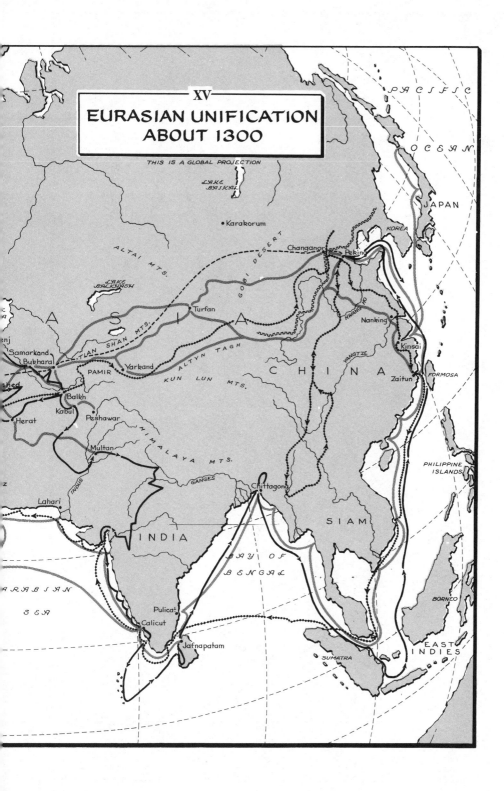

XV

EURASIAN UNIFICATION ABOUT 1300

THIS IS A GLOBAL PROJECTION

PACIFIC
OCEAN

LAKE BAIKAL

JAPAN

• Karakorum

KOREA

ALTAI MTS.

GOBI DESERT

Changanor   Peking

LAKE BALKHASH

Turfan

A S I A

TIAN SHAN MTS.

HWANG   Nanking

Samarkand
Bukhara

PAMIR   • Yarkand

ALTYN TAGH

C H I N A

Kinsai

KUN LUN MTS.

YANGTZE

Zaitun

FORMOSA

Balkh

Kabul

Peshawar

HIMALAYA MTS.

Herat

Multan

INDUS

GANGES

Chittagong

PHILIPPINE
ISLANDS

Lahari

I N D I A

SIAM

ARABIAN

SEA

BAY   OF

BENGAL

BORNEO

Pulicat

Calicut

Jafnapatam

SUMATRA

EAST
INDIES

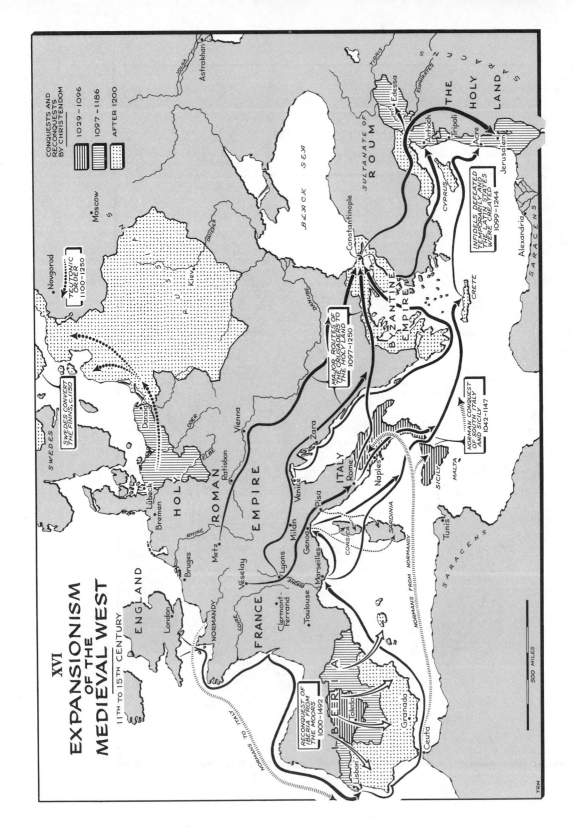

XVI

EXPANSIONISM
OF THE
MEDIEVAL WEST

11TH to 15TH CENTURY

CONQUESTS AND
RECONQUESTS
BY CHRISTENDOM

1029–1096
1097–1186
AFTER 1200

SWEDES CONVERT
THE FINNS, c.1150

TEUTONIC
ORDER
1100–1250

MAJOR ROUTES OF
THE CRUSADERS TO
THE HOLY LAND
1097–1250

NORMAN CONQUEST
OF SOUTHERN ITALY
AND SICILY
1042–1147

INFIDELS DEFEATED
THE TEMPORARY LANDS
THE LATIN STATES
WERE CREATED
1099–1244

RECONQUEST OF
IBERIA FROM
THE MOORS
1000–1492

500 MILES

SWEDES

Novgorod

Astrakhan

Moscow

Kiev

VOLGA

DNIEPER

P R U S

OD ER

ELBE

Danzig

Lübeck

Bremen

HOLY

ROMAN

EMPIRE

Ratisbon

Vienna

DANUBE

RHINE

Metz

ENGLAND

London

NORMANDY

LOIRE

FRANCE

Clermont-
Ferrand

Vézelay

Toulouse

Lyons

RHONE

Marseilles

Milan

Genoa

Pisa

Venice

Zara

ITALY

Rome

Naples

CORSICA

SARDINIA

NORMANS FROM NORMANDY

NORMANS TO ITALY

Bruges

Lisbon

Toledo

IBERIA

Granada

Ceuta

Tunis

SARACENS

SARACENS

MALTA

SICILY

BLACK SEA

Constantinople

BYZANTINE

EMPIRE

SULTANATE OF
ROUM

CRETE

CYPRUS

TIGRIS

EUPHRATES

Edessa

Antioch

Tripoli

Acre

Jerusalem

Alexandria

THE

HOLY

LAND

SARACENS

TRM

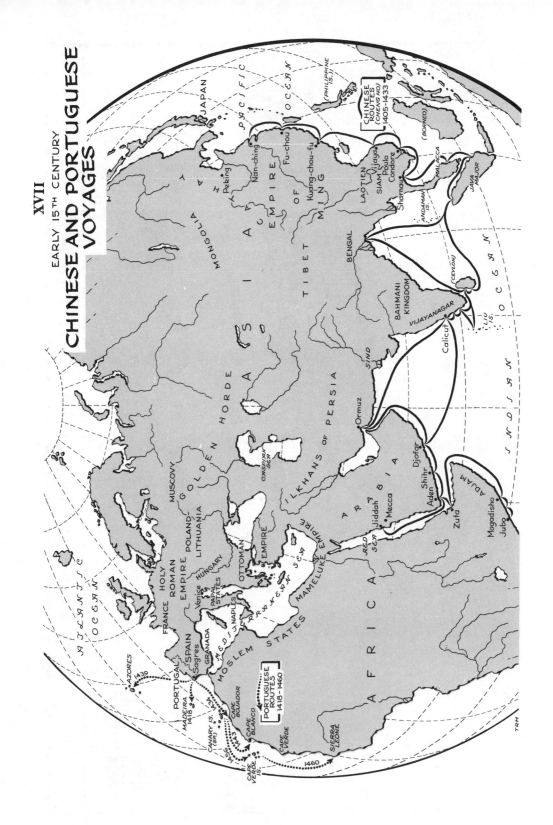

XVII

EARLY 15TH CENTURY

CHINESE AND PORTUGUESE VOYAGES

CHINESE ROUTES (CHENG HO) 1405-1433

PORTUGUESE ROUTE 1418-1460

ATLANTIC OCEAN
PACIFIC OCEAN
INDIAN OCEAN

JAPAN
MONGOLIA
MING EMPIRE
Peking
Nan-ching
Fu-chou
Kuang-chou-fu
TIBET
ASIA
LAOTIEN
SIAM
Shanau
Poulo Condore
(PHILIPPINE IS.)
(BORNEO)
MALACCA
JAVA MAJOR
ANDAMAN IS.
(CEYLON)
LIU IS.
BENGAL
BAHMANI KINGDOM
VIJAYANAGAR
Calicut
SIND
Ormuz
ILKHANS OF PERSIA
GOLDEN HORDE
MUSCOVY
POLAND-LITHUANIA
HUNGARY
HOLY ROMAN EMPIRE
FRANCE
Venice
PAPAL STATES
OTTOMAN EMPIRE
NAPLES
GRANADA
SPAIN
CASPIAN SEA
MEDITERRANEAN
MOSLEM STATES
MAMELUKE EMPIRE
ARABIA
RED SEA
Jiddah
Mecca
Aden
Shihr
Djofar
Zufa
AFRICA
Mogadisho
Jubo
ADJAM
SIERRA LEONE
CAPE VERDE
CAPE VERDE IS.
CAPE BLANCO
CAPE BOJADOR
CANARY IS. (SP.)
1433
1436
MADEIRA 1418
PORTUGAL
Sagres
AZORES
1430
1460

TRM

249

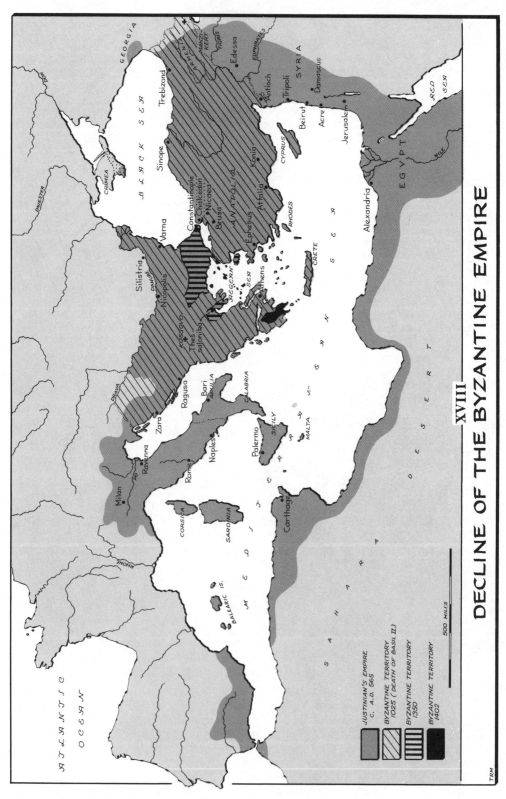

DECLINE OF THE BYZANTINE EMPIRE

XVIII

Legend:
- JUSTINIAN'S EMPIRE c. A.D. 565
- BYZANTINE TERRITORY 1025 (DEATH OF BASIL II)
- BYZANTINE TERRITORY 1350
- BYZANTINE TERRITORY 1402

500 MILES

TRM

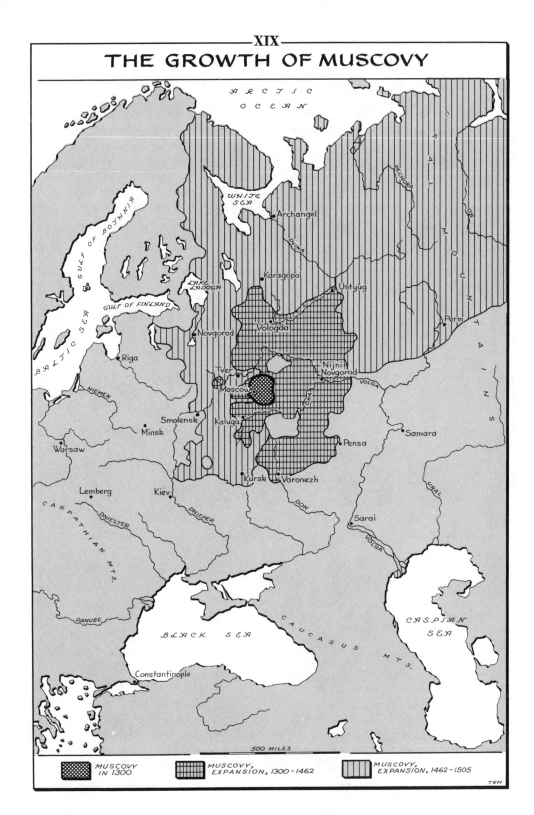

XIX

THE GROWTH OF MUSCOVY

ARCTIC OCEAN

URAL MOUNTAINS

PECHORA

OB

GULF OF BOTHNIA

WHITE SEA

Archangel

DVINA

LAKE LADOGA

Karagopol

Ustyug

GULF OF FINLAND

Perm

BALTIC SEA

Novgorod

Vologda

Riga

NIEMEN

Tver

Nijni Novgorod

Moscow

VOLGA

OKA

Smolensk

Kaluga

Minsk

Warsaw

Pensa

Samara

Lemberg

Kursk

Voronezh

Kiev

DNIESTER

DNIEPER

DON

URAL

Sarai

VOLGA

CARPATHIAN MTS.

DANUBE

BLACK SEA

CAUCASUS MTS.

CASPIAN SEA

Constantinople

500 MILES

| | MUSCOVY IN 1300 | | MUSCOVY, EXPANSION, 1300–1462 | | MUSCOVY, EXPANSION, 1462–1505 |

TRM

251

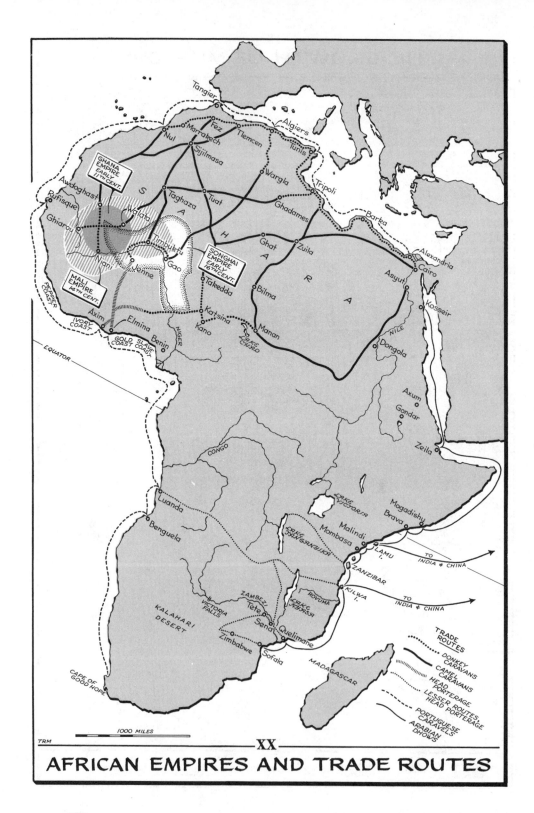

GHANA
EMPIRE
EARLY
11TH CENT.

SONGHAI
EMPIRE
EARLY
16TH CENT.

MALI
EMPIRE
14TH CENT.

Tangier
Algiers
Fez
Marrakech
Nul
Tlemcen
Sijilmasa
Tunis
Wargla
Tripoli
Awdoghast
Rufisque
Taghaza
Tuat
Ghadames
Barka
Ghiarou
Walata
S
A
H
A
R
A
Ghat
Zuila
Alexandria
Timbuktu
Niani
Jenne
Gao
Cairo
Asyut
Kosseir
PEPPER COAST
Axim
Takedda
Bilma
Dongola
NILE
Elmina
Benin
Katsina
Kano
Manan
LAKE CHAD
IVORY COAST
GOLD COAST
SLAVE COAST
NIGER
Axum
Gondar

EQUATOR

Zeila

CONGO

Luanda
Benguela
LAKE VICTORIA
LAKE TANGANYIKA
Mombasa
Malindi
Mogadishu
Brava
LAMU I.
INDIA & CHINA
ZANZIBAR
KILWA I.
INDIA & CHINA

KALAHARI
DESERT
VICTORIA FALLS
ZAMBEZI
Tete
Sena
Quelimane
LAKE NYASA
ROVUMA
Zimbabwe
Sofala
MADAGASCAR

CAPE OF
GOOD HOPE

1000 MILES

TRM

XX

AFRICAN EMPIRES AND TRADE ROUTES

TRADE
ROUTES
DONKEY
CARAVANS
CAMEL
CARAVANS
HEAD
PORTERAGE
LESSER ROUTES:
HEAD PORTERAGE
PORTUGUESE
CARAVELS
ARABIAN
DHOWS

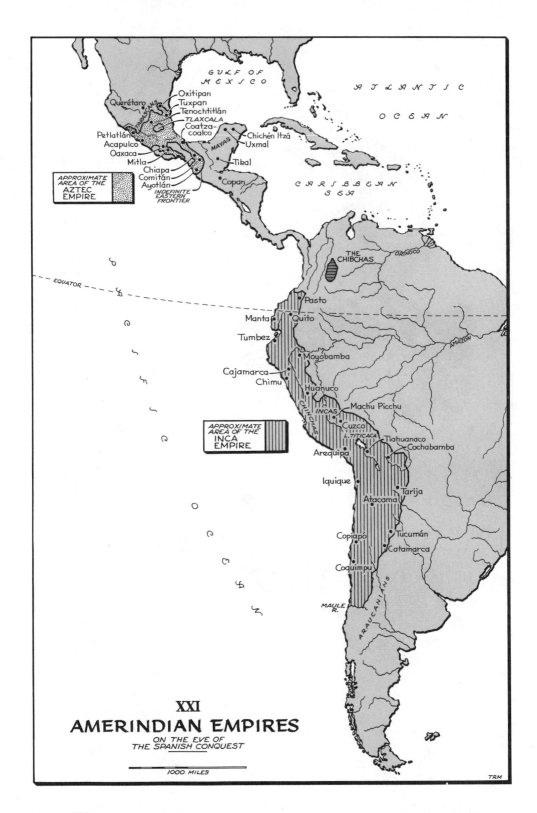

GULF OF
MEXICO

ATLANTIC

OCEAN

Querétaro
Oxitipan
Tuxpan
Tenochtitlán
TLAXCALA
Coatza-
coalco
Petlatlán
Acapulco
Oaxaca
Mitla
Chiapa
Comitán
Ayotlán
INDEFINITE
EASTERN
FRONTIER

Chichén Itzá
Uxmal

MAYAS

Tikal

Copan

CARIBBEAN

SEA

APPROXIMATE
AREA OF THE
AZTEC
EMPIRE

THE
CHIBCHAS

ORINOCO

EQUATOR

Pasto
Manta
Quito
Tumbez
Moyobamba
Cajamarca
Chimu
Huanuco
INCAS
Machu Picchu
Cuzco
L. TITICACA
Tiahuanaco
Cochabamba
Arequipa
Iquique
Atacama
Tarija
Copiapó
Tucumán
Catamarca
Coquimpu
MAULE
R.

AMAZON

CHINCHAS

APPROXIMATE
AREA OF THE
INCA
EMPIRE

PACIFIC

OCEAN

ARAUCANIANS

XXI
AMERINDIAN EMPIRES
ON THE EVE OF
THE SPANISH CONQUEST

1000 MILES

TRM

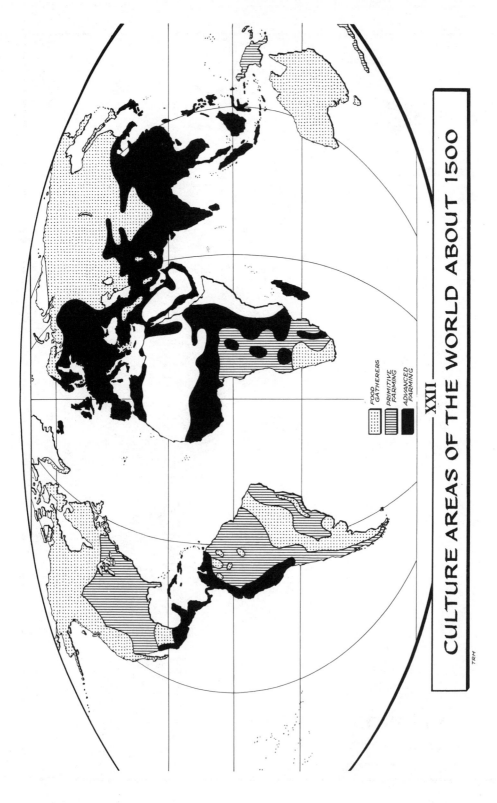

CULTURE AREAS OF THE WORLD ABOUT 1500

FOOD GATHERERS

PRIMITIVE FARMING

ADVANCED FARMING

XXII

TRH

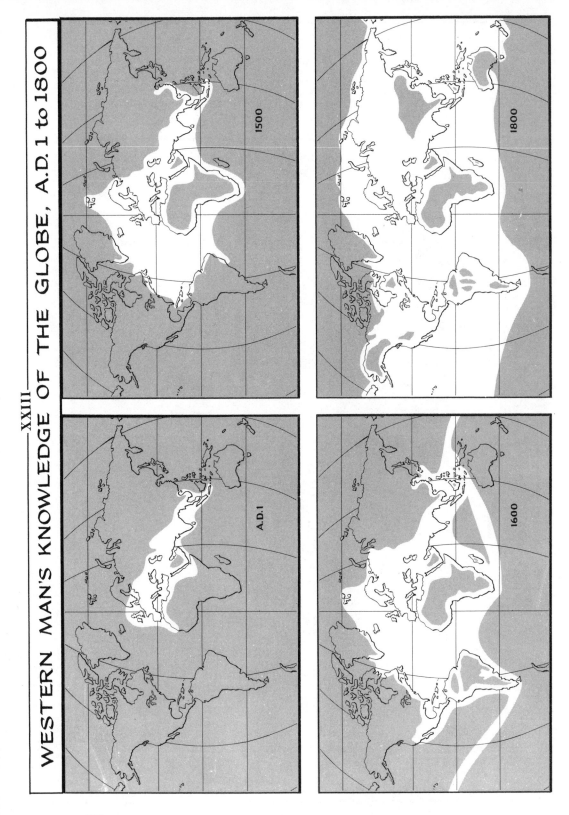

A.D. 1

1500

1600

1800

255

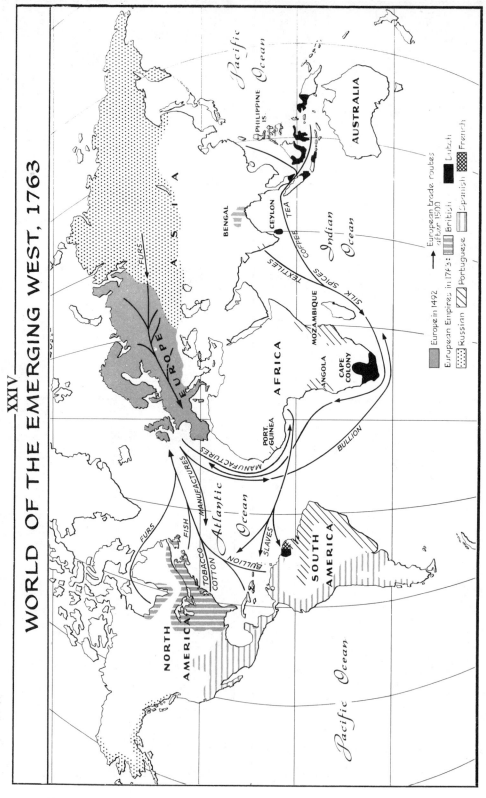

Legend:

European trade routes after 1500

Europe in 1492

European Empires in 1763:

British

Dutch

French

Russian

Spanish

Portuguese

PHILIPPINE IS.

AUSTRALIA

A S I A

FURS

BENGAL

CEYLON

TEA

COFFEE

SPICES

SILK

TEXTILES

Indian Ocean

EUROPE

AFRICA

MOZAMBIQUE

ANGOLA

CAPE COLONY

PORT. GUINEA

BULLION

MANUFACTURES

Atlantic Ocean

MANUFACTURES

SLAVES

BULLION

FURS

FISH

TOBACCO

COTTON

NORTH AMERICA

SOUTH AMERICA

Pacific Ocean

Pacific Ocean

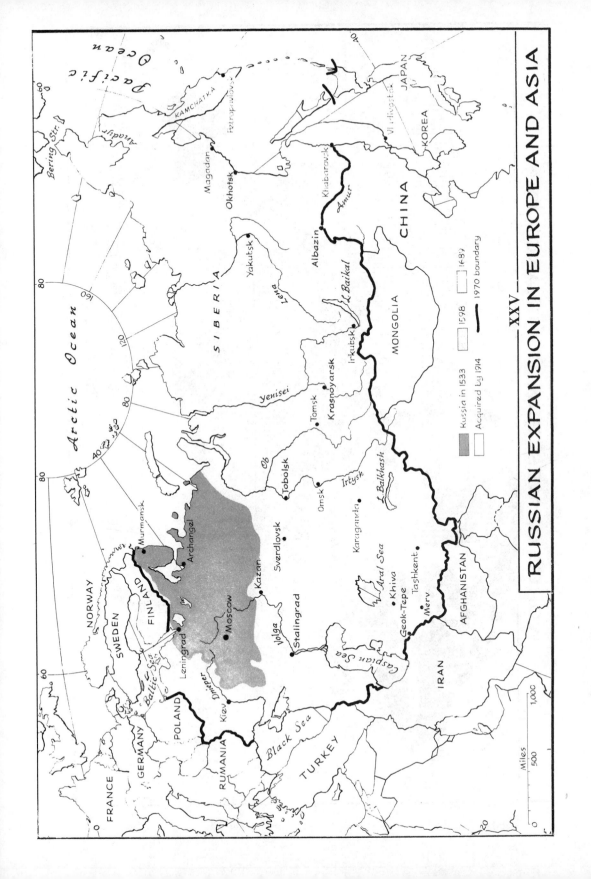

RUSSIAN EXPANSION IN EUROPE AND ASIA

XXV

Russia in 1533

Acquired by 1914

1598

1689

1970 boundary

Arctic Ocean

Pacific Ocean

Bering Str.

KAMCHATKA

Anadyr

Magadan

Okhotsk

Petropavlovsk

Khabarovsk

Amur

Vladivostok

JAPAN

KOREA

CHINA

MONGOLIA

Albazin

L. Baikal

Irkutsk

Yakutsk

Lena

SIBERIA

Yenisei

Tomsk

Krasnoyarsk

Ob

Tobolsk

Omsk

Irtysh

L. Balkhash

Karaganda

Aral Sea

Khiva

Tashkent

Merv

Geok-Tepe

AFGHANISTAN

IRAN

Caspian Sea

Sverdlovsk

Kazan

Volga

Stalingrad

Moscow

Archangel

Murmansk

Leningrad

Dnieper

Kiev

Black Sea

TURKEY

RUMANIA

POLAND

GERMANY

FRANCE

NORWAY

SWEDEN

FINLAND

Baltic Sea

Miles

500

1,000

60

80

80

160

120

80

40

60

20

40

60

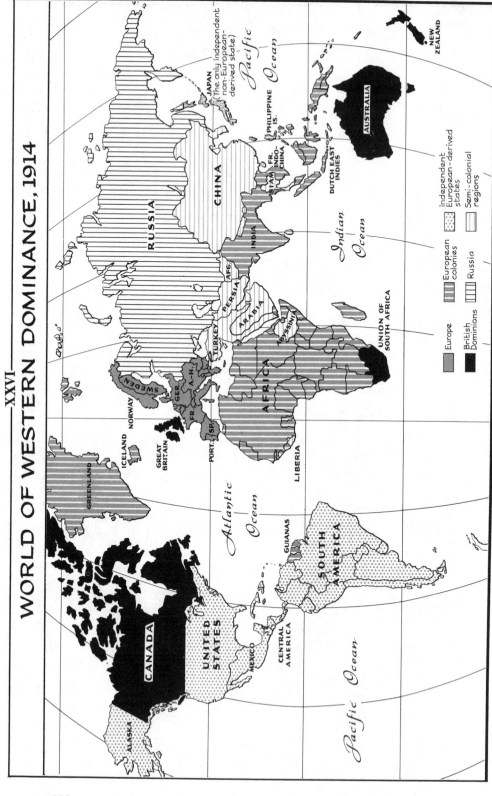

XXVI

WORLD OF WESTERN DOMINANCE, 1914

JAPAN
(The only independent
non-European-
derived state)

CHINA

RUSSIA

AUSTRALIA

NEW
ZEALAND

PHILIPPINE
IS.

FR.
INDO-
CHINA

SIAM

DUTCH EAST
INDIES

INDIA

AFG.

PERSIA

ARABIA

TURKEY

SWEDEN

NORWAY

ICELAND

GREENLAND

GREAT
BRITAIN

PORT.

SP.

FR.

A-H.

GER.

ABYSSINIA

AFRICA

UNION OF
SOUTH AFRICA

LIBERIA

*Indian
Ocean*

*Pacific
Ocean*

*Atlantic
Ocean*

GUIANAS

SOUTH
AMERICA

CENTRAL
AMERICA

MEXICO

UNITED
STATES

CANADA

ALASKA

*Pacific
Ocean*

Europe

British
Dominions

European
colonies

Russia

Independent
European-derived
states

Semi-colonial
regions

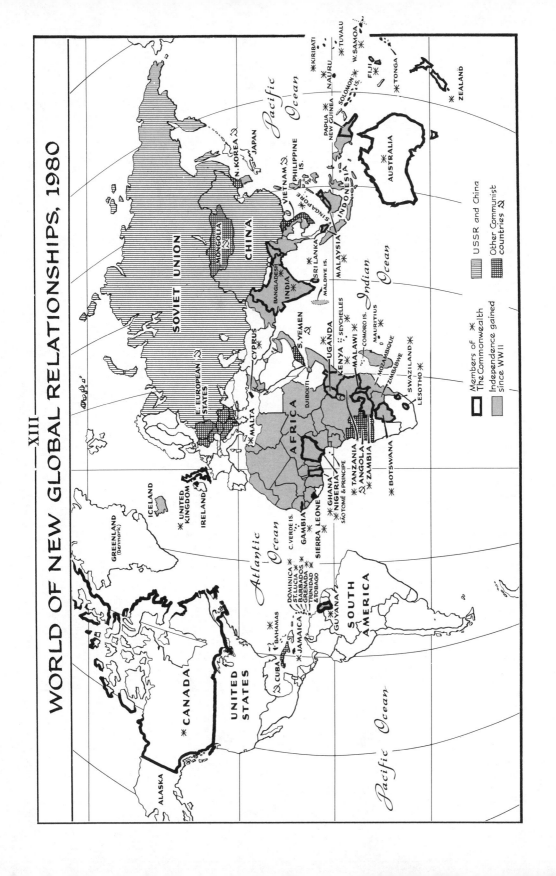

XIII

WORLD OF NEW GLOBAL RELATIONSHIPS, 1980

ALASKA

CANADA

UNITED STATES

GREENLAND (Denmark)

ICELAND

UNITED KINGDOM

IRELAND

Atlantic Ocean

Pacific Ocean

CUBA
BAHAMAS
JAMAICA
DOMINICA
ST. LUCIA
BARBADOS
GRENADA
TRINIDAD & TOBAGO

SOUTH AMERICA

GUYANA

C. VERDE IS.
GAMBIA
SIERRA LEONE
GHANA
NIGERIA
SÃO TOMÉ & PRÍNCIPE

SOVIET UNION

E. EUROPEAN STATES

MONGOLIA

CHINA

N. KOREA

JAPAN

VIETNAM

PHILIPPINE IS.

SINGAPORE

INDONESIA

MALAYSIA

SRI LANKA

MALDIVE IS.

BANGLADESH

INDIA

CYPRUS

MALTA

S. YEMEN

DJIBOUTI

AFRICA

UGANDA
KENYA
TANZANIA
ANGOLA
ZAMBIA
MALAWI
ZIMBABWE
MOZAMBIQUE
BOTSWANA
SWAZILAND
LESOTHO

SEYCHELLES

COMORO IS.

MAURITIUS

Indian Ocean

PAPUA NEW GUINEA

AUSTRALIA

SOLOMON IS.
NAURU
KIRIBATI
TUVALU
W. SAMOA
FIJI
TONGA

ZEALAND

Pacific Ocean

Members of The Commonwealth ✴

Independence gained since WWII

USSR and China

Other Communist countries

Part V

World Of The Emerging West, 1500–1763

During much of the medieval period the Western Europeans felt isolated and threatened on the western tip of Eurasia. Situated as they were at the terminal of the classic invasion route—the endless expanse of steppe lands stretching from north China across the length of Eurasia to the Danube valley in Central Europe—they had been traditionally vulnerable to attack from the east. Hence the long succession of nomadic invaders—Huns, Germans, Avars, Magyars, Mongols, and Turks—who used their unmatched mobility to break into the centers of civilization whenever imperial weakness gave them the opportunity.

The age-old pattern was reversed in early modern times by the emergence of a dynamic new West with superior technology, particularly in armaments and naval shipbuilding. This gave the Western Europeans the same mobility and superiority on the oceans of the world that had been enjoyed hitherto by the nomads on the steppes of Eurasia. The result was a fundamental alteration in the configuration of world affairs. All Eurasia now was enveloped by a gigantic European pincers. One arm was the Russian thrust overland across Siberia to the Pacific, and the other the West European expansion around Africa to India, Southeast Asia, and China. At the same time other Westerners, beginning with Columbus, ventured westward across the Atlantic, discovering the New World and circumnavigating the globe.

It is true that during these same decades, Turkish janissaries, like many of their Asian predecessors, were pressing up the Danube valley and besieging Vienna in the heart of Europe. But in the context of the new global historical stage, this was but a minor operation of only local importance. What was truly significant in the perspective of world history was the initial Iberian expansion overseas, the later activities of the Northwest Europeans, and the simultaneous overland expansion of the Russians to the Pacific. These are the subjects considered in the following chapters of Part V.

chapter 18

West European Expansion: Iberian Phase, 1500–1600

The two countries of the Iberian peninsula, Spain and Portugal, took the lead in the expansion of Europe in the sixteenth century. This seems paradoxical on first thought. The Iberian peninsula for centuries had been a Moslem stronghold. A large number of Moors and Jews were left behind in the country, giving it ethnic and religious diversity. And it is well known that after the sixteenth century the Iberian countries declined rapidly and that throughout modern times they have been quite insignificant. What, then, is the explanation for the short-lived but brilliant expansion of Spain and Portugal during the sixteenth century? This chapter is concerned first with the roots of Iberian expansionism, then with the process of empire building in the East and in the New World, and finally with the causes and results of Iberian decline at the end of the sixteenth century.

I. ROOTS OF IBERIAN EXPANSIONISM

Religion was an important factor in European overseas expansion, but nowhere was it so important as in the Iberian peninsula. Both the Spaniards and the Portuguese were urged on by memories of their long anti-Moslem crusade. To other peoples of Europe, Islam was a distant menace, but for the Iberians it represented a traditional and ever-present enemy. Most of the peninsula at one time had been under Moslem rule, and now, in the

263

fifteenth century, Granada in the south was still a Moslem stronghold. Furthermore, the Moslems were in control of the nearby North African coast, while the growing Turkish seapower was making itself felt throughout the Mediterranean. Other Europeans were Crusaders by fits and starts, but, for the devout and patriotic Iberian, the struggle against Islam combined religious duty and patriotic necessity (see Map XVI, "Expansionism of the Medieval West").

Prince Henry the Navigator first won fame in 1415 for his gallant role in the capture of the town and fortress of Ceuta across the Straits of Gibraltar. Likewise Queen Isabella, moved by intense religious conviction, was determined to wipe out Moslem Granada and to carry the war into the enemy's territory in North Africa, as the Portuguese had done at Ceuta. Isabella began her crusade against Granada in 1482, and she pressed on, village by village, until final victory in 1492. Immediately thereafter, the Spaniards crossed the straits and captured the city of Melilla. In this same year, 1492, a royal decree required all Jews in Spain to accept the Catholic faith or leave the realm. Ten years later a similar decree was issued against the Moslems remaining in Castile. At the time of the discoveries, the Iberians took their crusading spirit with them across the oceans where they found more Moslems to exterminate and new heathens to save from idolatry.

The Iberians were lured overseas also by four groups of islands—the Canaries, the Madeira, the Azores, and the Cape Verde—stretching westward across the Atlantic and southward down the coast of Africa. These were highly attractive, partly because they were fertile and productive, but also because they provided strategic bases and ports of call. After much local fighting and several appeals to the pope, the Canaries were recognized as Spanish, and the other three island groups as Portuguese. Throughout the fifteenth century, Spanish and Portuguese sailors had been discovering these islands stretching a quarter of the way across the Atlantic. It was natural that they should assume there were more islands awaiting discovery and exploitation. The agreement that Columbus reached with Isabella in 1492 stated that he should head an expedition "to discover and acquire islands and mainland in the Ocean Sea."

It was Portugal, however, rather than Spain, that took the lead in overseas enterprise during the fifteenth century. One reason for Portugal's head start was its small size and its location on the Atlantic coast, surrounded on three sides by Spanish territory. This effectively saved the Portuguese from the temptation to squander their resources in European wars. Thanks to the leadership of Prince Henry, they turned instead to seafaring projects. The other reason was Portugal's superior knowledge of navigation, gained primarily from the Italians. Lisbon was on the route of the Genoese and Venetian sea traffic with Flanders that sailed through the Straits of Gibraltar. The Portuguese took advantage of this to lure Italian captains and pilots into the royal navy. Prince Henry followed up by employing talented seamen, including Italians, Catalans, and even a Dane. Furthermore, Henry's work was continued by the crown following his death, so that the Portuguese became the most knowledgeable of all Europeans in seamanship and geography.

Portugal's interest in exploration quickened following the capture in 1415 of the port of Ceuta in North Africa. Moslem prisoners gave information about the ancient and profitable trade across the Sahara with the Negro kingdoms of the Sudan. For centuries the Sudan had provided ivory, slaves, and gold in return for various manufactured goods and salt. Since Western Europe in general and Portugal in particular were then suffering from a serious shortage of bullion, Prince Henry was intrigued by the possibility of sending his captains down the African coast and tapping the gold trade. In short, Henry's original objective was confined to Africa and did not extend to the East.

A major step forward in early Portuguese exploration was taken when Prince Henry's captains passed the desert coast in 1445 and found below it a fertile, green land. By the time of Henry's death, the coast had been explored down to Sierra Leone, and a number of coastal stations had been established so that the Portuguese were able to get at least a part of the caravan trade that they sought.

Meanwhile, even before Henry's death, Portuguese aspirations had come to include India as well as Africa. Europe at this time was blocked from access to the East by the Moslem power that controlled all of North Africa and the Middle East. The Mediterranean was for the Europeans a prison rather than a highway. Therefore, with the exception of the Venetians, who profited as middlemen, the Europeans eagerly sought a new route "to the Indies where the spices grow." Prince Henry had not thought of India when he first began his operations, but as his ships crept further and further down the African coast, it was natural that his horizon should expand from the African caravan trade to the Indies spice trade. From then on, the discovery and the domination of the spice route was the prime objective of Portuguese policy.

II. COLUMBUS DISCOVERS AMERICA

In view of Portugal's pioneering work in the theory and practice of maritime navigation, it is paradoxical that the first great discovery—that of the New World—was made under Spanish auspices. It is even more paradoxical that the reason for this outcome is that the Portuguese were more advanced in their geographical knowledge than the Spaniards and realized that Columbus was wrong in his calculations. By the fifteenth century informed people knew that the world was round. The question was not the shape of the world but its size, and the relationship of the continents to the oceans. By combining Marco Polo's estimate of the east-west extent of Asia, which was an overestimate, his report of the distance of Japan from the Asian mainland—15,000 miles—an extreme overestimate, and Ptolemy's estimate of the circumference of the globe, which was an underestimate, Columbus concluded that less than 3000 miles of ocean separated Europe from Japan. Accordingly, he believed that the shortest and easiest route to Asia was by a short voyage across the Atlantic, and this was the project that he proposed before various courts. The Portuguese, thanks to Prince Henry, had more practical experience and were better informed of the most advanced knowledge of the day. They were convinced that the globe was larger than Columbus held, that the oceans were wider, and that the shortest route to the Orient was around Africa rather than across the Atlantic. For this reason the Portuguese king turned Columbus down when he applied for financial assistance in 1484. Two years later Columbus was at the Spanish court where, after a preliminary rejection, he finally won the support of Queen Isabella.

On August 2, 1492, Columbus set sail from Palos with three small ships manned by reliable crews with capable and seasoned officers. By mid-October he had landed at one of the Bahaman Islands, which Columbus named San Salvador. One of the supreme ironies of world history is that Columbus was convinced until the end of his life that he had reached Asia. He was certain that San Salvador was very near to where Japan ought to be, and the next step was to find Japan itself. When he sailed southwest to the mainland of the New World, he believed that he was somewhere near the Malacca Straits. The fact that Columbus persisted in his delusion had momentous consequences: it spurred on further exploration of the Americas until the great prizes in Mexico and Peru were discovered. If

COLUMBUS DISCOVERS THE NEW WORLD

On his return from his first voyage, Columbus described his discoveries in a letter to Gabriel Sanchez (March 1493). The letter shows how anxious Columbus was to convince people that he had discovered valuable lands, and that he was ready to strip those lands of their riches and to make their "honest" and affectionate people into slaves. *

As I know that it will afford you pleasure that I have brought my undertaking to a successful result, I have determined to write you this letter to inform you of everything that has been done and discovered in this voyage of mine.

On the thirty-third day after leaving Cadiz I came into the Indian Sea, where I discovered many islands inhabited by numerous people. I took possession of all of them for our most fortunate King by making public proclamation and unfurling his standard, no one making any resistance. . . . The inhabitants of both sexes of this and of all the other islands I have seen, or of which I have any knowledge, always go as naked as they came into the world, except that some of the women cover parts of their bodies with leaves or branches, or a veil of cotton, which they prepare themselves for this purpose. They are all, as I said before, unprovided with any sort of iron, and they are destitute of arms, which are entirely unknown to them, and for which they are not adapted; not on account of any bodily deformity, for they are well made, but because they are timid and full of terror. They carry, however, canes dried in the sun in place of weapons, upon whose roots they fix a wooden shaft, dried and sharpened to a point. But they never dare to make use of these, for it has often happened, when I have sent two or three of my men to some of their villages to speak with the inhabitants, that a crowd of Indians has sallied forth; but, when they saw our men approaching, they speedily took to flight, parents abandoning their children, and children their parents. This happened not because any loss or injury had been inflicted upon any of them. On the contrary, I gave whatever I had, cloth and many other things, to whomsoever I approached, or with whom I could get speech, without any return being made to me; but they are by nature fearful and timid. But, when they see that they are safe, and all fear is banished, they are very guileless and honest, and very liberal of all they have. No one refuses the asker anything that he possesses; on the contrary, they themselves invite us to ask for it. They manifest the greatest affection toward all of us, exchanging valuable things for trifles, content with the very least thing or nothing at all.

Finally, to sum up in a few words the chief results and advantages of our departure and speedy return, I make this promise to our most invincible Sovereigns, that, if I am supported by some little assistance from them, I will give them as much gold as they have need of, and in addition spices, cotton, and mastic, which is found only in Chios, and as much aloes-wood, and as many heathen slaves as their Majesties may choose to demand. . . .

As these things have been accomplished, so have they been briefly narrated. Farewell.

CHRISTOPHER COLOM,
Admiral of the Ocean Fleet.

Lisbon, March 14th.

* Reprinted from *Old South Pamphlets,* vol. 2, no. 33 (Boston: Directors of the Old South Work, 1897).

Columbus and his backers had realized that they had stumbled on a great continental barrier between Europe and Asia, they might have turned away from what appeared to be an unprofitable wilderness, especially since Portugal's Vasco da Gama had in the meantime opened up the profitable Cape route to India.

III. PORTUGAL IN ASIA

The Portuguese had been making considerable profit from their trade along the African Guinea Coast. Coarse pepper, gold, ivory, cotton, sugar, and slaves now entered European commerce through Portugal. Prince Henry's successors continued his work of opening up the West African coast. A breakthrough occurred in 1487 when Bartholomeu Dias, while sailing along the coast, was caught by a gale that blew his ships south for thirteen days out of sight of land. When the wind moderated, Dias steered for the West African coast but discovered that he had already passed the Cape without knowing it. He landed at Mossel Bay on the Indian Ocean, and wanted to explore further, but his weary and frightened men forced him to return. On the homeward passage he first sighted the great cape, and named it the Cape of Storms. It was the Portuguese king who, upon Dias's return, renamed it the Cape of Good Hope. But the king did not follow up on this rounding of the Cape because of political and financial complications. The result, as noted, was that Columbus was the first to reach the New World, which he insisted in claiming as the Orient.

The more knowledgeable Portuguese were dubious from the beginning, but they now hastened to open and secure the Cape route to India. On July 8, 1497, Vasco da Gama sailed from Portugal with four ships, and at the end of May 1498 he entered Calicut harbor. Da Gama did not receive a warm welcome in Calicut. The resident Arab merchants were naturally alarmed by the threat to their traditional monopoly and did their best to throw obstacles in the way of the European intruders. Furthermore, the Portuguese trade goods—mostly trinkets and woolen cloth—were unsuitable for the Indian market. The fact is that the Portuguese had completely underestimated the level and sophistication of Indian civilization. Thus, da Gama had difficulty trading in Calicut not only because of the hostility of the resident Arab traders but also, and more important, because Portugal (and all Europe) produced little at this time that was of interest to the Eastern peoples. European manufactures were generally inferior in quality and higher in price than the goods produced in the East.

With much effort da Gama collected a cargo of pepper and cinnamon and cleared for home, arriving in September 1499. The cargo proved to be worth sixty times the cost of the entire expedition. Dazzling horizons opened up before the delighted Portuguese, and King Manuel assumed the titles "Lord of the Conquest, Navigation, and Commerce of Ethiopia, Arabia, Persia, and India." These titles were taken quite seriously. The Portuguese were determined to monopolize the trade along the new route and to exclude, not only other Europeans, but also the Arabs and other Eastern peoples who had traded in the Indian Ocean for centuries. To enforce their claims, the Portuguese resorted to ruthless terrorism, particularly when they encountered the hated Moslems. Da Gama, on a later voyage, found some unarmed vessels returning from Mecca. He captured the vessels and, in the words of a fellow Portuguese, "after making the ships empty of goods, prohibited anyone from taking out of it any Moor and then ordered them to set fire to it."[1]

Such was the nature of the epoch-making meeting of two Eurasian cultures when they came face to face for the first time after millennia of regional isolation. The Europeans were the aggressive intruders. They were the ones who seized the initiative and retained it until gradually, but inexorably, they emerged the masters in every quarter of the globe. This unprecedented domination of the world is at first difficult to understand. Why was Portugal, with a population of approximately 2 million, able to impose its will on highly civilized Asiatic countries with much greater human and natural resources?

One reason was that the Portuguese had the great advantage of being ready to use the vast bullion supply that was soon to start pouring in from the New World. The flood of bullion from the treasures of the Aztec and Inca empires and from the Mexican and Peruvian silver mines came just in time to finance Portugal's trade with the East. Without this windfall the Portuguese would have been very seriously restricted, because they had neither natural resources nor manufactured goods that were of interest to the Eastern peoples.

Another reason for the triumph of the Portuguese was the disunity of the Indian subcontinent. When the Portuguese arrived upon the scene, northern India was controlled by the new Mogul invaders who were interested in conquest rather than trade, while southern India, and especially the Malabar Coast, was under the control of petty Hindu rulers who were fighting one another. By contrast, the Portuguese and their European successors had a singleness and continuity of purpose that more than counterbalanced their inferiority in resources. The Europeans obviously were not united; they were riddled with political and religious dissension. But on one point they were all agreed—the need to expand eastward in order to reap profits and to outflank Islam. In pursuit of this objective the Europeans demonstrated a determination to succeed that was stronger than the will of the Asiatic peoples to resist. When da Gama returned from his historic voyage, the Portuguese court was prepared to follow up promptly. It had a detailed plan for organized trade, involving the establishment of trading posts in the Malabar ports and the sending of annual fleets under royal charter.

The Portuguese were successful also because of the superiority of their naval power. They had developed efficient new naval artillery that enabled them to use ships as floating batteries rather than as transports for boarding parties. The gun, not the foot soldier, was now the main instrument of naval warfare, and the guns were employed against the enemy's ships rather than against its men. It was these new developments that made it possible for the Portuguese to smash Moslem naval power in the Indian Ocean, and to win a profitable Asiatic empire.

The architect of this empire was the great Alfonso de Albuquerque, governor-general from 1509 to 1515. His policy was to smash the Arab trade network by capturing control of the narrow sea passages leading to and from the Indian Ocean. He seized the islands of Socotra and Hormuz, which were the keys to the Red Sea and the Persian Gulf, respectively. In India he took the city of Goa located in the middle of the Malabar Coast. He made Goa his main naval base and general headquarters, and it remained a Portuguese possession until 1961. Further to the east he captured Malacca, commanding the strait through which all commerce with the Far East had to pass. Two years later, in 1513, the first Portuguese ship to reach a Chinese port put into Canton. This was the first recorded European visit to China since Marco Polo's day. The Portuguese were given the right to establish a warehouse and a settlement at Macao, a little downstream from Canton, and from there they carried on their Far Eastern operations.

The Portuguese Empire in Asia was small in actual extent, made up of only a few islands and coastal posts. But these possessions were so strategically located that they gave the Portuguese command of trade routes spanning half the globe. Each year Portuguese fleets sailed down the African coast, which was dotted with stations for provisioning and refitting the ships. After they rounded the Cape, they put in at Mozambique in East Africa, another Portuguese possession. Then they sailed with the monsoon across to Cochin and Ceylon, where they loaded the spices that had been brought in from the surrounding territories. Further east was Malacca, which gave them access to the trade of East Asia and for which they served as middlemen and carriers. Thus, the Portuguese profited from purely Asian trade—between China and Japan and the Philippines, for example—as well as from the trade between Europe and the East.

With this network of trading stations and strong points, Albuquerque had broken the traditional monopoly of the Arab merchants in the Indian Ocean. In doing so he was competing with the Venetian merchants for the "spiceries" that they had customarily obtained in the ports of the Levant. The Venetians no longer found the spices they had bought for centuries in Alexandria and other Levant ports. Instead, the spices were now being shipped on the longer, but cheaper, ocean route to Lisbon. This explains why in 1508 the Egyptians, with full Venetian support, sent a naval expedition to help the Indian rajas drive the Portuguese interlopers out of the Indian Ocean. The effort failed, but the Turks, who conquered Egypt in 1517, continued the campaign against the Portuguese and sent several fleets during the following decades. They were all unsuccessful, and the spices continued to flow around the Cape to Europe.

Yet it should not be assumed that the old routes through the Middle East fell into complete disuse. In fact, after the initial dislocation, the old routes regained much of the lost trade for a variety of reasons. One reason was that there were some corrupt Portuguese officials who were willing, when bribed, to allow Arab shipping to enter the Red Sea and the Persian Gulf. The Arabs and Venetians thus were able to compete successfully with the Portuguese throughout the sixteenth century. It was not until the following century, with the appearance in the Indian Ocean of the more efficient and economically powerful Dutch and English, that the old Italian and Arab middlemen were completely displaced. The traditional Middle Eastern trade routes then gave way to oceanic routes.

IV. DIVISION OF THE WORLD

When the Europeans began to expand overseas, they adopted the convenient doctrine that they had the right to take the lands of non-Christians without regard for the native peoples concerned. Another doctrine that was adopted, at least by Portugal and Spain, was the right of the pope to give sovereignty to any lands not possessed by a Christian ruler. As early as 1454, Pope Nicholas V issued a decision granting to the Portuguese title to the territories they were discovering along the African coast toward India. When Columbus returned from his voyage, convinced that he had reached the Indies, the Spanish court feared Portuguese counterclaims and therefore pressed Pope Alexander VI for recognition of Spanish sovereignty. On May 4, 1493, Pope Alexander defined a dividing line running 100 leagues west of the Azores and Cape Verde Islands, and granted all lands to the west of it to Spain and to Portugal all lands to its east. On June 7, 1494, Spain and Portugal negotiated an agreement, the Treaty of Tordesillas, moving the line 270 leagues further west. This change gave Portugal a claim to Brazil in the New World.

The riches that Portugal reaped from the spice trade after da Gama's voyage goaded the other European countries into a frantic search for another route to the Indies. The successive failures of Columbus to find Cathay did not kill the hope of reaching Asia by sailing west. It might still be possible to thread a way between the various masses of in-hospitable land so far discovered. This was the aim of a new class of professional explorers that appeared in the early sixteenth century. Mostly Italians and Portuguese—the best-informed and the most experienced explorers at that time—they were ready to carry on explorations for any monarch willing to finance them. The Italians included Amerigo Vespucci who sailed for Portugal and Spain, John Verrazano who sailed for France, and the two Cabots, father and son, who sailed for England. The Portuguese included Juan Diaz de Solis, Juan Fernandez, and Ferdinand Magellan, all of whom sailed for Spain.

Magellan was the only one who found the passage to Asia. Spain sent him out because, with regular spice cargoes arriving in Lisbon, the Spanish realized that they were being beaten in the race for the Spice Islands. They claimed that the line of demarcation defined by the Tordesillas Treaty ran right round the globe. So they sent Magellan west to find Asia, hoping that he would find that at least some of the Spice Islands were on the Spanish side of the line.

In one of the great epics of seafaring, Magellan set out from Seville on September 10, 1519, with a fleet of five ships, each about 100 tons. On September 3, 1522, one surviving ship limped back into Seville harbor, the others having been lost during the rounding of the stormy Cape Horn and the long journey across the Pacific, and also in clashes with natives in the Philippines. Yet the single cargo of spices was valuable enough to pay the expense of the entire expedition.

The Spaniards sent out another expedition which reached the Spice Islands in 1524. But it was a disastrous failure because the Portuguese were too firmly established to be challenged profitably. Furthermore, the Spanish king was desperately in need of money at this time to finance his war with France. So in 1529 he signed the Treaty of Saragossa with Portugal. In return for 350,000 ducats, he gave up all claims to the Spice Islands and accepted a demarcation line fifteen degrees east of them. This treaty marked the end of a chapter in the history of discovery. The Portuguese held on to the Spice Islands until they lost them to the Dutch in 1605, while the Spaniards continued to show interest in the Philippines and eventually conquered them in 1571, even though the islands were east of the line stipulated by the Saragossa Treaty. Long before this, however, Spain shifted its attention to the New World, where great treasures had been found equal in value to the spices of the East.

V. CONQUISTADORS AND NEW SPAIN

The year 1519, in which Magellan left Seville on his famous voyage around the world, was also the year in which Hernando Cortes left Cuba on his equally famous expedition against the Aztec Empire. In doing so, Cortes began what might be termed the age of the *conquistadors*. The preceding decades, from 1500 to 1520, had been the age of the ex-plorers, when numerous navigators under various flags probed the entire length of the Americas in search of a passageway. In the thirty years that followed, a few thousand Spanish adventurers won the first great European overseas empire.

One of these soldiers of fortune, a typical product of the Iberian crusading tradition, was Hernando Cortes, an unsuccessful law student and the son of a respectable family. In 1504 he arrived in Hispaniola, and six years later he participated in the conquest of Cuba. Distinguishing himself during this campaign, he was selected to head an expedition to Yucatan to investigate reports of civilized city dwellers living in the interior. In March

1519, Cortes landed on the mainland coast near present-day Veracruz. He had only six hundred men, a few small cannon, thirteen muskets, and sixteen horses. Yet with this insignificant force he was to win fabulous riches and become master of an exotic, highly advanced empire.

Cortes began by scuttling his ships to show his men that they had no hope of returning to Cuba in case of setbacks. Then, after some fighting, he reached agreements with various tribes that were hostile to their Aztec overlords. Without the food, the porters, and the fighting men provided by these tribes, Cortes could not have won the victories he did. By playing upon the superstitions of Montezuma, the Aztec war-chief, Cortes was able to march peacefully into the capital, Tenochtitlán. He was graciously received by Montezuma, whom he treacherously took prisoner and kept as a hostage. But the Indians were vastly superior in numbers, and their priests stirred them up to rebellion. The Spanish policy of destroying native temples provoked an uprising during which Montezuma was killed. Cortes fought his way out of the capital by night, losing a third of his men and most of his baggage in the process. He recovered from this setback because his Indian allies remained loyal, and he received reinforcements from Cuba. A few months later Cortes returned and laid seige to the capital with a force of 800 Spanish soldiers and at least 25,000 Indians. The fighting was bitter and dragged on for four months. Finally, in August 1521, the surviving defenders surrendered their city, which was almost entirely reduced to rubble. Today, Mexico City stands in its place, with hardly a trace left of the original Aztec capital.

Even more audacious was the conquest of the Inca Empire by a Spanish expedition comprising 180 men, 27 horses, and 2 cannon. The leader was Francisco Pizarro, an illiterate and a drifter who was the illegitimate son of a Spanish officer. After preliminary explorations from which he learned the general location of the Inca Empire, he set forth in 1531, with his four brothers, on his great adventure. After a long delay in crossing the Andes, Pizarro reached the deserted city of Cajamarca on November 15, 1532. The following day the Inca ruler, Atahuallpa, who was curious about these strange ''men with beards,'' paid a formal visit to Pizarro. In imitation of Cortes, Pizarro captured the unarmed and unsuspecting emperor and massacred many of his followers. The emperor paid an enormous ransom for his freedom—a room 22 feet by 17 feet piled 7-feet deep with gold and silver articles. Pizarro seized the booty, and with customary treachery and bigotry, executed Atahuallpa. The Inca Empire now was left leaderless, and the Indian population, used to paternalistic regimentation, offered little resistance. A few weeks later Pizarro entered and looted the capital, Cuzco. The next year, 1535, he left for the coast, where he founded Lima, still the capital of Peru.

The triumphs of Cortes and Pizarro inspired other conquistadors to march through vast areas of both the American continents in search of more booty. They found nothing comparable to the Aztec and Inca treasures, but they did determine the major configuration of all South America and of a large part of North America. By the middle of the sixteenth century they had followed the Amazon from Peru to its mouth. By the end of the century they were familiar with the entire coastline of South America, from the Gulf of California south to Tierra del Fuego and north to the West Indies. Likewise in North America, Francisco de Coronado, in his search for the fabled Seven Cities of Cibola, traversed thousands of miles and discovered the Grand Canyon and the Colorado River. Hernando de Soto, who had been prominent in the conquest of Peru, explored widely in the southeast of what was to become the United States. He landed in Florida in 1539, made his way north to the Carolinas and west to the Mississippi, and followed that river from its junction with the Arkansas River to its mouth. These men, and many others like them, opened up the New World for the Spaniards in the same way that La Salle and Lewis and Clark opened it for the French and English-speaking peoples.

By 1550 the conquistadors had completed their work. The way was now clear for the Spaniards to proceed with the development of their overseas possessions. Since the native populations were not so dense or so highly organized as those of Africa and Asia, it was possible for the Iberians to settle in considerable numbers in the New World and to impose their cultures. Thus they built up Europe's first true colonial empire—something quite different from the purely commercial empires in Africa and Asia.

The swashbuckling conquistadors were effective as empire builders but quite ineffective as empire administrators. They could not settle down. They fell to fighting among themselves, and their ranks were decimated by feuding and warfare. The Spanish crown replaced the conquistadors with bureaucrats who imposed royal authority and royal justice.

At the top of the imperial administrative structure was the Council of the Indies, located in Spain and closely supervised by the crown. It made all important appointments and exercised general jurisdiction over colonial affairs. Supreme authority in the New World was entrusted to two viceroys who sat in Mexico City and Lima, respectively. The official in Mexico City headed the viceroyalty of New Spain, which was made up of all the Spanish territories in North America together with the West Indies, Venezuela, and the Philippines. The Lima official presided over the viceroyalty of Peru, which was made up of the remaining Spanish possessions in South America. These two vast viceroyalties were subdivided into smaller units ruled by *audiencias,* or courts. Audiencias were staffed by professional lawyers who usually had no excessive family pride or military ambition and therefore made ideal royal servants. In the sixteenth century there were ten such audiencias in the New World.

A basic problem of Spanish administration in the Americas was the treatment of the Indians. The crown granted to deserving conquistadors, known as ''protectors,'' or encomenderos, the right to draw specified tribute from assigned Indian villages and also to levy forced labor. In return, the encomenderos were required to give military service and to pay the salaries of the parish clergy. The provision for forced labor obviously opened the door to abuse, so it was modified in the mid-sixteenth century. The natives still could be made to work, but by public officials rather than private encomenderos, and official wage rates had to be paid to the laborers so recruited. Needless to say, these safeguards were not always enforced. The colonies were too far from Madrid and too isolated from each other. Yet the fact remains that the Spaniards discussed seriously and conscientiously the problem of exploitation for which there were no precedents.

The all-important fact for the economy of the Spanish colonial empire is that, with the work of native labor, a great flood of gold and silver poured in from the mines of Mexico and Bolivia. The law required that all precious metals be taken to the royal offices to be stamped and taxed at the rate of one-fifth their value, the royal quinto. Between 1503 and 1660 Spain received from America a total of 18,600 registered tons of silver and 200 registered tons of gold. Unregistered bullion smuggled into Spain has been variously estimated at from 10 to 50 percent of the total.

Apart from mining, the principal occupations in Latin America were agriculture and stock raising in the haciendas, and plantation monoculture in the tropical coastlands. The haciendas employed Indian labor and produced foodstuffs for their own use and for sale to nearby cities and mining settlements. The plantations were quite different, employing mostly imported African slaves and producing only one crop for the European market. The first plantations were evolved for the growing of sugar on the Atlantic islands—the Azores, Madeiras, Cape Verdes, and Canaries. Later this institution was further developed, first in the sugar plantations of Brazil and the West Indies, and subsequently in the tobacco, cotton, and coffee plantations of North and South America.

VI. IBERIAN DECLINE

During the sixteenth century the Iberian countries led Europe in overseas enterprise and won vast riches from the Eastern spice trade and from the New World silver mines. But by the end of the century they were rapidly slipping back from their respective positions of primacy. The French, the Dutch, and the English were poaching with increasing success in Portugal's Eastern empire and in Spain's American colonies. One reason for the Iberian decline was their involvement in the religious and dynastic wars of the sixteenth and seventeenth centuries. Spanish manpower and treasure were squandered by Charles V and Philip II to fight the religious wars against the Protestants, the recurring campaigns against the formidable Turks, and the dynastic struggles against rival royal houses, especially the French. In waging these campaigns the rulers of Spain fatally overextended themselves. They attempted to play the leading role on land as well as on sea. Their actions were in striking contrast to the successful strategy pursued later by England of remaining on the periphery of continental affairs and intervening only when the balance of power was seriously threatened. British strategy enabled them to concentrate their efforts on the defense and development of their colonies. But Spain, like France, focused on the Continent and was continually involved in its wars. The end result was that the British were able to build a great worldwide empire, while the Spaniards lost economic, and then political, control of their empire.

Although the Iberian states definitely were weakened by foreign entanglements, a more important cause for their continued decline was the fact that they had become economic dependencies of Northwest Europe. They had been so before they began their overseas expansion, and they remained so afterwards. As a result they were unable to exploit the economic opportunities offered by their newly won empires, and their empires, like the mother countries, fell under the domination of the Northwest European states and became their colonies or semicolonies.

The economic dependence of the Iberian countries was a part of the general shift of the economic center of Europe in the late Middle Ages from the Mediterranean basin to the north. The reason for the shift was the accelerating productivity of Northern Europe (see Chapter 14), which enabled the new mass trade of the Baltic–North Sea area (grain, lumber, fish, and coarse cloth) to surpass the traditional luxury trade of the Mediterranean (spices, silks, perfumes, and jewelry). As the European economy grew and living standards rose, the mass trade catering to the general population increased much more rapidly than the luxury trade for the wealthy few.

Northern commerce was controlled by the Hanseatic League, which played the same role in the Baltic and North Sea as Venice and Genoa did in the Mediterranean. In the sixteenth century the Hansa was dislodged by the Dutch who built such a large and efficient merchant marine that they soon dominated the Atlantic seaboard. Formerly the Atlantic trade had been controlled by the Venetians and Genoese sailing northward with luxury commodities. But now it was controlled by the Dutch sailing southward with bulk cargoes. In this new trade pattern, the dependent economic status of the Iberian states was evident in their exports, which were almost exclusively raw materials—wine, wool, and iron ore from Spain, and African gold and salt from Portugal. In return the Iberians received back their own wool, which had been manufactured abroad into cloth, as well as metallurgical products, salt, and fish. Thus the Iberian states, like the Italian, were declining at this time from the status of developed to underdeveloped societies relative to the burgeoning capitalist economies of Northern Europe.

The economically backward Iberian states were able to take the lead in overseas expansion only because of a fortunate combination of favorable geographic location, maritime technology, and religious drive. But their expansion was not based upon economic strength and dynamism, which explains why the Iberian states could not exploit their new empires effectively. They lacked the shipping necessary for imperial trade, and also the industries to supply the manufactured goods needed in the Spanish American colonies. It is true that Spanish industry for a few decades was stimulated by the expanding overseas market for manufactures. But the industrial growth stopped about 1560, and chronic decline then set in.

Paradoxically enough, one reason for the decline was the great inflow of treasure which produced a sharp inflation. Prices rose approximately twice as high in Spain as in Northern Europe, and Spanish wages lagged only slightly behind the soaring prices, while wages in the rest of Europe were kept far down. The inflation penalized Spanish industry and made its products too expensive to compete in the international market.

At least as important as the price and wage inflation was the ruinous influence of the Spanish aristocrat, or *hidalgo,* on the national economy and on national values. Although the aristocrats, together with the higher churchmen, comprised less than 2 percent of the population, they owned 95 to 97 percent of the land. It follows that the peasants, about 95 percent of all Spaniards, were almost all landless. The remaining 3 percent—clerics, merchants, and professional men, many of whom were Jews—were not a middle class in any economic or social sense. They were completely overshadowed by the nobility, who had social status and prestige. And because the nobility looked down upon careers in commerce or industry as demeaning for any gentleman, this prejudice became the national norm. Nor was this mere empty vanity, for the hidalgo had all the advantages—honors, exemption from taxation, and territorial wealth, which was more secure than commercial or industrial riches. Consequently, the ambition of successful merchants was to acquire estates, buy titles, which were sold by the impoverished crown, and thus abandon their class and become hidalgos. The blighting influence of this hidalgo spirit was felt in all branches of the economy—in the favoritism shown towards sheep farming as against agriculture, in the expulsion of the industrious Jews and Moslems, and in the negative attitude of the Cortes (the Spanish parliament) towards commercial and industrial interests. As a result of these attitudes, the economic spurt that occurred in Spain in the first half of the sixteenth century ended in failure.

This failure made it impossible to overcome the traditional Iberian economic backwardness and subservience to Northwest Europe. It also doomed the Iberian colonial possessions to a corresponding backwardness and subservience. First the Dutch and then the British controlled most of the carrying trade with the Spanish and Portuguese colonies. The Northwest Europeans also were soon supplying up to 90 percent of the manufactured goods imported by Brazil and Spanish America, as well as a high proportion of similar goods consumed in the Iberian peninsula itself. The merchant guild of Seville enjoyed a monopoly of all trade with the colonies, in which foreigners were forbidden by law to participate. But it was the foreigners who possessed the shipping and the manufactured goods needed in the colonies. Inevitably the Spanish merchants exported under their own name goods that belonged to foreign firms and were of foreign manufacture. Also through an elaborate set of pretenses, foreign merchants and financiers became members by proxy of the Seville guild. Thus the legal members conducted a vast commission business for foreigners that soon surpassed their own legitimate trade. The end result is apparent in the following complaint of a contemporary Spaniard: "All that the Spaniards bring from the Indies after long, prolix, and hazardous navigations, and all that they harvest with blood and labour, foreigners carry off to their homelands with ease and comfort."[2]

It is ironic that the net effect of Spanish overseas enterprise was to fuel the booming capitalist economy of Northwest Europe, while in the Iberian peninsula it provided just enough wealth to forestall the basic institutional reforms that were long overdue. This is the root cause for the sudden and irreversible decline that followed so soon after the few decades of imperial glory.

SUGGESTED READING

E. W. Bovill, *Caravans of the Old Sahara* (Oxford University Press, 1933); C. R. Boxer, *The Portuguese Seaborne Empire 1415–1825* (Hutchinson, 1969); R. T. Davies, *The Golden Century of Spain, 1501–1621* (Macmillan, 1954); and his *Spain in Decline, 1621–1700* (Macmillan, 1957); K. M. Panikkar, *Asia and Western Dominance* (Day, 1954); J. H. Parry, *The Age of Reconnaissance: Discovery, Exploration and Settlement 1450–1650* (World, 1963); and his *The Spanish Seaborne Empire* (Knopf, 1966); G. V. Scammel, *The World Encompassed: The First European Maritime Empire* (University of California Press, 1981); S. J. and B. H. Stein, *The Colonial Heritage of Latin America* (Oxford University Press, 1970).

chapter 19

West European Expansion: Dutch, French, British Phase, 1600-1763

In the period between 1600 and 1763 Spain and Portugal were overtaken and surpassed by the powers of Northwestern Europe—Holland, France, and Britain. This development was of great significance for the entire world. It made Northwestern Europe the most influential and dynamic region of the globe. And the countries of Northwestern Europe were to dominate the world—politically, militarily, economically, and, to a certain degree, culturally—until 1914. Their practices and institutions became the models for peoples everywhere.

The domination of the world by Northwestern Europe did not actually materialize until after 1763. But it was during the years between 1600 and 1763 that the basis for domination was laid. These were the years when the British gained their first foothold in India, when the Dutch drove the Portuguese out of the East Indies, when all the Northwestern powers set up stations on the coasts of Africa, and when the British and the French became the masters of North America above the Rio Grande and controlled much of the commerce of the Iberian possessions south of it.

This chapter will analyze the roots of Northwest European primacy, and the struggles of Holland, France, and Britain for leadership, culminating in 1763 with the emergence of Britain as the dominant colonial power of the world.

I. EARLY NORTHWEST EUROPEAN EXPANSION

Northwestern Europe did not rise from utter obscurity to the leading position in continental commerce and in overseas enterprise. As noted in the preceding chapter, the foundation was laid during the late Middle Ages when the economic center of Europe shifted from the Mediterranean basin northward, and the principal trade routes likewise shifted from the Mediterranean to the Atlantic. In addition to economic superiority, Northwestern Europe possessed a social structure and a cultural climate that were particularly responsive to economic interests. Far from regarding business enterprise with disdain, the patricians of Holland and the nobility of England, and even of France, were always ready to participate in any business venture that promised profit. Not only did gentlemen take part in commerce, but there was also much more class mobility in the north, where merchants and financiers often entered the ranks of the nobility. This favored a positive attitude toward economic enterprise, in contrast to the short-sighted hidalgo spirit that contributed so much to Iberian decadence.

Finally, Northwestern Europe was aided by a price-wage-rent differential. Prices rose 256 percent in England during the sixteenth and seventeenth centuries, while wages rose only 145 percent. Rents also lagged badly behind prices in Northwestern Europe. This meant that of the three main elements of society—the laborers, landlords, and entrepreneurs—the entrepreneurs were the ones who reaped golden profits during these centuries of inflation. Profits were plowed back into mining ventures, industrial establishments, and commercial enterprises, with the result that the economy of Northwestern Europe boomed ahead at an unprecedented rate. The famous British economist, John Maynard Keynes, has described the period from 1550 to 1650 as follows: "Never in the annals of the modern world has there existed so prolonged and so rich an opportunity for the business man, the speculator, and the profiteer. In these golden years modern capitalism was born." [1] That it was born in Northwestern Europe explains why the northwestern countries forged ahead of Spain and Portugal and attained a predominant position in world affairs, a position they were to retain until the outbreak of World War I.

The countries of Northwestern Europe were naturally envious of the lucrative empires of Spain and Portugal. But for a long time they refrained from poaching on these imperial preserves for fear of Iberian power. Accordingly, the English, the Dutch, and the French turned to the North Atlantic, which was beyond the limits of Iberian activity. Henry VII of England sent John Cabot out into the North Atlantic in 1496, the year of Columbus's second return. And Cabot discovered a resource that turned out in the long run to be even more valuable than the silver mines of the Spaniards: he found fish. The sea off Newfoundland was teeming with fish—probably the most important article of trade in fifteenth- and sixteenth-century Europe. Fish was the mainstay of the people in the winter and their diet on fast days throughout the year. The regular supply of immense quantities of cod was a great windfall for a continent where many people at that time lived near starvation level for part of every year. And the Newfoundland fisheries bred successive generations of mariners who were trained and fitted for ocean navigation. The ships that later probed the Arctic for a northeast or a northwest passage; the expeditions that began the settlement of North America; the English and the Dutch fleets that fought the armadas of Spain and Portugal—all these were largely manned by seamen trained in the hard school of the Banks fisheries.

The maritime states of Northwestern Europe were by no means satisfied with cod.

They still hankered after spices, but they were not yet prepared to challenge Portugal's mastery of the Cape route. So they began their long and fruitless series of expeditions in search of a northeast or northwest passage to the Orient. They reasoned that since the Tropics had proved passable, contrary to all expectations, the Arctic should be passable too. Hence the 1553 English expedition under Sir Hugh Willoughby and Richard Chancellor sought a northeast passage to China, only to be blocked by a wall of ice. This expedition did at least make a landing on the shores of the White Sea and established contact with the court of Tsar Ivan IV. The contact led to the founding of the Muscovy Company (1555) for direct trade between England and Russia. Other attempts to find a northeast passage proved futile.

Several expeditions seeking a northwest passage (John Davis 1585–87; Henry Hudson 1607–11; William Baffin 1615–16) had no better luck. But just as the efforts in the northeast brought about trade with Russia, so the northwest ventures discovered the Hudson Strait and Hudson Bay. Together they provided a back entrance to the richest fur-producing region of the New World.

The failure of the Northern Europeans to find new routes to the East drove them to encroach on the preserves of the Iberian powers. Since Portugal's eastern possessions were still too strongly guarded, the northerners struck first at the more vulnerable Spanish colonies in the Americas. English interlopers who were showing up in Spanish America at this time tried to carry on trade on a peaceful, commercial basis. They wanted not to plunder but to take advantage of the opportunities offered by the inability of the weak Spanish industry to meet the needs of the colonies. Of the two commodities most in demand in the Spanish colonies—cloth and Negro slaves—the English produced the first and could purchase the second in West Africa.

Sir John Hawkins won fame and fortune as the founder of the English slave trade because he was shrewd enough to see the possibilities of this situation and bold enough to act without regard for legal niceties. In 1562 he made his first voyage. He picked up slaves in Sierra Leone and exchanged them in Hispaniola (Haiti) for hides and sugar. The profits were so spectacular that Queen Elizabeth and several of her Privy Councilors secretly invested in his second voyage. He followed the same procedure as before and returned with a cargo of silver that made him the richest man in England.

The Spanish ambassador in London made strong protests against this contraband trade. Even though Hawkins had peacefully exchanged slaves for colonial commodities, the fact remained that it was illegal for foreigners to trade with the Spanish colonies. It was not piracy but it definitely was poaching. Hawkins nevertheless sailed out for a third time in 1567. This venture ended in disaster, with three of Hawkins's five ships sunk or captured. The other two, one commanded by Hawkins and the other by his cousin Francis Drake, reached England in 1569 in a disabled condition.

If the commerce could not be conducted peacefully and legally, it was bound to be carried on by other means. The opportunities for profit were too great for the English and the other northerners to refrain and forget. During the following decades, the Protestant sea captains visited the Spanish Indies as pirates and privateers rather than as peaceful, though illegal, traders. When King Philip of Spain sent his Armada against England in 1588, two of its most formidable adversaries were John Hawkins and Francis Drake. The defeat they inflicted on the Armada was, for them, sweet revenge for what they had suffered in the West Indies.

Formal war with Spain (which at this time had absorbed Portugal) removed any inhibitions that may have restrained the Protestant powers. They broke boldly and openly into the Iberian imperial preserves—into the Portuguese East as well as into Spanish America. And the more they penetrated, the more they were encouraged to go further as they found out how weak the Iberians were. The Dutch were the ones who were first able to exploit the opportunity afforded by Iberian decline. The seventeenth century was to be for Holland *Het Gouden Eeuw*—''the Golden Century.''

II. HOLLAND'S GOLDEN CENTURY

The remarkable rise of Holland to power and prosperity in the seventeenth century was in part a result of its favorable geographic location. Backed by the great hinterland of Germany, Holland was strategically located along the ancient trade routes of Europe running north-south from Bergen to Gibraltar, and east-west from the Gulf of Finland to Britain. Basic trade commodities were transported along these routes: herring and salt from Biscay, wine from the Mediterranean, cloth from Britain and Flanders, copper and iron from Sweden, and cereals, flax, hemp, timber, and wood products from the Baltic.

The Dutch began their rise to greatness by serving as the carriers of these commodities. Their merchant marine owed its start to the local coastal fisheries. The Dutch devised new methods of preserving, salting, and smoking, and exported their catch to all parts of Europe in return for corn, timber, and salt. With the building of the Spanish and Portuguese overseas empires, the Dutch picked up cargoes of the new colonial products in Seville and Lisbon and distributed them through Europe. In return, they supplied the Iberian countries with Baltic grain and naval stores. The Dutch transported these commodities in their *fluyt,* or flyboat, an inexpensive general carrier with enormous capacity. This slow and ugly but cheap and capacious boat was the mainstay of the Dutch merchant marine that came to dominate the seas of the world.

At the end of the sixteenth century the Dutch began to challenge Portugal's empire in the East. This first task was to collect reliable data to guide the navigators around the long Cape route. The Portuguese had taken the greatest precautions to keep such information from their rivals, but their navigation secrets gradually leaked out. The most important source of information for the northerners was the *Itinerario,* a geographical description of the world published in 1595 by the Dutchman Jan Huhghen van Linschoten. He had lived in India for seven years as a servant of the Portuguese archbishop of Goa, so that he was able to include in his book detailed sailing instructions for the Cape route.

Linschoten's work was used the year it was published to guide the first Dutch fleet to the East Indies. The losses were heavy during the two-and-a-half-year expedition. Only 89 of the original 289 men returned. But the trade was so lucrative that there were substantial profits despite the losses in manpower and equipment. The next expedition was more fortunate and cleared a profit of 400 percent. The Dutch now swarmed into the Eastern waters. No less than five fleets made up of twenty-two ships, sailed in the one year 1598. From the beginning they outmatched the Portuguese. They were better sailors, they could transport spices more cheaply in their fluyten, and their trade goods were cheaper and better constructed because their home industry was superior to that of the Iberian states.

By 1602 the Dutch amalgamated their various private trading companies into one great national concern, the Dutch East India Company. The English had organized their own East India Company two years earlier, in 1600, but they were no match for the Dutch. The subscribed capital of the English company was small, and the Dutch had the services of a governor-general of genius, Jan Pieterszoon Coen. He did for his country what Albuquerque had done for Portugal. During his term of office (1618–1629) he drove the Portuguese from the East Indies and made it possible for his successors to expel them from Malacca (1641) and from Ceylon (1658). Coen also harassed the English, chased them out of archipelago, and compelled them to retreat to their posts in India. Equally important was Coen's development of inter-Asiatic trade, much greater in volume than the traffic that rounded the Cape to Europe. The Portuguese had participated in this trade, but Coen went much further, establishing a base on Formosa (Taiwan) and from there controlling the commerce routes to China, Japan, and the Indies.

In later years, the Dutch East India Company established a network of fortified posts to enforce its trade monopoly. The posts made it necessary to have treaties with local rulers. Treaties led to alliances and alliances to protectorates. By the end of the seventeenth century the Dutch were actually administering only a small area, but numerous states making up a much greater area had become protectorates. Then during the eighteenth and nineteenth centuries the Dutch annexed these protectorates outright and built up a great territorial empire.

The export of spices to Europe diminished in value after about 1700, but the inter-Asiatic trade that Coen had developed made up for the shrinkage. Moreover, the Dutch developed a new economic resource at about that time when they introduced coffee bushes into the East Indies. In 1711 they harvested 100 pounds of coffee, and by 1723 they were marketing 12 million pounds. Thus, as Europe acquired a taste for coffee, the Dutch became the principal suppliers of this exotic beverage. Through these various means the Dutch East India Company managed to average annual dividends of 18 percent throughout the seventeenth and eighteenth centuries.

Dutch overseas activities were not confined to the East Indies, however. In the Arctic waters around Spitzbergen the Dutch virtually monopolized the whaling industry. In Russia they badly outdistanced the English Muscovy Company. They also dominated the rich Baltic trade so that they became the chief provisioners in Western Europe of the all-important naval stores—timber, pitch, tar, hemp for rope, and flax for canvas sailcloth.

Their merchant marine was by far the largest of the world, numbering 10,000 ships as early as 1600. Dutch shipyards were highly mechanized and could produce almost a vessel a day. Furthermore, the ships were economical to build and to operate, so that Dutch shipowners undercut their competitors. Thus, they served as the carriers between Spain, France, England, and the Baltic. Not until the eighteenth century were the English able to compete with the Dutch in merchant shipping.

In the New World, the Dutch founded the profitable but short-lived colony of New Amsterdam on Manhattan Island in 1612, and they also briefly held various islands and coastal strips in the West Indies. But the Dutch colony that proved to be the most durable of all was the small settlement established in 1652 on the Cape of Good Hope in South Africa. This was not a trading station but a true colony founded to provide fuel, water, and fresh provisions for the ships en route to the East. The colony soon proved its value. The fresh meat and vegetables it provided to Dutch and other ships helped keep down scurvy and saved the lives of thousands of seamen. Today the descendants of these Dutch peasants, or Boers, comprise two-fifths of the 3 million Europeans residing in South Africa.

During the eighteenth century Holland fell behind Britain and France in economic development and in overseas activity. One reason for this decline was the persistent efforts of the French and British governments to build up their merchant marines by discriminatory decrees against the Dutch. Examples of this legislation were the several Navigation Acts passed from 1651 onward. These provided that no goods should be imported into or exported from any English colony except in English ships—that is, ships built in England or an English colony and owned and at least three quarters manned by British or British colonials. The Dutch were weakened also by a series of exhausting wars—with Britain from 1652 to 1674 over mercantile disputes, and with France from 1667 to 1713 over the territorial ambitions of Louis XIV.

Perhaps the chief reason for the decline of the Dutch was that they lacked the resources of their rivals. The French had a large population, a flourishing agriculture, and a rich homeland with outlets on both the Atlantic and the Mediterranean. The English also had much greater natural resources than the Dutch and enjoyed the great boon of an insular location, which spared them the cost of periodic invasions. Furthermore, the English had behind them the rapidly growing wealth and strength of their overseas colonies, whereas the Dutch were backed by only one small and isolated settlement on the tip of South Africa. Thus we find that the value of British exports rose from £8 million in 1720 to £19 million in 1763, and that French exports increased from 120 million livres in 1716 to 500 million in 1789. The Dutch, who had already reached their peak, were simply incapable of matching such growth. In the final analysis, Holland gave way to Britain and France in the eighteenth century for the same reason that Britain and France were to give way to the United States and the Soviet Union in the twentieth.

III. ANGLO-FRENCH RIVALRY

The eighteenth century was marked by a struggle between Britain and France for colonial supremacy. The two countries were in face-to-face rivalry throughout the globe—in North America, in Africa, and in India.

In North America, the British and French possessions had many characteristics in common. They were settled at about the same time. They were located on the Atlantic seaboard and in the West Indian islands. The native populations were relatively sparse and primitive so that the British and the French, unlike the Spanish, could not hope to live off native labor, although they did depend on Negro slave labor in the sugar islands. Since the British and French found no precious metals, they had to support themselves by agriculture, fishing, lumbering, commerce, and fur trading.

The English colonies fell roughly into three groups: Virginia and its immediate neighbors, which produced mostly tobacco; New England with its little groups of nonconformist settlements, which engaged in fishing, lumbering, commerce, and the fur trade; and the British West Indies, by far the most highly prized because of their extremely profitable sugar plantations. One characteristic of the English colonies, taken as a whole, was their large populations, which were much greater than those of the French. Their other chief characteristic was their political independence. Every colony had a governor, an executive council, and a judiciary, all appointed from England. Nearly every colony also had an elective legislative assembly, and as a rule it was at loggerheads with the appointive officials. Its most common quarrel with the London government was the insistence of the latter that all colonial products be sent to England in English ships. This seemed to the royal officers a reasonable requirement, since they in turn gave the colonies a monopoly of the home market for their products. But the colonial merchants and planters protested bitterly when they were not allowed to use the cheaper Dutch shipping and to export their products to more profitable non-English markets.

The French settlements in North America were outstanding because of their strategic location. The first French posts were established in Acadia, or Nova Scotia, in 1605, in Quebec in 1608, and in Montreal in 1642. Using the St. Lawrence River valley as their main base of colonization, the French took advantage of the incomparable inland water system to push westward to Lake Superior and southward to the Ohio River. In 1682 a French nobleman, La Salle, paddled down the Mississippi and laid claim to the whole basin, a claim that was soon backed with a string of forts along the waterways. Thus the English colonies along the Atlantic seaboard were effectively encircled by a great arc running from the Gulf of St. Lawrence to the Gulf of Mexico. The French also had the considerable advantage of discipline and cohesion. There were no obstreperous elective bodies in the French colonies. Paris appointed the governors, who were responsible for the defense of each colony, and the intendants, who handled economic affairs. These officials gave the orders, and their subordinates carried them out without question.

The French and English were neighbors also in the West Indies. The chief French possessions in this region were Martinique and Guadeloupe; the English were Jamaica, Barbados, and the Bahamas. These colonies were valuable as stations for trade with the Spanish and Portuguese colonies to the south, but their greatest asset was their tropical produce—sugar, tobacco, and indigo—which supplemented the economies of France and Britain.

India also was the scene of sharp Anglo-French conflicts, paralleling those in North America. The British had fallen back on the Indian subcontinent when they were driven out of the East Indies by the Dutch in the early seventeenth century. By the end of the century they had four major footholds in India: Calcutta and Madras on the eastern coast, and, on the western, Surat and Bombay. The French had organized an East India Company of their own in 1604, but it soon became inactive. It was revived in 1664, and by the end of the century the French were ensconced in two major posts—Chandarnagar near Calcutta, and Pondichéry near Madras.

During the seventeenth century all Europeans who resided and traded in India did so on the sufferance of the powerful Mogul emperors. The Moguls could easily have driven the Europeans into the sea if they did not behave themselves and humbly submit petitions for the privilege of carrying on their commercial operations. During the eighteenth century the situation was completely reversed because of the disintegration of the Mogul Empire. Emperor Akbar's successors persecuted the Hindu majority which led to disaffection and turmoil. Provincial governors began to assert their independence and to establish hereditary local dynasties. The Marathas, who represented Hindu nationalism in a vague and incipient sense, expanded from their capital of Satara, about a hundred miles south of Bombay on the west coast to within two hundred miles of Calcutta on the east. This disintegration of central authority gave the British and the French East India Companies the opportunity to transform themselves from mere commercial organizations to territorial overlords and tribute collectors. They built forts, maintained soldiers, coined money, and entered into treaties with surrounding Indian potentates. No central authority in India was able to stop this spread of British and French influence.

IV. ENGLAND'S TRIUMPH

Such, then, was the line-up of the rival British and French empires in India and the Americas. The duel between the two empires during the seventeenth and eighteenth centuries ended in an overwhelming British triumph. One reason was that France was less interested in overseas possessions than in European hegemony. Since the sixteenth century, the French Bourbons had concentrated primarily on gaining ground in Italy and on combating the Hapsburgs in Austria and Spain.

Another reason for Britain's triumph was that many more Englishmen than Frenchmen emigrated to the colonies. By 1688 there were 300,000 English settlers concentrated in the narrow piedmont region of the Atlantic coast compared to a mere 20,000 Frenchmen scattered over the vast areas of Canada and the Mississippi valley. The disparity arose in part from the refusal of Paris to allow the French Protestants, or Huguenots, to emigrate to the colonies, whereas Massachusetts was populated in large part by Nonconformists who left England because they could not accept Anglicanism. Another significant factor was the richness of the French soil compared to that of England. The peasant masses of France were deeply attached to their holdings and were able to earn enough so that they did not have to resort to emigration. In England, on the other hand, large-scale *enclosures* had been taking place for some time in order to produce more wool for the growing textile industry and more foodstuffs for the growing towns. Both these commodities could be produced more efficiently on consolidated, scientifically operated holdings than on the small, separate field strips inherited from the Middle Ages. Enclosures meant more productivity, but they also meant dispossessed peasants, and it was the peasants who provided the mass basis of the emigration from England to the colonies. At the time of the American Revolution the population of the English colonies amounted to no less than 2 million. The mass transplantation explains in large part why Britain was victorious over France in 1763, and why the American Republic defeated Britain two decades later.

The remarkable development of Britain's industry also contributed to its success in overseas competition. Its industrial growth during the century between 1550 and 1650 was to be surpassed only by its growth during the Industrial Revolution after 1760. England's growth advanced its overseas enterprises in various ways. It made more capital available for colonial development, an important consideration because both the English and the French colonies required heavy initial expenditures. Unlike the Spanish colonies, they had no bullion and no native labor force that could be exploited. The English and French promoters of colonization therefore had to transplant whole communities with a complete labor force of Europeans. They had to provide transportation, tools, seed, and equipment for all these people. This involved a heavy capital outlay, and generally it was more often forthcoming from London than from Paris. England's industries also provided cheaper and more durable goods, which gave English colonists and traders an advantage over their French rivals. In North America, for example, the English fur traders were able to offer the Indians cheaper and better blankets and kettles and firearms in return for their pelts. English industry, besides, was well equipped for naval construction. This fact, together with the greater awareness in English ruling circles of the importance of sea power, explains in large part the superiority of the British navy during the long series of Anglo-French wars.

The colonial and commercial rivalry between Britain and France was fought out in a series of four wars that dragged on for almost a century until England's great victory in 1763. All these wars had two phases, one European and the other overseas. The European revolved about dynastic ambitions, especially those of Louis XIV of France and Frederick the Great of Prussia. The overseas operations were fought over diverse issues—the balance of power in India, conflicting territorial claims in America, terms of trade in the Spanish colonies, and control of the world trade routes. The dichotomy between the European and overseas aspects of these wars was sufficiently marked so that each one was known by one name in Europe and another in America. Hence the wars have come down in history as the War of the League of Augsburg or King William's War (1689—1697), the War of the Spanish Succession or Queen Anne's War (1701—1713), the War of the Austrian Succession or King George's War (1743—1748), and the Seven Years' War or the French and Indian War (1756—1763).

The first three wars were not decisive overseas. In Europe they did settle important matters: Louis XIV was effectively checkmated, and Frederick the Great successfully seized the province of Silesia and catapulted Prussia into the first rank of European powers. But in America, where most of the overseas engagements were fought, there were only isolated and inconclusive campaigns. The French enjoyed the support of most of the Indian tribes, partly because their missionaries were far more active than the English, and also because the few French settlers did not represent so great a threat to the Indians as the steadily advancing tide of English settlement that was beginning to spill over the Appalachians. With their Indian allies, the French repeatedly harried and burned the English frontier villages. The English, on the other hand, used their superior manpower and naval strength to attack the French possessions in present-day Nova Scotia and Cape Breton Island that were vulnerable by sea.

The net result of these first three wars was that the British acquired Nova Scotia, Newfoundland, and the Hudson Bay territories. But these conquests did not settle the basic question of whether the French would retain Canada and the Mississippi valley, and thereby restrict the English to the Atlantic seaboard. This question was finally answered conclusively by the fourth war, which also settled the future of India.

This fateful struggle is known as the Seven Years' War because it was waged for seven years–between 1756 and 1763–in Europe. But in America it began two years earlier because of the growing rivalry for the possession of the Ohio valley. British colonials had already begun to stream westward through the mountains into the valley when in 1749 the British government chartered the Ohio Company, organized by Virginia and London capitalists for the colonization of the valley. But at the same time the French were constructing a line of forts in western Pennsylvania—Fort Presqu'Isle (Erie), Fort Le Boeuf (Waterford), and Fort Venango (Franklin). The Ohio Company countered the French by building a fort in 1754 at the strategic junction of the Monongahela and Allegheny rivers. The French promptly captured it, enlarged it, and christened it Fort Duquesne in honor of the governor of Canada. In the following year the British General Braddock arrived in America with a regular army to retake Fort Duquesne. But he refused to take the advice of his colonial officers on how to wage frontier warfare. His forces were badly defeated and he himself killed. The British reverses continued through 1756.

The turning point of the war came in 1757, largely because of William Pitt (the Elder) who then entered the British cabinet. Pitt concentrated his resources on the navy and the colonies, while subsidizing his ally, Frederick of Prussia, to fight on in Europe. His strategy was, as he put it, to win an empire on the plains of Germany, and he succeeded brilliantly. His reinforced navies swept the French off the seas, while the American colonists, stirred by his leadership, joined the British regulars to form a force of about 50,000 men. This huge army overwhelmed one French fort after another. The climax came with the siege of Quebec, the heart of French Canada and a great natural stronghold on the banks of the St. Lawrence. In the ensuing battle, the British and the French commanders, General James Wolfe and the Marquis de Montcalm, were killed. But the British veterans prevailed, and Quebec surrendered in September 1759. The fall of Montreal the following year spelled the end of the French colonial empire in America.

In India the success of the English was no less complete. The situation was quite dif-

GENERAL WOLFE CONQUERS NEW FRANCE

Captain John Knox, one of General Wolfe's officers, describes in the following selection the victory of General Wolfe over the French General Montcalm. This battle, fought on the Plains of Abraham at Quebec, made New France, or Canada, a British colony.*

We ... clambered up one of the steepest precipices that can be conceived, being almost a perpendicular, and of an incredible height. As soon as we gained the summit, all was quiet, and not a shot was heard. ... We then faced to the right, and marched towards the town by files, till we came to the plains of Abraham; an even piece of ground which Mr. Wolfe had made choice of. ... Weather showery; about six o'clock the enemy first made their appearance upon the heights, between us and the town; whereupon we halted, and wheeled to the right, thereby forming the line of battle. ... The enemy had now likewise formed the line of battle, and got some cannon to play on us, with round and canister-shot; but what galled us most was a body of Indians and other marksmen they had concealed in the corn opposite to the front of our right wing. ... About ten o'clock the enemy began to advance briskly in three columns, with loud shouts and recovered arms, two of them inclining to the left of our army, and the third towards our right, firing obliquely at the two extremities of our line, from the distance of one hundred and thirty—, until they came within forty yards, which our troops withstood with the greatest intrepidity and firmness, still reserving their fire, and paying the strictest obedience to their Officers: this uncommon steadiness, together with the havoc which the grape-shot from our field-pieces made among them, threw them into some disorder, and was most critically maintained by a well-timed, regular, and heavy discharge of our small arms, such as they could no longer oppose; hereupon they gave way, and fled with precipitation, so that, by the time the cloud of smoke was vanished, our men were again loaded, and, profiting by the advantage we had over them, pursued them almost to the gates of the town. ... Our joy at this success is inexpressibly damped by the loss we sustained of one of the greatest heroes which this or any other age can boast of—General James Wolfe, who received his mortal wound, as he was exerting himself at the head of the grenadiers of Louisbourg. ... Thus has our late renowned Commander ... made a conquest of this fertile, healthy, and hitherto formidable country, with a handful of troops only, in spite of the political schemes, and most vigorous efforts, of the famous Montcalm. ...

*Captain John Knox, *An Historical Account of the Campaigns in North America for the Years 1757, 1758, 1759, and 1760*. A. G. Doughty, ed. (Toronto: Champlain Society, 1914), II, pp. 94–103.

ferent from what it was in America, for neither the British nor the French government had territorial ambitions in India. This was true also of the directors of the English and French East India companies, who insisted that their agents in India attend strictly to business. They were interested only in profits, and they resented every penny or sou spent on noncommercial objectives. But it took a year or more to communicate with the agents in

India, so agents frequently took advantage of this fact to act independently and involve their companies in Indian affairs. They became involved because the disintegration of the Mogul Empire that was taking place at this time offered dazzling opportunities for personal financial profit and for empire building.

The first European to intervene on a large scale in Indian affairs was the French governor Joseph Dupleix who drilled native Indians along European military lines. The trained Indian troops, or sepoys, enabled him to back claimants to various Indian thrones. He could then build up a clientele of native rulers who were under obligation to him. But Dupleix was recalled to France in 1754 because the company feared that his aggressive tactic would lead to war with Britain. Yet war did come to India in 1756 with the outbreak of full-scale hostilities between Britain and France.

At the outset the French, thanks to Dupleix's activities, were in the stronger position. But in the end the British won a crushing victory. Again naval superiority was the deciding factor. Britain was able to transport troops, money, and supplies from Europe while preventing France from doing likewise. The British, too, had the inspired leadership of Robert Clive, a company official who had come out years before as a clerk. Clive possessed both outstanding military talents and an ability to understand Indian politics. In 1756, on hearing of the war in Europe, he marched on Bengal. With the support of Indian merchants who had become wealthy in the trade with Europe, Clive defeated the pro-French Moslem ruler at the Battle of Plassey in 1757. He put his own puppet on the throne and extorted huge reparations both for himself and for his company. During the rest of the war, thanks to the strong British navy, Clive was able to shift his forces at will from one part of India to another. At the same time he severed the communications of the French posts with each other and with France. The end came with the surrender in 1761 of the main French base at Pondichéry.

The overseas phase of the Seven Years' War was decided by the fall of Quebec in America and of Pondichéry in India. But the war dragged on in Europe until 1763, when the belligerents concluded the Peace of Paris. Of its American possessions, France retained only Guiana in South America, the insignificant islands of St. Pierre and Miquelon on the Newfoundland coast, and a few islands in the West Indies, including Guadeloupe and Martinique. Britain therefore received from France the whole of the St. Lawrence valley and all the territory east of the Mississippi, Spain had entered the war late on the side of France and was, therefore, compelled to cede Florida to Britain. As compensation, France gave it western Louisiana, that is, the territory west of the Mississippi River. In India the French retained possession of their commercial installations—offices, warehouses, and docks—at Pondichéry and other towns. But they were forbidden to build fortifications or make political alliances with the Indian princes. In other words, the French returned to India as traders and not as empire builders.

When the Treaty of Paris was signed, the British political leader Horace Walpole remarked, ''Burn your Greek and Roman books, histories of little people.'' This far-seeing observation points up the long-range, worldwide implications of the peace settlement. So far as Europe was concerned, the treaty allowed Prussia to keep Silesia and to become Austria's rival for the leadership of the Germanies. But of much more significance for world history was France's loss of North America and India. This meant that America north of the Rio Grande was to develop in the future as a part of the English-speaking world.

France's expulsion from India was also a historical event of global significance, for it meant that the British were to take the place of the Moguls there. Once installed in Delhi, the British were well on their way to world empire and world primacy. It was the incomparable base offered by the vast and populous subcontinent of India that enabled the British in the nineteenth century to expand into the rest of South Asia and then beyond to East Asia. For these reasons the 1763 settlement has profoundly affected the course of world history to the present day.

SUGGESTED READING

C. R. Boxer, *The Dutch Seaborne Empire 1600–1800* (Knopf, 1965); E. P. Hamilton, *The French and Indian Wars: The Story of Battles and Forts in the Wilderness* (Doubleday, 1962); J. H. Parry, *Trade and Dominion: The Overseas European Empires in the Eighteenth Century* (Praeger, 1971); H. I. Priestly, *France Overseas Through the Old Regime: A Study of European Expansion* (Appleton, 1939); G. V. Scammel, *The World Encompassed: The First European Maritime Empire* (University of California Press, 1981); W. B. Willcox, *Star of Empire: A Study of Britain as a World Power, 1485–1945* (Knopf, 1950); C. Wilson, *Profit and Power: A Study of England and the Dutch Wars* (Longmans, 1957); T. Woodrooffe, *Vantage at Sea: England's Emergence as an Oceanic Power* (St. Martin's Press, 1958).

Throughout Russian history one dominating theme has been the frontier; the theme of the struggle for the mastering of the natural resources of an untamed country, expanded into a continent by the ever-shifting movement of the Russian people and their conquest of an intermingling with other peoples.

B. H. Sumner,
A Short History of Russia

chapter 20

Russian Expansion In Asia

At the same time that Western Europeans were expanding overseas to all corners of the globe, the Russians were expanding overland across the entire length of Eurasia. The mastering of the continental expanses of Siberia is an epic story comparable to that of westward expansion across the United States to the Pacific. In fact, the ever-advancing frontier has left as indelible a stamp on the Russian character and Russian institutions as it has on the American. The Russians were not the only European peoples who were affected by a frontier. During the medieval period, large parts of Central and Eastern Europe were lightly populated. For centuries, various European peoples, and particularly the Germans, pressed a line of settlement eastward along the Baltic coast and down the Danube valley. But by the end of the Middle Ages, internal colonization no longer was a dominant movement. Overseas colonization took its place, and the peoples of Western Europe concentrated their energies on opening and exploring new frontiers in new worlds. The Russian people, by contrast, continued to expand overland into the vast Eurasian plain stretching out from their doorstep. This was a stupendous undertaking which continued for several centuries until the last of the Moslem khanates in Central Asia was subdued in 1895. It is not surprising, then, that the frontier has been a major factor throughout the course of Russian history, as it has been throughout American. In this chapter we shall examine the nature and the course of Russian expansion into Siberia and the Ukraine.

I. GEOGRAPHY OF RUSSIAN EXPANSION

In order to understand the remarkable Russian expansion across the plains of Eurasia we must understand the geography of those plains. A glance at the map shows their staggering proportions. Russia encompasses a sixth of the land surface of the globe and is larger than the United States and Canada and Central America combined. Another prominent characteristic of the Russian landmass is its remarkable topographical uniformity. It is in very large part a flat plains area. The Ural Mountains do run across the plains in a north-south direction, and they are commonly thought of as dividing the country into two separate parts—European Russia and Asiatic Russia. But the fact is that the Urals are a single, narrow, worn-down chain of mountains with an average altitude of only two thousand feet. Furthermore, they do not extend further south than the 51st parallel, leaving a wide gap of flat desert country stretching down to the Caspian Sea. This topographic uniformity helps to explain why the Russians were able to spread so rapidly from the Baltic to the Pacific.

The Eurasian plains that make up most of present-day Russia are surrounded by a natural boundary stretching from the Black Sea to the Pacific Ocean. This boundary consists of an uninterrupted chain of mountains, deserts, and inland seas: beginning with the Caucasus Mountains in the west, the Russian barrier continues east with the Caspian Sea, the Ust Urt Desert, the Aral Sea, the Kizil-Kum Desert, the three mountain ranges Hindu Kush, Pamir, and Tien Shan, the Gobi Desert, and the Great Khingan Mountains to the Pacific Ocean. The ring of mountains surrounding the Eurasian plains keeps out the moisture-laden winds from the Pacific and the warm monsoons from the Indian Ocean, and this explains both the desert climate of Central Asia and the cold, dry climate of Siberia. The whole expanse of Siberia, from the Baltic to the Pacific, has essentially the same continental type of climate, with short, hot summers and long, cold winters. The uniformity of climate, like that of topography, facilitated Russia's eastward expansion, for the frontiersman felt equally at home throughout the five-thousand-mile expanse of plains. The Central Asian deserts, on the other hand, seemed strange and forbidding. Also they were held by militarily powerful Moslem khanates in contrast to the weak tribes in Siberia. As a result, the Russians did not master the Central Asian deserts until 250 years after they had reached the Pacific further north.

Russian expansion was affected by river systems as well as by topography and climate. Because of the flat terrain, Russian rivers are generally long, wide, and unencumbered by rapids. Consequently they are invaluable as routes for commerce, colonization, and conquest. West of the Urals the outstanding rivers are the Western Dvina flowing into the Baltic, the Dniester, the Dnieper, the Don flowing south to the Black Sea, and the Volga flowing first east and then south to the Caspian. East of the Urals the Siberian plains are watered by four vast river systems: the Ob in the west, the Yenisei in the center, the Lena in the northeast, and the Amur in the southeast. Since the whole of Siberia tilts downward from the massive Tibetan ranges, the first three of these rivers flow northward into the Arctic, while the fourth makes its way eastward to the Pacific. These rivers, together with their numerous tributaries, provided a natural network of highways across the plains. Thus the Russian fur traders were able to make their way eastward with few portages to the Pacific Ocean, just as French and English fur traders in the New World made their way westward along similar riverways to the same ocean.

A final geographic factor in the pace and course of Russian expansion is the combination of soil and vegetation prevailing in various parts of the country. Four major soil-vegetation zones run in east-west layers across Russia. In the far north, along the Arctic coast, is the barren *tundra,* frozen the year round except for a six-to-eight week growing period in the summer. To the south of the tundra is the *taiga,* or forest belt. The largest of the four zones, it is 600- to 1300-miles wide and 4600-miles long. It includes a fifth of the total forest area of the world. The Russians felt at home in the forests and they were able to go across the whole of Eurasia without ever losing the familiar protecting covering.

On their southern edges the forests thin out, and the trees grow smaller until they give way completely to the open, treeless *steppe.* Here there is fertile black earth formed by millennia of decayed grass. Today it is the breadbasket of Russia, but for centuries it was a source of misery and woe. The steppe was the home of the marauding horse nomads of Central Eurasia. When these nomads were sufficiently strong, they struck out along the line of least resistance—sometimes westward into Central Europe or eastward into China. More frequently they attacked the vulnerable Russians in Eastern Europe. A major theme of Russian history is this continued conflict between the Slavic peasant of the forest zone and the Asiatic nomad of the steppe. At first the nomad prevailed, and the result was two centuries of Mongol rule over Russia. But in the end the Slavic forest dwellers became stronger, and they were able not only to win their independence but also to expand over the Eurasian plains.

The fourth zone, the desert, is the smallest in area, starting in China but extending westward only to the Caspian Sea. We have seen that for various reasons—inaccessibility, severe climate, and the military power of the native peoples—the desert zone was not engulfed by the Russian tidal wave until the late nineteenth century.

II. EARLY RUSSIAN EXPANSION

About 1500 years ago, the Russians began their advance eastward from their place of origin in the upper reaches of the Dniester, Dnieper, Neman, and Dvina rivers. From there they fanned out in a great arc. The broad plains beckoned them on to the Arctic shores in the north, to the Black Sea in the south, and to the Urals and beyond in the east. Their subsistence type of agriculture could not support a dense population, so they lived in scattered homesteads and small hamlets rather than in compact villages or towns. The few towns that did appear grew up as trade centers along main river routes. This was the case with Kiev on the Dnieper River which carried the north-south traffic, and with Novgorod on Lake Ilmen which commanded the east-west commerce. This long-distance trade provided the basis for the first Russian state, which developed in the ninth century after Christ. The center was Kiev, but the state remained a loose federation of principalities strung out along the river routes. Kiev itself was extremely vulnerable to invasion because it was located at the point where the forest zone gave way to the steppe. Consequently, it was forced to wage a continual struggle for existence against the nomad tribes. Russian colonists were unable to settle more than 150 miles south and east of Kiev, for the threat of invasion by the nomads hung over their heads like the sword of Damocles.

The sword descended in 1237 when the Mongols swept over the Russian lands as they did over most of Eurasia. The Mongols continued their devastating inroads into Central Europe, to the gates of Italy and France. Then they withdrew voluntarily, retaining only the Russian lands in Europe. Their sprawling empire did not survive long as an entity. It broke up into regional fragments. One fragment, the so-called Golden Horde, included the Russian territories. The capital of the Golden Horde, and of Russia also for the next two centuries, was Sarai, near present-day Volgograd. The age-old struggle between the forest and the steppe had been settled decisively with the victory of the steppe and its nomad peoples.

The Russians now surrendered their small enclaves on the steppe and withdrew into their forest fastnesses. There they were left alone so long as they recognized the suzerainty of the khan and paid him annual tribute. Gradually the Russians recovered their strength and developed a new national center—the principality of Moscow, located deep in the forest zone away from the dangerous steppe. Moscow had advantages other than its relative inaccessibility to the nomads. A number of rivers flowing in various directions came closest to each other in the Moscow region, so Moscow could profit from an inland water system. The principality also enjoyed the advantage of a line of rulers who were peaceful, frugal, and calculating. The rulers added to their possessions patiently and ruthlessly, until Moscow became the new national nucleus. Whereas at the opening of the fourteenth century the principality was made up of only about 500 square miles, by the mid-fifteenth century it had grown to 15,000 square miles. And a century later, during the reign of Ivan the Terrible (1533–1584), all the Russian principalities were brought together under Moscow's rule (see Map XIX, ''The Growth of Muscovy'').

This ''gathering of the Russian lands'' reversed the balance of power between the Russians and the Mongols, or Tatars as they were now more commonly known. Originally the Tatars had triumphed because they were united, in contrast to the strife-ridden Kievan state, and also because they were militarily more advanced with their fast-moving cavalry armies. But by the sixteenth century it was the Russians who were united under Moscow, while the Golden Horde had split into the three rival khanates of Kazan, Astrakhan, and the Crimea, as well as the khanate of the Siberian Tatars to the east of the Urals. Furthermore, the Russians were also pulling ahead in military techniques, because they were able to profit from the great advances being made in Western Europe, especially in firearms and artillery. Thanks to this military advantage, the Russians were able to overrun the whole Kazan khanate. They swept down the Volga valley and in 1556 captured Astrakhan. To consolidate their gains, the Russians built a series of fortified posts along the banks of the Volga to its mouth at Astrakhan. Thus the Russians became the masters of the great Volga basin and reached the Caspian Sea in the south and the Urals in the east. The way now was open for limitless Russian expansion beyond the Volga and the Urals (see Map XXV, ''Russian Expansion in Europe and Asia'').

III. CONQUEST OF SIBERIA

The crossing of the Urals and the conquest of Siberia were largely the work of the rough-and-ready frontier people known as the *Cossacks*. In many respects these men resembled the frontiersmen of the American West. Most of them were former peasants who had fled from Russia or Poland to escape the bonds of serfdom. Their refuge was the wild steppe country to the south, where they became hunters, fishers, and pastoralists. Just as their counterparts in America became half-Indian, so they became half-Tatar.

A typical product of this frontier environment was Yermak Timofeevich. At the age of twenty-one he was condemned to death for stealing horses, so he fled to the Volga where he became the leader of a band of river pirates. He preyed indiscriminately on Russian shipping and Persian caravans until government troops began to close in. Then he fled with his band up the Volga valley to the Kama tributary, where a wealthy merchant,

Grigori Stroganov, had been given vast land concessions. Stroganov's efforts to colonize his domain were being frustrated by nomad raids from across the Urals. The organizer of these raids was the militant Moslem leader of the Siberian Tatars, the blind Khan Kuchum. Faced with this predicament, Stroganov welcomed Yermak and his men and hired them to guard the settlements.

Yermak the robber now showed that he had in him the stuff of a great empire builder. He did for Russia in Siberia what Pizarro and Cortez had done for Spain in America. With the audacity of the conquistador, Yermak decided that the best defense was a daring offense. On September 1, 1581, he set out at the head of 840 men to attack Khan Kuchum on his own territory. Yermak, like his Spanish counterparts, had the great advantage of superior weapons. He was well equipped with firearms and cannon, and after stiff fighting he captured Kuchum's capital, Sibir. The Russians now gave the name of the city to the entire trans-Ural area, which became known as Sibir, or, in its Anglicized form, Siberia. The road to the Pacific lay open.

The pace of the Russian advance across Siberia was staggering. Yermak campaigned between 1581 and 1584—at the same time (1584) that Sir Walter Raleigh landed on Roanoke Island in North Carolina. Within half a century, by 1637, the Russians reached Okhotsk on the Pacific Ocean, covering a distance half as much again as that between the Atlantic and the Pacific coasts of the United States. During that same period the English colonists had not crossed to the other side of the Allegheny Mountains.

Various factors explain the rapidity of the Russian advance. The climate, the terrain, the vegetation, and the river systems were, as we have seen, all favorable to the invaders. The native peoples were handicapped by small numbers, inferiority of armaments, and lack of unity and organization. We must give credit also to the stamina and courage of the Cossacks who, like the coureurs des bois of French Canada, endured fantastic hardships and dangers in the wilderness. And the reason they did so may be summed up with one word—"fur." The sable lured them ever eastward, from river to portage and on to new rivers.

As the Cossacks advanced, they secured their communications by building fortified posts or *ostrogs,* which were like the blockhouses of the American frontier. Thus they advanced from Sibir to the Ob River, to the Yenisei, and to the Lena, which they followed down to the Arctic coast in 1645. Two years later they reached the shores of the Pacific where they built Okhotsk.

Up to this point the Russians had not encountered any power capable of stopping them. But when they pushed down into the Amur valley they more than met their match. There they came up against the outposts of the mighty Chinese Empire, which then was at the height of its strength. The Cossack Vasily Poyarkov led the way down the Amur in 1643-4. He was followed by a series of adventurers who captured the town of Albazin, built a string of ostrogs, and killed and pillaged in typical Cossack fashion. The Chinese emperor finally was sufficiently exasperated by these outrages on the fringe of his empire to send an expedition northward in 1658. The Chinese recaptured Albazin and cleared the Russians out of the whole Amur basin. After more skirmishes the two governments negotiated the Treaty of Nerchinsk (August 27, 1689). The frontier was fixed along the Stanovoi mountain range north of the Amur River, so that the Russians were forced to withdraw completely from the disputed river valley. In return, the Russians were given commercial privileges by which the subjects of both empires could travel freely across the frontier and buy and sell without hindrance. The trade that grew up in the following years was carried on by caravan and consisted of gold and furs, which the Russians exchanged for tea.

With the signing of the Nerchinsk Treaty, the first stage of the Russian expansion in Asia came to a halt. For the next 170 years the Russians observed the provisions of the treaty and stayed out of the Amur basin. They did not resume their advance southward until the mid-nineteenth century, when they were much stronger than in the days of Vasily Poyarkov, and the Chinese were relatively weaker.

IV. ADMINISTRATION AND DEVELOPMENT OF SIBERIA

The fur trade dominated Siberia throughout the seventeenth century. The government was the chief fur trader; indeed, fur was one of its most important sources of revenue. The government acquired furs by various means: it collected tribute, or tax, from the natives in furs, and it levied a 10 percent tax on the best furs from the Russian trappers and traders. In addition, it reserved the right to buy the best furs obtained by both the natives and the Russians. By 1586, the state treasury was receiving from these various sources 200,000 sables, 10,000 black foxes, and 50,000 squirrels, besides beavers and ermines. Furthermore, the government had a lucrative monopoly of the foreign trade in furs. Estimates of the revenue derived from Siberian furs in the mid-seventeenth century vary from 7 to 30 percent of the total income of the state. A leading student of this subject has concluded that "The government paid the administrative expenses in Siberia out of the fur trade, retained a large surplus, and added an immense region to the state."[1]

The impact of the Russian expansion on the Siberian tribes was as disastrous as the effect of the American expansion on the Indians. On the one hand, the Moscow government repeatedly instructed its officials to treat the natives with "clemency and kindness." On the other hand, it ordered the same officials to "seek profit for the sovereign with zeal."[2] Since the number of furs collected definitely affected official advancement, it is understandable that the welfare of the natives did not receive primary consideration. One effect of this fur-tribute system was that it checked the missionary activities of the Russian Orthodox Church. Converts were not required to pay tribute, so missionary work was discontinued for a long time. It was a luxury that the state treasury could not afford. As a result, Islam spread widely among the Tatar peoples on the southern fringes of the forest zone, and Buddhist Lamaism spread among the Mongol Buriat. Thus we see that a basic difference between the Russian expansion in Siberia and the Spanish in the Americas was the great difference in the intensity of Catholic and Orthodox proselytizing zeal. The Catholic church never would have allowed another creed to be propagated amongst the Indians of New Spain.

In the eighteenth century, the traders and trappers began to give way to permanent colonists in the area of the Yenisei. Some colonists were prisoners shipped off to Siberia in the same manner that prisoners from the Western European countries were shipped to America, Australia, and the French West Indies. Most of these prisoners were hardened criminals, but a considerable proportion were political offenders who were the most enlightened and cultivated strata of society. Other colonists were forced to go by official summons. Each region of European Russia was required to provide a certain number of peasants each year for the colonization of Siberia. These people were granted certain exemptions and state assistance so that they could get started in their new surroundings.

REFLECTIONS ON CROSSING SIBERIA

In 1908 a young Russian diplomat crossed Siberia by railway on route to the embassy in Peking. His thoughts are revealing of Siberia as a country and as a class-divided society.*

On my way to Peking I had to cross the whole of Siberia, Manchuria, and North China. No one can fail to be impressed by the journey through Siberia, especially the first time. The dimensions of Russia are staggering. You travel a day, you travel a week, you travel ten days, and you are still in Russia. Except for the Ural Mountains and a stretch near Lake Baikal, the country is absolutely flat. After you leave European Russia the population becomes very scarce; you pass hours and hours without seeing any village or habitation. Near the stations there are a few houses. Usually, when the express train arrives at the station, the entire local population comes to stare at the travelers. Especially in the evenings, when the train is brilliantly illuminated by electricity and the elegant figures of some inhabitants of Shanghai or other Far Eastern ports are visible inside, the travelers must appear to the local residents like men from another planet. What envy and dissatisfaction the exotic creatures in furs must provoke in the hearts of those doomed to spend their entire life in some miserable station!

I imagine a young girl who has not yet lost the capacity to dream waiting on the station platform. She hears the express approaching and sees it all illuminated. The train stops for five minutes. The passengers, looking like people from a fairy land, jump on the platform; they laugh and joke. There is a whistle, the train with its passengers disappears, and darkness, emptiness, and dullness reign again.

It is unjust that some should move from place to place in luxury, while others must remain in some forsaken place in misery. Small wonder that this should cause irritation and discontent. I am convinced that the Siberian express played an important part in the awakening of the population of Siberia and thereby hastened the coming of the revolution.

The sight of unlimited space and the absence of life begins to affect you, and the passengers prefer to pass their time in the diner, drinking endless glasses of tea and playing cards. . . .

* The Memoirs of Dmitrii Ivanovich Abrikossow, MS, 1, 191–194, as edited and translated by G. A. Lensen. Published with permission of the Archive of Russian and Eastern European History and Culture, Columbia University.

Most of the permanent settlers in Siberia were neither prisoners nor compulsory colonists but were peasants who emigrated voluntarily in order to escape creditors, military service, religious persecution, and, above all else, the bonds of serfdom. Whereas serfdom had developed and spread through European Russia in the sixteenth and seventeenth centuries, it did not take root in Siberia at any time. The explanation seems to be that serfdom existed primarily to satisfy the needs of the nobility who were essential for the functioning of the state. But the nobles did not migrate to Siberia, which offered no attractions comparable to those of Moscow and St. Petersburg. Consequently, Siberia escaped the nobility, and thus also escaped serfdom. The growth of population in Siberia to 1763 is given in the following figures:

Table 2. SIBERIAN POPULATION GROWTH*

	Natives	Russians and Foreigners	Total
1622	173,000	23,000	196,000
1662	288,000	105,000	393,000
1709	200,000	229,227	429,227
1763	260,000	420,000	680,000

*The Great Siberian Movement: Government and Peasant in Resettlement from Emancipation to the First World War, by Donald W. Treadgold (copyright © 1957 by Princeton University Press): part of Table 1, p. 32. Reprinted by permission of Princeton University Press.

It is significant that whereas only 420,000 Russians were living in Siberia by 1763, the population of the Thirteen Colonies had risen by the same date to between 1½ and 2 million, or about four times as many. In other words, the Russians, who had been much faster in exploring and conquering, were now much slower in colonizing. One reason was that Siberia could draw only upon Russia for immigrants, whereas the American colonies were receiving immigrants from several European countries. Even more important was the greater attractiveness of America for would-be colonists. Climatic conditions in Siberia were akin to those prevailing in Canada. It is no accident that by 1914 the populations of Canada and Siberia were about the same—8 million for Canada and 9 million for Siberia. But by that same year the United States, smaller in area than either Canada or Siberia, had grown to a population of 100 million.

V. CONQUEST OF THE UKRAINE

We noted earlier that Ivan the Terrible's conquest of Kazan and Astrakhan in the mid-sixteenth century left two independent khanates—that of the Crimean Tatars in the south, and of Kuchum's Tatars across the Urals. The latter were subdued in a few years by Yermak and his successors, but the Crimean Tatars held out until the end of the eighteenth century. One reason for their survival is that they enjoyed the powerful support of the Ottoman Empire. The khan at Bakhchi-sarai, the capital of the Crimean Horde, recognized the suzereignty of the Ottoman sultan in Constantinople and supplied him with cavalry forces in time of war. In return the sultan went to the assistance of the khan whenever he was threatened by the Christian infidels. Furthermore, the khan usually could play off against each other the various infidels who had conflicting claims to the Ukrainian steppes—that is, the Russians, the Poles, and the Cossacks. The khan was also greatly aided by the inaccessibility of his domain. The Perekop Isthmus guarding the approaches to the Crimean peninsula was 700 miles direct from Moscow, and far more in actual riding miles. The last 300 miles were across a particularly arid type of steppe country in which it was extremely difficult to find water and provisions for an invading army. Thus, the Russians were not able to undertake serious campaigning against the Crimean Tatars until their line of settlement had advanced sufficiently far south to provide them with a base for striking across the steppes.

These various factors explain why the Crimean khanate survived until the time of Catherine the Great in the late eighteenth century. The 250 years between Ivan the Terrible and Catherine the Great were years of bloodshed and anarchy on the Ukrainian steppes north of the Black Sea. The Ukraine was a wild no man's land in which Russians, Poles, Cossacks, and Tatars fought intermittently and in constantly changing combinations. Particularly devastating were the incessant Tatar raids that were, in effect, slave-hunting expeditions. In 1571 the Tatars burned Moscow itself. But after 1591 they never succeeded in crossing the Oka River in front of Moscow, and gradually their raids penetrated less and less far northward. Nevertheless, small bands of a few hundred men continued to harass the Russian peasantry, slipping through where they perceived an opportunity and retiring swiftly with their human booty.

Finally Catherine the Great was able to remove the Tatar thorn from the side of Russia. She succeeded where so many of her predecessors had failed because several factors were operating in her favor. One was the rapid decline of both Poland and Turkey, the two powers that hitherto had contested Russia's claims to the Ukraine. Russia, by contrast, was growing steadily stronger, partly because of its spectacular territorial expansion and also because of its strongly centralized government. Russia's power was particularly effective during Catherine's reign because the empress was a superb diplomat and skillfully took advantage of every opportunity afforded by the international situation. She concluded agreements with Joseph II of Austria and Frederick the Great of Prussia that enabled her to wage war against Turkey without becoming embroiled with any major European power. Furthermore, Catherine had the gift of selecting first-class advisers and generals. The most outstanding was General Aleksandr Suvorov, a military genius comparable to Napoleon, and a matchless instrument for Catherine's policies. Moreover, in the eighty years since Peter the Great's campaigns, the Russian peasantry had been unobtrusively and patiently advancing its line of settlement southward, so that Suvorov had a stronger base for operations than his predecessors.

Catherine fought two wars against the Tatars and the Turks. The first, between 1768 and 1774, gave Russia effective control of the Crimean peninsula. The Treaty of Kuchuk-Kainarji in 1774 severed the ties between Bakhchisarai and Constantinople and gave Russia several strategic strongholds in the Crimea. The second war, from 1787 to 1792, was marked, like the first, by spectacular victories won by Suvorov. In fact, his great triumphs created difficulties, because both Prussia and Austria became alarmed at the sweeping Russian advances toward the Mediterranean. Catherine, however, shrewdly took advantage of the outbreak of the French Revolution by pointing out to the Austrian and Prussian rulers that the revolutionary movement in Paris represented a far greater peril than Russian expansion in the Near East. Thus Catherine was able to press her war against the Turks until, in 1792, they accepted the Treaty of Jassy. This settlement gave to Russia the entire north shore of the Black Sea from the Kuban River in the east to the Dniester River in the west.

The whole of the Ukraine now was under Russian rule. The forest at length had triumphed over the steppe. The desert zone of Central Asia still held out, but it also was destined to fall under Muscovy's sway during the following century. In this manner a small duchy in Eastern Europe expanded through the centuries to become the world's largest state with dozens of minority peoples in addition to the original Slavs. Until 1917 this state was known as the Tsarist Empire; after the 1917 Bolshevik Revolution it became the Union of Soviet Socialist Republics.

SUGGESTED READING

T. Armstrong, *Russian Expansion in the North* (Cambridge University Press, 1965); V. Chen, *Sino-Russian Relations in the Seventeenth Century* (Nijhoff, 1966); R. H. Fisher, *The Russian Fur Trade, 1550–1700* (University of California Press, 1943); F. A. Golder, *Russian Expansion on the Pacific, 1641–1850* (Clark, 1914); R. J. Kerner, *The Urge to the Sea: The Course of Russian History* (University of California, 1942); L. H. Neatby, *Discovery in Russian and Siberian Waters* (Ohio University Press, 1973); D. W. Treadgold, *The Great Siberian Migration* (Princeton University Press, 1957).

chapter 21

Beginning Of Global Unity

The early modern period from 1500 to 1763 is one of the more critical periods in human history. It was at this time that the great discoveries disclosed new continents and thereby heralded the global phase of world history. During this period also the Europeans began their rise to world primacy because of their leadership in overseas activities. Certain global interrelationships that developed during these centuries naturally became stronger with the passage of time. Hence the years from 1500 to 1763 are the period when global unity got underway—the period of transition from the regional isolationism of the pre-1500 era to the European global hegemony of the nineteenth century. The purpose of this chapter is to analyze the precise nature and extent of the global ties that developed in various fields (see Map XXIV, "World of the Emerging West 1763").

I. NEW GLOBAL HORIZONS

The first and most obvious result of Europe's expansion overseas and overland was an unprecedented widening of horizons. No longer was geographic knowledge limited to one region or continent or hemisphere. For the first time, the shape of the globe as a whole was known and charted (see Map XXIII, "Western Knowledge of the Globe, A.D. 1 to 1800"). This new geographical knowledge was largely the work of the Western Europeans who had taken the lead in transoceanic exploration. Before the Portuguese began feeling their way down the coast of Africa in the early fifteenth century, Europeans had accurate information only of North Africa and the Middle East. Their knowledge concerning India was vague. It was still vaguer regarding Central Asia, East Asia, and sub-Saharan Africa. The very existence of the Americas and of Australia—let alone Antarctica—was, of course, unsuspected.

By 1763 the picture was altogether different. The main coastlines of most of the world had become known in varying degrees of detail, including the Atlantic coasts of the Americas, the Pacific coast of South America, the whole outline of Africa, and the coasts of South and East Asia. In certain areas European knowledge went beyond the coastlines. The Russians were reasonably familiar with Siberia, and the Spaniards and Portuguese with Mexico, Central America, and parts of South America. North of the Rio Grande the Spaniards had explored considerable areas in their futile search for gold and fabled cities, while further north the French and English ranged widely, using the canoes and the river-lake routes known to the Indians.

On the other hand, the Pacific coast of North America was largely unknown, while Australia, though sighted on its west coast by Dutch navigators, was almost wholly uncharted. Likewise, the interior of sub-Saharan Africa was almost completely blank, and so was Central Asia, about which the main source of information still was the thirteenth-century account of Marco Polo. In general, then, the Europeans had gained knowledge of most of the coastlines of the world during the period to 1763. In the following period they were to penetrate into the interior of continents and also to explore the polar regions.

II. GLOBAL DIFFUSION OF HUMANS, ANIMALS, AND PLANTS

The European discoveries led not only to new global horizons but also to a new global distribution of races. Prior to 1500 there existed, in effect, worldwide racial segregation. The Negroids were concentrated in sub-Saharan Africa and a few Pacific islands, the Mongoloids in Central Asia, Siberia, East Asia, and the Americas, and the Caucasoids in Europe, North Africa, the Middle East, and India. Today this pattern has been fundamentally altered to the point where half the people of African descent live outside Africa. By 1763 this radically different race distribution was clearly discernible. The Russians had begun their slow migration across the Urals into Siberia. Much more substantial was the mass migration to the Americas, voluntary in the case of the Europeans, involuntary with the Africans.

The influx changed the Americas from purely Mongoloid continents to the most racially mixed regions of the globe. Immigration of Africans continued to the mid-nineteenth century, reaching a total of 12 million slaves. European immigration also steadily increased, reaching a high point at the beginning of the twentieth century when nearly a million arrived each year. The net result is that the New World today is peopled by a majority of whites, with substantial minorities of blacks, Indians, mestizos, and mulatoes, in that order (see Chapter 22, section VII, and Map III).

The new global racial pattern that resulted from these depopulations and migrations has become so familiar that it is now taken for granted, and its extraordinary significance generally overlooked. What happened in the period to 1763 is that the Europeans staked out claims to vast new regions, and in the following century they peopled those territories—not only the Americas, but also Siberia and, eventually, Australia. We can see the vital importance of the redrawing of the racial map of the world if we imagined that the Chinese rather than the Europeans first reached and settled the underpopulated continents. In that case the proportion of Chinese to the total world population would probably be closer to three out of four rather than one out of four as it is now.

The intermixture of human races was accompanied inevitably by a corresponding intermixture of plants and animals. With a few insignificant exceptions, all plants and animals being utilized today were domesticated by prehistoric humans in various parts of the world. Their diffusion from their places of origin had proceeded slowly until 1500, when globe-spanning Homo sapiens began transplanting them back and forth amongst continents. An important contribution of the Old World was the various stockyard animals, especially horses, cattle, and sheep. The New World had nothing comparable. The llama and alpaca were of relatively little value. Old World grains also were important, especially wheat, rye, oats, and barley. The Spaniards, who loved their orchards, brought with them a large variety of fruits, as well as the olive and the European vine.

The American Indians in return contributed their remarkable store of food plants, particularly corn and potatoes, but also cassava, tomatoes, avocados, sweet potatoes, peanuts, and certain varieties of beans, pumpkins, and squashes. So important are these Indian plants that today they are responsible for about one-half of the world's total plant-food production. In addition to these food plants, the American Indians were responsible for two major cash crops: tobacco and cotton. They also contributed several native American drugs that are prominent in modern pharmacology: coca for cocaine and novocaine, curare used in anesthetics, cinchona bark (the source of quinine), datura used in pain relievers, and cascara for laxatives.

The interchange of animals and plants was not, of course, confined to Eurasia and the Americas. The entire globe was involved, as is illustrated strikingly in the case of Australia. Australia is now a leading world exporter of primary products such as wool, mutton, beef, and wheat, all commodities derived from species that were transplanted from elsewhere. The same is true of Indonesia with its great rubber, coffee, tea, and tobacco production, and of Hawaii with its sugar and pineapples.

III. GLOBAL ECONOMIC RELATIONS

By the latter part of the eighteenth century, a large intercontinental trade had developed for the first time in history. Before 1500, Arab and Italian merchants transported mostly luxuries from one part of Eurasia to another—goods such as spices, silk, precious stones, and perfumes. By the late eighteenth century the limited luxury trade had been transformed into a mass trade because of the exchange of new bulky necessities. Atlantic commerce especially became mass trade since the New World plantations produced huge quantities of tobacco, sugar, and later, coffee, cotton, and other commodities which were sold in Europe. Because the plantations practiced *monoculture,* they had to import all necessities such as grain, fish, cloth, and metal products. They also had to import their labor. This led to the flourishing triangle trade: rum, cloth, guns, and other metal products from Europe to Africa; slaves from Africa to the New World; and sugar, tobacco, and bullion from the New World to Europe.

Another important aspect of the new mass global trade of this era was the exchange of products between Western and Eastern Europe. Here again Western Europe received raw materials, especially bread grains, which were in great demand because of population increase and because much arable land had been converted into pasture. At Danzig, chief port for the Baltic grain trade, rye prices between 1550 and 1600 rose 247 percent, barley 187 percent, and oats 185 percent. This stimulated a great increase in the export of grains and other raw materials, so that the value of Polish and Hungarian exports to the West during these decades usually was double that of imports. Poland, Hungary, Russia, and ultimately the Balkans received textiles, arms, metal products, and colonial goods, and in return provided grain, cattle, hides, ship stores, and flax. They also provided furs, which were obtained by the Russians in Siberia in the same way that the Spaniards obtained bullion in the New World, namely, by exploiting native labor.

Europe's trade with Asia was not equal to the trade with the Americas or Eastern Europe for two principal reasons. One was that the European textile industries opposed the importation of cotton goods from various Asiatic countries. Since foreign cottons were immensely popular in Europe, because they were light, bright, inexpensive, and, above all, washable, they began to be imported in large quantities. Soon objections were raised by native textile interests and by those who feared that national security was endangered by the loss of the bullion that was drained away to pay for the textiles. These interests brought sufficient pressure to bear upon their respective governments to secure the passage of laws forbidding or reducing the importation of Indian cottons.

The other factor limiting European commerce with Asia was the difficulty of finding something that would sell in the Asiatic market. This problem dated back to classical times when the Roman Empire was drained of its gold to pay for Chinese silk and Indian textiles. Likewise in the sixteenth, seventeenth, and eighteenth centuries, Asia remained uninterested in European goods, and Europe was reluctant to send bullion to pay for the Asiatic produce it wanted. Europe did not solve this problem of trade with Asia until it developed power machinery at the end of the eighteenth century. Then the situation was reversed, for it was Europe that was able to flood Asia with cheap, machine-made textiles. But until that time, East-West trade was hampered by the fact that Asia was willing to receive bullion from Europe but would accept little else.

What was the significance of the new worldwide economic ties? First and foremost, international division of labor for the first time had been achieved on a significant scale. The world was on the way to becoming an economic unit. The Americas and Eastern Europe (with Siberia) produced raw materials, Africa provided manpower, Asia an assortment of luxury commodities, while Western Europe directed these global operations and concentrated more and more on industrial output.

The requirements of the new global economy raised the question of how to get a big enough labor supply in the raw-material-producing regions. The New World plantations met this by importing African slaves on a large scale. Hence African elements are most numerous today in precisely those areas that had been devoted to plantation agriculture—northern Brazil, the West Indies, and the southern United States. This was to leave a bitter legacy. These areas to the present day are wracked by basic problems dating back to the colonial period—the problems of race discrimination and of underdevelopment. The ongoing racial conflict in American ghettos and on Caribbean islands is the end result of over four centuries of transatlantic slave trade. Likewise the underdevelopment of all Latin America is simply a continuation of the economic dependency on Northwestern Europe of the Spanish and Portuguese colonies (and of Spain and Portugal themselves).

Whereas the price for the participation of the Americas in the new global economy was slavery, the price for Eastern Europe was serfdom. The basic reason was the same—namely the need for a plentiful and reliable supply of cheap labor to produce goods for the lucrative West European market. Heretofore the nobles in Poland and Hungary had required minimal labor from the peasants—three to six days a year—for there was no incentive to increase output. But when production for market became profitable, the nobles responded by drastically raising the labor obligations to one day a week, and by the end of the sixteenth century to six days a week. To make sure that the peasants would remain to perform this labor, laws were passed limiting their freedom of movement more and more strictly. Eventually they were completely bound to the soil, thereby becoming serfs, without freedom of movement, and subject to the exactions of the nobles.

Africa also was vitally affected by the new global economy. An estimated 12 million slaves ended up in New World plantations. But the horrors of the slave trade were such that approximately four times as many were captured originally in the African interior as eventually arrived in the Americas. This amounted to a drain of 48 million people, nearly all in the prime of their productive years. The 36 million casualties were sustained in the course of the overland march from the interior to the coast, and then during the dreaded trans-Atlantic crossing.

ADAM SMITH ON THE EXPANSION OF EUROPE

In his world famous *Wealth of Nations* (1778), Adam Smith paid considerable attention to the effect of colonies. He noted that they added to the wealth of the European countries, but not to that of Spain and Portugal that owned the colonies.*

The discovery of America, and that of a passage to the East Indies by the Cape of Good Hope, are the two greatest and most important events recorded in the history of mankind. Their consequences have already been very great: but, in the short period of between two and three centuries which has elapsed since these discoveries were made, it is impossible that the whole extent of their consequences can have been seen. What benefits or what misfortunes to mankind may hereafter result from those great events, no human wisdom can foresee. By uniting, in some measure, the most distant parts of the world, by enabling them to relieve one another's wants, to increase one another's enjoyments, and to encourage one another's industry, their general tendency would seem to be beneficial.

In the mean time, one of the principal effects of those discoveries has been to raise the mercantile system to a degree of splendour and glory which it could never otherwise have attained to. It is the object of that system to enrich a great nation rather by trade and manufactures than by the improvement and cultivation of land, rather by the industry of the towns than by that of the country. But, in consequence of those discoveries, the commercial towns of Europe, instead of being the manufacturers and carriers for but a very small part of the world, (that part of Europe which is washed by the Atlantic ocean, and the countries which lie round the Baltic and Mediterranean seas), have now become the manufacturers for the numerous and thriving cultivators of America, and the carriers, and in some respects the manufacturers too, for almost all the different nations of Asia, Africa, and America. Two new worlds have been opened to their industry, each of them much greater and more extensive than the old one, and the market of one of them growing still greater and greater every day.

The countries which possess the colonies of America, and which trade directly to the East Indies, enjoy, indeed, the whole show and splendour of this great commerce. Other countries, however, notwithstanding all the invidious restraints by which it is meant to exclude them, frequently enjoy a greater share of the real benefit of it. The colonies of Spain and Portugal, for example, give more real encouragement to the industry of other countries than to that of Spain and Portugal. In the single article of linen alone the consumption of those colonies amounts, it is said, but I do not pretend to warrant the quantity, to more than three millions sterling a year. But this great consumption is almost entirely supplied by France, Flanders, Holland, and Germany. Spain and Portugal furnish but a small part of it. The capital which supplies the colonies with this great quantity of linen is annually distributed among, and furnishes a revenue to, the inhabitants of those other countries.

*Adam Smith, *Wealth of Nations* (Edinburgh, 1838), p. 282.

The effect of the slave trade varied greatly from one part of Africa to the other. Angola and East Africa suffered severely because their populations were relatively sparse to begin with, and their economies were often close to the subsistence level. So even a small population loss was devastating. By contrast, West Africa was more advanced economically and hence more populous, so that the devastations of the slavers were not so ruinous. Considering the continent as a whole, the effect on the population was not as great as might be expected because the slaves were taken over a period stretching from 1450 to 1870, and from a total sub-Saharan population estimated at 70 to 80 million. Nevertheless, the slave trade had a corrosive and unsettling effect on the entire African coast from Senegal to Angola, and for four to five hundred miles inland. The appearance of the European slavers with their cargoes of rum, guns, and hardware set off a chain reaction of slave-hunting raids into the interior. Wars broke out among various groups for control of the lucrative and militarily decisive trade. Some like the Ashanti Confederacy and the Dahomey Kingdom, rose to ascendancy, while others like the Yoruba and Benin civilizations and the Congo kingdom, declined. The overall effect was definitely disruptive.

And yet the slave trade did involve trade as well as slavery. In return for their fellow countrymen whom the Africans themselves sold to the Europeans, they received, not only alcohol and firearms, but also certain useful and economically productive commodities, including textiles, tools, and raw materials for local smithies and workshops. A more important positive influence in the long run was the introduction of new food plants from the Americas. Corn, cassava, sweet potatoes, peppers, pineapples, and tobacco were brought in by the Portuguese and spread very rapidly from tribe to tribe. Therefore it is argued that the substantially larger number of people that could be supported with these new foods probably outweighed the manpower lost to the slave trade. On the other hand, the slave trade was not essential for the introduction of the new food plants. They were spreading rapidly during these centuries all over the globe. Slavery or no slavery, they doubtless would have reached the interior of Africa as they did the interior of China.

Of the various continents, Asia was the least affected, because it was sufficiently strong militarily, politically, and economically to avoid direct or indirect subjugation. Most of Asia was quite unaware of the persistent and annoying European merchants who were appearing in the coastal regions. Only a few coastal areas in India, and some of the islands in the East Indies, felt the impact of Europe's economic expansion. So far as Asia as a whole was concerned, its attitude was best expressed by the Emperor of China, Ch'ien-lung. He replied as follows to a 1793 message from King George III of Britain asking for the establishment of diplomatic and commercial relations:

> Swaying the wide world, I have but one aim in view, namely, to maintain a perfect governance and to fulfill the duties of the State: strange and costly objects do not interest me. . . . As your Ambassador can see for himself, we possess all things. I set no value on objects strange or ingenious, and have no use for your country's manufactures.[1]

Europe also was affected by the new global economy, but the effects in this case were all positive. The Europeans were the pioneer middlemen of world trade. They had opened the new oceanic routes and supplied the necessary capital, shipping, and technical skills. So it was natural that they should have profited most from the slave trade, the sugar and tobacco plantations, and the eastern commerce. Some of the benefits trickled down to the European masses, as is indicated by the fact that tea cost about £10 a pound when introduced in England about 1650 but had become an article of common consumption a century later. More important than the effect on living standards was the effect the new global commerce had in stimulating Europe's economy. As we will see later, the industrial revolution that began in the late eighteenth century owed much to the capital earned from overseas enterprises and to the growing demand for European manufactures in overseas markets.

It was during this period, then, that Europe forged ahead in the great ascent to global economic primacy. The overall results were positive, because global division of labor led to increased global productivity. The world of 1763 was richer than that of 1500, and the economic growth has continued to the present day. But from the beginning, Northwestern Europe, as the world's entrepreneur, got most of the benefits at the expense of the other regions. What this expense involved is apparent in the current conflict of races, in the gross discrepancy between rich and poor nations, and in the scars left by serfdom throughout Eastern Europe, and by slavery throughout the world.

IV. GLOBAL POLITICAL RELATIONS

Global political relations changed as fundamentally during the period to 1763 as did the economic. The Western Europeans were no longer fenced in on the western tip of Eurasia by an expanding Islam. Instead, they had outflanked the Moslem world in the south by winning control of the Indian Ocean. Meanwhile, the Russians had outflanked the Moslems in the north by their conquest of Siberia. At the same time, the Western Europeans, by their discovery of the New World, had opened up vast territories for economic exploitation and colonization. In doing so, they built up a tremendous reservoir of resources and power.

All this represented a basic and fateful change in the global balance of power—a change comparable to that which had occurred in the demographic balance. Hitherto the Moslem world had been the center of initiative, probing and pushing in all directions—into Southeast Europe, into sub-Saharan Africa, into Central and Southeast Asia. Now a new center had arisen which was able to operate on a global, rather than merely Eurasian, scale. From this new center, first in the Iberian peninsula and later in Northwest Europe, the routes of trade and of political influence radiated outward to envelop the entire world—westward to the Americas, south around Africa, and east to India and around Southeast Asia.

All these territories were not actually controlled by 1763. But there was effective domination of the underpopulated lands—the Americas, Siberia, and later Australia—even though their actual peopling on a continental scale had to wait till the nineteenth century. In Africa and Asia the Western Europeans obtained only coastal footholds during this period—with one exception: the Dutch penetrated the Cape and the East Indies. Elsewhere the native peoples were too strong and highly organized to allow a repetition of what happened in the Americas and Siberia.

In West Africa, for example, the Europeans could not penetrate inland because of climatic difficulties. They were prevented also by the coastal chiefs who jealously guarded their profitable position as middlemen between the interior tribes and the Europeans. In India the Europeans were kept at arm's length for 250 years following the arrival of Vasco da Gama in 1498. During those centuries they were allowed to trade in a few ports, but clearly and explicitly only on the sufferance of the native rulers. In China and Japan there was no chance at all of European territorial encroachment, as the Russians discovered when they entered the Amur valley.

V. GLOBAL CULTURAL RELATIONS

The imposition of European culture, like that of European political rule, depended on the state of the native societies. In the Americas, for example, European culture was transported bodily because the native peoples were either wiped out or pushed aside. Yet even the casual traveler in Latin America cannot fail to notice evidence of Indian cultural survivals. There is, for example, the use of adobe for building purposes, and of unmilled pine logs as beams, or vigas. Likewise the blanket, or serape, that is draped over the shoulders is of Indian origin, as is also the poncho, consisting of two blankets sewn together with a slit left open for the head. The Roman Catholicism currently practiced in much of Latin America is a blend of Christian and Indian beliefs and practices. Although the names of native gods have been dropped, the Indians assign the attributes of these gods to the Virgin Mary and the saints, expecting the images of the Catholic gods to cure disease, control the weather, and keep them from harm, as they believed their gods had done. Perhaps the most conspicuous evidence of Indian influence is to be found in the Latin American cuisine. Tamales, tortillas, and the various chili dishes are based on the two great Indian staples, beans and corn.

European influence upon the native cultures of Africa and Eurasia was slight in the period prior to 1763, except for the diffusion of new food plants, which, as noted, was of first importance. In West Africa the native chiefs confined the European traders largely to their coastal posts. In the old Middle Eastern, Indian, and Chinese centers of civilization, the native peoples, as might be expected, were not at all impressed by the culture of the European intruders. The Moslem Turks, who had the closest ties with the Christian Europeans, looked down upon them with the utmost contempt. Even in the seventeenth and eighteenth centuries, when the Turks were themselves on the downgrade, they did not hesitate to express their disdain for the Christian infidels. "Do I not know you," burst out the grand vizier to the French ambassador in 1666, "that you are a Giaour [nonbeliever], that you are a hogge, a dogge, a turde eater?"[2]

Likewise on the mainland of India, the native peoples reacted very negatively when the Portuguese, who were ensconced at Goa, introduced the Inquisition in 1560. Between 1600 and 1773, seventy-three victims were consigned to the flames because of their heretical views. The Indian population could not fail to see the inconsistency in a religion that imprisoned, tortured, and condemned to the flames people whose only crime was unorthodoxy. But at the same time it prevented widows from being burnt of their own free will as an act of sublime virtue. Furthermore, the lawless and boisterous behavior of European adventurers in India further lowered the Indian people's opinion of the Western Christians. An English clergyman, Mr. Terry, was told in 1616: "Christian religion devil religion; Christian much drink; Christian much do wrong; Christian much beat; Christian much abuse others."[3]

The Chinese reaction to the Europeans was relatively favorable at the outset because of the exceptional ability and intellectual attainments of the Jesuit missionaries. The Jesuits succeeded in winning some converts, including a few scholars and some members of the imperial family. But even the capable Jesuits, with their knowledge of astronomy and mathematics and geography, did not make much of an impression upon most Chinese scholars who rejected both Western science and Western religion. So far as the popular Chinese attitude to the Europeans at that time is concerned, it probably was reflected accurately in the proverb that the Chinese alone possessed two eyes, the Europeans were one-eyed, and all the other inhabitants of the earth were blind. Given this attitude, it is not surprising that, with the exception of certain specialized fields of learning such as astronomy, European influence on Chinese civilization prior to 1763 was very slight.

Although the Chinese, the Indians, and the Turks were unimpressed by the culture of the Europeans during this period, the Europeans, by contrast, were very much impressed by what they saw in Constantinople, in Delhi, and in Peking. They became familiar first with the Ottoman Empire, and their reaction was one of respect, admiration, and apprehension. As late as 1634, after the decline of the empire had set in, a thoughtful English traveler concluded that the Turks were "the only modern people great in action," and that "he who would behold these times in their greatest glory, could not find a better scene than Turkey."[4]

During the seventeenth century the Ottoman Empire lost prestige among Europeans. But at the same time European intellectuals were becoming fascinated with numerous detailed accounts of the fabulous civilization of far-off Cathay. They were entranced as they learned of China's history, art, philosophy, and government. China came to be held up as a model civilization because of its Confucian system of morals, its examination system for government service, its respect for learning rather than for military prowess, and its exquisite handicrafts, including porcelain, silk, and lacquer work. Voltaire (1694–1778), for example, adorned the wall of his library with a portrait of Confucius, while the German philosopher Leibniz (1646–1716) extolled the Chinese emperor K'ang-hsi as "the monarch . . . who almost exceeds human heights of greatness, being a god-like mortal, ruling all by a nod of his head, who, however, is educated to virtue and wisdom . . . thereby earning the right to rule."[5]

In the late eighteenth century, European admiration for China began to wane, partly because the Catholic missionaries were now being persecuted and also because the Europeans were beginning to be more interested in China's natural resources than in its culture. The shift in attitude is reflected in the sixteen volumes of the *Memoirs on the History, Sciences, Arts, etc., of the Chinese,* published in Paris between 1776 and 1814. The eleventh volume, which appeared in 1786, contained little but reports on resources that might interest traders—borax, lignite, quicksilver, ammoniac, horses, bamboo, and wool-bearing animals.

Just as European interest had shifted in the seventeenth century from the Ottoman Empire to China, so now in the late eighteenth century it shifted to Greece and, to a lesser extent, India. The classical Greeks became the great favorites among educated Europeans. "How can you believe," wrote a German scholar in 1778, "that uncultivated Oriental peoples produced annals and poetry and possessed a complete religion and morality, before the Greeks, who were the teachers of Europe, were able to read?"[6] A few European intellectuals became engrossed in Indian culture. The Hindu pandits, or learned men, were unwilling to impart their sacred lore to foreigners, but a few Europeans, mostly Jesuit fathers, acquired a knowledge of Sanskrit language, literature, and philosophy. The German philosopher Schopenhauer (1788–1860) fell as much under the spell of Hindu philosophy as Leibniz had under the Chinese. An English scholar, Sir William Jones, proclaimed before the Asiatic Society of Bengal in 1786 that "the Sanskrit Language, whatever be its antiquity, is of wonderful structure; more perfect than the Greek, more copious than the Latin, and more exquisitely refined than either."[7]

IV. EARLY MODERN PERIOD IN HISTORICAL PERSPECTIVE

The early modern period from 1500 to 1763 represents a halfway point between the regional isolationism of the preceding ages and the European world domination of the nineteenth century. Economically, it was a time when the Europeans extended their trading operations to virtually all corners of the globe, though they were not yet able to exploit the interiors of the great landmasses. Intercontinental trade reached unprecedented proportions, though still far below the volume it was to reach in the following centuries.

Politically, the world was still far from being a single unit. The great Seven Years' War which convulsed Europe did not affect the Americas west of the Mississippi, nor the interior of Africa, nor most of the Middle East, nor any of East Asia. The Europeans had secured a firm grip on Siberia, South America, and the eastern portion of North America, but they had as yet only a few territorial enclaves in Africa, India, and the East Indies. In the Far East they could venture only as merchants, and even in that capacity they had to submit to the most restrictive and arbitrary regulations.

Culturally, it was a period of widening horizons. Throughout the globe peoples were becoming aware of other peoples and other cultures. By and large, the Europeans were more impressed and affected by the ancient civilizations of Eurasia than vice versa. They felt a sense of wide-eyed wonder as they discovered new oceans and continents and civilizations. At the same time that they were scrambling greedily for booty and for trade, they exhibited a certain humility. They even underwent an occasional anxious searching of conscience, as in the case of the treatment of the Indians in Spanish America. But before this period had passed, Europe's attitude toward the rest of the world was noticeably changing. It was becoming coarser and harder and more intolerant. In the mid-nineteenth century the French sinologist Guillaume Pauthier complained that the Chinese civilization, which in the time of Leibniz had keenly interested European intellectuals, ''now scarcely attracted the attention of a select few. . . . These people, whom we daily treat as barbarians, and who, nevertheless, had attained to a very high state of culture several centuries before our ancestors inhabited the forests of Gaul and Germany, now inspire in us only a deep contempt.''[8] Part VI of this book will be concerned with why the Europeans came to feel themselves superior to the ''lesser breeds,'' and how they were able to impose their rule upon them.

SUGGESTED READING

P. D. Curtin, *The Atlantic Slave Trade: A Census* (University of Wisconsin Press, 1969); L. S. S. O'Malley, ed., *Modern India and the West* (Oxford University Press, 1941); J. H. Parry, *The Age of Reconnaissance: Discovery, Exploration and Settlement, 1450–1650* (World, 1963); A. G. Price, *The Western Invasions of the Pacific and Its Continents: A Study of Moving Frontiers and Changing Landscapes, 1513–1958* (Clarendon, 1963); A. Reichwein, *China and Europe: Intellectual and Artistic Contacts in the Eighteenth Century* (Knopf, 1925); E. Reynolds, *Stand the Storm: A History of the Atlantic Slave Trade* (Oxford University Press, 1982); S. J. and B. H. Stein, *The Colonial Heritage of Latin America* (Oxford University Press, 1970).

What It Means
For Us Today

REGIONAL AUTONOMY VERSUS GLOBAL UNITY

The significance of the period after 1500 is that it marked the beginning of the clash between regional autonomy and global unity. Before that date there was no conflict because there were no global contacts, let alone global unity. For tens of thousands of years, human beings had lived in regional isolation. When the first humans fanned out from their ancestral birthplace, presumably in Africa, they lost contact with their original neighbors. They repeated this endlessly as they spread in all directions until they inhabited all continents except Antarctica. For example, when the first Mongoloids crossed over from Northeast Siberia to Alaska, they pressed on throughout North and South America. They settled down in new communities in relative isolation. Over thousands of years they developed distinctive local languages and cultures and even physical types. This process went on all over the globe, so that, until 1500, racial segregation existed on a global scale. All blacks or Negroids lived in Africa, all whites or Caucasoids lived in Europe and the Middle East, all Mongoloids in East Asia and the Americas, and all Australoids in Australia.

This traditional regional autonomy began to give way to global unity when Western overseas expansion got under way about 1500. Races no longer were isolated because millions of people moved, willingly or unwillingly, to new continents. Since the Europeans took the lead in this global activity, it was they who dominated the newly united world. By the nineteenth century they controlled the globe politically with their great empires, and economically with their joint stock companies and corporations. They also enjoyed cultural domination, so that Western culture became the global model. It was equated with civilization, and non-Western cultures came to be regarded as inherently inferior. This Western hegemony was taken for granted by the nineteenth century, not only by Europeans but also by non-Europeans. It was assumed to be almost divinely ordained—a part of the natural order of things.

With the twentieth century, the pendulum has begun to swing once more towards regional autonomy. Europe needed four centuries (1500 to 1900) to build up its worldwide dominance. Today it is disintegrating in little more than four decades. The disintegration began after World War I and picked up speed after World War II. Political disintegration took the form of the end of empires. Economic disintegration occurred with the rise of Communist societies, beginning with the Soviet Union in 1917, and accelerating after World War II with the spread of communism to China, Southeast Asia, Africa, and Cuba. Cultural disintegration is even more widespread. Western culture no longer is regarded as synonymous with civilization, and non-Western cultures are not equated with barbarism.

Western culture today is being directly challenged, and even rejected, throughout the world. In November 1979, when American embassy personnel in Teheran were taken hostage, Western journalists submitted a number of written questions to the youthful captors. The latter replied as a group, and their answer included the following: "Western culture is a splendid means for the colonialists, a tool that alienates the nation from itself. By making a nation accept Western and American values, they make it submit to their domination." The captors also expressed distrust of Iranian intellectuals who were trained in the West and influenced by the West. "What need do we have for these decaying brains. Let them go where they want. These decaying brains are those intellectuals molded on Western models and they have no role in our movement and our revolution."[1]

Such views are not limited to young radicals. They are now shared by many non-Westerners of all political beliefs. An example is Carlos Fuentes, a leading Mexican novelist and former ambassador to France. In 1980, when the U.S. Teheran embassy personnel were being held hostage, Fuentes held a visiting fellowship at Princeton University. The events in Teheran reminded him of his youth and of Mexico's earlier revolution.[2]

> I see Teheran today and I could be seeing Mexico in 1915. We had Pancho Villa, Zapata, Lagos Chazaro. It was chaos and it took years to settle down, but something was being born. . . . If there is one thing that is happening around the world, it is the determination of peoples not simply to accept the two versions of inevitable progress—that of Western capitalism or Soviet socialism—but to find ways of combining the power of technology with the energy of their own traditions.

Fuentes concluded that for non-Westerners, acceptance of "the Western belief in the imperative of its own progress is the assassination of the past."

Rejection of Western domination of the globe is not surprising. Such domination was an historical aberration, produced by a peculiar combination of circumstances, and therefore bound to be temporary. But what is surprising is that the forces of regional autonomy are also awakening today *within* the leading states. National groups or subgroups, which have been asleep for decades or for centuries, are now stirring and demanding autonomy. In the United States, there are the minority groups: the blacks, the Spanish-speaking, and the native Indians. In neighboring Canada, the very existence of the Dominion is threatened by the separatist demands of the French Quebecois. Britain likewise is coping with would-be secessionists in Scotland, Ireland, and Wales. France is facing the same challenge from the Corsican, Breton, and Basque liberation fronts.

The demand for regional autonomy is not directed only against central authority in the West. In Iran, the popular revolt against Western influences is paralleled by regional uprisings against Teheran—uprisings by minorities such as the Kurds, Arabs, Baluchis, and Turkomen. Since these minorities comprise almost half of the total population of the country, Iran is much more threatened by the demand for regional autonomy than is any Western country. The same may be said of the Soviet Union, where dozens of non-Slavic minorities live. Since their birthrate is much higher than that of the Slavs, they also will soon constitute half of the total population. The precise degree to which the Soviet minorities are disaffected is not clear. A Soviet emigré historian Andrei Amalrik predicts, in his book *Will the Soviet Union Survive Until 1984?*, that the minorities will play an important role in the disintegration of the Soviet state, which he confidently expects and looks forward to.

Much of the turmoil of our age arises from the clash of two great contradictory forces. On the one hand, modern technology is uniting the globe as never before, thanks to modern communication media, multinational corporations, and world-encircling spaceships. On the other hand, the globe is being torn apart by the awakening of hitherto dormant masses who refuse to allow their pasts to be ''assassinated,'' and who instead are determined to create their own futures. The roots of this historic conflict of our age go back to the centuries after 1500 when Western explorers and merchants for the first time brought together all the peoples of the world. The fateful repercussions, both positive and negative, confront us to the present day. ''Encircled nationalisms,'' writes the Egyptian journalist Mohammed Heikel, ''have fortified themselves for a last-ditch stand in the battle for their future, not their past.''[3]

SUGGESTED READING

The revolt against Western domination is best summarized by E. Fischer, *The Passing of the European Age,* rev. ed. (Harvard University Press, 1948). Various aspects of the current worldwide challenge to central authority are analyzed in L. Kohr, *The Breakdown of Nations* (Routledge & Kegan Paul, 1957); D. Morris and K. Hess, *Neighborhood Power: The New Localism* (Beacon Press, 1975); C. Bezold, ed., *Anticipatory Democracy* (Random House, 1978); A. Amalrik, *Will the Soviet Union Survive Until 1984?* (Harper & Row, 1979), and H. C. d'Encausse, *Decline of an Empire: The Soviet Socialist Republics in Revolt* (Newsweek, 1979).

Part VI

World Of Western Dominance, 1763–1914

Basis of Dominance

The century and a half between 1763 and 1914 stands out in the course of world history as the period of European domination over a large part of the globe. In 1763 Europe was still far from being the master of the world. It had only coastal footholds in Africa and in Asia. But by 1914 the European powers had annexed the whole of Africa. And they had effectively established their control over Asia, either directly, as in India and Southeast Asia, or indirectly, as in the Chinese and Ottoman empires. The unprecedented expansion of Europe was made possible by the continuation and acceleration of the modernization process. This process was set in motion earlier by the Renaissance, Reformation, technological development, capitalist enterprise, state building, and overseas expansion (see chapters 14 and 15). These triggered a chain reaction in the form of the three great revolutions—scientific, industrial, and political—which gave Europe irresistible dynamism and power.

Two features of these revolutions might be noted at this point. One is that they were well under way before 1763. The English Civil War, a major phase of the political revolution, occurred in the 1640s. The scientific revolution took place primarily during the century and a half between the publication of Copernicus's *De revolutionibus orbium coelestium* (1543) and of Newton's *Principia* (1687). Likewise, the roots of the industrial revolution were planted in the sixteenth and seventeenth centuries, when the countries of Northwestern Europe "were seething with such genuinely capitalistic phenomena as systematic mechanical invention, company formation, and speculation in the shares of financial and trading concerns."[1] But the worldwide impact of none of these revolutions was fully felt until the nineteenth century. That is why we are considering them here rather than earlier in this book.

      The other point to note about the three great revolutions is that they did not run in parallel or independent lines. Scientific, industrial, and technological events were interdependent and reacted continuously one upon the other. Newton's discovery of the laws governing the movements of heavenly bodies and Darwin's theories of biological evolution both had profound effects on political ideas. Likewise, we could not conceive of modern nationalism without technological innovations such as printing and the telegraph. And contrariwise, politics affected science, as in the case of the French Revolution, which provided a powerful stimulus to scientific advance. Politics also affected economics, as was made clear by the English manufacturer John Wilkinson, who stated bluntly, "Manufacture and Commerce will always flourish most where Church and King interfere least."[2]

      The first two chapters of Part VI (subtitled, "Basis of Dominance") will concentrate on analyzing the nature and the unfolding of these three European revolutions. We shall then, in the following chapters of Part VI of this volume ("Impact of Dominance"), trace the effect of these revolutions on various parts of the globe. We shall see how they made possible the Europeanization of the Americas and of Australia, the partitioning of Africa, and the domination of Asia.

The so-called scientific
revolution . . . outshines
everything since the rise of
Christianity and reduces the
Renaissance and Reformation to
the rank of mere episodes, mere
internal displacements within
the system of medieval
Christendom. . . . It looms so
large as the real origin both of
the modern world and of the
modern mentality that our
customary periodisation of
European history has become an
anachronism and an
encumbrance.

Herbert Butterfield

The manufacturing system as it
exists in Great Britain, and the
inconceivably rapid creation of
immense towns under it,
are without previous parallel in the
history of the world.

Manchester Guardian,
November 17, 1832

chapter 22

Europe's Scientific And Industrial Revolutions

The material culture of the human race has changed more in the past two hundred years than it did in the preceding five thousand. In the eighteenth century people were living in essentially the same way as the ancient Egyptians and Mesopotamians. They were still using the same materials to erect their buildings, the same animals to transport themselves and their belongings, the same sails and oars to propel their ships, the same textiles to make their clothes, and the same candles and torches to provide light. But today metals and plastics supplement stone and wood; the railroad, the automobile, and the airplane have replaced the oxen, the horse, and the donkey; steam, diesel, and atom power drive ships in place of wind and manpower; many synthetic fabrics compete with the traditional cottons, woolens, and linens; and electricity has replaced the candle and become a source of power for many duties at the flick of a switch.

The origins of this great transformation are to be found in the scientific and industrial revolutions, the outstanding contributions of Western civilization to human development. In the light of historical retrospect it appears that these two revolutions are of even greater significance than the agricultural revolution of Neolithic times. The agricultural revolution made civilization possible, but once this great step forward was taken, agriculture had no further contribution to make. Science-technology, on the other hand, is cumulative by its very methodology. It contains within itself the possibilities of infinite advance. If we bear in mind the achievements of science-technology in the past few centuries and its present accelerating pace of development, we may appreciate, if not comprehend, its staggering potentiality and significance. Science-technology, furthermore, is universal. Based as it is upon an objective methodology, it has obtained general assent to its propositions. It is the one product of Western civilization that non-Western people generally respect and seek. In fact, it was science and its related technology that made it possible for Europe to dominate the world in the nineteenth century. And today the formerly subject peoples are striving to redress the balance by learning the mysteries of the West's great and unique contribution to humanity.

That is why the scientific and industrial revolutions are of basic significance for the study of world history. This chapter will trace the unfolding of these revolutions from their beginnings in early modern times until World War I.

I. ROOTS OF THE SCIENTIFIC REVOLUTION

The roots of science may be traced back to ancient Mesopotamia, Egypt, and China, to classical Greece, and to the medieval Moslem world. Yet the scientific revolution is a unique product of Western civilization. The reason seems to be that only in the West did science become part and parcel of general society. Or, to put it another way, only in the West were the philosopher-scientist and the artisan united so that they stimulated each other. And it was this union of science and society, of scientist and artisan, that contributed greatly to the unprecedented blossoming of science in the Western world.

In all human societies the artisans developed certain skills in hunting, fishing, farming, and in working with wood, stone, metal, grasses, fibers, roots, and hides. Through their observations and experiments they gradually improved their techniques and sometimes reached very high levels, as in the case of the Eskimos. Yet the degree of progress achieved by all premodern societies was sharply restricted. The reason was that the artisans were interested only in making pots or building houses or constructing boats and did not bother with underlying chemical or mechanical principles. They did not ask about the relationship between causes and their effects. In short, the artisans by definition concerned themselves with technological know-how rather than with scientific know-why.

The philosophers and the artisans undoubtedly did work together at certain times to produce the elaborate calendars, the navigation aids, and the everyday rituals of antiquity. But the fact remains that until recent times the tendency was toward compartmentalization—toward the isolation of the thinker from the worker. The great achievement of the West was to bring the two together. This fusion of know-how and know-why gave science the grounding and the impetus that was to make it the dominant force that it is today.

Why did this epochal development take place in the West? One reason was the humanistic scholarship of the Renaissance. Scholars and artists had access not only to Plato and Aristotle but also to Euclid and Archimedes, who stimulated the study of physics and mathematics. Even more important was the impetus for the biological sciences. Medical men studied the complete works of Hippocrates and Galen, and naturalists those of Aristotle, Dioscorides, and Theophrastus. However, the fruits of human scholarship could not have brought about the scientific revolution without the favorable social atmosphere in Western Europe. In this atmosphere, the gulf between artisans and scholars was narrowed. Artisans were not so despised during the Renaissance as they had been in classical and medieval times. Respect was given to the practical arts of spinning, weaving, ceramics, glass making, and, most of all, to the increasingly important mining and metallurgy. All these crafts in Renaissance Europe were in the hands of freemen rather than of slaves as in classical times. And the freemen were not so far removed, socially and economically, from the ruling circles as were the artisans of the Middle Ages. The higher status of the Renaissance craftsman allowed him to strengthen his ties with the scholar. Each had an important contribution to make. The craftsman had the old techniques of antiquity, and added the new devices evolving during the Middle Ages. The scholars likewise provided the facts, speculations, and procedures of rediscovered antiquity and of medieval science. The two approaches fused slowly, but in the end they produced an explosive combination.

Closely connected with this union of the craftsman and scholar was the corresponding union of labor and thought that was brought about by individual scholars or scientists. A strong prejudice existed in ancient times against combining creative learning and manual work. This prejudice, which presumably arose out of the ancient association of manual labor with slavery, persisted in medieval Europe even after slavery had almost disappeared. Medieval scholastic philosophers drew a distinction between the "liberal" and the "servile" arts, between work done with the mind alone and work that involved a change in matter. Poets, logicians, and mathematicians, for example, belonged to the first category, and sculptors, glaziers, and ironworkers to the second. This attitude held back progress, as was clearly evident in the field of medicine. The work of a physician did not change matter so it was regarded as "liberal," while that of a surgeon, by the same criterion, was considered "servile." Accordingly, experimentation was looked down upon, and vivisection was deemed illegal and repulsive.

When William Harvey (1578–1657) made his great discovery concerning the movements of the heart and blood, he did so because he resolutely turned his back on this scorn for manual work. Instead, for decades he carried on painstaking experiments of all types. He cut the arteries and veins of living things, from large animals to tiny insects, observing and recording with care and patience the flow of the blood and the motions of the heart. He also utilized the new magnifying glass to observe wasps, hornets, and flies. Today this procedure seems sensible and obvious, but in Harvey's time it definitely was not. It took much courage for Harvey to use in his time what is considered today to be normal scientific method.

Science was stimulated also by the discovery and the opening up of overseas lands. New plants, new animals, new stars, even new human beings and new human societies were found, and all these challenged traditional ideas and assumptions. Similarly, the growth of commerce and industry led to technological advances which, in turn, stimulated, and were stimulated by, science. Oceanic commerce created an enormous demand for shipbuilding and navigation. A new class of mathematically trained craftsmen made compasses, maps, and instruments. Navigation schools were founded in Portugal, Spain, Holland, and France, and astronomy was studied seriously because of its obvious utilitarian value. Likewise, the needs of the mining industry brought about advances in power transmission and pumps. This was the beginning of a new interest in mechanical and hydraulic principles. In the same way metallurgy was responsible for notable progress in chemistry. As mining operations expanded, new ores and even new metals, like bismuth, zinc, and cobalt, were discovered. Techniques for separating and handling these had to be found and corrected by painful experience. But in doing so, a general theory of chemistry began to take form, involving oxidations and reductions, distillations and amalgamations. Finally, the new knowledge in all these fields was both stimulated and circulated by the universities and the printing press. The latter was especially important in promoting literacy and spreading new ideas.

These achievements gave the scientists, or philosophers, a self-assurance and a confidence that they were the signs of a new age. In 1662 Charles II of England granted a charter for the establishment of "The Royal Society of London for Promoting Natural Knowledge." Its members, seeing the advantage of cooperation between technicians and scientists, coordinated the efforts in every occupation throughout the country to gather data that might advance scientific knowledge.

All Places and Corners are now busy and warm about this Work: and we find many noble Rarities to be every Day given in [to the Society] not only by the Hands of learned and professed Philosophers; but from the Shops of Mechanicks; from the Voyages of Merchants; from the Ploughs of Husbandmen; from The Sports, The Fishponds, The Parks, The Gardens of Gentlemen. . . .[1]

At first, science received much more from the mine and the workshop than they received from science itself. During this early period science was not an integral part of economic life and was used sparingly and sporadically. This was true even in the early phases of the industrial revolution in the late eighteenth and early nineteenth centuries. But by the end of the nineteenth century the situation changed. Science no longer was in a subordinate position: it had begun to transform old industries and even to create entirely new ones.

II. COURSE OF THE SCIENTIFIC REVOLUTION

As we might expect, the first major advance of modern science occurred in the field of astronomy, which was closely related to geography and to navigation. This advance was achieved in the sixteenth and seventeenth centuries, and the great names were Minolaj Kopernik or Copernicus (1473–1543), Galileo Galilei (1564–1642), and Isaac Newton (1642–1727). Copernicus took up the idea of some ancient philosophers that the sun, rather than the earth, was the center of the universe, and he then demonstrated that this provided a simpler explanation of the movement of the heavenly bodies than did the traditional Ptolemaic system. Galileo supported Copernicus empirically by using the recently discovered telescope to see what actually was in the heavens. "By the aid of a telescope," he reported, "anyone may behold that . . . the Galaxy is nothing else but a mass of innumerable stars planted together in clusters. Upon whatever part of it you direct the telescope straightway a vast crowd of stars presents itself to view. . . ."[2]

By far the most outstanding figure of this early stage of science was Newton, a towering figure comparable to Euclid and Einstein. In addition to his pioneering work in optics, hydrodynamics, and mathematics, he discovered the law of gravitation: "every particle of matter in the universe attracts every other particle with a force varying inversely as the square of the distance between them and directly proportional to the product of their masses."

Here was a sensational and revolutionary explanation that tore the veils from the heavens. Newton had discovered a fundamental, cosmic law, that could be proved mathematically and applied to all matter, from the minutest object to the universe at large. Nature indeed appeared to be a gigantic mechanical object operating according to certain natural laws that could be found by observation, experiment, and calculation. All branches of human knowledge could be broken down into a few, simple, uniform laws that rational persons could discover. People began to apply the analytical method of Newtonian physics to the entire field of thought and knowledge, to human society as well as to the physical universe.

The science that made the most progress during the first half of the nineteenth century was chemistry—partly because of its close association with the textile industry, which experienced such rapid growth during those decades. The Newton of chemistry was Antoine Lavoisier (1743–1794), whose law of the conservation of matter is comparable to the law of gravitation: ". . . although matter may alter its state in a series of chemical actions, it does not change in amount; the quantity of matter is the same at the end as at the beginning of every operation, and can be traced by its weight." Lavoisier's successors in the nineteenth century made discovery after discovery which had important practical applications: Justus von Liebeg for chemical fertilizers, W.H. Perkin for synthetic dyes, and Louis Pasteur for his germ theory of disease which led to the adoption of sanitary precautions and so brought under control old scourges like typhoid, diphtheria, cholera, and malaria.

As Newton dominated seventeenth-century science with his discovery of the laws governing the bodies of the universe, so Darwin dominated nineteenth-century science, for he discovered the laws governing the evolution of humanity itself. His doctrine of evolution holds that animal and vegetable species in their present diverse forms are not the fixed and unchangeable results of separate special acts of creation. They are different. They are capable of change. And they are the natural outcomes of a common original source. Darwin believed that the chief manner in which variation took place was by natural selection. He defined this process as follows:

> As many more individuals of each species are born than can possible survive, and as, consequently, there is a frequently recurring struggle for existence, it follows that any being, if it vary however slightly in any manner profitable to itself, under the complex and sometimes varying conditions of life, will have a better chance of surviving, and thus be naturally selected. From the strong principle of inheritance, any selected variety will tend to propagate its new and modified form.[3]

It may be hard to conceive of all the variety in nature as being the product of what appears to be such a slow process of change as that afforded by ''natural selection.'' Yet statistical calculations show that even if a mutation resulted in only a 1-percent better chance of survival, the change would establish itself in half the individuals of a species in a hundred generations. In other words, if 101 individuals with a particular mutation survived for every 100 without it, it would spread through the species in what is, biologically speaking, a short time. The details of Darwin's theories have been modified by later research, but virtually all scientists now accept the essentials of the doctrine. There was bitter opposition in certain quarters, particularly amongst church leaders. This was understandable, because Darwin was denying the act of divine creation. Just as the Copernican system of astronomy had deposed the earth from its central place in the universe, so Darwinism seemed to dethrone humankind from its central place in the history of the earth.

Despite the hostile reception in religious and other circles, Darwinism had profound repercussions upon Western society. The basic reason is that its emphasis on survival of the fittest and struggle for survival fitted in admirably with the temper of the times. In politics, during this period, Bismarck was unifying Germany by blood and iron. Nationalistic admirers in all countries believed that Darwinism offered them support and justification. They held that in politics, as in nature, the strongest are victorious, and that warlike qualities decide who will win in the international "struggle for survival." In economic life this was the period of free enterprise and rugged individualism. The upper and middle classes, comfortable and contented, stoutly opposed any state intervention for the promotion of greater social equality. They argued that they deserved their blessings and prosperity because they had proven themselves "fitter" than the shiftless poor. Furthermore, the absorption of smaller concerns by big business was a part of the "struggle for survival." The late nineteenth century was also the golden age of colonial expansion, and Darwinism was used to justify imperialism. The argument was that colonies were necessary for the prosperity and survival of a "great power." Also native peoples, judged in terms of worldly success, were weak, inferior, and in need of the protection and guidance of the superior and stronger Europeans.

The application of Darwin's theories to the social milieu is known as Social Darwinism. Darwin himself had never dreamt, let alone intended, that his findings would be exploited in this fashion. But the fact remains that they were, and the reason is that they seemed to offer scientific support for the materialism that spread over Europe at this time. Darwinism, in short, fitted in conveniently with Kipling's dictum

> That they should take who have the power
> And they should keep who can.

Another English writer, Hilaire Belloc, expressed the same sentiment in reference to the position of the Europeans in Africa:

> Whatever happens we have got
> The Maxim gun, and they have not.

III. SIGNIFICANCE OF THE SCIENTIFIC REVOLUTION

As the nineteenth century proceeded, science became an increasingly important part of Western society. At the beginning of the century science was still on the periphery of economic and social life. But by the end it was making basic contributions to the old-established industries, it was creating entirely new industries, and it was profoundly affecting the way of thinking as well as the way of living of Western man. Furthermore, the metamorphosis wrought by the scientific revolution affected the entire world in many ways, direct and indirect. It made Europe's domination of the globe technologically possible, and it determined to a large extent the nature and effects of this domination. Also it provided the basis for the West's intellectual predominance in the nineteenth century. European art or religion or philosophy did not affect non-Western peoples very much because they had made comparable contributions in these fields. But there was no such equality in science and technology. Only the West had mastered the secrets of nature and had exploited them for material advancement. This was an undeniable and persuasive fact. Non-Westerners no longer looked down upon Europeans as uncouth barbarians who happened to have a certain superiority in sailing ships and firearms. Reluctantly they recognized the importance of Europe's scientific revolution. And today the primary aim of former colonial peoples is to experience this unique revolution themselves. For all these reasons, the distinguished British historian, Herbert Butterfield, concludes that the scientific revolution

> . . . proved to be so capable of growth, and so many-sided in its operations, that it consciously assumed a directing role from the very first, and, so to speak, began to take control of the other factors—just as Christianity in the middle ages had come to preside over everything else, percolating into every corner of life and thought. And when we speak of Western civilization being carried to an oriental country, like Japan in recent generations, we do not mean Graeco-Roman philosophy and humanist ideals, we do not mean the Christianising of Japan, we mean the science, the modes of thought and all that apparatus of civilization which were beginning to change the face of the West in the latter half of the seventeenth century.[4]

IV. ROOTS OF THE INDUSTRIAL REVOLUTION

The term "industrial revolution" is frequently challenged because this "revolution" got under way before the eighteenth century, and, for all practical purposes, it has continued to the present day. Obviously, then, this was not a revolution in the sense of a spectacular change that began and ended suddenly.

Yet the fact remains that during the 1780s a breakthrough did occur in productivity, or, as economists now put it, there was "a take-off into self-sustained growth." More specifically, a mechanized factory system was created that produced goods in vast quantities and at rapidly diminishing costs, so it was no longer dependent on existing demand but could create its own demand. An example of this now common, but hitherto unknown phenomenon, is the automobile industry. The demand for automobiles that existed at the turn of the century did not create the giant automobile industry of today. Rather the capacity to build the cheap Model-T Ford, in large quantities, stimulated the modern mass demand for them.

The first question that arises in considering the industrial revolution has to do with its timing. Why did it occur in the late eighteenth century rather than a hundred or a thousand years earlier? The answer lies in large part in the remarkable economic growth of Europe following the great expansion overseas. This growth was so pronounced that it is commonly referred to as the "commercial revolution."

The commercial revolution was characterized in the first place by a change in the articles of world trade. Before the sixteenth century the most important items were spices from East to West, and bullion in the opposite direction. But gradually new overseas products became staples of consumption in Europe and grew in commercial importance. These included new beverages (cocoa, tea, and coffee), new dyes (indigo, cochineal, and brazilwood), new flavors (allspice and vanilla), and new foodstuffs (guinea fowl and turkeys, and a greatly increased supply of Newfoundland cod). The other main feature of the commerial revolution was the marked increase in the volume of trade. Between 1715 and 1787 French imports from overseas territories increased tenfold, and exports increased between seven- and eightfold. England's trade grew almost as spectacularly—in the period from 1698 to 1775 both imports and exports rose between 500 and 600 percent. Europe's general trade was growing, but colonial trade was accounting for a larger and larger portion of it. In 1698, for example, about 15 percent of England's seaborne trade was with its colonies, but by 1775 this figure had risen to 33 percent. Furthermore, the reexport of colonial goods was responsible for much of the increase of France's and England's trade with other European countries.

The commercial revolution contributed to the industrial revolution in several important respects. First, it provided large and expanding markets for European industries, particularly those producing textiles, firearms, hardware, ships, and ships accessories, including lumber, rope, sails, anchors, pulleys, and nautical instruments. To meet the demands of these new markets, industries had to improve their organization and technology. The commercial revolution also contributed the large amounts of capital necessary to finance the construction of factories and machines for the industrial revolution. The capital, in the form of profits, poured into Europe from all parts of the world—from the fur trade in Siberia and North America, from the silver mines of Mexico and Peru, from the African slave trade, and from the profits of the several East India Companies, West India Companies, Levant Companies, Africa Companies, and assorted others, including the Muscovy Company, the Hudson's Bay Company, and the various land settlement companies in the Americas.

Profitable commercial enterprise, together with the accompanying technological growth and institutional change, explains why the industrial revolution reached the ''take-off'' stage in the late eighteenth century. This raises the question of why the take-off occurred first in England. One important advantage enjoyed by Britain is that it had taken an early lead in the basic coal and iron industries. Because its forest reserves were being depleted, Britain early began using coal for fuel and for smelting iron. By the time of the French Revolution in 1789, Britain was producing about 10 million tons of coal per year, while France was producing 700,000 tons. England also pioneered in the development of the blast furnace which, in contrast to the old forges, could mass produce iron. In 1780 Britain's iron output had been a third that of France; by 1840 it was three times more. All this meant that Britain was pushing ahead in the production of goods for mass consumption. And there was a large and steady demand for these goods. France, on the other hand, specialized more in luxury commodities of limited and fluctuating demand.

England also had more fluid capital available for the financing of the industrial revolution. More profits from commerce poured into England than into any other country. English court and military expenditures were less than the French costs, so that English taxation was lighter and English government finances were in better condition. Furthermore, banking developed earlier and more efficiently in England, providing pooled funds for individual and corporate enterprise.

Noteworthy also is the impressive concentration of managerial talent in England. This is to be explained in part by the outstanding contributions of Nonconformists like the Darbys in the iron industry, Cookworthy in pottery, the Brights in cotton milling and in politics, and Dalton and Eddington in science. Freedom from convention and stress on personal responsibility produced a disproportionate quota of experiments and inventors among the Nonconformists, while their frugality led them to plow profits back into business rather than to squander them in luxurious living. The influence of the Nonconformists in England was enhanced by the influx of coreligionists from the continent. With the revocation of the Edict of Nantes in 1685, for example, France lost considerable managerial talent to England, especially in the textile industry.

Britain also had the advantage of a mobile and plentiful supply of labor. The great supply was made available by the earlier disintegration of the guilds and by the enclosing of the traditional strips of farmland. The end of the guilds, with their manifold restrictions, made it easier to introduce the putting-out system and to equip the factories with power machinery. The land enclosures began in the sixteenth century and continued for three centuries, reaching their height in the late eighteenth and early nineteenth centuries. The yeomen frequently were forced to sell out, because the enclosing of common and of waste lands left them no land for grazing and for fuel. The earlier enclosures were caused by the rising price of wool, so that the land was used mostly for grazing. In the later period the need to grow foodstuffs for the burgeoning cities was more important, so the enclosed land was cultivated according to the most up-to-date and efficient methods. Crop rotation replaced the wasteful old system of allowing fields to lie fallow. Superior seeds were developed, and cattle were improved by scientific breeding. Some agricultural machinery was developed, such as a horse-driven hoeing machine and an automatic drill for planting seeds.

Between 1714 and 1820, over 6 million acres of land were enclosed in England. This meant serious dislocation and distress. The poor peasants lost part or all of their land, and were forced to become tenants or day laborers, or else to seek employment in the cities. Socially minded people were appalled by this wholesale uprooting of England's yeomanry and spoke up against it. The process of enclosing the land was unsettling and unpleasant, but so far as the industrial revolution was concerned it fulfilled two essential functions—it provided labor for the factories and food for the cities. For this reason the enclosures may be considered a prerequisite to England's industrial supremacy in the nineteenth century. Enclosures did occur in certain other European countries, but to a much lesser extent. In France, for example, the French Revolution provided the peasants with more land, and thereby increased their attachment to their birthplaces and their unwillingness to pack up and move.

V. COURSE OF THE INDUSTRIAL REVOLUTION

Inventors seldom invent except under the stimulus of strong demand. Many of the principles on which the new inventions of the industrial revolution were based were known long before the eighteenth century, but they were not applied to industry because the incentive was lacking. This was the case, for example, with steam power. It was known in Hellenistic Egypt but was used merely to open and close temple doors. In England, however, a new source of power was urgently needed to pump water out of mines and to turn the wheels of the new machinery. The result was a series of inventions and improvements until finally a commercially practical steam engine was developed.

The pattern of demand leading to invention is plainly evident in the course of the industrial revolution. For example, the cotton industry was the first to be mechanized because cotton goods, which were originally imported from India, had become exceedingly popular with the British public. In fact, cotton was used so widely that the old and powerful woolen interests secured the passage of a law in 1700 prohibiting the importation of cotton cloth or goods. The law, however, did not ban the manufacture of cotton cloth. This created a unique opportunity for local industry, and enterprising middlemen soon were exploiting it. The problem was how to speed up the spinning and weaving enough to meet the demand of the large and protected home market. Prizes were offered for inventions that would increase output, and by 1830 a series of such inventions had completely mechanized the cotton industry.

Outstanding were John Kay's flying shuttle (1733) that speeded up weaving, Richard Arkwright's water frame (1769) that spun fine strong yarn between rollers, James Hargreaves' spinning jenny (1770), on which one person could spin eight, then sixteen, and finally over a hundred threads of yarn at once, and Samuel Crompton's spinning mule (1779), so called because it combined features of the water frame and of the jenny. All these new spinning machines soon were producing far more thread than could be handled by the weavers. A clergyman, Edmund Cartwright, sought to redress the balance by patenting in 1785 a power loom operated first by horses and after 1789 by steam. The contraption was clumsy and commercially unprofitable. But after two decades of improvement the most serious defects were remedied. By the 1820s the power loom had largely supplanted the handweavers in the cotton industry.

Just as inventions in spinning led to related inventions in weaving, so inventions in one industry encouraged people to invent machinery so that other industries could keep up. For example, the new cotton machines created a demand for more plentiful and reliable power than that provided by the traditional waterwheels and horses. The response was James Watt's multiple improvements on a primitive engine built by Thomas Newcomen about 1702. By 1800 some 500 Watt engines were in service, 38 percent being engaged in pumping water, and the remainder in supplying rotary power for textile mills, iron furnaces, flour mills, and other industries.

The historical significance of the steam engine can scarcely be exaggerated. It provided a means for harnessing and utilizing heat energy to furnish driving power for machines. Thus, it ended the age-old dependance on animal, wind, and water power. A vast new source of energy now was available. Before long it was possible to tap the other fossil fuels locked up in the earth—namely, oil and gas. In this way the trend began that has led to the present situation in which Western Europe has 11.5 times and North America 29 times as much energy available per capita as Asia. The meaning of these figures is obvious in a world where economic and military strength depends directly upon the energy resources available. Indeed, it may be said that Europe's domination of the globe in the nineteenth century is based more upon the steam engine than upon any other single device or force.

The new cotton machines and steam engines required an increased supply of iron, steel, and coal. The need was met by a series of improvements in mining and metallurgy—Abraham Darby's substitution of coal for coke in smelting iron ore, Henry Cort's "puddling" process for removing impurities in smelted iron, and the use of the Watt steam engine for operating the bellows and hammers, and for rolling and splitting. As a result of these various developments, by 1800 Britain was producing more coal and iron than the rest of the world together. Britain's coal output rose from 6 million tons in 1770 to 12 million tons in 1800 to 57 million tons in 1861. Likewise, its iron output increased from 50,000 tons in 1770 to 130,000 tons in 1800 to 3.8 million tons in 1861. Iron had become plentiful and cheap enough to be used for general construction purposes, and humanity had entered the Age of Iron as well as the Age of Steam.

The expansion of the textile, mining, and metallurgical industries created a need for improved transportation facilities to move the bulky shipments of coal and ore. This started a canal-building boom that gave England 2500 miles of canals by 1830. The canal era was paralleled by a great period of road building. After 1750 a group of road engineers—John Metcalf, Thomas Telford, and John McAdam—developed methods of building hard-surfaced roads that would bear traffic all through the year. Travel by coach increased from four miles an hour to six, eight, or even ten. After 1830 both roads and waterways were challenged by the railroad. The chief figure here was a mining engineer, George Stephenson. In 1830 his Rocket pulled a train thirty-one miles from Liverpool to Manchester at an average speed of fourteen miles per hour. Within a few years the railroad dominated long-distance traffic, for it could move passengers and freight faster

A RIDE ON AN EARLY RAILWAY

The world's first railway was opened in 1825, and the second, in 1830 between Liverpool and Manchester. A description of the second railway has been left by the actress Frances (Fanny) Kimble, who rode on it as a young girl in the year of its opening.*

My father knew several of the gentlemen most deeply interested in the undertaking [the Liverpool-Manchester railway], and Stephenson having proposed a trial trip as far as the fifteen mile viaduct, they, with infinite kindness, invited him and permitted me to accompany them; allowing me, moreover, the place which I felt to be one of supreme honour, by the side of Stephenson. . . . He was a rather stern-featured man, with a dark and deeply marked countenance. . . .

We were introduced to the little engine which was to drag us along the rails. . . . This snorting little animal, which I felt rather inclined to pat, was then harnessed to our carriage, and, Mr. Stephenson having taken me on the bench of the engine with him, we started at about ten miles an hour. The steam-horse being ill-adapted for going up and down hill, the road was kept at a certain level, and appeared sometimes to sink below the surface of the earth, and sometimes to rise above it. Almost at starting it was cut through the solid rock, which formed a wall on either side of it, about sixty feet high. You can't imagine how strange it seemed to be journeying on thus, without any visible cause of progress other than the magical machine, with its flying white breath and rhythmical, unvarying pace. . . . We were to go only fifteen miles, that distance being sufficient to show the speed of the engine. . . . After proceeding through this rocky defile, we presently found ourselves raised upon embankments ten or twelve feet high; we then came to a moss, or swamp, of considerable extent, on which no human foot could tread without sinking, and yet it bore the road which bore us. . . .

We had now come fifteen miles, and stopped where the road traversed a wide and deep valley. Stephenson made me alight and led me down to the bottom of this ravine, over which, in order to keep his road level, he has thrown a magnificent viaduct of nine arches, the middle one of which is seventy feet high, through which we saw the whole of this beautiful little valley. . . . We then rejoined the rest of the party, and the engine having received its supply of water, the carriage was placed behind it, for it cannot turn, and was set off at its utmost speed, thirty-five miles an hour, swifter than a bird flies (for they tried the experiment with a snipe). You cannot conceive what that sensation of cutting the air was; the motion is as smooth as possible, too.

*F. A. Kimble, *Record of a Girlhood,* 3rd ed. (London: Richard Bentley, 1879), pp. 158–60.

and more cheaply than was possible by road or canal. By 1838 Britain had 500 miles of railroad; by 1850, 6600; and by 1870, 15,500.

The steam engine was also applied to water transportation. The pioneer was Robert Fulton who in 1807 launched his *Clermont* on the Hudson River. By 1833 the *Royal William* steamed from Nova Scotia to England, and five years later the *Sirius* and the *Great Western* crossed the Atlantic in the opposite direction. They took 16 ½ and 13 ½ days respectively, or about half the time required by the fastest sailships. In 1840 Samuel Cunard established a regular transatlantic service, announcing beforehand dates of arrival and departure.

The industrial revolution produced a revolution in communication as well as transportation. Hitherto a message could be sent to a distant place only by wagon, postrider, or boat. But in the middle of the nineteenth century the electric telegraph was invented. In 1866 a transatlantic cable was laid, establishing instant communication between the Old and New Worlds.

The industrial revolution did not end with transatlantic steamships and cables. It continues to the present day, and certain stages are discernible in its evolution. The first stage lasted to the mid-nineteenth century and included, as noted above, the mechanization of the cotton industry, of mining and of metallurgy, and the development of the steam engine and its application to industry and transportation. The second stage in the latter part of the nineteenth century was characterized by the more direct application of science to industry and by the development of mass-production techniques. Whereas science at the outset had little effect upon industry, it gradually became an integral part of all large industrial enterprises. A spectacular example of the results of industrial research laboratories are the many coal derivatives that have been developed. Coal not only yielded coke and a valuable gas that was used for illumination. It also gave a liquid, or coal tar. Chemists discovered a veritable treasure trove in coal tar: hundreds of dyes, aspirin, saccharin, wintergreen, disinfectants, laxatives, perfumes, photographic chemicals, high explosives, and essence of orange blossom.

Whereas Germany led the world in the nineteenth century in applying science to industry, the United States was the pioneer in developing mass-production techniques. These were of two varieties. One was the making of standard interchangeable parts and the assembling of these parts into the completed unit with a minimum of handicraft labor. The classic example of this variety is Henry Ford's endless conveyor belt. Car parts traveled along the belt and were assembled into the Model T by workers who were transformed into cogs of the machines. The other production technique was the manipulation of large masses of material by means of advanced mechanical devices. The prime example of this method is the steel industry, whose productivity was described in justifiably boastful terms by the industry tycoon Andrew Carnegie:

> Two pounds of ironstone mined upon Lake Superior and transported nine-hundred miles to Pittsburgh; one pound and one-half of coal, mined and manufactured into coke, and transported to Pittsburgh; one-half pound of lime, mined and transported to Pittsburgh; a small amount of manganese ore mined in Virginia and brought to Pittsburgh—and these four pounds of materials manufactured into one pound of steel, for which the consumer pays one cent.[5]

VI. EFFECT OF THE INDUSTRIAL REVOLUTION ON EUROPE

Diffusion of Industrialization

During the nineteenth century the industrial revolution spread gradually from England to the continent of Europe. The pattern of diffusion depended on various factors such as supply of natural resources and the existence of a free and mobile working population, unencumbered by guild restrictions or feudal obligations. Belgium was the first country to be industrialized, so that by 1870 the majority of its population lived in cities and were directly dependent on trade or industry. After Belgium followed France, Germany, Austria-Hungary, Italy, and Russia. Meanwhile non-European countries were being industrialized, first the United States, and then the British Dominions and Japan. Latecomers enjoyed the advantage of newer and more efficient factories, so that Britain lost its original status as the "industrial workshop of the world." Table 3, listing the powers in the order of their industrial production, demonstrates the changes that have occurred in the world's industrial balance.

Increase of Population

Another effect of the industrial revolution on Europe was further increase in population, which had started earlier with the increased productivity in agriculture. In spite of the emigration overseas of millions of Europeans during the nineteenth century, the population of the Continent in 1914 was well over three times that of 1750. The reasons for this population explosion are economic and medical. The great increase of productivity in both agriculture and industry meant increased means of subsistence in terms of food, clothing, shelter, and other necessities of life. Famine in most parts of Europe west of Russia became a memory of the past. Even if crops failed, the new transportation facilities ensured adequate supply from outside. The population increase was due also to the advances of medical science and to the adoption of numerous public-health measures. There was little or no increase in the birth rate, but the death rate was sharply reduced by preventing or curing disease. Vaccination, segregation of infected persons, safeguarding of water supplies, knowledge of antiseptics—all these reduced the death rate in Northwestern Europe from at least 30 per 1000 persons in 1800 to about 15 in 1914. Thus Europe's population climbed steeply from 140 million in 1750 to 188 million in 1800, 266 million in 1850, 401 million in 1900, and 463 million in 1914. This rate of increase in Europe was so much higher than in the other regions of the world that it altered the global population balance (see Table 4).

Urbanization

The industrial revolution led also to an unprecedented urbanization of world society. The size of cities traditionally had depended on the amount of food that the surrounding land could produce. Thus the most populous cities were in the valleys and flood plains, like the Nile, the Fertile Crescent, the Indus, and the Hwang Ho. With the industrial revolution and the factory system, a mass influx flooded the new centers of industry. The large new urban populations could be fed because food supplies now were available from

Table 3. RANKING OF WORLD INDUSTRIAL POWERS, 1860–1980

1860	1880	1900	1980
Great Britain	United States	United States	United States
France	Great Britain	Germany	Japan
United States	Germany	Great Britain	Soviet Union
Germany	France	France	Germany

Table 4. ESTIMATED POPULATION OF THE WORLD*

	1650	1750	1850	1900	1950	1977
Millions						
Europe	100	140	266	401	572	738
United States and Canada	1	1	26	81	166	242
Latin America	12	11	33	63	164	342
Oceania	2	2	2	6	13	22
Africa	100	95	95	120	219	424
Asia	330	479	749	937	1368	2355
Total	545	728	1171	1608	2502	4123
Percentages						
Europe	18.3	19.2	22.7	24.9	23.0	18.0
United States and Canada	.2	.1	2.3	5.1	6.7	5.8
Latin America	2.2	1.5	2.8	3.9	6.3	8.3
Oceania	.4	.3	.2	.4	.5	.5
Africa	18.3	13.1	8.1	7.4	8.8	10.3
Asia	60.6	65.8	63.9	58.3	54.7	57.1
Total	100.0	100.0	100.0	100.0	100.0	100.0

These figures show that Europe's percentage of the total world population rose from 18.3 in 1650 to a high of 24.9 percent in 1900 and then dropped to 18 percent in 1977. But by the twentieth century most of the population of the United States, Canada, and Oceania was of European origin, and at least half of the population of Latin America was also. Accordingly, it is more meaningful to say that throughout the twentieth century, the percentage of Europeans and people of European origin had risen to about one-third of the world total. Adapted from A. M. Carr-Saunders, World Population (Oxford: Clarendon, 1936), p. 42; and United Nations Demographic Yearbooks.

all parts of the world. Technological and medical advances eliminated the plagues that previously had decimated cities, and even made city living relatively endurable and pleasant. The most important of these advances were plenty of pure water, the perfecting of centralized sewerage and waste-disposal systems, insurance of an adequate food supply, and prevention and control of contagious diseases. Cities all over the world grew at such a rate that by 1930 they included 415 million people, or one-fifth of the human race. This represents one of the great social transformations in human history, for city dwelling meant an entirely new way of life.

Increase of Wealth

The industrial revolution, with its efficient exploitation of human and natural resources on a worldwide scale, brought about an increase in productivity that is without precedent in all history. Great Britain, which was the first affected, increased its capital from 500 million pounds sterling in 1750 to 1500 million pounds in 1800, to 2500 million pounds in 1833, and to 6000 million in 1865. In the latter part of the nineteenth century the entire world felt the impact of the increasing productivity. The wool of New Zealand, the wheat of Canada, the rice of Burma, the rubber of Malaya, the jute of Bengal, and the humming

Table 5. RISE OF INDUSTRIAL PRODUCTION (1913 = 100)*

	1860	1870	1880	1890	1900	1910	1913
Germany	14	18	25	40	65	89	100
Great Britain	34	44	53	62	79	85	100
France	26	34	43	56	66	89	100
Russia	8	13	17	27	61	84	100
Italy	—	17	23	40	56	99	100
U.S.	8	11	17	39	54	89	100
World	14	19	26	43	60	88	100

*F. Sternberg, Capitalism and Socialism on Trial (New York: Day, 1951), p. 21.

factories of Western Europe and eastern United States—all these resources were enmeshed in a dynamic and constantly expanding global economy. The figures in Table 5 indicate the rate at which industrial production rose in the second half of the nineteenth century in Europe and throughout the world.

Distribution of Wealth

There has been much difference of opinion among authorities in recent years concerning the distribution of the wealth created during the industrial revolution. One group holds that all classes benefited to a greater or lesser extent, while the other maintains that a few made huge fortunes while the many were ruthlessly exploited and suffered declining standards of living.

There is no doubt that there was much exploitation and social disruption in the early days of industrialization. The tenant farmers were dispossessed, and the weavers and other handicraftsmen were wiped out by the irresistible competition of the new machine-made goods. These people, and others like them, faced the strain of moving to the city, finding employment, and adjusting to an unfamiliar environment and to strange ways of living and of working. They were completely dependent on their employers, for they had no land, no cottage, no tools, and no capital. In short, they had become mere wage earners and had nothing to offer but their labor.

When they found employment, they discovered that the hours were long. A sixteen-hour day was by no means rare. When the workers finally won the rights to divide their work into two twelve-hour shifts, they looked upon the change as a blessing. The long hours alone would have been tolerable, since they were no worse than the hours worked at home under the putting-out system. But the real hardship came in getting used to the discipline and monotony of tending machines in a factory. The workers came and went at the sound of the factory whistle. They had to keep pace with the movements of the machine, always under the strict supervision of an ever-present overseer. The work was monotonous—pulling a lever, brushing away dirt, mending broken threads. Employers naturally regarded their wage bill as an expense that should be kept as low as possible. Consequently, many of them, particularly in the textile industries, preferred to employ women and children, who were willing to accept smaller wages and were more willing to follow orders. Exploitation of woman and child labor reached such proportions that a number of parliamentary committees that conducted investigations found shocking conditions.

There is, however, another side to this question of the effect of the industrial revolution on the working class. In the first place, the parliamentary committees investigated only industries, such as mining and textiles, where conditions were worst. The shocking testimony of the witnesses who appeared before the committees was based on facts, but those facts were by no means applicable to English industry as a whole. Furthermore, the plight of the worker in early nineteenth-century England must be viewed in the light of contemporary rather than present-day standards. The fact is that the villages from which these workers came were in many respects as squalid as the cities. Rats and vermin infested the straw bedding, and the wind whistled through the thinly thatched roof and the poorly plastered walls. Day laborers in the countryside were so poorly paid that they kept crowding into the new industrial cities. Thousands of Irish also crossed over to fill the jobs opening up in the new factories. Furthermore, the population of England soared during these early days of the industrial revolution, a fact that does not jibe with the usual picture of the unrelieved and debilitating misery.

Although we cannot be sure of the effect of the industrial revolution on working-class living standards in the late eighteenth and early nineteenth centuries, we are quite certain that the standards rose substantially in the second half of the nineteenth century. The great increases in productivity together with the profits made from the huge overseas investments gradually benefited even the lower classes in Western Europe. After the "Hungry Forties," when there was much suffering from unemployment, the workers of Western Europe enjoyed general prosperity and rising living standards until World War I. Between 1850 and 1913, *real* wages in Britain and France almost doubled.

The marked rise in national income did not mean, of course, that all classes benefited equally. The proceeds of the general prosperity did trickle down somewhat, but they were mostly absorbed at the top. In Great Britain, for example, 4.93 percent of the persons over 25 years of age possessed over 60 percent of the wealth in 1911–1913. Likewise, in Prussia in 1911, 3425 individuals had an average wealth of 5,321,400 marks, whereas 1,608,050 individuals had an average of 23,295 marks. The discrepancy meant a corresponding discrepancy in manner of living. The poor no longer starved, but they did live in crowded tenements, they subsisted on monotonous diets, and they were restricted for their pleasure or relaxation to churches or to taverns. By contrast, the middle classes could afford better living quarters and food, attend the theater and concerts, and educate their children adequately. At the top, the wealthy with their town and country houses, their art collections, and their well-advertised sports activities and foreign travels, lived in a style that was all but incomprehensible to the masses at the bottom.

VII. EFFECT OF THE INDUSTRIAL REVOLUTION ON THE NON-EUROPEAN WORLD

Europeanization of the Earlier Empires

In the period before 1763 the European powers had only a few footholds in Asia and Africa. Their major holdings were in the Americas. After 1763 they established their political control over large parts of Asia and almost all of Africa. In the Americas and the British Dominions, they were able to do much more than this. Taking advantage of the sparse populations in those regions, millions of Europeans emigrated and filled up those relatively empty spaces.

The industrial revolution was largely responsible for the mass migrations. We have seen that increased productivity together with the advances of medical science led to a sharp increase in Europe's population in the nineteenth century. This created a population pressure that found an outlet in overseas migration. Railways and steamships were available to transport masses of people across oceans and continents, and persecution of one sort or another stimulated further emigration, as well as disasters such as Ireland's potato famine. These various factors combined to produce a mass migration unequaled in human history to that date. With every decade the tide of population movement increased in volume. In the 1820s a total of 145,000 left Europe, in the 1850s about 2.6 million, and between 1900 and 1910 the crest was reached with 9 million emigrants, or almost a million per year.

Before 1885 most of the emigrants came from Northern and Western Europe; after that date the majority were from Southern and Eastern Europe. By and large, the British emigrants went to the Dominions and the United States, the Italians to the United States and Latin America, the Spaniards and Portuguese to Latin America, and the Germans to the United States and, in smaller numbers, to Argentina and Brazil. From the perspective of world history, the significance of this extraordinary migration is that it was all directed to the New World and Oceania, with the exception of the large flow to Asiatic Russia and the trickle to South Africa. The result has been the almost complete ethnic Europeanization of Siberia, the British Dominions excepting South Africa, and the Americas. The Indian population in Latin America managed to survive but was left a minority.

The ethnic Europeanization of overseas territories led inevitably also to political, economic and cultural Europeanization. This process is described in chapter 30.

New Imperialism Conquers New Empires

The industrial revolution was largely responsible, not only for the Europeanization of overseas territories, but also for the creation of huge European colonial structures in Asia and Africa. The great wave of empire building after 1870 was known as the *"new imperialism."* It made a large part of the earth's surface into an appendage of a few European powers. The interrelationship of the new imperialism and the industrial revolution was manifested in a growing desire to obtain colonies that might serve as markets for the rising volume of manufactured goods. The several European and overseas countries that became industrialized during the nineteenth century were soon competing with each other for markets. In the process they raised tariffs to keep out each other's products. Soon it was being argued that each industrialized country must have colonies to provide "sheltered markets" for its manufactures.

The industrial revolution also produced surplus capital, which again led the Great Powers to seek colonies as investment outlets. The more capital piled up at home, the lower the profits fell and the greater the need to find better investment markets abroad. Vast amounts of capital were, in fact, invested in foreign countries, especially by Britain, France, and Germany. For example, Britain by 1914 had invested £4 billion abroad, a sum amounting to one-fourth of its total national wealth. Europe by 1914 had become the banker of the world. In the first half of the nineteenth century most overseas investments were made in the Americas and Australia—in the "white man's" world. But in the second half of the century they were made mostly in the nonwhite and relatively unstable countries of Asia and Africa. The thousands of small private investors and the large banking combinations that provided the capital naturally were anxious about its safety. They preferred "civilized" administration, preferably by their own respective governments, in the regions in which their investments were situated. This is how the need to invest surplus capital safety promoted the new imperialism. The industrial revolution also created a demand for raw materials to feed the machines. Many of these materials—jute, rubber, petroleum, and various metals—came from the "uncivilized" portions of the globe. In most cases heavy capital outlays were needed to secure adequate production of these commodities. Such investments, as we have seen, usually led to the imposition of political control.

The new imperialism was not entirely economic in its origins; it was not related exclusively to the industrial revolution. A variety of other factors also were operative at this time. One was the desire to strengthen national security with strategic naval bases such as at Malta and Singapore. Another was the need to secure additional sources of manpower, as the French did in North Africa. Still another factor was the influence of the missionaries, who were particularly active during the nineteenth century. Sometimes these missionaries were maltreated, or even killed, by the natives they were seeking to convert. Even though the missionaries themselves might be willing to tolerate such risks as acceptable for the sake of their cause, public opinion frequently demanded action. And it was not unknown for governments to use such incidents as pretexts for military intervention. Finally, the vogue of Social Darwinism, with its doctrines of struggle for existence and survival of the fittest, led naturally to ideas of racial superiority. The *white man's burden* was to rule over the "inferior" colored peoples of the earth. The great empire builder Cecil Rhodes was quite outspoken on this matter. "I contend that we are the first race in the world, and that the more of the world we inhabit the better it is for the human race. . . . If there be a God, I think what He would like me to do is to paint as much of the map of Africa British red as possible."[6]

The net result of these economic, political, and intellectual-psychological factors was the greatest land-grab in the history of the world, unequaled even by the conquests of Genghis Khan. In the generation between 1871 and 1900 Britain added 4¼ million square miles and 66 million people to its empire; France added 3½ million square miles and 26 million people; Russia in Asia added half a million square miles and 6½ million people, and Germany one million square miles and 13 million people. Even little Belgium managed to acquire 900,000 square miles and 8½ million inhabitants. These conquests, along with the existing colonial possessions, created a fantastic and unprecedented situation in which one small portion of the globe dominated all the rest.

The industrialized European powers not only owned these vast colonial territories outright. They also dominated those economically and militarily weak areas that, for one reason or another, were not actually annexed. Examples are China, the Ottoman Empire, and Persia, all of which were nominally independent, but which, in fact, were constantly harried, humiliated, and controlled in various direct and indirect ways. Latin America also was an economic appendage of the Great Powers, though in this region military action by Europe was discouraged by the Monroe Doctrine. The doctrine, however, did not preclude repeated armed intervention by the United States Marine Corps to "restore law and order." The great Russian Empire was also dominated economically to a very large extent by Western Europe, but in this case the military strength of the Tsarist regime was great enough to prevent foreign economic influence from extending into other areas. Thus we see that Europe's control extended not only over its farflung empires but also over the equally extensive dependent regions. In fact, more European capital was invested in the dependent countries than in the colonies.

Investments were safeguarded through various devices and pressures such as military missions that trained the local armed forces, financial missions that supervised and usually controlled local finances, and extraterritorial and capitulatory arrangements that gave special privileges to Europeans residing or doing business in these areas. If necessary as a last resort, there were always the Marines in the New World or the gunboats in the Old. In this manner most of the earth's surface and most of the world's population had by 1914 come under the direct or indirect domination of a few European countries including Russia, and of the United States. This was a development without precedence in human history. Today, in the late twentieth century, much of the global turmoil represents the inevitable reaction to this European domination.

Impact of the New Imperialism

Why should we label the great European expansion of the late nineteenth century the "new imperialism?" Imperialism, after all, was not something new. If it be defined as "the rule or control, political or economic, direct or indirect, of one state, nation or people over similar groups. . . . ,"[7] then imperialism is as old as human civilization. Certainly the Romans were imperialistic, having conquered, and for centuries ruled, large parts of Europe and the Near East. And many other empires in all parts of the globe, both before and after the Romans, were conquered by all types of peoples.

Yet the term "new imperialism" is justified, because the late-nineteenth-century European expansion was quite unique in its impact upon the colonial and dependent territories. Rome exploited its possessions simply and directly by plundering and by collecting tribute, chiefly in the form of foodstuffs, but its exploitation did not particularly affect the economic life and structure of the colonies. They continued to produce pretty much the same foodstuffs and handicrafts in the same ways as in the past. To compare this imperialism with the later version that overran and remade entire continents is like comparing a spade to a steam shovel. The traditional imperialism involved exploitation but no basic economic and social change. The tribute merely went to one ruling clique rather than another. The new imperialism, by contrast, forced a thorough transformation of the conquered countries. This was not so much deliberate policy as it was the inevitable impact of the dynamic industrialism of Western Europe upon the static, self-contained agrarian regimes of Africa and Asia. In other words, Europe's industrial capitalism was far too complex and expansionist to stop with a simple tribute relationship with the colonies.

At the outset, the European conquerors certainly did not hesitate to plunder and to levy tribute. The British did so in India, as the Spaniards had earlier in Mexico and in Peru. But after this initial phase, Europe's dynamic economy began in various ways to enfold and refashion the colonial economic and social structures. This happened because, as we have seen, industrialized Europe needed sources of raw materials and markets for its surplus capital and manufactures. Thus the historic role of the new imperialism was to carry the industrial revolution to its logical conclusion—to enable the industrial nations, or industrial capitalism, to operate on a worldwide scale. The global operation of industrial capitalism resulted in much more extensive, coordinated and efficient use of the material and human resources of the globe. Certainly world productivity rose greatly when European capital and skills were combined with the raw materials and labor power of the underdeveloped regions. The combination produced, for the first time, an integrated global economy. In fact, world industrial production increased three times between 1860 and 1890, and seven times between 1860 and 1913. The value of world trade grew from 641 million pounds in 1851 to 3024 million pounds in 1880, to 4025 million pounds in 1900, and to 7840 million pounds in 1913.

Everyone agrees that this increase in the size of the cake was a great advantage. But there is much dispute over the question of how the cake is sliced. The colonial peoples have felt that in the past they have had less than their due share. The total amount that they have received obviously has increased, otherwise their rising populations could not have been supported. For example, a British economist has shown that in 1949 European companies engaged in mining in mineral-rich Northern Rhodesia sold their output for a total of £36.7 million. Of this, they spent only £12.5 million in Northern Rhodesia, which meant that two-thirds of the money was transferred abroad. Moreover, of the £12.5 spent in Northern Rhodesia, £4.1 million was paid to Europeans living and working there. Only £2 million out of the £36.7 million went to the Africans working in the mines. And yet these workers were receiving an average of £41 a year compared to an average income of £27 a year per adult African male in the colony.[8]

Under these circumstances it is understandable that colonial peoples are not very impressed by increased productivity or by the wages paid by foreign companies. They are more impressed by the wretched level at which they subsist, especially in comparison with Western levels. They also resent being cast in the role of hewers of wood and drawers of water, even in regions where there are human and material resources for industrial development.

There is an obvious parallel here between the reaction of Western workers to industrial capitalism and of colonial peoples to the new imperialism. Both have been dissatisfied with their lot, and both have supported movements designed to bring about radical change. But a basic difference is that the colonial peoples are ranged not against employers of their own nationality but rather against foreign rulers. Accordingly their movement of protest, at least in the first stage, was not socialism but rather a range of Western political doctrines—liberalism, democracy, and, above all, nationalism.

We turn now to consider these isms, which make up Europe's political revolution. An understanding of this revolution is as essential for world history as an understanding of the industrial revolution. Because of Europe's political revolution, the world, as we shall see, was affected by Western ideas and slogans and political institutions as well as by Western cottons and railways and banks.

SUGGESTED READING

C. Cipolla, *The Economic History of World Population* (Penguin, 1962); J. G. Crowther, *Scientists of the Industrial Revolution* (Cresset, 1962); W. C. Dampier, *A Shorter History of Science* (Harcourt Brace Jovanovich, 1957); A. R. and M. B. Hall, *A Brief History of Science* (New American Library, 1967); D. S. Landes, *The Unbound Prometheus* . . . . (Cambridge University Press, 1969); A. G. R. Smith, *Science and Society in the Sixteenth and Seventeenth Centuries* (Thames & Hudson, 1973); L. L. Snyder, ed., *The Imperialism Reader* (D. Van Nostrand, 1962); A. Thompson, *The Dynamics of the Industrial Revolution* (Arnold, 1973); E. P. Thompson, *The Making of the English Working Class* (Gollancz, 1963).

When individuals and nations have once got in their heads the abstract concept of full-blown liberty, there is nothing like it in its uncontrollable strength.

G.W.F. Hegel

chapter 23

Europe's Political Revolutions

Europe's domination of the world in the nineteenth century was based, not only on its industrial and scientific revolutions, but also on its political revolution. The essence of the political revolution was the end of the concept of a divinely ordained division of people into rulers and ruled. Government was no longer regarded as something above the people, and the people as something below the government. Instead the political revolution for the first time in history, at least on a scale larger than the city-state, called for the identification of government and people. The masses were awakened and activized so that they not only participated in government but considered it their inherent right to do so. In this chapter we shall consider the general pattern of this political revolution, its origins in the English, American, and French revolutions, and its varied manifestations and worldwide impact during the nineteenth century.

I. PATTERN OF THE POLITICAL REVOLUTION

The political revolution, like the economic, developed in several stages. We noted that the economic revolution began in England and then spread to the Continent and to the United States, and later to other parts of the globe. Likewise, the political revolution got under way with the English Revolution in the seventeenth century, developed much further with the American and French revolutions that followed, then affected the whole of Europe during the nineteenth century, and finally involved the entire globe during the twentieth.

The parallel course in the spread of the two revolutions was not accidental; indeed, the two were intimately related. The economic revolution was in large degree responsible for the political, because it created new classes with new interests and new ideologies that rationalized their interests. We will see this more clearly as we trace briefly the general course of the economic and political revolutions.

During the early medieval period, there were three well-defined social groups in Western Europe: the nobility who constituted a military aristocracy, the clergy who formed an ecclesiastical and intellectual elite, and the peasants who labored to support the two upper classes. With the development of commerce, the profile of the medieval social order began to be changed by the appearance of a new element, the urban *bourgeoisie*. As this class grew in wealth and numbers, it became more and more discontented with the special privileges of the feudal orders and with the numerous restrictions that hampered the development of a free market economy. Accordingly, the bourgeoisie made a mutually beneficial alliance with the national monarchies. The kings obtained financial support from the bourgeoisie and so were able to assert their authority over the feudal orders. The bourgeoisie in return profited from the establishment of law and order throughout the royal domains. The alliance lasted until it became irksome for the constantly growing middle class. Then the middle class turned against the kings to free itself from royal restrictions on commerce, from a growing burden of taxation, and from restraints on religious freedom. These objectives were important factors in the English, the American, and the French revolutions. The success of these revolutions also meant the success of liberalism—the new ideology that provided a rationalization for bourgeois interests and objectives. In this sense liberalism may be defined as the particular program by which the growing middle class proposed to get for itself the benefits and control it was aiming for.

The middle class, with its creed of liberalism, was challenged in turn by the urban workers, or *proletariat*. With the industrial revolution of the late eighteenth century, the workers in the crowded cities became increasingly class conscious. More and more they felt that their interests were not identical with those of their employers and that their situation could be improved only by combined action on their part. So the workers, or rather the intellectuals who led them, developed a new ideology—*socialism*. Socialism directly challenged the liberalism of the bourgeoisie, calling for social and economic change as well as for political reform. We shall see that socialism was to become a major force in European affairs in the late nineteenth century, and in world affairs in the twentieth.

Europe's political revolution was powered not only by the dynamic creeds of liberalism and socialism, but also by *nationalism*—an ideology that cut across classes and activated great masses of people. Traditionally the first allegiance of these people had been to region or to church. In early modern times it had extended to the new national monarchs. But beginning with the English Revolution, and particularly during the French Revolution, increasing numbers of Europeans gave their loyalty to the new cause of the nation. The rise of national churches, national dynasties, national armies, and national educational systems, all combined to transform former ducal subjects and feudal serfs and town *burghers* into all-inclusive nations. The new national ideology spread during the nineteenth century from Western Europe, where it originated, to all parts of the Continent. Today, in the twentieth century, it is the driving force behind the awakening of formerly subject colonial peoples throughout the world.

These three creeds—liberalism, socialism, and nationalism—are the principal components of Europe's political revolution. Together they galvanized into action broader and broader strata of the peoples of Europe, giving them a dynamism and a cohesiveness unequaled in any other portion of the globe. In this way the political revolution, like the scientific and the commercial revolutions, contributed vitally to Europe's world domination. When the Europeans began to expand overseas, they encountered societies in which there was little rapport between rulers and ruled. The apathy of the masses—their lack of identification with their governments—explains why in region after region the Europeans were able to establish and to maintain their rule with little difficulty. India is perhaps the leading example of the extent to which lack of rapport between rulers and ruled made societies vulnerable. India was a society that had remained a disparate collection of peoples, religions, and conflicting provincial loyalties, and so was easy prey. For over a century and a half, the great Indian subcontinent, with its teeming millions, its splendid civilization, and its ancient historical traditions, was ruled with little difficulty by a comparative handful of British officers and officials. When the mutiny against British rule broke out in 1857, it was put down not only by British troops but also Indian. A correspondent of the London *Times* reported this fact with astonishment: "I looked with ever-growing wonder on the vast tributary of the tide of war which was running around and before me. All these men, women, and children, with high delight were pouring towards Lucknow to aid the Feringhee [Europeans] to overcome their brethren."[1]

But European political and economic domination inevitably meant the diffusion of European political ideas. Just as the entire globe felt the impact of Stephenson's locomotive, of Fulton's steamship, and Gatling's machine gun, so it felt the impact of the Declaration of Independence, of the Declaration of the Rights of Man and Citizen, and of the Communist Manifesto. The worldwide convulsions that are the hallmark of our present age are the direct outcome of these heady documents.

II. ENGLISH REVOLUTION

The first phase of Europe's political revolution was the English Revolution of the seventeenth century. The roots of the upheaval in England rest in the conflict between Parliament and the Stuart dynasty. The conflict degenerated into an open civil war from which Parliament emerged victorious. The Tudor dynasty which preceded the Stuart was generally popular, particularly with the middle class and the gentry. It brought the warring noble families under central control. It severed the ecclesiastical ties with Rome by establishing a national Anglican church, and in the process distributed extensive lands and other properties that had belonged to the Catholic institution. It also built up the navy and pursued an anti-Catholic foreign policy that met with popular approval.

The first Stuart king, James I (1603–1625), and his son and successor, Charles I (1625–1649), soon dissipated this fund of good will. They tried to impose the doctrines and ritual of the Anglican church on all the people, thereby alienating their Nonconformist, or Puritan, subjects. They also tried to rule without Parliament but ran into difficulties because Parliament controlled the national purse. They tried to get around this obstacle by selling monopolies in the export and import trades, in domestic commerce, and in many fields of manufacturing. This produced considerable revenue, but it also antagonized the bourgeoisie, which demanded that "all free subjects be inheritable to the free exercise of their industry."[2]

The crisis came when the Scots rose in rebellion against Charles's attempt to impose Anglican religion upon them. In order to get funds to put down the uprising, Charles was forced to call upon Parliament. And this "Long Parliament," which met in 1640, ignored his requests for money and instead made a number of far-reaching demands. They called for the execution of the chief royal advisers and the complete reorganization of the Anglican church. Charles refused to submit, and in 1642 fighting broke out between the royalist Cavaliers and the Puritan Roundheads.

England did not settle down again for almost half a century, not until the so-called Glorious Revolution in 1688. The stirring events of those decades made up the English Revolution which went through five stages. The first, from 1642 to 1645, was the civil war. The royalists were routed in the civil war by the famous New Model Army that Oliver Cromwell had organized. During the second stage, from 1645 to 1649, a situation developed that was to be repeated with certain variations during the French Revolution in 1792 and the Russian Revolution in 1917. A split occurred between the moderate and radical elements among the victorious Puritans. The moderates, led by Cromwell, prevailed over the radicals, led by John Lilburne. When Charles was executed in 1649, Cromwell emerged as the head of an English republic, which was known as the Commonwealth.

Cromwell and his Puritan followers ruled England with great efficiency and much Godliness during the third stage from 1649 to 1660. During this time, the various feudal rights were suppressed and the religious question settled. Cromwell died in 1658 and was succeeded as Lord Protector of the Commonwealth by his son Richard. The latter was a nonentity, and furthermore the country was weary of the restricted and austere life under the Puritans. Accordingly, the Stuarts were placed back on the throne, and from 1660 to 1688 England went through the fourth stage, which is known as the Restoration.

The Stuart kings, Charles II (1660–1685) and James II (1685–1688), did not and could not undo the reforms of the republic. But they did try to revive personal rule. This effort, together with their subservience to the French crown and their encouragement of Catholicism, made them increasingly unpopular. Finally James II was overthrown with the Glorious Revolution of 1688, which marks the fifth and last stage of the English Revolution. The new ruler was William of Orange, son-in-law of James II. In 1689 William accepted a Bill of Rights which expressed the essential principles of parliamentary supremacy. The bill provided that no law could be suspended by the king, no taxes raised or army maintained except by Parliament's consent, and no subject arrested and detained without legal process. Such provisions did not mean that England had become a democracy. It was not until the establishment of universal suffrage in the late nineteenth century that this goal was attained. But the settlement in 1689 did establish once and for all the supreme authority of Parliament, and in doing so it ended the English Revolution that had begun almost half a century earlier.

From the viewpoint of world history, the major significance of the English Revolution is that it defined the principles of liberalism and put them to work. This was natural, because the English Revolution was essentially a middle-class affair. The merchants and the lesser gentry who supported Parliament had two principal ends in view—religious toleration and security of person and property. But there was no unanimity of opinion on the Puritan side concerning these matters. Many conflicting views were expressed and passionately debated. In the case of religion, for example, a veritable flood of new sects appeared, including the Congregationalists, the Baptists, and the Quakers. At the same time, the Presbyterians strove to establish their church as a national organization that could exercise its discipline upon all citizens. These religious differences obviously had to be reconciled or else Parliament's victory would be undone and the state itself might founder. It was under these circumstances that the basic liberal doctrine of religious toleration was worked out and established. On grounds of principle as well as of expediency it came to be generally agreed that it was both immoral and ineffective to coerce people into belief. It is true that the Anglican church remained the official, state-supported church, and that its members were favored in the filling of government posts and in other respects. But, by and large, the principle was established that liberty of conscience should be granted to all Christians who did not threaten public order or interfere with other people's worship.

The question of the rights of person and of property also aroused fierce controversy. This question divided the right- and left-wing elements among the Puritans even more sharply than did the religious issue. The split occurred gradually, as the common soldiers of the New Model Army came to feel that their interests were being ignored by their officers and by Parliament. Their feelings were articulated by the *Levellers,* a name of opprobrium given to a mass movement drawn chiefly from the lower middle class and from agricultural tenants. It is true that legislation passed by the House of Commons for the establishment of the Commonwealth included basic Leveller doctrine: "The People are, under God, the Original of all just Power," and the Commons "being chosen by, and representing the People, have the supreme Power in this Nation."[3]

If Parliament was thus willing to accept the principle of the sovereignty of the people, then what was the issue dividing Parliament and the Levellers? The answer is in the definition of the word "people." Cromwell and his followers held that the "people" who should participate in the election of the Commons were those with a "real or permanent interest in the kingdom"—that is, property owners—whereas the Levellers maintained that "any man that is born in England ought . . . to have his voice in election of burgesses [members of Parliament]."[4] Thus, the issue was between constitutional parliamentary government and democratic government. Many of those who favored democratic government did so with the intention of using their votes to bring about social reform. And fear of such reform motivated Cromwell and his followers in their resolute opposition to the Levellers.

The fact is that there were two revolutions under way in seventeenth-century England. The first was the political revolution of the lesser gentry and the bourgeoisie, who were interested in winning the civil and religious freedom necessary to make their way in the world. The second was the social revolution of the lower middle class and the tenant farmers, who had a vision of a community of small-property owners, with complete religious and political equality, and with generous provisions for the poor. The social revolution failed in England in the seventeenth century, as it was to fail in France in the eighteenth. In both cases the protagonists lacked the numbers, the organization, and the maturity necessary for victory. Their time was to come in the late nineteenth century, when the industrial revolution had spawned a large and class-conscious urban proletariat. The proletariat was to evolve its own ideology—socialism—distinct from, and in opposition to, the liberalism of the bourgeoisie.

III. ENLIGHTENMENT

The next stage in Europe's political revolution, following the upheaval in seventeenth-century England, was the so-called *Enlightenment* that manifested itself during the century before the French Revolution of 1789. The term Enlightenment owes its origin to the fact that the leaders of this movement believed that they lived in an enlightened age. They viewed the past largely as a time of superstition and ignorance and thought that only in their day were human beings at last emerging from darkness into sunlight. Thus, one basic characteristic of this age of Enlightenment was the idea of progress, an idea that was to persist into the twentieth century. With the Enlightenment, it began to be generally assumed that the condition of humanity would steadily improve, so that each generation would be better off than that which came before.

How was this unceasing progress to be maintained? The answer was simple and confident: by the use of humankind's reasoning powers. The faith in reason was the other basic feature of the Enlightenment. Indeed, the two key concepts were progress and reason. And the exponents of these concepts were a highly articulate group known as the *philosophes*. Not to be confused with formal philosophers, the philosophes were not profound or systematic thinkers in any particular field. They were mostly literary men or popularizers—more journalists than philosophers. They were closer to H. G. Wells and G. B. Shaw than to G. E. Moore and A. N. Whitehead. Like Wells and Shaw, the philosophes were generally opposed to the existing order, and they wrote plays, novels, essays, and histories to popularize their ideas and to show the need for change.

Much influenced by the law of gravitation that Newton had demonstrated, the philosophes believed in the existence of natural laws that regulated, not only the physical universe, but also human society. Acting upon this assumption, they proceeded to apply reason to all fields in order to discover the natural laws that operated. They subjected everything—all persons, all institutions, all traditions—to the test of reason. This would be a rigorous ordeal for any society in any period, but it was particularly rigorous for France's ancien régime, past its prime and creaking in many joints. Thus the philosophes subjected the old regime in France, and throughout Europe, to a barrage of devastating criticism. More important, they evolved a set of revolutionary principles by which they proposed to effect a wholesale reorganization of society. Of particular interest to us are their specific proposals in three areas—economics, religion, and government.

Their key slogan in economics was laissez faire—let the people do what they will, let nature take its course. This opposition to government intervention was a reaction to the rigid regulation of economic life generally known as *mercantilism*. In the early period of state building, mercantilism had been accepted as necessary for national security. But by the eighteenth century it seemed superfluous, and damaging. The classic account of laissez faire was made by the Scotsman Adam Smith in his famous work, *An Inquiry into the Nature and Causes of the Wealth of Nations* (1776). He argued that individuals are motivated by self-interest so far as their economic activities are concerned; that the national welfare is simply the sum of the individual interests operating in a nation; and that each man knows his own interest better than does any statesman.

In religion the key slogan was ''Ecrasez l'infame!''—''Crush the infamous thing!,'' or stamp out religious fanaticism and intolerance. The philosophes rejected the traditional belief that God controls the universe and arbitrarily determines the fate of humanity. Instead, they sought a natural religion that followed the dictates of reason. The outcome was a variety of radical departures from religious orthodoxy. Some became outright atheists, denying the existence of God and denouncing religion as a tool of priests and politicians. Others became agnostics who neither affirmed nor denied the existence of God. The majority were deists, willing to go along with the proposition that God existed and had created the universe but insisting that, after the act of creation, God allowed the universe to function according to certain natural laws and refrained from intervention. Thus the deists were able to have their cake and eat it too. They could accept God and the teaching of Christianity, and at the same time reject supernatural features such as the virgin birth, the resurrection, the divinity of Christ, and the divine inspiration of the Bible. The important point to note is that all these new dogmas—atheism, agnosticism, deism—reflected the unprecedented growth of skepticism regarding "revealed" or "supernatural" religion. For the first time since the triumph of Christianity in Europe, a definite break had occurred with the Christian tradition.

In government, also, the philosophes had a key phrase—the "social contract." The contract theory of government was not new. The English political theorist John Locke had formulated it in his *Essay on Civil Government* (1690), in which he defined government as a political contract between rulers and ruled. But the French philosopher Jean-Jacques Rousseau transformed it into a social rather than a political contract. For him it involved an agreement amongst the people themselves. In his major political work, *The Social Contract* (1762), Rousseau viewed government as simply a "commission," and thus he justified revolution as a restoration to the sovereign people of its rightful power.

This brief survey suggests the significance of the Enlightenment for Europe's political revolution. The slogans "ecrasez l'infame!," "laissez faire," and "social contract" were subversive of traditional institutions and practices. Furthermore, they represented a challenge to the status quo, not only in France, but throughout Europe and even in overseas lands. In fact, the philosophes thought of themselves, not as Frenchmen or Europeans, but as members of the human race. They thought and acted in global rather than Western terms. They sought to discover social laws that had universal application, like Newton's laws of the physical world.

If the philosophes did not discover fixed laws governing all humankind, their writings did influence thinking people in many parts of the world. Their greatest immediate success was in persuading a number of European monarchs to accept at least some of their doctrines. These monarchs still held to the theory that they ruled by divine right, but they changed their ideas about the purpose of their rule. Governmental authority was still to be the prerogative of the kings, but now it was to be used for the benefit of the people. Hence these rulers were known as *benevolent despots*.

The best known of these benevolent despots were Frederick the Great of Prussia (1740-1786), Catherine the Great of Russia (1762-1796), and Joseph II of the Hapsburg Empire (1765-1790). Catherine was perhaps the most articulate, frequently mouthing typical slogans of the Enlightenment, such as, "All citizens ought to be equal before the law," "Sovereigns are made to serve their people," and "It is dangerous for a country to be divided into a few large estates." But Catherine and her fellow sovereigns did not merely talk about reform. Catherine improved the administrative and educational systems of her country substantially; Frederick did much to advance agriculture in Prussia; while Joseph II, the most sincere and conscientious of the *enlightened despots,* wore himself out during his reign trying to remold his empire in accord with the new principles. Yet in spite of their royal authority, these rulers had a very modest impact. Their successors frequently undid their work, while the clergy and the aristocrats were relentless in their fight against the reforms that menaced their vested interests.

IV. AMERICAN REVOLUTION

We should not overrate the role of the benevolent despots in putting the doctrines of the Enlightenment to work. For the Enlightenment did not have much effect on the masses of the people in Europe until the outbreak of the French Revolution in 1789. But before then a revolution had broken out in England's Thirteen Colonies, and this revolution was to offer a laboratory demonstration of the new doctrines in action.

We noted earlier (Chapter 19, section III) that a leading characteristic of the Thirteen Colonies was their political independence. Their elective assemblies were continually at loggerheads with the governors and the other officials sent out from London. We also noted that Britain decisively defeated France in the Seven Years' War and, by the Treaty of Paris of 1763, acquired France's colonies north to the Arctic and west to the Mississippi. Both the British and the Americans felt considerable pride in the magnitude of their joint victory. But the victory created new problems at the same time that it settled old ones. One new problem was the growing spirit of defiance in the Thirteen Colonies now that the danger of a French attack had been removed. Another was the decision of the British government, following its acquisition of vast new colonial territories, to tighten its imperial organization. This tightening might have been feasible at an earlier date, but now, after the elimination of the French danger, the colonists were convinced that they were able to take care of themselves and had every right to do so. Thus the American Revolution arose basically out of the conflicting claims of British imperial authority and American colonial self-government.

The steps leading to the Revolution are well-known and need not be related in detail. First there was the Proclamation of 1763 prohibiting settlement west of a line drawn along the crests of the Appalachians. This was intended as a temporary measure to preserve peace until an orderly land policy could be worked out, but the prospective settlers and speculators assumed that they were to be excluded forever for the benefit of a few British fur traders. Then there was a series of financial measures—the Sugar Act, Quartering Act, Stamp Act, and Townshend Duties—designed to shift a part of Britain's heavy tax load to the American colonists. These levies seemed reasonable to the British, especially since they had spent a great deal of money to defeat the French in the recent war and estimated that they would have to spend even more in order to protect the American frontiers in the future. But the colonists were all affected by these imports and unanimously opposed them. They called an intercontinental congress which organized a boycott of British goods to last until the financial measures were repealed. But then another series of ill-considered measures by the British government started a fresh storm that was to lead to revolution.

THOMAS PAINE ON THE AMERICAN REVOLUTION

Thomas Paine's *Rights of Man* (1791) is an eloquent appraisal of the American Revolution. It was written as a reply to Edmund Burke's negative *Reflections on the French Revolution*. Paine was typical of his time in looking forward to more revolutions that would open "a new era to the human race."*

What Archimedes said of the mechanical powers, may be applied to Reason and Liberty: "Had we," said he, "a place to stand upon, we might raise the world."
The revolution of America presented in politics what was only theory in mechanics. So deeply rooted were all the governments of the old world, and so effectually had the tyranny and the antiquity of habit established itself over the mind, that no beginning could be made in Asia, Africa, or Europe, to reform the political condition of man.

Freedom had been hunted round the globe; reason was considered as rebellion; and the slavery of fear had made men afraid to think.

But such is the irresistible nature of truth, that all it asks, and all it wants, is the liberty of appearing. The sun needs no inscription to distinguish him from darkness; and no sooner did the American governments display themselves to the world, than despotism felt a shock, and man begin to contemplate redress.

The independence of America, considered merely as a separation from England, would have been a matter but of little importance, had it not been accompanied by a revolution in the principles and practice of governments. . . .

If universal peace, civilization, and commerce, are ever to be the happy lot of man, it cannot be accomplished but by a revolution in the system of governments. All the monarchical governments are military. War is their trade, plunder and revenue their objects. While such governments continue, peace has not the absolute security of a day. What is the history of all monarchical governments, but a disgustful picture of human wretchedness, and the accidental respite of a few years repose? Wearied with war, and tired with human butchery, they sat down to rest, and called it peace. This certainly is not the condition that Heaven intended for man.

The revolutions which formerly took place in the world, had nothing in them that interested the bulk of mankind. They extended only to a change of persons and measures, but not of principles, and rose or fell among the common transactions of the moment. What we now behold, may not improperly be called a "*counter revolution.*" Conquest and tyranny, at some early period, dispossessed man of his rights, and he is now recovering them. And as the tide of all human affairs has its ebb and flow in directions contrary to each other, so also is it in this. Government founded in a *moral theory, on a system of universal peace, on the indefeasible hereditary Rights of Man,* is now revolving from west to east, by a stronger impulse than the government of the sword revolved from east to west. It interests not particular individuals, but nations, in its progress, and promises a new era to the human race.

*Thomas Paine, *Rights of Man* (London, 1792), pp. 1–5.

The sequence of the dramatic events is familiar—the East India Company's tea monopoly, the Boston Tea Party, and the Coercive, or Intolerable, Acts intended as punishment for the vandalism in Boston harbor. At the same time, in 1774, Parliament passed the Quebec Act, providing a governmental system for the conquered French Canadians and drawing the boundaries of Quebec to include all the territories north of the Ohio River—that is, the present states of Wisconsin, Michigan, Illinois, Indiana, and Ohio. Much can be said in defense of the Quebec Act, but the American colonists denounced it as another Intolerable Act that blocked their westward expansion for the benefit of the Catholic French Canadians. The First Continental Congress met in Philadelphia in September 1774 and organized another boycott against British goods. Fighting began the next year when British troops set out from Boston to seize unauthorized stores of weapons at Concord. It was during this operation that someone fired at Lexington Green the "shot heard round the world." The outcome was that the British troops found themselves besieged in Boston. When the Second Continental Congress met the following month, in May 1775, it had a full-fledged war on its hands and proceeded to raise an American army.

Congress was still reluctant to make the final break with the mother country. But sentiment for independence grew with the spread of fighting. In January 1776, Thomas Paine published his incendiary pamphlet *Common Sense*. It was read everywhere in the colonies, and it contributed substantially to Congress's decision on July 4, 1776, to adopt the Declaration of Independence. Once military operations got fully under way, the decisive factor proved to be France's aid to the revolutionaries. During the first two years of the war France was not officially involved, yet it poured great amounts of munitions into the colonies. Nine-tenths of the arms used by the Americans in the crucial battle of Saratoga in 1777 were of French origin. The following year France signed an alliance with the insurgents and declared war on Britain. Holland and Spain joined France, while most of the other European powers formed an Armed Neutrality to protect their commerce from Britain's naval power. The help of the French Navy and of a French expeditionary force of 6000 men contributed substantially to the victories of George Washington's forces and to the final British surrender at Yorktown in 1781. The peace treaty signed at Paris in 1783 recognized the independence of the American republic, whose frontiers were to extend west to the Mississippi.

From the viewpoint of world history the American Revolution is significant not because it created an independent state but because it created a new and different type of state. The Declaration of Independence proclaimed, "We hold these truths to be self-evident: that all men are created equal." Now the American people, both during and after the Revolution, passed laws to make this declaration true in real life as well as on paper. They seized and distributed the large estates owned by the Tories. They extended the franchise until all men (but not women) had the right to vote. Many state governments passed laws forbidding the importation of slaves. Established churches were abolished, and freedom of religion became the law of the land. All Thirteen States adopted constitutions which included Bills of Rights that guaranteed the natural rights of citizens.

These changes were not so far reaching and fundamental as those that were brought about later by the French and Russian revolutions. These later revolutions, and particularly the Russian, involved much more social and economic reorganization. Nevertheless the American Revolution had a profound impact in its time. The establishment of an independent republic in the New World was widely interpreted in Europe as meaning that the ideas of the Enlightenment were practicable—that it was possible for people to establish a state and a workable system of government based on the rights of the individual. Thus America became a symbol of freedom and of opportunity, envied as a new land, free from the burdens and chains of the past.

V. FRENCH REVOLUTION

Roots of Revolution

The French Revolution looms much larger on the stage of world history than the English or the American revolutions. It brought about more economic and social change, and influenced a larger portion of the globe, than did the earlier upheavals. The French Revolution marked, not only the triumph of the bourgeoisie, but also the full awakening of the masses. Middle-class liberalism came to the fore, but so did nationalism with its appeal to the people in all sections of society. And "the people," long in the wings, now strode out to the front of the stage, and have remained there ever since.

Why did this great change take place in France? The basic reason is that France, the home of the Enlightenment, was not ruled by an enlightened despot until the advent of Napoleon. Consequently, France was a country of such gross inefficiency and inequality that the machinery of government creaked to a standstill. The breakdown of government gave the ambitious and dissatisfied bourgeoisie a chance to make its successful bid for power.

The old regime in France was aristocratic in its organization. All Frenchmen belonged legally to an "estate," or order of society, and this membership determined their legal rights and privileges. The First Estate comprised the clergy, who numbered about 100,000 out of a total population of 24.5 million. The Second Estate consisted of the nobility, who totaled about 400,000. The Third Estate included everyone else—over 20 million peasants and about 4 million urban merchants and artisans. Thus, the first two estates made up only about 2 percent of the total population. Yet they owned about 35 percent of the land and enjoyed most of the benefits of government patronage. Despite these disproportionate advantages they were exempted from almost all taxes, which, indeed, they thought were beneath their station.

The burden of taxation consequently fell upon the Third Estate, and especially upon the peasants. The peasants accounted for over 80 percent of the population but owned only 30 percent of the land. Furthermore, the peasants were required to pay a tithe to the church, an assortment of feudal dues to the nobles, and a land tax, an income tax, a poll tax, and various other imposts to the state. This tax load was particularly heavy because the general price level had risen 65 percent between 1720 and 1789, while the prices of farm goods lagged far behind.

The artisans in the cities were also discontented, because their wages had risen only 22 percent during those same decades. The bourgeoisie, by contrast, were not so badly off in the matter of taxes because they could protect themselves better than the artisans and the peasants. Furthermore, most businessmen profited from the rising prices and from the fivefold increase in French trade between 1713 and 1789. Yet the bourgeoisie were thoroughly dissatisfied with the old regime. They resented being snubbed by the nobility, treated as second-class subjects by the crown, and excluded from the higher posts in the bureaucracy, church, and army. In short, the bourgeoisie wanted political power and social prestige to match their growing economic importance.

Aristocratic Revolution

Such was the nature of the old regime in France when the great upheaval began. The French Revolution, like others before and after, started moderately and became progressively more radical. In fact, it began, not in 1789 as a bourgeois revolution, but in 1787 as an aristocratic revolution. Then it moved to the left through bourgeois and mass phases until a reaction occurred that brought Napoleon to power.

The aristocrats began the revolution because they wanted to regain the political power they had lost to the crown during the sixteenth and seventeenth centuries. The king's intendants had replaced the noble governors, and the king's bureaucracy controlled all levels of government throughout the country. The power of the monarchs was reflected in the fact that they had not bothered to call the Estates-General, or national parliament, since 1614. It is understandable then that, when Louis XVI found himself in financial straits after the heavy expenses incurred in supporting the American Revolution, the nobles tried to seize the opportunity to regain power.

The nobility and the clergy forced the issue in 1787 when Louis attempted to levy a uniform tax on all landed property without regard to the social status of the holder. The privileged orders branded the new tax illegal and said that only the nation as a whole sitting in the Estates-General could institute so sweeping a change. The pinch for money became so acute that the king finally gave way and summoned the Estates-General to meet in the spring of 1789. The nobility assumed that they would be able to control this body and thereby regain a dominant position in the government. But their assumption proved completely wrong. The meeting of the Estates-General led, not to the triumph of the nobility, but rather to the unleashing of an elemental revolutionary wave that was to sweep away established institutions and ruling classes in France and in much of Europe.

Bourgeois Revolution

The Estates-General that met in Versailles on May 5, 1789, did not represent the people of France. Rather it represented the three estates into which they traditionally had been divided. From the beginning the Third Estate was the most dynamic and decisive. It had the advantage of numbers. There were 600 representatives in the Third Estate as against 300 each in the other two. Actually, the Third Estate outnumbered the other two combined, because a certain number of clergy were ready to throw in their lot with the lower orders. There were also a few liberal-minded noblemen, like the Marquis de Lafayette, who already had fought for the revolutionary cause in America and sided with the Third Estate. The middle-class representatives also had some ideas. They knew that they wanted to change the old regime, and, from their reading in the works of the philosophes, they had at least a general idea of how they should bring about the change. They also had the ready cash that the government needed so desperately, and they did not hesitate to use this potent weapon to get the concessions they wanted.

The commoners won their first victory by pressuring King Louis to transform the Estates-General into a National Assembly. This was a vital change because, so long as decisions were made on the basis of estates, the Third Estate would be in a perpetual minority of one amongst three. But as soon as the representatives of all three estates combined to form a National Assembly, the commoners, with their allies in the other two camps, would have a majority. The king's concession did not represent a change of heart. His real intentions became apparent when, on July 11, he dismissed Jacques Necker, the minister who was regarded as most favorable to reform. At the same time several regiments of loyal troops were quietly transferred to Versailles. The rumor spread that the king was preparing to dissolve the Assembly by force. Furthermore, it seemed that nothing could prevent him from doing so. He had the bayonets, while the commoners had only words and resolutions. But at this critical point the commoners in the National Assembly were saved by an uprising of the common people in Paris. The masses intervened decisively, initiating the third, or mass, phase of the revolution.

Mass Revolution

The masses that now saved the revolution in France were not the riffraff of the streets. In fact, they were the lesser bourgeoisie, made up of shopkeepers and heads of workshops. They were the ones who circulated news and organized demonstrations, while their illiterate journeymen and clerks followed their leadership. The revolutionary outburst followed the dismissal of Necker. Mobs roamed the streets, demanding cheaper bread and parading busts of Necker draped in mourning. On July 14, they stormed and razed the Bastille, an ancient royal castle in Paris used as a prison. The event was of little practical significance, since the Bastille by this time was little used. Nevertheless, the Bastille stood in the eyes of the populace as a symbol of oppression, and now this symbol was destroyed. That is why Bastille Day continues to be celebrated in France as Independence Day is in the United States.

The fall of the Bastille marks the appearance of the masses on the historical stage. Their intervention had saved the bourgeoisie, and the middle class was forced henceforth to rely on the street mobs to supply a "dose of revolution" at crucial moments. There were to be a good many such moments in the years to come, as the bourgeoisie waged its struggle for power against the king, against the privileged orders, and, eventually, against the old order in all Europe.

Mass revolution occurred in the countryside as well as in Paris. The peasants took up arms, incited by their long-standing grievances and by the stirring news of the storming of the Bastille. In many parts of the countryside they tore down fences, seized lands, and burned manor houses. Faced with this revolutionary situation, the nobles and the clergy in the National Assembly made a virtue of necessity and voted with the commoners to abolish feudalism. During the famous "August Days" of 1789, legislation was passed that ended all feudal dues, the privilege of tax exemption, the right of the church to collect tithes, and the exclusive right of the nobility to hold office. Outstanding among the numerous other important measures decreed by the Assembly were the confiscation of church lands, the reorganization of the judicial and administrative systems, and the adoption of the Declaration of the Rights of Man and Citizen.

The Declaration set forth certain fundamental principles concerning liberty, property, and security—"Men are born, and always continue, free and equal, in respect of their rights. . . . The Nation is essentially the source of all sovereignty . . . law is an expression of the will of the community . . . liberty consists in the power of doing whatever does not injure another. . . ." The final clause showed that the bourgeoisie had not lost control of the direction of the revolution: "The right to property being inviolable and sacred, no one ought to be deprived of it, except in cases of evident public necessity, legally ascertained, and on condition of a previous just indemnity." This Declaration was the essential message of the revolution. Printed in thousands of leaflets, pamphlets, and books, and translated into other languages, the Declaration carried the revolutionary slogan of "Liberty, Equality, Fraternity" throughout Europe, and eventually to all the world.

King Louis was by no means willing to accept either the sweeping reforms of the Fourth of August or the revolutionary principles of the Declaration. Once more it was the Paris mob that overcame the royal opposition. Early in October a hungry crowd, composed chiefly of women, raided bread stores in Paris and then marched on the royal palace in Versailles. Under the pressure of the mob, Louis agreed to move the court to Paris. The royal family took up residence in the Tuileries (a palace in Paris), where they became virtual prisoners, and the National Assembly settled down in a nearby riding school. These turbulent October days assured the ratification of the decrees of August. They also increased the influence of the Paris mob tremendously. Both the royal family and the Assembly were now vulnerable to mass action.

War and Terror

Although the king in Paris was virtually powerless, many of the clergy and nobles were determined to regain their lost estates and privileges. Some of them fled abroad, where they worked to enlist the aid of foreign powers in a war against the revolutionary regime in

France. Their efforts were successful. War began in April 1792, with Austria and Prussia ranged against France. At first the poorly prepared French were routed, but thousands of volunteers flocked to the colors in a wave of national patriotism. At the same time the Paris mob swung into action against the unpopular Louis and his hated Austrian queen, Marie Antoinette. Under pressure from the mob, the Assembly suspended the king on August 10 and called for the election of a National Convention.

The Convention, elected by universal franchise, met on September 21, 1792, and was brilliantly successful in meeting its most pressing problem—the defense of the country against the Austrian-Prussian invaders. The combination of revolutionary élan and popular support proved irresistible. The Prussians and the Austrians were driven back across the frontier. In 1793 Britain, Holland, and Spain joined the coalition against France. The revolutionaries responded with their famous levée en masse. The people rose to the defense of their country. Fourteen armies were put into the field, under the command of young generals who had risen from the ranks. Inspired by the revolutionary slogan "Liberty, Equality, Fraternity," the French citizen armies swept everything before them. By 1795 the enemy coalition had been smashed.

Meanwhile, the Convention was shifting more and more to the left, partly because it had been elected by universal franchise, and also because of the revolutionary fervor engendered by the war effort. By June 1793 the Girondists had been displaced by the more radical Jacobins. The dominant organ of government now was the Committee of Public Safety. With revolutionary zeal and passionate patriotism, this Committee appointed and discharged generals, spurred the masses to heroic action, conducted foreign policy, legislated on countless matters, and crushed the opposition by means of a ruthless Reign of Terror. Thousands were charged with treason, or merely with insufficient patriotism, and were subjected to the "national razor," as the guillotine was called.

But the Terror got out of control, and the revolution began "devouring its own children." In the unceasing struggle for power, one after another of the revolutionary leaders followed Louis and Marie Antoinette to the guillotine. Equally disturbing for the bourgeoisie was the growing social radicalism of the revolution. The *sans-culottes* (literally, those who lacked the kneebreeches of genteel society) were pressing hard for a more egalitarian state. Corresponding to the Levellers of the English Revolution, they demanded a more equitable division of the land, government regulation of prices and wages, and a social-security system. Such measures were quite beyond the plans of the French bourgeoisie. So, like their counterparts in England, they worked to halt the leftward course of the revolution. In England, the outcome was the defeat of the Levellers and rule by Cromwell. In France, the sans-culottes were brought under control, first by a Directory of five in 1795, and then by Napoleon Bonaparte in 1799.

Napoleon

Napoleon won fame as a brilliantly successful general in Italy and used his reputation and popularity to overthrow the Directory. He governed France as First Consul from 1799 to 1804, and as Emperor from 1804 to 1814. Two features of his fifteen-year rule of France are noteworthy for our purposes: his domestic reforms, which consolidated the gains of the revolution, and his military campaigns, which provoked a nationalist reaction in neighboring countries and eventually brought about his downfall.

So far as domestic policies are concerned, Napoleon may be compared to the enlightened despots. He was interested in technical efficiency rather than abstract ideas. He ruled the country autocratically, but he ruled it efficiently. He codified the laws, centralized the administration, organized a system of national education, established the Bank of France, and reached an agreement with the Papacy concerning church-state relations in France. These solid achievements of Napoleon made him generally popular. There were die-hards who hankered for the restoration of the old regime or who thought that Napoleon had betrayed the revolution. But the majority hailed him for ending the disturbances and instituting an honest and energetic government.

Napoleon squandered this goodwill by waging war unceasingly. Since he was a military genius, he was fabulously successful. By 1810 he reached the height of his fortunes. He had extended France's frontiers across the Rhine to Lubeck and across the Alps to Rome. The rest of Europe consisted of dependent satellites or allies. Britain alone remained independent and implacably hostile.

In all his conquered territories Napoleon put some of the basic principles of the French Revolution into practice. He abolished feudalism and serfdom, recognized the equality of all citizens, and instituted his famous law codes. These innovations disturbed and alienated vested interests everywhere, but there was also widespread support for them in many quarters. The bourgeoisie and many intellectuals responded favorably to them, but the fact remains that it was foreign rule and that, where necessary, it was imposed by force. Napoleon's non-French subjects eventually grew tired of the requisitioning, the taxes, the conscription, and the wars and rumors of wars. French rule usually meant a higher quality of administration, but the time came when people were more impressed by the Frenchness of the administration than by its quality.

In other words, people had become nationalistic, and their nationalism had developed as a movement of resistance against Napoleon's domination. This explains the unrest in Italy, the armed resistance in Spain, and the growing national unity in Germany. Most vital for Napoleon was the bitter resistance of Russians of all classes when he invaded their country in 1812. Resistance, as much as ice and snow, was responsible for the catastrophic destruction of his Grand Army. Starting from the frozen plains of Russia, the course of Napoleon's career ended precipitously, and inevitably, on the island of Elba. Thus the ideology of the French Revolution backfired upon its originators. The people Napoleon had "offended" were people who had first been awakened and enthused by the slogan "Liberty, Equality, Fraternity." Then they had turned against their teachers when the very principles they had espoused were betrayed by them.

The Congress of Vienna, which met in 1815 to redraw the map of Europe after Napoleon's downfall, was guided by three principles—legitimacy, containment, and compensation. By the principle of legitimacy, the monarchs of France, Spain, Holland, and the Italian states were restored to their thrones. By the principle of containment, the states bordering France were made as strong as possible. Holland was given Belgium; Austria received Lombardy and Venetia; and Prussia received lands along the Rhine as well as part of Saxony. The victorious allies compensated themselves by taking various territories—Norway went to Sweden; Malta, Ceylon, and the Cape of Good Hope to Britain; Finland, Bessarabia, and most of Poland to Russia; and Dalmatia and Galicia (as well as Lombardy and Venetia) to Austria. In anticipation of later events it should be noted that Germany and Italy remained disunited. Germany consisted of the loose Germanic Confederation of thirty-nine states. Italy was simply a "geographic expression." It was made up of nine states, all of them dominated by Austria because of its commanding position in Lombardy and Venetia.

VI. NATIONALISM

What is the significance for world history of the three great revolutions we have studied—the English, the American, and the French? The best answer to this question was given by an illiterate Greek guerrilla chieftain who led his countrymen in revolt against the Turkish overlord in 1821.

> According to my judgement [he declared], the French Revolution and the doings of Napoleon opened the eyes of the world. The nations knew nothing before, and the people thought that kings were gods upon the earth and that they were bound to say that whatever they did was well done. Through this present change it is more difficult to rule the people.[5]

In this simple language the guerrilla leader summarized the essence of the English and the American, as well as the French, revolutions. We have seen how the eyes of the world were opened by the Levellers and the Minutemen and the sans-culottes. The opening of eyes represented a profound political revolution. It marked the beginning for the first time in history of active and institutionalized mass participation in government. The revolution expressed itself in numerous isms which flourished during the nineteenth century. In the remainder of this chapter we shall concern ourselves with three of them—nationalism, liberalism, and socialism—the three which have since exerted the most influence on the course of European and of world history.

Nationalism is a phenomenon of modern European history. It did not exist in recognizable form in the Middle Ages. At that time the universalism of the Roman Empire lived on in the Catholic church, to which all Western Christians belonged, in the Latin language, which all educated people used, and in the Holy Roman Empire, ramshackle structure though it was. Consequently, mass allegiance to a nation was, during those centuries, unknown. Instead, most people considered themselves to be first of all Christians, second, residents of a certain region such as Burgundy or Cornwall, and only last, if at all, French or English.

Three developments gradually modified this scale of allegiances. One was the rise of vernacular languages and the use of these languages for literary expression. Another was the break-off from the Catholic church of several national churches. Finally, the Western European dynasties built and consolidated several large, homogeneous, independent states—England, France, Spain, Portugal, and Denmark. These developments laid the basis for the rise of nationalism, though until the late eighteenth century the nation was identified with the person of the sovereign. Luther, for example, regarded "the bishops and princes" as "Germany," while Louis XIV stated that the French nation "resided wholly in the person of the king."

Nationalism did not assume its modern form until the eighteenth century, when the Western European bourgeoisie came to share or obtain full power. They did so in the name of the nation, so that the nation no longer was the king, his territory, and his subjects. Rather it was now composed of citizens (only propertied citizens until the late nineteenth century) "who inhabited a common territory, possessed a voice in their common government, and were conscious of their common (imagined or real) heritage and their common interests."[6]

This modern form of nationalism received its greatest boost during the French Revolutionary and Napoleonic period. In order to survive the onslaught of the old regimes of Europe, the revolutionary leaders were forced to mobilize national armies—armies of politically conscious citizens ready and eager to fight for their fatherland. The French Revolution contributed to the development of nationalism in several other ways. It required all French citizens to speak French—"the central or national language"—in place of the numerous regional dialects. It established a network of public elementary schools for the purpose of teaching French and love of country. The French Revolution also stimulated the publication of newspapers, pamphlets, and periodicals that were cheap and popularly written, and, therefore, that were effective in leaving their imprint upon the whole nation. And it inaugurated such nationalist rites and symbols as the national flag, the national anthem, and national holidays. All these developments enabled nationalism to overcome the people's traditional commitments to religion and to region.

We noted earlier that this passionate identification with one's nation spread from France to neighboring countries. It did so by the natural diffusion of nationalist ideology. Its spread was also a reaction to French aggression and domination. Nationalism was further stimulated by the industrial revolution which, with its new media for mass communication, brought about a more effective and all-embracing indoctrination of citizens. Thus nationalism became a prime factor in European history in the nineteenth century, and in world history in the twentieth. But nationalism changed in character as the nineteenth century passed. It began as a humane and tolerant creed, based on the concept of the brotherhood rather than the rivalry of the various nationalist movements. But in the latter part of the century it became increasingly chauvinistic and militaristic because of the influence of Social Darwinism and the success of Bismark in uniting Germany by Machiavellian diplomacy and war, or, as he put it, by "blood and iron."

Nationalism manifested itself strongly immediately after 1815 because the territorial settlement of that year left millions of peoples either disunited or under foreign rule. This was the case with the Germans, the Italians, the Belgians, the Norwegians, and the numerous nationalities of the Hapsburg and Ottoman empires. The inevitable result was a series of nationalist revolts that broke out in all parts of Europe after 1815. The Greeks revolted successfully in 1821, winning their independence from Turkish rule. The Belgians did likewise in 1830, breaking away from Dutch domination. The Italians, after futile uprisings in 1820, 1830, and 1848, established an independent and united state between 1859 and 1871. The Germans, under the leadership of Prussia, built their German Empire after defeating Austria in 1866 and France in 1870–71.

The principle of nationalism had triumphed in Western Europe by that final date. But in Central and Eastern Europe the Hapsburg, Tsarist, and Ottoman empires remained "prisons of nationalities." The inmates of these prisons, however, were becoming increasingly ungovernable as nationalist movements succeeded all around them. The rulers of the three empires were aware of the consequences of nationalism for their multinational states and tried to check it by various restrictive measures and by deliberately playing one subject nationality against another. These measures were successful at first but could not prevail indefinitely. The first breaches in the imperial structures were made by the Balkan subjects of the Turks. By 1878 the Serbs, the Rumanians, and the Montenegrins had gained their independence, and in 1908 the Bulgarians did likewise. Much more significant was the assassination in June 1914 of the Hapsburg Archduke Francis Ferdinand by a young Serbian patriot, Gavrilo Princip. This was the fateful event that precipitated World War I, whose outcome was the destruction of all the empires of Central and Eastern Europe—the German, Austro-Hungarian, Russian, and Turkish. The peace treaties that terminated the war (discussed in Chapter 31, section

VII) were generally based on the principle of nationalism, so that several new states appeared—Poland, Czechoslovakia, Yugoslavia, and Albania—that expressed the independent existence of hitherto subject peoples. For better or for worse, nationalism had triumphed throughout Europe with the conclusion of World War I. And in the following decades, as we shall see in later chapters, the idea of nationalism began to awaken and spur to action the hundreds of millions of subject peoples in Europe's overseas possessions.

VII. LIBERALISM

Liberalism, whose central feature is the emancipation of the individual from class or corporate or governmental restraint, was the second great European doctrine to affect the globe. Its rise was intimately related to the rise of the middle class, although in Central and Eastern Europe, where that class was weak, liberalism was espoused by enlightened members of the nobility. Still, liberalism developed in its classic form in Western Europe, and it has remained essentially a middle-class movement in its theory and source of support.

Liberal doctrines were first clearly formulated and implemented during the English Revolution. At that time, these doctrines were primarily those of religious toleration and of security of person and of property against the arbitrariness of the crown. Specifically, carrying out these doctrines involved parliamentary control of government, the existence of independent political parties, and the recognition of the need for, and the rights of, opposition parties. On the other hand, the franchise was limited by property qualifications, so that the lower middle class and the workers, who made up most of the population, were left voteless. Thus, liberalism in seventeenth-century England advanced middle-class interests.

Liberalism was further defined and applied as the American Revolution brought about substantial advances in restricting slavery, extending religious toleration, broadening the franchise, and establishing constitutional government. The federal Constitution adopted in 1791 was based on the principle of the separation of powers in order to prevent tyranny—by having the executive, legislative, and judicial powers check and balance each other. The Bill of Rights guaranteed freedom of religion, speech, press, and assembly. And the American Constitution, like the English settlement, carefully safeguarded the interests of the propertied classes: by limiting the franchise and by providing for the indirect election of the president and the senators, and for the election of the various branches of the government for different periods of time. These arrangements were designed to prevent a radical popular movement from getting control of the entire government at any one time and introducing dangerous changes.

Even more advanced in its liberal tenets than the American Revolution was the French. Its Declaration of the Rights of Man and Citizen is the classic statement of eighteenth-century liberalism, proclaiming in ringing phrases the liberties of the individual. But French liberalism, too, was primarily a bourgeois movement. The Declaration, like all of the several constitutions adopted by the French revolutionaries, stressed the rights of property as "inviolable and sacred." And Napoleon's famous codes, which proved to be the most durable and influential, specifically forbade the organization of trade unions and the waging of strikes.

We may conclude that the liberalism that emerged from the English, American, and

French revolutions took the institutional form of constitutional parliamentary government and was concerned about equal civil rights, though not equal political and social rights. As the nineteenth century passed, liberalism, like other historical movements, changed appreciably in character. It could not continue to concern itself mainly with bourgeois interests at a time when the masses were becoming more assertive as a result of increasing education and trade-union organization. Consequently, there was a shift from the early, classical liberalism to a more democratic variety. Equality before the law was supplemented by equality before the ballot box. By the end of the nineteenth century manhood suffrage had been adopted in most of the Western European countries. Even the hallowed principle of laissez faire was gradually modified. Hitherto intervention by the government in economic and social matters had been regarded as mischievous and futile meddling with the operation of natural laws. This theoretical proposition, however, did not jibe with the facts of life so far as the workers were concerned. Civil liberties and the right to vote did not relieve them from the poverty and insecurity produced by unemployment, sickness, disability, and old age. So they used their voting power and union organization to press for social reforms. Under this pressure a new *democratic liberalism* developed which recognized the responsibility of the state for the welfare of all its citizens. Thus the Western European countries, led by Germany, adopted social-reform programs, including old-age pensions, minimum-wage laws, sickness, accident, and unemployment insurance, and regulation of hours and conditions of work. These reforms of democratic liberalism were the prelude to the welfare state that has become the hallmark of our own age.

Despite this adjustment to a changing world, liberalism has steadily lost ground since the end of the nineteenth century. The chief reason seems to be that it has failed to win the support of the emerging working class. By and large, the workers have turned to various brands of socialism, either of the Marxist or the Christian variety. Thus the liberals in country after country have been squeezed between the conservatives on the right and the socialists on the left.

VIII. SOCIALISM

Socialism is the antithesis of the classical liberalism of the eighteenth and early nineteenth centuries. Liberalism emphasizes the individual and the individual's rights, socialism the community and its collective welfare. Liberalism represents society as the product of natural laws and is skeptical of advancing human welfare artificially by legislation. Socialism, by contrast, holds that humankind, by rational thought and action, can determine its own social system and social relationships. Furthermore, socialism maintains that human nature is primarily the product of social environment. Accordingly, contemporary evils may be eliminated by establishing a society specifically designed to promote collective well-being rather than individual profit and to instill cooperative social attitudes and patterns of behavior rather than competitive ones. In short, socialism stresses society and planned social change rather than the individual and laissez faire.

Plans for the reorganization of society are by no means peculiar to our modern age. Ever since the rise of civilization, political and economic power has been concentrated in the hands of a few. This has led prophets and reformers of all periods to advocate plans promoting social justice and equality. In the classical world, for example, Plato in his *Republic* called for an aristocratic communism, a dictatorship of communist philosophers.

In the medieval period the English peasant leader John Ball declared to his followers, "My good people,—things cannot go well in England, nor ever will, until all goods are held in common, and until there will be neither serfs nor gentlemen, and we shall all be equal."[7] The turmoil and the passions of the English and French revolutions naturally stimulated more schemes for the promotion of the common welfare, but the final outcome, as we have seen, was the triumph of the relatively conservative Cromwell and of Napoleon.

A vigorous new school of social reformers—the *Utopian Socialists*—appeared in the early nineteenth century. Outstanding were two Frenchmen, Henri de Saint-Simon (1760–1825) and Charles Fourier (1772–1837), and the English industrialist Robert Owen (1771–1858). Their proposals varied widely, but they had one basic characteristic in common. They concentrated their attention on the principles and on the precise workings of their projected model communities. But they never seriously faced the problem of how these were to take the place of the existing society. Fourier sat in his room at noon every day for twelve years waiting in vain for responses to his newspaper appeals for support. These reformers definitely did not think in terms of revolution or of class warfare. In fact, they scarcely thought at all about how their elaborate blueprints might be put into practice. It is for this reason that they are known as Utopian Socialists.

Karl Marx (1818–1883), the father of modern socialism, differed fundamentally from the Utopian Socialists in almost every respect. He was as materialistic in his outlook as they were idealistic. He spent most of his life studying the historical evolution and the precise functioning of the existing capitalistic society while Utopians prepared blueprints of model communities. Marx was firmly convinced from his study of history that class struggle offered the only means of social change, while Utopians looked for the support of wealthy benefactors.

The doctrine of class struggle is best summarized in the *Communist Manifesto* which Marx wrote in 1848 with Friedrich Engels.

> The history of all hitherto existing society is the history of class struggles. Freeman and slave, patrician and plebeian, lord and serf, guildmaster and journeyman, in a word, oppressor and oppressed, . . . carried on an uninterrupted . . . fight that each time ended, either in a revolutionary re-constitution of society at large, or in the common ruin of the contending classes.[8]

The idea of classes with conflicting interests was by no means new with Marx. But what was new, and immensely significant, was the proposition that it is through class struggle that humanity has passed from one type of social organization to another.

The inevitability of class struggle was argued by Marx on the basis of his theory of surplus value. According to this theory the worker who provides the labor receives in the form of wages substantially less than the price charged the consumer for the final product. Marx argued that this represents the Achilles's heel of capitalism, because the workers as a class cannot purchase with their wages what they produce. In the long run this will lead to overproduction, or, as the Marxists put it, to underconsumption due to inadequate purchasing power because of inadequate wages. Thus, the result is the closing of factories, unemployment, a further decline of purchasing power, and, at length, a full-scale depression. Furthermore, Marx believed that these depressions would become increasingly frequent and severe until finally the unemployed proletariat would be driven in desperation to revolution. In this way capitalism would be replaced by socialism as feudalism earlier had been by capitalism. And the new socialist society would be depression-proof because, with government ownership of the means of production, there could be no private employers, no profits, and hence no lack of purchasing power.

The course of events since the mid-nineteenth century when Marx wrote his books has not followed the precise pattern that he forecast. The poor have not become poorer in the advanced capitalist countries. Rather the workers have become increasingly affluent and hence increasingly satisfied with the existing state of affairs. Despite this, Marx's doctrines have exerted tremendous influence throughout the world, and today they represent one of the most vital forces shaping the course of history. The reason is to be found in the nature and the appeal of his doctrines. In the first place they gave the workers everywhere a feeling of self-confidence, a conviction that time was on their side. For did not the theory of surplus value prove that the collapse of capitalism was inevitable? Marxism also made the workers active and militant, because the theory of class struggle held that socialism was to be won not by the assistance of philanthropic benefactors but rather by the efforts of the workers themselves. Finally, Marxism gave workers throughout the world a sense of brotherhood and cohesion by stressing international class ties rather than national allegiance. The last sentence of the *Communist Manifesto* reads, "Workers of the world, unite!"

Marx played an important role in the establishment in 1864 of the International Workingmen's Association, or, as it is commonly called, the First International. This body was committed to Marx's program of the seizure of power by the workers in order to reorganize society along socialist lines. It attracted considerable attention with its propaganda and its participation in various strikes. But it disintegrated in 1873, largely because its membership included an undisciplined and constantly feuding assortment of romanticists, nationalists, and anarchists, as well as socialists.

In 1884 the Socialist, or Second, International was established in Paris. This was a loosely knit organization affiliated with the numerous Socialist parties that had appeared by this time in various countries. The Second International grew rapidly, so that by 1914 it included the Socialist parties of twenty-seven countries with a total membership of 12 million workers. The Second International was much more moderate in its doctrines and its actions than the First. The reason for the shift in emphasis was that the major constituent parties were themselves turning away from simon-pure Marxism to what was termed revisionism. A number of factors explain this shift in emphasis. One was the gradual extension of the franchise in the Western European countries, which meant that the workers could use ballots rather than bullets to attain their objectives. Another was the steady rise after 1850 in European living standards, which tended to make workers more willing to accept *capitalism.* The German revisionist leader Eduard Bernstein expressed the new viewpoint when he declared that Socialists should "work less for the better future and more for the better present." The new strategy, in other words, was to make immediate gains by gradual reform measures rather than to strive for a socialist society by revolution. Not all Socialists were willing to go along with this revisionism. Some of them remained true to what they considered to be the teachings of Marx, so that most Socialist parties split into "orthodox" and "revisionist" factions. The revisionists, however, were more in tune with the temper of the times and usually controlled their respective parties. Indeed, they were able to organize powerful trade-union movements and to win millions of votes in electoral contests. In fact, the German, the French, and the Italian Socialist parties had by 1914 a larger number of seats in their respective national assemblies than any other political parties.

When World War I began in 1914, the Second International paid the price for its *Revi-*

sionism: the majority of its members proved to be nationalists first and Socialists second. They responded to the exhortations of their respective national governments, with the result that millions of workers died fighting on both sides of the trenches. Thus the Second International was torn asunder, and although it was revived after the war, it never attained its former strength and prestige.

Socialism, however, did not peter out with the disintegration of the Second International. In fact, it was during World War I that the Russian Socialists, or Bolsheviks as they were called, succeeded in seizing power and establishing the first proletarian government in history. Furthermore, the Bolsheviks organized the Third, or Communist, International to challenge the Second, or Socialist, International. We shall consider later the nature and the activities of the Communist regime in Russia and of the international Communist movement. Suffice it to note here that Marxism is today a central force in world affairs, rivaling nationalism in its dynamism and in its universal appeal.

SUGGESTED READING

M. Ashley, *England in the Seventeenth Century* (Penguin, 1952); R. Gay, ed., *The Enlightenment: A Comprehensive Anthology* (Simon & Schuster, 1973); L. H. Gipson, *The Coming of the Revolution, 1763–1775* and J. R. Alden, *The American Revolution, 1775–1783,* both in the "New American Nation" series (Harper & Row, 1954); C. Hill, *The World Turned Upside Down: Radical Ideas During the English Revolution* (Viking, 1972); G. Lefebvre, *The Coming of the French Revolution* (Random House, 1957); G. Lichtheim, *The Origins of Socialism* (Praeger, 1969); R. R. Palmer, *The Age of the Democratic Revolution: A Political History of Europe and America, 1760–1800* (Princeton University Press, 1959, 1964); J. R. Pennock, *Liberal Democracy: Its Merits and Prospects* (Holt, Rinehart & Winston, 1950); B. C. Shafer, *Nationalism: Myth and Reality* (Harcourt Brace Jovanovich, 1955); J. Sigmann, *1848: The Romantic and Democratic Revolutions in Europe* (Harper & Row, 1973).

Impact of Dominance

Now that we have considered the three revolutions that made it possible for Europe to dominate the globe in the nineteenth century, we can turn to the domination process itself. We shall examine precisely how this domination manifested itself in the various parts of the world. Let us first consider the Eurasian lands. There we can see a certain pattern both in the timing and the unfolding of Europe's impact.

The timing was determined by three principal factors. The first was geographic location, which explains why Russia, for example, felt Europe's dynamism long before China or Japan. The second was the attitude of the local population, and particularly of the local ruling class, toward what the West had to offer. Peter the Great's ardent westernism, for example, ensured the early acceptance of Western thought and technology in Russia, while the rigid isolationist policies of China and Japan contributed to the exclusion of Western influence from those countries until the second half of the nineteenth century. The third factor was the strength and cohesion of the local societies. Where there was weakness and disunity, Western penetration and control came early, as in the case of India. Where there was strength and unity, as in the case of China, the West was kept at arm's length for a long time.

The nature of the actual impact itself, reminds one of a pebble that falls into a pool and makes a series of ever-expanding circles. Western intrusion was at first usually confined to some single specific area, but invariably it had repercussions in other fields, and these in turn caused further ripples until the entire society was affected. Precisely this point has been made by Sir Henry Maine, the English jurist and historian who served in India between 1862 and 1869:

> It is by indirect and for the most part unintended influence that the British power [in India] metamorphoses and dissolves the ideas and social forms underneath it, nor is there any expedient by which it can escape the duty of rebuilding upon its own principles that which it unwillingly destroyed . . . we do not innovate or destroy in mere arrogance. We rather change because we cannot help it. Whatever be the nature and value of that bundle of influences which we call Progress, nothing can be more certain than that, when a society is once touched by it, it spreads like a contagion.[1]

Specifically, the contagion from the West usually began in the military field. Non-Europeans were most impressed and alarmed by the West's superior military technology and strove to learn the secrets of this technology as soon as possible. This happened in region after region—in Russia, in the Middle East, in China, and in Japan. But Western arms required the development of certain industries, so that the original military objectives led to new objectives in the economic field. We shall see that for various reasons there was substantial industrialization in the nineteenth century in Russia and Japan, but comparatively little in the Middle East, in India, and in China. Modernization in tools led inevitably to modernization in ideas and values. Arms and factories required schools and science. One thing borrowed from the West inexorably required the borrowing of something more. Military and economic change produced intellectual change, and also social and political change. A new merchant and industrial class appeared which challenged the traditional society and ruling groups—and eventually also challenged Western domination. This explains the intellectual ferment and the revolutionary movement that opposed Tsardom in Russia, British control in India, and Manchu rule in China.

The general pattern noted here overlooks innumerable nuances and exceptions—the virtual absence of a native Moslem middle class amongst the Turks, the fateful disparity in the Japanese and Chinese responses to the West, the significance of total European political domination in India, compared to the semicontrol in China, and the relative lack of foreign control in Russia and Japan. In the following chapters we shall analyze the details of these individual developments in each of the regions of Eurasia. Succeeding chapters will analyze the even greater influence that the West had beyond Eurasia—in sub-Saharan Africa, the Americas, and Australia.

For three hundred years Russia has aspired to consort with Occidental Europe; for three hundred years she has taken her most serious ideas, her most fruitful teachings, and her most vivid delights from there.

Peter Y. Chaadayev

Russia

In a way, it is paradoxical to consider Europe's impact upon Russia, for Russia, after all, is a part of Europe, and the Russian people are a European people. But Russia lies on the fringe of Europe and provides a great buffer zone between that continent and Asia. Because of this location the historical experience of the Russian people has been quite different from that of other Europeans, and the culture they have developed is correspondingly different. As a result, Russian thinkers have tormented themselves generation after generation with the basic issue of national orientation and national goals.

Russia's relationship with the West has generally been that of passive recipient. Only in the past century and a half has Russia been able to repay the West, at first with the creations of its great writers and composers, and later with the economic-planning techniques and the social stimuli generated by the Bolshevik Revolution. But until the twentieth century, Europe's impact on Russia was much greater than the reverse, and this influence has been a central factor in the development of the country.

I. RUSSIA AND EUROPE TO 1856

The first Russian state developed around the principality of Kiev in the ninth century after Christ. This early Russian state had numerous commercial and diplomatic ties with the rest of Europe. But during the following centuries two crucial developments combined to isolate Russia. One was Prince Vladimir's decision about A.D. 990 to adopt the Byzantine Orthodox form of Christianity rather than the Roman Catholic. The differences between the two religions were not very substantial at the time. But during the following decades the development of the doctrine and practice of papal supremacy finally led in 1054 to the schism between the two churches. Russia inevitably became involved in the resulting feud between the Catholic and Orthodox worlds. This was particularly so after the fall of Constantinople to the Turks (1453), which left Russia as the only independent citadel of Orthodoxy. These events made the Russians self-satisfied, self-righteous, and self-isolated, and they ignored and scorned the great changes that were transforming the rest of Europe.

The other development that cut Russia off from the West was the Mongol invasion in 1237. The Mongols did not interfere with the affairs of their Russian subjects so long as the latter accepted the domination of the khan and paid him annual tribute. Nevertheless, Mongol domination severed most of the remaining ties between Russia and the rest of Europe. This rupture, which persisted during the two centuries of Mongol rule, came at a time when the West was experiencing the Renaissance, the Reformation, the overseas expansion, and the commercial revolution. But isolated Russia remained largely unaffected by these profound economic and cultural movements. Furthermore, the Mongols left their own imprint upon Russian society. Their ideas and administrative usages paved the way for the establishment of the semi-Oriental absolutism of the later Muscovite tsars. It is also noteworthy that approximately 17 percent of the Moscow upper class at the end of the seventeenth century was of non-Russian or Eastern origin.

When the Russians rid themselves of the Mongols in the fifteenth century, the Muscovite civilization that came to light was quite different from anything in Western Europe. It was a homogeneous civilization in the sense that the Orthodox religion shaped and colored people's outlook and actions. But it was also a civilization largely devoid of the commerce, the industry, and the science that had made the West so dynamic and expansionist. More emancipated and far-seeing Russian leaders soon perceived that their economic and technological backwardness represented a threat to their national security. Thus it was that the Russians in the sixteenth century, like the Turks and the Japanese and the Chinese in later centuries, began to borrow from the West as a measure of self-defense. And what they were primarily interested in borrowing was military technology.

There was nothing academic or abstract about this policy. Rather, it was a matter of life or death, for Russia was surrounded by the powerful Swedes, Lithuanians, and Poles in the west, and by the Turks and Crimean Tatars in the south. It is significant that when Tsar Ivan IV (1553–1584) proposed a military alliance and even suggested marriage to Queen Elizabeth of England, the King of Poland hastily wrote to Elizabeth and begged her to reject the proposition. "Up to now," he wrote, "we could conquer him [the Russian] only because he was a stranger to education and did not know the arts."[1] Thus the neighbors of Russia were deliberately trying to prevent that country from getting Western arms and techniques. The Russians, on their part, naturally tried to break the isolating encirclement, and they did so with increasing success. During the seventeenth century they employed many foreign military officers who were left unemployed when the Thirty Years' War ended.

Tsar Peter the Great (1682–1725) accelerated the process of westernization tremendously. With his iron will and herculean energy he issued over 3000 decrees, many in his own hand, and almost all inspired by him. He reorganized his administration and armed forces along Western lines, established industries to support his armies, imported thousands of foreign experts of various types, sent droves of young Russians to study abroad, and set up a number of schools, all of them utilitarian in character. He founded schools of mathematics and navigation, admiralty schools, war department schools, ciphering schools, and, at the summit, the Academy of Sciences. Peter also shattered all precedent by traveling through Western Europe to study foreign institutions and practices at first hand.

In all these various ways Peter succeeded in large part in reaching his goal of opening a "window to the West." Furthermore, he opened this window in a literal sense by defeating Sweden and acquiring frontage on the Baltic Sea. Here he built his new capital, St. Petersburg—the symbol of the new Russia, as Moscow was of the old.

Peter's work was continued by the gifted and colorful Catherine the Great (1762–1796). Catherine regarded herself and her court as media for the Europeanization of Russia. She was much more intellectual than the pragmatic Peter, and she energetically patronized literature, art, the theater, and the press. She was not an original thinker, but she readily absorbed the ideas of others, especially the philosophes. In fact, she prided herself on being an enlightened despot and often quoted the maxims of the Enlightenment. During her reign the higher Russian nobility became Europeanized. They had worn beards and flowing Oriental robes during Peter's reign, but under Catherine they aped the court of Versailles in their speech, clothes, dwellings, and social functions. Their children were brought up by French governesses, learned French as their mother tongue, and then picked up only enough Russian to manage the servants. Thus the Europeanization of Russia was no longer confined to technical matters, but it was limited to the upper class as it had been under Peter. Indeed, the gulf between the Europeanized upper crust and the peasant masses who were bound to the estates as serfs was becoming wider and more ominous.

This division between a favored ruling class and the exploited serfs who made up the great majority of the total population scarcely jibed with the principles of the Enlightenment that Catherine quoted so often. But Catherine was too much a realist to be unduly concerned about the discrepancy between theory and reality. She knew that she depended upon the nobles for her position and never seriously challenged their interests and privileges. On the contrary, she turned violently against the teachings of the philosophes when the French Revolution broke out. She denounced the revolution as "an irreligious, immoral, anarchical, abominable, and diabolical plague, the enemy of God and of Thrones. . . . As for the people and its opinion, that is of no great consequence."[2]

Catherine could afford to dismiss so lightly the views of "the people," but it was to be different with her successors. This was especially true after the great Russian victory over Napoleon's Grand Army. Between 1815 and 1818 a Russian army of occupation was stationed in France. These events naturally made a deep impression on public opinion in Russia. For most Russians, their feelings of superiority and condescension toward the West were reinforced, but many of the officers of the occupation army were much impressed by the relatively free Western society in which they had lived for four years. They absorbed the liberal and radical ideas in contemporary France and were profoundly influenced by them. When they returned to Russia in 1818, they found the Tsarist autocracy intolerable.

Sentiments such as these explain the so-called Decembrist Revolt that broke out in December 1825 upon the death of Alexander I. The leaders were mostly army officers who wished to westernize Russia by abolishing serfdom and the autocracy. The revolt failed miserably because there was no mass support. The Russians at this time lived under conditions so utterly different from those prevailing in Western Europe that they simply were not ready for Western political ideas and institutions. More specifically, Russia lacked the commerce, the industry, and the middle class that had played so decisive a role in the political evolution of the West. Instead, there were at the bottom the bound and inert serf masses—the "dark people," as they were called—and at the top the nobility and the court. Consequently, there was no mass support for the reforms and for the Western type of society desired by the Decembrists.

The meaning of these basic differences between Russia and the West divided Russian thinkers into two groups, the Westerners and the Slavophils. The Westerners deplored the differences, interpreting them as a product of Russia's slower rate of development. Accordingly, their hero was Peter the Great, and they urged that other rulers match Peter's heroic efforts to goad Russia to catch up with the West. The Slavophils, on the other hand, rejected the Westerner's basic assumption of the unity of human civilization. They maintained that every state embodies and expresses the peculiar national spirit of its people and that, if an attempt is made to model one state after another, the inevitable result will be contradiction and discord. They held that the differences between Russia and the West were fundamental and inherent, and reflected profound dissimilarities in national spirit rather than degrees of advance. Accordingly these Slavophils idealized the homogeneous Muscovite society of the period before Peter, and they regarded that westernizing Tsar as the archenemy of Russian civilization and national unity. Far from considering Western society as superior, they rejected it as being materialistic, irreligious, and torn by dissension and revolution.

II. RUSSIA AND EUROPE, 1856–1905

The issue between the Slavophils and the Westerners was settled, not by persuasion of one side by the other, but rather by the irresistible pressure of the rapidly developing and expanding Western society. This pressure was dramatically illustrated by the Crimean War (1854–1856) between Russia and a number of Western powers, of which the most important were Britain and France. The war was fought on Russian soil—in the Crimean peninsula—and yet Russia was defeated and forced to accept the humiliating Treaty of Paris. This treaty required Russia to scrap its naval units in the Black Sea and its fortifications along the Black Sea coast. It also forced Russia to surrender certain small but strategic territories along the Danube.

The Crimean defeat was a severe shock for the Russian nationalists and Slavophils. Unlike many Westerners who had warned of Russia's impending defeat because it had not kept up with the West, the Slavophils had predicted that the superiority of Russia's autocratic institutions would lead to a victory comparable to that of 1812 over Napoleon. Actually the Crimean defeat unveiled the corruption and backwardness of the old regime. Russia's soldiers had fought as gallantly in 1855 as in 1812. But the odds were hopelessly against them. They had rifles that shot only a third as far as those of the Western armies. They had only sailing ships to use against the steamships of the British and the French. They had no medical or commissariat services that were worthy of the name. And the lack of railways in the Crimean peninsula forced them to haul military supplies in carts, and to march on foot for hundreds of miles before reaching the front. In short, the war was lost because, as the Westerners had warned, "Europe has been steadily advancing on the road of progress while we have been standing still."

The revelation of the bankruptcy of the old regime led to its modification. The first change was the emancipation of the serfs, who had been intensely restless even before the war. In fact, over 500 peasant disturbances had broken out during the three decades of Nicholas I's reign between 1825 and 1855. With the disaster in the Crimea, the mounting pressure of the serfs became irresistible, and Nicholas's successor, Alexander II, accepted emancipation as the only alternative to revolution. His Emancipation Decree (March 1, 1861) freed the serfs and divided the land that they tilled between themselves and the noble proprietors. The proprietors were paid with government treasury bonds for the land that was distributed among the peasants. In return, the peasants were required to compensate the government by paying redemption dues for forty-nine years. This was a great turning point in Russian history, even greater than the 1863 Emancipation Proclamation in American history. Numerically, emancipation in the United States concerned only the Negro minority, whereas in Russia it involved the overwhelming majority of the population. The repercussions of the freeing of the serfs were so far reaching that a series of other reforms were unavoidable. These included the reorganization of the judiciary and of the local government.

During the decades following the Crimean War, Western Europe further undermined the old regime in Russia by contributing decisively to the industrialization of the country. Of the total of £500 million invested in Russian industry in 1917, just over one-third were made up of foreign investments. Western capital controlled 50 percent of coal and oil output, 60 percent of copper and iron ore, and 80 percent of coke. The number of factory workers rose from 381,000 in 1865 to 1.6 million in 1890, and to 3 million in 1898. By 1913, Russia was producing as much iron and three-fourths as much coal as France.

These developments meant that the Russia of 1914 was much more similar to Europe than the Russia of the Decembrists of 1825. But, as the Slavophils had warned, the growing similarity brought about certain divisions and conflicts within Russian society. One of these was the growing unrest and rising political consciousness among the peasants. The peasants had been far from satisfied with the terms of the Emancipation Decree, which, they felt, had left too large a proportion of the land to the nobles. During the following decades, as the peasants grew rapidly in numbers, their land hunger grew correspondingly, and they became increasingly dissatisfied. Another source of grievance for the peasants was the intolerably heavy tax load. They paid not only redemption dues for the land they had received in 1861 but also an assortment of local taxes. In addition, they bore much of the cost of Russia's industrialization, because high protective tariffs forced up the cost of the manufactured goods they bought. The extent and the intensity of peasant discontent was shown by the increasing frequency of violent peasant outbreaks against landlords and unpopular government officials.

Peasant disaffection found political expression in the Socialist Revolutionary party which was organized in 1901. Since no political parties were allowed in Russia prior to the 1905 Revolution, the Socialist Revolutionaries had to operate as an illegal underground group. The main plank of their platform was the distribution of state and noble lands amongst the peasantry. In two important respects they differed from the various types of Marxist socialists. In the first place, they regarded the peasantry rather than the urban proletariat as the main revolutionary force in Russia. In the second place, they advocated and practiced individual acts of terrorism, rather than relying on mass organization and pressure. Within the Socialist Revolutionary party was the highly secret Fighting Organization which directed the terroristic activities. The success of the Organization may be gauged from its long list of illustrious victims, including governors of provinces, ministers of state, and even the Tsar's uncle, Grand Duke Sergei.

The unrest of the peasants was matched by that of the urban proletariat who had appeared with the growth of industry. The early days of industrialization in Russia, as elsewhere in Europe, involved gross exploitation of labor: sixteen-hour working days, low wages, child labor, and abominable working and living conditions. Under these conditions the Russian workers, like those of Central and Western Europe, came under the influence of Marxist doctrines. Thus a Social Democratic party was organized in 1898 just as similar Socialist parties had been established elsewhere in Europe. And like the other Socialist parties, that of Russia split into revisionist and orthodox factions, or, as they were called in this instance, the Mensheviks and the Bolsheviks.

The split occurred during the second party congress held in London in 1903. The issues concerned party membership and party discipline. Vladimir Lenin, the leader of the orthodox faction, maintained that because of the repressive Tsarist autocracy, the Social Democratic party had to operate very differently from other Socialist parties. Membership should be open, not to any sympathizer who paid dues, but only to a small group of full-time professional revolutionaries. And this select membership was to function according to the principle of *"democratic centralism."* Any major issue facing the party was to be discussed freely by the members until a decision was reached democratically by a vote. But then the "centralism" part of the principle became operative. Every party member, regardless of his or her personal inclinations, was required on pain of expulsion to support undeviatingly what was now the "party line."

Only with such rigid discipline, Lenin maintained, could Russian Socialists carry on effectively their underground operations. Lenin won the support of most of the delegates to the 1903 congress, so that his followers henceforth were known as *Bolsheviks,* after the Russian word for "majority," and his opponents as *Mensheviks,* or "minority." It should be noted, however, that the Bolsheviks remained a small group until the outbreak of World War I. Then the chaos and misery produced by the defeats at the front gave the Bolsheviks the opportunity to use their superior organization to mobilize and lead the disaffected masses.

In addition to the peasants and the urban workers, there was in Russia at the turn of the century a middle class that also was becoming increasingly discontented with the Tsarist regime. The political organization reflecting the views of this group was the Constitutional Democratic party, commonly known under the abbreviated title of Cadets. The program of this party, founded in 1905, resembled that of the English Liberals: a constitutional monarchy balanced by a parliamentary body similar to Britain's House of Commons. The Cadets included many of Russia's outstanding intellectuals and businessmen. When the Tsar was forced to accept an elected assembly (Duma) following the 1905 Revolution, the Cadets played a leading role in its deliberations because of their knowledge of parliamentary procedures. And yet the Cadets never won a mass following comparable to that of the Social Democrats or the Socialist Revolutionaries. One reason was that the middle class was relatively small in Russia, thanks to the retarded development of commerce and industry. The middle class was further weakened because so much of the national economy was controlled by foreign interests. And the Cadets were peculiarly vulnerable to the pressures of the Tsarist autocracy, because, with their middle-class background, they were less willing to meet force with force.

Such, then, was the West's impact upon Russia by the turn of the century. The intrusion of the West had undermined a distinctive and homogeneous society; and the repercussions of the resulting stresses and dissensions were to culminate in the great revolutions of 1905 and 1917. Before considering these upheavals, we shall survey Russian policies in Asia up to the time of the Russo-Japanese War, which set the stage for the 1905 revolution.

III. RUSSIA AND ASIA TO 1905

Just as the relations between Russia and Europe were determined largely by the economic and technological superiority of Europe, so the relations between Russia and Asia were determined by the superiority of Russia. This superiority had enabled Russia between the sixteenth and eighteenth centuries to overcome the tribespeople of Siberia and to expand eastward to the Pacific. But in the southeast the Russians had been halted by the strong Chinese empire and forced to accept the Nerchinsk Treaty (1689) confining them to the territory north of the Amur valley (see Chapter 20, section III).

During the eighteenth and nineteenth centuries the Russians resumed their advance to the east and the south, rounding out their empire by acquiring Alaska, the Amur valley, and Central Asia. The addition of Alaska involved simply a continuation of the earlier trans-Siberian push into relatively empty territories. But in the Amur valley the Russians prevailed over the Chinese empire, and in Central Asia they imposed their rule upon ancient Moslem khanates. These successes were made possible by Russia's steady technological progress. Russia's technology, though inadequate vis-à-vis the West, and indeed derived from the West, was nonetheless sufficient to give the Russians a decisive advantage in their relations with the Chinese in East Asia and with the Moslems in Central Asia. Thus, the Russians continued to extend their imperial frontiers, until they were stopped by powers that were technologically equal or superior—that is, by the Americans in Alaska, by the British in India and Persia, and by the Japanese in Manchuria.

Alaska

The Russian advance to Alaska got under way during the reign of Peter the Great. The westernizing Tsar was as much interested in the Far East as in Europe, so he selected Captain Vitus Bering, a naval officer of Danish extraction, to lead expeditions to the American continent in 1728 and 1740. Bering sailed eastward across the sea that bears his name, explored the Aleutian Islands, and also landed on the coast of Alaska. Russian merchants followed on the heels of the explorers, attracted by the profitable trade in sea-otter skins. The merchants first exploited the Aleutian Islanders and then established posts along the Alaskan coast. In 1799 the various private trading companies combined to form the Russo-American Company. The outstanding Russian leader in Alaska was Alexander Baranov, who directed operations energetically and autocratically for a generation. His chief problem was transporting supplies from Siberia across one of the world's stormiest and foggiest seas. Accordingly, Baranov sent expeditions down the American coast to establish settlements where fresh supplies could be grown for the Alaskan posts. In November 1811, Fort Ross was established on the Russian River north of San Francisco, and by 1819 the Russians had a chain of nineteen settlements on the American coast.

This expansion led to friction with Spain and with the United States. In fact, the presence of the Russians in the northwest Pacific was partly responsible for the proclamation of the Monroe Doctrine in 1823. In the end, the Russians decided to give up their American holdings. The decline in the fur trade had brought the Russo-American Company to the point of bankruptcy. And the Russians feared that Alaska was too distant to be defended against American expansionism. Anticipating that they would lose the territory sooner or later, they sold it to the United States in 1867 for $7 million, or less than two cents per acre.

Amur Valley

Meanwhile, the Russian activity in North America had reawakened Russian interest in the Amur valley. The Russians needed an outlet on the Pacific Ocean to serve as a base for supplying their American settlements. They had the port of Okhotsk, but this was altogether inadequate. It was frozen every year until June and was almost continually fogbound. Consequently, the Russians once more looked longingly toward the broad and navigable Amur River from which they had been ousted by the Nerchinsk Treaty in 1689.

Russian interest was further sharpened by the so-called Opium War of 1839–1842 between Britain and China (see Chapter 27, section I). As a result of the war, Britain annexed Hong Kong and acquired a predominant influence in the Yangtze valley. The Russians now resolved to establish themselves in the Amur valley lest the British next gain control of the mouth of the river and block their natural outlet to the Pacific. In little more than a decade, the Russians gained all their objectives in this vital region. One reason for their success was the ambition and energy of young Count Nikolai Muraviev, who was appointed governor-general of Eastern Siberia in 1847 at the age of 38. Another reason was the weakness of China, by that time a hollow shell compared to the powerful Chinese empire that had expelled the Russians from the Amur valley in the seventeenth century.

Count Muraviev was given extensive viceregal powers, but he went beyond them and sent out exploratory expeditions that planted the Russian flag on foreign soil. One of his officers, Captain (later Admiral) Nevelskoi, established the fortress of Petropavlovsk on the Kamchatka peninsula. He explored and occupied Sakhalin Island after ousting Japanese settlers, launched steamships on the Amur River, encouraged Russian colonists to settle in the Amur valley, and founded a number of posts along the coast between the mouth of the Amur and the Korean frontier. The Russians were able to expand so easily because the entire region was a no man's land over which the Chinese had only a vague suzerainty and no control whatsoever. In fact, the Chinese court was quite unaware of the Russian measures, and it was the Russian government itself which, in May 1851, informed the Chinese of what had taken place.

Five years later, in 1856, hostilities broke out once more between China and Britain. The Chinese again were badly beaten and forced by the Tientsin Treaties (1858) to open more ports to Western merchants and to make other concessions. Muraviev seized the opportunity to warn the Chinese of the danger of British control of the Amur and to propose joint Russo-Chinese defense of the region. The outcome was the Aigun Treaty (1858) by which Russia obtained the left bank of the Amur to the Ussuri River. Beyond the Ussuri Russia and China were to exercise joint sovereignty over both banks of the river to the ocean.

Muraviev now explored carefully the newly won territories and discovered that the formation of ice on the lower Amur was such that control of both banks was essential for navigation purposes. He also found a magnificent harbor on the coast near the Korean frontier. Despite the provisions of the Aigun Treaty, he founded a city there (1860) which he significantly named Vladivostok, or Lord of the East. Meanwhile, China had become embroiled in further trouble with the Western powers, and in 1860 Peking was occupied by Anglo-French forces. The Russian minister in Peking, Count Nikolai Ignatiev, offered his services as an intermediary and succeeded in getting the allies to evacuate the capital under conditions that were not too unfavorable for China. In return for this service the Chinese government negotiated the Treaty of Peking (1860) giving Russia both banks of the Amur from the Ussuri to the sea, and the entire coastal area from the mouth of the Amur to the Korean border. With the winning of these new far-flung frontiers (which exist to the present day), Russian expansion in the Far East came to a halt. It was not resumed again until the beginning of the twentieth century, when Tsar Nicholas II attempted to penetrate south into Korea and Manchuria, and thereby started a disastrous war with Japan.

Central Asia

In the meantime, the Russians had also been penetrating into Central Asia, although their advance in this region did not begin until the second quarter of the nineteenth century. The delay was partly because of the lack of economic incentives comparable to the profitable fur trade in the north. But there were other reasons: The climate and vegetation of Central Asia were quite different from that to which the Russians were accustomed. Immediately to the south of Siberia was the steppe country where the Kazakh nomads lived. Still further south began the great desert, dotted with rich oases that supported the ancient Moslem khanates of Bukhara, Khiva, and Kokand. Much stronger militarily than the scattered Siberian tribes, these khanates were able to keep the Russians at arm's length until the late nineteenth century.

During the three decades between 1827 and 1854 the Russians made their first advance into Central Asia by conquering the Kazakh steppes to the Syr Darya River. They hoped that the river would serve as a permanent natural frontier, but this was not to be. The ambition of local commanders, far away from the capital and eager for glory and promotion, frequently forced the government's hand and presented it with a fait accompli. The constant harassment of marauding bands also led the Russians to press further in spite of misgivings in St. Petersburg and protests from Britain.

One after another, the legendary centers of Central Asian Moslem civilization fell to the advancing Russians—Tashkent in 1865, Bukhara in 1868, Khiva in 1873, Geok-Tepe in 1881, and Merv in 1884. These thrusts greatly alarmed the British in India, and there were recurring crises and rumors of war. But the century passed without open conflict, primarily because the distances were so great and the means of transport so limited. Instead of going to war, the British and the Russians struggled to control intervening states, particularly Persia and Afghanistan.

Russian rule changed Central Asia significantly. On the positive side the Russians abolished the widespread slavery and slave trade, freeing 10,000 slaves in Samarkand and its environs alone. The Russians also built railways—notably the Orenburg-Tashkent line—which helped them both to subjugate and to modernize the area. Thanks to the cheap transportation and the growing demands of the Russian textile industry, cotton cultivation increased spectacularly. In 1884, 300 desiatinas (1 desiatina = 2.7 acres) were planted to cotton on Russian initiative; by 1899, cotton acreage had jumped to 90,000 desiatinas. The Russians also introduced certain agrarian reforms, including a reduction of peasant tax and labor obligations to the state and to landlords.

On the other hand, the Russians' systematic expropriation of Kazakh grazing lands led to a decrease in the size of herds and to widespread famine. The Russians did nothing for the education of the natives, leaving this almost entirely to the Moslem mullahs. In other areas, such as the judiciary and local government, they were less active than the British were in India. The net result was that prior to the Bolshevik Revolution, which brought as many changes to Central Asia as to other regions of the Tsarist empire, the mass of Kazakhs, Kirghizes, Turkomans, Uzbeks, and Tajiks were little affected by the coming of the Russians. Despite the railway building and the spreading cotton cultivation, conquerors and conquered lived in different worlds, separated by barriers of language, religion, and customs.

Manchuria and the Russo-Japanese War

In the 1890s Russian interest was shifting from Central Asia to the Far East. The Trans-Siberian railway, which was slowly nearing completion, presented new opportunities for Russian economic and political expansion. Count Sergei Witte, the newly appointed minister of finance, presented a report to Tsar Alexander III (November 6, 1892) in which he stated that the Trans-Siberian line would supersede the Suez Canal as the principal trade route to China. He foresaw Russia in the position of arbiter between Asia and the Western world and advocated a Russo-Chinese alliance as the best means for attaining that position.

The outbreak of the Sino-Japanese War in 1895 (see Chapter 27, section I) paved the way for the alliance that Witte favored. China again was easily defeated, and it repeatedly requested Britain and the United States to mediate. Their refusal forced China to accept the Treaty of Shimonoseki (April 17, 1895), by which China ceded to Japan the Formosa and Pescadores Islands, and the Liaotung peninsula. But Russia, together with Germany and France, now intervened and compelled the Japanese to restore the peninsula.

This assistance impressed the Chinese who, in the following year, signed a secret treaty with Russia. It provided for mutual assistance in case of Japanese aggression, and it also granted a joint Russo-Chinese Bank a concession for the construction of the Chinese Eastern Railway across Manchuria to Vladivostok. The bank, nominally a private concern, was actually owned and operated by the Russian government. By the outbreak of the Russo-Japanese War in 1904, it had built a total of 1596 miles of railway in Manchuria.

Russia's next advance in the Far East was in 1898, with the negotiation of a twenty-five-year lease of the Liaotung peninsula, including strategic Port Arthur. And two years later the Russians took advantage of the disturbances during the Boxer Rebellion to occupy the entire province of Manchuria. This steady encroachment of Russia alarmed the Japanese, who had ambitions of their own on the mainland of Asia. Since they were in no position to stop the Russians singlehanded, they decided to strengthen themselves by securing an ally. On January 30, 1902, they concluded a military alliance with Britain, and, with this backing, they resolved to settle accounts with Russia. In July 1903, the Japanese proposed that Russia should recognize their "preponderant interests" in Korea, and in return they would recognize Russia's "special interests in railway enterprises in Manchuria."

The Russians were divided concerning the Japanese offer. The finance minister, Count Witte, favored acceptance because he was interested in economic penetration rather than in political annexation with its dangers of war. But influential Russian adventurers with vast timber concessions in northern Korea wished to involve their government in order to advance their personal fortunes. Russian military circles wanted to obtain a base along the Korean coast because of the great distance between their existing bases at Port Arthur and Vladivostok. And certain Russian politicians, concerned by the mounting revolutionary wave in the country, favored a "little victorious war" that would serve as a lightning rod for the popular unrest. There was no doubt in their minds, or in those of the military, that Russia would win in a war with Japan.

This group of adventurers, militarists, and politicians had their way. They secured the dismissal of Witte and virtually rejected the Japanese offer. Assured by their alliance with the British, and apprehensive about the near-completion of the Trans-Siberian railway, the Japanese struck promptly and decisively. On February 5, 1904, they broke off negotiations, and three days later they attacked the Russian fleet at Port Arthur without a formal declaration of war.

In the campaigns that followed, the Japanese David consistently defeated the Russian Goliath. The single-track Trans-Siberian railway proved quite inadequate to supply Russian armies fighting several thousand miles from their industrial centers in European Russia. In the first stage of the war, the Japanese surrounded Port Arthur and, after a siege of 148 days, captured the fortress on December 19, 1904. The second stage consisted of a series of battles on the plains of Manchuria. The Japanese were victorious here also, driving the Russians north of Mukden. These campaigns, however, were not decisive, because the Russian armies remained intact and were reinforced and strengthened as communications improved. But on the sea the Japanese won an overwhelming triumph that led to the beginning of peace negotiations. On May 27, 1905, the Russian Baltic fleet arrived at the Tsushima Straits between Japan and Korea after sailing a distance equivalent to more than two-thirds the circumference of the globe. It was attacked at once by a Japanese fleet that was superior both in numbers and in efficiency. Within a few hours virtually all the Russian units had been sunk or captured. The Japanese merely lost a few destroyers.

With this debacle the Russians were ready to discuss peace, especially since the war was very unpopular at home and the 1905 Revolution had started. The Japanese also wanted peace negotiations because, although they had won the victories, their still meager resources had been strained by the burden of the war. On September 5, 1905, the Treaty of Portsmouth was signed, by which Russia acknowledged Japan's "paramount political, military, and economic interests" in Korea, surrendered all preferential or exclusive concessions in Manchuria, and ceded to Japan the southern half of Sakhalin Island and the lease of the Liaotung peninsula. In this way the Japanese halted Russia's expansion in the Far East. Not until four decades later, when the Japanese were disastrously defeated in World War II, was Russia able to recover the territories lost at Portsmouth.

IV. FIRST RUSSIAN REVOLUTION
AND AFTERMATH, 1905–1914

While the Russo-Japanese War was being fought in the Far East, revolution was spreading behind the lines within Russia. The revolution had its roots in the chronic disaffection of the peasants, the urban workers, and the middle class. This disaffection was aggravated by the war with Japan, which was unpopular to begin with and became increasingly so after the string of defeats. Finally there occurred the so-called "Bloody Sunday" of January 22, 1905. The Imperial Guard fired on an unarmed crowd of several thousand persons who were marching peacefully carrying a petition to the Winter Palace in St. Petersburg. Between 75 and 1000 were killed, and 200 to 2000 wounded. The discrepancy in the figures is due to the fact that some eyewitnesses reported only the Sunday casualties, while others included casualties that occurred in the next two days as the disturbance continued on in the capital.

Bloody Sunday irreparably smashed the benevolent ''Little Father'' image of the Tsar that so many Russians had traditionally cherished. Citizens throughout the empire turned against the regime setting off the great Russian Revolution of 1905. This upheaval passed through three stages before the imperial government was able to reassert its authority. The first, between January and October 1905, was the rising wave of revolution. All classes and interests came out against the autocracy. The subject nationalities demanded autonomy, peasants pillaged houses and seized estates, city workers organized councils—or soviets—for revolutionary action, university students everywhere walked out of their classrooms, and the sailors of the Black Sea fleet mutinied and seized their ships. The Tsar had no alternative but to yield, so he issued his famous October Manifesto (October 30). It promised freedom of speech, press, and assembly, and also granted Russia a constitution and an elective national assembly, or *Duma.*

During the second stage of the revolution, between October 1905 and January 1906, the uprising continued at high pitch, but the revolutionaries no longer were united. The moderates, consisting mostly of middle-class elements, accepted the October Manifesto, while the radicals, including the Social Democrats and the Socialist Revolutionaries, demanded that a constituent assembly, not the Tsar's ministers, should prepare the new constitution. In order to gain their ends the radicals tried to prolong the revolution by organizing more strikes and disturbances. By this time, however, the government was getting stronger and was able to hit back. The signing of the Portsmouth Treaty with Japan on September 5, 1905, freed many troops, and they were sent home to restore order. A timely loan of $400 million from Paris and London greatly strengthened the faltering Tsarist government. Consequently, it was able to crush a dangerous workers' revolt that raged in Moscow between December 22 and January 1. Meanwhile, the moderates, alienated by the prolonged violence, were swinging over to the government's side. Thus by the beginning of 1906 the crest of the revolutionary wave had passed.

The third stage of the revolution, from January to July 21, 1906, was that of Tsarist consolidation of power. Government forces hunted down radicals and rebellious peasants, in some cases burning whole villages. On May 6 the government issued the so-called Fundamental Laws by which the Tsar was proclaimed autocrat and retained complete control over the executive, the armed forces, and foreign policy. The elective Duma was to share legislative power with an upper chamber, while its budgetary power was closely restricted. When the Duma did meet on May 10, it refused to accept the Fundamental Laws and criticized the government violently. A deadlock ensued, and the Tsar dissolved the Duma on July 21. The liberal Duma members retaliated by calling on the country to refuse to pay taxes. But the response was feeble. The fact is that by this time the revolutionary tide had ebbed, and the First Russian Revolution had run its course.

Although the revolution failed, it left its imprint on the course of Russia's history. Russia now had a constitutional regime, even though the Duma had little power. A second Duma was elected in February 1907, but it proved to be even more defiant than the first. The government then restricted the franchise so drastically that the third and fourth

A POLITICAL PRISONER IN SIBERIA

When caught by the Tsarist police, Russian revolutionaries usually were sentenced to Siberia. One of these was Leo Deutsch who was imprisoned for sixteen years until he escaped in 1902. In the following passage he describes how he was prepared for the long journey to Siberia.*

First of all, I was taken into a room where was stored everything necessary to the equipment of a convict under sentence. On the floor lay piles of chains; and clothes, boots, etc., were heaped on shelves. From among them some were selected that were supposed to fit me; and I was then conducted to a second room. Here the right side of my head was shaved, and the hair on the left side cut short. I had seen people in the prison who had been treated in this fashion, and the sight had always made a painful impression on me, as indeed it does on everyone. But when I saw my own face in the glass a cold shudder ran down my spine, and I experienced a sensation of personal degradation to something less than human. I thought of the days—in Russia not so long ago—when criminals were branded with hot irons.

A convict was waiting ready to fasten on my fetters. I was placed on a stool, and had to put my foot on an anvil. The blacksmith fitted an iron ring round each ankle, and welded it together. Every stroke of the hammer made my heart sink, as I realized that a new existence was beginning for me.

The mental depression into which I now fell was soon accompanied by physical discomfort. The fetters at first caused me intolerable pain in walking, and even disturbed my sleep. It also requires considerable practice before one can easily manage to dress and undress. The heavy chains—about 13 lbs. in weight—are not only an encumbrance but are very painful, as they chafe the skin round the ankles; and the leather lining is but little protection to those unaccustomed to these adornments. Another great torment is the continual clinking of chains. It is indescribably irritating to the nervous, and reminds the prisoner at every turn that he is a pariah among his kind, "deprived of all rights". . . .

My own clothes I gave away to the warders, and any possessions of value—watch, ring, cigarette-case—I sent by post to relations. I kept only my books. I had been given a bag in which to keep a change of linen; and into it I also put a few volumes of Shakespeare, Goethe, Heine, Molière, and Rosseau, thus completing my preparations for travelling.

Evening came. The officer in command of the convoy appeared in the prison courtyard with his men and took the party in charge. . . .

We were then arranged in processional order. The soldiers surrounded us; the officer lifted his cap and crossed himself.

"A pleasant journey! Good-bye!" called out the prison officials.

"Thanks. Good-bye!" cried the officer. He then gave the signal to start, and off we marched at a slow pace to the station.

* Leo Deutsch, *Sixteen Years in Siberia* (London: John Murray, 1903), pp. 95–97.

Dumas elected in 1907 and 1912 were acceptably conservative and subservient. Nevertheless, the absolutist Tsarist autocracy ended with the October Manifesto, and, after World War I began, the Duma came increasingly into its own until it was swept away by the Bolshevik Revolution.

The events of 1905 are important also because of their contribution to Russian revolutionary experience and tradition. Soviets were organized in the cities and proved their value as organs for revolutionary action. It is true that after 1906 a lull seemed to set in, but it was only a brief respite. The number of workers on strike declined from one million in 1905 to 4000 in 1910. But by 1912, the number had risen again to one million, and it remained at that level during the next two years. Then all discord ceased abruptly with the outbreak of World War I. But with the catastrophic defeats at the front, new storm clouds gathered, and the Tsarist regime entered a new time of troubles from which it never emerged. Thus, the Russian Revolution of 1905 stands out as a dress rehearsal for the world-shaking revolutions of 1917.

SUGGESTED READING

E. E. Allworth, *Central Asia: A Century of Russian Rule* (Columbia University Press, 1966); E. E. Bacon, *Central Asia Under Russian Rule: A Study in Culture Change* (Cornell University Press, 1966); W. L. Blackwell, *The Beginnings of Russian Industrialization, 1800–1860* (Princeton University Press, 1968); M. Malia, *Russia Under Western Eyes: From Peter the Great to Khrushchev* (John Wiley, 1964); R. A. Pierce, *Russian Central Asia, 1867–1917: A Study in Colonial Rule* (University of California Press, 1960); D. W. Treadgold, *The West in Russia and China:* Vol. I, *Russia 1472–1917* (Cambridge University Press, 1973).

It is not open to question that all
social changes in the Near East
during the past century or so
have arisen, directly or indirectly,
from the impact of our Western
society and the penetration of
Western techniques and ideas.

H. A. R. Gibb

chapter 25

The Middle East

The West's influence on the Middle East was quite different from its influence on Russia, and the response of the Middle Eastern peoples was just as different. Different peoples, religions, and cultures were involved, to be sure, but there was also a different political and social organization. The Ottoman Empire, which embraced most of the Middle East during the nineteenth century, remained a hodge-podge of peoples and religions and conflicting loyalties. It was organized as a theocracy on the basis of ecclesiastical communities rather than ethnic groups. These communities, the most important of which were the Greek Orthodox, Roman Catholic, and Jewish, were allowed considerable autonomy under their respective ecclesiastical leaders. Thus for centuries the various Moslem peoples (for example, Turks, Arabs, Albanians, and Kurds) and the various Christian peoples (for example, Serbs, Greeks, Bulgars, and Rumanians) lived side by side in semiautonomous and self-sufficient communities. Individual non-Moslems did suffer discrimination regarding dress, behavior, living areas, and higher taxes. Yet each community was allowed its own church, language, schools, and local government, so long as it accepted the sultan's authority and paid taxes to the imperial treasury.

The significance of this loose imperial organization is that Western ideas and pressures encountered a variety of cultures and conditions. Consequently, the West did not have a uniform impact on the Ottoman lands. Therefore, in analyzing the nature of that impact, it is essential to take into account the marked variations in regional conditions and re-

373

sponses. For this reason we shall now consider, not the Ottoman Empire as a whole, but rather its three main regions in turn—the Balkan peninsula with its predominantly Christian population, Asia Minor with its ruling Moslem Turkish population, and the provinces south of Asia Minor with their Moslem Arab peoples.

I. BALKAN CHRISTIANS

The Balkan peoples were affected earlier and more profoundly by the West than any of the other ethnic groups of the Ottoman Empire. Mostly Christians, they were more receptive to the Christian West than were the Moslem Turks and Arabs. The territorial contiguity of the Balkan lands to the rest of Europe made it easier for persons and goods and ideas to converge upon the Balkan peninsula from across the Danube and the Adriatic, Mediterranean, and Black seas. The increasing demand for food imports in Western Europe stimulated agriculture in the Balkans, especially the cultivation of the new colonial products, cotton and maize. The export of these commodities in turn contributed to the growth of a class of native Balkan merchants and mariners. The expansion of trade also stimulated the demand and output of handicraft products. Important manufacturing centers appeared in various parts of the peninsula, frequently in isolated mountain areas where the artisans could practice their crafts with a minimum of Turkish interference. Finally the rise of commerce and industry promoted the growth of a merchant marine along the Adriatic coast and amongst the Aegean Islands. The new Balkan mariners exported products such as cotton, maize, dyeing materials, wine, oil, and fruits, and brought back mostly colonial products and manufactured goods—spices, sugar, woolens, glass, watches, guns, and gunpowder.

The significance of this economic renaissance is that it created a middle class of merchants, artisans, shipowners, and mariners that was particularly susceptible and sympathetic to Western ideas and institutions. These people, by their very nature, were dissatisfied with Ottoman rule, which by this time had become ineffective and corrupt. Merchants and seamen who journeyed to foreign lands, and frequently resided there, could not help contrasting the security and enlightenment they witnessed abroad with the deplorable conditions at home. Very naturally they would conclude that their own future, and that of their fellow countrymen, depended upon the earliest possible removal of Turkish rule.

Serbian merchants in southern Hungary, Bulgarian merchants in southern Russia, and Greek merchants scattered widely in the main cities of Europe, all contributed to the intellectual awakening of their fellow countrymen. They did so by publishing books and newspapers in their native languages, by establishing schools and libraries in their home towns and villages, and by financing the education of their young men in foreign universities. All this meant not only more education but a new type of education. It was no longer primarily religious. Instead, it was profoundly influenced by the current Enlightenment in Western Europe.

Western influence in the Balkans became more directly political and inflammatory during the French revolutionary and Napoleonic era. Politically conscious elements were much impressed by the uprisings in Paris, by the slogan ''Liberty, Equality, Fraternity,'' and by the spectacle of Napoleon toppling over one dynasty after another. A contemporary Greek revolutionary testified: ''The French Revolution in general awakened the minds of all men. . . . All the Christians of the Near East prayed to God that France should wage war against the Turks, and they believed that they would be freed. . . . But when Napoleon made no move, they began to take measures for freeing themselves."[1]

The tempo of national awakening varied greatly from one Balkan people to another. The Greeks came first because of certain favorable circumstances: the numerous contacts with the West, their glorious classical and Byzantine heritage which stimulated national pride, and their Greek Orthodox church which embodied and preserved national consciousness. After the Greeks came the Serbs, who enjoyed a high degree of local self-government as well as the stimulating influence of the large Serbian settlements in southern Hungary. These advantages of the Greeks and the Serbs suggest the reasons for the slower rate of national revival among the other Balkan peoples. The Bulgars had no direct ties with the West and were located near the Ottoman capital and the solid Turkish settlements in Thrace and eastern Macedonia. The Rumanians suffered from a sharp social stratification which was unique in the Balkans and which produced a cultivated upper class and an inert peasant mass. The Albanians were the worst off, with their primitive tribal organization and their division among three creeds, Orthodoxy, Catholicism, and Islam.

These factors explain why, in place of a common Balkan revolution against Ottoman rule, there were separate uprisings ranging from the early nineteenth century to the early twentieth. The Greeks won complete independence from the Turks following a protracted War of Independence between 1821 and 1829. The Serbs had revolted earlier in 1804, but they only gained an autonomous status within the Ottoman Empire in 1815. It was not until 1878 that the Serbian Principality gained full independence and became the Kingdom of Serbia. The Rumanians came next, winning autonomy in 1859 and full independence in 1878. The Bulgarians followed later, gaining autonomy in 1878 and independence in 1908. Three of these Balkan peoples, the Serbs, Greeks, and Bulgarians, combined forces in 1912 to drive the Turks completely out of the peninsula. They were successful on the battlefield, and, despite a fratricidal war amongst the victors, the Turks were compelled in 1913 to surrender all their remaining territories in the Balkans with the exception of an enclave stretching around the Straits from Constantinople to Adrianople.

In this manner the imperial Ottoman frontiers shrank from the walls of Vienna in 1683 to the Danube in 1815, to the mid-Balkans in 1878, and to the environs of Constantinople in 1913. As the empire receded, independent Balkan states took its place—Greece, Serbia, Rumania, Bulgaria, and, in 1912, Albania. The West contributed decisively to this resurgence of the Balkan peoples by providing a revolutionary nationalist ideology, by stimulating the growth of a middle class that was ready to act on the basis of that ideology, and by sporadically helping the Balkan revolutionaries in their struggle against Turkish rule.

II. TURKS

The West affected the Turks much less and much later than it did the Balkan Christians. Various factors explain this difference. The most important of these probably were the Moslem religion of the Turks and their lack of a native middle class.

If the Christian faith of the Balkan peoples constituted a bond with the West, the Moslem faith of the Turks was a barrier. And it was a most formidable barrier because of the long history of antagonism and conflict between Christianity and Islam. The Turks also were little affected by the West because they never developed their own middle class.

They had no interest in, or respect for, commercial pursuits, so that the Ottoman bourgeoisie was largely Greek, Armenian, and Jewish. By contrast, the Turks were either peasants (who were generally apathetic), or teachers and judges in the Moslem ecclesiastical organization (which almost always meant that they were bitterly anti-Western), or else they were officeholders in the imperial bureaucracy (in which case they usually were interested only in retaining their posts and advancing in rank). The significance of this situation is apparent when we think of the vital role played by Greek, Serbian, and Bulgarian merchants in their respective countries. But there was no comparable group of Turkish merchants, so that the rare advocates of reform among the Turks found themselves without any following. They found themselves, in other words, in the same plight as did the Decembrists in Russia in 1825, and for the same reason.

The lack of mass support for reform was strikingly illustrated by the fate of Sultan Selim III. He was not the first sultan to recognize the need for reform in the empire, but he was the first to realize that the reform measures must look forward rather than backward. He was the first to consider reform in terms of borrowing from the West rather than returning to the days of Suleiman the Magnificent. His plans included the reorganization of administration, the revamping of education, and the complete transformation of the janissary corps.

The *janissaries,* who had once been the elite of the Ottoman infantry, by this time had degenerated to a worthless and insubordinate Praetorian Guard. This became apparent during the wars with Russia at the end of the eighteenth century, when, at the sight of the enemy, the janissaries were likely to break and run, pausing only to plunder their own camp. Several sultans had attempted in the past to curb or destroy this pernicious body. They all failed because the heads of law and religion, known collectively as the ulema, had sided with the janissaries. Important economic interests also opposed reform because they had been getting large sums from the imperial treasury over many decades in the guise of pay for janissary units that actually did not exist.

The powerful combination of military, religious, and economic vested interests explains why earlier sultans had failed to reform the janissary corps, and why Selim also was destined to fail, and to forfeit his throne and his life. In 1793, he took the decisive step of establishing a military force known as the New Regulations Army, a Western-type army with regulation uniforms, specified enlistment and recruitment procedures, European methods of training, and modern armaments. The New Army proved its superiority in several engagements, but this only intensified the fear and opposition of the janissaries and their allies. They spread rumors that the New Army was an invention of the Christian infidels and that Selim sponsored it because he no longer was the true defender of the Faith. Sufficient unrest was created so that the janissaries were able to force Selim to abdicate in May 1808. Two months later he was strangled when his supporters attempted to rescue him from his palace quarters where he was held captive.

In retrospect it is clear that Selim had tried to do what Peter the Great of Russia had accomplished a century earlier. He failed partly because he was not so forceful or decisive a personality as the Russian Tsar. But his failure was due even more to the fact that the janissaries, together with their allies in the ulema, the bureaucracy, and the court, comprised a much more powerful opposition bloc than any that Peter had faced. As a result, the Ottoman Empire seemed in 1808 to be as unchanging and as unchangeable as ever.

Yet during the course of the nineteenth century the Ottoman Empire, like the Russian, was penetrated, influenced, and controlled by the West in numerous direct and indirect ways. Of the several channels of penetration, the earliest, and in some respects the most effective, was the military. The Turks, like the Russians, found it necessary to adopt European military techniques for self-preservation. During the latter half of the nineteenth century the Western powers actively encouraged the Turks to modernize their military forces in order to block Russian expansion into the Middle East. But of the many young men who were sent abroad to study in foreign military academies, some inevitably learned about Western ideologies as well as Western military techniques. Thus it is not surprising that when the old Ottoman regime was finally overthrown in 1908, the coup was executed not by a political party or a mass movement but by an army clique.

In the field of religion, also, the West affected the Moslem Middle East. Missionaries were preaching and founding schools throughout the empire. By 1875 the American missionaries alone had 240 schools with 8000 pupils. Most of the latter were Armenians and other Christians, since proselytism amongst Moslems was forbidden. But a fair number of Turkish students were to be found in the foreign colleges scattered throughout the empire—colleges such as the American-operated Constantinople Women's College and Robert College (also in Constantinople), and the French Jesuit University of St. Joseph at Beirut. The Turks themselves by this time had established several institutions of higher learning, including the School of Medicine (1867), the Imperial Lycée (1868), the University of Constantinople (1869), the School of Law (1870), and the School of Political Science (1878). The Turkish press, too, was developing rapidly during these years. In 1859 there was only one official and one semiofficial weekly in the empire. By 1882 there were three daily papers and several weeklies.

At least as significant as this cultural impact was the West's economic penetration of the Ottoman Empire. In 1869 the Suez Canal was opened after ten years of construction by a European syndicate headed by a French diplomat and promoter, Ferdinand de Lesseps. The effect of the canal was to place the Ottoman Empire once more on the main trade route between Europe and Asia. At the same time the Ottoman government was falling hopelessly into debt to European governments and to private financiers. They contracted their first loan in 1854, and by 1875 their debts totaled £200 million sterling. Some £12 million sterling a year was required to meet annuities, interest, and sinking funds, a sum that amounted to a little more than half the total revenues of the empire. The load proved too heavy, and some of the interest payments were defaulted, whereupon in 1881 the European powers imposed the Ottoman Public Debt Administration. This body consisted mostly of foreign representatives and was entrusted with the revenues from various monopolies and customs duties for the service of the imperial debts.

In addition to this hold over Ottoman public finances, foreign interests had control over the Turkish banking and railway systems, irrigation works, mining enterprises, and municipal public utilities. The empire, besides, was still subject to the capitulations, or extraterritorial privileges, that foreigners had enjoyed in the Ottoman Empire since the fifteenth century. These privileges included exemption from the jurisdiction of Ottoman courts and from certain taxes, including personal imposts and customs tariffs. The latter were set at a very low level and could not be raised by the Ottoman government without the consent of the European powers, which, needless to say, was not forthcoming. Thus we may conclude that the Ottoman Empire, much more than the Russian, was in a semicolonial economic relationship with Europe.

The effect of all these Western pressures and controls cannot be measured precisely. But there can be no doubt that they gradually cracked the hitherto impregnable and monolithic Islamic structure. Canals, railways, banks, missionaries, schools, and newspapers form the background and also provide the explanation for a literary and intellectual awakening that occurred amongst the Turks in the latter half of the nineteenth century.

The best-known leaders of this awakening were Ibrahim Shinassi, Namik Kemal, and Abdul Hamid Ziya. These men did not agree on all issues, but they had all lived in Western Europe, and they had all been tremendously impressed by the thought and literature as well as the material achievements of the West. By 1865 a fairly well-defined group of young Western-minded writers had formed around the newspaper *Mushbir,* or *Herald of Glad Tidings.* The paper championed, among other things, the introduction of some form of constitutional representative government. This was too much for the imperial regime, which suppressed the paper in 1867. The editor and his colleagues were forced to flee to Paris and London, where they continued their journalistic attacks on the imperial regime.

Meanwhile, a few Turkish statesmen had realized that a comprehensive reform program along Western lines was essential for the survival of the empire. Outstanding were Reshid Pasha (1802–1858) and Midhat Pasha (1822–1884), both of whom served as grand viziers and issued numerous reform decrees. In May 1876, Midhat took advantage of a financial crisis at home and a revolution in the Balkan provinces to force Sultan Abdul Aziz to abdicate. He then prepared a constitution providing for an elected parliament, a bill of rights, and an independent judiciary. The new sultan, Abdul Hamid II, was forced to accept the constitution, but he had no intention of abiding by it. In January 1877, he dismissed Midhat from office and banished him from Constantinople. The only signs of protest were a few placards on walls. Turkish reformers still were faced with a mass inertia comparable to that which had doomed the Russian Decembrists in 1825. Consequently, Abdul Hamid was able to rule as the unchallenged master of his empire for the rest of the century.

During those decades Abdul Hamid kept himself in power by relentlessly combating the disruptive forces of nationalism and constitutionalism. To this end he discouraged travel and study abroad, maintained a great host of informers, and enforced a strict censorship of the press. Periodically his agents flushed out small groups of disaffected elements who usually fled to Paris for refuge. There they published periodicals and pamphlets criticizing the Hamidian autocracy and thus became popularly known in Western Europe as the *Young Turks.* These Turkish exiles were joined by revolutionary leaders of the various subject peoples under Abdul Hamid, including Arabs, Greeks, Armenians, Albanians, Kurds, and Jews. Representatives of all these nationalities held a congress in Paris in February 1902 with the aim of organizing a common front against the autocracy. But they quickly discovered that they agreed on nothing except that they all disliked the sultan. One group wanted Turkish predominance and centralized rule, while another favored a decentralized empire with full autonomy for the subject peoples.

While the exiled intellectuals were quarreling in Paris, reform-minded Turkish army leaders were taking decisive measures to break the Sultan's grip on the empire. Most of them had studied in the West or had contact with Western military missions within the empire. They had come to realize that the Sultan's rigid policy was obsolete and dangerous. They organized the Ottoman Society of Liberty with headquarters in Saloniki. Army officers were the backbone of this body, though they were greatly aided by other groups, and particularly by the Jews who were the most numerous and wealthy element in Saloniki. The Society of Liberty was organized into cells of five, so that no one knew more than four fellow members.

These conspirators openly revolted in July 1908. They telegraphed an ultimatum to the sultan threatening to march upon Constantinople unless the 1876 constitution were restored within twenty-four hours. Abdul Hamid was advised by his State Council to comply with the ultimatum, so he proclaimed the restoration of the constitution. The news of the Sultan's capitulation was greeted with wild rejoicing. Christians and Turks embraced one another in the streets. This euphoric atmosphere did not last long. The

THE SICK MAN OF EUROPE

During the nineteenth century the Ottoman Empire was known as the "sick man of Europe." Why it was sick is evident in the following account by the British merchant and diplomat Sir Charles Eliot. He describes his efforts to interest the Vali (Governor) of Karakeui in development projects, and the Vali's negative response.*

I suppose I might be described as a concession hunter or a commission agent. The essence of my trade is to make Orientals buy what they don't want—anything from matches to railroads. I bribe them to purchase my wares and they bribe me to put down in the bill (which the Ottoman Government pays) a much larger sum than I have actually received. So we both make money. . . .

"If you would only develop," [I told him,] "the commercial and material resources of your Empire, Christians and Turks would have a common interest. The Christians would want to support your Empire as the source of their prosperity.

"We Turks," [replied the Vali] don't know how to make money; we only know how to take it. You want to introduce a system in which Christians will be able to squeeze all the money out of us and our country and keep it. Who profit by all these concessions for railways, harbours, and quays? Franks, Jews, Greeks, and Armenians, but never a Moslim. Do you remember that railway I helped you to build from Durograd to Moropolis? Franks travel by it, Greeks and Armenians sell the tickets, and in the end all the money goes to the Jews. But what Turk wants the railway, and how much has any Turk made out of it?"

I might have said, "Exactly as much as passed into your Highness's pockets when the concession was arranged," but I forbore from this obvious retort and let the Vali go on. "This country is a dish of soup," he said, "and no one has any real intention except to eat it. We eat it in the good old-fashioned way with a big spoon. You bore little holes in the bottom of the soup-bowl and drain it off with pipes. Then you propose that the practice of eating soup with spoons should be abolished as uncivilised, because you know we have no gimlets and don't understand this trick of drinking through pipes."

"But surely your Highness has had experience yourself of the advantages which Osmanlis may obtain from commercial enterprises and—"

"Oh, I have had a suck at the pipe," said the Vali, "but, after all, I prefer eating with the spoon."

*Charles Eliot, *Turkey in Europe*, 2nd ed. (London: Edward Arnold, 1908), pp. 94–97.

issue of centralization versus decentralization that had divided the exiles in Paris now had to be faced as an urgent matter of policy rather than of theory. There were also conservative elements who distrusted all Young Turks, as the new leaders were generally called. The dissension came to a head on April 12, 1909, when the conservatives staged a counterrevolution in Constantinople and seized control of the capital. The Young Turks gathered their forces in Macedonia, marched on Constantinople, captured the city after a few hours' fighting, and then compelled Abdul Hamid to abdicate. The new sultan, Mohammed V, according to his own account had not read a newspaper in ten years. Accordingly, he served as a compliant figurehead for the Young Turks who now were the undisputed masters in Constantinople.

During the few years before the outbreak of World War I they tried to strengthen and modernize their empire, but with little success. They attempted a policy of centralization and Turkification. They tried to promote loyalty to the Ottoman Empire and the Ottoman Sultan rather than to the several minority nationalisms. But the more the Turks persisted, the more opposition they aroused. It was too late to deny the inexorable awakening of Albanians, Arabs, Greeks, Bulgarians, and other subject peoples. Thus the result was a vicious circle of repression and revolt. The Albanians took up arms in 1910, and two years later the Balkan states formed a league and turned upon the Turks. Meanwhile, Italy had invaded the African province of Tripolitania in 1911. The Young Turks thus found themselves almost continually at war until 1914, when they decided to throw in their lot with that of the Central Powers.

It is apparent, then, that the efforts of the Turks to adjust to the West had proven ineffective. Because of religious and historical traditions they had been more resistant to the West than the Russians, and for that very reason ended up much more vulnerable. Failing to develop their own industry, their armed forces remained dependent on Western arms as well as Western instructors. Indeed, the Ottoman Empire survived to World War I because of the conflicting interests and policies of the Great Powers rather than because of its own strength.

III. ARABS

Like the Balkan Christians, the Arab peoples were under Ottoman rule for four centuries. But they did not regard Ottoman rule as an onerous foreign yoke. In the first place, Ottoman administration in the early period was efficient and generally acceptable. The Arabs, who as Moslems thought in theocratic rather than secular, Western terms, regarded the Turks more as fellow Moslems than as foreigners. Consequently they felt a genuine affinity with the Moslem Ottoman Empire of which they were a part. In modern times this feeling was enhanced as a result of the aggressiveness of the Europeans who conquered ancient Moslem kingdoms in North Africa and Central and South Asia. Faced with such a formidable threat, the Arabs very naturally regarded the Turks as protectors, who—though they became increasingly corrupt and oppressive in the later period—were nevertheless still preferable to the infidels. These considerations explain why the Arabs lagged far behind the Balkan Christians in receptiveness to Western influences and in the development of nationalist aspirations.

The West's impact upon the modern Arab world may be said to begin on the day in 1798 when Napoleon landed in Egypt with his army of invasion. Napoleon's real objective had been to strike at Britain's position in the East, but, after Admiral Nelson destroyed his fleet near Alexandria, Napoleon gave up his objective and returned home. Yet his expedition had a lasting effect on Egypt, for it was more than a military affair. It was also a cultural incursion by the West into the heart of the Arab world. Napoleon brought with him the first printing press to reach Egypt, and he was accompanied by scientists who deciphered the ancient hieroglyphic writing, and engineers who prepared plans for joining the Mediterranean and Red Seas.

Napoleon also smashed the power of the established ruling class in Egypt during his brief campaign in that country. This paved the way for the rise to power of an Albanian adventurer of genius, Mehemet Ali. The historical significance of Mehemet Ali is that he was the first Middle Eastern potentate who sensed the significance of Western technology and used it efficiently to serve his purposes. His achievements were numerous and re-volutionary. He started the modern system of irrigation; introduced the cultivation of cotton, which quickly became the country's greatest resource; reopened the harbor of Alexandria; encouraged foreign trade; sent students to study abroad; opened schools of all varieties, though he himself was illiterate; and established a School of Translation, which translated into Arabic about 2000 European books between 1835 and 1848. Mehemet Ali also engaged foreign experts who helped him build the first modern army and navy in the Middle East. He even tried valiantly to build a modern industrial struc-ture in Egypt—and did erect a considerable number of factories in Cairo and Alexandria. These enterprises, however, eventually failed because of domestic deficiencies and the opposition of the European powers.

These accomplishments transformed Egypt into a formidable power. Mehemet easily overran Arabia, the Sudan, the island of Crete, and the entire Levant coast that today in-cludes Israel, Lebanon, and Syria. His plan was to create an Arab Empire out of the Ot-toman provinces south of Asia Minor. But this was not acceptable to Britain, which preferred the weak Ottoman Empire rather than a strong Arab Empire on the routes to India. Mehemet was forcefully compelled to surrender all his possessions except Egypt, where he remained the hereditary and autonomous ruler. Great Power interests had postponed the realization of Arab unity and independence and would continue to do so for over a century.

Thanks to Napoleon's expedition and to Mehemet Ali's herculean efforts, Egypt became by far the most significant bridgehead for Westernism in the Arab world. After 1870 Syria, which included the entire Levant coast at that time, rivaled Egypt as a center for Western influence. One reason was the flourishing commerce between Syria and Europe, including the large number of Syrian merchants who engaged in business ac-tivities abroad. These merchants had the same catalytic effect upon their countrymen at home as the Balkan merchants had in earlier decades. Another reason was the extensive missionary-educational activity carried on mostly by the French Jesuits and the American Presbyterians. They established schools in Syria that trained Arab students and printed and distributed Arab books. In this manner the Syrian Arabs rediscovered their past and learned about Western literature, ideology, and technology.

This stimulus from the outside was responsible for the earliest manifestations of Arab nationalism. The leaders at the outset were mostly Christian Arabs, since the Moslems did not enroll in the missionary schools until a later date. In 1860 Butros el Bustani, a con-vert to Protestantism, began publication of his newspaper *Nafir Suriya (Syrian Trumpet)*. Ten years later he founded a political, literary, and scientific journal, *El Jenan (The Shield)*. Its motto was "Love of our country is an article of faith"—a nationalistic sentiment hitherto unknown in the Arab world.

Bustani and the other pioneer nationalists could not carry on political agitation openly because of the repressive measures of the Ottoman authorities. Consequently, the first avowedly political activity was the organization of a secret revolutionary society in 1875 by five students at the Protestant College. They drew up a national program which included demands for self-government, freedom of the press, and the adoption of Arabic as an official language. Turkish officials conducted an investigation and attempted to uncover the secret society's leadership. The society became alarmed and dissolved their organization in 1878. Then they made their way to Egypt, where the imperial agents had little control and where conditions were more promising for modern-minded Arabs.

The Western-educated Syrian intellectuals published newspapers and magazines which acquainted Egyptians with liberal and scientific French and British currents of thought. At the same time the deciphering of the hieroglyphs, the establishment of museums, and the development of Egyptology stimulated an awareness of Egypt's ancient history and a pride in its achievements. This budding nationalism was further aroused by the growing Western domination of the country. The domination was imposed because Khedive Ismail's heavy borrowing on the European money markets had led to bankruptcy and ultimately to foreign military intervention and rule. During the sixteen years of Ismail's reign the funded debt rose from £3 million to £68 million. The Egyptians, like the Turks, were unaccustomed to the wiles of unscrupulous international financiers and were mercilessly fleeced. Loans that normally brought 6 or 7 percent elsewhere were made to the Egyptians at anywhere between 12 and 27 percent.

By 1876 Ismail was bankrupt and was forced to accept an international Public Debt Commission. This body saw to it that all obligations were promptly met, but the country was bled white in the process. The total revenue in 1877 amounted to £9,543,000, of which £7,473,000 had to be paid out for the service of the debt, and other amounts, for fixed obligations such as the annual tribute to the Sultan. Only a little over £1 million was left for the administration of the country, a sum that was patently inadequate.

Under these circumstances a nationalist revolt broke out in 1882 under the leadership of an Egyptian army officer, Ahmed Arabi. It was directed partly against foreign intervention in Egyptian affairs and partly against the khedive and the Turkish oligarchy that monopolized all the senior posts in both the army and the bureaucracy. After some rioting and loss of life in Alexandria, a British fleet bombarded the fortifications of Alexandria in July 1882, and two months later an expeditionary force landed in Egypt and defeated Arabi. The expeditionary force remained to become an army of occupation. Egypt was still nominally a Turkish province, but Britain now controlled the country in every respect—economically, politically, and militarily.

These events naturally provoked strong antiforeign sentiment in Egypt, but it was directed more against the Westerners than against the Turks. At this time only a handful of Christian Arab leaders wished to break away from Constantinople. The Moslem masses were still largely apathetic, while the small minority of politically conscious Moslems simply wanted autonomy within the Ottoman imperial structure.

With the Young Turk revolt of 1908 it appeared that this desire would be satisfied. The Arabs, like the other peoples of the empire, welcomed the revolt with unrestrained enthusiasm. But the enthusiasm proved short-lived, for the Young Turk leaders soon resorted to severe Turkification measures in a desperate attempt to hold the empire together against foreign military aggression and internal nationalist subversion. The Arabs resented this repression, as did the Balkan Christians. Yet the great majority of Arabs still aspired to autonomy rather than independence.

Such were the sentiments of the great majority of Arabs until the outbreak of World War I. Then the decision of the Young Turk leaders to throw in their lot with the Central Powers changed the situation overnight. It precipitated a chain reaction of events that culminated in the great Arab Revolt of 1916, and finally in the disappearance of the Ottoman Empire after World War I.

SUGGESTED READING

F. Ahmad, *The Young Turks* (Oxford University Press, 1970); R. H. Davison, *Reform in the Ottoman Empire, 1856–1876* (Princeton University Press, 1964); C. E. Dawn, *From Ottomanism to Arabism: Essays on the Origins of Arab Nationalism* (University of Illinois Press, 1973); A. Hourani, *Economic History of the Middle East 1800–1914* (University of Chicago Press, 1966); B. Lewis, *The Middle East and the West* (University of Indiana Press, 1964); L. S. Stavrianos, *The Balkans Since 1453* (Holt, Rinehart & Winston, 1958).

India is the one great non-Western society that has been, not merely attacked and hit, but overrun and conquered outright by Western arms, and not merely conquered by Western arms but ruled, after that, by Western administrators. . . . India's experience of the West has thus been more painful and more humiliating than China's or Turkey's, and much more so than Russia's or Japan's.

Arnold J. Toynbee

chapter 26

India

Prior to the appearance of the British, India had been invaded time and time again—by the Aryans, Greeks, Scythians, Turks, and Moguls. Each of these invaders left its mark on the great subcontinent, contributing in varying degrees to the evolution of India's traditional society. The historical role of the British was to disrupt and remold this traditional society. The other invaders wrought changes mostly at the top, but the British impact was felt down to the level of the village. The reason for this difference between the British and their predecessors is to be found in the dynamic and expansive nature of British society, which consequently undermined the comparatively static and self-sufficient society of India. To understand this process of penetration and transformation it is necessary first to study the character of the traditional Indian society. Then we shall consider the nature of the British impact and the Indian reaction to it.

I. INDIA'S TRADITIONAL SOCIETY

The basic unit of traditional Indian society was the village, as it was in most of the rest of the world, including Europe, in the preindustrial period. Within the village it was not the individual that mattered, but rather the joint family and the caste. This group form of organization was a source of social stability but also of national weakness. Loyalty to the family, to the caste, and to the village was the primary consideration, and this prevented the formation of a national spirit.

The land was regarded by immemorial custom as the property of the sovereign, who was entitled to a share of the gross produce or its equivalent. This constituted the land tax that was the main source of state revenue and the main burden of the cultivator. The share paid to the state varied from period to period from a sixth to a third or even half. Usually the responsibility for making this payment, whether in produce or in money, was collective, resting upon the village as a unit. Peasants had hereditary right to the use of the land so long as each paid their share of the taxes.

Transportation and communication facilities were primitive, so the villages tended to become economically and socially self-sufficient. Each village had its potter, who turned out on his wheel the simple utensils needed by the peasants; its carpenter, who constructed and repaired the buildings and ploughs; its blacksmith, who made axes and other necessary tools; its clerk, who attended to legal documents and wrote out correspondence between people of different villages; its town herdsman, who looked after the cattle and returned them at night to the various owners; its priest and its teacher, who frequently were combined in the same person; and its astrologer, who indicated the auspicious time for planting, for harvesting, for marriages, and other important events. These artisans and professionals served their villages on something akin to a barter basis. They were paid for their services with grain from the cultivating households or with tax-free village land for their own use. These hereditary and traditional divisions of occupation and function were turned into obligations by the caste system.

The political structure of the village consisted of an annually elected council of five or more, known to this day as the *Panchayat* (''Pancha'' meaning ''five''). The Panchayat, which normally consisted of caste leaders and village elders, met periodically to dispense local justice, to collect taxes, to keep in repair the village wells, roads, and irrigation systems, to see that the craftsmen and other professionals were provided for, and to extend hospitality to travelers passing through the village and furnish them with guides. The village had little contact with the outside world apart from the payment of the land tax and the irregular demand for forced labor. The combination of agriculture and hand industry made each village largely independent of the rest of the country except for a few indispensables like salt and iron. Consequently, the towns that existed in traditional India were not industrial in character. Rather, they were religious centers such as Benares, Puri, and Allahabad, political centers such as Poona, Tanjore, and Delhi, or commercial centers such as Mirzapur on the trade route from central India to Bengal.

Some Indian writers have romanticized this traditional society, painting an idyllic picture of village life continuing peacefully generation after generation in its slow and satisfying rhythm. It is true that the existence of group organizations such as the joint family, the caste, and the village council provided the peasants with both psychological and economic security. Each individual had recognized duties, rights, and status in his native village. If the central government was sufficiently strong to maintain order and to keep the land tax down to the customary sixth of the harvest, then the peasant masses did lead a peaceful and contented existence. But as often as not the central government was too weak to keep order, and the villagers were mercilessly fleeced by greedy tax collectors and by robber bands. This was the case in the seventeenth century when the Mogul imperial structure was disintegrating. Yet even in such trying periods the Indian village was not transformed in any basic respect. Individual regions were ravaged, but eventually the cultivators returned to resume their traditional institutions and their traditional ways of life.

II. BRITISH CONQUEST

The Indian village was relatively unchanging and self-sufficient until the coming of the British. But before examining the impact of these Western intruders we shall consider the reasons why they were able with comparatively little difficulty to conquer the whole of India during the late eighteenth and nineteenth centuries. This is a real question, because for 250 years after Albuquerque had captured Goa early in the sixteenth century the Europeans had been able only to cling to a few stations along the coasts. Then within a few decades the balance of power shifted decisively and the whole of the Indian subcontinent fell under British rule.

One reason for this outcome was the decline of Mogul power and authority. This enabled Moslem warlords and provincial governors to declare their independence and establish personal dynasties in various regions. At the same time the Hindus asserted themselves by organizing the powerful Maratha confederacy with its center in the city of Poona. The Marathas won control of the entire Deccan and then, about 1740, began to invade northern India with the intention of displacing the declining Moguls. Thus India was in an anarchical state in the eighteenth century, with various officials seeking to convert their posts into hereditary princedoms and plotting with any power, whether Indian or foreign, in order to realize their ambitions. The British consequently were able to play off one Indian prince against another until they became the masters of the entire peninsula. This was altogether different from China, where the Manchu imperial structure remained intact and compelled all foreigners to deal directly with the emperor in Peking.

Another important factor that contributed substantially to the vulnerability of India was the rise of a powerful merchant class whose economic interests were bound up with those of the Western companies. These companies were allowed to trade relatively freely in India (they were almost entirely excluded in China). During the sixteenth century India's economy was little affected by the trade because it was confined largely to spices and textiles. But in the seventeenth century various commercial crops such as indigo, mustard seed, and hemp, as well as saltpeter, were exported in large quantities. Bengal was the center of this trade, and in that province there now arose wealthy native merchants who dominated the local economy and who were becoming increasingly restless under the corrupt and inefficient rule of the Mogul officials. One of these merchants, Jagat Seth, bought the allegiance of the generals who supposedly were under the orders of the nawab, or governor, of Bengal. At the Battle of Plassey (1757) these generals refrained from fighting against the British, who lost only sixty-five men in that fateful encounter. As one Indian historian has put it, Plassey was "a transaction, not a battle."

The British now were the actual rulers of Bengal, though they continued to recognize puppet nawabs as a matter of form. In 1764, after defeating the Mogul's forces, the East India Company was granted the Diwani, or the right of tax collection, in the rich provinces of Bengal, Bihar, and Orissa. This opened up many opportunities for profit making and outright extortion, and the English agents exploited them to the full. By raising the taxes, controlling the trade, and accepting numerous "gifts" from native officials, they amassed fortunes for themselves and their superiors in London.

The foothold in Bengal gave the British the base and the resources necessary for further expansion in India. At that time there were four other contenders for the Mogul domains—the French, the Moslem rulers of Mysore and of Hyderabad, and the Maratha Confederacy. The French were eliminated during the course of the Seven Years' War, as they were forced to surrender virtually all their posts in India by the Treaty of Paris of 1763 (see Chapter 19, section IV). Then during the American Revolution the British were challenged in India by a coalition of the three principal native powers. The governor-general, Warren Hastings, managed to hold out and later took the offensive. By 1800 only the British and the Marathas were left, and during the following years the British gradually prevailed because of dissension within the Maratha Confederacy. By 1818 the back of the Marathas had been broken, though some fighting continued with them as well as with the Sikhs in the Punjab.

After they had established themselves in the heart of the subcontinent, the British began pushing northward in a search of natural frontiers. To the northeast, in Himalayan Nepal, they defeated the Gurkhas who henceforth fought on the side of the British. Likewise to the northwest they finally defeated the proud Sikhs of the Punjab. Thus by the middle of the nineteenth century the British were the masters of all India, from the Indus to the Brahmaputra, and from the Himalayas to Cape Comorin. A few major kingdoms still survived, including Kashmir, Hyderabad, Baroda, and Travancore, but these were now dependent territories, isolated from each other, and powerless against the might of Britain.

III. BRITISH RULE

We have seen that the East India Company was at first outrageously exploitive in its administration of the Indian territories it controlled. The excesses aroused public opinion in Britain and prompted Parliament to pass acts in 1773 and 1784 that placed the company under the supervision of the London government. The company continued to trade, and its servants and soldiers continued to govern and fight in India, but it functioned under the watchful eye of Parliament and the British government. This arrangement continued, with various modifications, until the Indian Mutiny of 1857.

The mutiny was not the national movement or war of independence that some Indian writers have called it. Rather it was primarily a military outbreak that was exploited by certain discontented princes and landlords whose interests had been harmed by the British. Lord Dalhousie, the governor-general between 1848 and 1856, had dispossessed many princes and aroused uneasiness and suspicion amongst those who remained. Other groups, too, were dissatisfied: Conservative elements of the Indian population were deeply disturbed by the introduction of the railway and telegraph, the opening of Western-type schools, the aggressive activities of certain Christian missionaries, the legalization or remarriage by widows, and the abolition of practices such as infanticide and suttee, or the self-cremation of widows on their husbands' funeral pyres. The Sepoys, as the Indian soldiers serving in the British forces were called, were disaffected because of prolonged campaigning in distant lands and the refusal of extra allowances for such service. The spark that set off the uprising was the introduction of cartridges that were greased with cow and pig fat, obnoxious to both the Hindus and the Moslems. All these factors combined to make the mutiny assume the proportions of a popular uprising in certain scattered regions.

When the mutiny began on May 10, 1857, the British were caught by surprise and forced to go on the defensive. But the revolt did not spread throughout the country. It was confined largely to the north. Even there most of the important native states remained loyal to the British and gave invaluable assistance. Thus after about four months the British were able to counterattack, and, by July 1858, the mutiny had been crushed. Both sides were guilty of brutality. The Indians murdered many captives, and the English burned down villages and indiscriminately killed the inhabitants.

A month after the suppression of the Indian Mutiny, Parliament passed the India Act ending the rule of the East India Company and substituting that of the crown. Henceforth India was ruled by a vast hierarchy with its base in India and its apex in London in the person of the secretary of state for India. This official was a member of the cabinet and generally was allowed a free hand by his colleagues. The top official in India was the governor-general, or viceroy, acting as the direct representative of the crown, and usually appointed for a five-year term. The viceroy was assisted by an executive council of five members, none of them Indian until 1909. Beneath these top officials was the famous Indian Civil Service which collected the revenues, maintained law and order, and supervised the judicial system. Prior to 1919 almost all the members of this small but elite group consisted of British graduates of Oxford and Cambridge. The civil service in turn supervised a subordinate provincial service that was exclusively Indian in personnel. It was through these Indian officials in the lower ranks of the bureaucracy that the authority of the government penetrated to the masses.

The efficiency of British rule in India is reflected in the fact that in 1900 there were a total of 4000 British civilian administrators in the country compared to 500,000 Indian. And in 1910 the Indian army comprised 69,000 Britishers and 130,000 Indians. It should be noted that Britain's position in India was based not only on the army and the bureaucracy but also on the surviving Indian princes. Prior to the Indian Mutiny the British often had no compunction about taking over principalities when it suited them to do so. But this policy was reversed following the mutiny, so that India remained thenceforth a crazy-quilt pattern of some 550 native states intermingled with British Indian provinces. The reason for this change of policy was made clear in 1860 by Lord Canning, the first viceroy following the mutiny: "If we could keep up a number of Native States without political power, but as royal instruments, we should exist in India as long as our naval supremacy was maintained."[1]

IV. BRITISH IMPACT

The British impact upon India was felt first in the economic field, and naturally so since the British arrived in India in search of markets and commodities. Particularly after they became masters of the country, the British affected its economy decisively, especially by their taxation and trade policies. Since they were unfamiliar with the Mogul revenue system and lacked experienced personnel, the British decided with their Permanent Settlement of 1793 to recognize the former imperial tax farmers and district revenue officers as English-type landlords, or zamindars. The "permanent" feature of this arrangement was that the annual sum expected of the zamindars was frozen at £3 million, while they were free, as landlords, to raise the rents they collected from the peasants. This was easy to do as land values were rising and the peasants now were tenants-at-will rather than hereditary cultivators of village lands. By World War II the landlords were collecting 12 to 20 million pounds annually, leaving them a huge surplus which, unlike their English counterparts, they did not use to improve their holdings. Nevertheless the British preserved this arrangement because, as Governor-General William Bentinck observed, it "created a vast body of rich landed proprietors deeply interested in the continuance of British Dominion and having complete command over the mass of the people."[2] This Permanent Settlement was confined to the Ganges basin. Elsewhere the British either collected the land taxes directly or from village communities. Their levies were not heavier than those of the Mogul period, but they had to be paid in cash, and there was less chance now of evading payment.

As regards trade, there was a strong demand in the nineteenth century for Indian raw materials such as jute, oilseeds, wheat, and cotton. These commodities were transported to the seaports by a newly built railroad network totaling 4000 miles by 1870 and 41,000 miles by 1939. The opening of the Suez Canal also facilitated the export of Indian raw materials by reducing the distance traversed by freighters between London and Karachi from 10,800 to 6100 miles. Thus India became one of the world's important sources of raw materials. And because of the high prices commanded by these materials, India was left with a favorable balance of trade throughout the nineteenth century.

The resulting capital surplus could have been used to develop modern industry. The fact that this was not done doomed India to its present critical state of underdevelopedness. Britain made no attempt to encourage manufacturing in India and, in certain crucial areas such as textiles, actively discouraged it. Thus there was no chance to erect tariffs to protect Indian infant industries against the tidal wave of cheap machine-made products from British factories. Indian economic historians describe this as a case of "aborted modernization." India had entered the world market and earned large sums of capital with no structural change in its outmoded national economy. In place of the economic modernization that had occurred in Europe, the British and their associates "skimmed cash crops off the surface of an immobilized agrarian society."[3]

Meanwhile, thanks to Western medical science, health measures, and famine-relief arrangements, India's population rose from 255 million in 1872 to 305 million in 1921. Similar population growth had occurred earlier in Europe but had been absorbed by new factories in the cities. Since no such industrialization occurred in India, the new extra millions could only fall back on agriculture. They naturally put a terrible overpressure on the land. And this remains to the present day one of the most acute problems of the Indian economy—and indeed of most Third World economies since they also suffer from "aborted modernization," and for the same reason.

British rule affected India profoundly in intellectual matters as well as economic. The impact began in 1823 when the British appointed a Committee on Public Instruction to determine educational policy. The committee split between the "Anglicists" who wished to encourage an English type of education, and the "Orientalists" who favored a traditional education based on Sanskrit, Arabic, and Persian. The deadlock was broken in 1835 when Committee President Thomas Babington Macauley issued his famous Minute on Education. This adopted the Anglicist position, concluding that "English is better worth knowing than Sanskrit or Arabic. . . ." Macauley added that

it is impossible for us, with our limited means, to attempt to educate the body of the people. We must at present do our best to form a class who may be interpreters between us and the millions whom we govern; a class of persons, Indian in blood and color, but English in taste, in opinions, in morals, and in intellect.[4]

Macauley worked hard to implement his recommendation as soon as it was officially adopted. During the following decades a national system of education was worked out. It consisted of universities, training colleges for teachers, high schools, and vernacular elementary schools designed for the masses. Between 1885 and 1900 the number of students in colleges and universities rose from 11,000 to 23,000, and those in secondary schools, from 429,000 to 633,000. At the same time the introduction of the printing press greatly stimulated intellectual life in India. Sanskrit works became public property rather than the jealously guarded monopoly of *Brahmins*. And newspapers appeared published in the various modern Indian languages as well as in English.

These developments affected the intellectual climate of India profoundly. They did not touch the masses, who remained completely illiterate. Nor, at first, did they reach the Moslems, who remained generally hostile to the new schools and books. Thus, English education became almost the exclusive possession of a small Hindu upper class. But this was enough to start off a chain reaction that has continued to the present day. English education created a new class of Indians familiar with foreign languages and cultures, and committed to liberal and rational ideologies. This Western-educated class used European ideology to attack British domination and to organize a nationalist movement that eventually culminated in an independent India.

V. INDIAN NATIONALISM

Britain's intellectual impact stimulated an upsurge and a creativity in Indian thought and culture that is commonly known as the Indian Renaissance. To appreciate the significance of this movement, we should note that when the British arrived upon the scene *Hinduism* was in a rather depressed and demoralized state. During the preceding seven hundred years of Moslem domination, Hinduism had been looked down upon as the idolatrous religion of a subject race. It lacked prestige, organization, and active leadership. But when the British overthrew Mogul rule, Hinduism for the first time in seven centuries was on a par with Islam. And when the British opened their schools, the Hindus, unlike the Moslems, flocked to them eagerly. By so doing, they benefited in two ways: they filled the posts in the new bureaucracy, and they experienced an intellectual revival because of their Western contacts.

The stimulus of the West provoked three types of reaction or three schools of thought amongst the Hindus, although the lines were by no means clear-cut and there was much overlapping. The first was wholeheartedly and uncritically pro-Western and antitraditional: everything Western was accepted as superior and preferable.

The second reaction was one of complete rejection. The West was admittedly stronger, but its ideas were subversive and its customs repugnant. No true Indian, Hindu, or Moslem should compromise with the evil West. Rather one should withdraw so far as possible from contact with the foreigner and live one's own life in the traditional way. Proponents of this view regarded caste rule as unchangeable, accepted the authority of the Hindu classics without reservations, and opposed such reforms as the abolition of suttee or of infanticide.

The third and most common reaction to the West represented a compromise between blind worship and outright rejection. It accepted the essence of Western secularism and learning, but it also sought to reform Hinduism from within and to preserve its basic truths while ridding it of corruptions and grossly unhuman practices. The outstanding leader of this school of thought was Ram Mohan Roy, widely venerated as "The Father of Modern India." Born in 1772 in a devout Brahman family of Bengal, he broke with his parents over the spectacle of his sister's torture on the funeral pyre of her husband. An insatiable student, he mastered Persian, Arabic, and Sanskrit, and then learned English and entered the service of the government. He was fascinated by Western thought and religions, and he studied Greek and Hebrew in order to read the Scriptures in the original. Roy rejected formal doctrinal Christianity but accepted its humanitarian message. Roy also reinterpreted Hinduism in his Brahmo Samaj, or Society of God, a new reformed sect of Hinduism which he founded. The Samaj was a synthesis of the doctrines of the European Enlightenment with the philosophical views of the Upanishads. Roy was above all a rationalist who believed that Hinduism rested squarely upon reason. This principle established, he proceeded both to prune current Hindu practices and to borrow freely from the West. Thus he left his followers a creed that enabled them to face the West without losing their identity or their self-respect.

Ram Mohan Roy was the pioneer leader not only of India's religious renaissance but also of its political awakening, or nationalist movement. This was a new phenomenon in India. Hitherto there had been cultural unity and regional loyalties but no all-Indian feeling of patriotism. Nationalism developed under British rule for several reasons. One was the "superiority complex" of the English—their conviction that they were a racial elite and divinely ordained to rule India permanently. This racism, which was particularly strong following the mutiny, manifested itself in all fields—in the army and the bureaucracy, where Indians could not rise above certain ranks regardless of their qualifications, and in social life, where Indians were excluded from certain hotels, clubs, and parks. Under these circumstances it was inevitable that the Indians should counter with the gradual development of a sense of cultural and national consciousness.

The British also stimulated nationalism by imposing an unprecedented unity upon the Indian peninsula. For the first time the whole of India was under one rule. The British also forged a physical unity with their railways and telegraph and postal services. Equally important was the linguistic unity that followed the adoption of English as the common speech of the educated.

The British system of education introduced the whole body of Western literature and political thought into the country and thereby furthered Indian nationalism. The principles of liberalism and nationalism, of personal freedom and self-determination, inevitably were turned against the foreign British rule. The Indian leaders used not only Western political principles but also Western political techniques. Newspapers, platform oratory, pamphleteering, mass meetings, and monster petitions—all were used as grist for the nationalist mill.

Among the early Indian nationalist leaders, three are especially noteworthy. The first is Dadabhai Naoroji (1825–1917), an Indian businessman who lived for many years in London and who, in fact, was elected in 1892 to the House of Commons on the Liberal ticket. Naoroji emphasized the drain of India's wealth to Britain, and he secured the appointment of a parliamentary commission to investigate the financial administration of British India. M. G. Ranade (1842–1901), another distinguished leader, was disqualified from entering active politics because he was a judge, so he concentrated on social and economic reform. After careful study of India's problems, he concluded that the greatest need was for rapid industrialization under British auspices, and he bent his efforts towards the realization of this goal. Ranade's disciple was G. K. Gokhale (1866–1915), who also was interested primarily in economic problems. As a member of the Legislative Council he raised the cry, "No taxation without representation," and his annual speeches on the imperial budget forced many tax reductions and financial reforms.

All these men were "moderates," in the sense that they accepted British rule and sought merely to win certain concessions. Accordingly, they cooperated in supporting the Indian National Congress founded in 1885. The expressed aim of this body was to obtain parliamentary government, which was considered to be compatible with loyalty to Britain.

This first generation of Indian nationalists, then, were admirers of Great Britain and apostles of cooperation. But after 1890 these "moderates" were challenged by the extremists led by Bal Gangadhar Tilak (1856–1920), the "father of Indian unrest." Tilak was a militant crusader who sought to transform the nationalist cause from an upper-class to a popular mass movement. This may explain his dogmatic support of many Hindu social customs. He even went so far as to organize a cow-protection society and to support child marriage. Yet at the same time he fought for a minimum wage for labor, freedom for trade-union organization, creation of a citizen army, universal franchise, and free and compulsory education without distinction as to sex. Tilak won followers throughout the country with slogans such as, "Educate, Agitate, and Organize," "Militancy, not mendicancy," and "Freedom is my birthright and I will have it."

Tilak was aided in his crusade by a series of famines and plagues in the 1890s that gave impetus to the growing sense of grievance. Indian militancy was also aroused by the revolution in Russia in 1905 and by Japan's defeat of Russia in the same year. The latter event was particularly exciting because it was taken as a refutation of the claim of Western superiority. At this point the Indian government passed in 1905 an act for the partition of Bengal into two provinces: the new East Bengal with 18 million Moslems and 12 million Hindus, and the remaining Bengal with 42 million Hindus and 12 million Moslems. The government's aim was to improve administration, for the original province had been too large, and the area east of the Ganges had been neglected. But to the Indian nationalists it appeared that, by dividing Bengal into predominantly Moslem and predominantly Hindu sections, the British were following a policy of divide and rule. This issue united the nationalists throughout the country more than ever before. They fought the government very effectively with the slogans "Swaraj," or self-government within the British Empire, and "Swadeshi," or boycott of British goods. The strong feelings aroused by the Bengal issue enabled the extremists to control the 1906 meeting of the Indian Congress and to secure a majority vote in favor of Swaraj and Swadeshi. Some of the nationalists went further, and, following the example and methods of the underground in Ireland and Russia, resorted to acts of terrorism.

Widespread though it was, this nationalist movement was predominantly Hindu. Under the leadership of Sir Sayyid Ahmad Khan, the Moslems had for the most part stayed out of the Indian Congress. They foresaw that if the Congress's demand for representative government were satisfied, the Moslems would suffer as a permanent minority. The Moslems also were alarmed by the increasing strength and militancy of Hindu nationalism, particularly since some of the most ardent Hindu patriots referred to the Moslems as "foreigners." In self-protection the Moslems organized the Moslem League, which, like the Indian Congress, held annual meetings. The British naturally

INDIA FOR THE INDIANS

B. G. Tilak was an early Indian nationalist who demanded that the British get out and raised the slogan "India for the Indians." This nationalist feeling is clear in the following selection from a speech by Tilak in 1906.*

One fact is that this alien government has ruined the country. In the beginning, all of us were taken by surprise. We were almost dazed. We thought that everything that the rulers did was for our good and that this English government has descended from the clouds to save us from the invasions of Tamerlane and Chingis Khan, and, as they say, not only from foreign invasions but from internecine [civil] warfare. We felt happy for a time, but it soon came to light that the peace which was established in this country did this....—that we were prevented from going at each other's throats, so that a foreigner might go at the throat of us all. *Pax Britannica* [British peace or rule] has been established in this country in order that a foreign government may exploit the country. That this is the effect of this *Pax Britannica* is being gradually realised in these days. It was an unhappy circumstance that it was not realised sooner.... English education, growing poverty, and better familiarity with our rulers, opened our eyes and our leaders....

Your industries are ruined utterly, ruined by foreign rule; your wealth is going out of the country and you are reduced to the lowest level which no human being can occupy. In this state of things, is there any other remedy by which you can help yourself? The remedy is not petitioning but boycott. We say prepare your forces, organize your power, and then go to work so that they cannot refuse you what you demand.... Every Englishman knows that they are a mere handful in this country and it is the business of every one of them to befool you in believing that you are weak and they are strong. This is politics. We have been deceived by such policy so long. What the new party wants you to do is to realize the fact that your future rests entirely in your own hands. ... We shall not give them assistance to collect revenue and keep peace. We shall not assist them in fighting beyond the frontiers or outside India with Indian blood and money. We shall not assist them in carrying on the administration of justice. We shall have our own courts, and when time comes we shall not pay taxes. Can you do that by your united efforts? If you can, you are free from tomorrow....

* B. G. Tilak, *His Writings and Speeches* (Madras: Ganesh and Co., 1923), pp. 55–67.

welcomed and supported the League as a counterweight to the Congress. The League's existence, however, did not result from British machinations, but rather from the error of many nationalist leaders such as Tilak who based their campaigns on a revival of Hinduism. The formation of cow-protection societies, for example, undoubtedly aided the nationalist movement. But it also alienated Moslem Indians who naturally felt apprehensive about their future in a Hindu-controlled India.

Meanwhile, the spread of terrorism and the growing dissatisfaction of even the ''moderates'' convinced the British government that some concession was necessary. Accordingly, in 1909 the secretary of state for India, Lord Morley, and the viceroy, Lord Minto, presented the so-called Morley-Minto Reforms. These provided that a very small group of Indian voters, selected on the basis of high property, income, or education qualifications, should elect a majority of the members in the Legislative Councils of the provincial governors and a minority of members in the viceroy's Legislative Council. A specified proportion of the legislative seats were reserved for Hindus and Moslems, and Moslem representation was weighted very considerably. For example, to become an elector, the Moslem had to pay income tax on an income of 3000 rupees a year, the non-Moslem on an income of 300,000 rupees. Furthermore, even where an elective majority existed, as in the provincial councils, the British government could, and was prepared to, override any opposition. Thus the reforms were in no way designed to introduce responsible government. Rather they were intended to split the opposition by apparently permitting representative government but leaving full power and final decisions in British hands.

The strategy succeeded quite well. The moderate nationalists, who had regained control of the Congress, passed a resolution expressing ''deep and general satisfaction at the Reform proposals.'' They were further placated when the British made several more concessions in 1911. The British annulled the unpopular partition of Bengal, released certain political prisoners, and granted substantial sums for educational purposes. Thus although individual acts of terrorism continued sporadically, India was relatively tranquil between 1910 and 1914.

Throughout this period, the nationalist movement was confined largely to the intellectuals. True, the National Congress had grown remarkably during the quarter-century following its establishment in 1885. Its membership was drawn from all parts of British India rather than from Bengal and a few cities on the west coast, as was originally the case. Yet the fact remains that it was almost exclusively a middle-class movement of lawyers, journalists, teachers, and merchants. These people were more familiar with John Stuart Mill, Herbert Spencer, and Charles Darwin than with the misery, grievances, and aspirations of the masses of their own countrymen in the villages. Not unnaturally, there was little rapport between the nationalist leaders and the illiterate peasants. The gulf persisted until bridged by Mohandas Gandhi in the postwar period. And Gandhi succeeded because he sensed the essentially religious outlook of his people and preached, not political abstractions, but religious concepts to which he gave a political meaning (see Chapter 32, section IV).

In conclusion, the impact of the West on India was quite different from its impact on Russia or the Middle East. In the case of Russia, the West exerted decisive cultural and economic influence, but Russia remained politically and militarily strong and independent. The Near East, on the other hand, was dominated economically and militarily by the West, yet, because of strategic considerations, the Ottoman Empire managed to retain its independence until World War I. India, by contrast, was conquered outright by Britain during the late eighteenth and nineteenth centuries. British rule lasted for nearly two centuries in Bengal and for more than one century in the Punjab. Consequently India did not have the privilege of picking and choosing those features of European civilization that were most appealing. It was subjected to the Western impact more indiscriminately than any other major region of Asia.

SUGGESTED READING

See bibliography for Chapter 6. Also see the following: P. Griffiths, *The British Impact on India* (Macdonald, 1952); M. D. Lewis, ed., *The British in India: Imperialism or Trusteeship* (D. C. Heath, 1962); R. P. Masani, *Britain in India* (Oxford University Press, 1961); L.S.S. O'Malley, *Modern India and the West* (Oxford University Press, 1941); J. R. McLane, *Indian Nationalism and Early Congress* (Princeton University Press, 1977), and his *Political Awakening in India* (Prentice-Hall, 1970); S. A. Wolpert, *Tilak and Gokhale: Revolution and Reform in the Making of Modern India* (University of California Press, 1962); P. Woodruff, *The Men Who Ruled India*, 2 vols. (J. Cape, 1954–1955).

The historian who grasps the true secret of Japan's success in rapid Westernization has a key to modern Far Eastern history.

John K. Fairbank

chapter 27

China
And
Japan

The Far East was the last major region of Eurasia to feel the impact of expanding Europe. Various factors explain why China and Japan followed behind Russia, the Near East, and India in this respect. First, and most obvious, is the fact that the Far East, by definition, is that portion of the Eurasian continent that is farthest removed from Europe. China and Japan do not touch upon Europe, as did the Russian and Ottoman empires. And they are much further to the east and north than India. Probably more significant than geographic isolation was the political unity of the two Far Eastern countries. In China and Japan the European intruders were not able to employ the divide-and-rule policy that had proven so effective in India. There were no independent local potentates who could be enlisted against the central governments in Peking and Tokyo. And, thanks to the rigid seclusion policies of both these governments, there were no native merchants ready to collaborate with the Europeans.

Consequently, the Far Eastern countries were able to limit their contact with Europe to a mere trickle of closely supervised trade. But in the mid-nineteenth century the situation changed suddenly and drastically. First China and then Japan were forced to open their doors and to accept Western merchants, missionaries, consuls, and gunboats. Both of the Far Eastern countries were fundamentally affected, though in very different ways. Japan adopted and used the instruments of Western power. It was able to exploit them for self-defense and, later, for aggrandizement. China, by contrast, was unable to reorganize itself to meet the Western challenge. But it was too large and cohesive to be conquered outright, like India and the countries of Southeast Asia. So China remained in an uncomfortable and unstable state until World War I, and even for some decades thereafter.

I. OPENING OF CHINA

Over a period of 4000 years the Chinese people developed a unique and self-contained society at the extreme eastern end of the Eurasian landmass. This society, like others in Asia, was based on agriculture rather than trade and was governed by landlords and bureaucrats rather than by merchants and politicians. It was a distinctly self-centered and self-assured society that regarded the rest of the world as inferior and subordinate.

The Chinese first came into direct contact with the West when the Portuguese appeared off the southeast coast in 1514. After the Portuguese came the Dutch and the British, who also arrived by sea. The Russians in the north came overland to the Amur valley. The Chinese resolutely kept all these intruders at arm's length (see Chapter 13, section IV). They restricted commercial relations to a few ports and refused to establish diplomatic relations on a full and equal basis.

The Chinese were forcefully jarred out of their seclusion and complacency by three disastrous wars; the first with Britain in 1839–1842, the second with Britain and France in 1856–1858, and the third with Japan in 1895. Britain was able to take the lead in opening up China because it had a powerful base in India as well as control of the seas. Britain's main objective in forcing the issue was to remove the many obstacles that the Chinese placed in the way of trading operations. The immediate issue that started hostilities between Britain and China was the trade in opium. European sailors had introduced opium smoking in China in the seventeenth century, and the habit spread rapidly from the ports. The demand for opium solved the British problem of paying for Chinese products. Hitherto the British had been forced to pay mostly in gold and silver, because the Chinese were little interested in Western goods. But now the market for opium reversed the balance of trade in favor of the British. The Peking government issued decrees in 1729 and 1799 prohibiting the importation of opium, but the trade was so profitable that Chinese officials could be bribed to permit smuggling.

The first Anglo-Chinese War, or Opium War as it is frequently called, broke out when the Chinese attempted to enforce their prohibition of the opium traffic. The emperor appointed as special imperial commissioner a man of proven integrity and firmness, Lin Tse-hsu. Lin seized 20,000 chests of opium worth $6 million and destroyed them at a public ceremony. Complications following this action led to a clash between Chinese war junks and British frigates, and war began in November 1839. During the hostilities that followed the hopeless military inferiority of the Chinese became obvious. With a squadron of ships and a few thousand men, the British were able to seize port after port at will. The Chinese fought valiantly. Their garrisons often resisted to the last man. But the odds were much more uneven than they had been between the conquistadors and the Aztecs. European warships and artillery had improved immeasurably between the sixteenth and nineteenth centuries, while Chinese military technology had stagnated at a level little above that of the Aztecs. In 1842, the Peking government capitulated and accepted the Treaty of Nanking, the first of a long series of unequal treaties that were to nibble away much of China's sovereignty.

FIRESHIPS AND MONKEYS

During the 1839 Opium War, the Chinese with their old-fashioned weapons had no chance against the British with their steam warships and artillery. This was proven when they tried to recapture the city of Ningpo. The resulting fiasco is described below by the British historian Arthur Waley, who uses contemporary Chinese sources. *

There were a great many literary men on the [Chinese] General's staff, and ten days before the attack commenced (January 31st) he ordered them to compose announcements of victory. Thirty of these were sent in, and the General arranged them in order of merit. The first place went to Miu Chia-ku who had composed a detailed and vivid account of the exploits of the various heroes. Second on the list was Ho Shih-ch'i (a fairly well-known calligrapher) who sent in a vast composition, full of classical tropes and brilliant felicities.

The signal for the general attack was to be the setting alight of the fire-rafts which were to be let loose upon the English ships and, drifting against them, would set fire to them before they could weigh anchor. . . . The English ships' boats put out long before the blazing rafts arrived, took them in tow—a ticklish operation during which several sailors were badly burnt—and beached them. A second contingent of fire-rafts at a point some miles away was also prematurely ignited as soon as the flames were seen rising from the other rafts; but when less than half of this second contingent had been launched the Chinese irregulars in charge were attacked by boats put out from English warships, and fled.

Someone suggested that fire-crackers should be tied to the backs of a number of monkeys, who would then be flung on board the English ships. The flames would spread rapidly in every direction and might with luck reach the powder-magazine, in which case the whole ship would blow up. Nineteen monkeys were bought, and at the time of the advance were brought in litters to the advanced base. After the failure of the Chinese attack they accompanied the retreating armies to Tz'u-ch'i. "The fact is," says Pei, "that no one ever dared go near enough to the foreign ships to fling them on board, so that the plan was never put into effect." During the panic that ensued after the defeat of the remaining Chinese troops on the heights behind Tz'u-ch'i, the people fled from the town, including a Mr Feng in whose charge the monkeys had been put. There was no one to care for them, and they eventually died of starvation in Mr Feng's deserted front lodge.

* A. Waley, *The Opium War Through Chinese Eyes* (London: George Allen & Unwin, 1958), pp. 165, 169, 170.

By the Nanking Treaty China ceded the island of Hong Kong and opened five ports to foreign trade—Canton, Foochow, Ningpo, Amoy, and Shanghai. British consuls could be stationed at these ports, and British merchants could lease land for residential and business uses. China also agreed to a uniform tariff fixed at 5 percent ad valorem, to be changed only by mutual agreement. This provision deprived China of tariff autonomy and hence of control over its national revenue. Furthermore, a supplementary treaty concluded the following year granted Britain extraterritoriality in criminal cases, and it also included a most-favored nation clause assuring Britain any additional privileges that China might grant other powers in the future.

The Nanking Treaty did not end the friction between the Chinese and the Europeans. The latter wanted more concessions in order to increase trade, while the Chinese felt that the treaties already had granted too many privileges to the Europeans. It is not surprising, then, that hostilities began again in 1856. The occasion this time was the imprisonment by Chinese officials of the Chinese crew on board a Chinese ship flying the British flag. When the Peking government refused to release the crew, the British bombarded Canton. The French also entered the war, using the murder of a French priest as a pretext. The Anglo-French forces proved irresistible, and in June 1858 the Chinese were compelled to sign the Tientsin Treaties. But they refused to carry out the provisions, and the Anglo-French forces renewed the attack. They captured the capital and forced China to sign the Peking Conventions in 1860. The Tientsin and Peking agreements opened several more ports on the coast. In the interior, they redefined and extended extraterritoriality, and they permitted the establishment of foreign legations in Peking and of Christian missions throughout the country. We should recall that it was at this time that the Russians took advantage of China's difficulties and used diplomatic means to get large areas in the Amur valley and along the Pacific Coast (see Chapter 24, section III).

The third defeat suffered by China was the most humiliating, for it was at the hands of the small neighboring kingdom of Japan. We shall see later in this chapter that the Japanese, in contrast to the Chinese, had been able to adapt Western technology to their needs and to build an efficient military establishment. Thus they accomplished what no other Oriental state had been able to achieve thus far. Japan now pressed certain shadowy claims in Korea. Traditionally, the Koreans had recognized the suzerainty of China, but they had also periodically paid tribute to Japan. Thus when China sent a small force to Korea in 1894 in response to an appeal for aid in suppressing a revolt, the Japanese also landed a detachment of marines. The two forces clashed, and war was formally declared by China and Japan in August 1894. The Chinese armies again were easily routed, and in April 1895 Peking was forced to accept the Treaty of Shimonoseki. Its terms required China to pay an indemnity, recognize the independence of Korea, cede to Japan the island of Formosa, the Pescadores Islands, and the Liaotung peninsula, and open four more ports to foreign commerce. Some of the European powers were not at all pleased with the appearance of a new rival for concessions in China. Accordingly, Russia, France, and Germany joined in a demand that the strategic Liaotung peninsula be returned to China, a demand to which Japan yielded reluctantly.

The Japanese war was a shattering blow to the pride and complacency of China. The great empire had been shown up as completely helpless at the hands of a despised neighbor who was equipped with modern instruments of war. Furthermore, the European powers during the preceding years had been taking advantage of China's weakness and annexing outlying territories that traditionally had recognized Peking's suzerainty. Russia took the Amur valley, the Maritime Provinces, and for a while occupied the Ili region in Central Asia. France seized Indochina, Britain took Burma, and Japan—since it had established its predominance in Korea by defeating China—proceeded to annex the country outright in 1910. In addition to these territorial acquisitions, the Western states divided up China proper. They set up spheres of influence in which the political and economic primacy of the respective powers was recognized. Thus Yunnan and the area bordering on Indochina became a French sphere, Canton and the Yangtze valley and the large area in between was a British sphere, Manchuria was Russian, Shantung was German, and Fukien Japanese.

The humiliations and disasters that China experienced in the latter half of the nineteenth century forced the traditionally self-centered Middle Kingdom to undertake a painful self-searching and reorganization. We will now trace the course of this process, noting how the Chinese slowly and grudgingly tried to follow the Western model, first in the military field, then in the economic, later in the social and intellectual, and finally in the political.

II. MILITARY AND ECONOMIC IMPACT

Lin Tse-hsu, the Chinese commissioner who had tried to stem the flow of opium and who had borne the brunt of the first British attack, realized the superiority of foreign arms. In a letter to a friend he described the impossibility of coping with British warships and concluded that "ships, guns, and a water force are absolutely indispensable." But Lin was by no means willing to broadcast these views. "I only beg you to keep them confidential," he required his friend. "By all means, please do not tell other persons."[1]

His aversion to publicity indicated that he feared a hostile reaction among his colleagues and superiors. This fear was fully justified. The scholar-officials who ruled China remained, with a few exceptions, profoundly hostile and scornful of everything Western. The shock of defeat compelled them to take certain measures toward imitating Western arms and techniques. But in actual practice they did little more than go through the motions. Even if they had sincerely wanted to imitate the West, which fundamentally they did not, the mandarins were hopelessly incompetent in mechanical matters. Thus China did little during the interwar years of 1842 to 1858 to face the challenge of European expansionism.

The second defeat at the hands of the Western powers forced a few forward-looking Chinese intellectuals to reconsider their traditional values and policies. Their response was what they called the "self-strengthening" movement. The phrase itself is from the Confucian *Classics* and was used in the 1860s to mean the preservation of Chinese civilization by grafting on Western mechanisms. In this regard the leaders of China now were ready to go beyond purely military matters to include railroads, steamship lines, machine factories, and applied science generally. This "self-strengthening" movement was doomed to failure because the basic assumption on which it rested was false. Westernization could not be a halfway process; it was all or nothing. Westernization in tools led inevitably to westernization in ideas and institutions. So Western science could not be used to preserve a Confucian civilization; rather it was bound to undermine that civilization.

For example, the China Merchants Steam Navigation Company was established in 1872 to build steamships for transporting rice from the Yangtze delta to the capital in the north. The steamer fleet needed coal, so the Kaiping coal mines were opened north of Tientsin in 1878. To transport this coal, China's first permanent railroad began operations in 1881. This integrated complex of enterprises had a sound economic basis and should have prospered. But its directors were motivated, in the traditional Chinese fashion, more by family than by corporate considerations. They appointed needy relatives and greedy henchmen to the various posts, with the result that the entire undertaking fell heavily into debt and eventually passed to foreign control.

China's failure to build up its economy and its armed forces led inevitably to increasing Western penetration and control. Numerous loans were made to the Peking government, frequently under pressure and on conditions that gave the creditors control over segments of China's economy. Another means of economic influence were the concessions in various Chinese ports that were held by the European powers. Most important was the "international settlement" of Shanghai which developed into a sovereign city-state in which Chinese laws did not apply and Chinese courts and police had no jurisdiction. These concessions profoundly affected China's economy, which traditionally had been self-sufficient and land-based. But now it was becoming increasingly dependent upon the foreign-controlled coastal cities, and particularly upon Shanghai. The Western powers also dominated the great inland waterways as well as the coastal ports. They maintained fleets of gunboats that patrolled the Yangtze River between Shanghai and Chunking, a distance of 1500 miles across the heart of China. In fact, Britain maintained an officer with the revealing title of "Rear-Admiral Yangtze"!

III. SOCIAL AND INTELLECTUAL IMPACT

In the late-nineteenth and early twentieth centuries, the Chinese response to the West's challenge broadened from the military and economic spheres to the social and intellectual. One reason for the shift was that the extension of foreign business into the interior of the country stimulated the growth of a Chinese merchant class, which soon took over the distribution of Western goods. Later, Chinese manufacturers began to establish match factories, flour mills, cotton mills, and silk-spinning factories. These new economic leaders tended to be an independent political force. They disliked European domination because of the privileges it conferred upon foreign business competitors. But they also had little use for the reactionary imperial court in Peking, which neither offered effective resistance to the foreigners nor showed any understanding of the nature and needs of a modern economy. Thus, these Chinese merchants felt no more loyalty toward the Manchu regime in Peking than the Indian merchants had felt earlier for the Mogul regime in Delhi. Consequently it was they who provided the dynamism behind the revolutionary nationalist movement that developed at the turn of the century. It was not accidental that the first antiforeign boycotts were organized in the coastal cities, and that the 1911 revolution that overthrew the Manchu dynasty also broke out in those cities.

The perilous situation of China also affected the ruling scholar-bureaucrats, though they were pushed in the direction of reform rather than revolution. Because of the official positions and vested interests, they wanted only "change within tradition." They still held that China's Confucian civilization could be renovated to meet modern needs. An outstanding exponent of this view was the fiery Cantonese scholar K'ang Yu-wei (1858–1927), who startled his colleagues with his study *Confucius as a Reformer*. This iconoclastic work depicted Confucius as a champion of the rights of the people, rather than of imperial authority.

Advocacy of people's rights and of their participation in government was something new for China. Hitherto the Western concepts of democracy and nationalism had been conspicuously absent. Instead, the emphasis had been on the family, and, so far as a broader allegiance was concerned, it took the form of "culturalism" rather than nationalism. By culturalism is meant identification with the native cultural tradition, which was viewed simply as the alternative to foreign barbarism. China's ruling scholar-bureaucracy was steeped in this tradition, and many of its members still avowed that it was "better to see the nation die than its way of life change."[2] But against the standpatism of this traditional culturalism the reform leaders now accepted revolutionary Western concepts. "What does nationalism mean?" asked one of these reformers.

It is that in all places people of the same race, the same language, the same religion, and the same customs, regard each other as brothers and work for independence and self-government, and organize a more perfect government to work for the public welfare and to oppose the infringement of other races. . . . If we wish to promote nationalism in China, there is no other means of doing it except through the renovation of the people.[3]

IV. POLITICAL IMPACT

The new reform spokesmen in China were able to win a hearing following the defeat at the hands of the Japanese in 1895. They gained the ear of the young emperor, Kuang-hsü, who momentarily broke away from the influence of the empress dowager, Tz'u-hsi. The latter had determined China's policy since 1860, but now the reformers won the emperor over to their side. So impressed was he by their oral and written presentations that in the summer of 1898 he issued a series of sweeping reform decrees that are collectively called the Hundred Days Reform. Numerous sinecures were to be eliminated, the provincial governments were to be more centralized under Peking, new schools were to disseminate European learning, Western-style production methods were to be encouraged, and a national conscript army was to be organized along Western lines. These measures never got beyond the paper stage. The empress, with the support of the military, deposed the unfortunate emperor, declared herself regent, rescinded all the reform decrees, and executed six of the reform leaders.

The collapse of the Hundred Days Reform gave the reactionaries full power. In their zeal they actively channeled social and political discontent against the foreigners. Antiforeign secret societies, incited by court reactionaries and provincial governors, organized local militias to combat foreign aggression. Chief among these societies was the I Ho T'uan, or Righteous Harmony Fists, popularly termed Boxers. With official connivance the Boxers began to attack foreigners, and by 1900 numerous Chinese Christians and foreigners had been killed in north China. When European naval detachments began to land at Tientsin, the Boxers declared war on all foreigners and besieged the foreign legations in Peking. Within a few months, international armies relieved the legations, and the Imperial Court fled from the capital. Once more China was forced to accept a peace with humiliating terms, including further commercial concessions and payment of an indemnity of $333 million.

The fiascos of the Hundred Days Reform and of the Boxer Rebellion dramatically demonstrated the futility of trying to modernize China by reform from above. The alternative was revolution from below, and this did take place in 1911, when the Manchu dynasty finally was overthrown and its place taken by a republic.

The leader and ideologist of the revolutionists was Dr. Sun Yat-sen (1866–1925). Compared to the reform leaders who had hitherto been prominent, Sun was a strange and anomalous figure. He was not one of the upper-class literati; in fact, his training was as much Western as Chinese. He was born in the Canton delta, which had been subject to foreign influence longer than any other area in China. At the age of thirteen he joined his brother in Honolulu where he remained five years and completed a high-school course in a Church of England boarding school. Then he went to Queen's College in Hong Kong, and after graduation he enrolled in the Hong Kong Medical College and received his medical degree in 1892. Thus Sun acquired an excellent scientific education that he could have used to acquire wealth and status. Instead he identified with the poor and always felt a passionate concern for their welfare. "I am a coolie and the son of a coolie," he declared on one occasion. "I was born with the poor and I am still poor. My sympathies have always been with the struggling mass."[4]

With such sentiments, he did not remain long in professional practice. The defeat by Japan in 1895 convinced him that the government of his country was rotten to the core and that nothing short of a revolution would provide the remedy. At a conference held in Tokyo in 1905 Sun founded the T'ung-meng-hui, or League of Common Alliance. Its program called for a republican government elected by "the people of the country" and also for the division of the land amongst the peasantry. It is significant that no one had earlier raised the issue of land distribution as a possible element in self-strengthening or reform. No one, before Sun, had proposed the notion that the peasant masses might be transformed into literate, property-owning, and politically active citizens.

Sun Yat-sen derived his main support from Chinese merchants overseas. Within the country only a few students and merchants were influenced by his ideas, while the mass of the population remained illiterate and apathetic. When the revolution came in 1911, it was partly the work of landlord gentry and commercial interests in the provinces, which were opposed to the belated efforts of the Manchu regime to nationalize railway construction. The provincial leaders fomented strikes and riots, ostensibly on the ground that nationalization would lead to foreign control, but actually because they feared they would lose the profits. In any case, the revolutionists exploited the discontent and worked effectively amongst students and soldiers. A small-scale republican uprising in Canton was suppressed, but on October 10, 1911, an accidental explosion in a revolutionist bomb factory at Hankow led to mutiny among nearby imperial troops. Despite lack of coordination, the revolutionary movement spread rapidly throughout the country. Sun Yat-sen, who was in the United States at the time, hurried back, and on December 30, 1911, a provisional revolutionary assembly elected him president of the United Provinces of China.

Sun was unable to control the country even though he was the nominal leader. Actual power was in the hands of an able and ambitious imperial official, Yuan Shih-k'ai (1859–1916), who commanded the most effective army in China. Rather than risk a civil war that would invite foreign intervention, Sun, in February 1912, yielded the presidency to Yuan, and the latter agreed to work with a parliament and a responsible cabinet. This arrangement, however, did not really settle the basic question of what form of government would replace the fallen Manchu regime. Yuan was all for Western military technology and administrative methods. But he regarded Western political institutions, including control of the executive by representatives of the people, as antithetical to China's traditions and certainly antithetical to his personal ambitions.

Sun Yat-sen founded a new political party, the *Kuomintang,* or National Peoples' party, which won a majority of seats in the National Assembly elected in April 1913. But this setback did not really restrict Yuan, for he had the backing of the army and of bureaucracy. Furthermore, the foreign powers preferred to back the strongman Yuan, just as they had backed the Manchu dynasty in earlier years. Yuan resorted to severe repression to consolidate his position, which led Sun to stage an armed uprising in the summer of 1913. The move was premature and Yuan suppressed the revolt with ease.

Sun fled to Japan with his principal followers, and Yuan made preparations to fulfill his ill-concealed ambition to establish himself as emperor. In October 1913, he had himself elected permanent president. Then he ordered the dissolution of both the Kuomintang and the parliament. With the opposition out of the way, he engineered ''spontaneous'' requests that he fulfill his duty to his country and become emperor. In December 1915, Yuan announced that he would assume the title of emperor on January 1, 1916.

His plans were upset by a revolt which broke out in Yunnan in December 1915 and quickly spread. Yuan found it necessary first to postpone and finally, in March 1916, to abandon the restoration of the monarchy. Humiliated and embittered, he died in June of the same year. After his death the army commanders who had served under him divided the country amongst themselves. These warlords paid little attention to the republican government that nominally ruled from Peking. Rather, they pillaged the countryside mercilessly and dragged China down to a brutalizing anarchy. These early years of the republic, up until 1926, marked one of the worst periods in the history of China.

Several factors account for this wretched outcome of several decades of response to the West. First there is the sheer size of China, which for many years left the interior of the country unaffected by Western contact. The interior functioned as a vast reservoir, out of which tradition-minded civil service candidates continued to appear for several decades. The bureaucracy that they formed consisted of intellectuals who were steeped in the Confucian *Classics* and who consequently placed much greater emphasis upon ethical principles than upon the manual arts or the technology of warfare. This ruling class was further inhibited by the fact that, apart from Buddhism, China had little or no tradition of borrowing from abroad. Thus it is not surprising that, although China did change in the second half of the nineteenth century, the tempo of its change was far below that of other countries that responded to the West. Finally the young Western-trained Chinese also were partly to blame. Some of them played leading roles in the early days of the republic, but they tried to set up in China carbon copies of the institutions they had observed abroad, especially in the United States. What they established naturally had no meaning for the Chinese people and quickly crumbled before the realities of Chinese politics.

V. JAPAN IN SECLUSION

Historians have presented several explanations for the difference between the Chinese and the Japanese response to the challenge of the West. The physical compactness of the Japanese islands facilitated both the forging of national unity and the spread of new values and new learning throughout the country. It also made the country vulnerable to, and aware of, foreign pressures, unlike the vast interior provinces of China that for long were inaccessible to Western influences. Furthermore, Japan's long tradition of borrowing from the great Chinese cultural world made similar borrowing from the Western world in the nineteenth century less jarring and painful. Japan had adapted selected aspects of Chinese culture with the slogan ''Japanese spirit and Chinese knowledge.'' Now it borrowed what it wished from the West with the slogan ''Eastern morale and Western arts.'' Also Japanese government and society were pluralistic in structure in comparison with the monolithic features of the Chinese Empire. The clan tradition and regional particularism of Japan were reinforced by geographic separation due to the broken mountainous terrain. The merchant class in Japan had more autonomy and economic strength, and, as we shall see, it was rapidly extending its power at the critical moment of the West's intrusion. The military elements in Japan were at the top of the social ladder, rather than at the bottom, as was the case in China. This meant that Japan had a ruling class that was much more sensitive and responsive to Western military technology than were the Chinese literati. In sum, geography, cultural traditions, and pluralistic organization combined to make Japan more vulnerable to Western intrusion than China, and quicker to respond to that intrusion.

Despite these basic differences, Japan, like China, remained in seclusion until the mid-nineteenth century. The Tokugawa shoguns severed one by one the ties between Japan and the Western world. By the mid-seventeenth century the sole remaining contact was the handful of Dutch traders who were confined to the islet of Deshima (see Chapter 13, section VII). The aim of the Tokugawa leaders was to keep Japan isolated and unchanging in order to perpetuate their regime. But despite their efforts, certain developments did occur that gradually altered the balance of forces in the country and undermined the status quo. The long peace enforced by Tokugawa rule stimulated population growth, economic expansion, and the strengthening of the merchant class. The population jumped from 18 million in 1600 to 26 million in 1725. Cities grew disproportionately, Edo approaching the million mark by 1700, and Osaka and Kyoto each reaching 300,000. The population spurt increased the demand for commodities and encouraged merchants and rich peasants to invest surplus capital in new forms of production, including the domestic, or putting-out, system. They provided materials and equipment for peasants and craftsmen, and marketed the finished products. It appears that in certain areas this industrial development had reached the level of factory organization by the end of the Tokugawa period. Regional specialization based on available raw materials and local skills became widespread, so that particular areas were noted for their lacquerware, pottery, textiles, or rice wine.

Rising production led to wide-scale exchange of goods, which in turn led to the development of a money economy. At first money was imported from China and Korea, but in the seventeenth century a gold mint was established. The aristocrats became dependent on brokers to convert their rice into money, and upon merchants to satisfy their consumption needs. In these transactions the aristocrats lost out because the merchants manipulated the prices through monopolies, and because the price of rice failed to keep up with the soaring costs of other commodities. The aristocrats, besides, had acquired a taste for luxuries and tended to compete with each other in ostentatious living. The net result was that they generally became indebted to the merchants, even though the merchants ranked far below in the social scale. In time the merchant families bought their way into the aristocracy by intermarriage or adoption. These families then dominated not only the economy but also the art and literature of the eighteenth and early nineteenth centuries.

We should note that these changes affected not only the top levels of the aristocracy but also the samurai, whose services were not so much in demand during this long period of peace. The mass of the peasants also suffered severely with the lag in the price of rice. Many of them migrated to the cities, but not all were able to find employment, for the growth of the national economy was not keeping pace with the growth of population.

Thus Japanese society was in a state of transition. It was experiencing profound economic and social change, which gave rise to political tensions. These tensions were reaching the breaking point when Admiral Perry forced Japan's doors open to trade. One reason the Japanese proved so ready to reorganize their society under the impact of the West was precisely that many of them were all too aware that their society needed reorganizing.

On July 8, 1853, Commodore Matthew Perry cast anchor in Edo Bay and delivered a letter from President Fillmore asking for trading privileges, coaling stations, and protection for shipwrecked Americans. Within a week he sailed away after warning that he would be back for an answer the following spring. When he returned in February 1854, he made it clear that the alternative was a treaty or war. The Japanese yielded and on March 31 signed the Treaty of Kanagawa. Its terms opened the ports of Shimoda and Hakodate for the repair and provisioning of American ships, provided for proper treatment and repatriation of shipwrecked Americans, permitted the appointment of consular representatives if either nation considered it necessary, and promised most-favored-nation treatment for the United States.

In accordance with the provisions of this treaty, the United States sent Townsend Harris, an unusually able man, as the first consul to Japan. With his extraordinary tact and patience, Harris gradually won the confidence of the Japanese and secured the Commercial Treaty of 1858. This opened four more ports to trade, provided for mutual diplomatic representation, gave to Americans both civil and criminal extraterritoriality, prohibited the opium trade, and gave freedom of religion to foreigners. Soon after signing these two treaties with the United States, Japan concluded similar pacts with Holland, Russia, Britain, and France. Thus Japan, like China before it, now had to suffer the intrusion of the West. But its response to that intrusion was altogether different from that of the Middle Kingdom.

VI. MODERNIZATION OF JAPAN

The first effect of the Western encroachment was to produce a crisis that precipitated the downfall of the Tukogawa Shogunate. With the signing of the treaties the shogun was subject to conflicting pressures: on the one hand from the foreign powers, which demanded implementation of all the provisions, and on the other from the Japanese population, which was strongly antiforeign. The popular sentiment was exploited by the anti-Tokugawa clans, especially the Satsuma, Choshu, Hizen, and Tosa, often referred to as the Satcho Hito group. Between 1858 and 1865, attacks were made upon Europeans and their employees with the slogan "Honor the Emperor! Expel the barbarians!" With the death in 1867 of both the emperor and the Tokugawa shogun, the way was clear for the so-called Meiji Restoration. The Tokugawa clansmen were shorn of their power and fiefs, and their place was taken by the Satcho Hito clans, which henceforth controlled the government in the name of the new Meiji emperor. It was the young samurai in the service of these clans who now provided Japan with the extraordinary leadership that made possible successful modernization. In contrast to China's literati, Japan's new leaders realized that they were retarded in certain fields, and they were willing and able to do something about it.

This is not altogether surprising if we note that even during their centuries of seclusion the Japanese leaders had gone out of their way to keep informed of developments in Europe. In fact, the Dutch were allowed to continue trading primarily so that they could be questioned concerning the outside world. Both the Shogunate and the clans promoted military industry and maintained schools for the study of foreign languages and foreign texts. The general level of knowledge rose to the point where, in the natural sciences, physics was separated from chemistry and, in medicine, students were trained in special fields such as surgery, pediatrics, obstetrics, and internal medicine. In the Nagasaki naval school, instruction was given in navigation and gunnery only after a solid base had been laid in mathematics, astronomy, and physics. In other words, the Japanese all along had been much more appreciative of, and responsive to, Western culture. In the light of this background, it is understandable why the Japanese acted quite differently from the Chinese once the Westerners forced their way in.

Japan's new leaders were interested only in those features of Western civilization that enhanced national power. In the field of religion, for example, the Meiji statesmen supported Shinto as the state cult because it identified the national character with the emperor and held that the emperor was descended from the Sun Goddess. In other words, Shinto stimulated national unity and patriotism, and these attributes were properly deemed necessary if Japan were to hold its own in the modern world. In education, it was explicitly stated that the objective was the furtherance of state interests rather than the development of the individual. Compulsory elementary education was required because the state needed a literate citizenry. Large numbers of foreign educators were brought to Japan to found schools and universities, and thousands of Japanese studied abroad and returned to teach in the new institutions. But the entire educational system was kept under close state supervision to ensure uniformity of thought as well as of administration.

In military affairs the Japanese abolished the old feudal levies and organized modern armed forces based on the latest European models. They built a conscript army with the aid of a German military mission, and a small navy under the guidance of the British. The Meiji leaders foresaw that the new military forces required a modern economy to supply their needs. Accordingly, they secured the establishment of the needed industries by granting subsidies, purchasing stock, or forming government corporations. The government leaders were careful to support, not only light industries such as textiles, but also heavy industries such as mining, steel, and shipbuilding, which were necessary to fill military needs. Once these enterprises were founded, the government generally sold them to various favored private interests at extremely low prices. In this way a few wealthy families, collectively known as the Zaibatsu, gained a stranglehold on the national economy that has persisted to the present.

The Japanese also overhauled their legal system. This was in such a bad state when the Westerners appeared that their demand for extraterritoriality was understandable. The laws were chaotic and harsh, individual rights were disregarded, the police were arbitrary and all-powerful, and prison conditions were revolting. In 1871 a judicial department was organized, and in the following years new codes were adopted and a distinction made between judicial and administrative powers.

At the same time various political innovations were made in order to provide Japan with at least the trappings of parliamentary government. A cabinet and a privy council were first established, and then, in 1889, a constitution was adopted. This document promised the citizens freedom from arbitrary arrest, protection of property rights, and freedom of religion, speech, and association. But in each instance the government was given authority to curb these rights when it so desired. The constitution provided Japan with a parliamentary facade while preserving oligarchic rule and emperor worship. Indeed, the first article of the constitution provided that "the empire of Japan shall be reigned over and governed by a line of Emperors unbroken for ages eternal." And the third article likewise stipulated that "the emperor is sacred and inviolable."

With the adoption of the constitution and of the legal reforms, the Japanese were in a position to press for the abolition of the unequal treaties. They could fairly argue that Japan now had taken its place in the ranks of civilized nations and that there was no longer any need for *extraterritoriality* and for the other infringements on their sovereignty. After prolonged diplomatic efforts they were able in 1894 to persuade Britain and the United States to end extraterritoriality and consular jurisdiction in five years. In the same year the Japanese won their unexpected and spectacular victory over the Chinese Empire. Henceforth there could be no more question of treating Japan as an inferior country, and the other powers soon followed Britain and the United States in yielding their special privileges. By 1899 Japan had gained legal jurisdiction over all foreigners on its soil, and, in doing so, it became the first Asian nation to break the chains of Western control.

VII. EXPANSION OF JAPAN

After it had modernized itself, Japan embarked on a career of expansion on the mainland. This is not surprising in view of Japan's warlike tradition and the immense prestige that its military leaders enjoyed from earliest times. Furthermore, the Far East was then a hotbed of international rivalry, and the practical-minded leaders of Japan drew the obvious conclusion: each people must grab for themselves. Their first expansionist move was in Korea where, as noted earlier in this chapter, the Japanese defeated the Chinese and then annexed Korea in 1910.

After their victory over China, the Japanese were faced by the much more powerful Russia which was advancing southward into Manchuria and Korea. We described earlier (Chapter 24, section III) Japan's offer for a compromise settlement, Russia's refusal of the offer, Japan's attack and victory over Russia, and the Portsmouth Treaty (September, 5, 1905) by which Japan won the southern half of Sakhalin Island and Russia's Liaotung leasehold, as well as recognition of its special interests in Korea.

In retrospect this war stands out as a major turning point in the history of the Far East, and even of the world. Certainly it established Japan as a major power and altered the balance of forces in the Far East. But much more significant is the fact that for the first time an Asian state defeated a European state, and a great empire at that. This had an electrifying effect on all Asia. It demonstrated to millions of colonial peoples that European domination was not divinely ordained. For the first time since the days of the conquistadors the white man had been beaten, and a thrill of hope ran through the nonwhite races of the globe. In this sense the Russo-Japanese War stands out as a landmark in modern history; it represents the prelude to the great awakening of the non-European peoples. Today that awakening is convulsing the entire world.

SUGGESTED READING

See bibliographies in chapters 7 and 13. See also the following: W. Franke, *China and the West* (Blackwell, 1967); N. Jacobs, *The Origin of Modern Capitalism and Eastern Asia* (Hong Kong University Press, 1958); F. V. Maulder, *Japan, China and the Modern World Economy* (Cambridge University Press, 1977); G. B. Sansom, *The Western World and Japan* (Knopf, 1950); H. Z. Schiffrin, *Sun Yat-Sen and the Origins of the 1911 Revolution* (University of California Press, 1969); Ssu-yu Teng and J. K. Fairbank, *China's Response to the West: A Documentary Survey, 1893–1923* (Harvard University Press, 1954); Y. C. Wang, *Chinese Intellectuals and the West, 1872–1949* (University of North Carolina Press, 1966); M. C. Wright, ed., *China in Revolution: The First Phase 1900–1913* (Yale University Press, 1968).

chapter 28

Africa

Europe's impact on sub-Saharan Africa was felt considerably later than that upon Eurasia. The European powers fastened their rule upon India, the East Indies, and much of North Africa, before they expanded south of the Sahara. France acquired Algeria in 1830 and Tunisia in 1881, while England occupied Egypt in 1882. European penetration southward generally came later because of various reasons, including adverse climate, prevalence of disease, geographic inaccessibility, and the superior organization and resistance of the Africans compared to the American Indians or the Australian aborigines (see Chapter 16, section I). Also there was a lack of exploitable riches to lure Europeans into the interior, as in the case of the bullion of Mexico and Peru. Thus sub-Saharan Africa, apart from certain coastal regions, remained largely unaffected by Europe until the late nineteenth century. In the last two decades of that century, however, the European powers made up for lost time. They partitioned virtually the entire continent and exploited its material and human resources. By 1914 the African peoples had, in many respects, come under European influence even more than had the Asians, though many villagers in the interior regions continued to live as before and to be little influenced by the European intruder.

I. SLAVE TRADE

For centuries the most valuable of African resources for Europeans were the slaves, but these could be obtained at coastal ports, without any need for penetration inland. Although the slave stations were restricted to the coast, the slave trade nevertheless had profound repercussions upon considerable areas of sub-Saharan Africa. The trade began in 1442 when two captains of Prince Henry the Navigator took twelve African slaves to Lisbon. It is true that slavery already was an established and widespread institution in Africa. Prisoners of war were enslaved, as were also debtors or individuals guilty of serious crimes. But these slaves usually were treated as part of the family; they had clearly defined rights, and their status was not necessarily hereditary. In Europe, by contrast, slavery was a very different institution and had a very different history. From the beginning it was primarily economic, so that slaves were worked to death in mines during classical times. This impersonalism was reinforced by racism when the Europeans became involved in the African slave trade on a large scale. Perhaps as a subconscious rationalization they gradually came to look down upon Negroes as inherently inferior, and therefore preordained to serve their white masters. Rationalization also may have been involved in the Europeans' use of religion to justify the traffic in human beings. Enslavement, it was argued, assured the conversion of the African heathen to the true faith as well as to civilization.

In this self-satisfying spirit the Portuguese shipped thousands of African slaves to their homeland. This was but a petty prelude to the new and fateful phase of the slave trade that began in 1510 when the first shipload of African slaves was shipped to the New World. The venture was highly successful, for there was urgent need for labor in the Americas, especially on the sugar plantations. The market for slaves was almost limitless, and several other countries entered the slave trade to share in the rich profits. Portugal dominated the trade in the sixteenth century, Holland during most of the seventeenth, and Britain in the eighteenth. The West African coast was dotted with about forty European forts which were used for defense against the rival trading nations and for storing the slaves while awaiting shipment across the Atlantic.

Thanks to the prevailing trade winds, the "middle passage" across the Atlantic to the New World was normally swift and brief. Nevertheless, the average death rate during the trip ranged from 10 to 55 percent, depending on the length of the voyage, the chance occurrence of epidemics, and the treatment accorded the slaves. This treatment almost invariably involved inhuman crowding, stifling heat, and poor food. Even greater casualties were suffered earlier, during the overland march to the coast. Raiding parties plundered villages and broke up families in their search for strong young men and women. The captives were then driven from dawn to dusk in the blazing heat and pouring rain, through thick jungles or over dry plains. The survivors who reached the coast were driven naked into the market like cattle. Then they were branded with the name of the company or buyer and herded into the forts to await shipment across the ocean. It is not surprising that in supplying American plantations with some 12 million slaves, Africa suffered an estimated loss of about four times that number of people (see Chapter 21, section III, for the overall effects on Africa).

Despite these horrors, Europeans continued to buy and sell Africans for over four centuries. The profits were so great that powerful vested interests strongly opposed any proposals for control or abolition. There were first of all the African chiefs who received as much as £20 to £36 for a single able-bodied slave. These African leaders played a vital role in the slave-trade operations. Their participation was essential for the Europeans who were confined to the coastal areas and who suffered mortality rates of 25 to 50 percent. Not only did the African middlemen reap handsome profits from the trade, but they also were violently opposed to all abolition proposals. Indeed, riots against Europeans were organized on African soil in defiance of the abolition movement!

The plantation owners in the Americas likewise supported the slave trade, especially the Barbados planters who held an important bloc of seats in the British Parliament in the eighteenth century. There were European vested interests also that championed the slave trade, both amongst the traders and the various merchants at home who provided the rum and the manufactured goods. According to one estimate, Britain shipped to Africa manufactures valued at one million pounds a year, and the other European countries sent an equal amount for the same purpose. The return on this outlay was so extraordinarily high that in the eighteenth century the prosperity of cities such as Liverpool and Bristol depended heavily on this traffic. The famous abolitionist leader William Wilberforce properly observed that "interest can draw a film over the eyes so thick that blindness itself could do no more."[1]

Despite these formidable obstacles, a small group of reformers campaigned vigorously for abolition. In 1787 they established in England the Society for the Abolition of the Slave Trade. In 1823 they founded the Anti-Slavery Society to end the institution of slavery as well as the slave trade. These abolitionists were aided by the progress of the industrial revolution, which was rendering slavery obsolete. Advancing technology called for overseas markets rather than for a cheap supply of human power. In fact, the abolitionists argued that the slave trade was inefficient and insisted that a more profitable "legitimate" trade could be developed in Africa.

The first success of the abolitionists was a law in 1807 providing that no British ships could participate in the slave trade and prohibiting the landing of slaves in British colonies. Finally, in 1833 Parliament passed a decree completely abolishing slavery on British territory and providing 20 million pounds as compensation for the slaveholders. The British government went further and persuaded other European countries to follow its example in allowing British warships to seize slave ships flying other flags. At one period, a fourth of the whole British navy was patrolling the coasts of Africa, Cuba, and Brazil with a force of 56 vessels manned by 9000 sailors. In twenty years these patrol ships captured over 1000 slavers and set free their human cargoes. Needless to say, many traders continued to slip through the blockade, lured on by the fortunes awaiting them in the Americas. Complete success was not possible until the various countries in the New World gradually abolished slavery as an institution—as did Haiti in 1803, the United States in 1863, Brazil in 1888, Cuba at about the same time, and so forth.

While the slave trade was being stamped out on the west coast of Africa, it continued to be carried on by the Arabs in Central and East Africa, though on a much smaller scale. The Arabs had been engaged in this trade long before the appearance of the Europeans, and they continued through the nineteenth century and even into the twentieth. The captives were marched across the Sahara to North African fairs, or they were taken to east-coast ports and then shipped to Zanzibar, Madagascar, Arabia, Turkey, Persia, and even India. This traffic was much more difficult to suppress than that on the west coast. Despite British naval patrols in the Red Sea and the Indian Ocean, it persisted until World War I and later.

II. AGE OF EXPLORATION

The agitation for the abolition of slavery contributed directly to the exploration and opening up of the "Dark Continent." The abolitionists hoped to curtail the slave trade by pushing into the interior where the slaves were captured. There they hoped to develop "legitimate" or regular commerce that would replace the traffic in slaves. At the same time, a growing fad for geography made Europeans intensely curious about unexplored lands. These factors all combined to bring to Africa in the nineteenth century a number of remarkable and colorful explorers.

The systematic exploration of the continent began with the founding of the African Association in 1788. It was headed by the noted British scientist, Joseph Banks, and its purpose was "to promote the cause of science and humanity, to explore the mysterious geography, to ascertain the resources, and to improve the conditions of that ill-fated continent." The association's attention was directed first to the problem of the Niger. As yet the river was only a name. Even before the beginning of the European slave trade rumors had circulated about fabulous cities on the banks of a great river called the Niger. No one knew where it rose or where it ended. To solve the mystery, the association in 1795 sent out a Scottish physician, Mungo Park. He and most of his companions fell victims to the dread African diseases. Not until 1830 did Richard Lander unlock the mystery of the Niger by following it to its mouth. In doing so, Lander proved that the so-called Oil Rivers, long known to Europeans as a source of palm oil and slaves, made up the delta of the Niger. The exploration of West Africa was furthered the most during the 1850s by Dr. Heinrich Barth. This remarkable German visited the most important cities of the western Sudan and then crossed the Sahara and returned to England in 1855. His journey is one of the greatest feats in the history of African travel.

Interest shifted to East Africa after a disastrous trading expedition up the Niger proved that commercial opportunities were scanty there. The big question in East Africa was the whereabouts of the source of the Nile. Hostile natives, vast marshes, and innumerable rapids had defeated all attempts to follow the river upstream to its headwaters. In 1856 two Englishmen, John Speke and Richard Burton, started inland from the African east coast. They discovered Lake Tanganyika, and, with Burton ill, Speke pushed on another two hundred miles to discover Lake Victoria. On a second trip (1860–1863) Speke saw the White Nile pouring from Lake Victoria at Ripon Falls, and then followed the great river to Khartoum and on through Egypt to the Mediterranean.

Head and shoulders above all the other explorers stands the figure of the great David Livingstone. He had trained himself originally to become a medical missionary in China, but the outbreak of the Opium War diverted him to Africa where he landed at Capetown and worked his way northward. In 1849 Livingstone crossed the Kalahari Desert to see what fields for missionary enterprise lay beyond. He discovered Lake Ngami where he heard that the country ahead was populous and well-watered, in contrast to the desert he had just crossed. In 1852 he set forth on the great journey that was to take him first to the Atlantic and then back across the continent to the Indian Ocean, which he reached in 1856. Livingstone then returned to England, and there, at Cambridge University, he delivered his historic address that stimulated interest in Africa throughout the Western world.

Between 1857 and 1863 Livingstone headed an expedition that explored the Zambezi region, and in 1866 he set forth again to settle various questions concerning the source of the Nile. Disappearing into the African bush, he was unable to send word to the outside world for five years. Finally the New York *Herald* sent Henry M. Stanley, a famous foreign correspondent, to find Livingstone. Stanley did find him in 1871 on Lake Tanganyika in one of the memorable episodes of African exploration. Although Livingstone was weak and emaciated, "a mere ruckle of bones" in his own words, he refused to return home with Stanley. Instead he continued his explorations until May 1, 1873, when his followers found him dead in a praying position beside his cot.

Stanley was so inspired by Livingstone's character and career that he returned to Africa to solve some of the problems left by "the Good Doctor." He discovered that the Lualaba River, thought by Livingstone to flow into the Nile, instead became the Congo, which flowed westward to the Atlantic. Stanley arrived in Boma on the west coast on November 26, 1877, exactly 999 days after leaving Zanzibar. The last of the four great African rivers had at last been traced from source to mouth.

Two years later, in 1879, Stanley was again on the Congo River, but this time he was functioning as the agent for King Leopold of Belgium rather than as an explorer. The age of African exploration had given way to the age of African partition.

III. PARTITION OF AFRICA

Prior to 1870 the European powers had insignificant holdings in Africa. They consisted mostly of seaports and fortified trading stations, together with bits of adjacent territory acquired as adjuncts to trade rather than as bases for territorial expansion. With the termination of the European slave trade, most of these coastal footholds were virtually abandoned since the legitimate trade was not great enough to support them. European statesmen during this early period repeatedly stated their opposition to the acquisition of colonies.

After 1870 a combination of factors (see Chapter 22, section VII) produced a reversal of this anticolonial attitude. Colonies now were regarded as assets for the mother country, and the continent of Africa, being unoccupied and defenseless, became the focus of imperialist aspirations. The leader of the imperialist drive in Africa was King Leopold of Belgium. At the outset he was interested primarily in East Africa. But with Stanley's exploration of the Congo basin in 1876–1877, Leopold at once saw the potentialities of this great central region. In fact Stanley himself saw the opportunity, but he was unable to enlist support in England. So in 1878 Stanley entered Leopold's service, and the following year he returned to the Congo. Between 1879 and 1880 Stanley signed numerous treaties with chiefs, handing over no less than 900,000 square miles to the International Association of the Congo, a new organization set up under Leopold's direction. The chiefs had no way of knowing that signing the pieces of paper and accepting token payments meant permanent loss of their tribal lands. An African chief traditionally was entrusted with his people's land. His selling was like a mayor's selling "his" city hall. Yet this was the standard procedure all over the continent, and repercussions are being felt to the present day.

The immediate effect of Leopold's machinations was to jolt the other European leaders to action. The French already had sent their famous explorer, Count de Brazza, to the lower Congo, and he was able to acquire for his country the lands to the north of the river. The Germans also entered the race, obtaining in 1884 South-West Africa, Togoland, and the Cameroons. Now the Portuguese joined in, especially since they claimed on the west coast both sides of the Congo mouth, and inland indefinitely. Britain never had been willing to recognize these Portuguese claims, but now it changed its mind in hopes of checking the aggressive Belgians and French. So an Anglo-Portuguese Convention was signed on February 26, 1884, recognizing Portuguese sovereignty over the mouth of the Congo and providing for Anglo-Portuguese control of navigation on the river.

The treaty was furiously denounced by the other powers, so an international conference was held in Berlin in 1884–1885 to prepare rules for the further acquisition of African territories. It was agreed that no power should annex land or establish a protectorate without first giving notice of intent; that recognition of territorial claims must depend on effective occupation; and that disputes were to be settled by arbitration. The conference also recognized the rights of Leopold's International Association of the Congo to much of the Congo basin, to be known as the Congo Free State. Finally, high-sounding declarations were made about uplifting the natives, spreading the Gospel, and stamping out slavery. All these were to be conspicuous by their absence in the so-called Free State.

Now that an international code for territorial aggrandizement was agreed upon, the entire continent was partitioned in less than two decades. In the Congo, Leopold bought out in 1887 all non-Belgian interests in order to eliminate possible criticism of his enterprise. Then he reimbursed himself by reserving a crown district of the richest rubber lands, ten times the size of Belgium. Here, as elsewhere in the Congo, special monopolies for the exploitation of natural products, including rights of native labor, were awarded to commercial concerns. Leopold was a heavy stockholder in most of these. His profits, therefore, were derived both from the stipends paid to the state by the concessionaries and from the dividends earned in the course of their immensely successful operations. In the final analysis, the fortunes that were made in the Congo were extracted by ruthless exploitation of the native peoples. So unbelievably brutal were the various methods of forced labor that the population of the Congo declined by one-half (from 20 to 10 million) between 1885 and 1908 when it was ruled by Leopold.

If the Africans did not bring in the required amount of rubber and ivory, they were mutilated or shot. Mutilation meant chopping off a hand or a foot or both. To prove that they were doing their job properly, the bosses of the labor gangs brought to their superiors baskets full of human hands. And because the climate was hot and humid, the hands were sometimes smoked in order to preserve them. News of these atrocities leaked out, and Leopold was forced to hand over his Congo possessions to the Belgian government in 1908. What had been private property now became a Belgian colony. The government took measures to end the atrocities, though a modified form of forced labor did continue. Leopold, the mercenary promoter to the end, induced the Belgian parliament to compensate him handsomely for his "sacrifice" of the Congo.

In the rest of West Africa the French were the most active. Starting from their old trading posts on the Ivory Coast, in Dahomey, and on the north bank of the Congo, they conceived a grand plan for pushing inward and founding a French West African Empire that would stretch from Algeria to the Congo and from the Senegal to the Nile or even the Red Sea. Since the Germans and the British also had footholds along the west coast, the French had to outflank their rivals in a race for the hinterland. By and large they were successful. Only the British in Nigeria and the Germans in the Cameroons were able to expand significantly into the interior. All the rest of West Africa, together with the vast Sahara, became a great French domain ruled from Paris.

In East Africa the Portuguese had held Mozambique since the sixteenth century, and France had claims to Madagascar. The chief rivals for the remaining territory were the Germans and the British. At the end of 1884, while the Berlin Conference was in session, a young German colonial enthusiast, Dr. Carl Peters, landed secretly in East Africa. Within ten days he had persuaded the local chiefs to sign away more than 60,000 square miles, an area almost one-third the size of his own homeland. The following year the German government proclaimed a protectorate over the region obtained by Carl Peters. The German activities aroused the British who proceeded to sign treaties giving them the territory in the Kenya area. In 1886 and 1890 the British and the Germans signed agreements settling their claims in East Africa. The Germans retained the huge area known as the German East Africa Protectorate, to be named Tanganyika after 1919. The British kept their East Africa Protectorate, later to be known as Kenya Colony, together with a protectorate over Uganda.

Meanwhile, the Italians had belatedly joined the scramble for African territory. They managed to obtain two barren colonies on the Red Sea coast, Eritrea and Somaliland, and later, in 1896, they gambled for higher stakes by sending an army to conquer the kingdom of Ethiopia. The Christian Ethiopians were able to resist more effectively than the people in most other parts of Africa. Their Emperor Menelik had an army of 80,000 men trained by French officers and armed with French weapons. He was able to defeat the small Italian army of 10,000, and his kingdom remained free from European rule. But, except for the small republic of Liberia, on the west coast, by 1914 Ethiopia was the only independent state on the whole continent. Even Liberia, set up in 1822 as a settlement for freed American Negroes (named from the Latin ''liber,'' meaning ''free''), became a virtual United States protectorate in 1911 because of bankruptcy and internal disorders.

Meanwhile, on the southern tip of the continent the British were roused to action by the establishment of a German protectorate in South-West Africa and by Portuguese plans for the linking of Angola on the west coast to Mozambique on the east. The British took control of three areas—Basutoland, Bechuanaland, and Swaziland—all of which were made into native reservations and placed under British commissioners. North of the Limpopo River the British were attracted by rich goldfields and healthy plateau lands that were suitable for white colonization. In 1889 the British government granted a charter to the British South Africa Company whose field of operations was defined as ''to the north and west of the South African Republic, and to the west of the Portuguese dominions.'' Settlers began to move in, and in 1890 the town of Salisbury was laid out on the beautiful and salubrious plateau between the Limpopo and the Zambesi. After World War I the British company gave up its charter, and its lands were organized as the two colonies of Northern and Southern Rhodesia.

The British also had difficulties in South Africa proper, where a long smoldering feud with the Boer settlers flared up into full-scale war in 1899. After the war the British granted self-government to the Boers in the Orange Free State and the Transvaal, and in 1907 these two colonies joined with Natal and Cape Colony to form the Dominion of the Union of South Africa.

The net result of this unprecedented territorial aggrandizement was the partitioning of the entire continent of Africa among the European powers. The only exceptions, as noted above, were the fragile states of Liberia and Ethiopia.

IV. EUROPE'S IMPACT

Economic

Since economic motives were prominent in the partitioning of Africa, it is not surprising that drastic economic changes followed the partitioning. Europe no longer was content with boatloads of slaves at the coastal ports. The industrialized West no longer needed human slaves; technology had replaced them with an abundance of machines. Instead the West had need for the raw materials found in the interior of Africa, and it now had the technological means to extract these materials.

The first important step in the exploitation of Africa's resources came with the discovery of diamonds in Kimberly (1867) and gold in the Witwatersrand (1884). Equally great mineral wealth was discovered in the Rhodesias (gold and copper) and in the Congo (gold, copper, and diamonds). Many portions of the west coast yielded rich supplies of such tropical forest products as palm oil, rubber, and ivory. European and American companies bought vast plantations in such regions as the Congo, the Cameroons, and French Equatorial Africa. One example was the Firestone Corporation, which in 1926 was given a 90-year lease on 100,000 acres of land in Liberia.

Not only did foreign companies lease large tracts of land, but foreign settlers took over much of the good agricultural land. Explorers had reported that some of the interior plateaus had fertile soil as well as a pleasant climate. Consequently, European settlers flocked in, particularly to Southern Rhodesia and East Africa. Before long they had gained possession of the most desirable agricultural properties in these regions.

In order to transport the minerals and the agricultural commodities now being produced, the Europeans proceeded to build a network of railways in Africa as they already had done in Asia. These railways were designed to facilitate the export of produce rather than to stimulate general economic development. The expansion of production and the construction of transportation facilities stimulated trade to the point where the traditional barter system gave way to a monetary system. No longer did the Africans exchange slaves, golddust, feathers, and ivory for the Europeans' salt, glassware, cloth, rum, and gin. By the end of the nineteenth century there was fairly widespread use of English silver coins and of Austrian and American dollars.

All of these economic developments naturally had profound effects upon the native peoples. The inhabitants of the temperate plateau areas were affected most by the loss of the lands taken by white settlers. In some cases whole districts were reserved for exclusive white use, and the land could not be tilled by the Africans, even though it sometimes lay fallow. Consequently, the Africans were forced to work for wages on the white man's plantations, while some even "squatted" on the land of the white farmers for whom they worked to gain the privilege of tilling a small plot for themselves. In other regions the Africans found it necessary to leave their families and go to work in the mines. If the Africans refused to provide the labor needed for the plantations and mines, various types of forced labor were used. The most common was the levying of a head tax compelling the African to work in order to earn the money to pay the tax. These various developments reduced the traditional economic self-sufficiency of Africans. No longer did they work simply to feed themselves and their family. They were involved more and more in a money economy and so were affected by world economic conditions. Thus the effect of Europe's economic impact was twofold: to entangle the Africans in a worldwide money economy, and to subordinate them—directly or indirectly—to the white man, who was everywhere the "boss."

Cultural

Together with traders, investors, and European settlers came the European missionaries. They had a profound effect upon African culture because they were the first Europeans who consciously sought to change it. The others affected it only indirectly and incidentally, as when they forced Africans to leave their ancestral villages to work in cities or mines. But missionaries came with the avowed purpose of changing the African way of life. They used three instruments to carry this out: education, medicine, and religion.

Schools offering a Western education and Western ideals were an integral part of every mission station. These schools were particularly influential, since most colonial governments left the job of educating to the missionaries. In many respects the mission schools were constructive in their influence: Often they taught the pupils how to build better houses, improve their agricultural methods, and observe the rudiments of hygiene and sanitation. They also taught reading and writing in African as well as European languages. The missionaries reduced the African languages to writing, and so laid the foundations for native African literature. The great majority of those Africans who chose literary careers were educated in missionary schools.

On the other hand, these schools inevitably had a subversive influence on the African people; they often taught that the traditional way of life was primitive and wrong. In time the students listened less to their parents and elders and more to their European teachers, whom they learned to respect. In addition, the mission schools used European books that taught more about Europe than about Africa. Early history textbooks used in the French colonies began with lessons dealing with "our ancestors the Gauls." Missionary education encouraged individualism, which was contrary to the communal African way of life. It is not surprising that Africans subjected to several years of this type of education were usually loathe to return to their villages. Instead they looked for jobs with the colonial governments, missions, or private business, and so moved further away from their traditional culture.

The missions also brought medical knowledge and facilities that saved the lives of many Africans. But besides saving lives, medicine also forced Africans to question their traditional ideas of what caused illness and death. The white man had the power to make people well even after the proper petitioning of spirits had not worked. So traditional religion no longer could be counted upon to meet all emergencies and to provide all the answers. Even though the majority of Africans clung to their old faiths, traditional religion was no longer as effective as it previously had been in holding together the African's whole way of life.

Political

Europe's imprint was as marked in the political field as it was in the economic and cultural fields. When the boundaries of the various colonies were drawn, no attention was paid to the indigenous people concerned. Hence they often found themselves under the rule of two or even three European powers. Some of the Somali, for example, were ruled by the French, others by the British, still others by the Italians, and a number even found themselves within the boundaries of Ethiopia.

Once the boundaries had been settled, the problem of organizing some administrative system arose. The European governments did not have enough manpower to rule all the peoples of the vast African continent directly. So they resorted to various forms of indirect rule; administration was conducted through tribal chiefs who were allowed to retain some of their authority. Usually the British allowed the chiefs more leeway than did the French, but even the French could not control everything because their African possessions were so vast and their supply of officials was so limited.

MEDICAL DOCTOR AND RAIN DOCTOR

Western missionaries in Africa brought a new culture as well as a new religion. The clash between old and new is illustrated in the following argument between David Livingstone (medical doctor) and a native rain doctor.*

R.D.—*You* ought not to despise our little knowledge, though you are ignorant of it.

M.D.—I don't despise what I am ignorant of; I only think you are mistaken in saying that you have medicines which can influence the rain at all.

R.D.—That's just the way people speak when they talk on a subject of which they have no knowledge. When we first opened our eyes, we found our forefathers making rain, and we follow in their footsteps. You, who send to Kuruman for corn, and irrigate your garden, may do without rain; *we* cannot manage in that way. If we had no rain, the cattle would have no pasture, the cows give no milk, our children become lean and die, our wives run away to other tribes who do make rain, and have corn, and the whole tribe become dispersed and lost; our fire would go out.

M.D.—I quite agree with you as to the value of the rain; but you cannot charm the clouds by medicines. You wait till you see the clouds come, then you use your medicines, and take the credit which belongs to God only.

R.D.—I use my medicines, and you employ yours; we are both doctors, and doctors are not deceivers. You give a patient medicine. Sometimes God is pleased to heal him by means of your medicine; sometimes not—he dies. When he is cured, you take the credit of what God does. I do the same. Sometimes God grants us rain, sometimes not. When he does, we take the credit of the charm. When a patient dies, you don't give up trust in your medicine, neither do I when rain fails. If you wish me to leave off my medicines, why continue your own?

M.D.—I give medicines to living creatures within my reach, and can see the effects though no cure follows; you pretend to charm the clouds which are so far above us that your medicines never reach them. The clouds usually lie in one direction, and your smoke goes in another. God alone can command the clouds. Only try and wait patiently; God will give us rain without your medicines.

R.D.—Mahala-ma-kapa-a-a!! Well, I always thought white men were wise till this morning. Who ever thought of making trial of starvation? Is death pleasant then?

M.D.—Could you make it rain on one spot and not on another?

R.D.—I wouldn't think of trying. I like to see the whole country green, and all the people glad; the women clapping their hands and giving me their ornaments for thankfulness, and lullilooing for joy.

M.D.—I think you deceive both them and yourself.

R.D.—Well, then, there is a pair of us (meaning both are rogues).

The above is only a specimen of their way of reasoning, in which, when the language is well understood, they are perceived to be remarkably acute. These arguments are generally known, and I never succeeded in convincing a single individual of their fallacy, though I tried to do so in every way I could think of. Their faith in medicines as charms is unbounded. The general effect of argument is to produce the impression that you are not anxious for rain at all; and it is very undesirable to allow the idea to spread that you do not take a generous interest in their welfare.

* D. Livingstone, *Missionary Travels and Researches in South Africa* (London: J. Murray, 1857), pp. 22–25.

On the surface, then, the Africans retained their traditional political institutions. They still had their councils of elders, their laws, their courts, and their chiefs. But in practice this political structure was undermined. The chiefs could be appointed or removed by the local European administrators, and their decisions no longer had the force of law since tribespeople could go over their heads to the European officials whose word was final.

Perhaps the most important factors undermining the traditional political systems were the economic and cultural changes brought about by European rule. Since chiefs often were thought to get their authority from the tribal gods, their political power was backed up by their religious leadership. Obviously both their religious leadership and political power were weakened when the people were converted to a new religion or when their faith was shaken in the old. Likewise, people who gained money wealth by working in cities or mines acquired a status and independence that would have been inconceivable had they remained in their villages. In some cases these newly rich people actually had more prestige and power than the old chiefs.

The most serious and direct challenge to the traditional tribal authorities came from the class of Western-educated Africans that gradually developed in almost all the colonies. They tended to challenge not only the native chiefs but also the European officials. They did so because they had imbibed in Western schools certain political ideas such as individual liberty and political freedom, and they saw no reason why the principles of liberalism and nationalism should apply in Europe but not in Africa. They were also goaded into political agitation by the discrimination they frequently encountered in government and private employment. Usually they were not allowed to be more than poorly paid clerks in European firms or very minor officials in the colonial administration. Again they could not see why, when they had the required education and experience, they should be kept in subordinate positions simply because their skins were dark. These educated Africans therefore became the first nationalists; they laid the foundations for the powerful nationalist movement of the twentieth century.

Conclusion

The above survey indicates that in many basic respects Europe left a much deeper imprint on Africa than on Eurasia. There was no parallel in Eurasia to the draining of African manpower through the slave trade. With the exception of Southeast Asia, there was also no parallel to the loss of agricultural lands, even though the loss was limited to East Africa and South Africa. Likewise, there was no parallel in Eurasia to the virtually total European domination of transport, finance, foreign trade, mining, and manufacturing. Finally, there was no parallel, with the exception of the Philippines, to the widespread diffusion of European Christianity and European languages, and to the ever-growing cultural influence of the European missionaries with their schools and their medical facilities.

The basic reason for this contrast in degree in European influence is that there was a corresponding contrast in the level of general development attained in Africa and in Eurasia. This contrast prevailed in all fields—in the sophistication of cultures, in the development of economics and technologies, and, consequently, in the density of populations. It was this contrast that made sub-Saharan Africa infinitely more vulnerable to European missionaries, entrepreneurs, and settlers.

And yet this very underdevelopedness of sub-Saharan Africa provided a natural resistance at the village level (as distinct from the European-influenced urban centers). In most parts of the continent prior to 1914, the interior villages retained their economic self-sufficiency and their integrated traditional cultures, which made them largely impervious to the West. Though we acknowledge the decisive impact of Europe in certain basic respects, we must still realize that many of the villages of sub-Saharan Africa remained relatively unchanged in their traditional patterns of life.

SUGGESTED READING

P. D. Curtin, *The Atlantic Slave Trade: A Census* (University of Wisconsin Press, 1969) and his *Africa and the West: Intellectual Responses to European Culture* (University of Wisconsin Press, 1972); B. Davidson, *Black Mother: The Years of the African Slave Trade* (Little, Brown, 1981); T. Hodgkin, *Nationalism in Colonial Africa* (New York University Press, 1957); M. Perham and J. Simmons, *African Discovery: An Anthology of Exploration* (Faber, 1942); E. Reynolds, *Stand the Storm: A History of the Atlantic Slave Trade* (Oxford University Press, 1982); H. Schiffers, *The Quest for Africa: Two Thousand Years of Exploration* (Odhams, 1957); H. A. Wieschoff, *Colonial Policies in Africa* (University of Pennsylvania Press, 1944).

Afterwards the Spaniards resolved to go and hunt the Indians who were in the mountains [of Cuba], where they perpetrated marvellous massacres. Thus they ruined and depopulated all this island which we beheld not long ago; and it excites pity, and great anguish to see it deserted, and reduced to a solitude.

Bartolome De Las Casas, 1552

The disappearance of these people [Australian aborigines] before the white invaders is just as certain as the disappearance of wolves in a country becoming civilized and populous.

James Stephen, 1841

chapter 29

The Americas And The British Dominions

Even more far-reaching than Europe's impact upon Asia and Africa during the nineteenth century were its effects upon the Americas and the British Dominions. The section titles of this chapter, then, refer not to "impact," but to outright *Europeanization*.

Europeanization involves more than just political domination or cultural penetration. It involves actual biological replacement, the physical substitution of one peoples by another—as happened in the relatively empty territories of the Western Hemisphere and the South Pacific. The scanty indigenous populations were either wiped out or pushed aside, and tens of millions of European emigrants swarmed in and occupied the lands of the native peoples. With them the Europeans brought their political institutions, their ways of earning a living, and their cultural traditions. Thus the ethnic Europeanization of overseas territories was followed inevitably by political, economic, and cultural Europeanization.

I. ETHNIC EUROPEANIZATION

In Chapter 22, section VII, we explained why Europe was able to supply so many emigrants, and why these millions of people were willing to leave their ancestral homes and brave unknown dangers in far-off continents. The thin ribbons of European settlement that existed in 1763 had stretched by 1914 to cover entire continents, including Australia and New Zealand, which had still been untouched at the earlier date.

Tables 6, 7, and 8 show that the majority of European emigrants went to the Americas. This is natural, since the earliest European colonies were established in the Americas. Also those continents offered much greater natural resources and economic opportunities. However, since the first European settlements were in Central and South America, it is surprising that so many more of these emigrants settled in North America.

The basically different character of the Spanish and Portuguese colonies, compared to the English explains why there were so many North American immigrants. The Spaniards and the Portuguese settled in territories with relatively dense Indian populations. Although estimates of the number of Indians in the Americas before the coming of the Europeans vary tremendously, it is agreed that the Indian populations were concentrated in what came to be Latin America. These native peoples supplied all the labor that was needed, so European settlers were not required for that purpose. Accordingly, emigrants to the Spanish and Portuguese colonies in the Americas were mostly soldiers, members of the clergy, government officials, and a few necessary craftsmen.

Table 6. RACIAL DISTRIBUTION IN THE AMERICAS (IN MILLIONS)*

	White		Black		Indian
	1835	1935	1835	1935	1935
North America	13.8	124.3	2.6	12.4	1.8
Central America	1.9	6.9	2.7	8.4	21.4
South America	2.9	40.9	4.5	18.7	29.2
TOTAL	18.6	172.1	9.8	39.5	52.4

*See Table 8.

Table 7. RACIAL DISTRIBUTION IN AFRICA*

	Whites		Africans
	1835	1935	1935
Mediterranean countries[a]	20,000	1,660,000[b]	30,000,000
Union of South Africa	66,000	1,950,000	6,600,000
Rest of South Africa[c]	3,000	190,000	12,200,000
Rest of continent	1,000	100,000	87,700,000
Islands	45,000	100,000	4,500,000
TOTAL	135,000	4,000,000	141,000,000

*See Table 8.
[a] Egypt, Libya, Tunis, Algeria, Moroccos, Spanish North Africa, Tangier.
[b] Includes only the settlers of European origin.
[c] Angola, S.W. Africa, Rhodesias, Nyasaland, Bechuanaland, Basutoland, Swaziland, Mozambique.

Table 8. RACIAL DISTRIBUTION IN OCEANIA*

	Date	Whites	Natives
Australia	June, 1935	6,674,000	81,000
New Zealand	Dec., 1935	1,486,000	76,000
Papua (Australia)	June, 1933	1,000	275,000
Fiji Islands (Br.)	Dec., 1934	5,000	107,000
New Guinea (Austr.)	June, 1935	4,000	679,000
Other islands (15)	1930s	109,756	464,525
TOTAL (of 19 areas)		8,279,756	1,682,525

*R. R. Kuczynski, Population Movements (Oxford: Clarendon, 1936), pp. 91, 95, 102–3, 118, by permission of The Clarendon Press, Oxford.

North of the Rio Grande, by contrast, the Indian population was relatively sparse and provided no reservoir of labor power. The English along the Atlantic Seaboard and the French on the banks of the St. Lawrence had to do their own work, whether it was cutting the forests, plowing the cleared land, or fishing the coastal waters. Under these circumstances North America wanted all the settlers it could get, and so the British North American colonies were opened to immigrants of all races, languages, and faiths. By 1835 there were 4.8 million European settlers in all of Central and South America as against 13.8 million in North America.

In the second half of the nineteenth century, European emigration steadily increased, reaching its height between 1900 and 1910 when almost a million people left each year. This unprecedented flood poured into every continent, so that Australia, South Africa, and South America now were peopled by substantial numbers of Europeans, although North America continued to be the main beneficiary.

OKLAHOMA LAND RUSH

A vivid example of how the Indian lands were flooded by Europeans was the opening for settlement of the Cherokee Strip in Oklahoma in 1893. The following description is by one of the participants, Billy McGinty.*

I had already slipped over into the Strip and picked out the place I aimed to file on. A hundred and sixty acres on the bank of Camp Creek; land sloping down so pretty you could run furrows smooth and straight as ribbons. Dig up the brush and you could set out enough peach trees to keep a whole country in fruit. I'd sow seed and reap money. Then I'd find me a spry girl and raise myself a crop of kids on that stretch. . . .

Day of the Run, I beat the roosters up. . . . By eight o'clock, four hours till starting time, men and horses were packed in so close lightning couldn't have cut them loose.

Men cursed and snarled at each other like dogs, as they tried to cut in their wagons ahead of others. Fist fights broke out along with dog fights.

Eleven fifty. Ten minutes until hell would break, and every minute like a year of your life. Eleven fifty-five, but the soldiers on guard not noticing that my horse's front hoofs were already two inches across the line.

Eleven fifty-nine. And now the talk was like the buzz of wild bees starting to swarm, as the official starter stepped on the line. He had his watch in one hand and his gun in the other. He looked at the watch and lifted the gun.

He fired one shot in the air. Wheels cracked! Whips popped! Hoofs thundered! The Run was on. . . .

All around me, wheel matched distance with saddle and man with man. Wagon was crashing against wagon. Horse's hides were raw red from being whipped to make them run faster. Drivers were standing up in wagons and buggies, lashing their own teams and those of other men when they crowded too close. . . .

Just before we reached the creek, I jumped off at the stretch I had picked out.

I grabbed rocks and sticks to mark off my hundred and sixty. . . . When I had put down the last marker, I cut a branch from a cottonwood and stuck my bandanna on it. For the law said you had to put up some kind of a banner when you had finished staking a place.

Then I stood up and looked out over that first piece of ground I had ever called my own. My heart was pounding as loud as the hoofs I had left behind.

"You're somebody now, Bill," I said to myself. "You got the finest horse, and you staked the finest claim. You outrode 'em all and, by thunder, you'll outfarm 'em all". . . .

* Billy McGinty, "Plow Fever," in Harold Preece, *Living Pioneers* (New York: Thomas Y. Crowell, 1952), pp. 190–201.

So far as the specific sources of immigration were concerned, the Latin American countries were peopled, as might be expected, mostly by emigrants from the Iberian peninsula, although considerable numbers also came in the late nineteenth century from Italy and Germany. The great majority of the emigrants to North America were, until 1890, from Northwestern Europe. After that date, approximately one-third came from Northwestern Europe, and the remaining two-thirds came from Eastern and Southern Europe. In the case of the British Dominions, immigration restrictions limited the supply largely to the British Isles. After World War I, and especially after World War II, the Dominions liberalized their immigration policies in order to attract more people into their wide open spaces.

The net result of these migrations has been the ethnic Europeanization of the Americas and the British Dominions. These areas have become largely European in population, although there are certain important exceptions, such as the native Indian strain remaining predominant—58 percent of the total population in Central America, and comprising one-third of the total population of South America. The substantial Negro element introduced into the Americas as a result of the slave trade is another exception to ethnic Europeanization. It is estimated that approximately 12 million slaves survived the trans-Atlantic passage and reached the New World. Their descendents today comprise about

10 percent of the total population in North America, 30 percent in Central America, and 21 percent in South America. South Africa represents the third exception to ethnic Europeanization; there the native Africans outnumber the whites (whether of Boer or British origin) by more than three to one.

II. POLITICAL EUROPEANIZATION

Ethnic Europeanization was accompanied by political Europeanization. The Americas and the British Dominions adopted constitutional governments of various forms. They also had European-derived law codes—Anglo-Saxon law in the United States and the British Dominions, Roman law in Latin America and Quebec.

Political Europeanization took many forms, reflecting original differences in the European mother countries as well as different conditions existing in the overseas lands. For example, Latin America and Britain's Thirteen Colonies won their political independence through armed revolution in the late eighteenth and early nineteenth centuries. By contrast, the British Dominions gained self-government in the late nineteenth century by acts of the British Parliament. Therefore they have remained within the British Commonwealth of Nations to the present day, recognizing the suzereignty of the British crown and, at the same time, enjoying full self-rule.

Another example of diversity within political Europeanization is the successful unification of the Thirteen Colonies and their eventual expansion from the Atlantic to the Pacific, as the United States of America. Latin America, by contrast, experienced political fragmentation. One reason was that mountain and jungle barriers separated one region from another. Also the lack of communication facilities left some parts of Latin America in closer contact with Europe than with each other. In addition Spain had discouraged contacts amongst its American colonies during the centuries of its rule. And after independence, ambitious political leaders preferred prominence in a small state to obscurity in a large union. For all these reasons, the original eight Spanish colonies in Latin America ended up as eighteen separate countries.

A final example of the variety of political Europeanization is the political stability of the United States and the British Dominions as against the never-ending coups in Latin America. Whereas the United States has kept its 1787 Constitution to the present day, the Latin American states have adopted an average of nearly ten different constitutions each. Almost all the "revolutions" responsible for these constitutions have been revolutions in name only. A true revolution is one that produces a fundamental change in a system, a basic reorganization of the social and political order. Most of the so-called "revolutions" in Latin America have simply involved the replacement of one military dictator by another without fundamental changes in the existing order. A procession of military and civilian leaders have succeeded each other, with little attention being paid to the wishes of the people or to the needs of the countries involved.

In conclusion, political Europeanization involved the transplanting of European political institutions to overseas lands. But in the process of transplanting there was adaptation and change. A Canadian or Australian political leader would be quite lost today if he or she were suddenly to become head of an American political party with its precarious balance of sectional interests, nationality blocs, and big-city machines. That same political leader would have been even more bewildered by Latin American politics and their unceasing succession of constitutions and caudillos.

III. ECONOMIC EUROPEANIZATION

Europeanization prevailed as much in the economic as in the political field. So far as the European powers were concerned, their economic objectives and methods were basically the same at the outset. All believed in the mercantilist doctrine of subordinating colonial economies to those of the mother countries. Despite this common mercantilist background, the various European settlements soon developed distinctive economies that differed in many respects from each other.

The economic development of Latin America, as noted in Chapter 18, section VI, was determined by several factors: the availability of abundant bullion and native labor, both of which were lacking in British and French America; the development of single-crop plantations based on African slave labor; and the economic backwardness of the Iberian states, which was transmitted to their colonies. The end result was that Latin America never achieved balanced economic growth. Instead there was chronic subservience to Northwestern Europe and later to the United States.

The economic history of the Thirteen Colonies was basically different. Strengthened by the fact that land was more plentiful than labor, the English colonists worked out their own economic institutions and practices. In the warm, rich, southern colonies, settlers found their best crops were tobacco, rice, and indigo. In the middle colonies—Pennsylvania, New Jersey, Delaware—grain grew well, and this area quickly became the breadbasket of the colonies. Most of New England also turned to agriculture, but the long winters and rocky soil were a severe handicap. So they also resorted to other occupations, mainly fishing, shipping, and manufacturing.

We see, then, that the economy of the Thirteen Colonies was much more diversified than that of Latin America, and it was more dynamic because native laborers, held down to a level of bare subsistence, did not form its basis. In place of Indian serfs and African slaves who toiled century after century (using the same tools and techniques), there were in the Thirteen Colonies clipper ships sailing the seven seas, a string of factories along the river fall line, and individual frontierspeople who, with rifle and ax, won homesteads in the wilderness and steadily pushed the line of settlement westward.

The same contrasting pattern of economic development continued after independence. After the mid-nineteenth century, there was a worldwide demand for Latin American foodstuffs and industrial raw materials—for Argentina's meat and grain, Chile's nitrate and copper, Mexico's gold and silver, Brazil's coffee and rubber, and Bolivia's tin. And so Latin America entered the world economy as it had never done before. On the other hand, this economic growth was in many respects one-sided and unhealthy. Most Latin American countries experienced booms in one or two commodities, while the rest of their economies remained static. The semifeudal hacienda system of land tenure and labor relations remained virtually unchanged, so the mass of people continued to exist as peons at subsistence level. And foreign economies penetrated and controlled most of the profitable enterprises, whether railways, public utilities, or mining properties. The benefits of this economic expansion, instead of being widely spread as they were in the United States, enriched only a small number of foreign and native landlords and merchants. This produced social unrest that was responsible for the political instability noted above.

In the United States, by contrast, there was rapid and diversified economic growth, especially after the Civil War. The war itself stimulated a vast industrial expansion, and this continued in the following decades with the opening of the West and the building of transcontinental railroads. Great quantities of foodstuffs and various raw materials were hauled by railroads and steamships to the burgeoning urban centers of eastern United States and Western Europe. At the same time, the millions of immigrants provided an abundant supply of cheap labor and further expanded the domestic market for American industrialists and farmers. The net result was that the U.S. economy spurted ahead in the second half of the nineteenth century at a rate unequaled to that time: In 1860 the United States was ranked fourth in the industrial nations of the world; by 1894 it was the first. Between 1860 and 1900 the number of industrial establishments increased three times, the number of industrial wage earners four times, the value of manufactured products seven times, and the amount of capital invested in industry nine times.

Like Latin America, the British Dominions also lagged behind the United States in rate of economic growth. The cause in this case, however, was not a semifeudal social system but rather inferior natural resources compared to those of the United States. The Dominions do possess abundant resources, but it was not profitable to exploit them until the mid-twentieth century when air transportation made them accessible and when more readily available resources in other countries had been depleted. This happened after World War II, with the result that manufactures and extractive industries have been booming in the Dominions in recent decades. But during the nineteenth century their economic development was modest, based mainly as it was on the export of foodstuffs and minerals, usually to the mother country.

In conclusion, Europe provided much of the manpower, the capital, the technology, and the markets for the economic development of the overseas lands. Between 1820 and 1830, 36 percent of all American exports went to Britain, and 43 percent of all American imports came from Britain. European capital—mostly British, Dutch, and German— poured into the United States during the nineteenth century, especially in the building of railways. By 1914 total foreign investments amounted to no less than 7.2 billion dollars. And in the comparatively underdeveloped Latin American countries, European investments dominated the national economies to a much greater degree than they did the American.

IV. CULTURAL EUROPEANIZATION

Cultural Europeanization inevitably accompanied the ethnic, political, and economic Europeanization, and this was true almost as much of the regions that won independence as of those that remained within the British Commonwealth. In Latin America the predominant cultural pattern is Spanish, with the exception of Portuguese Brazil; this pattern is evident in the Spanish language spoken by the majority of the people, and in the Roman Catholicism they profess. One sees it also in architectural forms such as the patio or courtyard, the barred window, and the house front that is flush with the sidewalk. Town planning, based on the central plaza rather than on the main street, is equally revealing. Much of the clothing is Spanish, including the men's broad-rimmed hats of felt or straw, and the women's cloth head coverings—mantilla, head shawl, or decorative scarf. In family organization the typical Spanish pattern of male dominance and close supervision of girls is followed, as is the tendency to regard physical labor as undignified and unsuitable for gentlemen.

Although Latin American culture is basically Spanish or Portuguese, a strong Indian influence prevails, especially in Mexico, Central America, and the northwestern part of

South America where the Indians make up a large percentage of the total population. This influence (see Chapter 21, section V), is evident in cooking, clothing, building materials, and religious practices. Latin American culture also has a considerable African element, brought over by the millions of slaves imported to work on plantations. This African influence is strongest in the Caribbean area where most of the slaves settled, although examples of their influence can be found in most parts of Latin America.

The culture that developed in the United States was less influenced by the native Indian population than was Latin American culture. The main reason is that the Indians were fewer in number and less advanced. Nevertheless, Indian influence was not altogether negligible: 25 states bear Indian names; at least 300 Indian words are now part of the English language; and many Indian inventions such as moccasins, canoes, toboggans, and snowshoes are in common use.

Likewise, the United States has been less influenced by African culture than have certain Latin American states in the Caribbean area. Still, the influence here has been considerable; blacks make up nearly 12 percent of the total population of the country compared to the one-half of one percent made up of Indians.

Despite these Indian and African elements, American culture is overwhelmingly European in origin, even though its European characteristics were drastically modified during the process of transplantation and adaptation. As late as 1820, fully 80 percent of all books in the United States were imported from Britain, and by 1830 the figure was still as high as 70 percent. So far as European intellectuals were concerned, American culture was nonexistent. This condescension was generally accepted by the Americans themselves. "All through life," wrote Henry Adams, "one had seen the American on his literary knees to the Europeans."[1]

Toward the end of the nineteenth century some change in this attitude began to be noticeable. Walt Whitman and Mark Twain were fully and truly American. Significant also was the publication in 1888 of James Bryce's appreciative masterpiece, *The American Commonwealth.* As the century closed, European intellectuals were becoming increasingly aware of a growing galaxy of American stars: John Dewey, William James, Oliver Wendell Holmes, Thorstein Veblen, and William Dean Howells. Yet Europe's tutelage remained hard to shake. At the end of the century, Henry Cabot Lodge still would write, "The first step of an American entering upon a literary career was to pretend to be an Englishman in order that he might win the approval, not of Englishmen, but of his own countrymen."[2]

Europe's cultural influence was stronger in the Dominions than in the United States or Latin America. One reason was the preservation of the imperial bonds, which caused more interaction with the mother country. Also, with the exception of South Africa, a much larger percentage of the peoples of the Dominions were of European origin than was the case in the United States and Latin America, with their substantial black and Indian elements. This does not mean, however, that the Dominions all developed a uniform culture. Distinctive local environments created distinctive cultures.

Canada's cultural development, for example, has been molded by two overriding factors. One is the French Canadian bloc that makes up one-third of the total population of the country. So determined are the French Canadians to preserve their identity in a predominantly Anglo-Saxon continent, that by the 1980s, separatism became a major threat to the unity of the Canadian Dominion.

The other major factor influencing Canadian culture is the American colossus to the south. This is evident in every aspect of national life, whether it be investments controlling jobs and national resources, or the magazines, novels, and radio and television programs that mold everyday life. The Canadian government has been concerned to the point of creating royal commissions and taking various measures to preserve national culture. This problem of American cultural intrusion exists also in Australia and New Zealand, though not as acutely as in Canada. Geographic isolation provides some cushion, as does also the greater ethnic homogeneity of those two Dominions.

We may conclude, then, that the cultural Europeanization of the Americas and the British Dominions has been both pervasive and enduring. A European need only visit New York, Mexico City, Montreal, or Melbourne, and then visit Cairo, Delhi, Tokyo, or Peking, to sense the reality and the extent of the overseas diffusion of his culture.

SUGGESTED READING

R. A. Billington, *Land of Savagery, Land of Promise: The European Image of the American Frontier* (Norton, 1981); E. Fisher, *The Passing of the European Age* (Harvard University Press, 1948); W. B. Hamilton, ed., *The Transfer of Institutions* (Duke University Press, 1964); L. Hanke, ed., *Do the Americans Have a Common History?* (Columbia University Press, 1964); L. Hartz, *The Founding of New Societies* (Harcourt Brace Jovanovich, 1964); P. Sharp, ''Three Frontiers: Some Comparative Studies of Canadian, American and Australian Settlements,'' *Pacific Historical Review,* XXIV (1955), pp. 369–77; W. P. Webb, *The Great Frontier* (Houghton Mifflin, 1952); W. F. Wilcox, et al., *International Migrations,* 2 vols. (National Bureau of Economic Research, 1929, 1931).

chapter 30

Consolidation Of Global Unity

The period between 1763 and 1914 stands out in world history as the period when Europe became master of the entire globe, whether directly or indirectly. Europe's domination was evident not only in the political sphere—in the form of great colonial empires—but also in the economic and cultural spheres. On the other hand, the decade before 1914 also witnessed the first serious challenges to Europe's predominance. The most significant challenge was the aforementioned defeat of Russia by Japan. The contemporary revolutions in Turkey and Persia, and the underground rumblings in various colonial or semi-colonial regions were also noteworthy. Let us now consider Europe's political, economic, and cultural predominance, and then the early challenges to this predominance.

I. EUROPE'S POLITICAL DOMINANCE

Between 1500 and 1763 Europe had emerged from its obscurity and gained control of the oceans and the relatively empty spaces of Siberia and the Americas. But so far as Asia and Africa were concerned, Europe's impact was still negligible at the end of the eighteenth century. In Africa there were only a string of slave-trading stations along the coasts and an insignificant settlement of Boers on the southern tip of the continent. Likewise, in

430

India the Europeans were confined to their few coastal trading posts and had not yet begun to have a substantial effect upon the vast hinterland. In East Asia the Westerners were rigidly restricted to Canton and Deshima despite their pleas for further contacts. If by some miracle the relations between Europe on the one hand and Africa and Asia on the other had been suddenly severed in the late eighteenth century, there would have been little left to show for the three centuries of interaction. A few ruined forts and churches would have been almost the only reminders of the intruders who had come across the sea. Everyday life would have continued along traditional lines as in the past millennia.

By 1914 this situation had changed fundamentally. Europe's impact had grown immeasurably, both in extent and in depth. Vast portions of the globe—the United States, Latin America, Siberia, and the British Dominions—had been Europeanized. Europeans had migrated to those territories in droves, displacing to a greater or lesser degree the native peoples. It is true that by 1914 the United States and Latin America had won political independence, while the British Dominions were self-governing. Nevertheless, as we have seen, the Dominions had become Europeanized. They were intimately related to Europe as regards ethnic composition, economic ties, and cultural institutions.

Vast territories, including the entire continent of Africa, with the exception of Liberia and Ethiopia, and the greater part of Asia, had become outright colonial possessions of the European powers. Of the 16,819,000 square miles in Asia, no less than 9,443,000 square miles were under European rule. These included 6,496,000 square miles under Russia, 1,998,000 under Britain, 587,000 under Holland, 248,000 under France, 114,000 under the United States, and a paltry 193 for Germany. In contrast to these tremendous colonial territories, Japan, the only truly independent Asian nation in 1914, accounted for a mere 161,000 square miles.

The remaining portion of the globe, apart from these colonial possessions and the Europeanized territories, consisted of countries that were nominally independent but actually semicolonial. These semicolonial countries included the great Chinese and Ottoman empires as well as such smaller states as Iran, Afghanistan, and Nepal. All these countries were dominated by European economic and military power. They were allowed to retain a nominal political independence simply because the European powers could not agree on the details of their dismemberment.

In this way the entire globe had come under Europe's domination by 1914. It was the extraordinary climax of the long process started half a millennium earlier when Portuguese captains began to feel their way down the coast of Africa. One peninsula of the Eurasian landmass was now the center of the world, with a concentration of power altogether unprecedented in past history (see Map XXVI, "World of Western Dominance, 1914").

II. EUROPE'S ECONOMIC DOMINANCE

The fact that by 1914 Europe's domination was unprecedented not only in extent but also in depth was evident in the economic control that Europe exercised. Europe had become the banker of the world, providing the capital needed for building transcontinental railroads, digging interoceanic canals, opening mines, and establishing plantations. Moreover, Europe had also become the industrial workshop of the world. By 1870 Europe was responsible for 64.7 percent of the world's total industrial output. The only rival was the United States with 23.3 percent. Even though the United States had forged ahead by 1913 to 35.8 percent, Europe's factories in that year still turned out 47.7 percent of the world's total production.

The effect of Europe's great outpouring of capital and technology was an unprecedented global economic unity: By 1914 over 516,000 kilometers of cables had been laid on ocean beds, as well as a vast network of telegraph and telephone lines on the land surface of the globe. By 1914 over 30,000 ships with a total tonnage of 50 millions carried goods from one part of the world to another. Several canals were built to facilitate world commerce. The most important were the Suez (1869), which shortened the route between Western Europe and India by 4000 miles, and the Panama (1914), which reduced the distance between New York and San Francisco by almost 8000 miles. Continents were opened for economic exploitation by the construction of several transcontinental railroads. The first in the United States was completed in 1869, the first in Canada in 1885, the trans-Siberian in 1905. The Berlin-to-Bagdad and the Cape-to-Cairo railroads were almost completed by 1914.

The economic integration of the continents led to a spectacular increase in overall global productivity. World industrial production multiplied no less than six times between 1860 and 1913, while the value of world trade increased twelve times between 1851 and 1913. Europe, as might be expected, benefited the most from this economic leap forward. Statistics are not available for conditions all over the globe, but it is estimated that the difference in per capita income between colonial or semicolonial regions and the European metropolitan countries was roughly 3 to 1 in 1800. By 1914 it had increased to about 7 to 1.

III. EUROPE'S CULTURAL DOMINANCE

The everyday life of the peasant masses in colonial territories had been drastically affected by the shift from a traditional natural economy to a money economy. Money had been used in the earlier period but only in a peripheral manner, and production had been carried on by the peasant households primarily to satisfy family needs. A few commodities might have been sold in the local market, but not for the purpose of making a profit. Rather the aim was to get a little money to meet tax obligations and to buy a few essentials such as salt and a little iron. Frequently the transactions and obligations were met by simple barter, and no money changed hands. But a new market economy was introduced when the Europeans appeared with their railroads, their machine-made goods, and their insatiable demands for foodstuffs and industrial raw materials. Before long the peasants found themselves producing for an international market rather than for themselves and their neighbors, which in turn meant that they became subject to global economic fluctuations. And they were at the mercies of merchants and money-lenders who now flourished in the new economy. The transition from a closed and static natural economy to a dynamic money-and-market economy was beneficial so far as productive capacity was concerned, but certainly its initial effects were disruptive and uncomfortable.

The way of thinking as well as the way of life was affected by Europe's intrusion. However, this intellectual change primarily involved the small upper class in the colonial world rather than the peasant masses. It was the few members of the thin upper crust who knew some Western language, who read Western newspapers and books, and who were familiar with European history and current politics. The initial response to this exposure to the alien culture was often an enthusiastic, uncritical admiration of everything Western. But it was usually followed by a reaction against the West and an attempt to preserve and foster at least some elements of the traditional culture. The ambivalent response to Western culture is clearly expressed in the following reminiscence written in 1925 by a prominent Indian:

Our fore fathers, the firstfruits of English education, were violently pro-British. They could see no flaw in the civilization or the culture of the West. They were charmed by its novelty and its strangeness. The enfranchisement of the individual, the substitution of the right of private judgement in the place of traditional authority, the exaltation of duty over custom, all came with a force and suddenness of a revelation to an Oriental people who knew no more binding obligation than the mandate of immemorial usage and of venerable tradition. . . . Everything English was good—even the drinking of brandy was a virtue; everything not English was to be viewed with suspicion. . . . In due time came the reaction, and with a sudden rush. And from the adoration of all things Western, we are now in a whirlpool that would recall us back to our ancient civilization and our time-honored ways and customs untempered by the impact of the ages that have rolled by and the forces of modern life.[1]

IV. WHITE MAN'S BURDEN

The political, economic, and cultural dominance of Europe at the turn of the century naturally led Europeans to assume that their primacy arose from the superiority of their civilization and that this in turn reflected their superiority as a race. It was confidently believed that God had created people unequal. He had made the whites more intelligent so that they could direct the labor and guide the development of the inferior races who had broad backs and weak minds. Hence the concept of the white man's burden—a preaching that cloaked the imperialism of the times with a mantle of idealistic devotion to duty. In the well-known lines of Rudyard Kipling, written appropriately at the end of the century (1899):

Take up the White Man's Burden—
Send forth the best ye breed—
Go bind your sons to exile
To serve your captives' need. . . .[2]

On all continents the European masters accepted the homage of the "lesser breeds" as part of the divine nature of things—as the inevitable outcome of the "survival of the fittest." In India they were addressed respectfully as "sahib," in the Middle East as "effendi," in Africa as "bwana," and in Latin America as "patron." Under these circumstances it is scarcely surprising that Europeans came to view the world with a myopia and a self-centeredness that today seems incredible. Most spectacular was the supreme self-confidence and aggressiveness of Cecil Rhodes, who was ahead of his time in dreaming of other planets to conquer: "The world is nearly parcelled out, and what there is left of it is being divided up, conquered, and colonized. To think of these stars that you see overhead at night, these vast worlds which we can never reach. I would annex the planets if I could; I often think of that. It makes me sad to see them so clear and yet so far."[3]

V. FIRST CHALLENGES TO EUROPE'S DOMINANCE

In 1914 Europe's global domination seemed to be unassailable and eternal. But in the clearer light of retrospect one can easily perceive the lurking threat of a colonial world slowly awakening and striking the first blows against Western domination.

Throughout history, whenever a weaker society has been threatened by one more vigorous and aggressive, there have been two contradictory types of reactions: the first reaction is to sever all contact with the intruding forces, withdraw into isolation, and seek refuge in traditional beliefs and practices; the second is to try instead to adopt as many features of the alien society as are necessary to meet it on equal terms and thus to resist it effectively. The first reaction represents retreat and escapism; the other, adjustment and adaptation. The slogan of the first is "Back to the good old days"; that of the second is, "Learn from the West in order to fight the West."

There were many cases during the nineteenth century of both types of reaction to the Western intrusion. Classic examples of the escapist variety were the Indian Mutiny in 1857–1858 and the Boxer Rebellion in 1900 (see Chapter 26, section III, and Chapter 27, section IV, for details). Both the mutiny and the rebellion were bitter, bloody affairs, yet neither of them seriously challenged Europe's supremacy because they were essentially negative revolts, seeking to oust the hated Europeans by force in order to restore the good old days. But the power of Western arms and the dynamism of Western economic enterprise were irresistable. It was an entirely different matter, however, when native peoples began to adopt Western ideas and technology in order to use them against the West.

ASIANS CHEER JAPANESE VICTORY OVER RUSSIANS

The spectacle of a small Asian kingdom defeating a great European power excited colonial peoples everywhere. The Chinese republican leader Dr. Sun Yat-sen described the excitement of those days in the following speech he delivered in 1924 in Tokyo.*

Thirty years ago . . . men thought and believed that European civilization was a progressive one—in science, industry, manufacture, and armament—and that Asia had nothing to compare with it. Consequently, they assumed that Asia could never resist Europe, that European oppression could never be shaken off. Such was the idea prevailing thirty years ago. It was a pessimistic idea. Even after Japan abolished the Unequal Treaties and attained the status of an independent country, Asia, with the exception of a few countries situated near Japan, was little influenced. Ten years later, however, the Russo-Japanese war broke out and Russia was defeated by Japan. For the first time in the history of the last several hundred years, an Asiatic country has defeated a European Power. The effect of this victory immediately spread over the whole Asia, and gave a new hope to all Asiatic peoples. In the year of the outbreak of the Russo-Japanese war I was in Europe. One day news came that Admiral Togo had defeated the Russian navy, annihilating in the Japan Sea the fleet newly despatched from Europe to Vladivostock. The population of the whole continent was taken aback.

Britain was Japan's Ally, yet most of the British people were painfully surprised, for in their eyes Japan's victory over Russia was certainly not a blessing for the White peoples. "Blood," after all, "is thicker than water." Later on I sailed for Asia. When the steamer passed the Suez Canal a number of natives came to see me. All of them wore smiling faces, and asked me whether I was a Japanese. I replied that I was a Chinese, and inquired what was in their minds, and why they were so happy. They said they had just heard the news that Japan had completely destroyed the Russian fleet recently despatched from Europe, and were wondering how true the story was. Some of them, living on both banks of the Canal had witnessed Russian hospital ships, with wounded on board, passing through the Canal from time to time. That was surely a proof of the Russian defeat, they added.

In former days, the coloured races in Asia, suffering from the oppression of the Western peoples, thought that emancipation was impossible. We regarded the Russian defeat by Japan as the defeat of the West by the East. We regarded the Japanese victory as our own victory. It was indeed a happy event. Did not therefore this news of Russia's defeat by Japan affect the peoples of the whole of Asia? Was not its effect tremendous?

*Sun Yat-sen, *China and Japan* (Shanghai: China United Press, 1941), pp. 142–143.

The Japanese were the first Asian people to succeed in carrying out the policy of resistance by adaptation. As we have seen, they defeated the weak Chinese Empire in 1894–1895, and then the mighty Russian Empire in 1904–1905 (see Chapter 27, section VII, for details). The triumph of a small Asian kingdom over a giant European power marks a turning point in recent world history. It was an event that sent a tremor of hope and excitement throughout the colonial world. Just as influential as the outcome of the Russo-Japanese War was the great Russian Revolution, stimulated in part by the war (see Chapter 24, section IV). The news that the Tsarist autocracy was on the verge of downfall was as exciting to oppressed peoples everywhere as the reports from the battlefields of Manchuria. A Britisher who was in Persia at this time sensed an undercurrent of aroused emotions and expectations in all the colonial lands. In a letter of August 1906 he reported:

It seems to me that a change must be coming over the East. The victory of Japan has, it would appear, had a remarkable influence all over the East. Even here in Persia it has not been without effect. . . . Moreover, the Russian Revolution has had a most astounding effect here. Events in Russia have been watched with great attention, and a new spirit would seem to have come over the people. They are tired of their rulers, and, taking example of Russia, have come to think that it is possible to have another and better form of government . . . it almost seems that the East is stirring in its sleep. In China there is a marked movement against the foreigners, and a tendency towards the ideal of "China for the Chinese." In Persia, owing to its proximity to Russia, the awakening would appear to take the form of a movement towards democratic reform. In Egypt and North Africa it is signalized by a remarkable increase in fanaticism, coupled with the spread of the Pan-Islamic movement. The simultaneousness of these symptoms of unrest is too remarkable to be attributed soley to coincidence. Who knows? Perhaps the East is really awakening from its secular slumber, and we are about to witness the rising of these patient millions against the exploitation of an unscrupulous West.[4]

This analysis proved prophetic. It was borne out by the 1905 Persian Revolution, the 1908 Young Turk Revolution, the 1911 Chinese Revolution, and by the heightened unrest and terrorism in India. We may conclude that although Europe's global hegemony in 1914 seemed irresistible and everlasting, it was actually being challenged at many points and in many ways. In some cases the challenge was direct, as in India and in Central Asia where a few pioneer nationalists were beginning to demand independence from Britain and Russia. In other cases the challenge was made indirectly against the weak Ottoman and Manchu dynasties because they had failed to resist Western aggression. In the pre-1914 period the European Powers were able to suppress the opposition, either by direct force or, as in China, by supporting the conservative Yuan Shih-kai against the radical Sun Yat-sen. Yet this early opposition did represent a beginning—the birth of the nationalist movements that, after World War I and especially after World War II, were to sweep everything before them.

SUGGESTED READING

H. C. d'Encausse and S. R. Schram, *Marxism and Asia* (Lane, 1969); E. Fischer, "Rebellion Against the European Man in the Nineteenth Century," *Journal of World Affairs,* II (1954), pp. 363–80; C. J. H. Hayes, *A Generation of Materialism, 1871–1900* (Harper & Row, 1941); I. Spector, *The First Russian Revolution: Its Impact on Asia* (Prentice-Hall, 1962).

What It Means
For Us Today

MARX TURNED UPSIDE DOWN

Karl Marx assumed that revolution would occur in the industrialized countries before it did in the colonies. He noted that Western capitalists were investing their surplus money in the colonies where higher profits could be made. Like all the Socialists of his time, Marx assumed that these investments would continue and that the colonies would become industrialized capitalist countries like their mother countries in Western Europe. Marx wrote in his famous work, *Das Kapital* (1867): "The industrialized developed country only shows the less-developed country the picture of its own future."

Marx also expected that as the colonies became industrialized and prosperous, the old manufacturing centers of the West would fall behind and suffer unemployment. This in turn would eventually force the suffering Western workers to rise in revolt and establish Socialist societies. Marx therefore concluded that revolution would come first in the West. In fact, in a letter to his friend Friedrich Engels (October 8, 1858), he expressed the fear that, when Europe became Socialist, the prosperous colonies would remain capitalist and would attack and "crush" the newly born Western socialism.

Today, more than a century later, we see that what has happened is the exact opposite of what Marx had feared. Revolution has come, not in the West, but in the former colonies, now known as the Third World. Thus history has turned Marx upside-down. Why has it done so?

One reason is that Western workers won the right to vote and the right to organize in unions. They used these rights to increase their wages and to organize the welfare state which provided help in case of accident, illness, or unemployment. Western workers therefore were more satisfied, and they became reformers rather than revolutionaries. A second reason is that the colonies, or the Third World, did not become industrialized. Western manufacturers did not want competition from overseas, so they actively opposed the establishment of industries in the colonies. As a result, the colonies remained producers of raw materials for Western factories and importers of manufactured goods made in Western factories. The trouble with this arrangement is that, after 1880, world prices for raw materials fell steadily, while the prices of manufactured goods rose steadily. Between 1880 and 1938, the amount of manufactured goods that Third World countries received for a set quantity of raw materials fell by over 40 percent.

This unfavorable trend in the "terms of trade," as the economists call it, is partly responsible for the serious economic problems of the Third World today. Other factors also have contributed to these problems, as noted above, in Chapter 22, section VII. The end result has been the widening gap between rich countries and poor—between the developed First World and the underdeveloped Third World. The ratio of per capita income between these two worlds has increased as follows:

```
1800 –  3:1
1914 –  7:1
1975 – 12:1
```

These figures explain why history has turned out the exact opposite of what Marx had expected. Before Marx, all the great revolutions had occurred in the West—the English, American and French revolutions. But in the twentieth century, all the great revolutions have been in the Third World: 1917-Russia; 1949-China; 1959-Cuba; 1975-Indochina; 1976-Portuguese Africa; 1979-Iran and Nicaragua; 1980-Zimbabur.

Instead of the capitalist Third World crushing socialism in Europe, it is the Socialist Third World that is exporting revolution to Europe. For example, during the time that the Portuguese military was attempting to subdue insurgency among its colonial possessions, some of its officers were won over to the revolutionary ideology of the African guerrillas they were fighting. Thus the years of colonial war in Africa culminated in the overthrow of dictatorship in Portugal by the Armed Forces Movement. Marx would have been surprised, indeed, to have heard Admiral Antonio Rosa Coutinho lecture a group of businessmen that "the Armed Forces Movement considers itself a liberation movement like those in Africa, and seeks not only formal independence but total liberation of the people."[1]

The course of future world history will depend on whether the gap between rich countries and poor continues to widen, or whether it is gradually closed. So far it has widened, and, if this continues, then the Third World will remain the center of world revolution. Robert McNamara made this point in a speech in 1966 when he was secretary of defense. He noted that in 1958 there had been 58 uprisings in various parts of the world, and that only one of these had been in a country with a per capita income of over $750. McNamara concluded: "There can be no question but that there is an irrefutable relationship between violence and economic backwardness. And the trend of such violence is up—not down."

SUGGESTED READING

The most useful and readable work on this subject is by R. L. Heilbroner, *Marxism: For and Against* (Norton, 1980). Also noteworthy is D. McLellan, *Marxism after Marx* (Harper & Row, 1980); and R. N. Carew Hunt, *The Theory and Practice of Communism* (Pelican, 1963). The following works interpret Marxism and the Soviet experiment as new approaches for the development of underdeveloped countries: R. Daniels, *The Nature of Communism* (Random House, 1962); and A. Ulam, *The Unfinished Revolution* (Westview, 1960).

Part VII

World Of Western Decline And Triumph, 1914–

The decades since 1914 have witnessed at one and the same time the decline and triumph of the West. Indeed these two seemingly contradictory trends have reinforced each other. The unprecedented integration of the globe led to the proliferation of Western technology, ideas, and institutions at an accelerating pace. But it was precisely this proliferation that undermined the global hegemony of the West that had appeared so invulnerable prior to 1914. Colonial peoples were selectively adopting Western civilization to better resist the West. For this reason, world history since 1914 is the history of the decline, and also of the triumph, of the West.

The combination of these two trends explains the turmoil of the world in which we live today. It takes only a glance at newspaper headlines and television screens to recognize that Peking and Cairo and New Delhi are now as prominent in international affairs as Paris and London and Washington. And everywhere, the hitherto silent masses are taking over the historical stage and shouting demands that would have been inconceivable a few decades ago.

chapter 31

World War I: Global Repercussions

In the autumn of 1914, as one European country after another was being dragged into the holocaust of World War I, the British foreign secretary, Earl Grey, remarked, "The lamps are going out all over Europe." His comment was indeed fully justified, and to a much greater degree than he could have foreseen. World War I was destined to bring down in ruins the Europe with which Earl Grey was familiar. It wiped out the centuries-old Hapsburg, Hohenzollern, Romanoff, and Ottoman dynasties. In their places there appeared new leaders, new institutions, and new ideologies that aristocrats such as Earl Grey only dimly understood. The Europe of 1918 was as different from that of 1914 as the Europe of 1815 had been different from that of 1789.

World War I also marked the end of the Europe that had dominated the globe so completely and abnormally during the nineteenth century. By the end of the war Europe's control had manifestly weakened and was everywhere being challenged. In one way or another the challenges were successfully resisted in most parts of the world. But the respite lasted only two decades, for the Second World War completed the undermining process begun by the First and left the European empires everywhere in shambles.

From the viewpoint of world history as well as European history, World War I stands out as a historic turning point. The purpose of this chapter is to analyze the roots, the course, and the global repercussions of this fateful event.

I. ROOTS OF WAR

In analyzing the forces that triggered World War I, historians distinguish between background causes that had been operative for some decades and immediate causes that came into play during the hectic weeks following the assassination of the Archduke Francis Ferdinand on June 28, 1914. The four most important background factors are: economic rivalries, colonial disputes, conflicting systems, and irreconcilable nationalist aspirations.

Considering first the economic rivalries, most of the major European powers became involved in tariff wars and in competition for foreign markets. For example, Italy and France waged a tariff war between 1888 and 1899, Russia and Germany between 1879 and 1894, and Austria and Serbia between 1906 and 1910. The most serious economic rivalry developed between Britain and Germany because of the latter's extraordinarily rapid rate of industrialization in the late nineteenth century. In 1870 Britain produced 31.8 percent of the world's total industrial output, compared to Germany's 13.2 percent. By 1914 Britain's share had dropped to 14 percent, while Germany's had risen slightly to 14.3 percent, or a shade greater than that of Britain. This German spurt meant stiff competition for Britain in overseas markets. It is impossible to define precisely the political repercussions of this economic rivalry, but it did strain the relations between the two countries. It further contributed to international tension by stimulating competition in naval armaments. In both countries it was argued vociferously that it was essential to build up naval strength in order to safeguard trade routes and merchant shipping. The kaiser's determination to have a big navy, as well as the most powerful army, contributed significantly to the final outbreak of war.

Economic rivalries also fomented colonial disputes, for additional colonies were eagerly sought after in order to ensure protected overseas markets for surplus capital and manufactures. Since the Germans did not enter the colonial race until after their national unification in 1871, they were particularly aggressive in their demands for an empire equal to their growing economic strength. The Pan-German League pointed to the substantial colonial possessions of small countries like Portugal, Holland, and Belgium and insisted that Germany also must have its "place in the sun." But in almost every part of the globe the Germans found themselves blocked by the far-flung possessions of the British, whom they bitterly accused of "dog in the manger" selfishness.

The competition for colonies, however, was by no means restricted to Britain and Germany. Almost all the major powers were involved in the scramble for empire in the late nineteenth century, so they repeatedly clashed in one region or another: Britain and Germany clashed in East Africa and South-West Africa; Britain and France, in Siam and the Nile valley; Britain and Russia, in Persia and Afghanistan; and Germany and France, in Morocco and West Africa.

The colonial rivalries in turn contributed to the forging of conflicting alliance systems that were in large part responsible for the coming of war. These systems began in 1879 when the German chancellor, Otto von Bismarck, concluded the Dual Alliance with Austria-Hungary. This was a defensive pact, designed to protect Germany against the French, who aspired to recover the Alsace-Lorraine provinces lost in 1871. It was also meant to protect Austria-Hungary against the Russians, with whom they continually clashed in the Balkans. In 1882 the Dual Alliance became the Triple Alliance with the addition of Italy. Again the objective was defensive: to protect Italy against France because of sharp conflict over Tunis. The Triple Alliance, then, was definitely not aggressive in intention or in its provisions. Germany and Austria-Hungary were both satisfied powers interested primarily in preserving the existing state of affairs on the Continent.

But from the other side of the fence the Triple Alliance seemed quite different. For France and Russia it was an overwhelming bloc that dominated Europe and left them isolated and vulnerable. Furthermore, France and Russia both had serious difficulties with Britain over colonial issues in several regions. The result was the Franco-Russian Alliance, concluded in 1894 with the double purpose of countering the Triple Alliance and resisting Britain in colonial disputes. The Franco-Russian Alliance became the Triple Entente with the signing of the Anglo-French Entente in 1904 and the Anglo-Russian Entente in 1907. Both of these arrangements were essentially colonial in nature. Britain and France, for example, agreed to recognize their respective interests in the Nile valley and Morocco, while Britain and Russia likewise agreed to divide Persia into spheres of influence.

Thus all the major powers now were aligned in rival alliance systems, with disastrous results for international relations. Whenever any dispute of consequence arose, the members of both blocs felt compelled to support their respective allies who were directly involved, even if they were doubtful about the issues. Otherwise they feared that their alliances would disintegrate, leaving them alone and exposed. Each dispute consequently was magnified into a major crisis involving, willy-nilly, all the members of both alliances.

The final background cause was the rising nationalist aspirations of Europe's subject minorities. This was difficult enough in Alsace-Lorraine, where the French remained unreconciled to German rule. But it was a nightmare in Central and Eastern Europe, where the multinational empires were in danger of being literally torn to pieces by the growing demand for self-determination. In the Hapsburg Empire, for example, the ruling Austrians and Hungarians were confronted by the awakening Italians and Rumanians as well as the many Slavic peoples: Czechs, Slovaks, Ruthenians, Poles, Slovenes, Croats, and Serbs. Very understandably, the Hapsburg officials decided that firm measures were necessary if the empire was to survive. This was especially true regarding the militant Serbs who were clamoring for unification with the independent Serbia across the Danube. Hence the stiff terms sent to Belgrade when the Archduke was murdered by a Serb patriot at Sarajevo. But behind Serbia was Russia, and behind Russia were France and Britain. Austria-Hungary, likewise, was backed by Germany and, theoretically, by Italy. Thus the combination of national self-determination and conflicting alliance systems drove the European powers to the holocaust.

II. SARAJEVO

On June 28, 1914, Archduke Francis Ferdinand and his wife were assassinated in Sarajevo, the capital of the recently annexed province of Bosnia. The murder was committed by a young Bosnian Serb student named Gavrilo Princip. He was not alone in carrying out the murder but was backed up by the secret Serbian organization Ujedinjenje ili Smrt, or "Union or Death," popularly known as the Black Hand. Founded in Belgrade in 1911, the Black Hand had as its avowed aim the realization of "the national ideal: the union of all Serbs." The Serbian government was not behind this society, which indeed was regarded as dangerously radical and militant. But this did not prevent the Black Hand from organizing an underground revolutionary organization that conducted an effective campaign of agitation and terrorism.

The unfortunate Francis Ferdinand played into the hands of these Serb revolutionaries by agreeing to pay an official visit to the Bosnian capital. When the archduke and his duchess began their procession on the radiant Sunday morning of June 28, no less than six assassins, armed with bombs and revolvers, were waiting along the designated route. As fate would have it, the procession stopped at the very corner where Princip was stationed. He drew his revolver and fired two shots, one at Francis Ferdinand and the other at General Potiorek, the Governor of Bosnia. The second shot went wild and hit the duchess instead. Before medical aid arrived, both the archduke and his wife were dead.

Now the alliance system began to operate relentlessly and fatally. First Germany assured Austria-Hungary of full support regardless of what course it decided upon. On July 23, Austria presented Serbia with a stiff ultimatum, which included demands for explanations and apologies, suppression of anti-Austrian publications and organizations, participation of Austrian officials in the inquiry regarding responsibility for the crime, and judicial proceedings against those accessory to the plot. The Serbian reply on July 25 accepted nearly all the terms but refused the demand that Hapsburg officials participate *within* Serbian territory in the investigation of the crime. Austria promptly broke off diplomatic relations, and on July 28 it declared war on Serbia.

Russia now retaliated and ordered full mobilization on July 30. The next day Germany sent a twelve-hour ultimatum to Russia demanding that mobilization be stopped. When no reply was received, Germany declared war against Russia on August 1 and against Russia's ally, France, on August 3. On the same day Germany began actual hostilities by invading Belgium. This aggression was given as the reason for Britain's declaration of war on Germany on August 4. Thus the great powers of Europe were at each other's throats five weeks after the murders at Sarajevo.

III. EUROPEAN PHASE OF THE WAR, 1914–1917

1914: War of Attrition in the West

World War I began with peoples on both sides confidently expecting a brief and victorious war. Instead, they soon found themselves embroiled in a prolonged and brutalizing ordeal that took unprecedented toll of material wealth and human lives. The explanation for the bloody stalemate that gutted European civilization is to be found in the failure of traditional war strategy. The general staffs of all the European armies had for years been carefully preparing for war against any neighbor or combination of neighbors. The Germans had a plan devised in 1905 by their chief of staff, Count Alfred von Schlieffen. The Schlieffen Plan called for a speedy and overwhelming attack upon France before turning against the slow-moving Russians in the east. The bulk of the German forces were to be concentrated in the north and were to attack through Belgium and Luxembourg in a vast wheeling movement that would roll up the French army to the east of Paris and thus end the war in thirty days.

On August 4 this plan went into operation when German forces crossed the frontier of Belgium, whose neutrality Germany itself had guaranteed, and rushed through Belgium and northern France. They reached the Marne River, and by September 2 were at Chantilly, only 25 miles from Paris. Now the tide unexpectedly began to turn when the French counterattacked through a 30-mile-wide gap between the advancing German armies. Outnumbered 4 to 3, and exhausted by their long advance, the Germans retreated to the natural defense line of the Aisne River. The opposing armies now began a series of flanking and counterflanking movements that ended only when the battle front extended from the coast of Flanders to the frontier of Switzerland.

This line did not shift by more than ten miles in either direction during the next three years despite repeated offensives that took a ghastly toll in lives. The reason for the bloody deadlock was that from the beginning of the war defensive weapons proved superior over offensive. The traditional mode of attack was the massed infantry charge supported by a preliminary artillery barrage. But this was of no avail against the combination of deep trenches, barbed wire entanglements, ingenious land mines, and machine-gun nests. Thus the casualties on the western front during the first four months were 700,000 Germans, 850,000 French, and 90,000 British. Contrary to the plans of all general staffs, the struggle in the west now became a war of position and attrition.

This was not the case on the Russian and Balkan fronts, where vast distances and scanty transportation facilities necessitated a fluid war of movement. The Russians led off with a surprisingly fast and powerful offensive into East Prussia, designed to relieve the pressure on the French in the west. The strategy worked, for the Germans transferred four divisions from Belgium to the east. Before they reached their destination, the issue had been decided by smashing victories over two Russian armies advancing into East Prussia. The German commanders, Hindenburg and Ludendorff, used their superior railway network to concentrate their forces against first one Russian army and then the other. By the middle of September, East Prussia was cleared of its invaders.

On the Balkan front the Austrians meanwhile were suffering humiliating setbacks. General Potiorek, who had barely escaped Princip's bullet in Sarajevo, was impatient to destroy ''the viper's nest.'' On August 12 he crossed the Drina River into Serbia with 250,000 men. But he was met by a Serbian army of 350,000, of whom 90 percent were seasoned veterans of the Balkan Wars of 1912–13. In less than two weeks the Serbs had forced the Austrians back across the river with a loss of one-third of their numbers. Potiorek returned to the attack in September and succeeded in taking Belgrade on December 2. But again the Serbians counterattacked, and by the end of the same month had cleared their country of the invaders.

1915: Russian Retreat in the East

The 1915 campaigns were dominated by the decision of the new German commander-in-chief, Erich von Falkenhayn, to reverse the Schlieffen Plan. In view of the stalemate on the western front he concentrated his forces on the east in an effort to knock out the Russians. Combined German and Austrian armies attacked with stunning effect on May 1, advancing by the end of the summer an average of 200 miles. In addition to military casualties totaling 2.5 million men, Russia lost 15 percent of its territories, 10 percent of its railways, 30 percent of its industries, and 20 percent of its civilian population. The Tsarist regime suffered a blow from which it never was able to recover.

At the same time the Western Powers were attempting to force the Straits in order to knock out Turkey and open a supply route to Russia. When Turkey joined the Central Powers on November 2, 1914, the Straits automatically were closed to the Allies, thus making it difficult to ship much-needed supplies to Russia. Accordingly, on March 18, 1915, a squadron of fourteen British and four French battleships steamed into the Straits with guns blazing. Heavy losses from mines and coastal artillery forced the Allied ships to withdraw. An attempt then was made to take the Straits by landings on the Gallipoli beaches, but only shallow footholds were secured in the face of withering machine-gun fire. The Turks held on to the heights above the beaches until the Allies finally faced facts and withdrew permanently in January 1916.

The failure at the Straits together with the disaster on the Russian front persuaded Bulgaria to join the Central Powers on October 14, 1915. This intervention spelled the end for the Serbs. An overwhelming number of German, Austrian, and Bulgarian divisions attacked Serbia on October 6 from three sides. By the end of the year the entire country was occupied.

To counterbalance these setbacks in the Balkans, the Allies were strengthened by the decision of Italy to join their cause. Although the Italians technically had been allies of the Central Powers, they decided at the outset of the war to remain neutral. The bulk of the Italian people favored this course, especially since it was Austria that held the "unredeemed" lands across the Adriatic. The Allies now freely offered these lands to Italy, together with additional territories at the expense of Turkey. The bait was effective, and on April 29 Italy signed the Treaty of London agreeing to enter the war in one month in return for these territorial promises. Actually Italy's intervention scarcely affected the course of the war, apart from compelling the Austrians to divert a few divisions from the eastern front.

1916: Verdun and the Somme

By 1916 the Central Powers had reached the height of their military fortunes. They controlled the continent of Europe from Hamburg to the Persian Gulf, yet they were not able to force a peace settlement on the Allies. To secure such a settlement, the Germans in February 1916 launched an all-out attack on the key French fortress of Verdun. The British counterattacked with an offensive to the northwest at the Somme. But the defense again proved superior to the offense. The two 1916 drives cost about 850,000 German casualties and about 950,000 British and French. Yet neither side was able to advance more than seven miles.

Meanwhile the Russians, to everyone's surprise, made a successful offensive on the eastern front. The Austrians had thinned their lines in Galicia in order to reinforce an attack against Italy. Consequently, when General Brusilov started what was intended at first to be merely a feint to relieve the pressure on Verdun, the Austrian front "broke like a pie crust" for a distance of 200 miles. The Russians poured all reserves into the gap and overran the province of Galicia.

The failure of the Germans at Verdun and the unexpected success of the Brusilov offensive encouraged Rumania to intervene in the war on the side of the Allies on August 27, 1916. The Central Powers now decided to make an object lesson of Rumania, as a warning to other neutrals who might be thinking of following its course. German, Austrian, Bulgarian, and Turkish forces descended in full speed and overwhelming force. By the end of the year the Rumanians had lost two-thirds of their country, including their capital.

The involvement of Rumania in the war left Greece as the only neutral in the Balkans. That country was fairly evenly divided on the issue of neutrality or intervention. The most prominent statesman, Eleutherios Venizelos, was all for joining the Allies, but King Constantine, who was the kaiser's brother-in-law, insisted on neutrality. The deadlock was broken in 1917 when the Allies decided that Greek assistance was essential to succeed in Macedonia, where they had been fighting inconclusively against the Bulgars. Accordingly, the Allies resorted to various extralegal measures, such as seizing the Greek fleet, blockading Greek ports, and even landing troops at Piraeus. Finally, on June 27, 1917, Greece entered the war on the Allied side, and so paved the way for the 1918 offensives in Macedonia that knocked Bulgaria out of the war.

1917: Bloodletting and Defeatism

Meanwhile, the terrible bloodletting was continuing unabated on the western front. Whereas in 1916 the Germans had assumed the offensive at Verdun, now in 1917 the Allies took the lead. The cautious General Joffre was replaced by the audacious General Nivelle who preached with persuasive fervor of a new type of lightning offensive that would bring victory with few casualties. Despite the opposition of many military leaders, both French and British, Nivelle's aggressive strategy was accepted.

The Germans at the same time had replaced Falkenhayn with their eastern-front team of Hindenburg and Ludendorff. After the shattering experience of the previous year at Verdun and the Somme, they decided to go on the defensive on the western front and to open unrestricted submarine warfare at sea. They hoped thereby to starve England into submission, leaving France isolated on the Continent. They were well aware that submarine warfare involved the risk of American intervention, but they gambled that England would be broken before American aid could become effective.

We shall see shortly that this gamble came within an ace of being won, though in the end it brought disaster. But the defensive strategy on land paid off handsomely. In order to consolidate and strengthen his front lines, Hindenburg withdrew his forces to a new fortified position (the Hindenburg Line) that was straighter, shorter, and more heavily fortified. The withdrawal badly upset Nivelle's offensive plans, but he persisted in going through with them. French, British, and Canadian troops went over the top as scheduled, but they suffered one of the bloodiest defeats of the war. Hindenburg's defensive strategy served the Germans well. They inflicted 400,000 casualties on the Allies, while incurring only 250,000 themselves.

By this time the peoples of Europe were enduring the fourth year of the most devastating and murderous war in history. Despite all the sacrifices and grief, no end was yet in sight. War weariness and defeatism appeared not only in the trenches but also amongst the civilians in both camps. One of the most spectacular manifestations was the passage of a Peace Resolution by the German Reichstag on July 19, 1917, by a vote of 212 to 126. In Austria-Hungary the death of the respected old Emperor Francis Joseph on November 21 brought to the throne the young Emperor Charles who began secret peace overtures. Likewise in England, a former foreign secretary, Lord Lansdowne, wrote an open letter prophesying the collapse of Western civilization unless some way was found to end the conflict.

IV. GLOBAL PHASE OF THE WAR: 1917 RUSSIAN REVOLUTION

1917 proved to be the year of decision because of two fateful developments—the Russian Revolutions and the intervention of the United States. These events changed the character of the war—from an essentially European affair fought over primarily European issues, to a war of global proportions. The American intervention and the Russian Revolutions also introduced a new ideological element that immediately had worldwide effects. Wilson's Fourteen Points and Lenin's revolutionary slogans were universal and disruptive in their impact, unlike limited European issues such as the fate of Alsace-Lorraine or of the Hapsburg subject nationalities. It was in 1917, then, that the transition occurred from the European to the global phase of World War I.

Roots of Russian Revolution

Russians of all classes rallied behind their government when war with Germany began on August 1, 1914. In contrast to the Japanese War of 1904–1905, this conflict was popular with the masses of the people, who were convinced it was a war of defense against the aggression of their traditional German enemies. The only exception to this closing of ranks came from the extreme left-wing Bolsheviks. Their leader, Lenin, branded the war as an imperialist struggle over markets and colonies. There was no reason, therefore, why the workers of the world should sacrifice themselves in such a conflict. Instead, Lenin called upon them to turn against the imperialist instigators of war: "Turn the imperialist war into a class war!" This, however, was the only discordant note in 1914, and at that time it was unnoticed and insignificant. The Bolsheviks were a tiny faction within Russia, and their outstanding leaders were in exile abroad, including Lenin, who was in Switzerland, and Trotsky, who was in New York.

Not only were the Russians united against the Germans, they were also confident that they would win the war in short order. But instead of quick victory, Russia suffered disastrous defeats. The most densely populated and highly industrialized provinces of the empire were lost to the Central Powers. The disasters of 1915 proved to be the beginning of the end of the Tsarist regime.

One reason why Russia never recovered from the military setbacks is that it simply lacked the economic strength to wage modern warfare against first-class industrial powers. Russian factories were incapable of supplying the needed quantities of arms, munitions, and supplies. This economic weakness became much worse with the loss of the industrialized portions of the empire in 1915. In addition, Russia's war effort was handicapped by incompetent military leadership. When hostilities began, Tsar Nicholas selected his uncle, Grand Duke Nicholas, to serve as commander in chief. The Grand Duke was regarded by all as unqualified for the position.

The Russians were handicapped also by political quarrels on the home front. The Duma and the imperial bureaucracy were constantly feuding over their respective jurisdictions and prerogatives. Both of them, in turn, clashed with the military in assigning responsibility for the shortage of war supplies and, ultimately, for the defeats at the front. This discord might have been minimized and controlled if there had been strong leadership at the top. Unfortunately, Tsar Nicholas was a well-meaning but weak and vacillating ruler with limited intelligence and imagination. The final outcome was the destruction of his family, the ending of the Tsarist regime, and the victory of the Bolsheviks.

March Revolution

In actuality, two revolutions occurred in Russia in 1917: the first, in March, ended Tsarism and created a Provisional Government, while the second, in November, toppled the Provisional Government and substituted Soviet rule. The first revolution was an unplanned affair that took everyone by surprise. Strikes and riots broke out in Petrograd on

March 8 because of the desperate shortage of food and fuel due to poor transportation facilities. The authorities ordered the army to restore order, but, instead, the soldiers mutinied and sided with the demonstrators. The Tsar, always distrustful of the Duma, suspected it of complicity and ordered its dissolution on March 11. The Duma leaders refused to obey the order, and the Tsar discovered that he no longer could enforce obedience. The realization of powerlessness was to all intents and purposes the revolution itself. Russia no longer had a functioning government. This was the situation legally as well as factually when Tsar Nicholas abdicated on March 15 in favor of his brother Michael, and when Michael in turn gave up the throne the following day.

Some new structure had to be erected quickly lest the radical elements in the streets take over. On March 12 a Provisional Government was organized to administer the country until a Constituent Assembly could be elected. The new government was headed by the liberal Prince Georgi Lvov and included the Cadet leader Professor Paul Miliukov as minister for foreign affairs and Alexander Kerensky, the only Socialist, as minister of justice. This was a bourgeois, liberal, middle-of-the-road cabinet, which favored reform up to a certain point. In fact, it did proclaim freedom of speech, press, and assembly; it declared an amnesty for political and religious offenses; recognized the legal equality of all citizens without social, religious, or racial discrimination; and passed labor legislation, including the eight-hour day. Despite its record of reform, the Provisional Government never sank roots in the country. For eight months it strove desperately but in vain to provide an adequate administration. At the end of that time the new government was not overthrown; rather, it collapsed as helplessly as the Tsarist regime had in March.

Between Revolutions

The period between March and November 1917 was one of struggle for power between the Provisional Government and the *soviets*. In this struggle the Provisional Government was fatally handicapped because from the beginning it refused to consider the two things that most Russians wanted—peace and land. Prince Lvov and his ministers insisted that such a fundamental reform as redistribution of land must wait for a Constituent Assembly that would be truly representative of the people and would have the authority to decide on such a basic issue. Likewise, the government refused to end the war because Russia had certain commitments to its allies that could not be denied. These arguments were sensible and understandable, but politically they were suicidal. While the government was pleading for patience, the soviets were winning over the masses by demanding immediate peace and immediate distribution of land.

The origin of the soviets goes back to the 1905 Revolution when the workers elected councils, or soviets, to coordinate their struggle against Tsarism. Although suppressed at that time, the soviets had proven their value as organs for agitation and direct action. Very naturally, soviets reappeared with the crisis precipitated by the World War. Because of their origin and composition, they had none of the Provisional Government's squeamishness about waiting for elections before proceeding with peace negotiations and land distribution. Without hesitation or reservations they gave voice to popular needs, and in doing so attracted more and more mass support. Thus the soviet movement mushroomed throughout the country, developing virtually into a grass-roots government that continually challenged that in Petrograd. Village soviets were organizing seizures of nobles' estates; city soviets were behind the unceasing demonstrations and riots in the streets; while the soldiers' soviets were gradually usurping the authority of the officers to the point where they had control of all weapons and countersigned all orders before they could be executed.

At the beginning, the delegates elected to the soviets were predominantly Socialist Revolutionaries and Mensheviks. The Bolsheviks remained relatively insignificant until the return of their leaders from Switzerland. On April 16, Lenin arrived in Petrograd and issued his famous "April Theses" demanding immediate peace, land to the peasants, and all power to the soviets. Lenin was almost alone in calling for a second revolution at once. Time, however, was on his side, for the longer the war continued, the more the public discontent mounted, and the more popular Lenin's demands became. Slogans that seemed bizarre in April were to sound perfectly reasonable half a year later. By late 1917 many were ready to fight for "all power to the soviets" in order to be rid of the Provisional Government that stood in the way of the much-desired peace and land.

An early indication of shifting public opinion was the forced resignation of Foreign Minister Miliukov on May 17. His insistence that Russia remain in the war made him so unpopular that he was dropped and a new Provisional Government formed under Lvov and Kerensky. It remained in office until July 20, when Kerensky, who had been steadily emerging as the strongman, organized a new government with himself as premier. By this time the temper of the country had swung so far to the left that the new ministers were mostly Socialist Revolutionaries and Mensheviks. Gone were the days when the Cadets were regarded as the radicals of Russian politics. Now Kerensky was cooperating with the Mensheviks and the Socialist Revolutionaries in order to withstand Lenin and his Bolsheviks.

Bolshevik Revolution

Kerensky declared that his main objective was "to save the revolution from the extremists." In an effort to halt the growing seizure of estates, he warned that the future Constituent Assembly would not recognize land transfers made after July 25. He also tried to restore some discipline in the armed forces by reintroducing the death penalty for certain offenses. These measures naturally made Kerensky very unpopular with the Bolsheviks and other radicals. Unfortunately for him, he did not thereby attract the support of the military men and other conservatives. They regarded him as a weak, loud-mouthed politician and demanded that he take immediate steps to crush the soviets. When he refused to do so, a certain General Lavr Kornilov staged an army revolt against Kerensky with the avowed aim of freeing the government from soviet domination.

The effect of Kornilov's revolt was precisely the opposite from that which was intended. It was the soviets that took the lead in organizing resistance against Kornilov and in conducting propaganda amongst his troops until many deserted. Thus Kornilov was defeated primarily by the soviets, and Kerensky consequently found himself under their domination. Furthermore, by this time the Bolsheviks were becoming increasingly influential within the soviets as public opinion veered more and more to the left. By October the Bolsheviks had a majority in both the Petrograd and Moscow soviets. Lenin now decided that the time had come to overthrow Kerensky and bring about the socialist revolution. But his own party still was not ready for the final plunge. It feared that it would not be able to retain power even if it were able to topple the Provisional Government. Lenin replied that 240,000 Bolshevik party members could govern Russia in the interest of the poor against the rich as easily as 130,000 landlords previously had governed in the interest of the rich against the poor. Finally, after threatening to resign, Lenin persuaded the central committee of his party to vote for revolution, and the date was set for November 7.

The actual revolution was anticlimactic. With almost no resistance the Bolshevik forces seized key positions in Petrograd—railway stations, bridges, banks, and government buildings. Blood was shed only at the Winter Palace, and casualties there totaled one Red soldier and five Red sailors. Kerensky managed to escape, and, after a futile attempt to organize resistance, he fled to exile abroad. Thus the Provisional Government fell with a humiliating casualness much like the end of Tsarism. There was no fighting, because Kerensky had as few dedicated supporters in November as Nicholas had had in March.

The easy victory of the Bolsheviks did not mean that they commanded the support of all the Russian people, or even the majority. This was demonstrated by the composition of the Constituent Assembly that was finally elected on November 25: Socialist Revolutionaries, 370; Bolsheviks, 175; Left Socialist Revolutionaries, 40; Cadets, 17; Mensheviks, 16; national groups, 86. The Assembly met in Petrograd on January 18, 1918, and, after holding one session, was dispersed by the Bolsheviks, who now had military power. Nevertheless, the make-up of the Assembly reveals the relative followings of the various parties at that time.

One of the first measures of the new Bolshevik government was to fulfill the promise of peace. On March 3, 1918, it signed the Brest-Litovsk Treaty with Germany. The treaty's severe terms required the surrender by Russia of Poland, the Baltic provinces, Finland, the Ukraine, and parts of the Caucasus. The areas surrendered involved 62 million people and 1¼ million square miles of territory, and they produced three-fourths of Russia's iron and coal. They also included half of its industrial plants and a third of its crop area.

LENIN PROCLAIMS THE NEW ORDER

The day after the overthrow of the Provisional Government, Lenin delivered a speech before the Petrograd Soviet in which he set forth the general objectives of his new regime. The text of this speech, given below, reveals the basic difference between the former Provisional Government and the new Bolshevik leaders, with their aim for ''socialist revolution'' within Russia and throughout the world.*

Comrades, the workmen's and peasants' revolution, the need of which the Bolsheviks have emphasized many times, has come to pass.

What is the significance of this revolution? Its significance is, in the first place, that we shall have a soviet government, without the participation of bourgeoisie of any kind. The oppressed masses will of themselves form a government. The old state machinery will be smashed into bits and in its place will be created a new machinery of government by the soviet organizations. From now on there is a new page in the history of Russia, and the present, third Russian revolution shall in its final result lead to the victory of Socialism.

One of our immediate tasks is to put an end to the war at once. But in order to end the war, which is closely bound up with the present capitalistic system, it is necessary to overthrow capitalism itself. In this work we shall have the aid of the world labor movement, which has already begun to develop in Italy, England, and Germany.

A just and immediate offer of peace by us to the international democracy will find everywhere a warm response among the international proletariat masses. In order to secure the confidence of the proletariat, it is necessary to publish at once all secret treaties.

In the interior of Russia a very large part of the peasantry has said: Enough playing with the capitalists; we will go with the workers. We shall secure the confidence of the peasants by one decree, which will wipe out the private property of the landowners. The peasants will understand that their only salvation is in union with the workers.

We will establish a real labor control on production.

We have now learned to work together in a friendly manner, as is evident from this revolution. We have the force of mass organization which has conquered all and which will lead the proletariat to world revolution.

We should now occupy ourselves in Russia in building up a proletarian socialist state.

Long live the world-wide socialistic revolution.

* F. A. Golder, ed., *Documents of Russian History, 1914–1917* (New York: Appleton, 1927), pp. 618–619.

In this manner Russia dropped out of World War I, and the new Bolshevik rulers proceeded to organize the Union of Soviet Socialist Republics.

V. GLOBAL PHASE OF THE WAR: AMERICAN INTERVENTION

When World War I began, President Wilson immediately called upon his fellow citizens to be strictly neutral. This met with general approval, for the great majority of Americans wished to stay out of the war. And yet, by 1917, Wilson himself was leading the country into war. Why this shift from neutrality to intervention within two and a half years?

One factor was the campaign for military preparedness. The National Security League, founded on December 1, 1914, was vigorously supported by military men, munitions makers, and politicians seeking an issue. They publicized the possibility of war with Germany and demanded compulsory military training and very substantial increases in the standing army and the navy. Wilson at first opposed this agitation, but for political reasons he could not ignore it altogether. In the end, he sponsored the National Defense Act of June 3, 1916, which doubled the standing army, reorganized the National Guard, and provided for the training of officers in colleges and summer camps. Two months later another bill authorized a three-year program for major expansion of the navy. The intensive agitation and publicity connected with this military preparedness helped to prepare the nation psychologically for intervention in the war.

Very similar was the effect of the armed American intervention into Mexico between March 1916 and February 1917. This was precipitated when Francisco (Pancho) Villa, a half-revolutionary and half-bandit, raided the border town of Columbus in New Mexico, leaving behind nineteen dead. Villa's aim was to provoke American intervention and thereby to discredit and overthrow President Carranza. Wilson responded by promptly ordering a punitive expedition under General John Pershing. Although over 100,000 men were sent across the border, it was impossible to pin down Villa and his followers. Nevertheless, this strange interlude contributed to the building up of a war spirit in the United States because it provided the thrills of military action without the grief and sacrifice.

Another factor operating in favor of intervention was the American financial and industrial commitment to the Allied cause. By the end of 1914 the House of Morgan was already "coordinating" Allied purchases of war material in the United States. To pay for these purchases the Allied powers first gave cash, then sold the bonds and stocks they held in the United States, and finally had to resort to large-scale borrowing. This situation inevitably generated pressures for American involvement in the war. Booming industries in the United States were dependent upon continued Allied orders, while American bankers had safes full of British and French IOU's that would become worthless if Germany emerged victorious.

Also noteworthy are the propaganda campaigns conducted by both the Allies and the Central Powers to influence American thinking. The Allies on the whole were more successful, partly because of superior skill and communication facilities, but also because their case was easier to justify and defend. British high-handedness on the seas paled before the German invasion and occupation of Belgium, and especially Germany's unrestricted submarine warfare against merchant shipping. The number of U-boats had risen so high that the German military believed, given a free hand, it could bring England to its knees within six months. This was the basic reason why the German government ordered unrestricted submarine warfare beginning on February 1, 1917, with full realization that it would lead almost inevitably to American intervention in Europe.

Wilson now cut diplomatic relations with Germany, but he still drew back from actual war. Wilson's restraint failed to halt what was now an inexorable drift to war. The publication, in March 1917, of the notorious Zimmermann telegram revealed German plans to involve Mexico in war against the United States if the latter joined the Allies. At the same time the Germans were torpedoing American ships and American lives were being lost. To cap it all, the Tsarist regime was now overthrown, and the United States recognized the new Russian Provisional Government on March 20. Without reservations the United States could now join a league of democratic powers battling the autocracies of Central Europe. By early April the United States did so, with the avowed aim of making the world "safe for democracy."

Wilson's address to the joint session of Congress on January 8, 1918, set forth specific and detailed war aims in the form of *Wilson's Fourteen Points*. Outstanding among these were "open covenants of Peace" as against secret diplomacy, freedom of the seas, removal of barriers to international trade, reduction of armaments, impartial adjustment to all colonial claims on the principle that the interests of the colonial peoples must have equal weight with the claims of colonial powers, and the application of the principle of self-determination in dealing with the various subject minorities in Central and Eastern Europe.

VI. ALLIED VICTORY

British and American naval experts are agreed that only a few more submarines would have enabled Germany to win the war. How close the decision was is evident in the figures on ship losses and ship construction presented in Table 9. These figures show that the Allies won out not only by stepping up ship construction but also by cutting down on ship sinkings. This was achieved by a variety of methods, including the development of an efficient convoy system, the camouflaging of merchant vessels, the use of depth bombs containing large charges of high explosives, and the invention of hydrophones, which made possible the detection of nearby submarines. Thanks to this variety of devices the Allies passed the danger point early in 1918, when the construction of new ships for the first time surpassed the tonnage destroyed.

Once the U-boat threat was overcome, the United States was able to make effective use of its enormous economic potential. How decisive this was is made clear in the statistics concerning the productivity of the belligerents shown in Table 10.

The intervention of the United States gave the Allies decisive superiority in manpower as well as in war supplies. In the month of March 1918, a total of 84,889 American soldiers reached the western front, and in July the number rose to 306,350. Thus a fresh

Table 9. ALLIED AND NEUTRAL SHIPS LOST AND CONSTRUCTED DURING WORLD WAR I (GROSS TONS)*

Period	Lost	Constructed
1915	1,744,657	1,202,000
1916	2,799,772	1,688,000
1917	6,623,623	2,937,786
1918		
1st quarter	1,146,920	870,317
2nd quarter	963,370	1,243,274
3rd quarter	892,546	1,384,130

* David Lloyd George, War Memoirs (Boston: Little, 1934), III, 132–33. By permission of the Beaverbrook Foundations.

Table 10. PRODUCTION OF THE BELLIGERENT POWERS (IN MILLIONS OF TONS)*

	August 1, 1914		September 15, 1914		1917	
	Allies	Central Powers	Allies	Central Powers	Allies	Central Powers
Pig Iron	22	22	16	25	50	15
Steel	19	21	16	25	58	16
Coal	394	331	346	355	851	340

*F. Sternberg, Capitalism and Socialism on Trial (New York: Day, 1951), pp. 166–67.

new army was made available to the Allied commanders each month. It is not surprising that during 1918 the Central Powers surrendered one by one.

The first to surrender were the Bulgarians, whose front crumbled when General Franchet d'Esperey, commander of the Allied forces in Saloniki, attacked in mid-September. On September 29, 1918, Bulgarian representatives signed an armistice, and on October 3 King Ferdinand abdicated in favor of his son Boris. Likewise in Turkey, British imperial forces were advancing victoriously in a two-pronged drive—one from Egypt up the Levant coast, and the other from the Persian Gulf up the Mesopotamian valley. At the same time an Allied force from Saloniki was marching upon Constantinople. Staggered by these setbacks and isolated by Bulgaria's surrender, the Turks accepted an armistice on October 30, 1918.

Most desperate was the position of Austria-Hungary. The numerous minorities were organizing national assemblies and proclaiming their independence. Even German-Austrians and Hungarians, who hitherto had ruled the empire, now were talking in terms of independent states of their own. At the same time the Italians were breaking through on the Piave, while Franchet d'Esperey was advancing up the Danube. On November 3 an Austro-Hungarian Armistice Commission accepted the terms of the Italian High Command, and on November 6 Count Michael Karolyi, a liberal Hungarian leader, signed a separate armistice at Belgrade in behalf of Hungary. The ancient Hapsburg Empire finally reached its end on November 11, when Emperor Charles abdicated.

Meanwhile, the German position on the western front had steadily deteriorated. With American soldiers pouring in, Marshal Foch, the Allied commander in chief, was able to strike where and as he pleased. German casualties were outstripping replacements, and deserters were crowding into depots and railroad stations. These setbacks, together with the news of their defecting allies, forced the Germans to begin armistice negotiations. A principal stumbling block was the kaiser's refusal to abdicate. His hand was forced, however, by mutiny in the German fleet at Kiel on November 3. The mutiny spread rapidly from port to port and then into the interior. The chancellor, Prince Max, forced the issue by announcing the abdication of the emperor November 9. Two days later the armistice was signed and fighting ceased on the western front.

Thus ended the First World War—a war that lasted four years and three months, involved thirty sovereign states, overthrew four empires, gave birth to seven new nations, took approximately 8.5 million combatant and 10 million noncombatant lives and cost $180.5 billion directly and $151.6 billion indirectly.

VII. PEACE SETTLEMENT

Separate peace treaties were signed with each of the Central Powers: the *Versailles Treaty* with Germany, June 28, 1919; the St. Germain Treaty with Austria, September 10, 1919; the Trianon Treaty with Hungary, March 22, 1919; the Neuilly Treaty with Bulgaria, November 27, 1919; and the Sèvres Treaty with Turkey, August 20, 1920. Three features of this overall peace settlement are significant for world history: the establishment of the *League of Nations,* the application of the principle of *self-determination* in Europe, and the failure to apply this principle outside Europe.

The League of Nations was organized in order to attain two basic objectives. The most important was to preserve the peace. Its members were to give each other mutual protection against aggression, to submit disputes to arbitration or inquiry, and to abstain from war until three months after arbitration. The secondary purpose of the League was to concern itself with health, social, economic, and humanitarian problems of international scope. For this purpose there were established specialized League bodies such as the Health Organization, the Committee on Intellectual Cooperation, and the International Labor Organization, as well as numerous temporary advisory commissions. By and large, the League succeeded brilliantly in its secondary functions. It proved invaluable in improving international labor conditions, promoting world health, combatting the narcotic and slave traffics, and coping with economic crises. But we shall see that the League was not able to keep the peace, and, since this was its chief aim, the failure spelled the end of the entire organization.

The post-World War I settlement was characterized also by the redrawing of European frontiers on the basis of the principle of self-determination. This policy, stated explicitly in the Fourteen Points, was officially implemented in the various peace treaties. The net result was a drastic revision of the map of Europe. Alsace-Lorraine was returned to France without question. Russia was deprived of most of its Baltic coastline by the establishment of the independent states of Finland, Latvia, Estonia, and Lithuania. An independent Poland was created, carved out of former Russian, German, and Hapsburg provinces; Czechoslovakia emerged from the former Hapsburg Empire. Yugoslavia also appeared, comprising prewar Serbia and Montenegro and various former Hapsburg territories inhabited by South Slavs. Rumania more than doubled in size as a result of its acquisitions from Austria-Hungary, Russia, and Bulgaria. Finally, from the remains of the old Hapsburg Empire, there emerged the two rump states of Austria and Hungary.

It does not follow that the principle of self-determination was invariably respected in the drawing of the new frontiers. Indeed, there were bitter protests concerning the sizable German minorities in Poland and Czechoslovakia, the Hungarian minorities in Yugoslavia, Rumania, and Czechoslovakia, and the Russian minorities in Poland, Czechoslovakia, and Rumania. The explanation is to be found partly in the fact that the numerous ethnic groups in Central and Eastern Europe were so inextricably mixed that no frontiers could be drawn without creating considerable minorities on one side or the other. The inevitable minorities, however, were substantially increased because frontiers sometimes were drawn to satisfy strategic considerations as well as nationalist aspirations. This was why the Sudeten Germans were left in Czechoslovakia, why the Tyrol Germans were left in Italy, and why the union of Austria and Germany was specifically forbidden by the St. Germain Treaty even though it would have been in accord with popular will, at least in the immediate postwar years. Yet despite these deviations, the new frontiers were infinitely more in accord with nationalist aspirations than the old. The number of the minority peoples was much smaller after World War I than before.

Although the peacemakers generally applied self-determination in Europe, they definitely did not do so outside Europe. This discrimination was clearly evident in Wilson's Fourteen Points, which specifically spelled out how the aspirations of the various European minorities were to be satisfied. By contrast, Point 5 declared that in the colonies "the interests of the populations concerned must have equal weight with the equitable claims of the government whose title is to be determined." The significant point here is the reference to the "interests" rather than to the "wishes" of the colonial peoples. Needless to say, it was the Europeans themselves who decided what these "interests" were, and the outcome was a modified form of imperial rule known as the mandate system.

Article 22 of the League Covenant referred to the inhabitants of the colonies taken from the Central Powers as "peoples not yet able to stand by themselves under the strenuous conditions of the modern world." The article accordingly provided that the ''tutelage of such peoples should be entrusted to advanced nations who, by reason of their resources, their experience, or their geographical position, can best undertake this responsibility . . . and that this tutelage should be exercised by them as Mandatories on behalf of the League.'' It is significant that this provision for ''tutelage'' under ''Mandatories'' was not extended to the colonies of the victorious Allies, whose inhabitants in many cases were at a similar level of development or lack of development.

The *mandates* article divided the foreign and overseas territories of Germany and the Ottoman Empire into Class-A, -B, and -C mandates. The category varied according to the level of development of the territory concerned. On this basis the former Ottoman possessions were put in Class A, and the German colonies in B and C. Of the Ottoman territories, Mesopotamia and Palestine were allotted to Britain as the Mandatory Power, and Syria and Lebanon to France. Of the German colonies, the greater part of Tanganyika went to Britain and the remainder to Belgium; Togoland and the Cameroons were divided between Britain and France; South-West Africa was allotted to the Union of South Africa; and Germany's Pacific islands north of the equator went to Japan, and those south of the equator to Australia and New Zealand.

The Mandatory Powers assumed specific obligations toward the inhabitants of the mandate territories. For fulfillment of these obligations they were accountable to the Permanent Mandates Commission and were required to report annually to the Council of the League of Nations. Though neither the Commission nor the League itself had authority to force a recalcitrant Mandatory Power to fill its obligations, it is significant that European states for the first time accepted certain specified procedures. The procedures varied according to the type of mandate. In the case of Class A, the Mandates article looked forward specifically to the granting of independence as soon as feasible. The duty of the Mandatory Power was merely ''the rendering of administrative advice and assistance . . . until such time as they [the people of the mandated territory] are able to stand alone. The wishes of these communities must be a principal consideration in the selection of the Mandatory.'' But for B- and C-Class mandates, there was no reference to eventual independence. The obligation rather was to provide administration in accord with the interests of the inhabitants.

Although the mandate system represented a certain improvement over the traditional division of colonial booty by the victors in a war, nevertheless it is strongly reminiscent of the 1815 settlement because it ignored national aspirations. We shall see that the inhabitants of the Ottoman territories did not want mandated status and were violently opposed to France as Mandatory Power. Their wishes were directly flouted when Syria and Lebanon were allotted to France. Even in the case of some of the Class-B mandates in Africa, there was acute dissatisfaction with the arrangements made. It is not surprising, then, that just as the ignoring of nationalist wishes in 1815 led to a long series of revolutions in Europe during the nineteenth century, so this mandate system was to lead to uprisings in the colonial world during the postwar years.

VIII. WORLD WAR I IN WORLD HISTORY

The overriding significance of World War I from a global viewpoint is that it began the undermining of Europe's supremacy—a process that was completed following World War II. The undermining was evident in at least three regards: the economic decline, the political crisis, and the weakening hold over the colonies.

Before 1914, Europe's economy was dependent to a considerable degree upon massive overseas investments, yielding massive annual returns. During World War I, however, Britain lost a quarter of its foreign investments, France a third, and Germany lost all. The reverse of this trend may be seen in the new financial strength of the United States. In 1914 the United States owed about $4 billion to European investors, but by 1919 the United States had become a creditor nation to the tune of $3.7 billion; by 1930 this had risen to $8.8 billion. The same pattern is evident in industry, for many European industrial areas were devastated, while American factories mushroomed spectacularly under the impetus of unlimited wartime demand. By 1929 the United States was responsible for no less than 42.2 percent of world industrial output, an amount greater than that of all the countries of Europe, including Russia. Thus, the economic relationships between Europe and the United States were reversed as a result of World War I. Europe no longer was the banker and the workshop of the world, as it had been during the nineteenth century. Leadership in both areas had crossed the Atlantic.

The war gutted Europe politically as well as economically. Prior to 1914 Europe had been the source of the basic political ideas and institutions of modern times. Their impact, as we have seen, had been felt in all corners of the globe. The holocaust of war, however, left Europeans demoralized and unbelieving. In all parts of the Continent the old order was being questioned and challenged. In a confidential memorandum of March 1919, the British premier, David Lloyd George, wrote, "There is a deep sense not only of discontent, but of anger and revolt, amongst the workmen against pre-war conditions. The whole existing order in its political, social and economic aspects is questioned by the masses of the people from one end of Europe to the other."[1]

In this revolutionary crisis, many Europeans looked for guidance to two non-Europeans, the American Wilson and the Russian Lenin. Wilson's Fourteen Points had stirred up a ferment of democratic hope and expectancy. When he stepped on the blood-soaked soil of Europe in December 1918, huge crowds greeted Wilson with delirious enthusiasm as "King of Humanity," "Savior," "Prince of Peace." They listened avidly to his plans for a future of peace and security.

At the same time another gospel of salvation was coming from the east. The millions of dead and wounded, the smoking ruins of cities and villages, made large masses receptive to the call for revolution and for a new social order. In imitation of the Bolshevik Revolution, soviets were set up in Berlin, Hamburg, and Budapest. Demonstrations were staged in the streets of London, Paris, and Rome. Wilson's confidante, Colonel House, wrote in his diary on March 22, 1919: "Rumblings of discontent every day. The people want peace. Bolshevism is gaining ground everywhere. Hungary has just succumbed. We are sitting upon an open powder magazine and some day a spark may ignite it."[2]

Finally, Europe's domination was undermined by World War I because of the repercussions in the overseas colonies. The spectacle of one bloc of European powers fighting another to the bitter end damaged the prestige of the white master irreparably. No longer was he regarded as almost divinely ordained to rule over colored subjects. Equally disruptive was the participation in the war of millions of colonials as soldiers or as laborers. Indian divisions fought on the western front and in Mesopotamia; many Africans in French uniform fought in northern France; and large numbers of Chinese and Indochinese served in labor battalions behind the lines. Needless to say, the colonials who returned home after such experiences were not likely to be as obedient to European overlords as before.

Revolutionary ideas in the colonies were also spread by propaganda associated with the conduct of the war. It is true that Wilson's Fourteen Points had referred only to the "interest" rather than to the desires of the colonial peoples. But this was an overfine distinction in a time of war. The revolutionary phrase "self-determination of peoples" left its imprint on the colonial world as well as upon Europe. Equally influential were the ideologies of socialism and communism. Before World War I, Asian intellectuals had been inspired by Western liberalism and nationalism. They had quoted Voltaire, Mazzini, and John Stuart Mill. But their sons now were likely to quote Marx, Lenin, or Harold Laski. Dr. Sun Yat-sen, on July 25, 1919, gave evidence of this shift when he declared, "If the people of China wish to be free . . . its only ally and brother in the struggle for national freedom are the Russian workers and peasants of the Red Army."[3]

All these repercussions of World War I on the colonial world inevitably had profound political consequences. One of the few who saw this clearly was the American black leader W.E.B. Du Bois, who in 1918 wrote the following remarkable forecast of the world to come.

> This war is an end and also a beginning. Never again will darker people of the world occupy just the place they had before. Out of this place will rise, soon or late, an independent China, a self-governing India, an Egypt with representative institutions, an Africa for the Africans, and not merely for business exploitation. Out of this war will rise, too, an American Negro with the right to vote and the right to work and the right to live without insult.[4]

SUGGESTED READING

L. Albertini, *The Origins of the War of 1914,* 2 vols., trans. and ed. I. M. Massey (Oxford University Press, 1953); H. W. Baldwin, *World War I: An Outline History* (Harper & Row, 1962); E. H. Carr, *The Bolshevik Revolution, 1917–1923,* 3 vols. (Macmillan, 1951–1953); M. Ferro, *The Great War, 1914–1918* (Routledge & Kegan Paul, 1973); R. W. Leopold, "The Problem of American Intervention, 1917: An Historical Retrospect," *World Politics,* II (1950), pp. 405–25; A. J. Mayer, *Politics and Diplomacy of Peace-making. Containment and Counterrevolution at Versailles 1918–1919* (Knopf, 1967).

chapter 32

Nationalist Uprisings In The Colonial World

World War I was followed by a wave of revolutions in the colonial territories. The roots of these revolutions go back to the pre-1914 years, but it was the war itself that provided the immediate stimulus. The final outcomes varied, with the Turks winning most of their objectives, while the Egyptians, Iraqis, Indians, and others won only modest constitutional concessions. These uprisings represent the prelude to the great upheavals that finally ended the European empires during the two decades following World War II.

I. TURKEY

The most spectacular and successful of all the post-World War I colonial revolts against European domination was that of the Turks. They had suffered disastrous defeat during the war, and had then been compelled to accept humiliating armistice and peace terms. Yet they bounced back, defeating their enemies in armed conflict and winning a new treaty with more favorable terms. Thus, of all the Central Powers, only primitive and despised Turkey was capable of turning upon the victorious Allies and forcing them to accept a revision of the peace settlement. To understand this extraordinary outcome it is necessary to review the tangled wartime diplomacy concerning the Ottoman Empire.

Wartime Diplomacy

Britain was the prime mover behind most of the diplomacy involving the Middle East during the war years. It was responsible for three sets of often conflicting agreements—with its own allies, with Arab representatives, and with the Zionists.

The agreements among the Allies consisted of four secret treaties: the Constantinople Agreement of March-April 1915, the Treaty of London of April 26, 1915, the Sykes-Picot Agreement of April 26, 1916, and the Saint-Jean-de-Maurienne Treaty of April 1917. These treaties allotted to Russia Constantinople, the Straits and a considerable portion of northeast Asia Minor; to Italy southwest Asia Minor; to Britain Mesopotamia and an enclave about Haifa and Acre; and to France the Syrian coast with the hinterland eastward to the Russian sphere. These secret treaties marked the death warrant of the Ottoman Empire, leaving to the Turks only 20,000 square miles in the northern section of their homeland. More important, these secret treaties were in direct conflict with certain agreements that Britain was concluding at this time with Arab representatives.

The leading figure among the Arabs was Emir Hussein of the Hashimite family, Keeper of the Holy Places and Prince of Mecca. When Turkey joined the Central Powers in November 1914, negotiations were begun between Hussein and Sir Henry McMahon, British high commissioner in Egypt. These resulted in a military alliance and an ambiguous political understanding. In return for an Arab revolt against the Turks, the British agreed to recognize the independence of the Arab countries south of the 37th latitude, including the Arabian peninsula. In the course of the correspondence, which dragged on between July 1915 and March 1916, McMahon stipulated that the agreement could not infringe upon unspecified French interests in Syria. Hussein replied that he would not consent to any Arab land becoming the possession of any power, meaning France. In order to avoid delay of the Arab revolt, this disputed point remained unclarified, with unfortunate results a few years later.

While the British Foreign Office was dealing with Hussein, the India Office was negotiating with Ibn-Saud, Sultan of the Nejd, whose territories were nearer the Persian Gulf. On December 26, 1915, an agreement was reached by which the India Office recognized Ibn-Saud's independence in return for his benevolent neutrality during the war. Though a different British government agency was involved, that did not alter the fact that contradictory commitments had been made to Ibn-Saud and to Hussein.

More ominous for the future was another conflicting commitment, this one to Lord Rothschild of the *World Zionist Organization*. Zionism was a nationalist movement that had developed among European Jews in the last quarter of the nineteenth century as a reaction against mounting anti-Semitism. The World Zionist Organization, established in Basle in 1897, had repeatedly but vainly sought permission from the Ottoman government to establish a Jewish settlement in Palestine, the Jewish biblical homeland. With Turkey's involvement in World War I, Zionist leaders in England and the United States seized the opportunity to press for an Allied commitment to create a Jewish commonwealth in Palestine after the end of the Ottoman Empire. The main government leaders in Britain gradually were won over to the Zionist position. On November 2, 1917, Lord Balfour wrote to Lord Rothschild that the British Government favored the establishment in Palestine of a "national home for the Jewish people . . . it being clearly understood that nothing shall be done which may prejudice the civil and religious rights of existing non-Jewish communities in Palestine. . . ." It is evident that this Balfour Declaration conflicted with both the Sykes-Picot and the Hussein-McMahon agreements.

In the end it was Britain and France who determined the Middle East peace settle-ment, for the United States was withdrawing into isolation, Russia was convulsed by civil war and intervention, while Italy was immobilized by internal dissension. The Treaty of Sèvres (August 10, 1920), then, was essentially of Anglo-French origin, and its provisions reflected that fact. France obtained Syria as a mandate, while Britain got Mesopotamia and Palestine, in addition to a protectorate over Egypt. The Dodecanese Islands were ceded to Italy, while Greece, thanks to the skillful diplomacy of its Premier Venizelos, ob-tained several Aegean islands, eastern Thrace, and the right to administer the Smyrna region for five years. After that its final disposition was to be determined by a plebiscite. Armenia and the Kingdom of Hejaz were recognized as independent. Finally, Soviet Russia, which was now in armed conflict with Allied interventionist forces, and which had published and repudiated the secret treaties signed by the Tsarist ministers, did not obtain Constantinople and the Straits. Instead, this strategic territory was left under Turkish sovereignty, though the Straits were to be demilitarized and placed under inter-national control.

These provisions, so contrary to the promises made to the Arabs and to the professed Allied principle of self-determination, aroused a wave of armed resistance throughout the Middle East. A combination of factors enabled the Turks to scrap the Sèvres Treaty al-together, while the Arabs won piecemeal concessions after ten years of stubborn struggle.

Republican Victory

The George Washington of modern Turkey is Mustafa Kemal, later known as Atatürk, or Foremost Turk. He won fame for his successful defense of the Dardanelles during the war, and, after the fighting ceased, he led the opposition to the Sèvres Treaty. He was per-fectly willing to surrender the Arab provinces of the old empire, but he refused to accept the cession of eastern Thrace, Constantinople, the Straits, or parts of Asia Minor. He traveled about in the Turkish hinterland, organizing resistance to the Allies and their puppet sultan in the capital. By September, 1919, Kemal had summoned a nationalist congress which adopted a National Pact consisting of six principles. These included self-determination, abolition of capitulations, security for Constantinople, and a new Straits settlement. In the elections of October 1919, Kemal's followers won a majority, and when parliament met in January 1920, it adopted the National Pact. Kemal now made the final break by summoning his nationalist deputies to Ankara in central Asia Minor. There, on April 23, 1920, they denounced the Sultan's regime and established a provisional govern-ment with Kemal as president.

The nationalists triumphed over seemingly overwhelming odds. One reason was the courageous and inspired leadership of Kemal. Another was the loyal support of the mass of the Turkish people, who were united to an unprecedented degree by the high-handedness of the Allies in Constantinople, and even more by the landing of Greek troops in Smyrna in the spring of 1919. Finally, Kemal exploited serious differences amongst the Allies to conclude separate treaties with them, thereby isolating the Greeks in Smyrna and paving the way for their defeat. The Allied dissension arose from the fact that both the French and the Italians felt, with justification, that the British and their Greek protégés had gotten the lion's share of the spoils in the Middle East. Accordingly, Kemal was able to sign separate treaties with France, Italy, and Russia, leaving only Britain and Greece to enforce the terms of the Sèvres Treaty. And Britain, because of its worldwide com-mitments and the state of public opinion at home, could do no more than maintain its ships in Constantinople and the Straits. In other words, the Greeks now were left alone in Smyrna to face the Turkish nationalist upsurge in Asia Minor.

Fighting between the Greeks and the Turks began at the end of March 1921. At first the Greeks met with weak resistance, because the opposition consisted of little more than guerrilla bands. But the population was so hostile that fully two-thirds of Greek man-power had to be used to guard transportation lines. The turning point came when the in-vaders reached the Sakarya River in the heart of Asia Minor. Kemal struck back, and the overextended Greeks were stopped dead and then pushed back. Retreat brought demoralization and eventually a stampede. By September 9, 1922, Kemal was riding triumphantly into Smyrna. Not only the Greek army, but also Greek civilians who had lived for centuries in the Smyrna region, were evacuated.

Kemal now was in a position to demand revision of the Sèvres Treaty. After long negotiations the Lausanne Treaty was signed on July 24, 1923. This returned to Turkey eastern Thrace and some of the Aegean islands. Also Turkey was to pay no reparations, and the capitulations were abolished in return for a promise of judicial reform. The Straits remained demilitarized, and open to ships of all nations in time of peace or war if Turkey remained neutral. If Turkey was at war, enemy ships, but not neutrals, might be excluded. Finally, a separate agreement provided for the compulsory exchange of the Greek minority in Constantinople for the Turkish minority in western Thrace and Macedonia.

New Turkey

The Lausanne Treaty represented a great personal triumph for Kemal. The decrepit Ot-toman Empire at long last was dead after half a millennium of checkered history. On October 29, 1923, the Turkish Republic was formally proclaimed with Kemal as presi-dent. Having created the new Turkey, Kemal now turned to the equally difficult task of creating new Turks. He ruthlessly swept away the outdated institutions of the past, as reform followed reform in a great torrent of change.

October 14, 1923—Capital of the Turkish state moved from Constantinople to Angora in the heart of Turkish Anatolia.
March 3, 1924—Caliphate abolished, and all members of the Ottoman dynasty banished from Turkey.
April 20, 1924—Adoption of a constitution providing for a president, premier, cabinet, and a grand national assembly elected quadrenially by indirect vote.
September 2, 1925—All religious orders and houses suppressed, and individuals prohibited from living as members of orders and from wearing the costumes or bearing the titles associated therewith.
January–February 1926—Introduction of new civil, criminal, and commercial law codes, based re-spectively on Swiss, Italian, and German systems.
August 17, 1926—Polygamy abolished.
November 3, 1928—Latin alphabet introduced in place of intricate Arabic script, the change being applied first to newspapers and then to books.
March 28, 1930—Place names changed: Constantinople to Istanbul; Angora to Ankara; Smyrna to Izmir; Adrianople to Edirne, and so forth.
December 14, 1934—Women given the right to vote and to sit in the assembly.

By the time of Kemal's death on November 10, 1938, the New Turkey was definitely established. The newness, however, was limited in its scope. A large proportion of the peasantry, which constituted the great majority of the population, still clung to their age-old Moslem ideas and customs. On the other hand, the new elite that governed the country had been Europeanized in its way of life and way of thought. The gap between peasants and the elite was to cause much trouble for Turkey after World War II.

II. ARAB MIDDLE EAST

While the Turks were successfully scrapping the Sèvres Treaty, the Arabs were stubbornly resisting the Mandatory Powers to which they had been assigned. Contrary to the Hussein-McMahon Agreement, Syria-Lebanon had been given as a mandate to France, Mesopotamia and Palestine had been made British mandates, and full British control had been established in Egypt. This high-handed parceling out of Arab lands was bound to lead to trouble, because the war itself had stimulated tremendous national sentiment among the Arabs.

A common pattern developed in the postwar struggle for independence. First, an explosion of defiance and armed revolt occurred during the years immediately following the peace treaties. Then Britain and France gradually restored order and reasserted their authority. Finally they granted varying degrees of autonomy, which did not entirely satisfy the nationalists, but which did preserve an uneasy peace until World War II.

In Egypt, the mandatory relationship, strictly speaking, did not exist. But the situation was essentially similar because Britain at the beginning of the war had repudiated the nominal Ottoman suzerainty and had declared the country a British protectorate. Immediately, the nationalist Wafd party organized violent opposition. In 1922 Britain proclaimed Egypt "an independent sovereign state" but reserved for itself control of foreign affairs and of external security, as well as protection of minorities and of foreign interests. The nationalists rejected this fake independence and continued the struggle. They won repeated electoral victories and also conducted a terror campaign. Finally in 1936 a compromise settlement was reached with the signing of a twenty-year alliance treaty. Britain undertook to end its military occupation of the country and to arrange for Egypt's admission to the League of Nations. In return, Egypt agreed to stand by Britain in time of war; to accept the British garrison stationed for the defense of the Suez Canal; and also to continue the joint British-Egyptian administration of the Sudan. Nationalist leaders were far from satisfied with this settlement. But they accepted it as the best available under the circumstances, and they waited for the first opportunity to abolish the hated remnants of foreign control.

Nationalist opposition in Iraq followed much the same course as in Egypt. A widespread armed revolt broke out in 1920. The British first restored order and then attempted to conciliate nationalist feeling by enthroning as king the third son of Hussein, Prince Faisal. The following year, in 1922, the British negotiated a treaty of alliance in which they retained such controls as they thought were needed to protect their interests. The nationalists remained dissatisfied and continued their agitation. Finally an alliance treaty was concluded in 1930, by which Britain agreed to end the mandate and to support Iraq's application for admission to the League of Nations. In return, Iraq agreed that Britain should maintain three air bases in the country and also should have full use of railways, rivers, and ports in time of war. In 1932 Iraq became a member of the League of

ARAB OPPOSITION TO MANDATES

Virtually all Arabs opposed the Allied plan for replacing the Ottoman Empire with Western-controlled mandates. This was made clear by the following memorandum adopted on July 2, 1919, by the General Syrian Congress (Syria at that time included present-day Syria, Lebanon, Jordan, and Israel). The rejection of this memorandum embittered Arab nationalists and contributed to the turmoil that grips the Middle East to the present day.*

1. We ask absolutely complete political independence for Syria. . . .

2. We ask that the Government of this Syrian country should be a democratic civil constitutional Monarchy on broad decentralization principles, safeguarding the rights of minorities, and that the King be the Emir Feisal, who carried on a glorious struggle in the cause of our liberation and merited our full confidence and entire reliance.

3. Considering the fact that the Arabs inhabiting the Syrian area are not naturally less gifted than other more advanced races and that they are by no means less developed than the Bulgarians, Serbians, Greeks, and Roumanians at the beginning of their independence, we protest against Article 22 of the Covenant of the League of Nations, placing us among the nations in their middle stage of development which stand in need of a mandatory power.

4. In the event of the rejection by the Peace Conference of this just protest for certain considerations that we may not understand, we, relying on the declarations of President Wilson that his object in waging war was to put an end to the ambition of conquest and colonization, can only regard the mandate mentioned in the Covenant of the League of Nations as equivalent to the rendering of economical and technical assistance that does not prejudice our complete independence. And desiring that our country should not fall a prey to colonization and believing that the American Nation is farthest from any thought of colonization and has no political ambition in our country, we will seek the technical and economical assistance from the United States of America, provided that such assistance does not exceed 20 years.

5. In the event of America not finding herself in a position to accept our desire for assistance, we will seek this assistance from Great Britain, also provided that such assistance does not infringe the complete independence and unity of our country and that the duration of such assistance does not exceed that mentioned in the previous article.

6. We do not acknowledge any right claimed by the French Government in any part whatever of our Syrian country and refuse that she should assist us or have a hand in our country under any circumstances and in any place.

7. We oppose the pretensions of the Zionists to create a Jewish commonwealth in the southern part of Syria, known as Palestine, and oppose Zionist migration to any part of our country; for we do not acknowledge their title but consider them a grave peril to our people from the national, economical, and political points of view. Our Jewish compatriots shall enjoy our common rights and assume the common responsibilities.

* *Foreign Relations of the United States: Paris Peace Conference, 1919,* vol. 12, pp. 780–781.

Nations, the first Arab country to gain that distinction. As in the case of Egypt, however, nationalist circles were still dissatisfied.

In Syria and Lebanon, the French were less flexible than the British and therefore less successful. Nationalist outbreaks occurred periodically. The most serious was in 1925, when the French were forced to shell Damascus in order to retain control. Finally in 1936 the French government negotiated treaties with Syria and Lebanon modeled after the Anglo-Iraqi treaty of 1930. Neither of these treaties, however, was ratified by the French Chamber of Deputies, so that the conflict remained unresolved when World War II began.

In Palestine the situation was unique because it quickly deteriorated into a bitter three-way struggle involving Britain, Arabs, and Jews. The Arabs maintained that the Balfour Declaration concerning a Jewish ''national home'' was in violation of prior commitments made to the Arabs in the McMahon correspondence. In 1921, Britain tried to appease the Arabs by setting apart the interior portion of the country as the independent state of Transjordan. This was exempt from all the clauses of the mandate concerning the establishment of a Jewish home. Furthermore, the British installed Faisal's elder brother, Abdullah, as ruler of Transjordan. This tactic was satisfactory so far as Transjordan itself was concerned. Abdullah always cooperated loyally with the British, particularly since the poverty of his country made him dependent on subsidies from London. Probably the most effective military unit in the Arab world was Transjordan's Arab legion, supported by British funds and led by the British General John Glubb.

In Palestine proper, however, the triangle conflict became increasingly fierce as Jewish immigrants poured in and the apprehensive Arabs struck back against both the Jews and the British. Article 6 of the mandate required Britain to ''facilitate'' Jewish immigration and to ''encourage close settlement by Jews on the land.'' But the same article also provided that ''the rights and position of other sections of the population'' were to be safeguarded. The British apparently felt at the time that the two orders were not necessarily contradictory. They expected that Jewish immigration would never reach such proportions as to threaten ''the rights and position'' of the Arabs. They could not have foreseen the repercussions of Hitler's rise to power in 1933. Jewish immigration jumped from 9553 in 1932 to 30,327 in 1933, to 42,359 in 1934, and to 61,854 in 1935. The total Jewish population in Palestine rose from 65,000 in 1919 to 450,000 in 1939.

So long as the Jewish influx had been modest, the Arabs had not raised serious objections. In fact they had welcomed the Jews with their money and energy and skills. The Arabs themselves had benefited substantially from the miracles the Jews had performed in restoring exhausted land, founding industries, and checking diseases. But when the stream of immigration became a torrent, the Arabs reacted violently.

Arab attacks against the Jews became increasingly frequent and serious. Highlights were the Wailing Wall disorders in 1929, the Arab ''National Political Strike'' in 1936, and the Arab Rebellion of 1938. The British response was to send out Royal Commissions following the major outbreaks. By the time of World War II several commissions had investigated the situation and had vacillated in their recommendations as they sought to satisfy three distinct and conflicting interests—the Jewish Zionist aspirations, Arab nationalist demands, and British imperial interests. The White Paper of May 1939, for example, proposed that Palestine become an independent state in ten years, and that definite limits be placed on Jewish immigration and land purchases. Both Arabs and Jews rejected the British proposals, and the Palestine controversy remained as far from settlement as ever when World War II began.

III. PERSIA

Persia had been divided by the 1907 Anglo-Russian Entente into British and Russian spheres of influence. When the first World War began in 1914, the shah announced an official policy of neutrality. Because he lacked the power to enforce this policy, the northern sections of the country were soon overrun by Turkish and Russian troops, and the southern by British. The authority of the Persian government scarcely extended beyond its capital of Teheran.

At the same time, Persian political life was becoming ever more anarchical. Cabinets rose and fell in hectic confusion until a coup d'état ensued in February 1921. The coup was engineered by Reza Khan, a colonel in the Persian Cossack Brigade that had been organized by the Russians before World War I. Reza was an austere, single-minded military man of exceptional courage and determination. Through sheer ability and concentration on military duties he rose from the ranks and won the respect and loyalty of his men. When the British compelled the Russian officers of the Cossack Division to resign their commissions in the fall of 1920, Reza moved into the power vacuum. By February 1921, he was strong enough to lead the coup that overthrew the government. From now on his rise was rapid, from commander in chief to minister of war to prime minister. In 1923, the ruler, Ahmad Shah of the Kajar dynasty, left Persia for the Riviera, and two years later, on December 15, 1925, Reza assumed the throne. He founded the Pahlevi dynasty which survived until the 1979 revolution which overthrew his son and successor.

Despite his eccentricities and excesses, Reza Shah's reign was like a breath of fresh air in the prevailing atmosphere of corruption and incompetence. Indeed, the shah was reminiscent of Kemal, whom he admired and imitated. His first move was to get rid of foreign military officers and build a unified and modern national army of 40,000, upon which he lavished much attention and money. With this military force at his command, the shah was able to resist undue foreign pressures and also to assert the central government's authority over tribal chieftains who had been virtually independent since the mid-nineteenth century.

Reza Shah also sought to modernize his country's economy. The most ambitious manifestation was the building of the trans-Iranian railroad. By the time of his abdication in 1941, a considerable number of factories had been built, including textile mills, cement plants, sugar refineries, and cigarette factories. Despite high protective tariffs, almost all operated at a loss because of the lack of overall planning and coordination.

Like Kemal, Reza Shah attacked various symbols of the past. He forbade the use of honorary titles, abolished the veil for women, and ordered men to wear European hats or caps. Above all else, nationalism was emphasized, and foreign influences were rooted out wherever possible. Arabic words were purged from the Persian language, and modern buildings were modeled after the Achaemenid style of architecture found in the ruins of the magnificent palaces of old. Typical of this nationalism was the adoption in 1934, in place of "Persia," of the name "Iran," harking back to Indo-European ancestors three millennia removed.

Reza Shah's reign ended abruptly with his abdication on September 16, 1941. During the preceding years he had been leaning increasingly toward Nazi Germany. Germany's share of Iranian trade rose to first place, while German technicians, teachers, merchants, and tourists increased steadily in numbers. With Hitler's attack on the USSR in June 1941, the shah received several joint Soviet-British notes requesting him to expel the Germans from Iran. His replies were considered unsatisfactory, and on August 25, 1941,

Soviet and British forces occupied the country. On September 16 Reza Shah abdicated in favor of his son, Mohammed Reza Pahlevi.

In retrospect, Reza Shah did not have as profound an impact on his country as Kemal did on Turkey. Kemal profited from a preceding military disaster of such magnitude that it made it easier to abolish outmoded institutions and practices. And the Turks, having been subject to Western influences longer, were more receptive to them. Nevertheless, Reza Shah stands head and shoulders above his predecessors, and his reign represents a major turning point in modern Iranian history.

IV. INDIA

At the turn of the century British rule in India seemed perfectly secure for the foreseeable future. In 1912, a great imperial durbar was held in Delhi to celebrate the coronation of King George V. Amidst pageantry and splendor, King George received the homage of India's princes and potentates without a voice being raised in dissent. In 1914, India rallied solidly behind Britain at war. The princes contributed generous financial aid, while no less than 900,000 Indians served in the British army as combatants and another 300,000 as laborers.

Only three decades after World War I British rule in India came to an end. One reason for this extraordinary outcome was the impact of the war itself—the influence of slogans about self-determination, and the unsettling effect of overseas service upon hundreds of thousands of soldiers who returned with new ideas and attitudes. Unrest was stimulated also by a series of disasters in the immediate postwar years. The failure of the monsoon in 1918 brought famine to many parts of India. The influenza epidemic of 1918–1919 killed no less than 13 million people! Another factor contributing to unrest was the repressive policy followed by Britain after the war which ended with the infamous Amritsar Massacre of April 13, 1919. Seeking to impress the people with the strength of the government, General Dyer ordered his troops to fire without warning on a crowded political meeting of unarmed civilians. Nearly 400 were killed and 1000 wounded. A committee of the House of Commons censured the general, who was relieved of his command. But the House of Lords supported Dyer, and £26,000 was raised for him by public subscription. A wave of bitter protest swept India, and Gandhi denounced the government as ''satanic.''

Gandhi was by all odds the outstanding figure in this postwar anti-British movement. The Indian Congress, organized in 1885, did not seriously threaten the British before 1914 (see Chapter 26, section V). It had remained essentially a middle-class movement with little support from village masses. Gandhi's great contribution was that he managed to break through to the villagers, establish rapport with them, and involve them in the struggle for independence. His message was simple and appealing. He pointed out that in 1914 the British were ruling 300 million Indians with a mere 4000 administrators and 69,000 soldiers. This was possible only because all classes of the population were cooperating with the British in one way or another. If this cooperation were withdrawn, British rule inevitably would collapse. The task, then, was to educate and prepare the people for satyagraha, or nonviolent passive resistance. Gandhi also called on the people to practice hartal, or boycott of British goods. In place of imported machine-made goods, Gandhi preached the wearing of homespun cloth. This would undermine the economic basis of British rule and also revive village industries. He himself wore a loin cloth of homespun material and publicly worked at his spinning wheel. The combination of satyagraha and hartal, Gandhi taught, would make possible the realization of swaraj, or home rule.

In an effort to forestall the gathering storm, the London government introduced on December 23, 1919, the Montagu-Chelmsford reforms establishing the administrative system known as "dyarchy." This left the central government in Delhi much the same as before, with an appointed viceroy and executive council, and a legislative assembly of 140 members, of whom 100 were elected by a very restricted vote. The dyarchy principle operated in the provincial governments, each of which consisted of an appointed governor and executive council, and of a legislative council which was 70 percent elective but for which only a rigidly limited group was allowed to vote. Important matters were "reserved" for the governor and his executive council; less important areas, such as sanitation, agriculture, medical relief, and education, were to be "transferred" to the Indian ministers. The theory was that more matters would be transferred from the "reserved" to the "transferred" list if this "dyarchy," or division of responsibility, proved workable.

The National Congress, led by Gandhi, rejected the British reform proposal. In September 1920, an all-out noncooperation campaign was launched. The response was impressive, but it gradually got out of hand. Gandhi insisted on strict nonviolence, yet strikes and riots broke out in many of the cities, while in the countryside the peasants rose up against landlords and moneylenders. The shocked Gandhi promptly ordered suspension of the noncooperation campaign, but he was nevertheless arrested and sentenced to six years' imprisonment. He was released after two years because of his precarious health, but the nationalist campaign had largely petered out by then.

Another nationalist leader, Jawaharlal Nehru, was now coming to the fore alongside Gandhi. The son of a wealthy lawyer, Nehru had been educated at Harrow and Cambridge and had been admitted to the bar in 1912. On his return, he plunged into the nationalist struggle for freedom and became a follower and admirer of Gandhi. Nehru, however, was very different from his mystical and ascetic leader. He was a Socialist and a firm believer in science and technology as the means for liberating humanity from its age-old misery and ignorance. Nehru nevertheless recognized Gandhi's extraordinary service in arousing India's peasantry. Even the National Congress, torn by personal rivalries and doctrinal disputes, was dependent on Gandhi. He returned to political life in December 1928 and persuaded Congress to accept a compromise resolution acceptable to both the radical and conservative elements. A few months later the British Labour Party defeated the Conservatives and formed a new government. The outlook seemed promising, for the Labourites consistently had criticized the Conservatives for being so late in giving self-government to India. The promise, however, was not realized; the decade 1930–1939 was a disappointment.

One reason was the increasing dissension between warring Hindu and Moslem blocs. The All-India Moslem League was founded as early as 1919, but for many years it had little following. Not only were the Moslems less than a quarter of the total population of the subcontinent, but the National Congress claimed it represented all Indians, regardless of religion. Indeed, the Congress did have a Moslem wing headed by the distinguished Abul Kalam Azad. Thus the Moslem League was of little significance until after 1935, when it came under the leadership of a Bombay lawyer, Mohammed Ali Jinnah. He offered to cooperate with the Congress on a coalition basis, but Congress rejected this and would deal only with Moslems who joined the party as individuals. Jinnah retaliated by appealing to the Moslem masses with the cry "Islam is in danger." The response was enthusiastic, for many Indian Moslems felt they had more in common with the rest of the Moslem world than with their Hindu neighbors. Jinnah's electoral successes made possible the future establishment of the independent Moslem Pakistan.

Meanwhile the viceroy, Lord Irwin, had announced in October 1929 that Britain definitely planned dominion status for India and that a conference would be held to make arrangements. The National Congress, however, passed a resolution on December 31, 1929, demanding complete independence. On March 12, Gandhi began another civil-disobedience campaign to force the British to get out of India. This incited widespread disorders, including attacks on government salt works, terrorist assaults on officials, and rioting by unemployed factory workers who were hard hit by the worldwide depression. On May 5, Gandhi was again arrested and imprisoned, along with some 60,000 of his followers.

Lord Irwin was aware that force alone offered no solution. After order had been somewhat restored, he released Gandhi on January 26, 1931, and resumed negotiations. Finally on August 2, 1935, the British Parliament passed the Government of India Act. It provided for new provincial arrangements that were implemented with the election of provincial legislatures in 1937. The nationalists (National Congress) gained control in seven of the eleven provinces and promptly proceeded to liberate political prisoners, restore civil liberties, and prepare agrarian reform.

In 1939 all this abruptly ended when the viceroy proclaimed that India was a participant in the new World War. Since the Indians were in no way consulted, the nationalist ministries in the seven provinces resigned. British governors then took over and governed by decree. Once again the nationalists raised the cry for complete independence, while the Moslems under Jinnah demanded that the subcontinent be partitioned into two states, one Hindu, and the other Moslem and to be called Pakistan.

V. CHINA

Although nominally independent, China experienced an anti-Western movement after World War I comparable to that of India. China entered the war in 1917 in hope of recovering Shantung province, which Japan had occupied in 1914. When the lost province was not restored by the peacemakers at Versailles, wild demonstrations broke out among the students and intellectuals in Peking. The protests soon spread to other cities, and the merchants joined by closing their shops. This developed into a boycott of Japanese goods attended by clashes with Japanese residents. The Western powers also were the targets of this violent outburst, because of their willingness to allow Japan to retain its booty on the mainland. Russia, by contrast, was regarded with sympathy and admiration, because the Soviet government had renounced Tsarist special privileges in China, as it also did at this time in Turkey and Persia.

These changes gave Dr. Sun Yat-sen the opportunity to make a fresh start with new policies and methods. After appealing in vain to the Western powers for aid against the provincial warlords who were carrying on as independent potentates, he turned to the Soviet government. He got a positive response and so began in 1921 the Kuomintang-Communist Entente that lasted to 1927. Dr. Sun and the able Russian representative,

Mikhail Borodin, together brought about three basic changes: they remodeled the Kuomintang Party along Communist lines, organized an efficient modern army, and developed a more effective and appealing political ideology.

In the reorganization of the Kuomintang, Sun exercised control through a Central Executive Committee elected by a Party Congress. For the first time the party was now able to function as a disciplined unit from headquarters to the smallest subdivision. At the same time a new army was being organized with the help of Russian arms and officers led by General Vasili Blücher. In May, 1924, the Whampoa Military Academy was established in Canton to train officers. Officially, its director was Chiang Kai-shek, Sun's chief of staff, who had just returned from a period of study at the Red Army Academy in Moscow, but its real head was Blücher.

Sun Yat-sen died in 1925, at the very time when the instruments had been forged to fulfill his ambitions. Although he did not live to see the warlords humbled and the country united, he is today recognized, both by the mainland Communists and the Taiwan Nationalists, as one of the creators of modern China. With Dr. Sun's death, Chiang Kai-shek became the leading figure in the Kuomintang. In May 1926, he assumed command of the "Northern Expedition," a campaign to unify China by crushing the warlords in the north. The Kuomintang forces, preceded by propaganda corps that included Chinese Communists, swept everything before them reaching the Yangtze by October. The capital was moved to Hankow, which was dominated by left-wing and Communist elements, the Chinese Communist party having been organized in 1921.

The military victories precipitated a split within the Kuomintang between the left wing in Hankow and the right wing under General Chiang. Chiang favored nationalism but not social revolution. He had become alarmed by the activities of the leftist propaganda corps that had been operating ahead of his divisions. Working among the peasantry and the city workers, these propagandists whipped up a revolutionary movement against the landed gentry, the urban bourgeoisie, and the Western business interests. Although Chiang had worked closely with his Russian advisers, he was definitely anti-Communist and determined to prevent the leftists from getting control of the Kuomintang.

The showdown between the incompatible forces of the Right and Left came when Nanking fell on March 24, 1927. As had happened in other cities, worker and student battalions were organized as the Kuomintang army approached. They waged a general strike and were able to take over control of the city during the interval between the departure of the warlord forces and the arrival of Chiang. The latter was not at all happy to be greeted by a revolutionary committee. With the backing of conservative elements in the Kuomintang and of financial interests in Shanghai, Chiang now carried out a bloody purge of Communists and their leftist allies. Borodin returned to Russia, and Chiang reorganized the Kuomintang so that he was the undisputed head. In June 1928, his armies took Peking, destroying the power of the northern warlords and completing the official unification of the country. The capital of the new China was moved to Nanking.

During the following decade the country made appreciable progress under Chiang's guidance. Railway mileage almost doubled, and that of modern roads quadrupled. Internal tariff barriers were abolished in 1932, and a unified currency was created for the first time. Significant progress was also made in governmental procedures, in public health, in education, and in industrialization. Equally striking were the government's successes in the diplomatic field. Control of the tariff was regained, some of the territories ceded to foreign nations were recovered, and many of the special privileges wrested by the

Western powers were returned. By 1943 extraterritorial rights had been surrendered by all foreign nations.

But there were serious gaps in Chiang's reform program, and these ultimately proved fatal. Badly needed land reform was neglected because the Kuomintang party in the rural areas was dominated by landlords who opposed any change. And Chiang's authoritarian, one-party government prevented the growth of democracy, so that opposition groups could not assert themselves by constitutional means; revolution was the sole alternative. Finally, the Kuomintang failed to develop ideas that could attract the support of the people. Nationalist appeals had little attraction for land-hungry peasants and poverty-stricken city workers.

These weaknesses of the Kuomintang regime might have been gradually overcome if it had been given a long period of peace. But it did not have this opportunity because of two mortal enemies, the Communists at home and the Japanese abroad. The Chinese Communist party was organized in Shanghai in July 1921, and in the following years branches appeared in all parts of the country. Many students and intellectuals joined the ranks, attracted by the call for action and the assurances of a classless and equitable society for the future. As we have seen, the Communists first cooperated with Sun Yat-sen and then broke with Chiang Kai-shek in 1927. Most of the Communist leaders were killed off by Chiang, but a number managed to escape to the mountainous interior of south China. One of their leaders was Mao Tse-tung, who now worked out a new revolutionary strategy in defiance of the Communist International in Moscow. He rejected the traditional Marxist doctrine that only the city proletariat could be depended upon to carry through a revolution. From first-hand observation in the countryside he concluded that the poor peasants, who made up 70 percent of the population, were "the vanguard of the revolution. . . . Without the poor peasant there can be no revolution." This was pure heresy in Moscow, but Mao went his way, organizing the peasants and building up a separate army and government in the south.

Chiang responded by launching five "bandit extermination campaigns," as they were called. The Communists managed to survive, thanks to the support of the peasants who were won over by the Communist policy of dividing large estates without compensation to the owners. The fifth campaign did succeed in dislodging the Communists, who were completely surrounded by the Kuomintang armies. Finally 90,000 managed to break through, and, of these, less than 7000 survived a 6000-mile trek of incredible hardship. During this historic "Long March" of 368 days (October 16, 1934, to October 25, 1935), they fought an average of almost a skirmish a day with Kuomintang forces totaling more than 300,000. Finally the Communist survivors reached the northwest provinces, where they dug in and established a base. Their land-reform policies again won them peasant support, so that they were able to build up their strength to the point where they became serious rivals of the Kuomintang regime in Nanking.

While Chiang was involved in this domestic struggle with the Communists, he was being attacked from the outside by the Japanese. We shall see later (Chapter 35, section I) that this aggression began with the occupation of Manchuria in 1931 and continued until, by the beginning of World War II, the Japanese were in control of the entire eastern seaboard. The combination of Communist subversion and Japanese aggression culminated in 1949 in Chiang's flight to Taiwan (Formosa), leaving Mao to rule the mainland from his new capital in Peking.

SUGGESTED READING

P. Avery, *Modern Iran* (Praeger, 1965); P. Balfour, *Ataturk: The Rebirth of a Nation* (Weidenfeld, 1964); N. S. Fatemi, *Diplomatic History of Persia, 1917–1923* (Moore, 1952); M. K. Gandhi, *An Autobiography: The Story of My Experiments with Truth* (Beacon, 1957); A. Hourani, *Arabic Thought in the Liberal Age 1798–1939* (Oxford University Press, 1962); G. Lenczowski, ed., *The Political Awakening in the Middle East* (Prentice-Hall, 1970); H. M. Sachar, *The Emergence of the Middle East 1914–1924* (Knopf, 1969); H. Z. Schiffrin, *Sun Yat-sen and the Origins of the 1911 Revolution* (University of California Press, 1969); *Toward Freedom: The Autobiography of Jawaharlal Nehru* (Day, 1941); J. E. Sheridan, *China in Disintegration: The Republican Era in Chinese History, 1912–1949* (Free Press, 1975).

chapter 33

Revolution And Settlement In Europe To 1929

At the same time that the colonial world was in the throes of national revolution, Europe itself was seething with social revolution. All over the Continent the old order was being questioned, partly because of the trauma of the World War, and partly because of the impact of the Russian Revolution. Thus, European history during the decade to 1929 was largely a history of struggle between revolutionary and counterrevolutionary forces. In Russia, communism emerged triumphant after years of civil war and intervention. In Central Europe the revolutionary forces were crushed and a variety of non-Communist regimes appeared, ranging from the liberal Weimar Republic in Germany to the rightist Horthy government in Hungary and to the fascist Mussolini state in Italy. Western Europe was spared such violent upheavals, but even here, the authority of traditional parliamentary institutions was being strained by economic difficulties, mass unemployment, and cabinet instability. By the late 1920s, some measure of order seemed to be returning to Europe. Prosperity was growing, unemployment was on the decline, and various international issues appeared to be resolved by the Dawes Plan, the Locarno Pacts, the Kellogg-Briand Pact, and the commitment of the Soviet Union to Five Year Plans rather than to world revolution. Europe was returning to a normal state, or so it seemed, until the Great Depression precipitated the series of domestic and international crises that were to culminate in World War II.

I. COMMUNISM TRIUMPHS IN RUSSIA

Course of Civil War

By signing the harsh Brest-Litovsk Treaty on March 3, 1918 (see Chapter 31, section IV), the Bolsheviks hoped that at last they would be able to turn from war to the more congenial task of building a new social order. Instead, they were destined to fight on for three more years against counterrevolution and foreign intervention. The counterrevolution was in part the work of members of the propertied classes—army officers, government officials, landowners, and businessmen—who for obvious reasons wished to be rid of the Bolsheviks. Equally ardent in their counterrevolutionary activities, however, were the various elements of the non-Bolshevik Left. Of these the Socialist Revolutionaries were by far the most numerous. They agreed with the Bolsheviks on the need for social revolution, but they bitterly resented the fact that the Bolsheviks had monopolized the revolution. They regarded the Bolshevik coup of November 7, 1917, as a gross betrayal, particularly because the Constituent Assembly elected on November 25, 1917, included only 175 Bolsheviks as against 370 Socialist Revolutionaries and 159 other assorted representatives. Accordingly, the non-Bolshevik Left took the lead in organizing underground opposition, while the rightist elements led armed forces in open revolt, beginning in the Cossack territories.

These anti-Bolshevik groups were encouraged and assisted by the Western powers, who were motivated by various considerations such as the strident Bolshevik campaign for world revolution. Both in Europe and in the colonial regions the Bolsheviks called on the "toiling masses" to "convert imperialist war into a class war." Many Western leaders naturally responded by seeking to crush these Marxist firebrands before they could ignite the smoldering tinder of revolution scattered throughout the world. Also, there was the problem of Allied materials that had been accumulated in Russia in high quantities—over 160,000 tons in Murmansk and 800,000 tons in Vladivostok. The Western powers were worried for fear that the Bolsheviks, willingly or unwillingly, might allow these supplies to fall into German hands. And there were economic motives behind the Allied intervention: Bolshevik nationalization of foreign properties and refusal to pay foreign debts naturally alienated powerful vested interests, and they used their influence to help the forces of intervention.

Under these circumstances several counterrevolutionary governments were set up soon after the Brest-Litovsk Treaty all along the borders of Russia—in the northern Archangel-Murmansk region, the Baltic provinces, the Ukraine, the Don territories, Transcaucasia, and Siberia. The Western powers provided these governments generously with funds and war materials, as well as with military advisers and small detachments of troops on certain fronts. At first the Bolsheviks suffered one reverse after another, simply because the old Russian army had disintegrated and there was nothing else to take its place. The commissar for defense, Leon Trotsky, gradually built up a new Red Army, which numbered about 500,000 men by the end of 1918. At times this force had to fight on two dozen different fronts, as revolts broke out in all parts of the country and Allied forces landed in coastal areas.

The chief opponents of the Bolsheviks in 1919 were Admiral Kolchak in Siberia, General Denikin in the Crimea and the Ukraine, and General Yudenich in Estonia. A common pattern is evident in their campaigns. Beginning with sudden attacks from their bases, they gained easy initial victories, came within reach of full victory, then were stopped, gradually pushed back, and finally routed. In March 1919, Kolchak captured the city of Ufa to the west of the Urals; in August, Denikin had advanced north to Kiev, and by October, Yudenich had penetrated to the very suburbs of Petrograd. Lenin's regime now was limited to the Petrograd-Moscow regions, an area about equal to the fifteenth-century Muscovite principality. However, by the end of 1919 the tides had turned: Denikin had been driven back to the Crimea, Yudenich to the Baltic, and Kolchak was not only forced back over the Urals, but was captured and shot.

It appeared early in 1920 that the ordeal was finally over. But another full year of fighting lay ahead, owing to the appearance of the Poles and renewed large-scale intervention by the French. The Poles, determined to extend their frontiers as far eastward as possible, took advantage of the confusion and exhaustion to invade the Ukraine in April 1920. The pattern of the previous year's operations was now repeated. The Poles advanced rapidly and took Kiev on May 7, but five weeks later they were driven out of the city, and by mid-July were back in their own territory. The triumphant Bolsheviks pressed on, reaching the outskirts of Warsaw on August 14. But the Poles, strongly supported by the French, stopped the advancing Russians and managed to push them back. The campaign ended in mid-October, and on March 18, 1921, the Treaty of Riga defined the Polish-Russian frontier that prevailed until World War II.

Meanwhile, General Wrangel, who had replaced Denikin, had overrun much of southern Russia with the generous assistance of the French. But after the Bolsheviks were through with the Poles, they turned their forces against Wrangel, driving him south to the Crimea. This peninsula, once the playground of tsars and grand dukes, was now crowded with a motley host of refugees—high ecclesiastics, Tsarist officials, aristocratic landowners, and the remnants of White armies. As many as possible were evacuated in French warships and scattered in ports from Constantinople to Marseilles; the remainder were left to the mercy of the victorious Red Army.

PEASANTS AND BOLSHEVIKS

C. R. Buxton, secretary to the British Labour party, visited Russia in June 1920. His report on the attitude of the Russian peasants explains why the Bolsheviks won out, even though they were a small minority of the total population.*

My host's name was Alexander Petrovich Emilianov. He was of the "middle" type of peasant, which formed the great majority of the village. About one-fifth of its people were considered "poor" peasants. Of "rich" peasants there were only four or five, I was told. . . .

Before the Revolution my host had had eight acres—about the average holding in that region. He had now no less than eighty-five. This was the tremendous fact that I had turned over and over in my mind as we bumped along. Tremendous, surely; for my host's case was a type, not only of thousands, but of millions of others. . . .

"Look there," said Emilianov, pointing out from the edge of the village field over the limitless rolling steppe. "All that was the land of the landlords (*barin*). . . .

"Who owned all this land?" I asked.

"All sorts of landlords. One was a Cossack. Two were Samara merchants. One was a German, Schmidt, who bought his from the Crown. Some was held by the Monks. One was an estate of Maria Feodorovna, the Tsaritsa."

"What has happened to them?"

"They are mostly gone," he replied in a matter-of-fact tone. "Some are in Samara. Most of them have left Russia, I suppose.". . .

"And what do the peasants think of it all now?" I asked Emilianov.

"It's a fine thing, the Revolution. Every one is in favour of it. They don't like the Communist Party, but they like the Revolution."

"Why don't they like the Communist Party?"

"Because they are always worrying us. They are people from the towns and don't understand the country. Commissars—powerful persons—are continually coming. We don't know what to do with them. New orders (*prikazi*) are always coming out. People are puzzled. As soon as you understand one of them, a different one comes along."

"What party do most people belong to here?"

"None at all. They are non-party (*bezpartini*)". . . .

The general attitude of the peasants, so far as I could judge, was that they owed much to the Soviet Government in the matter of the land; they approved of the "principle of everybody being equal"; they often talked of the "true" Communist as being an ideal sort of person. But they complained bitterly of the absence of necessities, of the compulsory contributions, and the worry of perpetual orders and appeals, often hard to understand. They considered that the Government was responsible for all these evils alike, and that the peasant was somehow in a position of inferiority to the townsman.

And yet, in spite of all these complaints, when the opportunity was offered them to choose between Kolchak on the one side and the Soviet Government on the other, the peasants do not seem to have had much hesitation. . . .

They were for the Revolution; and for the moment the Soviet power was the embodiment of the Revolution. They grumbled and cursed at it; but when the opportunity was offered to overthrow it, they said "No."

*C. R. Buxton, *In a Russian Village* (London: Labour Publishing Co., 1922), pp. 14–15, 19, 21, 26–27, 47–48.

The only foreign troops now left on Russian soil were the Japanese operating from Vladivostok. Originally there had been American and British as well as Japanese contingents in eastern Siberia, but the first two were withdrawn in 1920. The Japanese stayed on, hoping to keep control of these vast but sparsely populated regions by means of a puppet regime. The United States repeatedly brought diplomatic pressure on the Japanese to leave, and finally persuaded them to do so at the Washington Naval Disarmament Conference in 1922.

Significance of Bolshevik Victory

With the departure of the Japanese, the tragic period of civil war and intervention mercifully came to a close. Lenin's Communist party was now in control of the entire country. One reason for this unexpected outcome was Allied disunity and vacillation. Aside from certain passionately dedicated anti-Bolsheviks who occupied subordinate posts, the Allied leaders regarded the intervention as little more than a sideshow, and they supported it fitfully with varied and conflicting motives. Another reason for the triumph of the Bolsheviks was the disunity amongst the Whites (the counterrevolutionary Russian forces) who were bitterly divided by conflicting ambitions of individual leaders and by the basic incompatibility of the leftist Socialist Revolutionaries and the assorted right-wing elements. The Communists, by contrast, enjoyed certain advantages that proved decisive in the end. Their monolithic party organization imposed a cohesion and discipline that was unmatched on the other side. The Communist party was effectively supported by an efficient secret-police organization, the Cheka, that ruthlessly ferreted out opposition groups. The commissar of war, Leon Trotsky, skillfully combined the enthusiasm of proletarian volunteers with the indispensable technical knowledge of former Tsarist officers to forge a formidable new Red Army. Furthermore, this army enjoyed the substantial advantage of having internal lines of communication, in contrast to the tremendous distances separating the White forces from each other and from their sources of supplies in Western Europe and the United States. Finally, the Bolsheviks were generally more successful in winning the support of the peasant masses. This does not mean that the Russian peasants were won over to Marxist ideology; indeed, most of them were fed up with both the Reds and the Whites, and would rather have been left alone. But when forced to make a choice, they more frequently decided in favor of the Reds who, they thought, would allow them to keep the plots they had seized from the landlords.

In retrospect, the protracted civil war and intervention was a disaster for all parties concerned. It left the Russian countryside devastated from the Baltic to the Pacific, and the Russian people decimated by casualties, starvation, and disease. Equally serious was the poisoning of relations between the new Soviet state and the Western world. The Soviet leaders were confirmed in their Marxist fears of "capitalist encirclement," while Western statesmen took all too seriously the futile manifestos of the Communist International established in 1919. So deep and lasting was this mutual distrust that it poisoned international relations during the following decade and contributed significantly to the coming of World War II.

II. COMMUNISM FALLS IN CENTRAL EUROPE

Weimar Republic in Germany

While civil war was raging in Russia, the crucial question for Europe was whether communism would spread westward. Lenin and his fellow Bolsheviks assumed that if this did not occur, their cause would be doomed. In line with Marxist ideology, they could not conceive that their revolution might survive and take root in a single country, least of all in predominantly agrarian Russia. Accordingly, they followed closely and hopefully the course of events in Central Europe—especially Germany, which was clearly the key country. If it went Communist, the combination of German industrial strength and Russian natural resources would be unbeatable, and the future of the revolution would be assured.

At first it appeared that these Bolshevik hopes might be realized. The kaiser was forced to abdicate on November 9, 1918, following a mutiny in the navy and the spread of revolution from the Baltic ports into the interior (see Chapter 31, section VI). Workers' and

Soldiers' Councils, similar to the Russian Soviets, appeared in all the major cities, including Berlin. So strong was the revolutionary movement that it seemed possible that communism would engulf the Continent, at least to the Rhine. The final outcome, however, was not a Soviet Germany but the bourgeois Weimar Republic.

Several factors that escaped attention at the time explain this fateful outcome. One was the prosperity of prewar Germany, which left the working class relatively contented and in no mood for revolution. It is true that the German Social Democratic party in 1914 was the strongest party in Europe, but it was conservative, committed to social reform rather than to revolution. Equally important was the prosperity of the German peasants, so that the Bolshevik slogan "Land to the Peasants," which had been so effective in Russia, made very little impact on Germany. Also, the war had already ended at the time of the German revolution, again in contrast to the situation in Russia. The demand for peace, which probably helped the Bolsheviks more than anything else, was irrelevant in Germany. Furthermore, although the German army was defeated, it was far from being as demoralized and mutinous as the Russian army of 1917. The opponents of revolution in Germany were able to call upon reliable military forces when the showdown came.

A final factor of major significance was the split in the ranks of the German Socialists. The Majority Social Democrats, led by Friedrich Ebert and Philipp Scheidemann, had supported the German war effort from the beginning. They were relatively conservative, and so they now strenuously opposed the revolutionary Workers' and Soldiers' Councils. "I hate the social revolution," Ebert declared candidly, "I hate it like sin." At the other end of the spectrum was the Spartacist League, the counterpart of Lenin's Bolsheviks, led by Karl Liebknecht, of a well-known German Socialist family, and Rosa Luxemburg, of Polish-Jewish origin. The Spartacists, as might be expected, supported the Workers' and Soldiers' Councils and wished to establish a Soviet-type regime in Germany. Between the Majority Socialists and the Spartacists was the Independent Socialist party; it also favored a Soviet Germany but in addition wished to cooperate with the Majority Socialists.

When Prince Max announced the abdication of the kaiser, he himself resigned the chancellorship and handed the government over to Friedrich Ebert. The latter formed a cabinet, or council, of "Six Commissars," composed of three Majority Social Democrats and three Independent Socialists. The Spartacists chose to remain outside for the simple reason that they were interested only in forcing the revolution further to the Left. Philipp Scheidemann had proclaimed the establishment of the German Republic from the balcony of the parliament building, but Liebknecht at the same time had proclaimed a Soviet Germany from the balcony of the Imperial Palace a mile away. The great question now was which side would win.

The situation was comparable to that in Russia when the Provisional Government was established in March 1917. Ebert was very much aware of the outcome in that country and had no desire to be another Kerensky. Accordingly, on November 10, the day after the kaiser's abdication, he formed a secret alliance with General Wilhelm Groener, chief of the general staff, for the suppression of the Spartacists and the Workers' and Soldiers' Councils. Every night between 11:00 P.M. and 1:00 A.M., the two men talked on a special telephone linking the chancellory at Berlin and headquarters at Spa. With this powerful support, Ebert moved aggressively against the extreme Left. The Independent Social Democrats refused to go along and resigned from the cabinet, but this made little difference. On December 30, the Spartacists renamed themselves the Communist Labor party of Germany and made plans for revolt, but before these were completed, Karl Liebknecht and Rosa Luxemburg were arrested and shot "while trying to escape." Over a thousand of their followers were killed during the ruthless street fighting that followed. By mid-January 1919, the danger from the Left was over. On January 19, 1919, elections were held throughout Germany for a National Assembly rather than for a Congress of Soviets. The delegates elected were overwhelmingly of the moderate Left. The Assembly met in Weimar and elected Ebert the first president of the Republic, and Scheidemann the first chancellor.

The constitution adopted in July 1919 was unimpeachably democratic. Its provisions included universal suffrage, proportional representation, a bill of rights, and separation both of church and state and of church and school. But behind this new constitutional facade, much of the old Germany remained unchanged. The bureaucracy, the judiciary, and the police survived intact. In the universities, the most undemocratic and anti-Semitic faculties and fraternities continued untouched on the grounds of academic freedom. The new Reichswehr was the old imperial army in miniature. Except for the legal eight-hour day, virtually no social reforms were introduced. The industrial cartels and monopolies continued as before; the Junkers of east Prussia retained their landed estates, as did the kaiser and the various local rulers. In short, the German revolution had preserved more than it had changed. Power was left largely in the hands of the old ruling elements, which never accepted the new order. At first the Weimar Republic did succeed in stabilizing itself with foreign financial aid. But when the Great Depression undermined the foundations of the state, most of these unreconciled bureaucrats, army officers, and landed gentry turned upon the Republic and helped in its destruction.

Revolution and Reaction in Central Europe

The suppression of the Spartacists and the establishment of the Weimar Republic ensured that the rest of Central Europe would not go Communist. Nevertheless, for a number of years this part of Europe seethed with unrest and revolt. The peasant masses between the Baltic and the Aegean were politically awake and active to an unprecedented degree. One reason for the unrest was that millions of peasant army recruits had widened their horizons immeasurably as a result of their war experiences. They had observed, not only the differences between city and village life, but also the differences in living standards and social institutions among various countries. The peasants were also profoundly affected by the overthrow of the Hapsburg, Hohenzollern, and Romanoff dynasties. In the light of centuries-old traditions, this was a shock that aroused nationalist aspirations and class consciousness. Finally, the unprecedented destruction and suffering that took place during the long years of war aggravated the revolutionary situation, especially in the countries that had suffered defeat.

The precise manifestation of this revolutionary ferment varied from country to country according to local circumstances. The Communist parties did not play an outstanding role except in the case of Hungary, where in March 1919 a Soviet republic was established under the leadership of Bela Kun. It lasted less than a year because of the hostility of the peasants and the invasion of the country by Rumanian troops. When the Rumanians departed in February 1920, a right-wing government headed by Admiral Miklós Horthy was established with Allied support. Horthy remained in power for the whole interwar period, during which time Hungary was unique in Central Europe for the almost complete absence of agrarian or other reforms.

In most of the other Central European countries, agrarian or peasant parties were giving voice to popular discontent. The following peasant leaders assumed office in the post-war years: Aleksandr Stamboliski in Bulgaria in 1919, Stefan Radich in Yugoslavia in 1925, Wincenty Witos in Poland in 1926, and Iuliu Maniu in Rumania in 1928. Owing to their pacifism and distaste for violence, however, none of them was able to retain power for long. They were vulnerable to the entrenched military and bureaucratic elements that did not hesitate to seize power by force when their interests were threatened. Another reason for their failure was the increasing control that lawyers and urban intellectuals gained over the peasant parties. Under this leadership, the parties usually represented the interests of the wealthy peasants and had little contact with the great mass of poor peasants.

One after another the peasant leaders were ousted from office. Stamboliski was assassinated in 1923, and a dictatorship was established by King Boris. Radich was assassinated in 1928, and the following year King Alexander set up his dictatorship. In Poland, Witos lasted only a few days before he was removed by General Joseph Pilsudski, who dominated the country until his death in 1935. Maniu was eased out of office in 1930 by King Carol II, who made and unmade governments until forced to flee Rumania a decade later.

The same pattern prevailed in Austria and Greece where, for various reasons, agrarian parties never took hold. Yet Austria ended up with an authoritarian government under Chancellor Dollfuss in 1934, and Greece, with an avowedly fascist regime under General Metaxas in 1936. Thus, by World War II, the whole of Central Europe was under dictatorial rule, with one exception—Czechoslovakia. This country possessed certain advantages that explain its uniqueness: a high level of literacy; a trained bureaucracy inherited from the Hapsburgs; the capable leadership of Jan Masaryk and Eduard Benes; and a balanced economy that provided higher living standards and greater security than was possible in the predominantly agrarian countries to the east.

III. ITALY GOES FASCIST

While bolshevism, agrarianism, and traditional parliamentarianism battled for primacy in Eastern and Central Europe, an entirely new ism was coming to the fore in Italy—fascism, the outstanding political innovation in Europe in the postwar years. Bolshevism had a history going back at least to the Communist Manifesto of 1848, while agrarianism was taking political form with the appearance of peasant parties at the turn of the century. Fascism, by contrast, appeared unexpectedly and dramatically with Mussolini's march on Rome in October 1922.

Postwar conditions in Italy provided fertile soil for a violent, melodramatic, and anti-intellectual movement such as fascism. The Italy of 1919 had behind it only two generations of national independence and unity. Parliamentary government was, in practice, a morass of corruption in which party "bosses" manipulated short-lived coalition blocs. This unstable political structure was further weakened in the postwar years by serious economic dislocation. Many of the demobilized millions were unable to find jobs. Foreign trade and tourist traffic were declining in the aftermath of war. Emigration, which for decades had served as a safety valve and a source of overseas remittances, now petered out because of restrictive legislation in the United States and other countries. The popular unrest caused by this economic stress was aggravated by the slighting of Italian claims at the Paris peace conference. The resulting frustration and injured pride produced an inflammable situation.

This became evident with the November 1919 elections, which returned 160 for the Socialist party and 103 for the Catholic Popular party as against 93 and 58 respectively for the traditional Liberal and Radical parties. When parliament opened, the Socialists refused to greet the King and shouted "Long Live Socialism!" The climax came in September 1920, when workers throughout north Italy began taking over factories. Giovanni Giolitti, the old prewar political manipulator who had formed a cabinet in June 1920, decided to leave the "campers" in possession, partly because he did not know whether the soldiers would obey orders or join the workers. All the classical conditions for a revolution were present—except for the will to start one. The Socialist watchword at this time was "the revolution is not made. The revolution comes." Within two years this slogan was proven wrong by one who was ready to make revolution.

Benito Mussolini, the son of a Socialist blacksmith, first attracted attention during the Tripolitan War of 1911 by his inflammatory speeches in which he referred to the Italian flag as "a rag fit only to be planted on a dung heap." The following year he became editor of the official Socialist paper *Avanti!* When World War I began in August 1914, he was still a revolutionary and a pacifist, but the following month his great transformation took place, helped along by funds from the French government, which was anxious to secure Italy as an ally. Mussolini was able to start his own newspaper, *Il Popolo d'Italia,* in which he conducted a passionate intervenist campaign.

Called to battle in September 1915, Mussolini fought in the trenches for a few weeks until he was wounded and invalided out of the army. He languished in obscurity until 1919, when he formed his first "combat troops," and organized the Fascist party. Unity and authority were his watchwords against the political anarchy and social strife of the period. At the outset he attracted the support of only a handful of frustrated students and demobilized soldiers. But in the early twenties he forged rapidly ahead, partly because the passivity of the Socialists had created a vacuum that Mussolini promptly filled. Equally important was the substantial support that Mussolini was now receiving from industrialists, landowners, and other members of the propertied classes. Terrified by the widespread seizure of factories and estates, they now looked hopefully to the Fascist squadristi, or armed bands, as a bulwark against the dreaded social revolution. The government and the wealthy elements of society not only tolerated squadristi violence and terrorism but even secretly gave it their aid and support.

In the fall of 1922, Mussolini prepared for a coup by winning over both the monarchy and the church with specific assurance that their interests would be respected. Since the regular army and the police already had shown their benevolent neutrality, Mussolini proceeded with assurance to mobilize his Blackshirts for a widely publicized march on Rome. Prime Minister Luigi Facta asked King Victor Emmanuel to proclaim martial law, but the king refused and instead called on Mussolini to form a government. Thus only a token march on Rome by the Blackshirts was necessary, while Mussolini arrived anticlimactically in Rome on October 27 in a sleeping-car.

Parliament and the king gave Mussolini dictatorial powers until December 31, 1923, to restore order and introduce reforms. During this period he allowed a degree of liberty to the press, to the trade unions, and to the parliamentary parties. But at the same time he was gaining control of the state machinery by appointing prefects and judges of Fascist sympathies and organizing a voluntary Fascist militia. The showdown came with the elections of April 6, 1924. Through liberal use of the squadristi, the Fascist party polled 65 percent of the votes and won 375 seats, compared to the 35 they had previously held. Two months later a prominent Socialist deputy, Giacomo Matteotti, was found murdered. He had written a book, *The Fascisti Exposed,* presenting detailed case histories of hundreds of illegal acts of Fascist violence. It was widely suspected, and later proven, that Matteotti had been killed on orders from Mussolini himself. Most of the non-Fascist deputies walked out of the chamber, vowing not to return until the Matteotti affair had been cleared up. Mussolini faced a major crisis but managed to survive, thanks to the indecisiveness of the opposition and the unwavering support of the king.

By the fall of 1926, Mussolini felt strong enough to take the offensive. He declared the seats of the absent deputies vacant, disbanded the old political parties, tightened censorship of the press, and established an organization of secret police. Italy had become a one-party state, with the Chamber functioning as a rubber-stamp body for passing Fascist bills.

The new Fascist regime gradually evolved certain distinctive features. One was the corporative state in which deputies were elected as representatives not of geographical constituencies but rather of trades and professions. Theoretically it eliminated class conflict by bringing capital and labor together under the benevolent auspices of the state. Actually, only capital enjoyed true self-government, while labor was denied the right to strike or to select its own leaders. Neither the position of the workers nor that of the peasants was basically improved under the corporative state.

Another feature of Mussolini's Italy was the elaborate public-works program designed to provide employment and to erect impressive structures for the glorification of fascism. Monuments of the past were restored, and many cities were adorned with large new buildings, workers' tenements, and stadiums. Certain marshlands were drained and made available for cultivation. Tourists were particularly impressed by trains that ran on time and extensive new highways or autostrade.

IV. PROBLEMS OF DEMOCRACY IN WESTERN EUROPE

In Western Europe there were no upheavals comparable to the civil war in Russia or to the bitter clash between Right and Left in Central Europe. Democratic institutions had deeper roots in the West, and the prevailing social structures were healthier and enjoyed more popular support. In addition, the Western powers had been the victors rather than the losers in the war, a fact that further contributed to political and social stability. It does not follow, however, that Western Europe experienced no difficulties in the postwar years. There were many problems. The most serious were economic in nature, though with far-reaching social and political repercussions. The experiences of the two leading Western countries, Great Britain and France, illustrate this.

The chief problem in Britain was, by all odds, the severe and chronic unemployment. There was a short-lived boom immediately after the war when factories operated overtime to meet long-pent-up consumer demands. But the bust came in 1920, and by March of 1921 over 2 million people were out of work. Unemployment persisted through the 1920s, and the situation grew worse in the 1930s. Thus the Depression actually began in Britain in 1920 rather than in 1929, and continued without interruption to World War II.

These economic difficulties stemmed in part from World War I which, by stimulating the industrialization of such countries as the United States, Japan, and the British Dominions, reduced the overseas markets of British manufactures. The destruction of much of

Britain's merchant marine also caused the invisible revenues to be reduced, as did the fact that Britain was no longer the world's financial center. The Bolshevik revolution further hurt the British economy, wiping out an important market for manufactured goods as well as substantial investments. Finally there was the failure of the British themselves to keep up with the rest of the world in industrial efficiency. Initially, they had led the world in the industrial revolution, but now they lagged behind in modernizing their equipment. Because they tended to keep machines until they were worn out rather than until they had become obsolete, productivity per worker-hour lagged in comparison with other countries. For example, taking the year 1913 as 100, the output per worker-shift in British mines rose by 1938 to a mere 113, compared to 164 in the German mines, and 201 in the Dutch.

This combination of circumstances was responsible for the almost unrelieved depression that gripped Britain during the interwar period. Millions of families subsisted on state relief, or the ''dole'' as it was popularly called. A whole generation grew up without an opportunity to work. Such a situation was as unhealthy psychologically as it was economically. Eventually the unemployed became demoralized, depending on the dole without hope for the future.

These conditions inevitably caused political repercussions. Most important was the decline of the Liberal party as the workers turned increasingly to the Labour party in the hope of finding relief. Thus the economic crisis tended to polarize British politics, with the propertied classes generally voting Conservative, the workers supporting Labour, and the middle class fluctuating between the two. Each party had its panacea for the country's ills: the Conservatives called for protection; the declining Liberals, for free trade; and Labour, for a capital levy and for the nationalization of heavy industry. The net result was a succession of alternating Conservative and Labour ministries under Stanley Baldwin and Ramsay MacDonald. None was able to improve significantly the national fortunes. In the May 1929 elections the Labourites won a plurality of the seats, and MacDonald formed his second government with the backing of the Liberals. He could not have known that within half a year the country would be hit by the Great Depression that was to cripple Britain's economy still more, ultimately sweeping away MacDonald's new administration.

France, too, was plagued by economic difficulties in the postwar years, although in certain respects it was better off than most of its neighbors. France had a well-balanced economy, so that it was not as vulnerable as the predominantly agrarian or industrial countries. The peace settlement strengthened its economy by adding the Saar Basin with its coal mines, and the Alsace-Lorraine region with its textile industry and rich potash and iron-ore deposits. Conversely, France had been weakened by the loss of 1.4 million men in the prime of life, and by unprecedented destruction of property. The war on the western front had been waged mostly on French soil, causing 23 billion dollars worth of damage to villages, towns, factories, mines, and railways. Also France had financed the war by loans rather than taxes, which led to the depreciation of the franc after the war.

In contrast to Britain's two or three parties, France had several, so that a government's life depended on its ability to organize a bloc of these parties to secure majority support. This explains the relatively rapid turnover of governments in France compared to that in Britain. The leading parties, from Left to Right, were the Communists and Socialists, who represented mostly urban and rural workers; the Radical Socialists, who were in the center and were supported by the lower middle class; and various parties on the Right, such as the Republican Democratic Union and the Democratic Alliance, which were usually strongly Catholic and represented big business and high finance.

For five years after the end of the war, France was ruled by National Bloc ministries based mostly on the parties of the Right. The dominant personality during this period was Raymond Poincaré, who was determined to make the Germans pay the costs of reconstruction. His policy culminated in the French occupation of the Ruhr in 1923, an expensive operation that yielded little revenue. By early 1924 the franc had fallen from its prewar value of 19.3 cents to little more than 3 cents. The French public was alienated by this financial instability and by the Ruhr adventure, which aroused fears of renewed warfare. Accordingly, the May 1924 elections returned a majority for the Cartel des Gauches, or Left Bloc. Edouard Herriot, leader of the Radical Socialists, became premier with the support of the Socialists. In foreign affairs he ended the Ruhr occupation, agreed to a settlement of the reparations issue, and recognized the Soviet Union. But the financial dilemma remained unsolved, and on this matter the laissez-faire Radicals and the quasi-Marxist Socialists were unable to reach agreement. The Socialists demanded a capital levy, Herriot was opposed, and his government fell in April 1925. The franc immediately decreased in value; by the following year it was worth only two cents—one-tenth of its prewar value.

France now turned once more to the Right. In July 1926 Poincaré formed a National Union ministry of all parties except the Socialist and Communist. Poincaré adopted orthodox but stringent measures to reduce expenditures and increase revenues. By the end of 1926, the franc stood at 4 cents and was stabilized at that level. Since this was only one-fifth of its prewar value, the government had relieved itself of four-fifths of its debts, though this was achieved at the expense of French bondholders. The devaluation attracted many tourists, especially the Americans, and also facilitated the exportation of French goods. Poincaré's success enabled him to remain premier for three years, an interwar record. He retired in the summer of 1929, just in time to escape the economic cyclone that was to destroy the precarious stability he had achieved.

V. STABILIZATION AND SETTLEMENT IN EUROPE

Reparations Settlement: Dawes Plan

The period from 1924 to 1929 was one of peace and settlement in Europe. The negotiation in 1924 of the Dawes Plan, an agreement concerning reparations payments, was the first phase of this process of stabilization. Germany had been required by the Versailles Treaty to accept responsibility for the war and to promise to make payments for the losses sustained. No agreement was reached at Versailles concerning the amount and the schedule of payments. The Reparations Commission, a body that had been appointed to work out the details, decided in 1920 that the payments from Germany should be divided as follows: 52 percent to France, 22 percent to Britain, 10 percent to Italy, 8 percent to Belgium, and the remaining 8 percent to the other Allied powers. The following year the commission set the total German indemnity at $32 billion, to be paid both in cash and in kind (coal, locomotives, textile machinery, and other products of German factories and mines).

Some payments were made in 1921 and 1922, but at the same time Germany was undergoing a disastrous inflation. The mark, worth 25 cents in 1914, had fallen to 2 cents by July 1922, and a year later it was worthless—two and one-half trillion to the dollar. The Germans requested a two-year moratorium on payments. The French, convinced that the Germans could pay if they wished to, occupied the Ruhr industrial region in January 1923. The Germans responded with a general strike, so that the French were forced to spend more on the occupation than they got out of it. With the German economy prostrate and the French stymied, the reparations issue was deadlocked.

A commission of economic experts, headed by an American banker, Charles Dawes, was called in. On September 1, 1924, the so-called Dawes Plan was approved by both sides and went into effect. The plan called for annual payments beginning at $238 million and reaching a maximum of $595 million. These amounts were adjustable depending on the index of prosperity for a given year. In return, Germany was to receive a foreign loan of $200 million, and France was required to evacuate the Ruhr. This arrangement, like so many others, was to be swept away with the onslaught of the Great Depression. Even during the four years that it operated, up to September 1928, the Germans paid in cash and in kind only about half of what they borrowed from foreign markets, mostly American. Nevertheless, the Dawes Plan did ease tensions in Europe and prepare the way for the settlement of political issues.

Quest for Peace: Locarno Pacts

Theoretically, the League of Nations provided general security with Article 10 of the Covenant, which required member states "to respect and preserve against external aggression the territorial integrity and existing political independence of all members of the League." The difficulty was that the League lacked the power necessary to enforce this article. The League possessed no weapons and no armed force. Having experienced two German invasions in less than 50 years, France refused to entrust its security to a League without authority. First it proposed a British-French-American triple alliance that would guarantee Anglo-American aid to France in case of German aggression. When this plan failed because the United States Senate refused to ratify the treaty, France turned to the smaller European states that shared its interest in supporting the peace settlement and opposing treaty revision. It negotiated a formal military alliance with Belgium in September 1920, with Poland in 1921, and with Czechoslovakia in 1924. Czechoslovakia had already organized the so-called "Little Entente" with Rumania and Yugoslavia in 1920–1921 for the purpose of providing mutual aid in case of either an attack by Hungary or the restoration of the Hapsburg dynasty. Poland was attached to the Little Entente in 1921 through an alliance with Rumania in which the two guaranteed reciprocal help in the event of attack by Russia. France's relationship with the Little Entente enabled it, then, to extend its own alliance system to include Rumania in 1926 and Yugoslavia in 1927.

This alliance system was basically anti-German, its primary purpose being to protect France and its allies by isolating Germany. About 1925, however, Franco-German relations improved, thanks to the temporarily successful operation of the Dawes Plan, and also to the foreign ministers of the two countries, Aristide Briand of France and Gustav Stresemann of Germany. The two foreign ministers decided that the security of their respective countries could be enhanced by direct negotiations and agreements. They were encouraged by the British foreign minister, Sir Austen Chamberlain, who also brought the Italians around to this view. The outcome was a series of agreements known as the Locarno Pacts, signed in October 1925.

These provided that Germany should enter the League of Nations and become a permanent Council member. In return, Germany agreed not to seek treaty revision by force and to settle peacefully every dispute with France, Belgium, Czechoslovakia, and Poland. Germany did reserve the right to seek modifications of its eastern frontiers by peaceful means, but it recognized the permanence of its western frontiers. Germany, France, and Belgium undertook to respect for all time their mutual borders, and Britain and Italy guaranteed observance of this provision.

The Locarno Pacts led many to believe that peace at last was assured. In the afterglow of this optimism, the American secretary of state, Frank Kellogg, acting on a suggestion of Briand, proposed that nations pledge themselves to renounce war as ''an instrument of national policy.'' The proposal was implemented, and on August 27, 1928, the Kellogg-Briand Pact was signed. Since the pact only involved renunciation of war and made no provision for sanctions, it was quickly signed by over 60 countries. Although it depended exclusively on the moral pressure of world public opinion, the mere fact that so many countries signed contributed to a further lessening of international tension.

Equally promising were the improved relations with Germany. That country was admitted into the League of Nations in 1926 and was made a permanent member of the Council. Also, a further settlement was reached with Germany concerning the payment of reparations. The Dawes Plan had not stipulated the sum total of reparations that Germany should pay, so in 1929 a second commission of economic experts, under the chairmanship of another American financier, Owen Young, met in Paris and prepared a new payment schedule that was adopted early in 1930. The total amount to be paid by Germany was set at $8 billion, and the installment was to be extended over 58 years. In return for Germany's acceptance of the Young Plan, France evacuated the Rhineland in 1930, four years earlier than was required by the Versailles Treaty.

At the same time, a series of disarmament conferences was being held, partly because of the pressure of international public opinion, but also because the Allies had forced Germany to disarm with the expressed intention of initiating ''a general limitation in the armaments of all nations.'' However, no general limitation of armaments was achieved in the interwar period. The basic difficulty was that, given the absence of an international security system, each country sought security in its own armed forces. Some progress was made in limiting navies, partly because the number of naval powers was smaller than the number of military powers. But even here agreement was restricted to the ratio of tonnages in certain categories, instead of limiting the total tonnage.

Despite the failure in disarmament, there was a general feeling in the late 1920s that Europe had at last returned to normalcy: Germany and its former enemies appeared to be reconciled; French troops were out of the Rhineland, and the Germans were in the League; the problem of reparations appeared to be finally resolved; over 60 nations had renounced war ''as an instrument of national policy''; prosperity was on the rise, and unemployment was correspondingly declining. Even the news from the Soviet Union was encouraging, for that country had launched in 1928 a novel and grandiose Five Year Plan. Most authorities in the West regarded the Plan as impractical and doomed to failure, but at least it diverted the Russians from international adventures to internal economic development. Thus it was assumed that Europe now could settle back to enjoy decades of peace and prosperity as it had in the nineteenth century.

SUGGESTED READING

W. T. Angress, *Stillborn Revolution: The Communist Bid for Power in Germany, 1921–1923* (Princeton University Press, 1964); E. H. Carr, *The Bolshevik Revolution, 1917–1923* (Macmillan, 1951–1953); and his *International Relations Between the Two World Wars* (Macmillan, 1947); F. L. Carsten, *Revolution in Central Europe 1918–1919* (University of California Press, 1972); C. L. Mowat, *Britain Between the Wars, 1918–1940* (University of Chicago Press, 1955); H. Seton-Watson, *Eastern Europe Between the Wars, 1918–1941* (Cambridge University Press, 1946); D. M. Smith, *Mussolini's Roman Empire* (Viking Press, 1976); D. Thomson, *Democracy in France* (Oxford University Press, 1952); E. Wiskemann, *Fascism in Italy: Its Development and Influence* (Macmillan, 1969).

chapter 34

The Five Year Plans And The Great Depression

As the 1920s drew to a close, Europe seemed to be settling down to an era of peace, security, and relative prosperity. This comfortable prospect was, however, destroyed completely by the onset of the Great Depression. The resulting economic dislocation and mass unemployment undermined the foundations of the settlement that had been reached in the preceding years. Everywhere governments rose and fell under the pressure of mounting distress and discontent. Such political instability affected directly—and disastrously—the international situation. Some governments resorted to foreign adventures as a means for diverting domestic tension, while others ignored the acts of aggression because of their own pressing problems at home. Thus the Depression represents the Great Divide of the interwar period. The years before 1929 were years of hope, as Europe gradually resolved the various issues created by the First World War. By contrast, the years after 1929 were filled with anxiety and disillusionment, as crisis followed crisis, culminating finally in World War II.

The impact and significance of the Great Depression was heightened by Russia's Five Year Plans. At the same time that the West's economy was a veritable shambles, the Soviet Union was proceeding with its unique experiment in economic development. Although they were accompanied by rigid repression and mass privation, the Five Year Plans were substantially successful. The Soviet Union rose rapidly from a predominantly agrarian state to the second greatest industrial power in the world. This unprecedented achievement had international repercussions, particularly because of the economic difficulties besetting the West at the time.

And so the Five Year Plans and the Great Depression stand out in the interwar period, the one accentuating the other, and each having effects that are being felt to the present day.

I. FIVE YEAR PLANS

War Communism

As soon as the Bolsheviks found themselves the masters of Russia, they faced the challenge of creating the new socialist society about which they had preached for so long. They soon discovered that it was a challenge they were unprepared to meet. There was no model in past history to follow. At first there was little opportunity for experimenting because the struggle for survival took precedence over everything else. The so-called "War Communism" that prevailed between 1917 and 1921 evolved out of the desperate measures taken to supply the battle front with needed materials and manpower. One feature of War Communism was the nationalization of land, banks, foreign trade, and heavy industry. Another was the forcible requisitioning of surplus agricultural produce needed to feed the soldiers and the city dwellers. The original plan was to compensate the peasants with manufactured goods, but this proved impossible because almost all factories were producing for the front.

The ending of the civil war meant that the stopgap system of War Communism was no longer needed, so it was promptly dropped. The peasants were up in arms against confiscation without compensation. At the same time, the economy of the country was paralyzed, owing largely to the uninterrupted fighting between 1914 and 1921. Industry had fallen to 10 percent of prewar levels, while the grain crop declined from 74 million tons in 1916 to 30 million tons in 1919. The crowning disaster, was the widespread drought of 1920 and 1921, which contributed to the worst famine in Russia's history. Millions of people died of starvation, and millions more were kept alive only by the shipments of the American Relief Administration.

NEP to Gosplan

The practical-minded Lenin realized that concessions were unavoidable—hence the adoption in 1921 of the *New Economic Policy,* or NEP as it was commonly known, which allowed a partial restoration of capitalism. Peasants were permitted to sell their produce on the open market, and private individuals were allowed to operate small stores and factories. Both the peasants and the new businessmen could employ labor and retain what profits they made from their operations. Lenin, however, saw to it that the state kept control of title to the land and of what he termed "the commanding heights" (banking, foreign trade, heavy industry, and transportation). So far as Lenin was concerned, the NEP did not mean the end of socialism in Russia; rather it was a temporary retreat, "one step backward in order to take two steps forward."

The great question in the following years was how these "two steps forward" should be made. By 1926, industrial and agricultural production had reached pre-1914 levels. But the population had increased by 8 million since 1914, so the prewar per capita standards had not been reached. Even more disturbing was the growing strength of the well-to-do peasants, or *kulaks* (kulak means "the fist"), and their supporters. They were openly hostile to the Soviet regime because agricultural prices had fallen to just over half what they had been in 1913, while the prices for manufactured goods had nearly doubled. The kulaks, who produced most of the surplus foodstuffs, retaliated by reducing their output or keeping it from the market in order to force prices upward. Thus the Soviets found it increasingly difficult to feed the urban population; the hostile kulaks were in a position to starve the cities at will. Such was the unpleasant state of affairs more than a decade after the great revolution that was to have heralded the new Socialist society.

Lenin died in 1924, and his successor, Joseph Stalin, launched in 1928 the first of a series of Five Year Plans. These Plans were without precedent for they provided a blueprint and a mechanism for the reorganization and operation of a nation's entire economy. At the center was the State Planning Commission (*Gosplan*), appointed by the Council of Peoples Commissars, the Soviet counterpart of a Western cabinet. The function of the Gosplan to the present day is to prepare the plans on the basis of the general directives received from the government and the statistical data received from all parts of the country.

The government (actually the Communist-party leadership) makes the basic decisions, such as whether a particular Plan should concentrate on producing armaments or building up heavy industry or turning out more consumer goods or reducing grain crops in favor of industrial crops. With these directives as a guide, the Gosplan sets to work on the huge mass of statistical information that is constantly pouring into headquarters. All Soviet organizations—whether agricultural, industrial, military, or cultural—are required by law to provide the Gosplan with specified data concerning resources and operations. This mass of information is processed by a highly trained staff of statisticians, economists, and technical experts, who proceed to work out a provisional Five Year Plan. After consultation and countersuggestions from the organizations concerned, a final Plan is drafted. The first of these Five Year Plans, though primitive when compared with the current computer-prepared ones, consisted of a three-volume text of 1600 pages. It included tables and statistics that ranged over heavy industries, light industries, finance, cooperatives, agriculture, transportation, communications, labor, wages, schools, literature, public health, and social insurance.

Collectivization of Agriculture

Stalin once stated that the kulak resistance to collectivization of the land was the most dangerous challenge he ever encountered. Yet he had no choice but to force his plan on them, for collectivization was the foundation of the new economy he had blueprinted. The kulaks naturally opposed the collective farms for they had to enter on the same terms as the poor peasants who brought little with them. In some cases, the kulaks burned the buildings of the collectives, poisoned the cattle, and spread rumors to frighten away other peasants. The Soviet government retaliated by uprooting hundreds of thousands of kulak families from their villages, putting them in prisons and in Siberian labor camps. In the end, the government had its way, so that by 1938 almost all peasant holdings had been amalgamated into 242,400 collective farms, or kolkhozy, and 4000 state farms, or sovkhozy. The kolkhozy are cooperatives, whose members divide the profits at the end of the year on the basis of the amount and the skill of the work contributed. The sovkhozy, by contrast, are operated by the government, and its members are paid set wages as though they were factory hands.

The Soviet agricultural system has not worked well. With 50 percent more land being farmed, and with ten times more people working on it, the Soviet Union produces only three-fourths of the U.S. farm output. One reason for this difference is that the climate of the Soviet Union is much less favorable for agriculture than that of the United States. Another reason is that the Soviet government until recently has been more interested in developing industry and therefore has starved agriculture. Soviet farmers use only half as much machinery and fertilizer per acre as do the Americans. The chief difficulty with Soviet agriculture is that the farm workers have never been satisfied with collectivized farming. Government taxes have been so high, and agricultural prices so low, that at the end of the year they receive little for their work in the collective fields. Thus they prefer to work hard on their own private plots, and to sell any surplus produce on the open market for high prices. This explains why these plots, although less than 4 percent of Soviet cultivated land, produced in 1975 half its eggs, 35 percent of its meat, 63 percent of its potatoes, and 37 percent of other vegetables.

Although collectivization has not been successful from the viewpoint of production, it has nevertheless provided the essential basis for the Five Year Plans. It has eliminated the kulaks who at one time threatened the very existence of the Soviet regime. The peasants are no longer an independent political force, and Soviet authority is firmly established in the countryside. This, in turn, has enabled the Soviet government to foist much of the cost of industrialization upon the peasantry. Surplus produce has been taken off by the state in the form of tax levies and then exported in order to finance the cost of industrialization. Even though the peasants have been dragging their heels, the collectivist system of agriculture has enabled the government to squeeze enough out of them to feed the city dwellers and to help pay for the new industrial centers.

Growth of Industry

Whereas most of the farms are run as cooperatives, the factories are mostly owned and operated by the government. Besides providing industry with the necessary capital, the government also employs a combination of the ''carrot'' and the ''stick'' to stimulate maximum production. Both workers and managers are required to meet certain quotas on pain of fine or dismissal. On the other hand, if they surpass their quotas, they are rewarded with bonuses. Trade unions are allowed and recognized but are denied the basic right to strike—for strikes would be incompatible with the goals and functioning of the Soviet-planned economy. The purpose of a strike is to secure for the workers, in the form of higher wages, a larger proportion of what is produced. But the Gosplan has already decided how much will go to workers and how much to the government for reinvestment in industry.

In actuality, Soviet industry has grown as rapidly as it has because the government withdraws about one-third of the national income for reinvestment; in comparison, the United States withdraws about half that proportion. Furthermore, in a planned economy the government is able to allocate investment capital as it wishes. Thus about 70 percent of the total Soviet industrial output consists of capital goods, and 30 percent, of consumer goods, whereas in the United States the ratio is roughly the reverse. By the end of the first Five Year Plan, in 1932, the Soviet Union had risen in industrial output from fifth to second place in the world. This extraordinary spurt was due, not only to the increase of productivity in the Soviet Union, but also to the decline of productivity in the West that was brought about by the Depression. Nevertheless, Soviet gross national product, which included the lagging agricultural as well as the industrial output, increased 3 ½ during the quarter century between 1928 and 1952—a rate of growth surpassing that of any other country during this period. From the viewpoint of world balance of power, which was Stalin's main concern, the Soviet share of total global industrial output rose from 1.5 percent in 1921 to 10 percent in 1939 to 20 percent in 1966.

We should emphasize that Soviet economic growth has been achieved at the expense of the Soviet citizens, who have been forced to work hard for the future and to endure privation in the present, regardless of what their wishes might be. Consumer goods are scarce, expensive, and of poor quality. The *Gross National Product* (GNP—a statistical measure of total output of goods and services) of the Soviet Union has remained for the past several years at 46 to 48 percent of the GNP of the United States. And in per capita terms, the Soviet GNP is only about two-fifths that of the United States, because the Soviet work force is about one-fourth larger than the American.

Significance for World History

From the point of view of global impact, it is likely that the Gosplan will prove to be of greater significance than the Communist International. The Five Year Plans attracted worldwide attention, particularly because of the concurrent breakdown of the West's economy. Socialism was no longer a dream of visionaries; it was a going concern. The original skepticism in the West gave way to genuine interest and, in some cases, to imitation. Economic policies were influenced, consciously or unconsciously, by the Soviet success in setting priorities for the investment of national resources, which is the essence of planning. Some countries went so far as to launch Plans of their own, of varying duration, in the hope of alleviating their economic difficulties.

The Five Year Plans do not seem to have impressed the Western countries as much as the underdeveloped nations. Western visitors to Russia were struck by the shabby clothing, the monotonous diet, the wretched housing, and the scarcity of consumer goods. They were also appalled by the lack of individual freedom as reflected in the one-party political structure, the hobbling of trade unions, the regimentation of education, and the rigid control of all communication media. Soviet society, despite the achievements of the Five Year Plans, did not seem to most Westerners a Socialist paradise worth copying. On the other hand, most Westerners concede that without the industrial growth under the Five Year Plans, the Soviet Union would not have been able to contribute so much to Hitler's defeat in World War II.

Former colonial peoples in the underdeveloped world reacted very differently. To them, the Soviet Union was the country that succeeded in transforming itself within a generation from a backward agrarian state into the second greatest industrial and military power in the world. The institutions and the techniques that made this dramatic change possible were of vital concern to these peoples. Also noteworthy is the fact that the Soviet Union is a great Asian as well as European state. Its frontiers stretch from Korea, past Mongolia, Sinkiang, Afghanistan, and Iran, to Turkey. In almost all these regions, kindred people exist on both sides of the frontier, thus facilitating interaction and comparison of conditions. In most cases, the Soviet Union has fared well by comparison, thanks to the revivifying effect of the Five Year Plans on its eastern regions. The other side of the long frontier has had few counterparts to the substantial material advances made in the Soviet Central Asian republics: the 185-mile Ferghana irrigation canal, the 900-mile Turksib Railway, the new textile mills, the Karaganda coalfields, the Lake Balcha copper-smelting works, the fertilizer and farm-machinery plants, as well as the new health services and the rise in literacy from about 2 percent in 1914 to 75 percent in 1940, and to over 90 percent today. These statistics explain the following report by an American correspondent from Tashkent in Soviet Uzbekistan.

> What is it that gives Asian visitors to Tashkent such [favorable] impressions? It is the sight of a . . . huge Asian city with excellent health standards, education, sanitation, clean streets, rapidly improving housing, electric facilities, substantial if not fancy consumers' goods, an abundance of food, an abundance of work, a rapidly widening industrialization program and constantly improving agricultural productivity.
>
> Along with this they see equality of races under the law and the participation of large numbers of Uzbeks and other Central Asian peoples in government, industry and education.
>
> Against this background the Asian visitor is not likely to be too much influenced by Western arguments about democracy nor does the individual human factor impress the Asian visitor so strongly since he is more likely to know the mortality tables of his own country. . . .
>
> It is the Asian's conclusions that are important, since Tashkent has prime importance as a symbol for Asia rather than for Europe. [1]

II. THE GREAT DEPRESSION

Origins of the Crash

With the opening of the year 1929, the United States appeared to be flourishing. Businessmen, academic economists, and government leaders were all expressing confidence in the future. Their optimism proved unjustified; in the fall of 1929, the bottom fell out of the stock market, and a worldwide depression, unprecedented in its intensity and longevity, followed. The serious international economic imbalance that developed when the United States became a creditor nation on a large scale (following World War I) seems to have been one reason for this unexpected denouement. Britain had been a creditor nation before the war, but it had used the proceeds from its overseas investments and loans to pay for its chronic excess of imports over exports. The United States, by contrast, normally had a favorable trade balance, accentuated by tariffs that were kept at high levels for reasons of domestic politics. In addition, money poured into the country in the 1920s in payment of war debts, and the American gold hoard rose between 1913 and 1924 from $1.924 to $4.499 billion, or half the world's total gold supply.

This imbalance was neutralized for several years by large-scale American loans and investments abroad: between 1925 and 1928, the average annual total for American foreign investments amounted to $1.1 billion. In the long run, this, of course, intensified the imbalance and could not be continued indefinitely. As payments came due, debtor countries were forced to curtail imports from the United States, and certain branches of the American economy, especially agriculture, were hurt. In addition, some countries found it necessary to default on their debts, which shook certain financial firms in the United States.

As serious as the imbalance of the international economy was that of the American economy, the basic reason being that wages lagged behind the rising productivity. Between 1920 and 1929, hourly industrial wages rose only 2 percent, while the productivity of workers in factories jumped 55 percent. At the same time, the real income of the farmers was shrinking because agricultural prices were falling while taxes and living costs were rising. Whereas in 1910 the income per farm worker had been slightly less than 40 percent that of the nonfarm worker, by 1930, it was just under 30 percent. Such poverty in the countryside was a serious matter, because the rural population at that time was one-fifth of the total population.

The combination of stationary factory wages and falling farm income resulted in severe maldistribution of national income. In 1929, 5 percent of the American people received one-third of all personal incomes (compared to one-sixth by the end of World War II). This meant inadequate purchasing power for the masses, combined with a high level of capital investment by those who were receiving the high salaries and dividends. Production of capital goods during the 1920s rose at an average annual rate of 6.4 percent, compared to 2.8 percent for consumer goods. Eventually this led to the clogging of the economy; the low purchasing power was unable to support such a high rate of capital investment. As a result, the index of industrial production dropped from 126 to 117 between June and October 1929, creating a slump that contributed to the stock market crash that autumn.

The weakness of the American banking system was a final factor contributing to the crash of 1929. A great number of independent banking firms were operating, and some of these lacked sufficient resources to weather financial storms. When one closed its doors, panic spread, and depositors rushed to withdraw their savings from other banks, thus setting in motion a chain reaction that undermined the entire banking structure.

Worldwide Depression

The stock market crash in the United States began in September 1929. Within one month, stock values dropped 40 percent, and apart from a few brief recoveries, the decline continued for three years. During that period, United States Steel stock fell from 262 to 22, General Motors, from 73 to 8. Every branch of the national economy suffered correspondingly. During those three years, 5000 banks closed their doors. General Motors had produced 5.5 million automobiles in 1929, but in 1931 they produced only 2.5 million. The steel industry in July 1932 was operating at 12 percent of capacity. By 1933, both general industrial production and national income had slumped by nearly one-half, wholesale prices, by almost one-third, and merchandise trade, by more than two-thirds.

The Great Depression was unique not only in its intensity but also in its worldwide impact. American financial houses were forced to call in their short-term loans abroad; naturally, there were repercussions. In May 1931, the Credit-Anstalt, the largest and most reputable bank in Vienna, declared itself insolvent, setting off a wave of panic throughout the Continent. On July 13, the German Danatbank followed suit, and for the next two days all German banks were decreed on holiday; the Berlin Stock Exchange, the Börse, closed for two months. In September 1931, Britain went off the gold standard, to be followed two years later by the United States and nearly all the major countries.

The breakdown of the financial world had its counterpart in industry and commerce: the index of world industrial production, excluding the Soviet Union, fell from 100 in 1929 to 86.5 in 1930, 74.8 in 1931, and 63.8 in 1932, a drop of 36.2 percent. The maximum decline in previous crises had been 7 percent. Even more drastic was the shrinking of world international trade, from $68.6 billion in 1929 to 55.6 in 1930, 39.7 in 1931, 26.9 in 1932, and 24.2 in 1933. Again it might be noted that the maximum drop in international trade in the past had been 7 percent, during the 1907–1908 crisis.

Social and Political Repercussions

These economic catastrophies gave rise to social problems of corresponding magnitude. Most serious was the mass unemployment which reached tragic proportions. In March 1933, the number of people out of work in the United States was estimated conservatively at over 14 million, or a fourth of the total labor force. In Britain, the jobless were numbered at nearly 3 million, representing about the same proportion of the workers as in the United States. Germany was the worst off with more than two-fifths of trade unionists wholly unemployed, and another fifth on part-time work.

Unemployment on this scale drastically lowered living standards in all countries. Even in the wealthy United States there was wholesale misery and privation, especially in the beginning, when relief was left to private and to local agencies with inadequate funds. In England, where unemployment had been chronic through the 1920s, the situation now became even worse. A substantial proportion of a whole generation was growing up with little opportunity or prospect of finding employment. Some bitterly referred to their purposeless existence as a "living death." In Germany, with its higher percentage of jobless people, the frustrations and tensions were more acute. Eventually they made it possible for Hitler to triumph, for social dislocation on such a large scale inevitably had profound political repercussions.

Even in the United States, with its superior resources and its tradition of political stability, these were years of strange ideas and agitations. Various proposals were made for income redistribution, including the Townsend Plan for munificent old-age pensions and the Share-Our-Wealth movement of Senator Huey Long of Louisiana. Another manifestation of the political turbulence was Franklin Roosevelt's sweeping electoral victory in 1932. The New Deal that followed served as an escape valve for the political discontent and effectively neutralized the extremist movements.

POVERTY AMIDST PLENTY IN THE UNITED STATES

The Great Depression was unprecedented in its intensity, scope, and longevity. Its effect on the United States is described in the following testimony before a congressional committee in February 1932.*

During the last three months I [Oscar Ameringer of Oklahoma City] have visited, as I have said, some 20 states of this wonderfully rich and beautiful country. Here are some of the things I heard and saw: In the State of Washington I was told that the forest fires raging in that region all summer and fall were caused by unemployed timber workers and bankrupt farmers in an endeavor to earn a few honest dollars as fire fighters. The last thing I saw on the night I left Seattle was numbers of women searching for scraps of food in the refuse piles of the principal market of that city. A number of Montana citizens told me of thousands of bushels of wheat left in the fields uncut on account of its low price that hardly paid for the harvesting. In Oregon I saw thousands of bushels of apples rotting in the orchards. Only absolutely flawless apples were still salable, at from 40 to 50 cents a box containing 200 apples. At the same time, there are millions of children who, on account of the poverty of their parents, will not eat one apple this winter.

While I was in Oregon the *Portland Oregonian* bemoaned the fact that thousands of ewes were killed by the sheep raisers because they did not bring enough in the market to pay the freight on them. And while Oregon sheep raisers fed mutton to the buzzards, I saw men picking for meat scraps in the garbage cans in the cities of New York and Chicago. I talked to one man in a restaurant in Chicago. He told me of his experience in raising sheep. He said that he had killed 3,000 sheep this fall and thrown them down the canyon, because it cost $1.10 to ship a sheep, and then he would get less than a dollar for it. He said he could not afford to feed the sheep, and he would not let them starve, so he just cut their throats and threw them down the canyon.

The roads of the West and Southwest teem with hungry hitchhikers. The camp fires of the homeless are seen along every railroad track. I saw men, women, and children walking over the hard roads. Most of them were tenant farmers who had lost their all in the late slump in wheat and cotton. Between Clarksville and Russellville, Ark., I picked up a family. The woman was hugging a dead chicken under a ragged coat. When I asked her where she had procured the fowl, first she told me she had found it dead in the road, and then added in grim humor, "They promised me a chicken in the pot, and now I got mine." . . .

The farmers are being pauperized by the poverty of industrial populations and the industrial populations are being pauperized by the poverty of the farmers. Neither has the money to buy the product of the other; hence we have overproduction and underconsumption at the same time and in the same country.

* *Unemployment in the United States. . . . Hearings before a Subcommittee of the Committee on Labor,* House of Representatives, 72nd Congress, 1st Session (Washington: Government Printing Office, 1932), pp. 98–99.

Political developments in Britain and France during these years were generally the same as in the United States. Both countries were hit by political storms but managed to ride them out within the framework of their traditional institutions. The British Labour party, which had come into office in June 1929, was forced to give way in August 1931 to a new coalition, "National" government. This proved to be a mere facade for Tory rule, with the Conservatives making up the majority of the cabinet. Three years later, the aging and ailing MacDonald resigned in favor of Stanley Baldwin, and so Britain passed under virtual Conservative rule, though the coalition still existed nominally.

In France, too, the Left was forced out of office by the pressures of the Depression. It won the 1932 elections, and the Radical Edouard Herriot formed a government with Socialist support as had been done in 1924. The Radicals and the Socialists were hopelessly divided on the question of how to cope with the economic crisis. Herriot held office for only six months, and four other premiers followed in rapid succession. The showdown came in December 1933 with the Stavisky scandal involving a Russian-born promoter and a provincial pawnshop in a fraudulent bond issue. According to rumors, various important officials and politicians were implicated. Extreme rightist groups took advantage of the opportunity to stage street riots in an effort to overthrow the republic itself. Although they failed to do so, they did force the government to resign in February 1934. A number of conservative ministries followed, none of which proved capable of coping with the country's basic ills.

Much more dramatic and fateful was the rise of Hitler to power in Germany. When the Depression hit that country, its government was a Left-Center coalition led by the Socialist Chancellor Herman Müller, while the conservative old war hero Paul von Hindenburg was functioning as president. Like Socialist ministries elsewhere, the Müller ministry in Germany was undermined by dissension over how to cope with unemployment and other problems created by the Depression. The ministry was forced to resign in March 1930, and, from then on, Germany was ruled by parties of the Center and Right.

At first a coalition government was organized by Heinrich Brüning, an intelligent and upright, though cold and rigid, Centrist. Lacking a parliamentary majority, he fell back upon Article 48 of the constitution, which empowered the president, in case of emergency, to issue decrees that would have the force of law unless specifically rejected by majority vote of the Reichstag. The Reichstag did, in fact, vote against the first emergency decrees, but Brüning countered by persuading Hindenburg to dissolve the Reichstag and order new elections for September 1930. Thus Germany was ruled, well before the Hitler years, by legal but authoritarian presidential power. Brüning expected that a majority of the various Center and Right parties would be returned, enabling him to govern the country in regular parliamentary fashion. Instead, the elections marked the emergence of Hitler's National Socialist party as a national force.

The son of a minor Austrian customs official, Adolf Hitler went to Vienna early in life, aspiring to be a painter. According to his own account—which seems to be greatly exaggerated—he spent five miserable years working at the most menial jobs to keep body and soul together. From Vienna, Hitler drifted to Munich, where in 1914 he enlisted in a Bavarian regiment. At the end of the war, Hitler joined a struggling group called the National Socialist German Workers' party, of which he soon became the leader, or Führer. After making rabble-rousing speeches on nationalist and anti-Semitic themes, he joined Field Marshal Ludendorff in an uprising in Munich in 1923. It was easily put down by the police, and Hitler was imprisoned for nine months. There, at the age of thirty-five, he wrote *Mein Kampf*—"My Battle"—a long and turgid autobiographical reflection into which he poured his hatred of democracy, Marxism, and Jews.

Upon release from prison, Hitler resumed his agitation but with disappointing results. In the December 1924 elections, his Nazi party won only 14 seats and a mere 908,000 votes, and in May 1928 it won even fewer—12 seats and 810,000 votes, or 2.6 percent of the total number. The turning point came with the September 1930 elections when the Nazis won 107 seats and 6,407,000 votes, or 18.3 percent of the total. This avalanche of ballots did not come from the workers. The Socialist and Communist parties between them gained 13 more seats in 1930 than in 1928. Hitler was getting his newfound support from the middle-class elements that were looking desperately for safety in the fierce economic storm. (This is evident in Table 11, which shows the marked drop in the votes received from 1930 onward by all the Center and Right parties except the Catholic Centrum).

To the minor functionaries and bankrupt tradespeople, the Nazi platform offered

Table 11. REICHSTAG ELECTIONS, 1919–1933
(NUMBER OF DEPUTIES AND PERCENTAGE OF TOTAL VOTES*)

Party	1/19/19	6/6/20	5/4/24	12/7/24	5/20/28	9/14/30	7/31/32	11/6/32	3/5/33
Communist									
No. dep.	0	4	62	45	54	77	89	100	81
% vote		2.1%	12.6%	9.0%	10.6%	13.1%	14.6%	16.9%	12.3%
Social Democratic									
No. dep.			100	131	153	143	133	121	120
% vote			20.5%	26.0%	29.8%	24.5%	21.6%	20.4%	18.3%
Ind.									
No. dep.	22	84							
% vote	7.6%	17.9%							
Maj.									
No. dep.	165	102							
% vote	37.9%	21.6%							
Democratic									
No. dep.	75	39	28	32	25	20	4	2	5
% vote	18.6%	8.3%	5.7%	6.3%	4.9%	3.8%	1.0%	1.0%	0.8%
Centrum									
No. dep.	91	64	65	69	62	68	75	70	74
% vote	19.7%	13.6%	13.4%	13.6%	12.1%	11.8%	12.5%	11.9%	11.7%
Bavarian People's									
No. dep.	0	21	16	19	16	19	22	20	18
% vote		4.4%	3.2%	3.7%	3.0%	3.0%	3.2%	3.1%	2.7%
Economic									
No. dep.	4	4	10	17	23	23	2	1	0
% vote	0.9%	0.8%	2.4%	3.3%	4.5%	3.9%	0.4%	0.3%	
German People's									
No. dep.	19	65	45	51	45	30	7	11	2
% vote	4.4%	13.9%	9.2%	10.1%	8.7%	4.5%	1.2%	1.9%	1.1%
National People's									
No. dep.	44	71	95	103	73	41	37	52	52
% vote	10.3%	14.9%	19.5%	20.5%	14.2%	7.0%	5.9%	8.8%	8.0%
National Socialist									
No. dep.	0	0	32	14	12	107	230	196	288
% vote			6.5%	3.0%	2.6%	18.3%	37.4%	33.1%	43.9%

*Under the electoral system provided for in the Weimar Constitution, each party received approximately one representative for every 60,000 popular votes cast for its candidates. Various small parties, not listed here, were underrepresented in the Reichstag.

comfort and hope. It called for abolition of unearned income and "interest slavery," nationalization of all trusts, profit sharing in large concerns, and the death penalty for usurers and profiteers. At the same time, all patriotic Germans were promised the smashing of the Versailles chains and the persecution of the Jews, who were branded as being both exploiting financiers and materialistic Communists. It should be emphasized that Hitler had been campaigning on this platform for years, with little response. It was the Depression that transformed him from a loud-mouthed fanatic to the beloved Führer who supplied scapegoats for misery, and a program of action for individual and national fulfillment.

With the September, 1930, elections, the Nazis increased their Reichstag representation from 12 to 107, thus becoming the second largest party in the country. This unexpected outcome undermined parliamentary government in Germany because it denied a majority to both a Center-Right coalition desired by Brüning and a Center-Left coalition that had functioned under Müller. Consequently, Brüning had to rely for over two years on presidential decrees for all necessary legislation. The extent of his dependence on Hindenburg was demonstrated when he proposed legislation for the break-up of east Prussian estates; President Hindenburg, himself a Junker landowner, was strongly opposed, and forced Brüning to resign in May 1932.

The new chancellor, Franz von Papen, headed a weak coalition government with negligible Reichstag support, so he held new elections in July 1932, in the hope of strengthening his position. Instead, the Nazis were the big winners: their votes jumped to 13,799,000, or 37.4 percent of the total number, and their seats to 230. Hitler was now the head of the number-one party in the country, and since neither he nor the Communists would enter a coalition, no majority government support could be organized.

In November 1932, Papen held still another election in an attempt to break the deadlock. This time the Nazis lost 2 million votes and 34 seats in the Reichstag, reducing them to 196 deputies. They were still the strongest party in the country, but they could no longer pose as the irresistable wave of the future. Yet less than two months later, Hitler was the chancellor of Germany. One reason for this startling reversal was the large-scale financial support now given to the Nazi party by German business leaders, who were worried that millions of votes might shift to the Left if the party disintegrated. Hitler met with the Cologne banker Kurt von Schroeder on January 4, and, from then on, the supply of funds was no longer a problem. The other reason was the morass of intrigues and cabals that passed for government in Berlin at the time. The aged Hindenburg was now senile and could function lucidly for only a few hours each day. Persuaded to get rid of Papen, he appointed in his place General Kurt von Schleicher.

Schleicher canceled the cuts in wages and relief that Papen had made, revived plans for partitioning east Prussian estates, and began an investigation of illegal profits made by landowners through government agrarian legislation. Both the landowners and the businessmen denounced him bitterly, and they won over Hindenburg. Schleicher was vulnerable for the same reason that Brüning and Papen had been: inability to organize a majority in the Reichstag. So, on January 28, 1933, Schleicher was forced to resign, and two days later, Hitler became chancellor with a coalition cabinet of Nationalists and Nazis.

Within six months Hitler had regimented Germany. A new Reichstag was elected on March 5 following a campaign of unprecedented propaganda and terrorism. The Nazis received 288 seats and 5.5 million votes, but they still made up only 44 percent of the total. When the representatives met, Hitler declared the Communist seats null and void, and then made a deal with the Catholic Center that gave him enough votes to pass the Enabling Act on March 23, 1933. This gave him authority to rule by decree for four years. But by the summer of 1933, he had eliminated or leashed virtually all independent elements in German life—trade unions, schools, churches, political parties, communications media, the judiciary, and the states of the federation.

Thus Hitler became master of Germany, and by technically legal methods, as he never ceased to boast. The Depression had made his triumph possible, though by no means inevitable. The possibility was translated into actuality by a combination of other factors, including Hitler's own talents, the support afforded by assorted vested interests, and the myopia of his opponents who underestimated him and failed to unite in opposition.

International Repercussions

The British foreign minister, Sir Austen Chamberlain, comparing the international situation in 1932 with that of the Locarno era, observed:

> I look at the world to-day and I contrast the conditions now with the conditions at that time, and I am forced to acknowledge that for some reason or other, owing to something upon which it is difficult to put one's finger, in these last two years the world is moving backward. Instead of approaching nearer to one another, instead of increasing the measure of goodwill, instead of progressing to a stable peace, it has fallen back into an attitude of suspicion, of fear, of danger, which imperils the peace of the world. [2]

That "something" that Chamberlain could not identify was the Depression and its manifold repercussions, international as well as national. Various international agreements of the Locarno era became unworkable, particularly those concerning reparations and war debts. It soon became obvious that governments, pushed to the brink of bankruptcy by their slumping economies and mounting unemployment, would not be able to meet commitments undertaken a few years earlier. In July 1931, on the initiative of President Hoover, the powers agreed to a moratorium on all intergovernmental debts. The following summer, at the Lausanne Conference, the powers in fact, if not in theory, canceled German reparations entirely. Simultaneously, the payment of war debts to the United States came to an end, though a few token payments were made in the following years. And so the sticky old issue of reparations and war debts was finally swept away by the economic storms let loose by the Depression.

Another effect of the storms was to accentuate the ever-present economic nationalism to the point where it disturbed international relations. Self-protective measures by individual nations took such forms as higher tariffs, more rigid import quotas, clearing agreements, currency-control regulations, and bilateral trade pacts. These measures inevitably brought economic friction and political tensions among states. Various attempts were made to reverse the trend but without success. The World Economic Conference that met in London in 1933 was a dismal fiasco. "Autarchy," or economic self-sufficiency, gradually became a commonly accepted national goal.

Closely related was the petering out of disarmament efforts, which gave way to massive rearmament programs. The Disarmament Conference that met intermittently for twenty months, beginning in February 1932, was as futile as the Economic Conference. As the 1930s progressed, countries devoted more and more of their energies to rearming. The trend was impossible to stop because armament manufacturing provided jobs as well as imagined security. Unemployment in the United States, for example, was not substantially reduced until the country began to rearm on the eve of World War II. Likewise, Hitler quickly disposed of the unprecedented unemployment he faced by launching a gigantic rearmament program.

The armaments now being accumulated were bound sooner or later to be used, and their use required some justification. The most obvious was that of lebensraum, or living space. This was the term coined by Hitler, but similar expressions and arguments were employed by Mussolini in Italy and by the military leaders in Japan. The unemployment and general misery, according to this doctrine, arose from the lack of lebensraum. A few fortunate countries had seized all the colonies and underpopulated lands overseas, leaving the other nations without the natural resources needed to support their people. The obvious way out was to expand, by force if necessary, to remedy the injustices inflicted in the past. Such were the arguments used by the so-called "have-not" countries against the "haves."

The reasoning was obviously false in view of the fact that the Depression had devastated equally and impartially the United States, Canada, and Britain, along with Germany, Italy, and Japan. Nevertheless, the lebensraum ideology served to unite the people of the "have-not" countries in support of the expansionist policies of their respective governments. It also gave a superficial moral justification to aggression committed for the avowed purpose of providing food for the needy and work for the jobless. Indeed, certain elements even within the "have" countries accepted these rationalizations and defended the aggressions that followed.

Such, then, was the combination of forces behind the "suspicion," the "fear," and the "moving backward" that Chamberlain had observed in 1932. During the following years, these forces undermined completely the settlement that had been reached in the Twenties and precipitated one crisis after another, culminating finally in World War II.

SUGGESTED READING

A. Bulloch, *Hitler: A Study in Tyranny* (Harper & Row, 1952); J. K. Gilbraith, *The Great Crash, 1929* (Houghton Mifflin, 1955); H. Holborn, ed., *Republic to Reich: The Making of the Nazi Revolution* (Pantheon, 1972); C. P. Kindleberger, *The World in Depression, 1929–1939* (Allen Lane, 1973); A. Nove, *An Economic History of the U.S.S.R.* (Lane, 1969); W. L. Shirer, *The Rise and Fall of the Third Reich* (Simon & Schuster, 1960); C. K. Wilber, *The Soviet Model and Underdeveloped Countries* (University of North Carolina Press, 1970).

chapter 35

Drift To War, 1929-1939

The late 1920s were years of prosperity, stabilization, and settlement; the 1930s were years of depression, crises, and war. In Europe, the settled atmosphere of the 1920s was based on the French system of alliances, and in the Far East, on the Washington Conference agreements. The objective in each case was to preserve the status quo in the two regions. This objective was realized in the 1920s, but during the next decade everything was suddenly and decisively upset. New leaders appeared in Germany and Japan who were determined to revise the territorial settlement of World War I and who possessed the means and the will to do so. Their massive rearming programs and their breath-taking aggressions drastically altered the balance of power. No longer was the relatively weak Italy the only revisionist state attempting ineffectually to challenge the status quo. The Third Reich and Imperial Japan also gave strength to the revisionist drive, resulting in an entirely new balance of power. A triangle situation developed, with Britain, France, and their Continental allies supporting the status quo, Germany, Italy, and Japan driving for revision, and the Soviet Union, strengthened by the Five Year Plans, playing an increasingly important role. The interplay of these three forces explains the recurring crises of the 1930s and the final outbreak of World War II.

I. JAPAN INVADES MANCHURIA

The first major act of aggression was made by Japan, pursuing long-cherished territorial ambitions on the mainland. The Japanese had entered World War I promptly in order to exploit what appeared to be a golden opportunity. They took over with little difficulty the German islands in the Pacific and the German holdings on the Shantung peninsula. The Japanese also had ambitions on the mainland, as evident in their twenty-one demands on China (January 1915) and in their expeditionary force to Siberia, which remained there after the British and American troops left in 1920. These ambitions were, for the most part, unsatisfied. At the Paris Peace Conference Japan did retain control of the former German islands, but as Class-C mandates rather than as outright possessions. President Wilson strenuously opposed Japanese claims to the Chinese Shantung peninsula. As a compromise, Japan was confirmed in "temporary" possession of the peninsula, but it conceded that it was its "policy" to restore the territory to China at an unspecified date, "retaining only the economic priviliges [hitherto] granted to Germany."

At the Washington Naval Conference Japan formally renounced any territorial ambitions it might still have cherished. The nine powers at the conference signed a Nine-Power Treaty (February 6, 1922) guaranteeing the territorial integrity of China and reiterating the principle of the Open Door. At the same conference the United States, Britain, France, and Japan signed the Four-Power Treaty (December 13, 1921) by which they agreed to respect one another's rights in "insular possessions" in the Pacific and to settle any future differences by consultation. In addition, Japan, after energetic American mediation, agreed to restore Shantung to China and to evacuate its troops from Siberia. Both commitments were fulfilled in 1922.

Having finished with foreign adventures, at least for the time being, Japan now turned to domestic economic problems. Japan, like the United States, had prospered greatly during World War I, supplying munitions and merchant shipping. Between 1914 and 1920, the value of foreign trade increased almost four times. The prosperity, however, was poorly distributed, because of the unprecedented concentration of economic power in the so-called *Zaibatsu* (Zai means wealth; batsu, clique). This was the general name given to four giant family corporations (Mitsui, Mitsubishi, Sumitomo, and Yasuda) that by World War II controlled three-fourths of the combined capitalization of all Japanese firms. They held one-third of all deposits in Japan's private banks, three-fourths of all trust deposits, and one-fifth of all life-insurance policies. The peasants, comprising one-half the total population, were impoverished by high rents and heavy debts. Only 7 percent of these families owned five acres or more of land; the average holding was less than three acres. City workers suffered from high food prices, low wages, and lack of trade-union freedom.

The depressed living standards of the workers and peasants meant a severely restricted domestic market. Consequently, Japanese industry was particularly dependent upon foreign markets for the disposal of its products. This dependence spelled disaster with the coming of the Depression. Between 1929 and 1931, foreign trade decreased by almost 50 percent. The peasants, who had supplemented their meager incomes by silk cultivation, were badly hurt by the sharp slump in silk exports to depression-ridden America. City workers suffered correspondingly from unemployment.

Army leaders and other champions of territorial aggrandizement argued persuasively that the source of Japan's trouble was its dependence upon foreign markets. Japan should conquer an empire that would make it economically independent of the rest of the world.

506

Military spokesmen had been preaching this doctrine for years, but the ravages of the Depression now provided them with a responsive audience, as had happened with Hitler in Germany. The Japanese expansionists were not only motivated by economic considerations. They were also concerned about the growing strength of the Soviet Union and the increasing success of Chiang Kai-shek in unifying China. In addition, they were fully aware of the unemployment situation and other problems that were then engrossing the attention of Western statesmen. These calculations figured in the Japanese decision to attack the Chinese province of Manchuria in 1931.

On the evening of September 18, 1931, an explosion wrecked a small section of track on the Japanese-controlled South Manchuria Railway to the north of Mukden. Baron Shidehara, who was foreign minister in 1931, testified before the International War Crimes Tribunal in June 1946 that the incident had been staged by army officers who he had tried vainly to stop. His testimony is supported by the speed and precision with which the Japanese army swung immediately into action. Without declaring war, it captured Mukden and Changchun in the space of twenty-four hours and then fanned out in all directions. The taking of Harbin in late January 1932 signified the end of all organized resistance in Manchuria. In March 1932, the victors renamed their conquest Manchukuo, the ''State of Manchu.'' They needed a puppet emperor, so they dragged out of retirement Henry P'u Yi, the surviving head of the old Manchu dynasty that had fallen in 1911, and solemnly installed him as regent.

Meanwhile, the Chinese government had appealed to the League of Nations under Article 11, and to the United States under the Paris Pact (Kellogg-Briand Pact). The result was much deliberation but no practical aid. The League Council convened on September 19, October 13, and again on November 16 to discuss the Manchurian situation. On November 21, the Japanese delegation accepted the original Chinese proposal for an impartial commission of inquiry, but the members were not chosen until January 14, 1932, and they did not actually reach Mukden until April 21. By that time, Manchuria had become Manchukuo.

The League Commission, known as the Lytton Commission after its chairman Lord Lytton, submitted its report in October 1932. Carefully worded to avoid offending the Japanese, it denied that the Japanese aggression could be justified as a defensive measure and branded the new Manchukuo state a Japanese puppet regime. On the other hand, it refrained from ordering Japan to get out. Instead, the report proposed a settlement recognizing Japan's special interest in Manchuria and making that province an autonomous state under Chinese sovereignty but with the Japanese in control. On February 25, 1933, the League adopted the report, and the following month Japan withdrew from that body.

In retrospect, the Manchurian affair stands out as the first serious blow leveled at the League of Nations and at the entire diplomatic structure designed to maintain the status quo—the Versailles settlement, the Washington Conference agreements, and the Paris Pact. The ease with which Japan had acquired its rich new possession was not lost upon the revisionist leaders of Italy and Germany; Manchuria set off a chain reaction of aggressions that ultimately led to World War II.

II. DIPLOMATIC REACTIONS TO HITLER

The Japanese conquest of Manchuria was a rude challenge to the status quo in the Far East, but even more upsetting was Hitler's threat to the status quo in Europe. Hitherto the French system of alliances had dominated the continent with little difficulty. Mussolini had tried to organize a counter bloc, but his agreements with third-rate revisionist states such as Austria, Hungary, Bulgaria, and Albania were of little value. Likewise, the Soviet Union was cut off by the "cordon sanitaire" and, in any case, was engrossed in "building socialism in one country." Only Germany was left, and under Stresemann, this country had made peace with its wartime enemies when it accepted the Locarno Pacts and entered the League of Nations.

This comfortable situation was drastically altered when Hitler became chancellor in 1933. The Nazi leader had for some time been demanding more lebensraum for the German people. It is scarcely surprising that there were immediate diplomatic repercussions when the champion of lebensraum became the master of Germany. The first move was the revitalization of the Little Entente, which had been dormant for several years. In February 1933, Czechoslovakia, Yugoslavia, and Rumania established a permanent council of their foreign ministers to facilitate the coordination and implementation of their diplomatic policies.

Even Mussolini, who later was to form the Rome-Berlin Axis with Hitler, at first reacted strongly against his fellow dictator. In view of the substantial German minority in the South Tyrol, Mussolini was apprehensive of an expansionist Nazi regime with its slogan of "Ein Volk, ein Reich, ein Führer." Accordingly, he took the initiative in concluding the Four-Power Pact on July 15, 1933, with Britain, France, and Germany. The agreement confirmed the adherence of the signatories to the League Covenant, the Locarno Treaties, and the Kellogg-Briand Pact, and it also prohibited any changes in the Versailles Treaty without the consent of all four powers. This was a futile exercise, for Hitler repeatedly violated these commitments—without even a reference to his fellow signatories. In October 1933, he announced Germany's withdrawal from the Disarmament Conference and from the League of Nations. Although he did not immediately reveal his rearmament program, its existence, if not its pace and magnitude, became generally known.

These developments stimulated the formation of another regional bloc made up of Turkey, Greece, Rumania, and Yugoslavia, the last two with considerable German minorities. On February 9, 1934, the four countries signed the Balkan Pact which provided for cooperation to preserve the status quo in Southeastern Europe.

More significant than the formation of the Balkan Entente was the basic shift now occurring in Soviet foreign policy. Traditionally, the Soviet leaders regarded the League as an organization of imperialist powers. But with Hitler's rise to power, the apprehensive Russians began to view the League as a possible instrument for organizing collective resistance against anticipated Nazi aggression. This new attitude was encouraged by the French foreign minister Louis Barthou. A conservative in domestic matters, Barthou's simple and consistent objective in foreign affairs was to build up a coalition that would be strong enough to discourage Hitler from expansionist ventures. In addition to cementing the ties between France, the Little Entente, and Poland, Barthou now sought to add the Soviet Union to the status-quo bloc. It was due largely to his efforts that the League of Nations invited the Soviet Union to join its ranks and that the invitation was accepted on September 19, 1934.

The following month, in Marseilles, an assassin's bullets killed Barthou, along with King Alexander of Yugoslavia. It was a turning point in European diplomacy, for Barthou's successors followed a devious and ambivalent policy vis-à-vis Germany. This was particularly true of Pierre Laval, who concluded a pact with Mussolini on January 7,

HITLER, MUSSOLINI, AND LEBENSRAUM

Hitler and Mussolini both justified their conquests by claiming the need for *lebensraum,* or living space. They blamed their national problems on the lack of empire with resources and markets. This argument is made in the following statements by the two leaders.*

Hitler, 1930: If the German people does not solve the problem of its lack of space, and if it does not open up the domestic market for its industry, then 2000 years have been in vain. Germany will then make its exit from the world stage and peoples with more vigor will come into our heritage. . . .

Space must be fought for and maintained. People who are lazy have no right to the soil. Soil is for him who tills it and protects it. If a people disclaims soil, it disclaims life. If a nation loses in the defense of its soil, then the individual loses. There is no higher justice that decrees that a people must starve. There is only power, which creates justice. . . .

Parliaments do not create all of the rights on this earth; force also creates rights. The question is whether we wish to live or die. We have more right to soil than all the other nations because we are so thickly populated. I am of the opinion that in this respect too the principle can be applied: God helps him who helps himself.

Mussolini, 1933: . . . Fascism, the more it considers and observes the future and the development of humanity quite apart from political considerations of the moment, believes neither in the possibility nor the utility of perpetual peace. It thus repudiates the doctrine of Pacifism—born of a renunciation of the struggle and an act of cowardice in the face of sacrifice. War alone brings up to its highest tension all human energy and puts the stamp of nobility upon the peoples who have the courage to meet it. . . .

For Fascism, the growth of empire, that is to say the expansion of the nation, is an essential manifestation of vitality, and its opposite a sign of decadence. Peoples which are rising, or rising again after a period of decadence, are always imperialist. . . .

* *Voelkischer Beobachter,* May 7, 1930; and Benito Mussolini, "The Political and Social Doctrines of Fascism," *Political Quarterly* (July–September 1933), p. 356.

1935, in which the two agreed to cooperate in case of action by Hitler. They also settled various differences concerning their African possessions. France ceded to Italy certain desert territories adjoining the Italian colonies of Libya and Eritrea, and Mussolini, in turn, gave up claims in Tunis, where there was a considerable Italian population. However, a verbal understanding regarding Ethiopia was to lead to much controversy: Mussolini claimed that he had been promised a completely free hand in that country, while Laval insisted that the understanding had been limited to economic matters.

Two months later, on March 16, 1935, Germany formally renounced the clauses of the Versailles Treaty concerning its disarmament, reintroduced conscription, and announced that its army would be increased to 36 divisions. Britain, France, and Italy responded on April 11 at the Stresa Conference where they agreed on common action against the German menace. The "Stresa front" proved as futile as the Four-Power Pact two years earlier. Each of the signatories promptly proceeded to go its own way: Italy busied itself preparing to invade Ethiopia; Britain made a separate naval agreement with Germany on June 18 permitting the latter to build up to 35 percent of British strength; France concluded on May 2 a five-year alliance with Russia, each promising to aid the other in case of unprovoked attack. On May 16, Czechoslovakia signed a similar pact with Russia, though Russian aid to Czechoslovakia depended upon France also providing aid as required by the 1924 alliance.

In conclusion, Hitler's accession to power had stimulated within two years several new diplomatic groupings—the Balkan Entente, the revived Little Entente, the French-Russian alliance, and the Czech-Russian alliance—all designed to block any aggressive moves on the Führer's part. On the other hand, there were serious conflicts within this diplomatic line-up. The British-German Naval Pact was resented in Paris, the German-Polish Nonaggression Pact of January 1934 was not appreciated in Paris, and Laval basically distrusted his Soviet ally and preferred to make his own private deals on the side. With the outbreak of the Ethiopian crisis, these conflicts completely undermined the League of Nations and the entire post-World War I diplomatic structure.

III. ITALY CONQUERS ETHIOPIA

On October 3, 1935, Mussolini's legions invaded the independent African kingdom of Ethiopia. Behind this naked aggression were several motivations: the fascist yen for imperial glory, the hope that colonial expansion would relieve unemployment at home, and Mussolini's conviction that Laval had given him the green light and that opposition from other quarters would not be sufficient to stop him—an assumption that proved to be quite justified.

The pretext for the Italian aggression was reminiscent of the incident staged by the Japanese in Manchuria. On December 5, 1934, Ethiopian and Italian troops clashed at Walwal near the border between Italian Somaliland and Ethiopia. Emperor Haile Selassie offered to leave to an arbitration commission the question of whether Walwal was on Italian or Ethiopian territory. Mussolini refused to accept this. Instead he made various demands and prepared openly for invasion.

On October 3, 1935, the Italians began their invasion of Ethiopia. The League Council declared Italy the aggressor, and the Assembly voted for economic sanctions. These sanctions, which went into effect on November 18, 1935, included embargoes on arms, credits, and certain raw materials but did not include the key materials—oil, coal, iron, and steel. Despite such limitations, the sanctions did represent a significant beginning toward stopping the Italian advance. Also, world public opinion expressed itself overwhelmingly against Mussolini's aggression, and the Ethiopians resisted stoutly.

At this point, Laval squandered what chance there was of stopping the Italians. Early in December 1935 he persuaded the British foreign secretary, Sir Samuel Hoare, to accept a plan by which Italy would be given outright about half of Ethiopia and would control the remaining half of the country as a "zone of economic expansion and settlement." The two negotiators agreed to maintain secrecy until the plan had been submitted to the interested parties: Italy, Ethiopia, and the League. Laval, however, anticipated difficulties in Britain, so he leaked the plan to the French press. To his astonishment, the news of the deal aroused a storm of indignation in both London and Paris. Hoare was forced to resign and was succeeded by Anthony Eden. The following month, Laval also had to go, after a smashing defeat in the Chamber.

For a while it seemed like a clean sweep for the supporters of the League against aggression. But the basic issue still was whether the sanctions would be made effective by adding the key materials, particularly oil. Eden was in favor of doing so, but the new French foreign minister, Pierre Flandin, persisted in dragging his feet. Flandin's chief argument was that Mussolini would quit the League if oil sanctions were voted. He insisted that another attempt be made to reach a settlement. Since the British cabinet was not united behind Eden, Flandin had his way and effective sanctions were never enforced.

The death blow to any remaining hope of effective sanctions came with Hitler's occupation of the Rhineland on March 7, 1936. This was a fateful move with far-reaching repercussions (see the following section). It made the British and French governments even more sensitive to the German threat and more determined to placate Mussolini in order to keep him on their side and within the League of Nations. Consequently, the League Council voted on April 20, 1936, to continue the sanctions without oil, thus spelling the doom of the Ethiopian armies that in the meantime had been fighting the Italians.

The Ethiopian tribal leaders, in their suicidal pride and ignorance, scorned guerrilla warfare as unworthy and demeaning. Instead, they attempted to wage a war of position and were mercilessly bombarded, strafed, and even sprayed with mustard gas. After a campaign of seven months, the Italians triumphantly entered Addis Ababa on May 5, 1936. The same day, Mussolini proclaimed "a Roman peace, which is expressed in this simple, irrevocable, definite phrase—'Ethiopia is Italian.'" Four days later, the king of Italy assumed the title of "Emperor of Ethiopia." And so, at a cost of 3000 men and $1 billion, Mussolini had won an empire of 350,000 square miles, 10 million inhabitants, and rich natural resources.

So far as Europe and the rest of the world were concerned, the significance of the Ethiopian affair was that it undermined the League of Nations. Many small countries such as Greece, Rumania, and Yugoslavia had loyally supported the League during the crisis and enforced the sanctions against Italy. But their only rewards were heavy economic losses, and furthermore they were exposing themselves to the wrath of the triumphant Duce. The obvious moral was that, given the undependability of the leading Western powers, collective security was a delusion. Accordingly, the small countries henceforth looked only to their own interests and turned their backs on the League of Nations. Ironically, the sacrifice of the League did not keep Italy on the side of the Western powers against Germany, which had been the great objective of those who insisted on placating Mussolini. Instead, the appeasement had precisely the opposite effect. Both Mussolini and Hitler were impressed by their striking victories in Ethiopia and the Rhineland and saw the vast possibilities of coordinated, aggressive activities. The final outcome was not the isolation of Nazi Germany but the formation of the Rome-Berlin Axis.

IV. ROME-BERLIN AXIS

At the beginning of the Ethiopian crisis Hitler played a wait-and-see game. If Mussolini failed, a rival in Central Europe would be eliminated; if he won, then the collective security system would be undermined, and Hitler's lebensraum plans would be helped. On

March 7, 1936, Hitler dramatically ended this passive policy by sending a force of 35,000 marching into the Rhineland. The Versailles Treaty had stipulated that Germany should have no fortifications or armed forces on the left bank of the Rhine, nor in a zone of 50 kilometers from the right bank. Hitler's violation of this provision was a move of first-rate strategic significance: the French system of alliances was based on the accessibility of Central Europe to the French army; with the reoccupation of the Rhineland and the building of the Siegfried Line fortifications, which were immediately started, the French no longer had this accessibility. France was cut off from its allies, while Germany's strength was immeasurably increased because its vitals were no longer left vulnerable by a demilitarized Rhineland. In short, Hitler's Rhineland coup represented a tremendous upset in Europe's military and diplomatic balance of power.

We know now that the coup was based on bluff. The German army was not ready for serious war, so Hitler ordered that his divisions crossing into the Rhineland should retire without firing a shot if France even began to mobilize. Hitler, like Mussolini, was bluffing, and both men won because the French and British governments at this time were divided and unable to take decisive action.

The Rhineland coup served to bring together the hitherto antagonistic Führer and Duce. Mussolini deeply appreciated Hitler's role in distracting the attention of the League at a time when oil sanctions were still a possibility. Within a short time, the two dictators had formed a working partnership that quickly made a shambles of the existing diplomatic structure.

With the Austro-German accord of July 11, 1936, Hitler undertook to respect the integrity of Austria, thus removing the main source of discord between Rome and Berlin. A week later, civil war broke out in Spain, a tragic episode (see the following section) that was to drag on for three years. During that time Hitler and Mussolini worked together to overthrow the Spanish Republic. On October 24, 1936, the Rome-Berlin Axis was formally constituted. Italy and Germany agreed on general cooperation as well as on such specific issues as German recognition of Italian Ethiopia in return for economic concessions. The following month Japan associated itself with the Axis by concluding anti-Communist pacts with Germany and then with Italy.

And so by the end of 1936, the diplomatic balance was entirely different from what it had been when Hitler came into office. Italy and Germany now had a working partnership. France had lost its former hegemony and declined into relative isolation. Its old allies in Central Europe were drifting away, while the new alliance with the Soviet Union remained largely a paper creation. The French government distrusted the Soviet regime to the point of refusing to conclude the military convention needed to make their alliance fully effective. Likewise, the relations of the French and the British were far from being close or trustful. The distrust within the status-quo bloc, together with the crippling of the League of Nations, enabled the Rome-Berlin Axis during the next three years to score triumph after triumph with virtually no opposition.

V. SPANISH CIVIL WAR

The Spanish Civil War was of more than ordinary significance because it was essentially two wars in one—a deep-rooted social conflict generated by the decay and tensions of Spanish society, and a dress rehearsal for World War II arising from the clash of ideologies and of Great Power interests. Three principal elements made up Spain's traditional oligarchy: the large landowners, the army, and the church. The large landowners consisted of the old aristocracy and the wealthy upper middle class that had bought many estates. About 35,000 of these landowners possessed approximately 50 percent of the total arable land. Agricultural productivity in the country as a whole was very low, and the peasants, comprising 70 percent of the entire population, were as depressed as any in Europe. The landowners contributed nothing, being of the absentee type who squandered their incomes in Madrid or in foreign capitals.

The Spanish army was noteworthy for two reasons: the extraordinarily large number of officers in proportion to the number of rank and file, and the constant intervention of the military in the politics of the country. Indeed, the officers felt they had a right to supervise political affairs, and they acted accordingly; specifically, this meant the safeguarding of the status quo against all challengers, whether of the Republican Center or the parties of the Left.

The established Roman Catholic church, an enormously wealthy and influential institution, had lost its landed property in the early and mid-nineteenth century, but, in compensation, it had acquired industrial stocks and had received a substantial subsidy from the government, amounting to 2 percent of the annual budget in the 1920s. The bishops were nominees of the king, and some of them were members of the Senate; but most important of all, the church controlled most of the education of the country. In addition, the church exerted much influence through certain important newspapers, labor groups, and a variety of lay organizations. As had occurred in other countries where Catholicism played a similar role, this formidable power engendered a strong anticlerical movement in Spain. The widespread attacks on priests and nuns, and the wholesale destruction of church property during the Civil War, were by no means unique in Spanish history.

Such was the Spain that Alfonso XIII was called upon to rule when he ascended the throne in 1902. Between that date and the establishment of the Rivera dictatorship in 1923, there were 33 different cabinets as well as a liberal number of strikes, mutinies, and assassinations. Spain's neutrality during World War I brought relative prosperity, but this lasted only for the duration of the war; with the peace, the chronic ailments and disorders returned. These were accentuated during the 1920s by the disasters suffered by the Spanish armies in Morocco at the hands of the Rif. The resulting discontent paved the way for the military coup d'état of General Primo de Rivera in September 1923.

The new "strong man" admired Mussolini and imitated him in destroying the remnants of constitutional government, censoring the press, and restricting the universities. He also followed the Duce's example in building highways and staging international exhibitions. But these were merely surface gestures, for underneath, traditional Spanish society creaked on with its inequities and anachronisms. Finally, Primo de Rivera lost the support of the army and the king, and he was forced to resign in January 1930.

With the dictator gone, popular discontent was turned against the king himself. The Depression made the situation still more precarious, until at last Alfonso decided to restore the constitution and to hold municipal elections in April 1931. The vote went heavily against the regime, the Republicans carrying 46 of the 50 provincial capitals. The state of public opinion was evident, and Alfonso prudently left the country, as four of his predecessors had done since 1789.

A republic was proclaimed on April 14, 1931, and elections were held for a constituent assembly, or Cortes. When this body assembled in July, its members fell into three broad groupings: a conservative Right, a republican Center, and a left comprising Socialists, Stalinist and Trotskyite Communists, and Anarcho-Syndicalists. The Center and the

Left, which together comprised a large majority, combined to adopt a markedly liberal constitution that proclaimed complete religious freedom, separated church and state, secularized education, and nationalized church property.

The first prime minister under the new constitution, the able Republican Manuel Azaña, was supported also by the moderate Socialists, and laws were promptly passed to implement the provisions of the constitution: government subsidies to the church were abolished, certain monastic orders were banned, the pay of farm laborers was raised above the usual $.20 per day, a few large estates were divided among the peasants with partial compensation for the owners, hundreds of army officers were retired, and home rule was granted to the province of Catalonia. These typical middle-of-the-road reforms satisfied neither the Right nor the Left, so that the November 1933 elections for a regular Cortes returned a conservative majority. The bienio negro, the "black" two years of clerical reaction, followed. Autonomy for Catalonia was revoked and much of the legislation concerning the church and land distribution was either repealed or not enforced.

In preparation for the elections of February 1936, the parties of the Left and the Left-Center now banded together to form a Popular Front similar to that which had just appeared in France. The coalition won a narrow victory and Azaña formed a new Republican cabinet which the Left parties supported but did not enter. Catalan autonomy was restored and anticlerical measures along with mild social reform were resumed. In retrospect, the Republicans appear to have blundered in emphasizing anticlericalism rather than agrarian reform, which most Spaniards accepted. This policy alienated the fervent Catholics and much of the middle class. At the same time, the Great Depression, with its widespread unemployment, strengthened the extremist and weakened the moderate parties. To hold the desperate workers, the Socialists had to move steadily to the extreme Left; reacting to this, much of the middle class allied itself with the extreme Right—hence the mounting ideological passions and the polarization of political life to the point where parliamentary government became increasingly tenuous.

At this juncture, the Spanish rightists, with the connivance of Germany and Italy, and under the leadership of General Francisco Franco, raised the standard of counterrevolution. On July 17, 1936, the army in Morocco revolted, and the next day a number of mainland generals took up arms. The rebels, or self-styled Nationalists, quickly overran the southern and the western regions, and these sections of the country remained their main bases throughout the protracted struggle. Franco had hoped that, with the advantage of surprise, he would be able to capture quickly the main cities and fortresses and so gain control of the entire country. Instead, the struggle dragged on for almost three years with a savagery reminiscent of the sixteenth-century Wars of Religion.

After losing about one-half the country in the first few weeks of the revolt, the Loyalists rallied and managed to retain control of Madrid in the center, the Basque provinces in the north, and the highly developed east coast with the large cities of Barcelona and Valencia. The Loyalists were now in a strong position, for they had behind them the industrial centers, the most densely populated regions, and the capital, with its exceptionally large gold reserve. Despite these advantages, the Loyalists were eventually beaten, the main reason being that they were unable to obtain arms from abroad in quantities approaching those received by the Nationalists.

That such a turn of events should take place was paradoxical, because the Loyalists had both the money to import arms and the right to do so under international law, since they constituted the legal government of the country. The British and French governments, however, refused to allow the sale of arms to the Republican regime. They were inhibited by the sharp division of public opinion in their respective countries concerning the civil war, and they feared that an unrestricted flow of arms to the contending parties might escalate into a European war. Accordingly, Britain and France took the lead in sponsoring a nonintervention agreement, which was accepted by Germany, Italy, and the Soviet Union, as well as by several smaller countries.

The agreement provided that the signatories should refrain from shipping arms to Spain, but Germany and Italy violated their pledge from the beginning, and the Soviet Union soon was doing likewise. Italy sent not only arms but also regular army units, which rapidly increased in numbers as the war continued. According to official Italian sources, during the four months between December 1936 and April 1937, Mussolini dispatched 100,000 men along with 40,000 tons of munitions and 750 cannon. Russia, like Germany, sent no ground troops but did provide war materials of all types in addition to technical advisers and pilots. The Loyalists were also aided by the International Brigades, which first went into action in November 1936 in the defense of Madrid. The brigades consisted of volunteers—mostly young idealists from Britain, France, and the United States—as well as antifascist émigrés from Italy and Germany.

Foreign intervention affected the civil war in two important respects: it favored by all odds the Nationalists and was the decisive factor behind their victory; it also served to bring the Nationalists closer to fascism and the Republicans closer to communism, the latter trend being the more pronounced. At the outset, the Anarchists and the Socialists were predominant on the Republican side, with moderate Socialists filling the leading posts in the Loyalist administration throughout the civil war. But the Communists became increasingly dominant with the Loyalist dependence on Soviet war materials, and, by late 1937, the Russian-controlled International Brigades, Russian aircraft, and Spanish Communist generals were leading the Loyalist armies and dictating policy.

If the Loyalists had won, a new civil war might well have followed, with the Communists ranged against the Socialists, Anarchists, and Trotskyites. As it turned out, the Axis supplies of both ground troops and war materials proved irresistible, especially when Stalin decided to abandon the Spanish Republic. For two years there had been a stalemate, with the Nationalists controlling the agrarian western and southern regions, and the Loyalists, the more developed northern and eastern sections, together with the Madrid salient. But in mid-1938, the Soviet government decided to cut its losses and stop the aid to Spain, in view of the continued refusal of the Western democracies to end the nonintervention farce, thus enabling Franco's armies to break the stalemate. In late December 1938, the Nationalists began their great offensive against Catalonia; within a month they had taken Barcelona. Madrid and Valencia were now helpless, but they held out for two more months. With their fall in late March, the civil war ended.

For Spain, the long ordeal involved 750,000 casualties out of a population of 25 million, and one of every seven of the uninjured was left without shelter. For the Western powers, the civil war represented another stunning defeat. As in the case of Ethiopia, they had again shown themselves weak and vacillating in the face of Axis aggression, a pattern that had also manifested itself during the German annexation of Austria, which had occurred in the course of the Spanish Civil War.

VI. END OF AUSTRIA AND CZECHOSLOVAKIA

1938 was the year of the great bloodless victories of the Axis powers. At the center of these fateful developments was Neville Chamberlain, who succeeded Stanley Baldwin as British prime minister in May 1937. Little by little Chamberlain took over the direction of British foreign policy, even though Anthony Eden was his foreign secretary. "The truth," wrote Eden, "was that some of my seniors in the Cabinet . . . could not believe that Mussolini and Hitler were as untrustworthy as I painted them. After all, had not Mussolini defeated the reds and made the trains in Italy run on time?"[1] The basic problem, as Eden discovered, was that the conservatives in both Britain and France were motivated primarily by deep-seated distrust of Russia, and therefore by a determination to appease the dictators in order to gain time for rearmament. This conservative strategy explains in large part the stunning Axis victories of these years. Conservatives in Britain felt that they could do business with the dictators, and that this was preferable to "wooly" and "idealistic" projects based on the principle of collective security. Their counterparts in France likewise preferred to deal with Mussolini and Hitler rather than to turn to the Russians with whom they were nominally allied. The direct outcome of this way of thinking was the sacrifice of the independent states of Austria, Albania, and Czechoslovakia—a sacrifice that led, not to "peace in our time" as was fondly imagined, but to World War II.

On February 12, 1938, Hitler invited Austria's Chancellor, Kurt von Schuschnigg, to his Bavarian mountain retreat at Berchtesgaden. There the Führer demanded various concessions that would have seriously violated Austrian independence. Schuschnigg resisted by scheduling a plebiscite on March 13 on the following question: "Are you for a free and independent, German and Christian Austria?"

In the ensuing crisis, no Great Power went to the aid of Austria. France was caught between two ministries and had no government at all. Mussolini was resentful that he had not been forewarned, but his hands were tied by the Rome-Berlin Axis. Chamberlain informed the House of Commons on February 22 that "small weak nations" should not expect help from the League of Nations. On March 11, Schuschnigg, in the face of two ultimatums, was compelled first to cancel the plebiscite and then to hand over the chancellorship to the Nazi minister of interior, Dr. Artur von Seyss-Inquart. The latter, who had been in continual telephone communication with Berlin, now issued a statement that had been dictated from Berlin and that requested the German government "to send in German troops as soon as possible . . . to restore peace and order . . . and to prevent bloodshed." On March 13, decrees from Berlin and Vienna declared Austria a part of Germany, and the next day Hitler made his triumphant entry into the land of his birth. Thus Austria was taken over by telephone. The event was not mentioned in the League of Nations.

With Austria safely annexed, Hitler turned against the neighboring state of Czechoslovakia, a larger and much stronger country with an efficient modern army and a considerable industrial establishment. But the minority presence of 3 million Germans in the Sudeten borderlands made Czechoslovakia vulnerable to Nazi propaganda and subversion.

With the disappearance of Austria, the Sudeten problem became a serious menace for Czechoslovakia. The country was now surrounded on three sides by the enlarged Reich. Even more serious were certain indications that the British and French governments were ready to abandon Czechoslovakia as they had Austria. This soon became apparent when Hitler precipitated the Czechoslovak crisis on September 12 with an inflammatory speech in which he violently attacked President Benes for his "persecution" of the Sudeten Germans and warned that, "if these tortured creatures can find no rights and no help themselves, they will get both from us." The speech was followed by widespread rioting on the part of the Sudeten Germans. The Prague government proclaimed martial law, Nazi leaders fled to Germany, and Hitler concentrated troops along Czechoslovakia's frontier. Chamberlain feared that if Hitler actually invaded, a chain reaction might be unleashed that would embroil France and ultimately Britain. To avert this danger, Chamberlain and Daladier met with Hitler at Berchtesgaden on September 15.

Hitler boldly set forth his demand for annexation of the Sudeten areas on the basis of self-determination and indicated his readiness "to risk a world war" to attain his end. Chamberlain returned home and persuaded first his own cabinet, and then the French, to accept Hitler's terms. The two governments in turn urged acceptance upon the Czechoslovak government. When the latter resisted, they brought every pressure to bear, including the threat of desertion. Prague finally capitulated on September 21, in return for an Anglo-French guarantee for the new frontier.

The next day Chamberlain flew to Godesberg in the belief that he only needed to work out with Hitler the technical details for the transfer of the territories. Instead, the Führer made new demands: immediate surrender of the predominantly German areas without waiting for plebiscites and without any removal or destruction of military or economic establishments. In addition, Hitler now supported territorial claims on Czechoslovakia made by Poland and Hungary. These new demands precipitated an acute international crisis. Czechoslovakia ordered full mobilization, France called up 600,000 reservists, while the Soviet foreign minister, Maxim Litvinov, declared on September 21 before the League Assembly: "We intend to fulfill our obligations under the Pact, and together with France to afford assistance to Czechoslovakia by the ways open to us."

"This public and unqualified declaration," as Churchill pointed out, was treated by the Western powers with "indifference—not to say disdain." Instead, they acted on Mussolini's suggestion for a four-power conference of Britain, France, Germany, and Italy. The meetings were held in Munich on September 29, and, without either Czech or Soviet participation, it was decided that Hitler should be granted all his demands, the only modifications being the face-saving provisions that the Sudeten lands should be occupied in stages and that the final delimitation of the frontier should be determined by an international commission.

The Munich surrender was popular with the masses in both Britain and France. Chamberlain and Daladier were hailed as peacemakers by enthusiastic crowds. Loud cheers greeted Chamberlain when he declared, "I believe it is peace in our time." Hitler was gratefully believed when he avowed, "This is the last territorial claim I have to make in Europe." The events of the next year were to prove the worthlessness of such statements.

The first signs that further demands were in the offing was the gradual taking of substantial border regions of the Czechoslovak state. In accordance with the provisions reached at Munich, an international commission was appointed to determine the new frontiers. It soon became apparent that, despite their commitments, Britain and France had no interest in the proceedings of the commission. Accordingly, no plebiscites were held, and the decisions were made by two German generals who were members of the commission. In the end, Germany acquired 10,000 square miles of Czechoslovak territory with a population of 3.5 million, of whom about one-fifth were Czechs. At the same time, Poland seized the Teschen area with its rich coal fields, while Hungary occupied generous portions of Slovakia and Ruthenia. What remained of the Czechoslovak state now disintegrated into three fragments: an autonomous Slovakia, an autonomous Ruthenia, and the Czech provinces of Bohemia and Moravia.

The finale came in March 1939, when the puppet heads of the Czech and Slovak lands were summoned to Berlin to hear from Hitler the dissolution of their respective states. On March 15, German troops entered Prague. Bohemia and Moravia were declared a protectorate of the Reich, and Slovakia was also placed under German protection. Simultaneously, the Hungarians were allowed by Hitler to invade and annex Ruthenia in the east. So ended the state of Czechoslovakia, as well as the illusion that Hitler's objective was simply the redemption of German-populated lands. The partitioning of Czechoslovakia with its predominantly Slavic population was a rude awakening for those who had taken the Führer at his word. Chamberlain was particularly shocked, for as an orthodox British businessman, he had assumed that Hitler would keep the pledge that he had no further territorial ambitions in Europe. The breaking of this promise forced Chamberlain, as well as Daladier, to painfully reappraise their policy and to take a firmer stand when Hitler now turned upon Poland.

VII. COMING OF WAR

With Austria and Czechoslovakia taken, and with Spain and Hungary in the Axis camp, it was becoming apparent that the Western powers and the Soviet Union needed to work together in order to stem further aggression. "The key to a Grand Alliance," wrote Churchill, "was an understanding with Russia." The Russian government, for its part, was more than ready for such an "understanding." On March 18, it informed Berlin that it refused to recognize the partitioning of Czechoslovakia. Three days later, the Soviet government proposed a six-power conference (Britain, France, Russia, Poland, Rumania, and Turkey) to consider measures against future aggression. London replied that the proposal was "premature," and so it was not pursued further. But in the same month, Hitler forced Lithuania to hand over the city of Memel, and he sent stiff demands to Warsaw concerning Danzig and the Polish Corridor. Faced by the prospect of limitless German expansion, Chamberlain, on March 31, pledged Anglo-French aid to the Poles in the case of "any action which clearly threatened Polish independence." A week later this was expanded into a pact of mutual assistance. The next move of the Axis was Italy's invasion and conquest of Albania, which began on April 7. Again Britain and France countered by pledging on April 13 full support to Rumania and Greece in the event that their independence was clearly threatened. The following month, Anglo-Turkish and Franco-Turkish mutual assistance pacts were signed.

These commitments to various East European countries were worthless unless Britain acted in concert with the Soviet Union. As Churchill declared in the Commons on May 19, "Without an effective eastern front, there can be no satisfactory defence of our interests in the West, and without Russia there can be no effective eastern front."[2] Chamberlain finally opened negotiations with the Russians on April 15.

On the surface, both Russia and the Western powers favored the organization of a "Peace Front." However, given the current atmosphere, this was easier said than done. For example, on May 31, Vyacheslav Molotov, who had replaced Maxim Litvinov as Soviet foreign minister, declared that no Peace Front was possible unless Britain and France accepted the elementary principle of reciprocity and equal obligations. Specifically, he demanded that the border states of the Soviet Union—Finland and the three Baltic countries—must be given the same guarantees as had been extended to Poland, Greece, Rumania, and Turkey. But the Baltic states had concluded nonaggression pacts with Germany and refused any Soviet-Western guarantees. London took the position that this ended the possibility of guarantees, whereas the Russians interpreted it as legalistic quibbling and evading of the issue. Likewise, the Poles refused to agree to allow the Red army to operate on Polish territory in case of war. Soviet aid, they insisted, should be limited to the providing of war materials. From the Polish viewpoint this was understandable, but the Soviet Marshal Voroshilov retorted, "Just as the British and American troops in the past World War would have been unable to participate in military collaboration with the French armed forces if they had no possibility of operating in French territory, the Soviet armed forces could not participate in military collaboration with armed forces of France and Great Britain if they are not allowed access to Polish territory." [3]

Behind this sparring was the gnawing suspicion in London that the real objective of the Soviets was to obtain legal justification for marching into Poland and the Baltic states at their pleasure. The Russians, on their part, feared that if they agreed to go to war in the event of an attack on Poland and could not send their army into Polish territory to meet the advancing Germans, the latter would quickly overrun Poland and reach the Soviet frontier. Would Britain and France then wage serious war against Germany, or would they sit back and leave the Soviet Union to face the onslaught alone? Their apprehension was strengthened when, in July, two representatives of Chamberlain, acting on his instructions, broached to a German official in London the possibility of a British-German nonaggression pact that would enable Britain to rid itself of its commitments to Poland. Thus Chamberlain, who was not very happy about the guarantee to Poland, and was even less happy about the negotiations with the Soviet Union, was feeling out the Germans with a view to reviving his appeasement policy.

All of this was behind Stalin's fateful decision to turn to his hitherto mortal Axis enemies: On August 23 Russia and Germany signed a nonaggression pact and agreed to remain neutral if either were attacked by a third power. Significantly enough, the pact did not contain the so-called "escape clause," characteristic of Soviet nonaggression pacts with other countries, that would render the agreement inoperative if either party committed aggression against a third state. Perhaps this omission was related to a secret protocol in the pact stipulating that in the event of "a territorial or political rearrangement," Lithuania and western Poland were to come under the German sphere of influence, and the remainder of Poland, together with Finland, Estonia, Latvia, and Bessarabia, were to fall to the Russian sphere.

Now that he was protected on his eastern flank, Hitler felt free to strike. Early in the morning of September 1, 1939, without a declaration of war, German troops, tanks, and planes crossed Poland's frontier all along the line. On September 3, both Britain and France declared war on Germany. Mussolini, despite his oratory about the Axis "pact of steel," remained neutral. World War II had begun.

SUGGESTED READING

M. Baumont, *The Origins of the Second World War* (Yale University Press, 1968); A. D. Boca, *The Ethiopian War* (University of Chicago Press, 1969); D. F. Fleming, *The Cold War and Its Origins, 1917–1960,* 2 vols. (Doubleday, 1961); M. Gilbert, *The Roots of Appeasement* (Weidenfeld & Nicolson, 1966); G. Jackson, *The Spanish Republic and the Civil War, 1931–1939* (Princeton University Press, 1965); G. F. Kennan, *Russia and the West* (Little, Brown, 1960); L. Lafore, The End of Glory: *An Interpretation of the Origins of World War II* (Lippincott, 1970); A. J. P. Taylor, *The Origins of the Second World War* (Hamilton, 1961); T. Taylor, *Munich: The Price of Peace* (Doubleday, 1979); C. Thorne, *The Approach of War, 1938–1939* (St. Martin's Press, 1968); G. L. Weinberg, *Diplomatic Revolution in Europe, 1933–36* (University of Chicago Press, 1970).

chapter 36

World War II:
Global
Repercussions

When World War II began, Hitler had a definite schedule of conquest: first Poland, then the West, and finally Russia. He adhered to this schedule, and in doing so determined the course of World War II until Russia and the West became strong enough to seize the initiative.

The Second World War, like the First, began as a European conflict precipitated by the issue of minorities in Eastern Europe. During the first two years the campaigns were waged on European battlefields. Then Japan's attack on Pearl Harbor in 1941 transformed World War II into a global struggle, just as America's intervention in 1917 had transformed World War I. At this point, however, the similarity between the two wars ends. With Japan's lightning conquest of the entire East and Southeast Asia, World War II came to involve much more of the globe than the preceding war had included. The two wars also differed fundamentally in the strategy and weapons employed. During the first war, the defense, based on trenches and machine-gun nests, proved superior to the offense. During the second war the offense, based on tanks and planes, proved stronger than the defense. This explains the extraordinary fluidity of battle lines that characterized the later struggle. Whole countries, and even continents, changed hands back and forth—in striking contrast to the bloody stalemate on the western front between 1914 and 1918.

520

I. EUROPEAN PHASE OF THE WAR

Partitioning of Poland

In Poland the Germans demonstrated for the first time the deadly effectiveness of their new type of *blitzkrieg,* or "lightning war." First came waves of dive bombers, or Stukas, blasting communication lines and spreading terror and confusion. Then followed the armored tank divisions, or Panzers, smashing holes in the enemy lines, penetrating deeply into the rear, destroying transportation and communication facilities, and cutting the opposing forces into ribbons. Finally the lighter motorized divisions and the infantry moved in for the "mopping up" of the splintered and battered enemy forces, supported where necessary by air and artillery cover.

Unfortunate Poland, with its flat plains and obsolete army, was a "set-up" for this type of warfare. Within ten days the campaign had been virtually decided. The German tank-plane teams raced through the Polish countryside against declining resistance. The speed of the German advance forced Stalin to move in order to take over the territories he had staked out in his pact with Hitler. On September 17, the Red army crossed over into eastern Poland, and two days later it established contact with the triumphant Germans. On September 27, Warsaw fell. The Polish government leaders fled to Rumania and thence to France. Their country was partitioned two days later. The Germans took 37,000 square miles with 22 million people, and the Russians took 77,000 square miles with a population of 13 million. Within less than a month one of the largest countries of Europe had disappeared completely from the map.

The Soviet government now took advantage of the secret protocol of the Moscow Pact to strengthen its strategic position in the Baltic area. In September and October 1939, it compelled Estonia, Latvia, and Lithuania to accept Russian military bases on their territories. Lithuania, by way of compensation, received the long-desired district and city of Vilna, hitherto a part of Poland. The Soviets next demanded from Finland certain territories in the Karelian Isthmus and around Petsamo on the Arctic Ocean. The Finns refused, and, on November 30, the Red army attacked.

Finland appealed to the League of Nations, and that body expelled the Soviet Union from membership. The Finns resisted the Russian onslaught with unexpected success, repulsing repeated attacks on their Mannerheim Line. The Russians, who had grossly underestimated Finnish strength, brought up their regular forces with heavy artillery. By mid-March they cracked the Mannerheim Line and forced the Finns to sue for peace. The ensuing treaty gave the Russians somewhat more territory than they originally demanded, including the Petsamo region, the port of Viipuri, several islands in the Gulf of Finland, and a naval base at Hanko.

Poland to France

Meanwhile, the western front had been disconcertingly quiet. The British and the French had stood helplessly by while Poland was being partitioned. They could not enter the Baltic Sea which the Germans had sealed tight; their air forces were unable to operate across the breadth of the Reich; while their ground troops were confronted by the elaborate fortifications built by Hitler following his 1936 occupation of the Rhineland. Thus the French were forced to sit behind their Maginot Line, while the Germans made no move from behind their Siegfried Line or West Wall.

This surface calm proved deceptive. On April 9, 1940, the Wehrmacht suddenly erupted into action, sweeping through Denmark and making landings on the coast of Norway. The main objective was to gain control of the Norwegian fiords which could provide invaluable bases for German submarines and also safeguard the shipment of Swedish iron ore down the coast to Germany. The Danes could offer no resistance, but the Norwegians, with British support, fought back stubbornly. But by early June France itself was in mortal peril, so the Allied expeditionary forces sailed away, accompanied by the Norwegian government, which took refuge in London. The Germans set up their own administration in Norway under the collaborationist *Quisling,* whose name became a synonym for the self-seeking traitor.

The Allied setback in Norway was soon dwarfed by the stunning blitzkrieg that overran France and the Low Countries in seven weeks. On May 10 the Germans attacked Holland and Belgium, and two days later France. The Dutch defense collapsed in five days. The Belgians held out longer, but by May 28 King Leopold surrendered in person, and the Belgian army capitulated. Meanwhile the Germans had skirted the northern end of the Maginot Line, which had never been extended to the sea, and drove through the Ardennes Forest, smashing a fifty-mile breach in the French lines at Sedan. The Panzer divisions now raced westward to Abbéville, on the English Channel, and from there fanned out along the coast. The Allied armies in Flanders, mostly British, retreated to Dunkirk, the only port still free of the enemy. The prospects for evacuation appeared hopeless, with the harbor half destroyed and only a few miles of open beach. In fact, 366,000 were ferried back to Britain, though 13,000 dead and 40,000 prisoners were left behind, along with all the equipment.

With the completion of the Dunkirk evacuation on June 4, the agony of France began. On the following day the German forces resumed their advance southward. By June 13 Paris was occupied, undefended and abandoned by the government. The French premier, Paul Reynaud, who had succeeded Daladier in late March, was thoroughly demoralized and under the influence of appeasers within his cabinet. Originally he had planned to move his government to North Africa, but on June 16 he wearily resigned the premiership to Marshal Pétain. It was this "hero of Verdun" who, ironically, now sued for peace. On June 22, at Compiègne, the site of the signing of the 1918 German armistice, the French accepted the severe armistice terms, including release of all German prisoners of war, disbandment of French military forces, surrender of French warships, and occupation by Germany of slightly over half of France, including the principal industrial and food-producing areas and the entire French coastline down to the Spanish border.

The staggering impact of the German blitzkrieg is reflected in the incredibly low casualty figures. During the entire campaign the French lost about 100,000 men, the other Allies 20,000, and the Germans 45,000. These losses were less than half those sustained in single offensives during World War I. This speedy collapse by what was considered to be the strongest Western power came naturally as a most painful shock. Charges of treason and cowardice were leveled in explanation for the great disaster. Though these charges were not altogether unwarranted, other factors appear to have been more decisive. One was the effect of the Russo-German pact, which enabled Hitler to concentrate his forces on a single front. Perhaps most important was the German superiority in several fields, especially in the number of planes and tanks, and in the development of the new blitzkrieg technique. The French High Command was handicapped, not only by inadequate equipment, but even more by obsolete plans for waging World War II with World War I strategic concepts.

Battle of Britain

After Dunkirk and the fall of France, Hitler assumed that Britain would see reason and would come to terms. But he failed to reckon with the British people and with Winston Churchill. A born fighter and maverick, Churchill had taken the lead in demanding a firm stand against Axis aggression during the years of appeasement under Chamberlain. This record made him the natural successor to Chamberlain when the latter was forced to resign on May 10, 1940, because of his failure to mobilize the country for a war of survival. Churchill formed an all-party cabinet and quickly proved himself an incomparable war leader. With characteristic resoluteness and audacity he told his people—and the world; "We shall fight on the beaches. We shall fight on the landing grounds. We shall fight on the fields and in the streets. We shall fight in the hills; we shall never surrender."

Meanwhile, Hitler was marking time, unsure what the next step should be. The unexpectedly rapid fall of France had caught him by surprise. First he tried to make a deal with the British, for whom he always had genuine respect. When his overtures were ignored, Reichmarshal Hermann Göring unleashed his Luftwaffe, confident that it could subdue Britain by air attack alone, without resort to a hazardous sea crossing.

The ensuing air assault developed into the critical Battle of Britain, one of the major turning points of World War II. In this epic struggle in the skies, the Luftwaffe had the advantage of numbers—2670 planes against the Royal Air Force's 1475. But the RAF Spitfires and Hurricanes were more-advanced planes, because Britain had gone into mass production a couple of years later than Germany. The British also had the use of radar, a new invention that enabled enemy aircraft to be "sighted" fifty to a hundred miles before reaching their targets. With these advantages, a few thousand British and Dominion fighter pilots, with a scattering of Poles, Czechs, French, and Belgians, were able to repulse the Luftwaffe and thus end Hitler's chance for invading Britain.

Conquest of the Balkans

With his failure in the Battle for Britain, Hitler decided to invade Russia the following spring. Preparing for the projected invasion, Hitler sent troops into Rumania in October 1940 to prepare the Rumanian army to participate in the attack on the Soviet Union. At this point, when Hitler was occupying Rumania, Mussolini launched his blundering invasion of Greece. Il Duce, who for long had fancied himself the dean of the dictators, had become jealous of the spectacularly successful Führer. Although formally allied by the Axis Pact, Hitler had gone on from triumph to triumph without consulting or notifying his Italian partner. "Hitler always faces me with a fait accompli," complained Mussolini to his son-in-law and foreign minister, Count Ciano. "This time I am going to pay him back in his own coin. He will find out from the papers that I have occupied Greece." [1]

What Mussolini assumed would be an effortless occupation proved in fact to be a humiliating fiasco. On October 28, 1940, Italian troops crossed over from Albania into Greece, expecting a triumphal procession to Athens. But after pushing some distance across the Greek-Albanian frontier, they suffered a decisive defeat at the battle of Metsovo on November 11. Taking advantage of the difficulties of the ponderous Italian armored divisions in the mountains of Epirus, the Greeks invariably made for the high ground and from there cut off and surrounded the enemy below. By mid-November they had driven the Italians back across the frontier into Albania. In the following weeks they captured the large Albanian towns of Koritsa, Argyrokastron, and Porto Edda. For a while it appeared that Mussolini might even have to endure a Dunkirk in the Adriatic.

At this point Mussolini was rescued from his mortifying predicament by the intervention of his Axis ally. Hitler was not motivated by sentiments of loyalty to his partner; in fact, he was furious that the war had been extended to the Balkans. But he could not sit back and watch the Italians flounder, particularly because the British were landing air units in Greece, which could prove troublesome once his invasion of Russia was under way. So on April 6 he launched his Operation Marita for the conquest of both Yugoslavia and Greece.

As in Poland and France, the Panzer divisions and the Luftwaffe swept everything before them. The mountainous terrain of the Balkan peninsula did not prove an effective obstacle, as had been hoped, while the British ground and air units were too weak to halt the tide. By April 13, the Germans had entered Belgrade, and ten days later the British were evacuating their forces from southern Greece to Crete. The Germans then launched an airborne invasion of Crete, surprising the British who did not expect an air attack from the Greek mainland 180 miles to the north. Though they suffered heavy losses, the Germans finally gained complete control of the island by the beginning of June. Thus, with the Balkan peninsula completely subjugated, the Wehrmacht on June 22, 1941, smashed across the frontier into the Soviet Union.

II. GLOBAL PHASE OF THE WAR

Invasion of Russia

At first it seemed that Russia would collapse as quickly as had Poland and France. The Panzer divisions, in their now familiar fashion, smashed through the frontier defenses and drove deeply into the rear, encircling entire Soviet armies and taking hundreds of thousands of prisoners. By the end of the year the Wehrmacht had penetrated 600 miles eastward, overrunning the most industrialized and populous regions of the Soviet Union.

One reason for the German triumph, apart from the important factor of surprise, was numerical preponderance at the outset. Hitler struck with an army of about 3 million as against approximately 2 million on the other side. The Russians, of course, had huge reserves to draw upon, but the Luftwaffe bombing made it difficult to utilize them promptly and efficiently. The German forces also had the telling advantage of battle experience under varied conditions in Poland, France, and the Balkans. In addition, recent Russian publications have revealed hitherto unsuspected weaknesses in the Soviet armed forces. A large part of the Red air fleet had been concentrated on small fields near the frontier, where most of it was destroyed on the very first day. The Red army lacked sufficient antitank guns to cope with the massive Panzer onslaught that sometimes reached 100 tanks per kilometer. And whereas in 1941 most German infantrymen had Tommy guns, the Russians had only rifles. Finally it should be recalled that this was not a struggle between the Soviet Union and Germany, but rather between the Soviet Union and the European continent. This meant that the Red army had to cope with substantial Finnish, Rumanian, and Hungarian forces as well as German, and that Soviet armament plants were in competition with those of France and Czechoslovakia as well as Germany. Thus whereas Soviet steel output in 1941 was almost equal to Germany's, it was considerably less than half that of Germany and the rest of the Continent.

Hitler's strategy was to advance all along the thousand-mile front from Finland to Rumania, and to push eastward to a line running from Leningrad to Moscow to Kharkov to Rostov. The Red army was to be encircled and destroyed to the west of this line, so that the Wehrmacht would not need to overextend its lines to the Urals and beyond. Thanks to the factors indicated above, the Germans attained almost all their territorial objectives. They captured both Kharkov and Rostov, and almost completely encircled Moscow and Leningrad.

Despite these impressive gains, the 1941 German campaign failed in its basic strategic objectives. Neither Moscow nor Leningrad was taken, while the Red army, though badly mauled, remained intact. In fact, it was able on December 10 to launch a counteroffensive that broke the German pincers around Moscow and Leningrad, and also recaptured Rostov—the first city of any size that the Wehrmacht had taken and then been forced to surrender.

Pearl Harbor

At the beginning of the war, almost all Americans were determined to remain neutral. President Roosevelt, like Woodrow Wilson, publicly expressed this determination; "there will be no blackout of peace," he declared to the nation on September 3, 1939. But Hitler's unexpected victories, and particularly the fall of France, compelled American policy makers to question whether neutrality automatically afforded protection against involvement. If Hitler were to conquer England and then gain control of the Atlantic— eventualities that seemed by no means improbable at the time—might not the New World be next on the schedule of conquest?

These considerations led Washington to conclude that the best way to avoid involvement in the war was to give all aid short of war to those still fighting Germany. This explains the steady drift of the United States from neutrality to nonbelligerency with the Destroyers-Bases Agreement (September 2, 1940), and from nonbelligerency to undeclared war with the Lend-Lease Act (March 11, 1941), the signing of the Atlantic Charter (August 12, 1941), and the orders (August–September 1941) to provide naval escorts for all belligerent and neutral merchant vessels between Newfoundland and Iceland, and to shoot on sight any Axis warships in those waters.

While striving to limit Axis expansion in the West, President Roosevelt also had attempted to restrain Japan from aggression in the Pacific. Successive Tokyo governments, however, became increasingly bellicose in response to what appeared to be golden opportunities provided by the course of events in Europe. Hitler's victories had left almost undefended the rich French, British, and Dutch possessions in East and Southeast Asia. Accordingly, on September 27, 1940, Japan signed the Tripartite Pact with Germany and Italy. This recognized the hegemony of Germany and Italy in Europe and of Japan in Asia and called for full mutual aid if any of the signatories were attacked by the United States.

The Japanese, however, had no direct interest in the war in Europe. In pursuit of their own advantage, they concluded a treaty with Russia on April 13, 1941, in which each power pledged neutrality should the other "become the object of hostilities on the part of one or several third powers." When Hitler invaded Russia in June 1941, he pressed

Japan to join him and to attack from the east. The Japanese refused to oblige, distrusting German intentions in Asia. Furthermore, they perceived greener fields in Southeast Asia, which was seething with unrest and which offered obvious opportunity for them. By the summer of 1941 they had occupied bases in French Indochina, signed an alliance treaty with Thailand, and were demanding the oil and rubber output of the Dutch East Indies. The British were so hard-pressed in Europe that they had withdrawn from Shanghai and maintained only feeble forces in Hong Kong and Singapore. Thus the entire East and Southeast Asia appeared ripe for plucking if only the United States would not intervene.

Japan's leaders were divided on the question of relations with the United States. The army was ready to challenge Britain, France, and the United States directly, but the navy, the diplomats, and the industrialists mostly held back. The turning point came with the resignation, in October 1941, of the premier, Prince Fumimaro Konoye, who favored a settlement with the United States. He was succeeded by General Hideki Tojo, at the head of a cabinet of army and navy officers. Tojo decided to settle accounts with the United States, by diplomacy or by force, before the end of the year. The Japanese ambassador in Washington, Admiral Kichisaburo Nomura, joined by a special envoy, Saburo Kurusu, held an eleventh-hour series of conversations with Secretary of State Cordell Hull. The positions taken by the two sides were so far apart that a compromise was out of the question.

Just as the Japanese forced the issue against the Russians in 1904 by attacking Port Arthur without a declaration of war, so now on December 7, 1941, they struck at Pearl Harbor. Within a few hours five of the eight battleships in Pearl Harbor had been destroyed, as well as three cruisers and three destroyers. At the same time another Japanese task force destroyed most of the United States army's planes in the Philippines. In conformity with the terms of the Tripartite Pact, Germany and Italy declared war on the United States. Thus America was fully involved in the war, both in Europe and in Asia.

1942: Year of Axis Triumphs

During the year 1942, Germany, Italy, and Japan were almost everywhere victorious. Great offensives overran large parts of Russia, North Africa, and the Pacific, like a huge three-taloned claw grasping the Eurasian hemisphere. At the same time, German submarines and surface craft were threatening Allied communication lines, their toll averaging about 400,000 tons a month in 1942.

The most spectacular triumphs were won by the Japanese, who quickly conquered a vast Pacific empire, stretching from the Aleutians to Australia, and from Guam to India. The Japanese were successful partly because they struck at a time when France and Holland were occupied, Britain was struggling desperately for sheer survival, and the United States was only starting to convert from a peace to a war economy. Thus, the Japanese moved into a vacuum and filled it rapidly and easily. The Western powers' traditional treatment of their colonial subjects as providers of raw materials and consumers of manufactured goods also contributed to Japan's success. Profitable though this arrangement may have been for the mother countries, it left the colonial territories economically stunted, with all basic war materials now having to be transported several thousand miles from Europe or the United States. The traditional political policies of the colonial powers also boomeranged at this time of showdown: many Indians or Burmese or Indonesians saw no reason why they should fight in defense of regimes that they regarded as alien and oppressive. Instead, many took a plague-on-both-your-houses attitude, when they did not actively welcome and assist the Japanese invaders. The latter shrewdly exploited this sentiment with slogans such as ''Asia for the Asians.''

By Christmas, little more than two weeks after Pearl Harbor, the Japanese already had captured Guam, Wake, and Hong Kong. They invaded the jungles of the Malay peninsula, hitherto considered to be impregnable. Thanks to years of experience against guerrilla forces in China, the Japanese had trained their men to infiltrate around enemy positions and to attack on the flanks and the rear. These tactics proved so successful that by February 15, 1942, the great Singapore fortress fell, with a demoralized army of 80,000 British, Australian, and Indian troops surrendering to 50,000 Japanese. Essentially the same pattern was repeated in Burma and Indonesia. Japanese troops crossed the Burmese frontier on December 10, 1941. By April they had taken Rangoon and Mandalay, and mixed British, Indian, and Chinese forces were fleeing to India along obscure jungle trails. In Indonesia the Dutch commander in chief capitulated with his army at Bandung on March 8. Nor had the Japanese more trouble landing in the Philippines and capturing Manila on January 2. Thus, in five months, at a cost of only 15,000 killed and wounded, the Japanese had won an empire that had a population of over 100 million and that had supplied 95 percent of the world's raw rubber, 90 percent of the hemp, and two-thirds of the tin.

Meanwhile, on the Russian front, Hitler had launched another massive offensive in June 1942. Since Moscow and Leningrad had proven impregnable the previous year, he now directed his armies southward. His objective was to reach the Volga and the Caspian, thereby cutting the Soviet Union in two and depriving the Red army of its oil supplies from the Caucasus. As in 1941, the Panzer divisions at first rolled swiftly across the flat steppe country. Then they crossed the Don River and fanned out southeast toward the Caucasus oil fields and northeast toward Stalingrad on the Volga. By August 22, Nazi tanks had taken the Maikop oil center, though they fell short of the major oil fields at Grozny. The main tank forces then drove through to the Volga slightly to the north of Stalingrad. The amount of territory overrun by the Germans in 1942 was most impressive, and Hitler proclaimed that his troops on the banks of the Volga, in the heart of Russia, would never be dislodged.

In North Africa also, 1942 was a year of victory for the Germans. Under the dashing General Rommel, the Afrika Korps in March 1941 had driven the British back across Libya to the Egyptian border. In May 1942 Rommel resumed the attack, crossed into Egypt and reached El Alamein, a scant fifty miles from Alexandria. So confident was Rommel of complete victory that he selected a white stallion for his triumphal entry into Cairo.

On every front the Axis powers were at the height of their fortunes in 1942. In North Africa Rommel was preparing to strike for Cairo, in Russia the Wehrmacht had reached the Volga, in the Pacific the Japanese appeared to be ready to spring on Australia and India, while the shipping battle on the high seas remained close until the end of the year.

1943: Turning of the Tide

During the first three years of the war the Axis powers had everything their own way. The turning point began at the end of 1942 with the Russian victory at Stalingrad, the British breakthrough in Egypt, the Allied landings in French North Africa, the fall of Mussolini, the mounting aerial bombardment of Germany, and the defeat of Japanese fleets in the Pacific.

At Stalingrad the Russians had dug in with orders to defend the city to the last soldier. The battle for the city began on August 22. By mid-September the Germans had fought their way into the center, and there they bogged down. Their planes had reduced the city to a great sea of rubble. This, paradoxically, prevented the Germans from exploiting their tank superiority that had proven so effective in the open steppe. Instead of mobile warfare, the battle of Stalingrad became the Rattenkrieg (War of the Rats), as men fought hand to hand in cellars, on rooftops, in alleys and courtyards and sewers.

Meanwhile, Stalin had been preparing a vast winter counteroffensive. On November 19, 1942, it was launched under the direction of General Georgi Zhukov. Two new armies crossed the Volga from the east, one attacking to the north of Stalingrad and the other to the south. With this gigantic pincers operation the besiegers became the besieged. A German relief army from the southeast was thrown back with heavy losses, while the Russians progressively occupied more and more airfields, thereby immobilizing Göring's air transports. The Germans now were hopelessly stranded. The end came on February 3, 1943, with the surrender of 120,000 men, the miserable survivors of the original army of 334,000.

At the same time that the Russians were destroying the German army at Stalingrad, they launched a series of offensives at other points along the front. By the end of March, they had regained all the territory they had lost in 1942. In a desperate effort to check the relentless advance of the Red army, the Germans made an all-out attack on a Soviet salient at Kursk. Though they concentrated 160 tanks per mile, they gained only 20 miles, and this at a cost of 40,000 men, 1400 planes, and 3000 tanks. On July 12 the Russians counterattacked, quickly rewon their positions, and then rolled on. The Kursk battle marks the turning point in the Russo-German War. Henceforth the Russians had the initiative, and the Germans fought defensive actions to prevent their retreat from becoming a rout.

While the Germans were being forced back in Russia, they and their Italian allies were being driven out completely from North Africa. In late August 1942, Rommel attempted to resume his offensive into Egypt but was heavily repulsed. The British now had a new commander on this front, Sir Bernard Montgomery, a flamboyant personality but a strict disciplinarian and a cautious strategist. With the aid of new and heavier tanks from the United States, Montgomery unleashed his own offensive on October 23. After twelve days' hard fighting, the Germans and Italians were routed. As they fell back along the coastal road, they were harried by air and naval bombardment. By January 24, 1943, Montgomery had captured Tripoli, and the road to Tunisia lay open.

Meanwhile, Anglo-American troops had landed on November 7–8, 1942, at the other end of North Africa, in Morocco and Algeria. The strategy was to squeeze the Axis forces in a great pincers operation from east and west, and thus remove them once and for all from this theater. The Anglo-Americans drove toward Tunisia, which was to be subdued by Christmas. This plan was upset, however, as Hitler rushed reinforcements across the Mediterranean. The fighting was hard, and not until May 1943 was Tunisia subdued by the Allied forces. Following their conquest of North Africa, the Anglo-Americans pressed on to Sicily, which they invaded on July 10. The Sicilian capital, Palermo, fell on July 22, and, by mid-August, allied troops were following the retreating enemy across the Messina Straits to the mainland.

Mussolini paid for these disasters with his office and eventually with his life. King Victor Emmanuel III was persuaded by monarchists and Fascist dissidents to dismiss

Mussolini and to place him in prison. This was done on July 25, three days after the fall of Palermo. Supreme authority was now vested in the king and in Marshal Pietro Badoglio, the conquerer of Ethiopia. The latter concluded an armistice agreement with the Allies on September 3. At the same time, British troops landed at Calabria on the toe of the Italian peninsula, while Americans attacked at Salerno, south of Naples. The Germans responded promptly by seizing Rome and occupying the central and northern parts of the country. In a bold raid, Nazi parachutists rescued Mussolini from prison. The shopworn Duce established a ''Fascist Republic'' in northern Italy and proclaimed his intention of fighting to the bitter end. For the next year and a half Italy was to be a divided and war-wracked country; the Germans with their puppet Mussolini in the north, and the Allies with Badoglio's provisional government in the south.

Meanwhile, the soil of the Third Reich itself was being subjected to steadily increasing aerial bombardment. By 1943, round-the-clock bombing became possible, the British raiding by night and the Americans by day. More explosives were now dropped on German cities in one hour than had been loosed during the entire Battle of Britain.

At the same time, the Japanese were suffering reverses comparable to those of their Axis partners in Europe. After their spectacular victories in the first six months, the Japanese finally were stopped and then were pushed back at an accelerating pace. The basic reason for this shift in the course of the war was the overwhelming superiority of American resources and productivity. When the war began, the Japanese economy was roughly comparable to the French in productivity. But compared to the American it was paltry. The Japanese could not even begin to match the flood from American factories. The empire they had conquered had an abundant supply of raw materials, but they could not convert these into war goods. One reason was the decimation of their merchant marine by American planes and submarines, so that the Japanese found it increasingly difficult to keep supplies flowing to their factories at home as well as to their armed forces abroad. Equally serious was the weakness of Japanese heavy industry. Even if raw materials had been available in adequate quantities, Japan lacked the industrial resources to utilize them. Manpower also was in short supply, despite the 73 million people who were then crowded on the home islands. No less than 40 percent of this population was engaged in intensive rice cultivation, leaving no surplus for substantial expansion of industry. If Japan could have had a decade or two of peace to exploit its newly won territories, it might well have become a great world empire. But instead of peace, it was to suffer catastrophic defeat.

The first step on the long road to Tokyo was taken at Guadalcanal, where United States Marines landed on August 7, 1942. Slowly, and at heavy cost, American forces captured other enemy bases in the South Pacific. Very few Japanese were taken prisoners, for capture was considered a disgrace and was rarely accepted. Suicidal banzai charges by officers and soldiers refusing to surrender became almost a routine climax to the taking of Japanese positions. In the face of such resistance, the American counteroffensive rolled on. By mid-1944 Saipan and Guam in the Marianas were taken, bringing the Japanese home islands within range of the new B-29 superfortresses. It was the beginning of the end of Japan's brief hour of glory.

Liberation of Europe

Europe was liberated in 1944–1945 primarily by the Red army advancing from the east and by Anglo-American forces invading from the Normandy landing beaches in the west. Fighting also continued in Italy during this period, but it was peripheral compared to the campaigns in the north. In an attempt to end the Italian war quickly, the Allies in January 1944 made a landing at Anzio, only 30 miles from Rome and also attacked the German stronghold at the Monte Cassino monastery. Both operations failed, and the Italian campaign bogged down to a dreary stalemate. Not until June 5 did the Fifth American Army of General Mark Clark enter Rome, where it was tempestuously welcomed by its inhabitants. Rome was the first of the Continental capitals to be freed from Nazi rule, but this triumph was overshadowed by the Allied landings in Normandy on the following day.

The invasion armada from England was made up of 4000 merchant vessels and 700 warships. At 6:30 A.M. landings began, and by the end of the first day 326,000 troops and 20,000 vehicles reached the shore. Bitter fighting occurred at Omaha and Utah beaches, and for some hours the fate of the entire expedition hung in balance. Fortunately for the Allies, the German High Command suspected that the Normandy landings were only a feint and that the main attack would come at Calais, where the Channel was narrowest. Accordingly, the German armored forces were kept in reserve until it was too late to dislodge the invaders. By D-Day plus five, the beachheads had been merged along a front of sixty miles. From the beginning, it should be noted, the Allied forces received invaluable aid from the French underground bands (maquis), which wrecked bridges, cut communication lines, and derailed German troop trains.

The Allied plan of campaign was for the British and Canadian forces on the left to repel the main enemy attacks, while the American forces on the right, trained and equipped for mobility, broke out of the bridgehead and took the Germans in the rear. On July 25, the Americans, aided by 1500 heavy bombers that blasted a gap in the enemy lines, fought their way into open country at Saint-Lô. As they advanced, they trapped 100,000 of the enemy in the Cherbourg peninsula. By early August General George Patton was rushing headlong across northern France toward Paris. On August 15, a new American army under General Alexander M. Patch, with strong French reinforcements, landed on the Riviera beaches and advanced rapidly up the Rhone valley. Meanwhile, central France was being liberated by the maquis who descended from the hills and attacked enemy garrisons and communication lines. Belabored from all sides, the Germans now made a general withdrawal toward their own frontiers. On August 19, resistance forces began open insurrection in Paris, and six days later a French armored division and an American infantry division completed the liberation of the capital. General de Gaulle, now universally recognized as the leader of the French people, drove in triumph to Notre Dame.

While the Western powers were liberating France, the Red army was advancing rapidly from the East. Having driven the Wehrmacht from the Crimea and the Ukraine by the spring of 1944, it then began a general offensive against approximately 2 million Germans (compared to the 1 million facing the Allies in France and Italy). In the north the Russians knocked Finland out of the war by September. In the center they crossed both the old and new frontiers of Poland and drove to the gates of Warsaw. In the south they reached the mouth of the Danube in the heart of Rumania. Young King Michael of Rumania seized the opportunity to pull his country out of the war in September, thus opening the Balkan peninsula to the Red army. Bulgaria followed this example by suing for peace and reentering the war on the side of the Soviet Union. The German armies in the Balkans were now in danger of being trapped and began to pull out as fast as possible. Aided by the local Communist-led guerrillas, the Red army drove up the Danube valley until it was stopped in Hungary by stiffening German resistance.

At this point the Allies were caught off guard by a sudden offensive launched by the

Germans on December 16, 1944, in the Ardennes in Belgium. Using much heavy armor and helped by foggy weather that hampered Allied aerial counterattacks, the Germans carved out a salient or ''bulge'' fifty miles in depth and as broad at the base. They came uncomfortably close to capturing the key supply base of Antwerp, which would have upset the entire Allied plan of operations. Finally the weather cleared on December 24, and 5000 Allied planes pounded German supply lines, while Patton counterattacked from the south and Montgomery from the north. By the end of January 1945, the Germans had been forced back to their original positions, and thereafter they were forced steadily backward under relentless Allied pressure.

While the ''Battle of the Bulge'' was raging in the west, the Russians were advancing steadily in Poland and Hungary. Both Warsaw and Budapest were taken by February 1945, though only after bitter fighting that left the two capitals in ruins. Thanks to an exceptionally mild winter, the Red army was able to move into Austria and Germany. On April 13, the Russians took Vienna and in the north overran east Prussia and Silesia. By late March, they were fighting their way across the Oder, forty miles from Berlin.

Meanwhile, the American, British, Canadian, and French armies were making corresponding progress on the western front. After recovering from the shock at Ardennes they cracked the West Wall and fought their way through to the Rhine. There they discovered to their astonishment that the retreating Germans had neglected to blow up the Ludendorff railway bridge at Remagen, south of Bonn. The Allies swarmed over, and within a month they had conquered the Rhineland and taken a quarter-million prisoners. Seven allied armies raced through the collapsing Reich. They could have taken Berlin as the Red army still was on the Oder, and the Germans had concentrated their defenses against the Russians on the east, leaving the western approaches to their capital almost defenseless. General Eisenhower, the supreme Allied commander, decided against taking the prize for strategic and diplomatic reasons that have been questioned ever since.

Strategically, Eisenhower was worried about his supply lines, which were stretched dangerously thin during the race across the Reich. Diplomatically, he favored a clear line of demarcation between his troops and the Russians, which the Elbe neatly provided. In addition, Eisenhower had been receiving reports that the Nazis were planning their last stand in an Alpine redoubt, so he ordered Omar Bradley to stop at the Elbe and turn south. The reports about the redoubt proved unfounded, but at the time Eisenhower perforce accepted them at face value and acted accordingly.

Under these circumstances the Allied armies stood aside while Zhukov opened his final offensive against Berlin on April 16. Nine days later he had the capital surrounded. At the same time, on April 25, an American patrol linked up with the Soviet vanguard at the village of Torgau on the Elbe, cutting Germany in two. On the last day of April, Hitler and his companion, Eva Braun, committed suicide in a concrete bunker with shells thudding on all sides. On May 2, Berlin surrendered to the Russians. During the next week Nazi emissaries surrendered unconditionally to the Western powers at Rheims and to the Soviet Union in Berlin.

Meanwhile General Mark Clark was clearing the Germans out of Italy with the noteworthy assistance of Italian guerrillas, who harassed the enemy as the maquis did in France. A final offensive was launched on April 10, and within a fortnight the German lines had crumpled and the Allies streamed down into the Po valley and beyond to the Alps. In Milan and other industrial cities, the resistance fighters organized successful risings and won control before the Allies arrived. On May 2, the German commanders in Italy signed terms of unconditional surrender. Five days earlier Mussolini had been apprehended by guerrillas while attempting to escape to Switzerland and was summarily shot. His body, and that of his mistress, were hung up on display in Milan.

Surrender of Japan

The surrender of Germany made even bleaker the prospects for the Japanese in the Pacific. Already by mid-1944 their home islands were being bombed by superfortresses based on the Marianas. At the end of the year American forces landed in the Philippines, and, by late February 1945, they had forced the Japanese garrisons to surrender. More serious for the enemy were the losses of Iwo Jima, which was only 750 miles away from the Japanese homeland, and Okinawa, which was only 350 miles distant. Using these two islands as bases, American airmen now subjected Japan's crowded cities to the same storm of explosives that had racked Germany. The Japanese were even more vulnerable, for their flimsy wood and paper structures went up in flames like so much kindling. In nine months, from November 1944 to the surrender in September 1945, B-29 superfortresses made 32,000 sorties against Japan, or more than a hundred a day. The toll of dead or homeless Japanese soared beyond 8 million.

Now a series of unprecedented cataclysms forced the Japanese to surrender. On August 6, 1945, an American superfortress dropped an atomic bomb on Hiroshima, demolishing three-fifths of the city and killing 78,150 inhabitants. Two days later Russia declared war on Japan, and the Red army promptly drove across the frontier into Manchuria. Russia's invasion came exactly three months after Germany's surrender, fulfilling an obligation assumed by Stalin during his meeting with Roosevelt and Churchill at Yalta in February 1945. The final blow was the dropping of a second atomic bomb on August 9 upon the city of Nagasaki, with results as devastating as at Hiroshima. The extreme Japanese militarists still opposed a general surrender, but the emperor, on the advice of the cabinet and the elder statesmen, decided to capitulate. On August 14 the Allied ultimatum was accepted, the formal ceremony of surrender taking place on board the U.S.S. Missouri in Tokyo Bay on September 2 in the presence of General MacArthur, Admiral Nimitz, and ranking Allied officers.

HIROSHIMA

The dropping of an atomic bomb by the United States on Hiroshima on August 6, 1945, began a new era in the history of warfare and humanity. A study of the effect of the bomb was made by the U.S. Strategic Bombing Survey, and the following selection is taken from its report.*

The surprise, the collapse of many buildings, and the conflagration contributed to an unprecedented casualty rate. Seventy to eighty thousand people were killed, or missing and presumed dead, and an equal number were injured. The magnitude of casualties is set in relief by a comparison with the Tokyo fire raid of 9–10 March, 1945, in which, though nearly 16 square miles were destroyed, the number killed was no larger, and fewer people were injured. . . .

When the atomic bomb exploded, an intense flash was observed first, as though a large amount of magnesium had been ignited, and the scene grew hazy with white smoke. At the same time at the center of the explosion, and a short while later in other areas, a tremendous roaring sound was heard and a crushing blast wave and intense heat were felt. The people, even those who lived on the outer edge of the blast, all felt as though they had sustained a direct hit, and the whole city suffered damage such as would have resulted from direct hits everywhere by ordinary bombs. . . .

Such a shattering event could not fail to have its impact on people's way of thinking. . . .

Typical comments of survivors were:

"If the enemy has this type of bomb, everyone is going to die, and we wish the war would hurry and finish."

"I did not expect that it was that powerful. I thought we have no defense against such a bomb."

"One of my children was killed by it, and I didn't care what happened after that."

Other reactions were found. In view of their experiences, it is not remarkable that some of the survivors (nearly one-fifth) hated the Americans for using the bomb or expressed their anger in such terms as "cruel," "inhuman," and "barbarous."

". . . they really despise the Americans for it, the people all say that if there are such things as ghosts, why don't they haunt the Americans? . . ."

The reaction of hate and anger is not surprising, and it is likely that in fact it was a more extensive sentiment than the figures indicate, since unquestionably many respondents, out of fear or politeness, did not reveal their sentiments with complete candor. . . .

* U.S. Strategic Bombing Survey, *The Effects of the Atomic Bombs on Hiroshima and Nagasaki* (Washington, D.C.: Government Printing Office, 1946), pp. 3–5, 8–9.

III. WORLD WAR II IN WORLD HISTORY

World War II completed the undermining of Europe's global hegemony that had been started by World War I. Thus, in a general sense the two wars had a similar significance for world history. There were variations in detail, however, that are of prime significance for the contemporary scene. The Nazis and the Japanese militarists were infinitely more destructive of the old orders in Europe and Asia than the Hohenzollerns and the Hapsburgs had ever been. The Germans had overrun the entire continent of Europe; and the Japanese, the whole of East and Southeast Asia. But these vast empires proved short-lived. They disappeared in 1945, leaving behind two great power vacuums embracing territories of primary economic and strategic significance. It was the existence of these vacuums, as much as any ideological considerations, that was responsible for the outbreak of the Cold War and the inability to conclude a general peace settlement immediately after 1945.

Another difference between the two postwar periods was the successful upsurge of colonial subjects after 1945, in contrast to the enforcement of imperial authority after 1918. Within a period of two decades the far-flung European empires had all but disappeared. In this sense, these were decades of European decline, political and military. Yet at the same time, thanks to the accelerating unification of the globe, Western ideas and institutions and technology were spreading throughout the globe at an unprecedented pace. Thus the post-World War II years constitute, paradoxically, a period of European triumph as well as decline.

SUGGESTED READING

R. A. Divine, *Causes and Consequences of World War II* (Quadrangle, 1969); B. Liddell Hart, *History of the Second World War* (Putnam, 1970); M. B. Hoyle, *A World in Flames: A History of World War II* (Atheneum, 1970); J. Toland, *The Rising Sun: The Decline and Fall of the Japanese Empire* (Bantam, 1970); G. Wright, *The Ordeal of Total War 1939–1945* (Harper & Row, 1969); B. Whaley, *Codeword Barbarossa* (MIT Press, 1973).

chapter 37

End Of Empires

A major difference between World War I and World War II lay in their colonial aftermaths. Europe's hold over the colonial empires was weakened but not broken by World War I; indeed, the colonial holdings were expanded by the acquisition of Arab lands as mandates. After World War II, by contrast, an irrepressible revolutionary wave swept the colonial empires and ended European domination with dramatic speed. In 1939, the only independent states in sub-Saharan Africa were Liberia and South Africa, and they owed their independence to their atypical historical backgrounds. The one had been settled in the early nineteenth century by freed slaves, and the other was controlled by a resident European minority. Four decades later, the only significant colonies left in sub-Saharan Africa were under South Africa's shadow; South-West Africa, Bechuanaland, and Basutoland. Just as most of Europe's colonies had been swiftly acquired in the last two decades of the nineteenth century, so most of them now were lost in an equally short period following World War II. Between 1944 and 1980, a total of 90 countries had won their independence. These included about a third of the world's total population (see Table 12). After so many epoch-making triumphs and achievements overseas, the Europeans appeared in the mid-twentieth century to be retreating back to the small Eurasian peninsula whence they had set forth half a millennium earlier (see Map XXVII, "World of New Global Relationships").

Table 12 AFRICAN-ASIAN MARCH TO INDEPENDENCE

	Became Independent of	Year		Became Independent of	Year
Syria	France	1944	Jamaica	Britain	1962
Lebanon	France	1944	Rwanda	Belgium	1962
Jordan	Britain	1946	Trinidad & Tobago	Britain	1962
Philippines	United States	1946	Uganda	Britain	1962
India	Britain	1947	Western Samoa	N. Zealand	1962
Pakistan	Britain	1947	Kenya	Britain	1963
Burma	Britain	1948	Zanzibar[b]	Britain	1963
N. Korea	Japan	1948	Malta	Britain	1964
S. Korea	Japan	1948	Malawi	Britain	1964
Israel	Britain	1948	Zambia	Britain	1964
Sri Lanka (Ceylon)	Britain	1948	Gambia	Britain	1965
Indonesia	Netherlands	1949	Maldive Islands	Britain	1965
Libya	Italy	1952	Singapore	Britain	1965
Cambodia	France	1954	Guyana	Britain	1966
Laos	France	1954	Botswana	Britain	1966
N. Vietnam	France	1954	Lesotho	Britain	1966
S. Vietnam	France	1954	Barbados	Britain	1966
Sudan	Britain-Egypt	1956	South Yemen	Britain	1967
Morocco	France	1956	Mauritius	Britain	1968
Tunisia	France	1956	Swaziland	Britain	1968
Ghana	Britain	1957	Equatorial Guinea	Spain	1968
Malaya[a]	Britain	1957	Nauru	Australia	1968
Guinea	France	1958	Fiji	Britain	1970
Republic of the Congo	Belgium	1960	Tonga	Britain	1970
Somalia	Italy	1960	Bangladesh	Pakistan	1971
Nigeria	Britain	1960	Bahrein	Britain	1971
Cameroon	France	1960	Bhutan	Britain	1971
Mali	France	1960	Oman	Britain	1971
Senegal	France	1960	Qatar	Britain	1971
Malagasy	France	1960	United Arab Emirates	Britain	1971
Togo	France	1960	Bahamas	Britain	1973
Cyprus	Britain	1960	Grenada	Britain	1974
Ivory Coast	France	1960	Guinea-Bissau	Portugal	1974
Upper Volta	France	1960	Sao Tomé and Principe	Portugal	1975
Niger	France	1960	Mozambique	Portugal	1975
Dahomey	France	1960	Cape Verde Islands	Portugal	1975
Congo Republic	France	1960	Comoro Islands	France	1975
Central African			Seychelles	Britain	1976
Republic	France	1960	Djibouti	France	1977
Chad	France	1960	Dominica	Britain	1978
Gabon	France	1960	Solomon Islands	Britain	1978
Mauritania	France	1960	Tuvalu	Britain	1978
Sierra Leone	Britain	1961	Saint Lucia	Britain	1979
Tanganyika[b]	Britain	1961	Kiribati	Britain	1979
Algeria	France	1962	Zimbabwe	Britain	1980
Burundi	Belgium	1962			

[a] Combined in 1963 with Singapore, Sarawak, and Sabah (British North Borneo) to form the state of Malaysia with a population of 10 million.
[b] Tanganyika and Zanzibar combined in 1964 to form the United Republic of Tanganyika and Zanzibar, or Tanzania.

I. ROOTS OF COLONIAL REVOLUTION

One reason for the colonial revolution was the unprecedented weakening of the foremost colonial powers during the Second World War. France and Holland were overrun and occupied, while Britain was debilitated economically and militarily. Equally important was the growth of democratic, antiimperialist sentiment within the imperial countries themselves. Gone were the days when white men in the colonies confidently asserted, "We are here because we are superior." Now their presence was questioned, not only by their subjects but also by their own fellow citizens. Mussolini's attack on Ethiopia in 1935 was widely regarded in Western Europe as a deplorable throwback, while the Anglo-French assault on the Suez in 1956 aroused much popular opposition in both Britain and France. The end of the Western empires was due as much to the lack of will to rule as it was to lack of strength.

The short-lived Japanese Empire in Asia also contributed substantially to the colonial revolution. Western military prestige was shattered by the ease with which the Japanese drove the British out of Malaya and Burma, the French out of Indochina, the Dutch out of Indonesia, and the Americans out of the Philippines. The political foundations of Western imperialism were undermined by Japanese propaganda based on the slogan, "Asia for the Asians." We should note, however, that the Africans who escaped Japanese invasion also won freedom along with the Asians, thus pointing up the fact that, important as the Japanese impact was, it merely strengthened the great unrest and awakening that had been gathering momentum since the beginning of the century. The series of colonial uprisings following World War I reflected this growing movement (see Chapter 32): in the intervening years it had gained strength and purpose, with the growth of a Western-educated native intelligentsia. It was not accidental that the successful nationalist leaders were people who had studied in Western universities and observed Western institutions in operation—leaders like Gandhi, Nehru, Sukarno, Nkrumah, Azikwe, and Bourguiba.

The worldwide colonial awakening was further stimulated during World War II with the service of millions of colonials in both Allied and Japanese armies and labor battalions. Many Africans fought under the British, French, and Italian flags. Over 2 million Indians volunteered for the British forces, and an additional 40,000 Indian prisoners captured in Hong Kong, Singapore, and Burma signed up for the Japanese-sponsored Indian National army. When all these men returned to their homes, they inevitably regarded in a new light the local colonial officials and native leaders. Finally, the civilian populations were affected at this time, as during World War I, by the Allied propaganda regarding freedom and self-determination.

II. INDIA AND PAKISTAN

By far the most important single event in the colonial revolution was the winning of independence by India and Pakistan. More than a century of British rule had prepared India better than any other colony for self-rule. The Indian Civil Service had been largely Indianized; the universities had turned out generations of Western-educated leaders; and the Congress party had voiced and directed into the proper channels nationalist aspirations (see Chapter 26, section V). When Britain declared war on Germany on September 3, 1939, the viceroy, the Marquis of Linlithgow, on the same day proclaimed

India also to be at war. The Congress party protested bitterly, but the viceroy announced that basic changes were not feasible during the war. He did promise postwar dominion status, but Congress promptly rejected this offer and the deadlock continued.

With Japan's precipitous conquest of Southeast Asia in early 1942, Churchill sent to India on March 22 a cabinet member, Sir Stafford Cripps. Again major change was excluded for the duration of the war, but, as soon as it was over, India could become fully autonomous, with the right to secede from the Commonwealth. Congress turned down Cripp's offer and on August 7, 1942, passed a "Quit India Resolution" demanding immediate freedom, "both for the sake of India and for the success of the cause of the UN." Congress further threatened, if its demand was not met, to wage "a mass struggle on nonviolent lines." Britain's response was wholesale repression: over 60,000 people were arrested, including all the Congress leaders; 14,000 were detained without trial; 940 were killed; and 1630 were injured in clashes with the police and military.

It was a most critical moment for the Allies as well as for India. The Germans had by then reached the Volga and were only thirty miles from Alexandria, while the Japanese had overrun Burma. The gigantic German and Japanese pincers were separated only by India, which was seething with disaffection, and by the Arab countries, which sided more with the Axis than with the Allies. Britain's position in the subcontinent would have been precarious, if not impossible, had Congress made any preparations for armed revolt. Instead, under Gandhi's influence, only nonviolent resistance was offered.

During the remaining years of the war, the British stood firm in refusing to release the Congress leaders unless they modified their "Quit India" demand, which they refused to do. Meanwhile, Mohammed Jinnah, head of the Moslem League, took advantage of this hobbling of Congress to win India's Moslems to his organization and thus prepare the ground for an independent postwar Moslem state. A new and decisive turn in Indian affairs was taken with the Labour party victory in the British elections of July 1945. Labour traditionally had championed Indian freedom, and now Prime Minister Attlee acted swiftly for its materialization. Apart from his party's commitments and sympathies, the fact is that Attlee had little choice but to accept independence. Indian nationalism, inflamed by the wartime experiences, no longer could be repressed by sheer physical force, as became apparent when the government brought to trial at the end of 1945 some officers of the Japanese-sponsored Indian National army. These men immediately became national heroes, not because they had cooperated with the Japanese, but because their aim had been to oust the hated British. So strong was the feeling throughout the country that the trial had to be dropped. The truth was that Britain could no longer rule the country against the wishes of its people. Nor was there much inclination any longer to attempt to do so. The Indian Civil Service had become even more Indianized during the war, while British investments in India had shrunk drastically; and the British public had become weary of the never-ending Indian problem. Thus Attlee was now able to sever ties with the former jewel of the empire with relatively little opposition at home.

Admiral Lord Louis Mountbatten, who was sent as the new viceroy, concluded that no plan for preserving Indian political unity was feasible because of enmity between Congress and the Moslem League. He recommended partition, with the two governments each to have dominion status. By this time the Congress leaders had realized that partition was inevitable, so they accepted the plan. In July 1947, the British Parliament passed the Indian Independence Act, and on August 15, both Pakistan and the Union of India became free nations in the British Commonwealth.

III. SOUTHEAST ASIA

Southeast Asia, in contrast to India, was occupied by the Japanese during the war. A common pattern is discernible throughout the area during this brief occupation period between 1942 and 1945. In almost every country, widespread disaffection against Western rule had contributed substantially to the swift conquests of the Japanese. The latter then proclaimed, like the Germans, that their conquests inaugurated the beginning of a "New Order." The watchwords of this "New Order" were "Asia for the Asians," "Greater East Asia Co-Prosperity Sphere," and "no conquests, no oppression and no exploitation."

If these principles had been applied, the Japanese could have mobilized solid popular support in most of Southeast Asia. The Japanese military, however, had other plans, so that the principles remained propagandist slogans which soon sounded hollow and unconvincing. These military leaders viewed Greater East Asia, not as a "Co-Prosperity Sphere," but as a region consisting of satellite states held under varying degrees of control. The Japanese armed forces everywhere lived off the land as much as possible, frequently creating severe local shortages of food and supplies. Also they ruthlessly expropriated whatever foodstuffs and industrial raw materials were needed for the home islands. In return, the Japanese were able to offer little, since their economy was not strong enough to produce both war materials and consumer goods.

After the initial honeymoon period, relations between the Japanese and the local nationalists rapidly deteriorated. If the occupation had been prolonged, the Japanese undoubtedly would have been faced with serious uprisings. Fortunately for them, they were forced to pull out during 1945. In doing so, they did everything possible to create obstacles in the way of a restoration of Western rule. In Indochina they overthrew the Vichy regime and recognized Ho Chi Minh's provisional government; in Indonesia they handed over the administration to the nationalist leader Sukarno; and in many regions they distributed arms to local revolutionary groups.

It is not surprising that within ten years of the Japanese withdrawal, all Southeast Asia was independent. The manner in which the various countries won their freedom varied, depending upon the imperial rulers involved. The British, having been forced to face facts in India, were the most realistic in coping with Southeast Asian nationalism. In January 1948, they recognized Burma as an independent republic outside the Commonwealth, and in the next month they granted Ceylon full dominion status within the Commonwealth. Malayan independence, however, was delayed until February 1957. One reason for the delay was the country's mosaiclike ethnic composition. It included Malayans and Chinese—each a little over 40 percent of the total population—as well as Indians, Pakistanis, and a few Europeans. The Chinese were the prime movers behind a Communist uprising that began in 1948. The ensuing jungle warfare was very costly and dragged on until 1955. In 1963, Malaya combined with Singapore, Sarawak, and Sabah (British North Borneo) to constitute the new state of Malaysia. Tension between Malaya and the predominantly Chinese Singapore led in 1965 to the secession of Singapore, which became an independent state in the Commonwealth.

The French and the Dutch, whose subjects also demanded independence, were less adjustable and fared much worse. The Dutch were willing to grant Sukarno's nationalists some measure of self-government, but not enough to satisfy their demands. The negotiations broke down, and the Dutch resorted to armed force to reassert their authority. The war dragged on until 1947 when the Dutch finally recognized the independent United States of Indonesia. This legacy of armed conflict embittered the future relations between the two countries. Although a Dutch-Indonesian Union with a common crown existed for a few years, it ended when Sukarno withdrew in 1954. Relations became more strained in the following years because the Dutch refused to yield Netherlands New Guinea to the new republic. In 1957, in retaliation, Indonesia seized more than $1 billion worth of Dutch assets, and in 1960 it severed diplomatic relations with The Hague. Three years later Sukarno gained control over West Irian, thus liquidating the last remnant of an empire older than most of the British Empire.

The French in Indochina fought longer to retain their colony, but in the end they, too, were forced out. Indochina consisted of three nations: Vietnam, Laos, and Cambodia. Resistance against the restoration of French rule was led by the Vietminh, or League for the Independence of Vietnam. Though comprising many elements, the Vietminh was led by a Communist, Ho Chi Minh, who had lived in Paris, Moscow, and China. In 1945, after war's end, Ho Chi Minh proclaimed the provisional Republic of Vietnam. The French refused to recognize the new regime, and war ensued. Laos and Cambodia were easily reoccupied by the French, but an exhausting struggle dragged on in Vietnam.

With the advent of the Cold War, the United States backed up the French financially as a part of the policy of "containment." By 1954, most of northern Vietnam was in the hands of the Vietminh, and in the same year the French suffered a major defeat at Dien Bien Phu. The ensuing Geneva settlement recognized the independence of all Vietnam, divided the country temporarily at the 17th parallel, and called for supervised elections to be held in 1956 to reunify the country. This settlement in effect gave Ho Chi Minh half the country, and the expectation of the other half within two years since his resistance record had made him a national hero.

To avert this outcome the United States supported in the south the anti-Communist Catholic leader Ngo Dinh Diem. His policies aroused such fierce opposition amongst the peasants and the powerful Buddhist monks that in 1963 his regime was overthrown and a succession of coups followed until the rise to power, with Washington's support, of Nguyen Cao Ky and then of Nguyen Van Thieu. They were able to hold out in Saigon only because of accelerating American intervention, beginning with money and arms, and progressing to "advisers," combat troops, and, after the Tonkin Bay incident (August 1964), the bombing of North Vietnam. The bombing was designed to coerce Hanoi, which had been sending troops southward, to disengage and to recognize South Vietnam as a separate state. Although the bombing far surpassed World War II levels, and although over a half-million American troops were committed, victory remained elusive. The enemy's January 1968 Tet offensive strengthened the growing antiwar movement in the United States. Hence President Johnson's decision to end the bombing of North Vietnam and to begin peace talks in Paris.

His successor, President Nixon, had been elected on the promise of a plan to end the war. This plan involved withdrawal of American troops, a move that in any case had become unavoidable because of the growing disaffection of the troops and of the home population. But the Nixon plan also involved continued support to President Thieu, whose regime was thought to be essential for American interests. Accordingly it was buttressed with United States funds, arms, noncombative military personnel, and supportive bombing on a scale surpassing that of the Johnson administration. Despite the magnitude of the American assistance the position of the Thieu government remained so precarious that Nixon felt it necessary to launch incursions, supported by American troops and air-power, into Cambodia (April–June 1970) and into Laos (February–March 1971).

These moves provoked intense dissension and mass demonstrations in the United States. But at the same time Nixon was conducting secret diplomacy with China and the Soviet Union, culminating in his well-publicized visits to Peking (February 1972) and to Moscow (May 1972). In October 1972, on the eve of the presidential election, Nixon announced an American–North Vietnamese agreement for a ceasefire. But the announcement proved premature, as Nixon ordered the heaviest bombing of the entire war directed against North Vietnam's industrial heartland on December 18–30, 1972. Finally a ceasefire was signed in Paris on January 27, 1973 with terms essentially similar to those of the 1954 Geneva accords. Both agreements called for a temporary partition of Vietnam into a Communist North and a non-Communist South, for the determination of the future of South Vietnam by an election, for the neutralization of Laos and Cambodia, for the withdrawal from all Indochina of all foreign troops—French in 1954, American in 1973—and for the supervision of both settlements by a small and largely powerless international committee.

The cost of obtaining in 1973 what the United States had opposed in 1954 was the longest war in American history, 46,000 American deaths, 600,000 civilian and military deaths in South Vietnam, and an estimated 900,000 deaths in North Vietnam. Also there was incalculable damage to the American social fabric: among them, G.I. drug addiction, bitter domestic discord, and festering national problems neglected with the financial drain of Vietnam-war expenditures totaling 146 billion dollars. Nor did the 1973 Paris agreement finally end the fighting. The war dragged on until April 1975 when the demoralized Thieu regime collapsed like a house of cards before a north Vietnamese offensive.

IV. TROPICAL AFRICA

Just as the first postwar decade witnessed the liberation of Asia, so the second witnessed the liberation of Africa. During that decade, no less than 31 African countries won their independence; the few remaining colonies stood out painfully as obsolete hangovers from the past. The course of this nationalist awakening differed fundamentally from region to region because of the varying historical backgrounds and contemporary developments. Accordingly, the colonial revolution will be considered, not on a continentwide basis, but individually in tropical Africa, South Africa, and North Africa.

Nationalist movements of any significance did not appear in tropical Africa until after World War I. The form they assumed depended on the policies and administrative institutions established by the colonial powers. In British West Africa, authority was vested in the hands of governors who were appointed from London and who were advised by executive and legislative councils. The executive councils consisted entirely of British officials, but the legislative councils included a few African nominees. The African leaders in these colonies sought to convert the legislative councils into African parliaments, and then to convert the executive councils into African ministries responsible to such parliaments. In the French colonies, by contrast, authority was wielded to a much greater degree from Paris, and the French Africans tried to affiliate with the metropolitan parties in order to be in a position to influence decisions in the capital.

These strategies had little impact prior to World War II. Only a few Western-educated leaders were awake and active; the mass of the people were largely apathetic. The few nationalist organizations were more like debating societies than political parties, and they devoted more energy to sniping at the European administrators than to communicating with their own peoples. World War II drastically altered this traditional African pattern. In the first place, a tremendous economic expansion occurred during the war years because of the pressing demand for African raw materials and foodstuffs. This general economic upsurge led to a boom in the building of schools, the construction of roads, and the improvement of housing, sanitation, and medical services. At the same time, the Africans, observing a host of Asian peoples gaining their independence, naturally asked why they, too, should not be rid of the bonds of colonialism. The question became acute with the return of the war veterans, large numbers of whom had served for the French in Europe and for the British in Burma and the Middle East. All these factors combined to shake up and awaken tropical Africa out of its traditional lethargy.

The first outburst occurred on the Gold Coast in 1948, where the small farmers now had more income than ever before, but where consumer goods were in short supply and very expensive. They suspected the European traders of profiteering and organized a widespread boycott of their concerns. This was followed by rioting in the towns and general ferment in the countryside. A new leader now appeared who exploited this disaffection with startling success: Kwame Nkrumah had studied in American and English universities, where he had become converted to the Marxist socialism current among colonial students. Nkrumah quickly overshadowed the older West African nationalists by demanding immediate independence and organizing in 1949 the Convention People's party on a genuine mass basis.

In a general election held in 1951 under a new constitution, this party won an overwhelming majority. Nkrumah was in prison on election day, charged with sedition, but the British governor, sensing the trend of events, released Nkrumah and gave him and his colleagues leading posts in the administration. In the next few years the cabinet became all-African and was entrusted with full authority except for defense and foreign affairs. With this apprenticeship in self-government, it proved possible to make the transition to full independence without violence or dislocation. By 1957, thanks to the initiative of Nkrumah and the statesmanship of the British, the Gold Coast became the independent Commonwealth country of Ghana.

Once the colonial dam had been broken in Ghana, it was impossible to keep it from breaking elsewhere. Most decisive was the course of events in Nigeria, the most populous country in Africa, with its 35 million people. The three regions of the country—the North, the West, and the South—differed basically from each other in ethnic composition, cultural traditions, and economic development; this diversity led to serious interregional conflicts that delayed the winning of independence to 1960. The other British West African colonies, Sierra Leone and Gambia, followed in 1961 and 1963 respectively, their delay being due primarily to poverty and small size.

The British did not foresee how quickly their new colonial policy would affect the rest of tropical Africa. Repercussions were felt first in the surrounding French holdings where, in 1956, a "framework law" granted representative institutions to the twelve West African territories and to the island of Madagascar. Two years later the new de Gaulle regime, brought into power by the crisis in Algeria (see section VI, this chapter) decided to avoid a similar ordeal in tropical Africa. The sub-Saharan colonies were given the option of voting either for full independence or for autonomy as separate republics in the French "Community" that was to replace the empire. At first this strategy appeared to be successful; in the ensuing referendum, all the territories except Guinea, which was under the influence of the trade-union leader Sékou Touré, voted for autonomy. The arrangement, however, proved transitory. In 1959, Senegal and the French Sudan asked for full independence within the Community as the Federation of Mali. When this was granted, four other territories—the Ivory Coast, Niger, Dahomey, and Upper Volta—went a step further and secured independence outside the Community. By the end of 1960, all the former colonies of both French West Africa and French Equatorial Africa had won their independence.

In contrast to the smooth transition to independence in French and British West Africa, the Belgian Congo endured a bitter and costly struggle involving the Great Powers as well as Belgium and assorted Congolese factions. One source of this trouble was the rigid paternalistic character of Belgian rule. The educated native elite were few in number and inexperienced, while tribal alliances and rivalries remained prominent. Such was the situation when the French colonies across the Congo were given self-rule, thus stimulating latent hostility to European rule and bringing to the fore Patrice Lumumba, the only Congolese leader with any pretence to more than a regional following. His radical and nationwide approach to the problem of Congo independence won him a substantial following within his country as well as among pan-Africanists everywhere.

Early in 1959, after the Congo capital had been shaken by nationalist riots, the Belgians hastily decided that they could best protect their vast economic interests by allowing free elections and immediate independence. The predictable outcome was conflict and chaos. Lumumba became the first premier, but he found he could govern only with the help of Belgian army officers and civil-service officials. Some of the soldiers mutinied against the remaining officers, and attacks upon whites occurred in various parts of the country. At the same time, fighting broke out between tribes taking advantage of the opportunity to repay old scores. Most serious was the virtual secession of the rich mining province of Katanga, owing to an unholy alliance of local African politicians and Belgian mining interests. The Cold War now intruded when the Soviet Union threatened unilateral intervention under the guise of supporting the Congolese against a restoration of imperialist rule. Faced with the prospect of a Korea-like situation in Africa, the United Nations assumed the responsibility of policing the Congo with an international force consisting largely of Africans. After months of confused violence some semblance of order was restored, though not without the sacrifice of Lumumba, who was murdered by Katanga secessionists, and of the UN Secretary-General, Dag Hammarskjöld, who died in an airplane crash during a mediatory mission in the Congo.

Meanwhile, across the continent in East Africa, the nationalist cause was encountering much stiffer resistance because of the presence of white settlers in the salubrious highlands. In Kenya, the conflict between African and settler was particularly acute because of the settler's appropriation of much of the best farming land. This contributed to the uprising of the *Mau Mau,* a secret terrorist society made up of members of the Kikuyu tribe. Before the fighting was over, nearly 7000 Mau Mau had been killed, over 83,000 were in prison, and many more were held in temporary detention camps. The uprising, though it led to sickening excesses on both sides, did force the British to recognize the futility of attempting to follow a conciliatory policy in West Africa and a rigid one in the East. Accordingly, they released from prison the outstanding Kikuyu leader, Jomo Kenyatta. Like Nkrumah, he won a majority vote in an election and was allowed in 1963 to become premier. In the same year, Kenya became an independent state amidst wild re-joicing in Nairobi for the cherished Uruhu, or Freedom.

In neighboring Uganda, where the whites had not been allowed to take land, the issues were simpler and independence had been granted peaceably in 1962. Tanganyika, a Ger-man possession before World War I, had become a British mandate in 1922, with two seg-ments, Ruanda and Urundi, becoming Belgian mandates. All three territories were granted independence in 1962, with Julius K. Nyerere of Tanganyika playing a key role in the transition. Under his leadership, Tanganyika and Zanzibar combined in 1964 to form the republic of Tanzania.

The Central African Federation, comprising Southern Rhodesia, Northern Rhodesia, and Nyasaland, was organized to the south of Tanganyika in 1953. Though it was created with the declared objective of "racial partnership," the Federation was beset by crises and violence, the root cause being the political and economic domination of more than 9 million Africans by 300,000 Europeans, most of whom were living in Southern Rhodesia, a self-governing territory on the northern border of the Republic of South Africa. The nationalist movement made strong gains in Northern Rhodesia and Nyasaland, and, in 1962, both were given self-rule under African prime ministers. Be-cause Southern Rhodesia refused to follow suit and give Africans the vote, the Federation became impossible and was dissolved on January 1, 1964. Later in the year, Northern Rhodesia became fully independent as Zambia, and Nyasaland as Malawi.

The center of strife then shifted to Southern Rhodesia, now known as Rhodesia, where the black majority demanded the vote. The London government sought a compromise settlement looking towards gradual enfranchisement of the Africans. The white minority was adamantly opposed. Under the leadership of Prime Minister Ian Smith it rejected British rule in 1965 and became officially independent in 1970. The constitution of the new state of Rhodesia gave 50 seats in Parliament to the 230,000 whites, as against 16 seats to the 4.5 million Africans. By 1973, however, the black majority was organizing in-creasingly successful guerrilla attacks from Zambia. A major setback for the Smith regime was the collapse of Portuguese rule in 1975 in Mozambique, which now became another base for guerrilla attacks.

In March 1978 Smith negotiated an "internal settlement" and held elections which led to the establishment (June 1, 1978) of Zimbabwe-Rhodesia under Biship Muzorewa. The UN Security Council rejected this arrangement as camouflage for continued white domination. The guerrillas continued their armed struggle until December 1979 when they agreed to a cease fire and to new elections monitored by a Commonwealth contin-gent. The ensuing election (February 1980) gave an overwhelming majority to the Marxist leader, Robert Mugabe, whose guerrilla forces had been the most active. After seven years of armed resistance, in April 1980 the independent African state of Zimbabwe was born.

Meanwhile African nationalism had triumphed in the Portuguese colonies of Mozam-bique, Angola, and Guinea-Bissau. South Africa strongly supported Portuguese rule as a barrier against spreading African nationalism. Nevertheless insurrections broke out in all the colonies, and, as the colonial wars dragged on, the financial burden was too much for poverty-stricken Portugal. Forty percent of the budget was spent on the military, and army recruits were deserting and fleeing abroad like their American counterparts during the Vietnam War. Finally on April 12, 1974, Portugal's dictatorship was overthrown in a military coup. By the following year all three colonies were internationally recognized as independent states.

V. SOUTH AFRICA

The basic difference between tropical Africa on the one hand and North Africa and South Africa on the other is the relative absence of European settlers in the former region and their presence in large numbers in the latter two. This difference explains the brutal armed struggle that ravaged Algeria between 1954 and 1962, and the undercover conflict wracking South Africa to the present day. The colony of South Africa, as noted earlier, was established by the Dutch but came under British rule in 1814. The Dutch farmers, or Boers, rejected British rule and trekked northward, where they established the independent republics of the Transvaal and the Orange Free State. With the discovery in these republics of diamonds in 1871 and gold in 1886, the British made moves to annex them. The resulting Boer War (1899–1902) ended with the Boers accepting British sovereignty, but in return they were promised self-rule. This promise was fulfilled in 1909 when South Africa became a self-governing Dominion in the British Commonwealth.

A little more than half a century later, in May 1961, South Africa left the Commonwealth to become an independent republic. The main reason for the separation was the clash between South Africa and new African and Asian Commonwealth members, such as Nigeria and India, over the issue of *apartheid*. Apartheid involves two basic policies: the exclusion of all non-whites from any share in political life; and the confinement of the Africans to separate areas known as Bantustans—or preserves for the ''Bantu,'' as the Africans have been known. These Bantustans comprise only 14 percent of South Africa's land, while the Africans are 71.3 percent of South Africa's total population of 26 million (1980). The whites, by contrast, are only 16.5 percent, and the Afrikaners are a minority of two-fifths within the white minority. The other ethnic elements are the Coloreds or mixed race (9.3 percent) and the Asians (2.9 percent).

The Afrikaner minority controls South Africa partly because parliamentary representation is weighted in favor of the predominantly Afrikaner rural areas, and also because many English-speaking whites support apartheid for economic reasons. This is especially true of Labour, which fears competition in employment from non-whites if the latter are given equal opportunities. In fact, the first Afrikaner (Nationalist) government was able to take office in 1924 because of support from the South African Labour party.

It is generally agreed that apartheid is not a viable program, either economically or politically. If the Africans were in fact segregated on the proposed Bantustans, the entire economy of South Africa would collapse. Their labor, as well as that of the Coloreds and the Asians, has been essential for agriculture and commerce as well as mining and other industries. In addition, Bantustans have not been able to support even a third of the African population, and the government has been unwilling to spend the large sums needed to increase their absorptive capacity. Most important of all, the great majority of Africans have no desire to be isolated as separate ''tribal'' entities. Instead, they demand a fair share in the united South Africa of which they are an integral part. In this demand they are backed by the growing power of African nationalism in the rest of the continent.

South Africa tried to check African nationalism by giving substantial aid to Portugal and Rhodesia. Both efforts failed, so that South Africa now faces to the north the Marxist regimes in Angola, Zimbabwe, and Mozambique. When Robert Mugabe won the February 1980 election in Zimbabwe, the South African Prime Minister Pieter Botha said that he would accept the election result, but he also warned that he would use his ''full force'' if Zimbabwe became a base for guerrilla attacks.

More serious for South Africa than this external danger is the internal. Africans, Col-

545

oreds, and Asians all are showing a rising sense of "black consciousness." One manifestation is their rejection of the term "non-white" hitherto applied to them. In its place they substitute the term "black" as a positive assertion of worth. Another manifestation is the wave of strikes by black workers, 30 percent of whom are unemployed. Most alarming is the obvious popularity of the African National Congress, especially among students and trade unionists. After the mass killing of black demonstrators in Sharpeville (1960) and Soweto (1976), thousands of young Africans fled abroad for guerrilla training in Angola, Libya, and the Soviet Union. By 1980 South African officials estimated that 5000 trained guerrillas were infiltrating down from Angola alone. The growing number of bombings and shoot-outs in both urban and rural areas indicated that blacks, Coloreds, and Asians were abandoning peaceful marches, strikes, and boycotts for armed resistance. The *Rand Daily Mail* declared in June 1980 that South Africa had entered a "state of revolutionary war".[1]

Prime Minister Botha has tried to win over the opposition with various reforms. They allow the blacks to join legal trade unions and to take skilled jobs in mines and factories. They also permit blacks to participate in some sports with whites, and to mix with whites in some theaters, restaurants, hotels and parks. But at the same time Botha has stated flatly: "One man, one vote is out in this country. That is, never." Thus David Willers of the South African Institute of International Affairs concludes that the reforms amount to "merely rearranging the deck chairs on the Titanic. There's an amelioration of social and workplace apartheid, but they don't address themselves to the fundamental issue of political power."[2]

VI. NORTH AFRICA

In North Africa, as in Indochina, the French fought long and stubbornly to retain their possessions. A principal reason was the substantial number of French settlers in this region—250,000 in Tunisia, 400,000 in Morocco, and a million in Algeria. These colons, in league with powerful French economic interests in North Africa, bitterly opposed all proposals for self-rule and sabotaged a number of provisional moves in this direction made by certain Paris cabinets.

Tunisia and Morocco had the legal status of protectorates, which France claimed to administer in behalf of their traditional rulers. Both territories were governed autocratically—not even the resident Europeans were allowed political rights. This foreign domination stimulated movements for national liberation: in Tunisia, the Neo-Destour party, established in 1934 and led by Habib Bourguiba; and in Morocco, the Istiqlal party, founded in 1944 and given some support by Sultan Mohamed Ben Youssef.

Tunisia and Morocco won their freedom relatively easily following World War II. The French, determined to hang on to Algeria, were willing to accept losses elsewhere in order to concentrate on this prime objective. Accordingly, when armed resistance began in Tunisia in 1952, the French, after two years of guerrilla warfare, agreed to grant it autonomous status, and, having made this concession in Tunisia, they were ready to do likewise in Morocco. Sultan Mohamed, who had been exiled for his pro-Istiqlal sympathies, was allowed to return to his throne. He then demanded complete independence, which the French conceded on March 2, 1956. In the same month, Tunisia also became fully independent, with Bourguiba as president of the new republic.

The French now were able to deal with the crucial Algerian problem without distractions. Legally, Algeria was not a colony but an integral part of France, with representatives in the National Assembly in Paris. In practice, a double standard of citizenship prevailed in Algeria, so that the country was dominated economically and politically by the Europeans who comprised only one-tenth of the 10 million total population. On the other hand, the colons, like the Afrikaners at the other tip of the continent, did not regard themselves as mere colonists. Algeria was their homeland as much as that of the native Algerians. Their fathers and grandfathers had worked and died there, and they were resolved to defend their patrimony. This meant unalterable opposition to any concessions to the Algerian nationalists.

Armed revolt against French rule began in the fall of 1954. The French had been ousted from Indochina only four months earlier and were in no mood for compromise. With the enthusiastic approval of the colons and of the army officers, who were still smarting from the Indochina humiliation, the Paris government resolved to crush the uprising. The result was an exhausting, brutalizing struggle that dragged on until 1962. At its height, the French were forced to send 500,000 men into Algeria and to spend nearly $1 billion annually. The Algerians paid much more heavily in human terms, including a million dead, or one-ninth of their total numbers.

Although the French suffered little by comparison, they did pay a heavy price, in a manner much like that of the Americans in Vietnam a decade later. The imponderable cost of the psychological trauma experienced by French soldiers who were forced to participate in the bestialities of a repressive war of this type was very real. The clergy and many of the intellectuals in France spoke up with troubled consciences against the "dirty war." The government responded with arbitrary arrests and sporadic censorship of the press. Indeed, the heaviest cost for the French was the steady erosion of their personal liberties, culminating in the overthrow of the Fourth Republic itself.

In May 1958, a North African "Committee of Public Safety" seized power in Algeria in order to replace the Republic with an authoritarian regime that presumably would be more successful in holding the empire together. The demoralized National Assembly bowed to this show of force, especially since most of the armed forces were in Algeria. In June 1958, the Assembly voted full power to de Gaulle to rule France in whatever manner he wished for six months, and to prepare a new constitution for the country. Before the end of the year the Fourth Republic had given way to the Fifth, and political power had been shifted decisively from the legislative to the executive branch—specifically to the president.

President de Gaulle now used his unprecedented popularity to end the Algerian bloodshed, despite the opposition of the colons and the military who had made possible his rise to power. In March 1962, after a referendum in France had approved such a move, de Gaulle agreed to a cease-fire and to a plebiscite to determine Algeria's future. On July 3, 1962, he proclaimed the independence of Algeria after its people had voted overwhelmingly in favor of it. All of North Africa was now free for the first time since French soldiers had landed in Algeria in 1830. The granting of independence to Algeria marked the virtual end of a French African empire that once had covered nearly 4 million square miles and contained more than 41 million people.

VII. MIDDLE EAST

Because of unhappy experiences during the interwar years (see Chapter 32, section II), most politically conscious Arabs during World War II were either neutral or openly hostile to the Western powers. Hence the pro-Axis uprising in Iraq in May 1941 and the extremely reluctant assistance that King Farouk I of Egypt gave to the British despite his treaty obligations.

Although the Arab nationalists had been unable to satisfy their aspirations during World War II, the new postwar balance of power offered them a unique opportunity which they promptly exploited. Britain and France, who had dominated the Middle East before the war, now emerged drastically weakened. A power vacuum was created, which the United States and the Soviet Union attempted to fill. The Arabs skillfully took advantage of the Anglo-French weakness and the American-Russian rivalry to play off one side against the other, thus enabling them to win concessions that would have seemed preposterous only a few years earlier. The Arabs were further aided by their control over vast Middle East oil reserves, which appeared particularly indispensable to the fuel-hungry West during the postwar years.

In October 1944, the Arabs organized a League of Arab states to coordinate their policies and maximize their effectiveness. The Arab League won its first success against the French in Syria and Lebanon. In May 1945 a French expeditionary force landed in Beirut and proceeded to bombard Damascus in an attempt to cow the local nationalists. Such tactics had prevailed in the 1920s, but they did not work now. The Arab League Council promptly met and passed a resolution demanding the evacuation of all French forces. Churchill supported the Arabs, especially since World War II was not yet over; and he had no desire to cope with an aroused Arab nationalism in the Middle East. Under British pressure the French withdrew their troops, and, in July 1945, they accepted the end of their rule in the Middle East. As a result of the French withdrawal, the Arab states of Lebanon and Syria won their independence.

NASSER NATIONALIZES THE SUEZ CANAL

On July 26, 1956, Premier Nasser nationalized the Suez Canal. The following passages from his speech proclaiming the nationalization reflect Egyptian bitterness towards the Suez Canal Company of Paris and towards imperialism in general.*

Is history to repeat itself again with treachery and deceit? Will economic independence . . . or economic domination and control be the cause of the destruction of our political independence and freedom?

Brothers, it is impossible that history should repeat itself.

Today, we do not repeat what happened in the past. We are eradicating the traces of the past. We are building our country on strong and sound bases.

Whenever we turn backwards, we aim at the eradication of the past evils which brought about our domination, and the vestiges of the past which took place despite ourselves and which were caused by imperialism through treachery and deceit.

Today, the Suez Canal where 120,000 of our sons had lost their lives in digging it by corvee, and for the foundation of which we paid 8 million pounds, has become a state within the state. It has humiliated ministers and cabinets. . . .

Britain has forcibly grabbed our rights, our 44 per cent of its shares. Britain still collects the profits of these shares from the time of its inauguration until now. All countries and shareholders get their profits. A state within the state; an Egyptian Joint Stock Company.

The income of the Suez Canal Company in 1955 reached 35 million pounds, or 100 million dollars. Of this sum, we, who have lost 120,000 persons, who have died in digging the Canal, take only 1 million pounds or 3 million dollars! This is the Suez Canal Company, which was dug for the sake of Egypt and its benefit!

Do you know how much assistance America and Britain were going to offer us over five years? 70 million dollars. Do you know who takes the 100 million dollars, the Company's income, every year? They take it of course....

We shall not repeat the past. We shall eradicate it by restoring our rights in the Suez Canal. This money is ours. This Canal is the property of Egypt because it is an Egyptian Joint Stock Company.

The Canal was dug by Egypt's sons and 120,000 of them died while working. The Suez Canal Company in Paris is an imposter company. It usurped our concessions....

Therefore, I have signed today the following law which has been approved by the Cabinet: [Article 1 of the decree read, "The Universal Company of the Suez Maritime Canal (Egyptian Joint-Stock Company) is hereby nationalized. All its assets, rights and obligations are hereby transferred to the Nation...."]

* Mimeographed copy of speech from Egyptian Embassy, Washington, D.C.

In Egypt, the aim of the nationalist leaders after the war was to end or modify the 1936 treaty, which was the legal basis for Britain's control of the Canal Zone and of the Sudan. The Egyptians tried various measures, including direct negotiations, appeals to the UN Security Council, and desultory guerrilla activity. All proved futile, and the resulting frustration, together with the general resentment against the disastrous failure in the Palestine War, culminated in an army revolt in July 1952. General Muhammad Naguib assumed power and forced King Farouk to abdicate.

Naguib removed one of the sources of friction between Egypt and Britain when he concluded an agreement with Britain on February 12, 1953, by which the Sudanese were to be given a choice of independence, union with Egypt, or some other course. The decision was for independence, and in 1956 the Sudan joined the ranks of free nations. The remaining Egyptian grievance—the British presence at the Suez—was ended by Gamal Abdel Nasser, who displaced Naguib as head of the new Egyptian regime. After prolonged negotiations, Nasser signed an agreement with Britain on October 19, 1954, by which under certain stipulated conditions, the British garrison was to be removed and the British installations transferred to Egypt.

Arab nationalism was successful in Syria and Lebanon, and in Egypt and the Sudan, but it failed disastrously in Palestine. The mass extermination of Jews in Hitler-controlled Europe created strong pressures for opening up Palestine to the desperate survivors. In August 1945, President Truman proposed that 100,000 Jews be allowed to enter the mandate. In April 1946, an Anglo-American investigating committee reported in favor of the president's proposal. The Arab League responded by warning that it was unalterably opposed to such an influx, and that it was prepared to use force to stop it. The United Nations then sent a fact-finding commission to Palestine, and the General Assembly, after receiving the commission's report, voted on November 29, 1947, in favor of partitioning the mandate. On May 14 of the following year, the Jews invoked the partition resolution and proclaimed the establishment of a Jewish state to be called Israel. On the same day, President Truman extended recognition to the new state. The following day, the Arabs carried out their long-standing threat and sent their armies across the Israeli border.

The course of the war went contrary to expectations. The Arab armies lacked discipline, unity, and effective leadership. The Israelis, fighting literally with their backs to the sea, possessed all three qualities to a high degree. Not only did they repulse the Arab attacks from all sides, but they advanced and occupied more territory than had been awarded to them by the UN Assembly's resolution. After two abortive truces, the Israelis finally signed armistice agreements with the various Arab states between February and July 1949.

A peaceful settlement did not follow the cessation of fighting. The main reason is that the armistice agreements left Israel with more territory than had been allotted by the UN. The Arabs demanded that this extra territory be surrendered. Israel maintained that it was won in a war that the Arabs themselves started, and that the extra land was needed for the Jewish immigrants pouring in from all parts of the world.

This issue resulted in renewed warfare in 1956, 1967, and 1973. Israel attacked Egypt in 1956 to stop repeated border raids, and Britain and France joined in the attack because Nasser had nationalized the Suez Canal. Both the United States and the Soviet Union strongly opposed the invasion and forced the three aggressors to withdraw. Quite different was the outcome of the six-day Israeli blitz of June 5–10, 1967. Claiming that the surrounding Arab states were planning invasion, the Israeli forces quickly advanced to the Suez Canal and the Jordan River, and also occupied Jerusalem, the Gaza Strip, and Sharm el-Sheikh on the Tiran Strait. The UN Security Council on November 22, 1967, passed a resolution requiring withdrawal of the Israeli armed forces from the overrun territories and acknowledgement of the independence and integrity of Israel. The resolution remained inoperative because Israel demanded direct peace negotiations with the Arab states, while the latter demanded Israeli withdrawal before negotiations.

The deadlock persisted for six years, marked by an unending succession of attacks and counterattacks. On October 6, 1973, the fourth round in the Arab-Israeli struggle exploded with the Egyptians attacking across the Suez Canal and the Syrians into the Golan Heights. In successfully crossing the Suez canal and occupying a wide strip in the Sinai along the northern half of the Canal, the Egyptians destroyed the myth of Israeli invincibility, even though the Israelis counterattacked and occupied an equally wide strip of Egyptian territory along the southern half of the canal. On January 17, 1974, Egypt and Israel agreed that Israeli forces should withdraw to a north-south line roughly twenty miles east of the Canal, and that a UN buffer force should be installed between the two armies. On May 31, a similar agreement was signed by Israel and Syria concerning the Golan Heights.

It was hoped that these agreements would clear the way for a lasting peace, but this has not happened. The main reason is that the Palestinians demand independence. Until the 1967 war the Palestinians depended on the Arab states to win back their homeland from the Israelis. But the crushing defeat of the Arab armies in 1967 led the Palestinians to depend on their own efforts. They organized the *Palestinian Liberation Organization* (PLO), which made raids against Israel, though with little success. The National Charter of the PLO drawn up in 1968 demands the elimination of Israel and the substitution of a secular

Palestine. This has created a deadlock. In the late 1970s, the Israeli premier, Menachim Begin, referred to the West Bank by the old biblical names of Judea and Samaria. He considered the West Bank to be an inalienable part of Eretz Yisrael—the land of Israel—ceded to the Jews in the Bible. The resulting stalemate was summarized in a *New York Times* editorial (September 2, 1977):

> Because the PLO's leaders look upon acknowledgement of Israel's right to exist as their one diplomatic trump card, they will not play it—if at all—except in exchange for some sort of counter-recognition from Israel. And no such recognition is remotely likely, given Israeli Prime Minister Begin's evident conviction that the PLO can never be more than a terrorist body committed to Israel's destruction.

Egypt's President Anwar Sadat tried to break this stalemate with his famous peace trip to Jerusalem in November 1977. The outcome was the Egyptian-Israeli Peace Treaty of March 26, 1979, which provided that in stipulated stages the two countries would take several important steps: (1) establish full diplomatic relations; (2) Israel evacuates the Sinai within three years; (3) Egypt ends its economic embargo of Israel and allows Israeli shipping through the Suez Canal; (4) and the two countries negotiate on the future of Palestine with the aim of holding elections for local representative councils within one year.

The treaty temporarily lessened the danger of a Mideast war because the Arab states lost their most powerful member. On the other hand, the basic problem of Palestine remained unsolved. Begin has stated repeatedly that "there will never be a Palestinian state," and he has backed this up by planting new Israeli settlements on the West Bank. This is opposed, not only by the Palestinians, but also by the United Nations and in varying degrees by the various Arab governments. Thus the Middle East after the Egyptian-Israeli Treaty remains trapped in a state of neither war nor peace.

SUGGESTED READING

S. C. Easton, *The Rise and Fall of Western Colonialism* (Praeger, 1964); R. Emerson, *From Empire to Nation: The Rise to Self-Assertion of Asian and African Peoples* (Harvard University Press, 1960); R. Emerson and M. Kilson, ed., *The Political Awakening of Africa* (Prentice-Hall, 1965); R. Gibson, *African Liberation Movements* (Oxford University Press, 1972); W. Laqueur, ed., *The Israeli-Arab Reader* (Bantam, 1969); E. W. Said, *The Question of Palestine* (Times Books, 1980); L. L. Snyder, *The New Nationalism* (Cornell University Press, 1969).

chapter 38

Grand Alliance, Cold War, And Aftermath

World War I was followed by revolution in Central and Eastern Europe and by the threat of revolution in Western Europe. World War II stimulated no comparable disturbances. Revolutions did not convulse the Continent, despite the fact that the Second War inflicted greater material damage and political dislocation than the First. One reason was the sheer fatigue of the civilian populations. For six years they had been subjected to constant bombardment from the air, to wide-ranging ground operations, and to mass uprooting through flight, forced labor, or imprisonment. More than 15 million soldiers were killed, as well as 10 million civilians, including 6 million Jews. This was approximately twice the casualties and thirteen times the material damage of World War I. Those who survived had experienced unprecedented privation and dislocation. At the end of the hostilities, Allied armies and international relief agencies returned more than 12 million "displaced persons" to their homes, yet there still remained a hard core of more than a million—mostly anti-Communists from Eastern Europe—who refused to go home. The wholesale reshuffling of peoples, together with cold, hunger, and disease, left most Europeans too exhausted and dispirited to think of revolution.

Equally decisive was the occupation of all Europe by the forces of the victorious Allies. The Red army, no less than the British and the American, stamped out opposition and disorder. A revolution in the social structure did occur in Eastern Europe, but it was an imposed revolution directed from Moscow. The Communist parties throughout Europe

552

were obedient instruments of Soviet foreign policy rather than fomenters of indigenous revolutions. Thus, Russia and Britain and the United States effectively controlled developments in Europe after the downfall of Hitler. It was these powers that were responsible for the policies and events that gradually disrupted the wartime Grand Alliance and brought on the Cold War.

I. WARTIME UNITY

During the war years, the Western powers and the Soviet Union were forced to present a common front against the menace of a mortal enemy. Specific expressions of Allied cooperation were the twenty-year mutual-aid pact signed by Great Britain and the Soviet Union in May 1942, the American-Russian Lend-Lease Agreement of the following month, and the decision of the Russians in May 1943 to abolish the Communist International which they had established in 1919 to overthrow world capitalism. More important was the agreement reached by Britain and Russia in October 1944, when the advance of the Red army up the Danube valley was forcing the Germans to evacuate the Balkan peninsula, with Communist-led resistance fighters filling in the vacuum. The prospect of a Communist-dominated Balkans prompted Churchill to meet with Stalin in Moscow, where the two leaders quickly agreed upon spheres of influence in the disputed peninsula. Bulgaria and Rumania were to be in the Russian sphere, and Greece in the British; Yugoslavia was to be a buffer zone under joint British-Russian influence. Thus Churchill was forced, by the exigencies of an unfavorable strategic situation, to accept Soviet predominance in the northern Balkans in order to preserve Britain's traditional primacy in Greece.

At the same time that Churchill was bargaining with Stalin in Moscow, British troops were beginning to land in Greece. They advanced northward on the heels of the retreating Germans but found the Greek resistance forces preceding them in all the towns and cities. No opposition was offered by these forces, led by disciplined Communists who obediently followed the current Kremlin line. Despite the compliance of the Greek resistance forces, the fact remained that they were the preponderant military power in the country as the Germans withdrew. This was an intolerable situation for Churchill, who resolved to secure the disarming of the resistance forces in order to transfer state power to the legal royal government in Athens. Various disarmament formulas were proposed, but none satisfied both sides. This dispute precipitated an armed clash that developed into the bitter and bloody Battle of Athens. British and Indian troops were rushed in from Italy, and, after a month of fighting, the resistance forces withdrew from the Athens area.

On February 12, a peace agreement (the Varkiza Pact) was signed by which the resistance troops surrendered their arms in return for a promise of elections and a plebiscite on the question of the return of the king. Thus Churchill secured the sphere allotted to him in Moscow: Greece was to be on the side of the West during the postwar years. Equally significant was Stalin's eloquent silence while Churchill was dispersing the leftist resistance fighters. The British-Russian deal on the Balkans was in operation and was working.

The fighting in Athens had barely ceased when, in February 1945, Roosevelt, Churchill, and Stalin met at Yalta for the last of their wartime conferences. With the Allied armies converging upon Germany from all sides, the problems of a postwar settlement now had to be considered specifically and realistically. As regards the Far East, Stalin agreed to declare war against Japan within sixty days after the end of hostilities in Europe, and, in return, Russia was to regain various concessions and territories lost to Japan in 1905. The conference postponed decision on most issues concerning Germany, including reparations and frontiers, but did agree that the country should be divided into four occupation zones.

Most of the negotiating at Yalta concerned the newly liberated countries in Eastern Europe. Stalin was in a strong position in this area, for his armies had done the liberating and were in actual occupation. Given this context, the agreements that were made on Eastern Europe were, on paper, eminently satisfactory from the Western viewpoint. As regards frontiers, Russia was to receive the Polish territory east of a modified Curzon Line, which had been drawn after World War I but subsequently ignored. Poland was to be compensated with territory in east Germany; this was agreed upon in principle, though a final and specific decision was postponed. As regards the Polish and Yugoslav governments, Stalin agreed that the Communist regimes already established under Soviet auspices should be broadened by the admission of representatives from the West-oriented governments-in-exile. The latter were understandably apprehensive about this arrangement, which left the Red army and the Communist governments in physical and legal control. Their doubts were met, in theory, by a broad statement of policy known as the Yalta Declaration on Liberated Europe. This committed the three powers to assist the liberated peoples of Europe ''to form interim governmental authorities broadly representative of all democratic elements in the population and pledged to the earliest possible establishment through free elections of governments responsive to the will of the people. . . .''

Taken at face value, this declaration represented a substantial concession on the part of Stalin. Despite his domination of Eastern Europe he had consented to free elections that might well bring to office anti-Soviet governments. The substance of this concession, however, was negligible because it was interpreted very differently by the various signatories. The United States interpreted it literally—that is, free elections and no spheres of influence in Eastern Europe. The United States was free to take this position because it was not bound by the agreement reached by Churchill and Stalin in Moscow the previous October. Britain, on the other hand, was ambivalent about the declaration because the Moscow agreement had enabled it to secure its position in Greece. Yet the declaration was alluring, because, if literally enforced, it would give Britain a chance to regain positions in Rumania and Bulgaria that it had abandoned. Stalin, by contrast, clung to the Moscow agreement and regarded the declaration as mere window dressing. He had scrupulously kept quiet while the British crushed the Greek resistance forces, and now, in return, he expected the Western powers to respect his primacy in Eastern Europe. His concern for a Russian security zone as opposed to the American insistence on free elections was a chief cause for the disruption of the Grand Alliance in the months to come.

II. UNITED NATIONS AND PEACE TREATIES

Meanwhile the wartime Allies had been cooperating in the organization of the *United Nations.* The final charter was signed by the representatives of 50 nations at the conclusion of the conference held in San Francisco from April to June 1945. By 1980 UN membership had more than tripled, the majority of the newcomers being the newly independent states of Asia and Africa.

The UN, like its predecessor the League of Nations, was set up to accomplish two basic tasks: to preserve peace and security, and to cope with international economic, social, and cultural problems. The latter was entrusted to the *Economic and Social Council,* which set up numerous specialized agencies, including the International Labor Organization; Food and Agriculture Organization; UN Educational, Scientific, and Cultural Organization; World Health Organization; and International Monetary Fund.

Like the League of Nations, the UN has been quite successful in these various non-political activities. But again like the League, the UN has had a spotty record in its main job of keeping the peace. It has helped to prevent all-out war between the Great Powers by providing a medium for maintaining rapport. It has stopped fighting in areas such as Indonesia, and Kashmir, where vital interests of the major powers were not involved. But it was not able to forestall a series of local, or "brushfire," wars in Korea, Algeria, Vietnam, and the Middle East. Nor was there any consultation of the UN during the highly dangerous Cuban crisis of 1962. The basic difficulty of the UN, as of the League, was that in a world of sovereign states it could provide machinery for settling disputes but could not compel use of the machinery. Consequently, the major powers went their separate ways, organizing their rival security systems and reacting independently to each crisis.

Despite the drift to the Cold War, the foreign ministers of the victorious Allies did succeed in signing peace treaties on February 10, 1947, with Italy, Rumania, Hungary, Bulgaria, and Finland. All the treaties imposed reparations on the defeated countries, limited their armed forces, and redrew their frontiers. Italy lost the Dodecanese Islands to Greece, Saseno Island to Albania, small enclaves to France, and Venezia Giulia and the countryside surrounding Trieste to Yugoslavia. Its African colonies were placed under the temporary trusteeship of Great Britain, their ultimate status to be determined later.

In the Balkans, Bulgaria restored the Greek and Yugoslav territories that it had occupied, but it acquired southern Dobruja, which it had lost to Rumania in 1919. Rumania lost Bessarabia (which had been Russian from 1812 to 1918) and the northern Bucovina (inhabited largely by Ukrainians) to the Soviet Union, but it regained northern Transylvania, which Hungary had seized during the war. Other territorial changes in Eastern Europe not covered by the satellite treaties included the acquisition by Russia of the predominantly Ukrainian Carpathian-Ruthenia from Czechoslovakia, and of the three Baltic states—Latvia, Lithuania, and Estonia. Though Russia claimed the Baltic states on the ground that they had been a part of the Tsarist empire, the Western powers withheld official recognition of their annexation.

Perhaps these treaties will be remembered in the future for the fact that they sanctioned the new Communist regimes in Eastern Europe. Churchill had frequently declared during the war that he would not allow the Soviet zone to extend westward to a line from Stettin in the north to Trieste in the south. Yet this is precisely what the Western powers accepted when they signed the peace treaties at Paris. In doing so they recognized a new balance in Europe—a balance in which Bucharest, Sofia, and Budapest, along with Prague and Warsaw, now looked toward Moscow rather than toward Paris or Berlin.

The satellite treaties were not followed by corresponding pacts with the other enemy countries, and especially with Japan and Germany. The breakdown in peacemaking reflected the growing dissension between East and West. This, in turn, may be explained to a large degree by the immense power vacuums in Europe and Asia following the collapse of the German and Japanese empires. Vacuums are as unnatural and transitory in the political world as in the physical. They obviously were destined to be filled as soon as the fighting ceased. The question was how and by whom.

This vital question involved fundamental readjustments of power relationships. Under the best of circumstances such readjustments are difficult to arrange and fraught with danger, as evidenced by the crises following the Napoleonic Wars and World War I. Now, after World War II, the process of readjustment was made even more complicated and perilous by the addition of ideological issues to the traditional power struggle.

A region of major conflict was Eastern Europe, which Russia viewed as its security zone, and where it used its Red army to install "friendly" dependent governments. More serious was the East-West clash in Germany, which had been divided into four zones. When the occupying powers faced the concrete problems of administering the country, they discovered basic differences in aims and policies. The Russians wanted substantial reparations and also a social revolution that would transform their zone, and the whole nation if possible, into another dependent People's Democracy. For this reason they favored a centralized German state that would facilitate its eventual communization. The French, like the Russians, were determined to exact heavy reparations, but they preferred a loose federative union, which they regarded as less dangerous to their national security. The British and the Americans were with the French in favoring a federative state, but they opposed both the French and the Russians in economic matters.

The issue came to a head over reparations. It had been agreed at the Potsdam Conference in July 1945 that Russia was to receive $10 billion indemnity from Germany, to be collected from German foreign assets and through the removal of industrial equipment—from the Russian zone, and from the Western zones insofar as the equipment was not needed by the local economies. The Russians promptly proceeded to dismantle and ship East German factories to their own country, and also to tap current German factory output. The latter practice was a violation of the Potsdam agreement, as was also the refusal by the Russians to allow any inspection of the East German economy. In retaliation, the Americans and the British stopped the delivery of reparations from their zones in May 1946 and repeatedly raised the permitted level of German industry. The next step occurred in December 1946, when the British and the Americans combined their zones into an economic "Bizonia."

By early 1947 the four-power administration of Germany had broken up. In an effort to resolve the conflict, a Big Four conference was held in Moscow in March 1947. The Americans and the British insisted on the economic unification of Germany; the French and the Russians were opposed. After six weeks of futile wrangling, the conference adjourned. Its failure, together with the proclamation of the Truman Doctrine at the same time, mark the beginning of the Cold War.

III. COLD WAR IN EUROPE

The most dramatic manifestation of the oncoming Cold War was President Truman's intervention in the Greek Civil War in March 1947. Communist-led guerrillas had appeared the preceding fall in the mountains of northern Greece. One reason for the renewed civil strife was the wretched economic condition that drove many impoverished peasants to the rebel ranks. Another was the deteriorating international situation, which led the Soviet bloc to incite and aid the guerrillas against the British-supported Athens government. Finally there was the rightist persecution of political opponents despite the provision for amnesty and normal political procedures in the Varkiza Pact, which terminated the Battle of Athens.

TRUMAN DOCTRINE AND COLD WAR

When World War II ended, the wartime cooperation between Russia and the Western Powers gave way to the Cold War. The American view of the Cold War was set forth by President Truman in his speech to Congress (March 12, 1947) in which he enunciated the following principles, known as the Truman Doctrine.*

The gravity of the situation which confronts the world today necessitates my appearance before a joint session of the Congress.

The foreign policy and the national security of this country are involved.

One aspect of the present situation, which I wish to present to you at this time for your consideration and decision, concerns Greece and Turkey. . . .

The very existence of the Greek state is today threatened by the terrorist activities of several thousand armed men, led by Communists, who defy the Government's authority at a number of points, particularly along the northern boundaries. A commission appointed by the United Nations Security Council is at present investigating disturbed conditions in northern Greece and alleged border violations along the frontier between Greece on the one hand and Albania, Bulgaria, and Yugoslavia on the other.

Meanwhile, the Greek Government is unable to cope with the situation. The Greek Army is small and poorly equipped. It needs supplies and equipment if it is to restore the authority of the Government throughout Greek territory.

Greece must have assistance if it is to become a self-supporting and self-respecting democracy.

The United States must supply this assistance. . . .

Greece's neighbor, Turkey, also deserves our attention.

The future of Turkey as an independent and economically sound state is clearly no less important to the freedom-loving peoples of the world than the future of Greece. The circumstances in which Turkey finds itself today are considerably different from those of Greece. Turkey has been spared the disasters that have beset Greece. And during the war, the United States and Great Britain furnished Turkey with material aid.

Nevertheless, Turkey now needs our support. . . .

We must take immediate and resolute action.

I therefore ask the Congress to provide authority for assistance to Greece and Turkey in the amount of $400,000,000 for the period ending June 30, 1948. . . .

I am fully aware of the broad implications involved if the United States extends assistance to Greece and Turkey, and I shall discuss these implications with you at this time. . . .

The United States contributed $341,000,000,000 toward winning World War II. This is an investment in world freedom and world peace.

The assistance that I am recommending for Greece and Turkey amounts to little more than one-tenth of 1 percent of this investment. It is only common sense that we should safeguard this investment and make sure that it was not in vain.

* *Congressional Record*, 80th Congress, lst Session (Washington, D.C.: Government Printing Office, 1947), XCIII, 1980–1981.

These circumstances engendered considerable popular support for the insurrection, which spread from the northern mountains to the Peloponnesus and the larger islands. The situation became critical when on February 24, 1947, the British government announced that it could not afford the large-scale aid necessary to ensure victory over the rebel bands. Without further aid from London, the Athens regime probably would not have survived the year. President Truman met the emergency by proclaiming the doctrine named after him. Enunciating the principle that ''it must be the policy of the United States to support free peoples who are resisting attempted subjugation by armed minorities or by outside pressures,'' he stated that ''the very existence of the Greek state is today threatened,'' and requested Congress to appropriate $400 million for aid to Greece and Turkey. Thus Britain surrendered its century-old primacy in Greece, and the United States assumed the responsibility for preventing the extension of Communist influence in the eastern Mediterranean.

The task proved more onerous than anticipated despite lavish American military and economic aid to Athens. Both the 1947 and 1948 campaigns proved inconclusive. In 1949 the balance shifted decisively in favor of the government. The Tito-Stalin split led Marshal Tito to close the Yugoslav border and stop all aid to the guerrillas who had sided with Stalin. At the same time the Athens armies were being retrained by American officers to fight a mobile offensive war instead of garrisoning key towns and communication routes. Thus, in the fall of 1949 the national armies were able to drive the guerrillas from their mountain strongholds and to reach and seal the northern frontiers.

The counterpart to the Truman Doctrine in the economic sphere was the European Recovery Program, commonly known as the Marshall Plan. By the time of its termination on December 31, 1951, a total of $12.5 billion was spent in support of the West European economy. This extraordinary investment, together with the human and material resources of Europe, made possible a rapid recovery that raised production and living standards to above prewar levels. But from the viewpoint of East-West relations, the Marshall Plan marked the final step toward the *Cold War*. The offer of aid had been directed to all countries, irrespective of ideology. Moscow, however, interpreted the offer as an anti-Communist maneuver and ordered back the Czechs and Poles who had been inclined to respond. Instead, Moscow established, in January 1949, the Council for Mutual Economic Assistance (Molotov Plan), as the Eastern counterpart to the Marshall Plan.

Thus the line was drawn between the Communist and Western worlds. The Cold War now was in full swing, and for the next half decade one crisis followed closely on another in tragic sequence. In February 1948, the Communists eliminated the last bridgehead of Western influence in the Soviet sphere when they seized full control in Czechoslovakia. That small republic had tried to steer a middle course between East and West, but the attempt ended when the Communists used their control of the police and of their militant ''action committees'' to take over the government. The venerable President Eduard Benes, who had led his country also in the prewar period, was succeeded by the Communist leader Gottwald, and thus all of Eastern Europe, except Finland, was now in Communist hands.

Even more dramatic than the Communist takeover in Prague was the protracted Berlin Airlift crisis that began in June 1948. Having failed to dissuade the British and Americans from setting up a separate West German government, the Russians retaliated by cutting off railway and road access to the three Western sectors of Berlin. The Americans replied with an unprecedented airlift that supplied the food, coal, and other essentials needed by the 2 million people in the Western sectors. By the spring of 1949 the success of the airlift was apparent, and in May the Russians called off the blockade. In September, the Federal Republic was officially launched in West Germany, and in the next month the Democratic Republic was established in the East. Thus the Cold War had split Germany in two.

These various manifestations of Communist aggressiveness—the coup in Czechoslovakia, the Berlin blockade, and the continuing civil war in Greece—persuaded the Western powers that some defensive alliance system was necessary. Hence, the signing of the *North Atlantic Treaty* in Washington on April 4, 1949. The treaty included the United States, Canada, Britain, France, Belgium, the Netherlands, Luxembourg, Italy, Portugal, Denmark, Iceland, and Norway. These twelve original powers were joined later by Greece and Turkey (1951) and by West Germany (1955). The treaty provided that "an armed attack against one or more" of the signatories, in Europe, North Africa, or North America, "shall be considered an attack against them all."

Meanwhile, the Soviet Union had made corresponding political and military arrangements in Eastern Europe. Even before the end of the war Stalin had concluded mutual assistance pacts with Czechoslovakia, Yugoslavia, and Poland, and by 1948 similar pacts were signed with the former Axis satellites—Bulgaria, Rumania, and Hungary. In May 1955, a more formal and comprehensive military alliance was concluded between Russia and the East European countries. This was known as the *Warsaw Pact* and constituted the Eastern response to the North Atlantic Treaty. Thus Europe as well as Germany was cut in two by the Cold War—the Western half armed and organized under the aegis of the United States, and the Eastern, under that of the Soviet Union.

IV. COLD WAR IN THE FAR EAST

In 1950, the focus of the Cold War shifted from Europe to the Far East. By this time a balance had been reached in Europe between East and West. But in the Far East the balance was upset by a momentous development—the triumph of the Communists in China. Just as the Bolshevik Revolution was the outstanding by-product of World War I, so the Chinese Communist Revolution was the outstanding by-product of World War II.

Chiang Kai-shek had become the master of China in 1928, but from the outset his Kuomintang regime was threatened by two mortal enemies, the Communists within and the Japanese without. It was during the war years that Chiang's regime was irretrievably undermined. Chiang traditionally had depended on the support of the conservative landlord class and of the relatively enlightened big businessmen. The latter were largely eliminated when the Japanese overran the east coast, and Chiang was left with the self-centered and short-sighted landlords of the interior. His government became increasingly corrupt and unresponsive to the needs of a peasantry wracked and aroused by years of war. In contrast to the decaying Kuomintang, the Communists carried out land reforms in their territories, thereby winning the support of the peasant masses. They had a disciplined and efficient organization that brought order out of political and economic chaos in the areas under their control. Also their leadership in the anti-Japanese struggle won them popular support as patriots dedicated to ridding the country of foreign invaders and to restoring China's unity, pride, and greatness.

Such was the situation when Japan's surrender in August 1945 set off a wild scramble by the Nationalists and Communists to take over the Japanese-occupied parts of China.

The Communists occupied the countryside around the major cities, being helped by the Russians, who turned over to them the arms the Japanese had surrendered in Manchuria. The Nationalists, aided by the transportation services of the United States Navy and Air Force, won all the main cities, including Nanking, and also rushed troops north to Manchuria. The latter move was a strategic blunder. The Kuomintang forces found themselves in indefensible positions and were forced in the fall of 1948 to surrender to the Chinese Red army. A chain of comparable military disasters followed in quick succession. The Communist armies swept down from Manchuria through the major cities of north China. By April 1949, they were crossing the Yangtze and fanning out over south China. The Communist steamroller advanced even more rapidly in the south than in the north. By the end of 1949 it had overrun all of mainland China. Chiang fled to the island of Taiwan (Formosa), while in Peking the Communist leader, Mao Tse-tung, proclaimed the People's Republic of China on October 1, 1949.

These developments represented a setback for the postwar American policy of the containment of Communism on a global scale. In Japan, however, the postwar occupation was dominated by the United States. Japan, in contrast to Germany, was governed by a single Supreme Command of the Allied Powers, which included Allied representatives. The Supreme Commander, General Douglas MacArthur, and the bulk of the occupation forces were American. MacArthur's instructions were to disarm and demilitarize the country, develop democratic institutions, and create a viable economy. By 1951, when the occupation had attained most of these objectives, a peace treaty was concluded and signed by the United States and most of the Allies, with the notable exception of China and the Soviet Union, who considered the terms overly generous. The treaty restored Japanese sovereignty, but only over the four main islands. There were no military or economic restrictions, except that the United States was permitted to maintain military bases in Japan. The United States also gained trusteeship over the Ryuku and Bonin islands and over Japan's former Pacific mandates. Japan relinquished the Kuril islands and southern Sakhalin (which had been allotted to Russia) as well as Formosa, but the future disposition of these islands was left open. In effect, this treaty made Japan the main bastion of the American position in the Far East. In support of this bastion the United States spent about $2 billion in the first six years after the war. With the demand for a wide variety of goods during the Korean and Vietnamese wars, Japan made such remarkable economic progress that by 1970 it had become the third greatest industrial power in the world, surpassed only by the United States and the Soviet Union.

In the Far East, as in Europe, then, World War II was followed by Cold War. Russia backed Mao Tse-tung, albeit belatedly, while the United States vainly attempted to maintain Chiang Kai-shek as master of China. Conversely, in Japan the United States dominated the occupation and utilized it to further its interests, while the Soviet representatives impotently protested. Once the outcome had apparently been settled in both countries, there was hope, as expressed by Secretary of State Dean Acheson, for "the dust to settle" and for a balance to be reached, as had been done in Europe. The hope was shattered when in 1950 fighting broke out in Korea and the Cold War became hot.

The tragedy of Korea is that its location has made it a natural bridge between China and Japan. Repeatedly it has been fought over by the two countries, and occasionally by Russia also. Since 1895—and formally since 1910—Korea had passed under Japanese rule. Thereafter it was in effect a colony, though unique in that it was under Asian rather than European domination. During World War II, at the 1943 Cairo Conference, the

United States, Britain, and China declared that, "in due course," Korea should once more be free and independent. But a generation of Japanese rule had left Korea without the necessary experience for self-government. The victorious Allies decided, therefore, that for a period of not more than five years Korea, though independent, should be under the trusteeship of the United States, Russia, Britain, and China.

With the surrender of Japan, American and Russian troops poured into Korea. For purposes of military convenience the 38th parallel was set as the dividing line in their operations. The coming of the Cold War froze this temporary division in Korea as it did in Germany. The Russians set up in their zone a regime dominated by the Communist New People's party. In the south, the Americans leaned on English-speaking Koreans, who usually were members of the conservative upper class. In August 1948, a Republic of Korea was proclaimed in the south, with Dr. Syngman Rhee as president. A month later the North Koreans formed their People's Democratic Republic under Kim Il-sung. A UN commission attempted without success to mediate between the regimes headed by these two men. So strong were the feelings that the commission warned in September 1949 of the danger of civil war.

On June 24, 1950, civil war did begin, when North Korean troops suddenly crossed the 38th parallel in order to "liberate" South Korea. The next day the UN Security Council adopted an American resolution calling for an immediate ceasefire and the withdrawal of the North Koreans to the 38th parallel. On June 27 the Security Council asked UN members to "furnish such assistance to the Republic of Korea as may be necessary to repel the armed attack and to restore international peace and security in the area." Forty UN member states responded to the Security Council's appeal and provided supplies, transport, hospital units, and, in some cases, combat forces. But the main contribution, aside from that of South Korea, came from the United States, and General MacArthur served as commander in chief.

The course of the Korean War fell into two phases—the first before, and the second after, the Chinese intervention. The first phase began with the headlong rush of the North Korean forces down the length of the peninsula to within fifty miles of the port of Pusan at the southern tip. Then on September 14, 1950, an American force landed at Inchon, far up the coast near the 38th parallel, and in twelve days retook the South Korean capital, Seoul. The North Koreans, their communications severed, fell back as precipitously as they had advanced. By the end of September the UN forces had reached the 38th parallel, and on October 8 they crossed the 38th parallel and quickly occupied Pyongyang, the North Korean capital. By November 22 they reached the Yalu River, the boundary line between Korea and the Chinese province of Manchuria.

At this point the second phase of the Korean War began with a massive attack by Chinese "volunteers" supported by Russian-made jets. The Chinese drove southward rapidly in what looked like a repetition of the first phase of the war. Early in January 1951, they retook Seoul, but the UN forces now recovered and held their ground. In March, Seoul once more changed hands, and by June the battle line ran roughly along the 38th parallel. By mid-1951 it was apparent that a stalemate prevailed at the front. Large-scale fighting petered out, and armistice negotiations started. After two years of stormy and often-interrupted negotiations, an armistice agreement was concluded on July 27, 1953. The terms reflected the military stalemate. The line of partition between North and South Korea remained roughly where it had been before the war. The Western powers had successfully contained Communism in Korea and had vindicated the authority of the United

Nations. The Chinese had secured North Korea as a Communist buffer-state between Manchuria and Western influences. And meanwhile, most of the Korean countryside had been laid waste and about 10 percent of the Korean people had been killed.

V. RELAXATION OF THE COLD WAR

In 1953 the Cold War began to subside. One reason was the death in April 1953, of Joseph Stalin, who had become increasingly paranoid and inflexible in his later years. The younger men who succeeded him were ready for a relaxation of both the Cold War abroad and the dictatorship at home. At the same time, the new Eisenhower administration was replacing that of Truman in the United States. This also contributed to the international "thaw," for Eisenhower was able, in July 1953, to make a compromise peace in Korea, whereas Truman would have found this extremely difficult because of domestic political considerations. The following month the Soviet government announced that it also possessed the secret of the hydrogen bomb. Paradoxically, this strengthened the movement for a settlement, for it was known that the hydrogen bomb exploded by the United States at Bikini was 750 times more powerful than the Hiroshima atomic bomb, which had killed 78,000 people. All but the most fanatic Cold Warriors sensed that war no longer was a feasible instrument of national policy.

The deterring effect of the H-bomb was manifested during the 1962 Cuba crisis, precipitated when American air reconnaissance revealed that Russian missile bases were under construction in Cuba and that a large part of the United States soon would be within range. It became clear that neither country wanted war when Soviet vessels bound for Cuba altered course and the United States permitted a Soviet tanker to proceed when satisfied that it carried no offensive weapons. Finally, on October 28, Khrushchev announced that he had ordered Soviet missiles withdrawn and all Soviet bases in Cuba dismantled under UN inspection, in return for the ending of the United States blockade and a pledge not to invade Cuba.

Although the Cuban crisis ended peaceably, it was a very near thing—so near that it stimulated several agreements for the limitation of nuclear weapons: controls on tests of nuclear weapons (1963), prohibition of nuclear weapons in space (1967), Latin America made a nonnuclear zone (1967), nonproliferation of nuclear weapons beyond the nations already possessing them (1968), prohibition of emplacement of nuclear weapons on the seabed (1971), and prohibition of the use of biological weapons (1971). These agreements together helped to lessen substantially the international tensions of the Cold War.

VI. EUROPE ITS OWN MASTER

The slackening of the Cold War in turn lessened the rigidity of the opposing blocs and gradually undermined the American-Russian domination of the globe. The Western European states, no longer so apprehensive of the danger of Russian invasion, did not feel so dependent upon Washington and were more ready to formulate and pursue their own policies. To a lesser extent this was true also of the Eastern European states vis-à-vis Russia, which explains in part the Polish and Hungarian outbreaks in 1956. More spectacular and significant was China's breakaway from Russia, ending the hitherto monolithic unity of the Communist world.

The Western European states were able to become increasingly independent of the

United States not only because of the waning Cold War but also because of their own growing economic strength, which allowed them more maneuverability in political matters. West European prosperity was based on American aid under the Marshall Plan, on the introduction of American production and managerial techniques, and on the organization of the *Common Market.* Originally the Common Market comprised six members (Italy, West Germany, the Netherlands, Belgium, Luxembourg, and France), but in 1973 it was expanded to include also Britain, Ireland, and Denmark. Thus the Common Market now is a bloc of 195 million people, and an economic power comparable to the United States.

These factors together explain the remarkable growth of Western Europe from an economic dependency to an economic rival of the United States. During the two decades 1950–60 and 1960–70, per capita GNP increased by the following percentages: United States, 1.4 and 2.7; France, 3.6 and 4.7; Italy, 5.2 and 4.8; and West Germany, 6.8 and 3.8. Likewise between 1967 and 1977 the share of the major non-Communist powers in world exports of manufactured goods changed as follows: United States, 21.5 to 16.5 percent; West Germany, 19.3 to 20.5 percent; Japan, 8.1 to 15.4 percent; and Britain, 14.4 to 9.8 percent.

The change in economic relationships between Western Europe and the United States led to a corresponding change in political relationships. This was particularly true of France under de Gaulle, who pursued independent policies in every field. He rebuffed American policy makers by developing his own atomic weapons and aerial striking force. In order to be free to build up this independent military power, de Gaulle rejected the test-ban treaty signed in Moscow in 1963 by the United States, Britain, and Russia. Along the same lines, he extended full diplomatic recognition to Communist China on January 27, 1964, despite obvious American disapproval. Likewise all European members of NATO, except Portugal, refused to allow landing rights to American planes airlifting arms to Israel during the 1973 Mideast war. Henry Kissinger denounced the European behavior as "contemptible" and "jackal-like." Chancellor Brandt of Germany replied: "Europe has become self-confident and independent enough to regard itself as an equal partner in this relationship, and it is as such that it must be accepted. Partnership cannot mean subordination."[1]

While Western Europe was becoming independent of the United States, Eastern Europe was gaining a measure of autonomy from the Soviet Union. Here also the change was made possible by the American-Russian military stalemate and by the easing of the Cold War. An additional important factor in Eastern Europe was the change in leadership in the Soviet Union. The death of Stalin in 1953, and the eventual emergence of Nikita Khrushchev as his successor, marked the beginning of a new era not only in Soviet domestic affairs but also in the relations between the Soviet Union and its East European satellites.

The first anti-Soviet outbreak in Eastern Europe had occurred in 1948 when Tito successfully asserted the independence of his Communist state from Kremlin dictation. Thanks to strong popular support at home and to generous economic aid from the West, Tito was able to resist Soviet pressure and to establish Yugoslavia as a nonaligned state. The next break occurred in Poland where the "national" Communist leader, Wyadyslaw Gomulka, was able in 1956 to win a degree of autonomy, though not equal to the nonalignment of Yugoslavia. Poland enjoyed autonomy in domestic affairs but remained definitely a Communist state and a dependable member of the Warsaw Pact.

In contrast to this peaceful compromise reached in Poland, the nationalist-minded

Communists of Hungary provoked a violent confrontation in which they were crushed. Unlike the Poles who were content with autonomy within the Soviet orbit, the Hungarians demanded a Western-type democracy, completely free from commitments to Moscow or to the Warsaw Pact. The Russians, viewing this as an intolerable threat to their East European security system, sent their tanks into Budapest in 1956 and installed Janos Kadar as the new and dependable Communist leader. During the following years Kadar was able to evolve a relationship with Russia similar to that of Gomulka, while at home he attracted considerable popular support by easing controls and raising living standards.

This relaxation of Soviet political domination of Eastern Europe had its counterpart in the economic and cultural fields. Under Stalin, satellite states had been ruthlessly exploited by a variety of unequal trade treaties and development arrangements that operated in favor of the Soviet Union. After the 1956 turmoil in Poland, Hungary, and other Eastern European countries, this pattern was quickly changed. Trade treaties and development projects were renegotiated and made more equitable. Each country was allowed gradually to make its own decisions regarding the pace and course of economic development. Industries no longer had to be integrated with those of Russia or the other Communist countries. Instead the trend was toward more independent national development, more leeway to both industry and agriculture, and more trade with the West. Similar relaxation occurred in the field of culture with cultural agreements concluded with Western countries, less frequent jamming of foreign broadcasts, increase in tourism, greater freedom to foreign correspondents, and freer circulation of Western films, books, and periodicals.

In August 1968, this trend toward liberalization in Eastern Europe was abruptly reversed with the invasion of Czechoslovakia by the Soviet army together with East German, Hungarian, Polish, and Bulgarian units. The invaders ended the "democratic socialist revolution" launched in Prague in January 1968 by Alexander Dubcek. Perhaps the Russians were motivated by genuine concern that the new Czech regime might drift into the Western camp. Certainly they feared that the new freedom in Czechoslovakia might strengthen popular demand throughout Eastern Europe for similar freedom and thus endanger the existing Communist regimes. In any case, the Soviets justified the invasion with their so-called Brezhnev Doctrine, which reserved the right to invade any socialist neighbor that they considered to be abandoning their camp.

Despite the Czech invasion and the Brezhnev Doctrine, the Soviet position in Eastern Europe is far from being as dominating as during the Stalin era. Public opinion in Czechoslovakia remains overwhelmingly anti-Soviet. Yugoslavia continues on its course of independent neutralism between East and West. Rumania is relatively cautious because of its common border with the Soviet Union. Yet it has paraded before the world its cordial relations with the United States and China, and also it has refused to allow the Warsaw Treaty powers to conduct army maneuvers on its soil. During a 1976 conference of Communist parties, President Ceausescu of Rumania declared, "It is the sacred right of each nation to decide its own destiny without interference from the outside."[2]

VII. CHINA CHALLENGES RUSSIA

When the victorious Chinese Communists established their People's Republic in 1949, they were promptly recognized by the Soviet Union. A score of other countries, including Britain and India, did likewise. The United States, however, continued to treat Chiang

Kai-shek's exiled regime in Taiwan as the legal government of China. Peking therefore turned to Moscow and, in 1950, signed a thirty-year treaty of "friendship, alliance, and mutual assistance." Under the terms of the treaty, the Soviet Union helped China to build a large modern army and to begin an ambitious program of industrialization.

The Russo-Chinese alliance began to show signs of disruption in the late 1950s. Peking criticized Khrushchev indirectly with thinly veiled barbs against "Yugoslav revisionists," while Moscow spokesmen retaliated with attacks against "dogmatists" and "left infantilists." During the Twenty-second Soviet Party Congress in 1960, Khrushchev and Chou En-lai clashed openly, and the latter left the Congress and flew back to Peking. About this time the Russians recalled from China nearly all their technical experts. The Chinese charged later that the Russians had withdrawn 1390 experts and canceled 257 projects of scientific and technical cooperation. Worst of all, from the Chinese viewpoint, the Soviets refused to share their atomic weapons or the technical information and the resources necessary for their manufacture. Thus the quarrel between the two Communist giants grew to an outright schism, including name calling and open rivalry all over the globe.

The roots of this dramatic and fateful rift in the Communist world appear to be partly a conflict of national interests and partly a conflict of ideologies. The national issues arose from traditional material considerations such as frontier demarcation and different economic interests because of different levels of development. The Soviet Union has a land area two and a half times that of China, and a population density of 24 per square mile as against China's 190. The 2000-mile frontier separating the two countries has been drawn in precise detail in Soviet maps, whereas on Chinese maps certain sections have been depicted as "undemarcated," including the eastern margins of the Pamir highlands, some islands at the confluence of the Amur and Ussuri Rivers, and almost the entire frontier with Mongolia. These territories, formerly a part of the Chinese Empire, were annexed by Tsarist Russia during the nineteenth century; they now are claimed by Communist China. Many armed clashes have occurred along these disputed frontiers.

At the outset of the Russo-Chinese dispute, it appeared that ideological issues were more important than frontier lines. Years of revolutionary struggle in China had stimulated a new vision of human and social relations—a vision of an egalitarian Communist order in which the individual is motivated by the desire for social service rather than personal gain. Thus, although the Soviet-type Five-Year Plans were successful in furthering industrialization and raising productivity, Mao was unwilling to accept the increasing income differentiation and bureaucratic elitism on which these plans were based. This explains the Great Leap Forward of 1958 and the Cultural Revolution of 1966, with their slogans such as "organization without bureaucracy" and "serve the people." The Russians regarded this as utopian romanticism doomed to failure, which was one reason why they stopped their aid to China.

It is significant, however, that after Mao's death, his successors launched a "modernization" drive based on Soviet practices hitherto denounced as "revisionism." Examples of this basic shift within China are mass importation of industrial plants and technologies as against self-reliance; encouragement rather than discouragement of private family plots and rural fairs; "one-person management" in factories and universities as against collective administration by revolutionary committees; and more concern with scholastic aptitude and less with combining mental work with physical.

All this amounts to the revisionism practiced in the Soviet Union. It is not surprising, then, that Peking has ordered that the Soviet Union should not be criticized as being a revisionist society. Yet the disappearance of ideological issues between China and Russia has not led to a corresponding disappearance of political feuding between the two countries. In fact, post-Mao China has moved close to Japan and the United States and has called for a worldwide alliance against Soviet "hegemonism." Which suggests that conflicting national interests explain the Russo-Chinese feud more satisfactorily than do ideological issues.

SUGGESTED READING

D. F. Fleming, *The Cold War and Its Origins, 1917–1960,* 2 vols. (Doubleday, 1961); J. Freymond, *Western Europe Since the War* (Praeger, 1964); J. L. Gaddis, *The United States and the Origins of the Cold War* (Columbia University Press, 1973); J. Gittings, ed., *Survey of the Sino-Soviet Dispute* (Oxford University Press, 1969); H. R. Hunter, *Security in Europe* (Indiana University Press, 1973); G. F. Kennan, *Russia and the West* (Little, Brown, 1961); G. Kolko, *The Politics of War: The World and U.S. Foreign Policy 1943–1945* (Random House, 1969); W. LaFeber, *America, Russia and the Cold War* (John Wiley, 1968); R. Lowenthal, *World Communism: The Disintegration of a Secular Faith* (Oxford University Press, 1964).

The present international situation is one characterized by great disorder on the earth. . . . The US-Soviet contention for hegemony is the cause of world intranquility. It cannot be covered up by any false appearances they create, and is already perceived by an increasing number of people and countries. It has met with a strong resistance from the Third World. . . . The awakening and growth of the Third World is a major event in contemporary international relations.

Premier Chou En Lai, 1973

The Europeanization of Asia has produced the revolt of Asia against Europe.

Rene Grousset, 1941

chapter 39

Age Of "Great Disorder"

Premier Chou's above statement about "great disorder on the earth" is fully justified, as is proven daily by newspaper headlines and television broadcasts. Chou made this charge in 1973, yet by the end of the 1970s China was virtually allied to the United States. Within less than a decade, China had so shifted its position that it was blaming the Soviet Union for the global "disorder" and was clamoring for a worldwide alliance, including the United States, against "Soviet hegemonism." Chou's statement, therefore, is significant because it correctly notes the "disorder" of our age, and also because it unintentionally reflects that disorder through China's flip-flops, both in its domestic and foreign policies.

In this chapter we shall note in the first section the manifestations of disorder in today's fluctuating conflicts and alignments, and in the second section we shall trace the root cause of disorder to the simultaneous decline and triumph of the West.

I. GLOBAL CONFRONTATIONS

Before 1917 the peoples of the world had only one societal model—that of Western capitalism. After 1917 the Soviet Union provided a second model. With World War II a variety of new regimes emerged, while old ones developed along different lines. Thus capitalist societies today range in character from the United States to Sweden to Japan. Communist states span the ideological and geographic horizons from the Soviet Union, Vietnam and Cuba, to China, Albania and North Korea. Likewise the Third World encompasses states with historical traditions and ideological commitments varying from those of Mozambique, Mexico, and Oman to those of Nigeria, Brazil, and Pakistan.

Such are the heterogeneous and interacting historical forces that comprise the "great disorder" of our times. In addition to the centuries-old clash of the First World and the Third (North vs. South), there is the well-known post-World War II Cold War (West vs. East), and also the less conspicuous but increasingly ominous intrabloc conflicts (West vs. West, and East vs. East).

North Versus South

According to C. Fred Bergsten, former assistant secretary for internal affairs of the U.S. Treasury Department, the return on American investments in the Third World in 1976 was 25 percent, or more than twice the return on investments in developed countries. Thus the flow of dividends from the Third World to the United States in 1976 totaled $7 billion, whereas the flow of investments in the opposite direction amounted to only $2.8 billion. [1] This economic imbalance contributes to the growing gap between rich countries and poor, and to the corresponding conflict between the two sides.

Another reason for North-South conflict is the depletion of Third World resources by the First World. Before 1500, global trade was mostly in renewable luxuries such as spices, textiles, perfumes, and porcelain. Modern trade, by contrast, is largely in nonrenewable commodities such as minerals and oil, which flow from the Third World to the First. The level of consumption has risen so high that shortages of various commodities are becoming a serious problem. The depletion of Third World natural resources affects North-South relations in two ways.

One is that Third World countries will not be able to follow the Western model of economic development, for the simple reason that their resources will have already been used up by the wealthier countries. If all countries achieved American living standards and consumption levels, all known iron deposits would be exhausted in 40 years, copper deposits in 8 years, tin in 6 years, and petroleum in 5½ years.

The second result of the depletion of global resources is that the First World is becoming increasingly dependent on the Third. Japan and Western Europe import nearly all of their oil needs, while the United States, which was self-sufficient in oil in the 1960s, was by 1980 importing more oil than it was producing at home. American dependence on imported raw materials will increase from about 20 percent in 1970 to 30–50 percent by the year 2000. This growing dependence naturally concerns American policy makers. "The particular manner in which our economy has expanded," declared former Secretary of Defense Harold Brown in January 1980, "means that we have come to depend to no small degree on imports, exports and earnings from overseas investments for our material well-being. . . . A large-scale disruption in the supply of foreign oil could have as damaging consequences for the United States as the loss of an important military campaign, or indeed a war." Hence the formation of a Rapid Deployment Force which can be sent quickly to any part of the globe where American interests are endangered. And the danger can come as much from Third World instability as from Soviet expansionism. "International economic disorder," stated Brown, "could almost equal in severity the military threat from the Soviet Union." [2] Since the widening gap between rich countries and poor is likely to increase the frequency of Third World revolutions, the outlook is for a very busy Rapid Deployment Force in the coming decades.

West Versus West

The basic cause for the increasing tensions within the Western camp is the uneven rate of economic growth of its members. At the end of World War II the United States was by far the leading economic and military power of the world. But as noted in the preceding chapter, Japan and Western Europe overcame the American lead by the 1970s. Competition is increasing between the United States and its allies for foreign markets and raw materials. Current tensions within the Western camp are reminiscent of similar tensions amongst European states in 1914. Just as Britain then was being challenged by Germany, so the United States is challenged today by its competitive allies. And just as the British-German economic rivalry spilled over into armaments and diplomacy, so West vs. West conflicts today are becoming an important factor in international politics. With American trade unions demanding the exclusion of competing Japanese products, such as autos and television sets, the Japanese Prime Minister Ohira warned the U.S. Congress in the spring of 1979 that American protectionism could trigger a "catastrophic" chain reaction.

East Versus East

Conflict exists among Communist states as well as capitalist, and the root cause is the primacy of nationalism over Marxism, At one time Communists took seriously Marx's slogan, "Workers of the World Unite." But they became disillusioned after 1917 when the new Soviet government used the Communist parties to advance Soviet state interests rather than international communism. The issue came to a head when Brezhnev sought to justify his invasion of Czechoslovakia in August 1968 with the doctrine of "limited sovereignty." According to this thesis the Soviet Union can intervene in the internal affairs of another Socialist country whenever, in the Kremlin's judgment, it has strayed from the Socialist path. As noted in the preceding chapter, the Brezhnev doctrine has been challenged by various countries in Eastern Europe, and also by China.

The resulting feud between the Soviet Union and China has been most evident in Southeast Asia. After the American withdrawal in 1973, Peking feared Soviet domination in the region and therefore urged Washington to keep its forces there. The Vietnamese in turn believed the Chinese were trying to isolate them. Their suspicion was reinforced by the hostility of Washington, which opposed Vietnam's entry into the United Nations and enforced a trade embargo even after Hanoi had dropped its demand for war reparations. Vietnam therefore responded by signing on November 8, 1978, a treaty with the Soviet Union providing for increased Soviet economic aid and for mutual defense in case either was attacked.

The Soviet-Vietnam Treaty triggered a chain reaction of fast-moving events culminating in renewed warfare in Indochina. Peking ended all economic aid to Vietnam and stepped up its support for the Pol Pot regime in Cambodia, which launched border raids against Vietnam. The latter responded by invading Cambodia on December 25, 1978, with Vietnamese and Cambodian rebel troops, occupying the entire country. Whatever the provocation, Vietnam had done to a small Communist neighbor what the Soviet Union had done to Czechoslovakia. China's response was to invade Vietnam on

February 17, 1979, in order to ''teach a lesson'' to ''the Cuba of Southeast Asia.'' In the ensuing four-week war, China acknowledged 20,000 casualties and claimed to have inflicted 50,000 on Vietnam. The war was followed by futile peace negotiations, during which Peking threatened to ''teach a second lesson.'' A South Asian foreign minister has concluded from these events that, ''The big story of the past 30 years has been the East-West conflict, but the big story of the next 20 years is going to be the East-West conflict between China and Russia. That will affect everything from now on.''[3]

East Versus West

East-West relations have see-sawed from cooperation during World War II to Cold War after 1945, to detente during the Nixon-Kissinger years, to Cold War II under Carter-Brzezinski and Reagan-Haig. From Washington's viewpoint, detente was based on the assumption that the technological and economic backwardness of the Communist powers could be exploited by offering them trade treaties and corporate contracts. This ''bait,'' it was believed, would ''domesticate'' the Russians and the Chinese by integrating them into the global capitalist world order to the point where they would profit from it and therefore cooperate with it.

During the Carter administration, detente crumbled for various reasons. One was the opposition of increasingly powerful conservative circles in the United States. They regarded the Soviet Union as an aggressive imperialist power bent on world domination and as profiting from American weakness after Vietnam. These conservative elements paradoxically were encouraged by Peking, which sought to organize the already mentioned worldwide alliance against ''Soviet hegemonism.'' Detente also was undermined by Third World revolutionaries determined to destroy the global status quo on which detente was based. And when the Soviet Union gave aid to those revolutionaries, as it did in varying degrees in Angola, Mozambique, South Yemen, and Afghanistan, then the American response was the Rapid Deployment Force, the dropping of SALT II, and the boycott of the Moscow Olympic Games.

Yet the fact remains that revolutions in the Third World are the inevitable result of deteriorating local conditions. They would continue to erupt even if an impenetrable Chinese wall completely isolated all Third World countries. Thus a major contributor to global disorders, today and tomorrow, is that the unavoidable Third World revolutions are blown up into East-West confrontations. Some have been peacefully resolved in the past, and others will in the future. But the danger is that some eruption will get out of control and drag the world powers into World War III, just as Sarajevo dragged the European powers into World War I.

In conclusion, it is the simultaneous existence of Third World revolutions, of East-West rivalries, and of intra-West and intra-East discords that comprise the ''great disorder'' of our age.

II. DECLINE AND TRIUMPH OF THE WEST

If we view current global trends in the light of past world history, we can see that behind today's disorder is the decline and triumph of the West. Looking back over the five centuries covered by this book, certain stages in the evolution of global politics stand out clearly. Before 1500, the various regions of the world had coexisted in greater or lesser isolation. After Columbus and da Gama, this fragmentation began to give way to ever-increasing interaction and integration directed and exploited by Europe. By the nineteenth century, this trend had culminated in the unprecedented domination of the globe by a few European powers. The two world wars shattered this domination and replaced it with the bipolar predominance of Washington and Moscow. This lasted only two decades, before being replaced by the "great disorder" of our times—by the crisscrossing conflicts and alignments noted in the preceding section. The various regions of the world once more are becoming more independent, though by no means as much as in the pre-1500 period.

In one sense, this trend in current world affairs reflects the decline of Europe. London, Paris, and Berlin no longer dominate world news. No longer do they control world empires. Their armies and navies and alliance systems have ceased to dominate the globe. In 1860, for example, Western Europe was responsible for 72 percent of the world's total industrial output. By 1913 the percentage had dropped to 42; by the eve of World War II, to 30; and by 1960, to 25. It is self-evident that Europe's nineteenth-century global hegemony has ended, and ended forever. There is no possibility of Europe's regaining its colonial empires or reestablishing its former military and economic predominance.

Although Europe is suffering relative decline in its military, economic, and political power, its culture is sweeping the world as never before. Europe is entering a period of triumph as well as decline. Its ideas, techniques, and institutions are spreading throughout the globe more rapidly than at any time in the past. Fundamentally, this represents the diffusion of Europe's three great revolutions—the industrial, the scientific, and the political—which earlier had given it the power, the drive, and the knowledge to expand all over the world and to conquer the great colonial empires (see Chapters 22 and 23). But Europe's epochal success has boomeranged. The colonial empires, by their very existence, facilitated the diffusion of the three revolutions. The subject peoples, profoundly affected by these revolutions, reacted by selectively adopting some of their features in order better to resist the intruding West.

All countries today seek to have their own industrial revolutions in order to become economically developed and independent. Likewise all seek to master modern science because this is the key for advancing in technology and economic development. Finally Europe's political revolution also is sweeping the globe. People everywhere are becoming politically active; no longer are they accepting the old division of humanity into rulers and ruled. This political revolution is reflected each day in newspaper reports, as evident in the following headlines from *The New York Times:* [4]

GUEVARA STATUE UNVEILED IN WORKERS AREA IN CHILE (*Nov. 9, 1970*)
WORLD GYPSIES RESIST "GENOCIDE BY ASSIMILATION" (*June 18, 1971*)
LATVIANS PROTEST RUSSIFICATION (*Feb. 27, 1972*)
SHAH QUITS IRAN FOR INDEFINITE STAY (*Jan. 17, 1979*)
SOMOZA YIELDS POST: FLIES TO U.S. (*July 18, 1979*)
RHODESIA GUERRILLAS DOUBLE-TIME TO POLLS (*March 11, 1980*)
8,000 STUDENTS ROUTED BY TEAR GAS AT CAPE TOWN (*April 23, 1980*)
POLISH LABOR CRISIS: WORKERS LIST THEIR DEMANDS (*Aug. 18, 1980*)
BEIRUT STRIFE LEAVES 23 DEAD (*April 23, 1981*)

We may conclude that behind Europe's decline has been Europe's triumph. The one led naturally and inevitably to the other. If Europe has lost its place as the dominant force in the world, the basic reason has been the diffusion throughout the world of Europe's three great revolutions. Furthermore, this diffusion has continually been gaining in momentum, because for the first time it is affecting the masses of the people. ''It is true,'' stated President Nasser, ''that most of our people are still illiterate. But politically that counts far less than it did twenty years ago. . . . Radio had changed everything. . . . Today people in the most remote villages hear of what is happening everywhere and form their opinions. Leaders cannot govern as they once did. We live in a new world.''[5]

Nasser's ''new world'' is taking form all over the globe. It is the product of Western ideas and technology, and reflects both the triumph and the decline of the West.

SUGGESTED READING

I. Adelman and C. T. Morris, *Economic Growth and Social Equity in Developing Countries* (Stanford University Press, 1973); G. Barraclough, *An Introduction to Contemporary History* (Penguin, 1965); G. M. Foster, *Traditional Cultures and the Impact of Technological Change* (Harper & Row, 1963); M. Jansen, ed., *Changing Japanese Attitudes Towards Modernization* (Princeton University Press, 1964); D. Lerner, *The Passing of Traditional Society: Modernizing the Middle East* (Free Press, 1958); M. Mead, ed., *Cultural Patterns and Technical Change* (New American Library, 1955); L. S. S. O'Malley, *Modern India and the West: A Study of the Interaction of Their Civilizations* (Oxford University Press, 1941); F. Schurmann and O. Schell, *The China Reader,* Vol. 3, *Communist China* (Random House, 1967); H. Schiller, *Mass Communications and American Empire* (Beacon Press, 1971); L. S. Stavrianos, *Global Rift: The Third World Comes of Age* (Morrow, 1981).

What It Means
For Us Today

GOLDEN AGE OR DARK AGE?

"I am just as convinced as can be," states the geochemist Harrison Brown of the California Institute of Technology, "that man has it within his power today to create a world in which people the world over can lead free and abundant and even creative lives. . . . I am convinced that we can create a world which will pale the Golden Age of Pericles into nothingness."[1] On the other hand, the father of the atomic age, Albert Einstein, reached this dark conclusion: "The unleashed power of the atom has changed everything save our modes of thinking, and thus we drift to unparalleled catastrophe."[2] These opinions of two distinguished scientists point up the great paradox of our age. We are living in a time of unprecedented promise and also unprecedented perils.

The perils are obvious. They are broadcast daily on television, radio, and newspapers. One is race conflict, which has become a worldwide problem following the European overseas expansion. The expansion is responsible for the large degree of racial intermixture today in the Americas, and a lesser degree in Africa, Central Asia, and Siberia. Where there is intermixture, there is more likelihood of conflict than where there is little contact amongst the races. A good example is the case of England, where a considerable number of Indians, Pakistanis, and West Indians have immigrated since World War II. For the first time England is now experiencing serious outbreaks of racial violence.

573

It does not follow that racial intermixture leads inevitably to racial conflict. No part of the globe has more races living side by side than does Hawaii. Yet race relations there are relatively harmonious because racial discrimination is relatively minor. By contrast, in South Africa, where apartheid represents racial discrimination carried to the extreme, the entire country is a smoldering volcano.

Another major problem of our age is the widening gap between rich countries and poor. Many conferences have been held on this problem, yet the gap continues to grow. In October 1979 President Carter appointed a Commission on World Hunger, which concluded that, "The most potentially explosive force in the world today is the frustrated desire of poor people to attain a decent standard of living. The anger, despair and often hatred that result represent real and persistent threats to international order." The commission recommended "an authentic sharing of economic and political power among and within all nations." This recommendation has been made many times by many organizations, but with no significant result.

A final problem of our times is runaway science. On the night of July 9, 1962, on Johnston Island in the mid-Pacific, the United States detonated a hydrogen bomb with the explosive force of 2 million tons of TNT. The entire heavens lighted up and remained bright for fifteen minutes in a dazzling kaleidoscope of interweaving reds, purples, yellow-oranges, and whites. Natives on American Samoa, 2000 miles away, rushed panic-stricken into their homes or into churches to pray. When informed of the source of the terrifying celestial display, they commented, "Crazy white man."

Science admittedly is one of the great achievements of the human mind. But has it now become an uncontrollable menace? What about environmental pollution, depletion of natural resources, population explosion, and manipulation of the DNA molecule? The human species was the first to reverse the evolutionary process. Instead of adapting its genes to environment through natural selection, it changed environment to suit its genes. But today humans are able to change their own genes, and even to create new forms of life. Our generation marks the time when three billion years of evolution by natural selection are giving way to evolution by human selection. Are we opening a new Pandora's box, even more perilous than that which terrified Einstein?

And yet, for everyone of these problems there is also a promise. The distinguished historian, Arnold Toynbee, stated:

"Our age will be remembered chiefly neither for its horrifying crimes nor for its astonishing inventions, but for its having been the first age since the dawn of civilization, some five or six thousand years back, in which people dared to think it practicable to make the benefits of civilization available for the whole human race."[3]

The potentiality to which Toynbee refers has not been realized. But the important point is that it does exist, and for the first time in human history. Famine, disease and ignorance have been the scourges of the human race since its very beginning. Only today is the knowledge available to eliminate these scourges. Atomic power can destroy humanity, but it can also transform living conditions throughout the world. Rockets can be used for intercontinental warfare but also for transporting humans around the globe and to other planets. Heredity control raises frightening questions but also exciting possibilities. More specifically, scientists now look forward to the following achievements within the next few decades:

Self-guiding automobiles and atomic trains
Motor energy transmitted to airplanes via radio
Weather dams across the arctic seas to change world climate
Shallow seas turned into marine farms
Robot mining vehicles exploring deep under the earth's crust
Desalination process producing fresh water at competitive price
Nuclear fusion producing unlimited power
Far-reaching space exploration following the moon landing

We may conclude that this is an age of great problems and great opportunities—of great peril and great potential. This is not a cozy or soothing predicament. It is uncomfortable and unsettling. But this has been the case with all the great ages of the past. And inevitably so, for great ages, by definition, are ages of transition. They are times of rapid change, when old values and institutions are reluctantly cast aside and new ones gradually and painfully evolved. All the golden ages of the past were ages of tension and apprehension. This was true of Periclean Athens, of Renaissance Italy, and of Elizabethan England.

It is true also of our times, though with two important differences. One is that today's changes affect not merely a small island like England, or a small peninsula like Greece or Italy. Rather they affect the entire globe, and all of its inhabitants. The second difference is that both the promise and the perils are infinitely greater today than at any time in the past. Never before have humans perceived such a dazzling horizon opening before them. But also never before have humans known that behind that horizon lurks the mushroom cloud.

SUGGESTED READING

Like all ages of transition, this one also has stimulated a vast body of literature on the prospects for the human race. The following works in various disciplines range across the spectrum, from bright rainbows to dark clouds:

Sociology: Barrington Moore, Jr., *Reflections on the Causes of Human Misery* (Beacon Press, 1970); and D. Bell, *The Coming of Post-Industrial Society* (Basic Books, 1976).

Economics: R. L. Heilbroner, *An Inquiry into the Human Prospect* (Norton, 1974); and H. Henderson, *Creating Alternative Futures* (Berkeley Publishing Corporation, 1978).

History: A. J. Toynbee, *Change and Habit: The Challenge of Our Time* (Oxford University Press, 1966); and L. S. Stavrianos, *The Promise of the Coming Dark Age* (W. H. Freeman, 1976).

International Relations: R. Barnet, *The Lean Years: The Politics of the Age of Scarcity* (Simon & Schuster, 1980); and F. M. Lappé and J. Collins, *Food First: Beyond the Myth of Scarcity* (Houghton Mifflin, 1977).

Physical Science: J. Bronowski, *The Ascent of Man* (Little, Brown, 1973); and A. C. Clarke, *Profiles of the Future: An Inquiry into the Limits of the Possible* (Harper & Row, 1973).

Notes

WHAT IT MEANS FOR US TODAY

1. Albert Bandura, *Aggression: A Social Learning Analysis,* © 1973, pp. 113, 132. Reprinted by permission of Prentice-Hall, Inc., Englewood Cliffs, N.J.

CHAPTER 3

1. R. Linton, *The Study of Man* (Appleton-Century-Crofts, 1936), p. 353.

CHAPTER 5

1. Cited by F. M. Cornford, *Greek Religious Thought.* . . . (Dent, 1923), p. 85.
2. Cited by C. J. Sinter, *A History of Biology* (Schuman, 1950), p. 4.
3. Herodotus, *The Persian Wars* (trans., G. Rawlinson), Book VII, chap. 104.
4. Thucydides, *The Peloponnesian War* (trans., B. Jowett), Book I, chap. 22.
5. Cicero, *First Part of the Speech Against Gaius Verres at the First Hearing* (New York, 1928), chap. V.
6. A. Piganiol, *L'Empire Chrétien* (Presses Universitaires de France, 1947), p. 422.
7. From *The Birth of Europe* by Robert S. Lopez. Copyright © 1962 by Max Leclerc et Cie, Proprietors of Librairie Armand Colin. Copyright © 1966 translation by J. M. Dent & Sons Ltd. Reprinted by permission of the publisher, M. Evans and Company, Inc., New York, N.Y. 10017.

8. *Life of Marcellus,* from *Plutarch's Lives,* Vol. 3, trans. J. and W. Langhorne (London, 1821), pp. 119ff.

9. J. Levy, *The Economic Life of the Ancient World,* ed., J. G. Birain (University of Chicago Press, 1967), p. 99.

CHAPTER 8

1. J. M. Keynes, *Essays in Persuasion* (Harcourt, 1932), pp. 360–61.

2. A. H. M. Jones, "The Decline and Fall of the Roman Empire," *History,* XL (October, 1955), 220.

3. Cited by F. Klemm, *A History of Western Technology* (London: George Allen & Unwin, 1959), p. 23.

4. W. W. Rostow, *The Process of Economic Growth,* 2nd ed. (Belmont, Calif.: Wadsworth Publishing Co., 1962), pp. 311–12.

5. Cited by M. Hadas, *A History of Rome* (Doubleday, 1956), pp. 204–5.

6. From *The Birth of Europe* by Robert S. Lopez. Copyright © 1962 by Max Leclerc et Cie, Proprietors of Librairie Armand Colin. Copyright © 1066 translation by. J. M. Dent & Sons Ltd. Reprinted by permission of the publisher, M. Evans and Company, Inc., New York, N.Y. 10017.

WHAT IT MEANS FOR US TODAY

1. Adapted from J. Hawkes and L. Wooley, *Prehistory and the Beginnings of Civilization,* UNESCO History of Mankind, Vol. I (Harper & Row, 1936), p. 467; and V. Gordon Childe, *Man Makes Himself* (New American Library, 1951), p. 149.

2. E. R. Service, *The Hunters* (Prentice-Hall, 1966), p. 69.

CHAPTER 9

1. H. Yule, ed., *Cathay and the Way Thither,* Hakluyt Society, Series 2, XXXVII (London, 1914), pp. 152, 154.

2. Cited by J. Needham, *Science and Civilization in China* (London: Cambridge University Press, 1954), I, p. 219.

CHAPTER 10

1. Cited by A. Mieli, *La science arabe* (Brill, 1939), p. 376.

CHAPTER 11

1. Ibn Khaldun, *The Muqaddimah: An Introduction To History,* Trans. from the Arabic by Franz Rosenthal, Bollingen Series XLIII. Copyright © 1958 and 1967 by Princeton University Press. Excerpts reprinted by permission of Princeton University Press.

CHAPTER 12

1. Cited by S. Vryonis, Jr., *Byzantium and Europe* (Harcourt Brace Jovanovich, 1967), pp. 190–92.

CHAPTER 13

1. Cited by H. Yule, ed., *Cathay and the Way Thither,* Hakluyt Society, Series 2, XXXVII (London, 1914), p. 154.

2. Cited by L. C. Goodrich, *A Short History of the Chinese People* (Harper & Row, 1943), p. 200.

CHAPTER 14

1. Francis Bacon, *Novum organum,* Book I, Aphorism 129.
2. From *The Birth of Europe* by Robert Lopez. Copyright © 1962 by Max Leclerc et Cie, Proprietors of Librairie Armand Colin. Copyright © 1966 translation by J. M. Dent & Sons Ltd. Reprinted by permission of the publisher, M. Evans and Company, Inc., New York, N.Y. 10017.
3. Cited by L. White, "Dynamo and Virgin Reconsidered," *American Scholar* (1958), p. 192. Used with author's permission.

CHAPTER 15

1. J. H. Parry, *The Age of Reconnaissance* (Weidenfeld & Nicolson, 1963), p. 36.
2. Cited in manuscript by L. V. Thomas, *Ottoman Awareness of Europe, 1650–1800.*

CHAPTER 16

1. Cited by C. M. Cipolla, *European Culture and Overseas Expansion* (Pelican, 1970), p. 105.
2. Ibn Battuta, *Travels in Asia and Africa, 1325–1354,* trans. H. A. R. Gibb (Routledge, 1929), pp. 329–30.
3. Cited by T. Hodgkin, "Kingdoms of the Western Sudan," in *The Dawn of African History,* ed. R. Oliver (Oxford University Press, 1961), p. 43.
4. Basil Davidson, *Africa in History,* Revised Edition (New York: Macmillan, 1974).
5. T. Hodgkin, "Islam in West Africa," *Africa South,* II (April–June, 1958), p. 98.
6. Basil Davidson, op. cit., p. 125.
7. Cited by D. O. Dike, *Trade and Politics in the Niger Delta, 1830–1885* (Oxford University Press, 1956), p. 7.
8. Adam Smith, *Wealth of Nations* (Edinburgh, 1838), p. 286.

CHAPTER 17

1. R. M. Adams, "Early Civilizations, Subsistence and Environment," in *City Invincible,* ed. R. M. Adams and C. H. Kraeling (University of Chicago Press, 1960), p. 270.
2. Cited by A. G. Price, *White Settlers and Native Peoples* (Melbourne University, 1949), p. 121.

WHAT IT MEANS FOR US TODAY

1. Cited by UNESCO, *What is Race?* (Paris, 1952), pp. 85, 86.
2. F. Boas, "Racial Purity," *Asia,* XL (May, 1940), p. 231.
3. Cited by R. Benedict, *Race: Science and Politics,* rev. ed. (Viking Press, 1943), p. 7.
4. Ibid., p. 8.

CHAPTER 18

1. Cited by K. M. Panikkar, *Asia and Western Dominance* (Day, 1953), p. 42.
2. Cited by *The New Cambridge Economic History,* I (Cambridge University Press, 1957), p. 454.

CHAPTER 19

1. J. M. Keynes, *A Treatise on Money* (Harcourt, 1930), II, p. 159.

CHAPTER 20

1. R. J. Kerner, *The Urge to the Sea* (University of California Press, 1942), p. 86.
2. Cited by G. V. Lantzeff, *Siberia in the Seventeenth Century* (University of California Press, 1940), p. 105.

CHAPTER 21

1. Cited by F. Whyte, *China and Foreign Powers* (Oxford University Press, 1927), p. 38.
2. Cited by A. C. Wood, *A History of the Levant Company* (Oxford University Press, 1935), p. 230.
3. Cited by L. S. S. O'Malley, ed., *Modern India and the West* (Oxford University Press, 1941), p. 51.
4. H. Blount, "A Voyage into the Levant," in J. Pinkerton (ed.) *A General Collection of the Best and Most Interesting Voyages. . . . ,* X (London: 1808-1814), p. 222.
5. Cited by D. Lach, "Leibniz and China," *Journal of the History of Ideas,* VI (October, 1945), p. 440.
6. Cited by A. Reichwein, *China and Europe: Intellectual and Artistic Contacts in the Eighteenth Century* (Knopf, 1925), p. 152.
7. Cited by O'Malley, op. cit., p. 546.
8. Cited by Reichwein, op. cit., p. 151.

WHAT IT MEANS FOR US TODAY

1. *The New York Times,* November 30, 1979. © 1979 by The New York Times Company. Reprinted by permission.
2. Ibid., January 9, 1980. © 1980 by The New York Times Company. Reprinted by permission.
3. Ibid., February 4, 1980. © 1980 by The New York Times Company. Reprinted by permission.

PART VI

1. E. J. Hamilton, "American Treasure and the Rise of Capitalism (1500-1700)," *Economica* (November, 1929), p. 356.
2. Cited by C. E. Robinson, "The English Philosophes and the French Revolution." *History Today,* VI (February, 1956), p. 121.

CHAPTER 22

1. T. Sprat, *The History of the Royal Society of London, for the Improving of General Knowledge* (London, 1734), p. 72.
2. *Siderius nuncius,* trans. E. D. Carlos (1880). Cited by M. Nicolson, *Science and Imagination* (Cornell University Press, 1956), p. 15.
3. Charles Darwin, *Origin of Species,* Vol. 1 (New York, 1872), p. 3.
4. H. Butterfield, *The Origins of Modern Science, 1300-1800* (London: G. Bell & Sons, Ltd. 1957), p. 179, by permission of Bell & Hyman.)
5. Cited by L. Huberman, *We, the People,* rev. ed. (Harper, 1947), p. 218.
6. Ibid., p. 263.
7. W. L. Langer, *Diplomacy of Imperialism 1890-1902,* 2nd ed. (Knopf, 1935), p. 67.
8. P. Deane, *Colonial Social Accounting* (Cambridge University Press, 1953), p. 37.

CHAPTER 23

1. Cited by G. Wint, *The British in Asia* (Institute of Pacific Relations, 1954), p. 18.
2. Sir Edwin Sandys, in a speech in Parliament. Cited by H. J. Laski, *The Rise of Liberalism* (Harper, 1936), p. 117.

3. P. Zagorin, "The English Revolution, 1640–1660," *Journal of World History,* II (1955), p. 903.

4. A. S. P. Woodhouse, *Puritanism and Liberty* (Dent, 1938), p. 55.

5. T. Kolokotrones and E. M. Edmonds, *Kolokotrones, Klepht and Warrior* (London, 1892), pp. 127–28.

6. B. C. Shafer, *Nationalism, Myth and Reality* (Harcourt, 1955), p. 105.

7. Cited by D. W. Morris, *The Christian Origins of Social Revolt* (Allen, 1949), p. 34.

8. K. Marx and F. Engles, *Communist Manifesto* (League for Industrial Democracy, 1933), p. 59.

IMPACT OF DOMINANCE

1. H. S. Maine, *Village-Communities in the East and West* (Henry Holt, 1880), pp. 237–38.

CHAPTER 24

1. Cited by B. Pares, *A History of Russia* (Knopf, 1953), p. 117.

2. Cited by F. Nowak, *Medieval Slavdom and the Rise of Russia* (Holt, 1930), p. 91.

CHAPTER 25

1. C. Photios, *Apomnemoneumata peri tes Hellenikes Epanastaseos* [*Memoirs on the Greek Revolution*], Vol. I (Athens, 1899), p. 1.

CHAPTER 26

1. Cited by K. Goshal, *The People of India* (Sheridan, 1944), p. 129.

2. Cited in A. B. Keith, ed., *Speeches and Documents on Indian Policy, 1750–1921* (Oxford University Press, 1922), I, p. 209.

3. Cited by E. Stokes, "The First Century of British Colonial Rule in India: Social Revolution or Social Stagnation," *Past & Present,* (February, 1973), p. 153.

4. Cited by W. T. deBary, et al., *Sources of Indian Tradition* (Columbia University Press, 1958), p. 601.

5. D. Naoroji, *Speeches and Writings* (Madras, Natesan, N. D.), p. 2.

CHAPTER 27

1. S. Teng and J. K. Fairbank, *China's Response to the West: A Documentary Survey, 1839–1923* (Harvard University, 1954), p. 28. Reprinted by permission of the publishers. Copyright 1954 by the President and Fellows of Harvard College.

2. Cited by J. R. Levenson, *Confucian China and Its Modern Fate* (University of California Press, 1958), p. 105.

3. Cited by J. K. Fairbank, "China's Response to the West. Problems and Suggestions," *Journal of World History,* III (1956), p. 403.

4. Cited by J. K. Fairbank, *The United States and China* (Harvard University Press, 1958), p. 150.

CHAPTER 28

1. Cited by H. Russell, *Human Cargoes* (Longmans, 1948), p. 36.

CHAPTER 29

1. *The Education of Henry Adams: An Autobiography* (Constable, 1919), p. 319–20.
2. H. C. Lodge, *Studies of History* (Boston, 1884), p. 352.

CHAPTER 30

1. Surendranath Banerjea, cited in L. S. S. O'Malley, *Modern India and the West* (Oxford University Press, 1941), p. 766.
2. From ''The White Man's Burden,'' in *Rudyard Kipling's Verse. Definitive Edition* (New York: Doubleday).
3. W. T. Stead, *The Last Will and Testament of Cecil John Rhodes* (London, 1902), p. 190.
4. E. G. Browne, *The Persian Revolution of 1905-1909* (Cambridge University Press, 1910), pp. 120–23.

WHAT IT MEANS FOR US TODAY

1. *The New York Times,* June 30, 1975. © 1975 by The New York Times Company. Reprinted by permission.

CHAPTER 31

1. Cited by R. S. Baker, *Woodrow Wilson and World Settlement,* Vol. III (Doubleday, 1922), p. 451.
2. C. Seymour, ed., *The Intimate Papers of Colonel House,* Vol. IV (Houghton, 1928), p. 389.
3. Cited by K. M. Panikkar, *Asia and Western Dominance* (Day, 1953), p. 36.
4. Cited by R. Emerson and M. Kilson, ''The American Dilemma in a Changing World: The Rise of Africa and Negro American,'' *Daedalus,* Vol. 94 (Fall, 1965), p. 1057. Reprinted by permission of *Daedalus,* Journal of the American Academy of Arts and Science, Volume 94, 1965, Boston, MA.

CHAPTER 34

1. H. E. Salisbury, *The New York Times,* September 29, 1953. © 1953 by The New York Times Company. Reprinted by permission.
2. *London Times,* February 4, 1932.

CHAPTER 35

1. A. Eden, *Facing the Dictators* (Houghton, 1962), p. 636.
2. Winston S. Churchill, *The Second World War: The Gathering Storm* (Houghton, 1948), p. 376.
3. *The New York Times,* August 27, 1939.

CHAPTER 36

1. *Ciano's Diary, 1939-1943,* ed., Malcolm Muggeridge (Heinemann, 1947), p. 297.

CHAPTER 37

1. *The New York Times,* June 4, 1980. © 1980 by The New York Times Company. Reprinted by permission.
2. *Wall Street Journal,* July 27, 1979.

CHAPTER 38

1. Cited by M. Kaldor, *The Disintegrating West* (Allen Lane, 1978), p. 151.
2. *Los Angeles Times,* December 2, 1978.

CHAPTER 39

1. From letter by C. Fred Bergsten to *The New York Times,* January 12, 1977.
2. Mimeographed text released January 28, 1980.
3. Statement made to Dan Oberdorfer of *The Washington Post.* Published in *Los Angeles Times,* April 18, 1979.
4. © 1970, 1971, 1972, 1979, 1980, 1981 The New York Times Company. Reprinted by permission.
5. Cited by D. Lerner, *The Passing of Traditional Society: Modernizing the Middle East* (Free Press, 1958), p. 214.

WHAT IT MEANS FOR US TODAY

1. CBS Program, ''The 21st Century,'' May 21, 1967.
2. *The New York Times,* May 25, 1942.
3. A. J. Toynbee, ''Not the Age of Atoms but of Welfare for All,'' *New York Times Magazine,* October 21, 1951, p. 15. © 1951 The New York Times Company. Reprinted by permission.

Glossary

agriculture cultivating the soil, producing crops and sometimes raising livestock

ahimsa nonviolence, a concept of India

alienation estrangement or withdrawal where good relationships formerly existed

anarchy lawlessness or disorder due to lack of governmental authority

apartheid South African policy that excludes all non-whites from any share in political life and confines Africans to separate areas known as Bantustands (preserves for the Bantu Africans)

audiencas courts into which the huge viceroyalties of New Spain were divided

autarchic unit self-sufficient, independent economic unit

benevolent despots rulers such as Frederick the Great of Prussia (1740–1781), Catherine the Great of Russia (1762–1796), Joseph II of the Hapsburg Empire (1765–1790) who used their governmental authority for the benefit of the people

blitzkrieg new type of "lightning war" used by the Germans in World War II; first came dive bombers, then armored tank divisions called Panzers, and finally the lighter motorized divisions and infantry

Bolsheviks literally "majority" in Russian; Lenin's followers

bourgeoisie the middle class, e.g., merchants, industrialists, professionals, etc.

Brahmins one of the highest Hindu castes; theoretically their occupation was that of priest or teacher; see caste

Buddhism a movement which was begun by Guatama Buddha in India in the 5th century B.C., and which became a full-fledged religion that spread throughtout Asia

bureaucracy a body of non-elected workers in any unit of government; China developed a complex bureaucracy very early

burghers middle class townspeople

capitalism a system in which the desire for profits is the driving motive and capital is accumulated and used to make profits in a variety of ways

caste one of many hereditary groups in India that were originally based on color and occupation; there are four broad divisions with thousands of sub-divisions; despite efforts to abolish caste differences, they still exist in rural India

city-state independent cities that were leaders of a particular region

civilization a stage of development in which people have achieved all or most of the following: writing, arts and sciences, cities, formal political organization, social classes, taxation

class differentiation the development from a homogeneous to heterogeneous society in which there is an increasing gap between rich and poor classes of people; opposite of egalitarian society

Cold War name given to the series of crises after World War II that resulted from bad relations between the Communist and Western worlds

colonization establishment of settlements that are ruled by foreign countries

commercial agriculture agriculture in which most of the crops produced are sold for money rather than consumed by the family

commercial bonds ties based on the interchange of material goods; trade

Common Market an economic association with six original members: Italy, West Germany, Belgium, Netherlands, Luxembourg and France; then in 1973 Britain, Ireland and Denmark joined

Confucianism the name given to the teachings of Confucius and his followers; mainly a practical moral system concerned with problems of everyday life and emphasizing conformity, propriety, and social responsibility

conquistadors New World soldiers of fortune from Spain; Cortes, conqueror of the Aztec Empire, is one of the best known

Cossacks Russian frontiersmen, mostly former serfs, who fled to the wild steppe country and became hunters, fishermen, and pastoralists

culture the way of life of a society; the ideas, habits, arts and institutions which are passed on from generation to generation

cuneiform pictograph writings of ancient Mesopotamia; such writing is based not on the letters of an

NOTE: Glossary terms appear in italics in text.

583

alphabet but on symbols which represent words or ideas; see ideographic script

Cynicism   Greek doctrine which held that virtue is the only good; everything else—riches, honor, freedom, even life itself—is contemptible

daimyo   local lords in 16th century Japan who fought each other to extend their domains

democratic centralism   principle adopted by Lenin for the operation of the Social Democratic Party; major issues were discussed freely, and decision reached by democratic vote; once a vote was taken every party member had to support the "party line" or be expelled

democratic liberalism   doctrine that holds that the state is responsible for all its citizens; reforms of democratic liberalism were the prelude to the welfare state

demographic patterns   patterns of human population

dharma   a Hindu and Buddhist term that means morality, obligations to family and society and religious law

dialectics   a science evolved by Socrates in which provisional definitions were tested by questions until universally recognized absolute truths were reached

Duma   Russian elective national assembly created after the Russian Revolution of 1905 and swept away by the Bolshevik Revolution of 1917

dyarchy   dual system of government, as in Japan, where one family did the actual work of ruling while the emperor lived in luxurious seclusion and was responsible only for ensuring that his dynasty would continue forever

dynasty   a succession of rulers of the same family

Economic and Social Council   United Nations council whose task was fighting hunger and disease; set-up such agencies as the ILO, Food and Agriculture Organization, UN Educational, Scientific and Cultural Organization, World Health Organization, and International Monetary Fund

egalitarian society   a society with the least possible inequalities—social, economic or political—amongst its people

empire   a large area, usually including several countries or peoples, all under a single political authority

enclosures   land closed off in England in the 15th to 19th centuries; left yeomen without grazing land or land for woodcutting; between 1715 and 1820 over 6 million acres were enclosed

enlightened despots   see Enlightenment and benevolent despots

Enlightenment   movement dating from the century prior to the French Revolution of 1789; leaders believed they lived in an enlightened age of reason and progress in contrast to the previous times of superstition and ignorance

Epicureanism   Greek doctrine that defined philosophy as the art of making life happy, with pleasure (defined as serenity and avoidance of pain rather than indulgence) as the highest and only good

equal-field system   during the Sun and T'ang dynasties in China, the central government gave plots of about 19 acres each to all abled-bodied peasants; in practice, only free peasants and not even all of these, were given land

ethnic group   a group that retains its own national characteristics, language, religion, customs and institutions

ethnocentrism   regarding one's own cultural group as superior and scorning all things alien

Europeanization   term used to include political domination and cultural penetration by Europe as well as actual biological replacement of one people by another; as in the relatively empty territories of the Western Hemisphere and South Pacific that were inundated by European emigrants

extended family   two or more married couples and their children

extraterritoriality   right of foreigners to be exempt from the laws of a nation in which they are living, e.g., most ambassadors and diplomats are not subject to the laws of the nation in which they live but only to the laws of their own country

feudalism   a political system that flourished in Europe from about the 9th to the 15th century; a lord gave land to vassals who, in return, gave him military service

fiefs   feudal estates granted by kings or lords as reward for military service; see feudalism

fluyt   flyboat; a large, cheap Dutch merchant ship that was unarmed and had great capacity for carrying goods

food gatherer   a person who collects foods, e.g., picks fruits, nuts and plants, digs up roots and shellfish, catches fish

food producer   a peasant or farmer who grows food instead of gathering it

Gosplan   Soviet State Planning Commission that prepared plans on the basis of general directions from the government and statistical data received from all parts of the country

Gross National Product (GNP)   total output of goods and services of a country

habitat   one's physical environment where one normally lives and grows up

Hellenism Greek culture which spread through the Middle East with the conquests of Alexander the Great

helot member of the lowest social class of ancient Sparta

hierarchy organization into a series of orders or ranks with each one subordinate to the one above it

high culture ''upper class'' culture found in schools, temples and palaces of the cities and passed on by philosophers, theologians and literary men

hidalgo Spanish aristocrat who had most of the territorial wealth, was exempt from taxes, and looked down upon people engaged in commerce and industry

Hinduism major religion of India

hominids human-like ancestors of modern human beings who had a smaller brain that was less developed than that of humans

Homo sapiens ''thinking'' humans; includes all members of the human race

ideographic script writing in which symbols represent ideas or objects; found in early China, Mesopotamia and Egypt

imperialism the rule or control, political or economic, direct or indirect, of one state, nation or people over similar groups; see also new imperialism

incipient agriculture the long gradual phase during which people made the shift from partial to full dependence on agriculture

Islam the religion of the Muslims based on the monotheistic teachings of the prophet Mohammed; also a political system and a social code

janissaries Ottoman infantrymen

jus gentium ''law of the peoples''; a new body of law accepted by the Romans and applied to all peoples

jus naturale Roman legal concept that held that natural law was above that of mere custom

Koran bible of the Islamic faith; provided guidance for all phases of life, manners, hygiene, marriage, divorce, commerce and politics, crime and punishment, peace and war

kulaks well-to-do Russian peasants who were hostile to the Soviet regime; finally eliminated when agriculture was collectivized

Kuomintang Chinese National People's Party founded by Sun Yat-sen

lactation taboo birth control practice which forbade sexual intercourse while a woman was nursing a baby

latifundia large plantations that grew up in Italy in the 2nd century B.C.; worked by slaves and owned by absentee landlords

Law of Retarding Lead the best adapted and most successful societies have the most difficulty in adapting during a period of transition and change

League of Nations created by the Versailles Treaty; its two basic objectives were: 1) to preserve the peace, and 2) to concern itself with health, social, economic, and humanitarian problems of international scope; failed in its first objective but succeeded in its second

Legalists adherents of a Chinese doctrine very different from Confucianism or Taoism; practicing statesmen interested in strengthening the princes they served so that they could wage war and unite the country by force; all aspects of life were regulated in detail by laws that would promote the state's economic and military power

Levellers group drawn mainly from the English lower middle class agricultural tenants who favored a democratic government and social reform

low culture ''lower class'' culture found in the villages and passed on by word of mouth among illiterate peasants

mandates people of the colonies taken from the Central Powers after World War I were regarded as unable to stand on their own feet; their tutelage was entrusted to ''advanced nations'' who were to exercise their tutelage on behalf of the League of Nations; this tutelage was not extended to the colonies of the victorious allies

manor a self-sufficient village worked by feudal serfs who had certain rights and responsibilities but were not free to move away

Mau Mau secret East African terrorist organization made up of members of the Kikuyu tribe

Mawali non-Arab Moslems

Mensheviks literally ''minority'' in Russian; Lenin's opponents within the Russian Social Democratic Party

mercantile activities see commercial bonds

mercantilism early modern rigid regulation of economic life in contrast to no regulation of ''laissez faire'' policy

millennium one thousand year period

monoculture cultivation of a single crop

nationalism allegiance to the cause of the nation rather than to the church and region as before the 19th century

natural geopolitical center a natural central area whose location and physical features gave it regional leadership

natural selection an important part of the process of evolution; in the struggle for existence, the organisms whose genes are best adapted to the environment are selected and will survive and reproduce; the less well-adapted will die out

Neo-Confucianism a combination of Buddhism and Taoism with Confucianism; believe man is good and capable of becoming more perfect and evil is the result of neglect and defective education and can be corrected

New Economic Policy (NEP) plan adopted by the Soviet government in 1921 that made some concessions, e.g., that peasants were allowed to sell their produce on the open market, private individuals could operate small stores and factories and keep the profits

new imperialism the great European expansion of the late 19th century; differed from the old imperialist control of a state over another because it did not simply demand tribute but completely transformed the conquered countries

Nirvana the goal of Buddhism which is to end sorrow by stopping desire; done by following the ''eight-fold path''

North Atlantic Treaty Organization (NATO) a mutual defense organization consisting of the United States, Canada, and several western European countries who agreed that ''an attack on one or more of the signers is an attack upon all''

nuclear family married couple and their children

oligarchy government controlled by a small group

Orthodox Christianity Greek Christian religion which rejected leadership of the Pope and instead was under the Patriach of Constantinople

ostrogs fortified posts or blockhouses built by the Cossacks as they advanced eastward

Palestine Liberation Organization (PLO) an organization consisting of several Palestinian nationalist groups; all are opposed to Israel, but disagree as to how an independent Palestinian state should be created

Panchayat elected council of five or more, usually caste leaders and village elders, who governed the traditional Indian village

pastoral nomads people who make a living by domesticating animals and herding them from place to place in search of pastures

Pax Mongolica literally ''Mongol Peace''; during the short period of Mongol peace, overland trade flourished from the Baltic to the Pacific because the Mongols ruled the entire area and kept the peace

Pax Romana literally ''Roman Peace''; period brought about by Augustus and lasting for two centuries

philosophes a group who believed in the existence of natural laws that regulated the universe and human society

philosophical systems systems of ideas, beliefs and attitudes

pictographs early cuneiform writing consisting of conventionalized pictures representing objects

plebians common people

Pleistocene epoch a period of glacial and interglacial stages during which animals adapted to changing environmental conditions

polis see city-state

productivity the conversion of resources into goods and services needed by humans; increased by using better seeds and tools, moving to better land, improving economic organization, etc.

proletariat the working class in industrial societies, e.g., workers in factories, mines or the docks, etc.

Quisling a Norwegian who collaborated with Hitler and whose name became a synonym for the self-seeking traitor

rationalism a way of thinking based on logical thought and reason rather than on myths or traditional religion

Reformation basic upheaval that shattered the unity of Western Christendom; Martin Luther triggered the Protestant Reformation when he reacted against abuses in the Roman church

religious sanctions rewards and punishments to enforce rules of the religious elite

Renaissance literally ''new birth'' or ''revival''; an intellectual and cultural awakening that took place in Europe during the 15th to 17th centuries

Revisionism a movement among 20th-century socialists to adopt a ''revised'' strategy that depends on gradual reform instead of revolution to bring about a socialist society

sans culottes literally ''those who lacked the knee breeches of genteel society''; French revolutionists who wanted a more egalitarian state with equitable division of land, government regulation of prices and wages, and a social security system

savannas tropical or subtropical grasslands; treeless plains

scholasticism a philosophy that taught that seeking God was more important than understanding nature, theology was the queen of the sciences and one should turn to religion for succor and consolation in the face of material disaster

secular states states controlled by non-religious leaders (laymen), as opposed to states controlled by religious leaders

self-determination the principle that all peoples should have the right to self rule

shamans medicine men or sorcerers; individuals

in early cultures who were part-time specialists and who used magical arts for the common good

sheikhs Arabian elective tribal chiefs who were leaders in the time of war

Skepticism Greek doctrine that challenged the supremacy of reason and rationalism and adopted a questioning attitude

social homogeneity social equality that was a distinctive feature of Neolithic villages; all people shared equally in the ownership of land and other natural resources; see also egalitarian society

socialism ideology calling for social and economic change and political reform; the government owns and operates the means of production and the main parts of the economy, e.g., banks, mines, factories, railroads, foreign trade, etc.; emphasizes community and collective welfare rather than the individual

soviets workers' elected councils that originated in the Russian Revolution of 1905 and reappeared in the 1917 Revolution; soviets supplied the government with close rapport with the masses

steppe open, treeless plains with fertile black earth

stimulus diffusion a process that occurs when two different peoples first come in contact whereby they don't adopt one another's specific techniques or institutions completely but instead borrow underlying ideas or principles and adapt them to their specific needs; early civilizations often developed by this means

Stoicism Greek doctrine that accepted virtue as the highest good in life; people must put aside passion, unjust thoughts and self-indulgence and perform their duties rationally and selflessly

strategos generals in charge of both civil and military affairs in the Byzantine themes

subsistence security multiple crop agriculture providing a dependable food supply; if one crop failed peasants could depend on other crops for subsistence

taiga forest belt or zone

Taoism Chinese doctrine that stressed the importance of living naturally, conforming to nature's pattern; ambition was abandoned and honors and responsibilities rejected in favor of a meditative return to nature

technology the body of knowledge and skills evolved by humans to produce goods and services

thalassocracy civilization based on sea power, such as that of the Minoan civilization of Crete

themes provinces in the Byzantine empire

theocratically-controlled states states controlled by priests or other religious leaders

totem emblem or symbol of a particular group that

stood for it or imposed rules upon it; rules had to be observed to assure the well-being of the group

tribes inhabitants of villages of a given region identified and distinguished from others by their distinctive language and customs

tundra barren, frozen land along the Arctic coast

United Nations (UN) organization of nations set up in 1945 to carry out two basic tasks: 1) preserve peace and security, and 2) set-up international economic, social, and cultural programs; originally 50 charter members with membership doubling by 1980

Utopian Socialists school of social reformers who produced blueprints for the operations of their projected model communities but did not indicate how these principles could be put into practice in the larger society

veda old and sacred Hindu texts consisting of hymns, prayers and doctrines of Hindu divinities; similar to the Bible for Christians; veda means knowledge

Versailles Treaty treaty with Germany, signed on June 28, 1919, which ended World War I; this treaty, together with separate treaties with the other Central Powers, are signficiant for world history because they applied the principle of self-determination to Europe but failed to apply it in overseas colonies

Warsaw Pact formal military alliance concluded in May, 1955, between Russia and the East European countries

white man's burden theory that Europeans were a superior race who had the duty to direct the labor and guide the development of the inferior races; allowed Europeans to cloak their imperialism with a mantle of idealistic devotion to duty

Wilson's Fourteen Points specific, detailed aims including open diplomacy, freedom of the seas, removal of international trade barriers, armament reduction, application of the principle of self-determination to subject minorities in Central and Eastern Europe

World Zionist Organization nationalist Jewish movement established in Basle in 1897; wanted a Jewish commonwealth in Palestine after the end of the Ottoman Empire

Young Turks pioneer groups of Turkish nationalists who wanted a new modern government in place of the Ottoman Sultanate

Zaibatsu literally "wealth-clique"; general name given to four giant family corporations that by World War II controlled three-fourths of the combined capital of all Japanese firms, three-fourths of all trust deposits, and one-fifth of all life insurance policies

Acknowledgments

Grateful acknowledgment is made to the following authors and publishers for permission for quotation of the epigraphs:

Chapter 1, Clyde Kluckholn, *Mirror for Man* (New York: McGraw-Hill, 1949), p. 11; Chapter 2, R. J. Braidwood, "Near Eastern Prehistory," *Science,* vol. 127 (June 20, 1958), 1419-30; Chapter 8, Robert Lopez, *The Birth of Europe,* © 1962 by Max Leclerc et Cie, Prop. of Librairie Armand Colin and © 1966 trans. by J. M. Dent & Sons, Ltd., and published in 1967 by M. Evans and Co., Inc., New York, by arrangement with J. M. Dent & Sons, Ltd.; Chapter 9, Lynn White, Jr., "Tibet, India, and Malaya as Sources of Western Medieval Technology," *American Historical Review,* XLV (April 1960), 515, 526; Chapter 12, W. C. Bark, *Origins of the Medieval World* (Stanford: Stanford University Press, 1958), p. 66; Chapter 14, Lynn White, Jr., "Technology and Invention in the Middle Ages," *Speculum,* XV (1940), 156; Chapter 20, B. H. Sumner, *A Short History of Russia* (New York: Harcourt Brace Jovanovich, 1943), p. 1; Chapter 22, Herbert Butterfield, *Origins of Modern Science* (London: G. Bell & Sons, Ltd., 1957); p. 179; Chapter 24, Peter Chaadayev, *Apology of a Madman,* cited in H. Kohn's *The Mind of Modern Russia* (New Brunswick, N.J.: Rutgers University Press, 1955), p. 50; Chapter 25, H. A. R. Gibb, "Social Change in the Near East," in P. W. Ireland, ed., *The Near East* (Chicago: The University of Chicago Press; 1942), p. 43; Chapter 26, Arnold J. Toynbee, *The World and the West* (London: Oxford University Press, 1953); Chapter 27, J. K. Fairbank, "The Influence of Modern Western Science and Technology on Japan and China," from *Explorations in Entrepreneurial History,* VII, No. 4; Chapter 31; K. M. Panikkar, *Asia and Western Dominance* (London: George Allen & Unwin, Ltd., 1969); Chapter 34, Arnold J. Toynbee, *Survey of International Affairs,* 1931 (London: Oxford University Press, 1932) under the auspices of the Royal Institute of International Affairs, p. 1; and Chapter 39, René Grousset, *A History of Asia* (New York: Walker & Co., 1963).

Index

Abbasid caliphate, 137–41, 143, 144, 148, 155–56
Aborigines, 7, 8, 11, 20, 211, 213, 222–23
Abu Bakr, 134
Aeschylus, 66
Africa, 14, 15–16, 203–12, 252, 300, 301–3, 331–34, 409–20, 541–44
Agriculture, 7, 13–20, 27–28, 29, 41, 47, 50, 60–61, 83, 113, 168, 177, 182–83, 184, 199, 205–6, 210, 211, 215, 216, 218, 219, 220, 234, 254, 493–94
Ahimsa, 82
Alaric, 110
Alaska, 365–66
Albania, 352, 375, 518, 523–24
Albuquerque, Alfonso de, 268–69
Alexander II of Russia, 363
Alexander the Great, 52, 53, 54, 64, 69, 73, 87, 88, 237
Alexius Commenus, 158
Alienation, 8
Alphabet, 32, 52, 104, 199
American Indians, 9, 14, 22, 211, 212, 214–15, 216–21, 284, 300
American Revolution, 336, 341–44, 352
Americas, the, 14, 15, 16, 30–31, 213–21, 295, 301–3, 305, 330–31, 421–29
Amur Valley, 366–67
Anabaptists, 192, 193
Anarchy, 52
Ancient civilizations, 27–45
Animals, 14, 40–41, 300
Apartheid, 545, 574
Aquinas, Thomas, 171
Arabs, 31, 52, 112, 113, 132–37, 380–83, 411, 466–68, 547–51 (see also Islam)
Archimedes, 71, 80, 316
Aristophanes, 67
Aristotle, 79, 140, 171, 316
Artisans, 316–17
Aryans, 36, 44, 47, 82–85, 236
Ashoka, 87–88
Asia, 16, 267–69, 279–80, 288–97, 301, 303–4, 331–34 (see also names of countries)
Assyrians, 31, 42
Atahuallpa, 220–21, 271
Atatürk, Kemal, 464–66
Athens, 61–64, 67, 68, 69, 72
Atomic warfare, 532–33, 562
Attila, 110

Audiencias, 272
Augustus Caesar, 75–76
Australia, 221–23, 422, 423
Australopithecus, 5, 10, 230
Austria, 349, 446, 447, 448, 449, 457, 458, 483, 515–16
Autarchic units, 80
Avicenna (ibn Sina), 139
Aztec Empire, 216, 217–19, 220–21, 253, 268, 270–71

Babylonia, 236
Bacon, Francis, 179
Balfour Declaration, 463, 468
Balkans, 374–75, 523–24
Ball, John, 354
Baranov, Alexander, 365
Barbarian invasions, 106–12, 242, 243
Belgium, 332, 349, 351, 446, 455, 522, 531, 543
Belisarius, 110–11
Benevolent despotism, 341
Bentinck, William, 389
Bering, Vitus, 365
Bismarck, Otto von, 319, 351, 444
Blitzkrieg, 521, 522
Boers, 280, 415, 545
Bolsheviks, 364, 452–54, 460, 492
Bourguiba, Habib, 546
Boxer Rebellion, 402
Brahmans, 84, 85–86, 390
Brest-Litovsk Treaty, 453, 477
Brezhnev Doctrine, 564
Britain, Battle of, 523
British Empire, 286–87, 331–32, 384–94, 397–400, 413–17, 433, 463–72 (see also Colonial empires, end of)
Buddhism, 49, 52, 53, 54–55, 57–58, 86, 87–88, 94, 145, 149, 167, 168, 175, 176, 241, 293
Bulgaria, 375, 448, 449, 457, 483, 555, 559
Bullion, 264, 268, 283, 300, 301, 321
Burghers, 194–95, 336
Bushmen, 8, 13–14, 19, 205–6, 210, 232
Byzantine Empire, 53, 78, 103, 110–11, 112, 119, 154–63, 250

Cabot, John, 277
Caesar, Julius, 74, 75

Calvin, John, 192
Canada, 282, 283, 284, 285, 286, 428–29
Capitalism, 333–34, 354–55, 568–69
Carolingian dynasty, 111, 112
Carthage, 73
Caste system, 82, 84, 108, 145
Catherine the Great, 296, 341, 361
Catholic Church, 81, 110, 193, 305, 337, 338, 350, 373, 513
Ceylon, 56, 57
Chamberlain, Neville, 515–18, 523
Chancellor, Richard, 278
Chandragupta, I and II, 84, 87, 89
Charlemagne, 111, 181, 243
Charles I of England, 337, 338
Charles II of England, 318
Charles V, Emperor, 192, 193, 273
Cheng Ho, 179, 196, 249
Chiang Kai-shek, 473–74, 507, 559–60, 564–65
Ch'ien-lung, Emperor, 304
China, 14, 15, 16, 28, 30, 31, 37–38, 44–45, 47, 49, 50, 51, 52, 53, 56–57, 58, 92–102, 103, 112, 113, 124–26, 147–48, 164–77, 196, 198, 199, 239, 249, 292, 305, 306, 307–8, 366–67, 396–404, 472–74, 506–7 559–60, 561, 564–66, 569–70
Ch'in Empire, 108, 239
Chou dynasty, 45, 93–94, 98, 239
Chou En-lai, 565
Christianity, 53, 54–56, 58, 78, 88, 113, 162–63, 199, 210, 240–41 (see also Catholic Church; Protestantism)
Chu Hsi, 170–71
Churchill, Winston, 517, 518, 523, 532, 538, 553, 554
Cicero, 74, 77, 225
City-state, 60, 61, 65, 70, 72, 81
Civilization, meaning of, 26–27, 115–18
Class differentiation, 30, 37–38, 145
Classical civilizations, 46–58
Clovis, 110, 111
Coen, Jan Pieterszoon, 280
Coinage, 48, 89, 93, 104, 158, 199
Cold War, 533, 540, 543, 556–62, 570
Colonial empires, end of, 526–27, 535–51
Columbus, Christopher, 196, 264, 265–67, 269
Commercial bonds, 49–52, 121–24
Commercial revolution, 321–22
Common Market, 563

589

Communications revolution, 326
Communism, 353, 472–74, 480–82, 492–96, 515, 516–18, 559–70
Communist Manifesto, 337, 354, 355
Confucianism, 49, 94–96, 99–100, 112, 164–74, 175, 198, 306, 400, 401, 404
Congress of Vienna, 349
Conquistadors, 270–73
Constantine (Byzantine Emperor), 155
Constantine (Roman Emperor) 55, 77, 78, 79, 81
Copernicus, 318
Cortes, Hernando, 217, 218, 220, 270–71, 292
Cossacks, 291–92
Crete, 35–36, 40, 42, 50, 236
Crimean War, 362
Cromwell, Oliver, 338
Crusades, 127, 141, 158, 160, 195, 196, 248, 264
Culture, 7
Cuneiform, 32, 53
Currency, 101, 170, 180
Cynicism, 70
Cyrus, King, 42
Czechoslovakia, 352, 483, 558, 559, 564, 569

da Gama, Vasco, 196, 209, 267, 268
Daimyo, 177
Darius of Persia, 62, 87
Darwinism, 319–20, 332, 351
da Vinci, Leonardo, 189
Dawes Plan, 487–88, 489
Decembrist Revolt, 361–62
Declaration of Independence, 337, 344
Declaration of the Rights of Man and Citizen, 337, 347, 352
de Gaulle, Charles, 547, 563
de Lesseps, Ferdinand, 377
Democracy, 61–62, 68, 161, 334, 338, 339
Democratic centralism, 364
Democratic liberalism, 353
Demographic pattern, 10
de Soto, Hernando, 271–72
Dharma, 84
Dialectics, 67
Dias, Bartholomeu, 267
Diaz, Bernal, 218
Diocletian, 77, 78, 79, 81
Drake, Francis, 278
Du Bois, W. E. B., 461
Duma, 370, 372, 450, 451
Dupleix, Joseph, 286
Dutch, the, 256, 405, 406, 410, 539–40
Dyarchy, 175
Dynasty, 54

East India Companies, 279–80, 282, 285–86, 322, 386–88
East Indies, 276, 279–80
Eden, Anthony, 511, 516
Egalitarianism, 26, 115, 211
Egypt, 28, 30, 31, 33–35, 42, 50, 69, 74, 236 (*see also* Arabs)
Eisenhower, Dwight D., 531, 562
Elizabeth I of England, 278, 360

Emancipation Decree (Russia), 363
Emigration, 330–31, 421–25
Empire, 48
Enclosures, 283
Engels, Friedrich, 354
England, 55, 195, 256, 273, 274, 279–87, 322–30, 335, 337–39, 349, 352, 367, 485–86, 497, 498, 553–58 (*see also* British Empire; World War I; World War II)
Enlightenment, the, 339–41, 345, 361
Epicureanism, 70
Equal-field system, 165–66, 167
Eskimos, 8, 214
Ethiopia, 415, 509, 510–11
Ethnic group, 92
Ethnocentrism, 153, 171
Euclid, 71, 140, 316
Eurasia, 25–45, 46–118, 119–99, 240–41, 246–47, 289
Euripides, 64, 66–67
Europe (*see* Western Europe)
Europeanization, 421
Extended family, 17

Fascism, 483–85
Fentou, 21, 22
Ferdinand, Archduke Francis, 444, 445–46
Feudalism, 157–58, 176–77, 180, 347, 349
Finland, 458, 518, 519, 521, 524, 530, 555, 558
Fire, 5–6
Fishing industry, 277
Five-Year Plans, 491–96
Fluyt, 279
Food gatherers, 3–11, 19–20, 222, 254
Food growers, 12–22
Food plants, 300, 303
Fourier, Charles, 354
Fourteen Points, 450, 455, 458, 460–61
France, 195, 276, 281–87, 331, 332, 361, 399, 400, 413–14, 415, 417, 463–64, 478, 486–87, 556, 563 (*see also* Colonial empires; French Revolution; World War I; World War II)
Franco, Francisco, 514
Franks, 109, 110, 111
Frederick the Great of Prussia, 283, 284, 296, 341
French Revolution, 296, 336, 338, 344–49, 350–53, 374
Fur trade, 281, 283, 289, 292–93, 301, 322, 365–66

Galen, 71, 124, 126, 140, 316
Galileo Galilei, 318
Gandhi, Mohandus, 470, 471, 538
Genghis Khan, 128, 145–48
Genoa, 123–24, 161, 188, 264, 273
Germanic tribes, 55, 58, 77, 79, 103, 106, 108–11, 112, 113, 119, 242
Germany, 195–97, 326, 327, 328, 331, 332, 349, 351, 353, 399, 400, 413, 414, 415, 480–83, 497, 498, 511–12, 555–56, 558–59 (*see also* World War I; World War II)

Ghana, 207, 208, 252
Global relationships, 298–311, 430–36
Glorious Revolution, 338
Gokhale, G. K., 292
Gold, 206, 207, 208, 209, 211, 267, 271, 272, 274, 416, 496, 497 (*see also* Bullion)
Golden Horde, 290–91
Gosplan, 493, 495
Gracchus, Tiberius and Gaius, 75
Great Depression, 496–504, 506–7, 514
Great Wall of China, 147, 165, 239
Greco-Roman civilization, 59–81
Greece, 42–43, 48, 50–51, 52, 53, 60–71, 74, 79, 236, 307, 351, 375–76, 464–65, 483, 508, 511, 523–24, 553, 556, 558
Gross National Product, 495
Guilds, 177, 186, 322
Gupta Age, 83, 89–91, 106, 108, 110, 238

Habitat, 7
Haciendas, 272
Hammurabi, 31, 33
Han Empire, 46, 55, 98–102, 106–8, 112, 164, 165, 166, 167, 239, 241
Hannibal, 72, 73, 74
Hanseatic League, 186, 273
Hapsburg Empire, 351, 445, 457
Harun al-Rashid, 138
Harvey, William, 317
Hawkins, Sir John, 278
Hebrews, 42 (*see also* Jews)
Hellenism, 53–54, 55, 69–71, 74
Helots, 61, 64
Henry the Navigator, 190, 264–65, 267, 410
Heraclius, Emperor, 155, 156
Herodotus, 62, 66, 68, 100
Hesiod, 43, 66, 115
Hierarchy, 8, 116
High culture, 116–18
Hildalgo, 274, 277
Hindenburg, Paul von, 447, 449, 500
Hinduism, 44, 52, 57, 85–86, 89, 115, 144, 145, 150, 199, 307, 390–91
Hippocrates, 66, 140, 316
Hiroshima, 532–33
Hitler, Adolf, 500–503, 507–8, 509, 511–12, 516–18, 531
Hittites, 31, 41, 42, 47, 236
Ho Chi Minh, 539, 540
Holland, 279–81, 349, 539–40
Homer, 43, 66
Hominids, 4–6, 10, 230
Homo erectus, 5, 10, 230
Homo sapiens, 4–6, 10, 21, 230
Hsiung-nu barbarians, 107
Hsüan-tsang, 57, 90
Humanism, 188
Human nature, 21–22
Hundred Years War, 183
Hungary, 302, 458, 482, 517, 518, 524, 555, 559, 564
Huns, 103, 106, 108, 109–10, 112, 119
Hunters, 5, 6–9, 13–14, 19, 211, 214, 215, 222, 231, 233

590

Iberia (see Portugal; Spain)
Ibn Battuta, 122, 207, 209, 246–47
Ideographic script, 37
Ilkhanate, 149, 150, 151–52
Imperialism, New, 331–34
Inca Empire, 216, 217, 219–21, 253, 268, 271
India, 16, 28, 30, 31, 43–44, 47, 48, 49, 50, 51–52, 56, 57, 58, 69, 82–91, 103, 112, 187–88, 199, 238, 267–68, 276, 280, 282, 284–87, 306, 337, 384–94, 470–72, 537–38
Indochina, 539, 540
Indo-Europeans, 31, 39, 42, 44, 64–65, 71, 236
Indonesia, 539, 540
Industrial Revolution, 315–16, 321–34, 364, 431–32, 437–38, 571
Indus valley, 30, 31, 36–37, 40, 43–44, 236
Inventions, 100, 105, 114, 125, 179, 183, 198–99
Iran, 16, 106, 131, 310, 469–70
Iraq, 25, 131, 466, 468
Isabella of Spain, 264, 265
Islam, 52, 54, 119, 121, 124, 126, 127, 131–41, 151–53, 196, 206–7, 244, 263–64, 268, 293, 304–5
Israel, 467, 550–51
Italy, 236, 270, 349, 351, 415, 448, 457, 483–85, 509, 510–12, 515, 523–24, 528–30, 531, 555
Ivan the Terrible, 278, 295, 360

Janissaries, 376
Japan, 56, 174–77, 368–69, 399, 400, 404–8, 459, 479, 506–7, 525–27, 528, 529, 532–33, 537, 539, 553–54, 555, 560
Jesuits, 193, 306, 307
Jews, 138, 263, 264, 274, 373, 468 (see also Judaism; Zionism)
Jinnah, Mohammed Ali, 471–72, 538
Johnson, Lyndon B., 199, 540
Joseph II of Austria, 341
Judaism, 55, 58 (see also Jews)
Jus gentium, 77
Jus naturae, 77
Justinian the Great, 110–11, 155, 156, 162, 250

Katib Chelebi, 190–91
Kenyatta, Jomo, 543–44
Kerensky, Alexander, 451–53
Keynes, John Maynard, 104, 277
Khan, Sayyid Ahmad, 392
Khedive, 382
Khrushchev, Nikita, 562, 563, 565
Khufu (Cheops), 34
Kilwa city state, 209
Koine, the, 54
Koran, 133, 152
Korea, 56, 399
Korean War, 560–62
Kublai Khan, 123, 127, 128, 148, 149, 169, 245
Kulaks, 493, 494

Kuomintang Party, 403–4, 472–74, 559–60
Kushan Empire, 46, 238, 241

Labor supply, 301, 322, 323
Lactation taboos, 13
Laissez faire, 340, 353
Land enclosures, 322–23
La Salle, Robert Cavelier, 272, 282
Latifundia, 74
Latin America, 272–73, 301, 331, 422, 424–28
Laval Pierre, 508–9, 510, 511
Lavoisier, Antoine, 319
Law codes, 32, 33, 62, 77, 81, 162, 349, 352, 407, 425
League of Nations, 457–59, 488, 489, 507, 508, 510, 511
Lebanon, 459, 467, 468
Lebensraum, 509
Legalists, doctrines of, 96
Lenin, Nikolai, 364, 450, 452–54, 460, 461, 478, 479, 480, 492, 493
Leo Africanus, 208–9
Leo I, Pope, 110
Leo III (the Isaurian), 155
Leo III, Pope, 111
Leo X, Pope, 191
Leopold of Belgium, 413, 414
Levellers, 339, 348
Liberalism, 334, 336, 337, 338–39, 344, 352–53
Liebeg, Justus von, 319
Lilburne, John, 338
Linschoten, Jan Huyghen van, 279
Lin Tse-hsu, 397, 400
Livingstone, David, 412–13
Locarno Pacts, 488–89, 508
Locke, John, 341
Lombard League, 186
Louis XIV of France, 281, 283, 284
Louis XVI of France, 345–48
Low culture, 116–17
Ludendorff, Erich, 447, 449, 500
Lumumba, Patrice, 543
Luther, Martin, 191, 192, 193
Lvov, Prince Georgi, 451, 452

Macedon, 31, 65, 69, 71, 73, 74
Machiavelli, Niccolo, 195
Magadha, 83, 87, 89
Magellan, Ferdinand, 270
Magyars, 111, 112, 243
Maine, Sir Henry, 358
Malaysia, 539
Mali, 207, 252
Manchu dynasty, 96
Manchuria, 368–69, 532, 560, 562
Mandate of Heaven concept, 100–101
Mandates, League of Nations, 459
Manorial system, 180–81, 182
Mao Tse-tung, 474, 560, 565
Marco Polo, 122, 128–30, 146, 152, 169, 170, 246–47, 265
Marshall Plan, 558–63
Martel, Charles (the Hammer), 111, 126
Marx, Karl, 354–55, 461

Marxism, 437–38, 569
Mau Mau, 543
Maurya Empire, 83, 86–88, 238
Mawali, 137
Mayan Empire, 216–17, 253
Medicine, 35, 66, 139, 327
Meiji Restoration, 406–7
Mensheviks, 364
Mercantilism, 340
Merovingians, 110, 111
Mesopotamia, 25, 28, 30, 31–33, 34, 40, 42, 69
Metallurgy, 28, 37, 38, 41, 47, 83, 93, 97, 104, 121, 183, 199, 205–6, 210, 211, 220, 317, 322, 324
Metics, 69
Middle East, 14, 15, 16, 28, 37, 41, 42, 114, 199, 373–83, 462–70, 547–48
Millenium, 28
Ming dynasty, 122, 123, 170–74
Minoan civilization (see Crete)
Missionaries, 127, 157, 177, 181, 284, 293, 306, 332, 377, 381, 399, 416–17, 418
Mohammed, 132–34
Mohenjo-daro, 36
Monarchies, 194–95, 336
Mongol Empire, 52, 245
Mongolia, 56, 111
Mongoloids, 215, 232, 299, 309
Mongols, 39, 119, 121–22, 123, 124, 126–27, 145–49, 151, 169–70, 176, 290
Mongol-Turkish peoples, 39–40
Monoculture, 300
Monomotapa, 209
Monroe Doctrine, 365
Montcalm, Marquis de, 284, 285
Montezuma, 217, 220, 221, 271
Moslems, 103, 111, 112, 121, 124, 392–93 (see also Islam)
Muraviev, Nikolai, 366
Muscovy Company, 278, 280, 322
Mussolini, Benito, 483–85, 508–9, 510–11, 512, 517, 519, 531–32

Nanda dynasty, 83–84, 87
Naoroji, Dadabhai, 391
Napoleon I of France, 345, 348–49, 352
Nasser, Gamal Abdel, 548–49, 572
Nationalism, 191–92, 334, 336, 337, 344, 349, 350–52, 356, 390–94, 462–74, 503 (see also Colonial empires, end of)
Natural geopolitical center, 60
Natural selection, 4–5
Nazi Party, 500–503 (see also Hitler, Adolf)
Necker, Jacques, 346
Negroids, 232, 299, 309
Nehru, Jawaharlal, 471
Neo-Confucianism, 170–71, 173
Neolithic Age, 13, 16–19, 104, 115–16, 117
Nerchinsk, Treaty of, 292–93, 365, 366
New Economic Policy, 492
Newton, Isaac, 318–19
New Zealand, 422
Nicholas II of Russia, 367, 450, 451

Nile valley, 25, 31, 40 (*see also* Egypt)
Nixon, Richard M., 540–41
Nkrumah, Kwame, 542
Nomads, 16, 38–45, 97, 101, 102, 103, 106–12, 168, 290
Nonconformists, 322, 337
Normans, 112, 141, 157, 158, 248
North Africa, 203–4, 546–47
North Atlantic Treaty, 559, 563
Northwestern Europe, 276–87
Norway, 349, 351, 522
Nuclear family, 17

October Manifesto, 370, 372
Oligarchies, 61
Omar, Caliph, 134–36
Opium War, 397–98
Orthodox Church, 157, 161
Ostrogoths, 109, 111
Ottoman Empire, 150, 151, 161–62, 295, 306, 351, 373–83

Paine, Thomas, 242–43, 344
Pakistan, 472, 538
Paleolithic Age, 6–11, 13, 16, 22, 116, 221, 222
Palestine, 55, 459, 468
Palestine Liberation Organization, 550–51
Panchayat, 385
Papacy, 127, 152, 156, 181, 188, 191, 194, 269, 349, 360
Pasteur, Louis, 319
Pauthier, Guillaume, 307–8
Pax Britannica, 393
Pax Mongolica, 123, 124, 151, 196
Pax Romana, 51, 76, 81
Pearl Harbor, 526
Peloponnesian War, 68
Pepin the Short, 111
Pericles, 62–63
Perry, Matthew, 405–6
Persia, 31, 34, 42, 48, 51, 62, 69, 73, 103, 112, 131, 137, 236, 237 (*see also* Iran)
Persian Wars, 62, 64, 65
Peter the Great of Russia, 296, 360–61, 362, 365
Petrarch, 188
Philip of Macedon, 64, 69
Philip V of Macedon, 73
Philosophes, 340–41, 361
Phoenicians, 32, 42, 43, 50, 53, 73, 237
Pictographs, 32, 53
Pitt, William, 284
Pizarro, Francisco, 220, 221, 271, 292
Plato, 65, 67–68, 80, 140, 316, 353
Plebeians, 72
Pleistocene Age, 4, 6
Pluralism, Western, 180–81
Plutarch, 80
Poland, 302, 352, 478, 483, 517, 518–19, 521, 559, 563, 564
Polis, 60, 65, 66, 67, 70
Political revolutions, 335–56, 571
Polybus, 49
Population, growth, 10, 183, 184, 231

Portugal, 123, 195, 205, 209, 211, 212, 249, 256, 264–65, 267–70, 272, 278, 303, 306, 410, 413–14, 415, 422, 427, 438 (*see also* Colonial empires, end of)
Printing, 318
Proletariat, 336, 339
Protestantism, 192–94
Prussia, 349, 351
Ptolemy, 71, 140
Punic Wars, 73, 74, 75
Puritans, 338–39
Pygmies, 19, 205–6, 210, 232
Pyrrhus of Epirus, 72–73

Rabban Bar Sauma, 128, 246–47
Race conflict, 573–74
Races, 10–11, 19–20, 224–25, 232, 299–300, 309–10, 422–23
Ranade, M. G., 391
Reformation, the, 191–94
Religion, 18, 19, 28–29, 32–33, 34, 36, 37, 44, 45, 54–58, 65–67, 71, 78, 85–88, 89, 116–17, 126–27, 138, 140, 150, 152, 157, 161, 162, 166–67, 191–94, 215, 217, 219, 220, 263–64, 319, 322, 337, 338–39, 340–41, 347, 352, 375, 377 (*see also* names of religions)
Religious sanctions, 29
Renaissance, 188–91, 316–17
Retarding Lead, Law of, 199
Revisionism, 355–56
Reza Khan, 469–70
Rhazes (al-Razi), 139
Rhodes, Cecil, 433
Roman Empire, 46, 48–49, 51, 53, 71–81, 110, 113, 237, 240, 242
Roosevelt, Franklin D., 525, 532, 553
Rousseau, Jean-Jacques, 341
Roy, Ram Mohan, 391
Rumania, 351, 375, 448, 482, 483, 508, 511, 524, 530, 555, 559, 564
Russia, 148, 256, 257, 288–97, 332, 338, 349, 351, 359–72, 399, 400, 446, 447–48, 449–54 (*see also* USSR)
Russian Orthodox Church, 153, 163, 360
Russo-Japanese War, 368–69, 408, 434–35

Saint-Simon, Henri de, 354
Saladin (Salah ad-Din), 141
Sans-culottes, 348
Sarajevo, 445–46
Sargon the Great, 30, 31
Savannas, 5, 10, 204
Schlieffen Plan, 446, 447
Scholasticism, 152
Scientific revolution, 315, 316–21, 571
Scribes, 32, 53, 116
Secular states, 29
Seii-Tai-Shogun, 176
Selassie, Haile, 510
Selim III, 376
Seljuks, 144, 150, 158
Semites, 31, 39, 40, 42
Seneca, 105
Serbs, 351, 375

Serfdom, 109, 171, 180, 186, 294–95, 302, 304, 349, 361, 362, 363
Seven Years War, 284–86
Shamans, 8, 29
Shang, 37–38, 44–45, 236
Siberia, 214, 215, 289, 291–95, 304–5
Siddhartha, 56
Skeikhs, 132
Skepticism, 70
Slavery, 67, 69, 70, 74, 75, 79–80, 105, 182, 183, 206, 211, 218, 273, 278, 281, 296, 300, 301–3, 304, 317, 322, 344, 352, 367, 410–11, 412, 424–25, 428
Slavs, 55, 58, 106, 111, 112, 155, 157
Smith, Adam, 212, 213, 340
Social differentiation, 205
Social homogeneity, 18
Socialism, 334, 336, 337, 339, 353–56
Socrates, 65, 67, 68
Somme, Battle of, 448
Songhai, 207, 208, 252
Sophists, 67
Sophocles, 66
South Africa, 280, 423, 425, 545–46
Southeast Asia, 539–41
Soviets, 451–52
Spain, 110, 111, 136, 138, 141, 195, 217–21, 256, 264, 265–67, 269–75, 278–79, 349, 422, 425, 427, 512–15
Sparta, 61, 62, 63, 64
Spice trade, 265, 267–70, 272, 278, 279, 280, 321
Ssu-ma Ch'ien, 100
Stalin, Joseph, 493, 495, 515, 521, 528, 553–54, 562
Stanley, Henry M., 413
Steam engine, 324
Steppe, 290
Stimulus diffusion, 31
Stoicism, 70
St. Paul, 55, 171
Strategos, 156, 157
Stuart dynasty, 337–38
Submarine warfare, 455, 456
Subsistence security, 15
Sudan, 204, 206
Suez Canal, 377, 389, 548–49
Suffrage, 338, 353
Sui dynasty, 108, 110, 164, 165
Sukarno, 539
Sumer (*see* Mesopotamia)
Sung dynasty, 122, 168–69
Sun Yat-sen, 402–4, 434–35, 436, 461, 472–73, 474
Suvorov, Aleksandr, 296
Syria, 42, 51, 69, 459, 467, 468

Tacitus, 109
Taiga, 290
Tamerlane (Timur), 149–50
Tanala Kingdom, 26–27
T'ang dynasty, 112, 165–67
Taoism, 96
Tasaday, 21, 22
Tatars, 291, 295–96

Technology, 6, 10, 17, 28, 29–30, 34–35, 50, 70, 71, 77, 79–80, 81, 100, 103, 104, 105–6, 113, 118, 120, 121, 124–26, 140–41, 151–52, 153, 169, 173, 174, 177, 181, 182–83, 201, 205–6, 211, 220, 222 (*see also* Metallurgy)
Tehuacán, 15
Textiles, 17, 301, 323–24, 329
Thalassocracy, 35
Thebes, 64, 69
Themes, 156, 157
Theocratically-controlled states, 30
Thermopylae, Battle of, 62
Third World, 438, 568–69, 570
Thucydides, 3, 63, 64, 68
Tigris-Euphrates valley, 25, 27–30
Tilak, Bal Gangadhar, 392–93
Timbuktu, 208–9
Tojo Hideki, 526
Totem, 8
Tours, Battle of, 111
Trade, 35, 42–43, 47–48, 50–52, 60, 70, 76, 78, 83, 87, 88, 89, 93, 132, 138, 151, 156, 161, 162, 166, 168–69, 172–74, 181, 184, 198, 206, 207, 210, 212, 240–41, 246–47, 252, 256, 273–75, 300–304, 321–22 (*see also* Commercial bonds)
Tribes, 17
Triple Alliance, 444–45
Triple Entente, 445
Trotsky, Leon, 477, 480
Truman, Harry S, 549–50
Truman Doctrine, 556–58
Tundra, 290
Turco-Mongols, 106, 108, 143–53
Turks, 31, 119, 143, 144–45, 149–50, 151, 196, 305–6, 375–80, 447–48, 457, 462–66, 508

Ukraine, 295–97
Umayyad dynasty, 137, 139, 141
United Nations, 550, 554–56, 561
United States, 326, 332, 333, 426–27, 479, 492, 496–97, 498–99, 540–41, 556–63 (*see also* World War I; World War II)
Untouchables, 84–85
Urals, the, 289
Urbanization, 31, 61, 62, 74, 76, 83, 104, 188, 199, 327–28
USSR, 472–74, 477–80, 491–96, 508, 519, 552–66 (*see also* Russia; World War II)
Utopian Socialists, 354

Vandals, 109, 111
Venice, 123, 124, 158, 160, 161, 188, 264, 265, 269, 273
Verdun, Battle of, 448
Versailles Treaty, 457, 487, 508, 510
Vespasian, 105
Vietnam, 540–41, 569–70
Vikings, 103, 106, 112, 213
Villa, Francisco (Pancho), 455
Visigoths, 109–11, 136
Vladimir of Russia, 162, 360
Voltaire, 306, 461

Walpole, Horace, 286
Wang Mang, 101–2
Warsaw Pact, 559, 564
Wealth, distribution of, 329–30
Weimar Republic, 480–82
Western Europe, uniqueness of, 112–14, 179–86, 187–88, 195–97, 261–62, 313–14, 357–58, 421, 430–33, 570–72

William the Conqueror, 112
Willoughby, Hugh, 278
Wilson, Woodrow, 450, 454–55, 458, 460, 506
Witte, Sergei, 368, 369
Wolfe, James, 284, 285
World War I, 22, 310, 443–61
World War II, 22, 310, 520–34
World Zionist Organization, 463
Writing, 36–37, 97–98, 113, 118, 199, 216
Wu Ti, 99, 101

Xenophanes, 66

Yalta conference, 532, 553–54
Yellow River valley civilization, 30
Yermak, 291–92, 295
Young Turks, 378–80, 382–83
Yuan dynasty, 122, 169
Yuan Shih-k'ai, 403–4, 436
Yugoslavia, 352, 458, 483, 508, 511, 554, 563, 564

Za, 177
Zaibatsu, 407, 506
Zimmermann telegram, 455
Zionism, 463, 468
Zoroastrianism, 49, 58, 112, 136